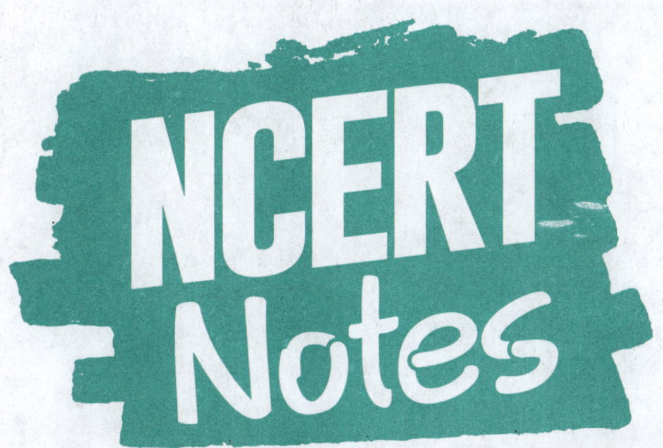

General Science

Class 6-12 (Old+New)

No.1
BEST SELLER

General Science

Class 6-12 (Old + New)

Authors
Digvijay Singh *(Physics)*
Abhishika Kaushik *(Chemistry)*
Juhi Bhatia *(Biology)*

ARIHANT PUBLICATIONS (INDIA) LIMITED

Administrative & Production Offices

Regd. Office

'Ramchhaya' 4577/15, Agarwal Road, Darya Ganj, New Delhi -110002
Tele: 011- 47630600, 43518550

Head Office

Kalindi, TP Nagar, Meerut (UP) - 250002
Tel: 0121-7156203, 7156204

Sales & Support Offices

Agra, Ahmedabad, Bengaluru, Bareilly, Chennai, Delhi, Guwahati, Hyderabad, Jaipur, Jhansi, Kolkata, Lucknow, Nagpur & Pune.

PRICE ₹280.00

PO No. : TXT-59-T071354-6-26

Published by Arihant Publications (India) Ltd.

For further information about the books published by Arihant, log on to www.arihantbooks.com or e-mail at info@arihantbooks.com

Follow us on    

NCERT are the Foundation in the Journey of IAS...

Civil Services Examinations are the most prestigious and coveted examinations in India. Being the toughest exam, it automatically consists of a vast and a detailed syllabus. Aspirants often find it difficult to cover the entire syllabus and lack a right direction for a proper and a systematic study for the exam.

The most important aspect of this preparation journey are the **NCERT books.** Every year approximately **35-40 questions** directly come from NCERT books.

NCERT books also play a key role in understanding the **Basic Concepts**; so that aspirants can easily form the basic foundation of the entire syllabus. But due to the demand for many NCERT books which are required for study, it becomes exhausting to cover each and every NCERT book.

NCERT NOTES SERIES presented by Arihant Publications covers complete text from Class 6th to 12th NCERT books in a comprehensive manner.

Features of Revised Edition

- Extra and relevant facts from exam point of view are covered from Tamil Nadu Board Books.
- Most important facts from NIOS books also compiled to enrich the content.
- Theory in each chapter is facilited with charts, tables, etc. to make the preparation easy and convenient.
- Exam focused last minute revision topics are also covered in the appendix.

The book is adorned with questions prepared by a team of experts along with a vital role played by the Project Management team with members: Mona Yadav (Project Manager), Prachi Parshuram (Project Coordinator), Manshi (Phy), Jyoti (Che) and Pooja Verma (Bio) (Proof Reading TL), Pradeep Chaudhary, (DTP TL), Bilal Hashmi, Rakesh Rawat and Ankit Tyagi (Cover and Inner designer).

We hope this book will help the aspirants to achieve their goals of clearing UPSC as well as State PCS exams. Your valuable suggestions have always inspired us to strive for useful, authentic and more trustworthy publications. So your inputs and suggestions are welcomed for subsequent editions.

We wish you all the very best for your preparation and journey!!

Authors

CONTENTS

PHYSICS

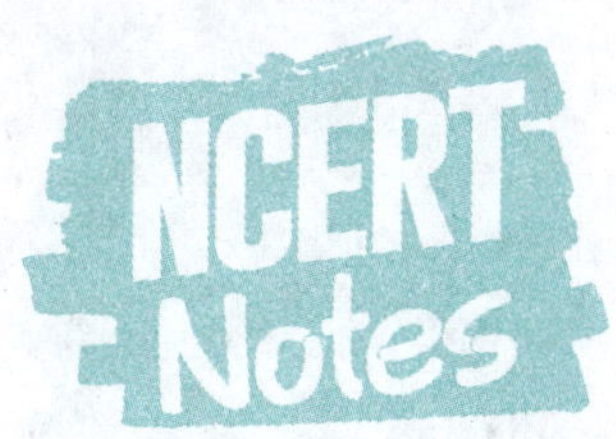

CHEMISTRY

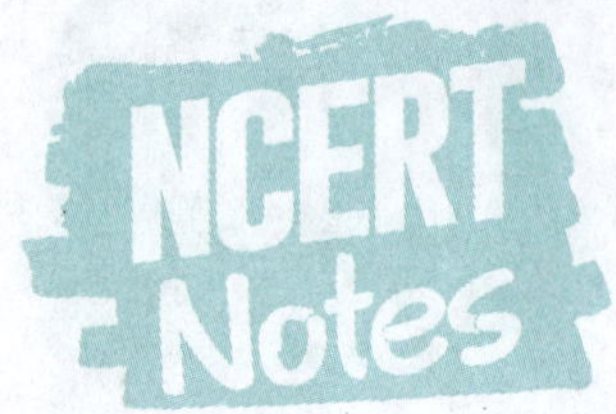

BIOLOGY

NCERT
Notes

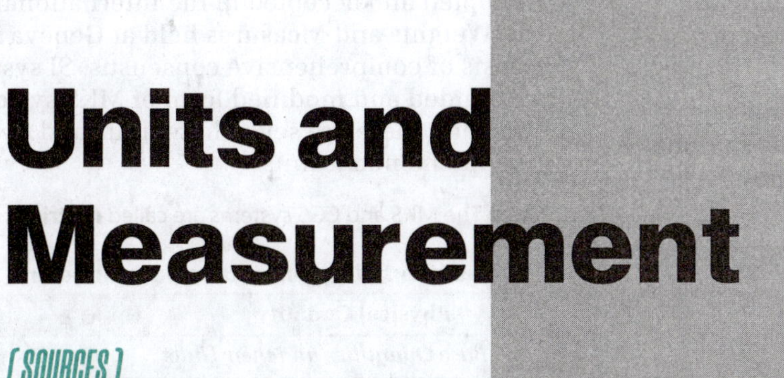

01

Physics

Units and Measurement

(SOURCES)

Class-VI NCERT Chap 7 (Motion and Measurement of Distances),
Class-XI NCERT Chap 1 (Units and Measurement),
Chap 3 (Motion in a plane),
Tamil Nadu Board (Class-IX), NIOS

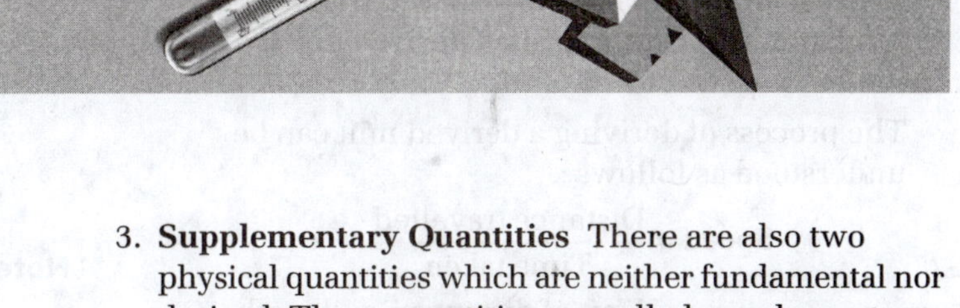

Measurement of any physical quantity involves comparison with a certain basic , arbitrarily chosen, internationally accepted reference standard called unit.

Physical Quantities

Those quantities which can be defined and measured are called physical quantities. e.g. Length, force, temperature, etc.

A physical quantity have a numerical magnitude and a unit. The laws of Physics can be described in terms of physical quantities.

Physical quantities are classified into following categories :

1. **Fundamental Quantities** These are the basic or base quantities which are independent of each other.
   e.g. Mass, temperature, length, time, current, amount of substance, luminous intensity, etc.
2. **Derived Quantities** These quantities are derived with the help of fundamental quantities.
   e.g. Momentum, area, volume, force, etc.
   $$\text{Volume} = \text{Length} \times \text{Breadth} \times \text{Height}$$
   $$= \text{Length} \times \text{Length} \times \text{Length}$$
   $$\text{Volume} = (\text{Length})^3$$
   Here, volume is derived quantity which is derived from the fundamental quantity 'length'.
3. **Supplementary Quantities** There are also two physical quantities which are neither fundamental nor derived. These quantities are called supplementary quantities. e.g. Plane angle and solid angle.

Scalar and Vector Quantities

On the basis of direction and their magnitude, physical quantities can be divided into following parts :

1. **Scalar Quantity** A physical quantity which has only its magnitude but no direction is called a scalar quantity.
   e.g. distance, energy, power, time, speed, volume, density, pressure, work, charge, electric current, temperature, specific heat, frequency, mass, etc.
2. **Vector Quantity** A physical quantity which has magnitude as well as direction is called a vector quantity. e.g. displacement, velocity, torque, position, acceleration, force, weight, momentum, impulse, electric field, magnetic field, current density, angular velocity, etc.

Measurement of Physical Quantities

To express the measurement of a physical quantity, the following two facts are essential :

1. **Standard Unit** It is the unit in which the quantity is measured. e.g. Metre is the unit of length. The unit should be precise and of convenient size.

2. **Numerical Value** The numerical value or the magnitude of the quantity i.e., the number of times that unit is contained in the given physical quantity.

   e.g. When we say that the length of a rod is 20 metres, it means that the unit of length is metre and the length of the rod is twenty times the magnitude of the metre.

Classification of Units

Units are classified into following categories :

1. **Fundamental/Base Unit** The units used for the measurement of fundamental or base quantities are called fundamental or base units. There are seven fundamental units i.e., kilogram, kelvin, metre, second, ampere, mole and candela.
2. **Derived Unit** The units of all other physical quantities can be expressed as combinations of the base units. Such units obtained from the fundamental units are called derived units. e.g. metre^2, metre^3, etc.

   The process of deriving a derived unit can be understood as follows :

$$\text{Speed} = \frac{\text{Distance travelled}}{\text{Time taken}}$$

$$\therefore \text{Unit of speed} = \frac{\text{Unit of distance i.e., length}}{\text{Unit of time}}$$

$$= \frac{\text{metre}}{\text{second}}$$

   In the above situation, the unit of speed is derived from fundamental unit. Therefore metre/second is a derived unit.

3. **Supplementary Unit** The units used for the supplementary quantities are known as supplementary units. e.g. Unit of plane angle and solid angle.

International System of Units

The common systems of measuring physical quantities are given below :

- **CGS System** (Centimetre Gram Second) In this system, the units of length, mass and time are centimetre, gram and second respectively. It is also called **Gaussian system**.
- **FPS System** (Foot Pound Second) In this system, the units of length, mass and time are foot, pound and second respectively. It is also called **British system**.
- **MKS System** (Metre Kilogram Second) In this system, the units of length, mass and time are metre, kilogram and second respectively.
- **SI System** (International System of Units) SI was adopted and accepted in the International Conference of Weights and Measures held at Geneva in 1960, on the basis of comprehensive consensus. SI system is extended and modified form of MKS system. In SI system, there are seven base units and two supplementary units.

Note The MKS and CGS systems are called **metric** or **decimal system.**

Base and Supplementary Quantities and their Units

Physical Quantity	Unit	Symbol
Base Quantities and their Units		
Length	metre	m
Mass	kilogram	kg
Time	second	s
Electric current	ampere	A
Temperature	kelvin	K
Amount of substance	mole	mol
Luminous intensity	candela	cd
Supplementary Quantities and their Units		
Plane angle	radian	rad
Solid angle	steradian	Sr

Note Both radian and steradian are dimensionless quantities.

Definitions of Fundamental Units

- **Metre** One metre is the length of the path travelled by light in vacuum during a time interval of 1/299, 792, 458 of a second.
- **Kilogram** On atomic scale, one kilogram is the mass of 5.0188×10^{25} atoms of C^{12} isotope.
- **Second** One second is defined as the time interval in which cesium. 133 atom completes 9192631770 vibrations in an atomic clock.
- **Ampere** One ampere is defined as the current which, when maintained in two straight infinite length parallel conductor of negligible cross-section and placed 1 m apart in vacuum, would produce a force equal to 2×10^{-7} newton per metre of length.
- **Kelvin** One kelvin is the fraction of 1/273.16 temperature of the triple point of water.
- **Mole** One mole is the amount of substance which contains as many elementary entities as there are atoms in 0.012 kg of carbon-12.
- **Candela** One candela is the luminous intensity, in a given direction, of a monochromatic source that emits radiation of frequency 540×10^{12} Hz and that has a radiant intensity in that direction of $\frac{1}{683}$ W per steradian.

Definitions of Supplementary Units

- **Radian** One radian is the angle subtended at centre of a circle by an arc equal in length to the radius of the circle.
- **Steradian** One steradian is the solid angle, subtended at the centre of a sphere by that area of the surface of the sphere which is equal to the square of the radius of sphere.

Physical Quantities, Formulae and Units

Physical quantity	Formulae	SI unit
Area	length × breadth	m^2
Volume	length × breadth × height	m^3
Density	$\frac{\text{mass}}{\text{volume}}$	kg m^{-3}
Speed or velocity	$\frac{\text{distance or displacement}}{\text{time}}$	ms^{-1}
Linear momentum	mass × velocity	kg-ms^{-1}
Acceleration	$\frac{\text{change in velocity}}{\text{time taken}}$	ms^{-2}
Force	mass × acceleration	N (newton)
Impulse	force × time	Ns
Pressure	force/area	Nm^{-2}
Work	force × distance	J (joule)
Energy (All types)	work	J (joule)
Moment of force	force × distance	N-m
Power	$\frac{\text{work}}{\text{time}}$	W (watt)
Surface tension	$\frac{\text{force}}{\text{length}}$	Nm^{-1}
Thrust	force	N (newton)
Coefficient of elasticity	$\frac{\text{stress}}{\text{strain}}$	Nm^{-2}
Moment of inertia (I)	mass (radius of gyration)^2	kg-m^2
Angular acceleration (α)	$\frac{\text{change in angular velocity}}{\text{time taken}}$	rad s^{-2}
Frequency (ν)	number of vibrations/ second	s^{-1} or Hz (hertz)
Planck's constant (h)	$\frac{\text{energy }(E)}{\text{frequency }(n)}$	J-s
Resistance (R)	$\frac{\text{potential difference}}{\text{current}}$	Ω (ohm)
Capacitance (C)	$\frac{\text{charge}}{\text{potential difference}}$	F (farad)
Specific resistance or resistivity (ρ)	$\frac{Ra}{l}$	Ω-m
Conductance (G)	$\frac{1}{R}$	Ω (ohm^{-1})
Electric flux	electric field × area	$Nm^2 C^{-1}$

Measurement of Length

The standard unit of length based on the metric system is a metre (m).

To measure long and short lengths, we use some special units, which are as follows :

Bigger Units of Length

- **Astronomical Unit** (AU) The average distance of the sun from the earth is known as one astronomical unit, i.e.,

$$1 \text{ AU} = 1.496 \times 10^{11} \text{ m}$$

- **Light year** (ly) The distance that light travels with a velocity of 3×10^8 m/s in one year is known as one light year, i.e.,

$$1 \text{ ly} = 3 \times 10^8 \times 365 \times 24 \times 60 \times 60 \text{ m}$$
$$= 9.461 \times 10^{15} \text{ m}$$

- **Parsec** The distance at which average radius of earth's orbit around the sun subtends an angle of 1 arc second is one parsec, i.e.,

$$1 \text{ parsec} = 3.08 \times 10^{16} \text{ m}$$
$$= 3.26 \text{ ly}$$

Smaller Units of Length

- 1 Decimetre $= \frac{1}{10}$ metre $= 10^{-1}$ metre
- 1 Centimetre $= \frac{1}{100}$ metre $= 10^{-2}$ metre
- 1 Millimetre $= \frac{1}{1000}$ metre $= 10^{-3}$ metre
- 1 Micrometre $= 10^{-6}$ metre
- 1 Nanometre $= 10^{-9}$ metre
- 1 Angstrom $= 10^{-10}$ metre
- 1 Fermi $= 10^{-15}$ metre
- 1 Decametre = 10 metre
- 1 Hectometre = 100 metre $= 10^2$ metre
- 1 Kilometre = 1000 metre $= 10^3$ metre
- 1 Megametre $= 10^6$ metre
- 1 Gigametre $= 10^9$ metre

Note (i) 1 Inch = 0.0254 m = 2.54 cm
(ii) 1 Yard = 3 foot = 0.9144 m
(iii) 1 Foot = 12 inch = 0.3048 m
(iv) 1 Nautical mile = 1852 m

Measurement of Mass

Mass is the basic property of matter which does not depend on the temperature, pressure or location of the object in space.

Different units for measuring mass are as follows :

Bigger Units of Mass

- 1 Quintal (qu) = 100 kg = 10^2 kg
- 1 Metric tonne (mt) = 1000 kg = 10^3 kg = 10 quintal
- 1 Mega gram (Mg) = 10^3 kg
- 1 Giga gram (Gg) = 10^6 kg
- 1 Tera gram (Tg) = 10^9 kg
- 1 Slug = 14.57 kg
- 1 Solar mass = 1.989×10^{30} kg
- 1 Chandrashekhar limit = 2.8×10^{30} kg

Smaller Units of Mass

- 1 Hectogram (hg) = 10^{-1} kg = 100 g
- 1 Decagram (dag) = 10^{-2} kg = 10 g
- 1 Gram (g) = 10^{-3} kg
- 1 Decigram (dg) = 10^{-4} kg = 10^{-1} g
- 1 Centigram (cg) = 10^{-5} kg = 10^{-2} g
- 1 Milligram (mg) = 10^{-6} kg = 10^{-3} g
- 1 Microgram (µg) = 10^{-9} kg = 10^{-6} g
- 1 Nanogram (ng) = 10^{-12} kg = 10^{-9} g
- 1 Picogram (pg) = 10^{-15} kg = 10^{-12} g
- 1 Atomic mass unit = 1.66×10^{-27} kg

Note 1 Carat = 200 mg

Measuring Mass

We commonly use the term 'weight' which is actually the 'mass'. The SI unit of mass is kilogram (kg).
e.g. We buy gold in gram or milligram, medicines in milligram.

There are different type of balance scale
(i) Common (beam) balance
(ii) Physical balance
(iii) Digital balance
(iv) Spring balance

Difference between Mass and Weight

	Mass	Weight
1.	It is a fundamental quantity.	It is a derived quantity.
2.	It has magnitude alone scalar quantity.	It has magnitude and direction vector.
3.	It is the amount of matter contained in a body.	It is the normal force exerted by the surface on the object against gravitational pull.
	Remains the same verywhere.	Varies from place to place.
	...asured using ... balance.	It is measured using spring balance.
	...kilogram.	Its unit is newton(N).

Important Prefixes and Symbols

Prefix	Symbol	Power of 10
Exa	E	18
Peta	P	15
Tera	T	12
Giga	G	9
Mega	M	6
Kilo	k	3
Hecto	h	2
Deca	da	1
Deci	d	– 1
Centi	c	– 2
Milli	m	– 3
Micro	µ	– 6
Nano	n	– 9
Pico	p	– 12
Femto	f	– 15
Atto	a	– 18

Measurement of Time

To measure any time interval we need a clock. The clock which is based on periodic vibrations produced in a cesium atom is called cesium clock or atomic clock. It is used in the national standards.

Some units based on this clock are as follows:

Bigger Units of Time

- 1 Minute (min) = 60 second
- 1 Hour (h) = 60 min = 3600 second
- 1 Day (D) = 24 h = 86400 second
- 1 Year (yr) = 365 days = 3.15×10^7 second

Note 1 Century (CE) = 100 yr

Smaller Units of Time

- 1 Millisecond (ms) = 10^{-3} second
- 1 Microsecond (µs) = 10^{-6} second
- 1 Shake = 10^{-8} second
- 1 Nanosecond (ns) = 10^{-9} second
- 1 Picosecond (ps) = 10^{-12} second

Practical Units

Other than SI units, some units retained for general use, are listed below :

Units of Area 1 Barn = 10^{-28} m^2
1 Hectare = 10^4 m^2

Units of Capacity 1 Litre (L) = 10^{-3} m^3
1 Gallon (Gal) = 3.7854 L (US)
= 4.546 L (UK)

Units of Pressure 1 Pascal (Pa) = 1 N/m^2
1 Bar (bar) = 10^5 Pa
1 Atmospheric pressure (atm)
$= 1.01 \times 10^5$ Pa

Units of Energy 1 Calorie (cal) = 4.184 J
1 Erg = 10^{-7} J
1 Kilowatt hour (kWh) = 3.6×10^{-6} J
1 Electron volt (eV) = 1.6×10^{-19} J

Unit of Power 1 Horse power (hp) = 746 W

Errors in Measurements

Generally measured value of a quantity is different from the true value of the physical quantity. The difference between the true value and measured value is called error.

Error = True value – Measured value

In general the errors in measurement can be broadly classified as (a) systematic errors and (b) random errors.

Systematic Errors

The errors that tends to be in one direction, either positive or negative.

(a) **Instrumental Errors** That arise from the errors due to imperfect design or calibration of measuring instrument, zero error in instrument etc. e.g. The temperature graduations of a thermometer may be inadequately calibrated.

(b) **Imperfection in Experimental Technique or Procedure** To determine the temperature of human body a thermometer placed under the armpit will always give a temperature lower than actual value of the body temperature. Other external conditions during the experiment may systematically affect the measurement.

(c) **Personal Errors** That arise due to an individual's bias, lack of proper setting of the apparatus or individual carelessness in taking observations without observing proper precautions etc.

Least Count Errors

Least count error is the smallest value that can be measured by the measuring instrument. The error associated with the resolution of the instrument is called the least count error.

Random Errors

The random errors are those errors, which occur irregularly and have are random with respect to sign and size. These can arise due to random and unpredictable fluctuations in experimental conditions.

Absolute Error, Relative Error and Percentage Error

Absolute Error

The magnitude of the difference between the individual measurement and the true value of the quantity. It is always positive.

$\therefore$ Absolute error, $a_1 = |\Delta a_1| = |a_m - a_1|$

$$|\Delta a_2| = |a_m - a_2|$$
$$\vdots$$
$$|\Delta a_n| = |a_m - a_n|$$

$\therefore$ Mean absolute error, $\Delta a_{mean} = \dfrac{|\Delta a_1| + |\Delta a_2| + \ldots . |\Delta a_n|}{n}$

Relative Error

It is the ratio of the mean absolute error to the mean value of the physical quantity i.e., $\delta a = \dfrac{\Delta a_{mean}}{a_{mean}}$

Percentage Error

It is the relative error expressed in percent.

Percentage error $= \delta a \times 100\% = \dfrac{\Delta a_{mean}}{a_{mean}} \times 100\%$

Combination of Errors

(i) **Error in Sum of Two Quantities** If a physical quantity (x) can be expressed as the sum of two physical quantities a and b as $x = a + b$, then error in x will be $\Delta x = \pm(\Delta a \pm \Delta b)$

(ii) **Error in Product of Two Quantities** If $x = a \times b$, then the fractional error in x will be $\dfrac{\Delta x}{x} = \pm \dfrac{\Delta a}{a} \pm \dfrac{\Delta b}{b}$.

(iii) **Error in the Division of Two Quantities** If $x = \dfrac{a}{b}$, then fractional error in x will be $\dfrac{\Delta x}{x} = \pm\left(\dfrac{\Delta a}{a} \pm \dfrac{\Delta b}{b}\right)$.

Hence, relative error in the result when two quantities are multiple on divided is the sum of the relative errors.

(iv) **Error in the Power of a Quantity** If $x = \dfrac{a^m b^n}{c^r}$, then the relative or fractional error in x will be

$$\frac{\Delta x}{x} = \pm\left(m\frac{\Delta a}{a} + n\frac{\Delta b}{b} + r\frac{\Delta c}{c}\right)$$

Significant Figures

Significant figures indicated the precision of measurement which depends on the least count of the measuring instruments.

Rules to Determine the Numbers of Significant Figures

- All non - zero digits are significant
- 235.75 has five significant figures.
- All zeros between two non-zero digits are significant.
- 2016.008 has seven significant figures.
- All zeros occuring between the decimal point and the non-zero digit are non-significant, provided there is only a zero to left of decimal point 0.00652 has three significant figures.
- All zeroes written to the right of a non-zero digit in a number written without a decimal are not significant figures.
- This rule does not work, if the zero is a result of the measurement 54000 two significant figures. 54000 m five significant figures.
- All zeroes occuring to the right of a non-zero digit in a number written with a decimal point are significant. 32.2000 has six significant figures.
- When a number is written in the exponential form, the exponential term does not contribute towards the significant figures 2.465×10^5 has four significant figures.

Rules for Arithmetic Operations with Significant Figures

In arithmetic operations involving significant, the answer is reported in such a way that it reflects the reliability of the least precise operation.

In Addition and Subtraction

For addition and subtraction, look at the decimal portion of the number. If follows the following procedure

(a) Count the number of significant figure in the decimal portion of each problem.

(b) Add or subtract in normal fashion.

In Multiplication or Division

The final result should retain as many significant figures as are there in the originial number with the least significant figures.

Rounding Off

Rule of Rounding Off the Uncertain Digits

(a) The preceding digit is raised by 1 if the uncertain digit to be dropped is more than 5 and its left unchanged if the latter is less than 5.

e.g. $x = 5.686$ is round off to 5.69 (as $6 > 5$)

$x = 3.462$ is round off to 3.46 (as $2 < 5$)

... uncertain digit to be dropped is 5, the preceding ... aised by 1 if it is odd and is left unchanged if it ... digit.

e.g. 7.735 is rounded off to three significant figure 7.74 as preceding digit is odd.

7.745 is sound off to 7.74 as preceeding digit is even.

Vernier Caliper and Screw Gauge

Vernier Caliper

- A vernier scale which is named after pierre vernier is defined as a visual aid to take an accurate measurement reading between two graduation markings on linear scale by using mechanical interpolation.
- It is used to calculate the internal and external diameters of follow cylinders.
- It is also used for the measurement of diameters of round objects with the half of the measuring jaws.

(a) **Least Count**

Least Count (LC)

$$= \frac{\text{Value of 1 main scale division}}{\text{Total number of vernier scale division}}$$

$$\therefore \quad LC = \frac{1\text{ mm}}{10} = 0.1\text{ mm} = 0.01\text{ cm}$$

(b) **Zero Error** Unscrew the slider and move it to the left such that both the jaws touch each other.

If they do not coincide, then the instrument is said to posses zero error. Zero error may be positive, negative.

Screw Gauge

- Screw gauge is an instrument that can measure the dimensions upto $\frac{1}{100}$ th of a millimeter or 0.041 mm.
- With the screw gauge it is possible to measure the diameter of a thin wire and thickness of thin metallic plates.
- The screw gauge works on the principle that when a screw rotates in a nut, the distance moved by the tip of the screw is directly proportional to the number of rotations

(a) **Pitch of the Screw** The distance moved by the tip of the screw for one complete rotation of the head. It is equal to 1 mm in typical screw gauge.

$$\text{Pitch} = \frac{\text{Distance moved by the pitch}}{\text{No. of rotation by head scale}}$$

(b) **Least count of a Screw Gauge** Least count of instrument (LC)

$$= \frac{\text{Value of 1 smallest scale reading}}{\text{Total No. of head scale division}}$$

$$LC = \frac{1\text{ mm}}{100} = 0.01\text{ mm}$$

Zero Error of a Screw Gauge

When the movable stud of the screw and the opposite fixed stud on the frame area brought into contact, if the zero of the head scale coincides with the pitch scale axis there is no zero error .

Dimensions of Physical Quantities

The dimensions of physical quantity are the powers to which the fundamental quantities mass, length, and time must be reaised to represent it.

e.g. momentum = mass × velocity

$$= \text{mass} \times \frac{\text{length}}{\text{time}}$$

$$\therefore \text{Dimension of momentum} = [M]\left[\frac{L}{T}\right] = [MLT^{-1}]$$

Hence, the dimensions of momentum are 1m mass, 1 in length and 1 in time.

Dimensional Formulae and Dimensional Equations

- The expression which shows how and which fundamental quantities represent the dimensions of a physical quantity is known as dimensional formula.
- e.g. The dimensional formula of the volume is $[M^0L^3T^0]$ and that of speed or velocity is $[M^0LT^{-1}]$.
- An equation obtained by equating a physical quantity with its dimensional formula is called the dimensional equation of the physical quantity.
- Dimensional equation of energy

By $E = W = \text{force} \times \text{displacement}$

$E = [M^1L^1T^{-2}]\,[L^1] = [ML^{-2}T^{-2}]$

Application of Dimensional Analysis

(i) To find the unit of a given physical quantity in a given system of units.

(ii) To convert a physical quantity from one system of unit to other.

(iii) To check the dimensional correctness of a given physical relation.

(iv) Deducing relation among the physical quantities.

Limitations of Dimensional Analysis

(i) To derive a physical relation, we must first know on what factors the given physical quantity depends and after that we can derive only the preliminary relations of the product type, such as $T = k\sqrt{\frac{l}{g}}$.

(ii) The value of dimensionless contact appearing in formula cannot be determined by this method.

Extra Facts From Tamil Nadu Board and NIOS

- The nearest star Alpha Centauri is about 1.34 per second from the Sun. Most of the stars visible to the unaided eye in the night sky are within 500 per second distance from the Sun.

02

Motion

[SOURCES]

Class-VI NCERT Chap 7 (Motion and Measurement of Distances),
Class-VII NCERT Chap 9 (Motion and Time),
Class-IX NCERT Chap 7 (Motion),
Class-XI NCERT Chap 2 (Motion in a Straight Line), Chap 3 (Motion in a Plane).

- In our daily life, we see some objects at rest and others in motion.
- We often perceive an object to be in motion when its position changes with time.
- There are also some situations in which the motion is inferred through indirect evidences. e.g. Motion of air by observing the movement of dust and movement of leaves and branches of trees.
- Similarly, the phenomena of sunrise, sunset are due to motion of the earth. Atoms, molecules, planets, stars and galaxies all are in motion.

Rest and Motion

- If a body does not change its position with respect to surroundings with the passage of time, it is said to be **'at rest.'**
  e.g. An object placed on the table is at rest, because its position with respect to the desk does not changes with time.
- When the position of an object changes continuously with respect to its surroundings with passage of time, then the object is said to be in **motion.**
  e.g. Car is moving on road, water is flowing in rivers etc.
- Further, an object may appear to be moving for one person and the same object may appear to be at rest for another person.
  e.g. When a bus is moving on a road, a person standing on the road finds the bus moving forward. However, a person inside the moving bus finds his fellow passengers at rest.

Types of Motion

According to the path travelled by the object, motion is divided into following types :

1. **Rectilinear Motion** When an object moves along in a straight line, then the object is said to be in rectilinear motion. e.g. An athlete running on a straight track.
2. **Circular Motion** When an object travels over a circular path, then the motion possessed by it is circular motion.
   e.g. The motion of earth around the sun axis.
3. **Rotational Motion** When an object rotates about a fixed axis, it is said to be rotational motion and the axis is called the axis of rotation.
   e.g. The rotation of earth on its axis.

   When a ball moves along the ground, it undergoes a rectilinear motion as well as rotational motion.
4. **Oscillatory Motion** When the object moves to and fro motion about its fixed position, then it is said to be in an oscillatory motion.
   e.g. Pendulum of a clock, motion of a child on a swing etc.

Some Basic Terms Related with Motion

Some basic terms related with motion are as follows :

Origin

To describe the position of an object, we need to specify a reference point called the origin. The reference point or origin is chosen according to our convenience.

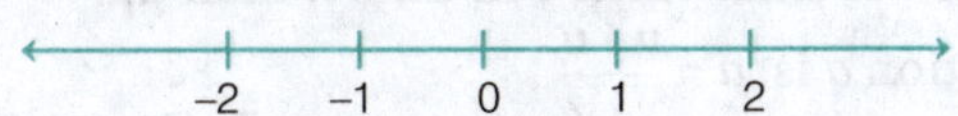

Here, the point $x = 0$ is the position of origin.

Distance

- The actual length covered by an object in a particular interval of time during motion is called distance or path length. It is a scalar quantity.
- The value of distance is always positive, it cannot be zero or negative. Its SI unit is metre (m).
  e.g. Suppose an object starts its journey from origin O. Let, the object go from O to B and come back to A along the same straight line.

40 km 100 km
O A B X

The total path covered by the object $= OB + AB$
$= 100 + 60 = 160$ km

Note Odometer is a device used to measure distance.

Displacement

- The shortest distance measured from the initial and final position of the object is called the displacement of the object in motion.
- It is a vector quantity with SI unit metre (m).
  e.g. Suppose an object starts from origin O, travels 5 km towards East, 5 km towards North and 10 km towards West.

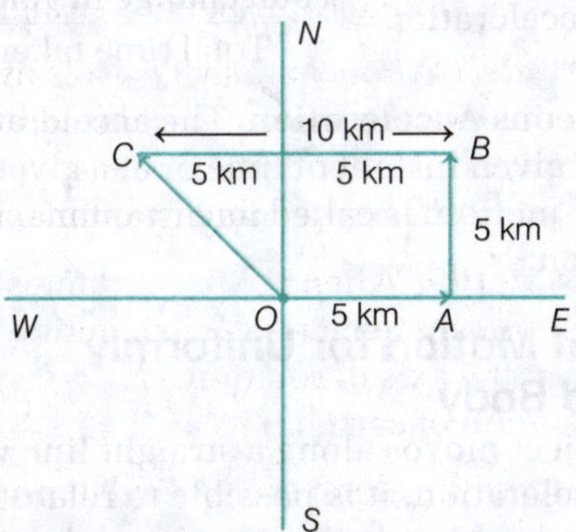

The distance travelled by the object is going from point O to point $C = OA + AB + BC = 5 + 5 + 10 = 20$ km

The displacement of the object from O to C = **OC**

where, $OC = |\mathbf{OC}| = \sqrt{5^2 + 5^2}$

$= 5\sqrt{2}$ km

Distinction between Distance and Displacement

Distance	Displacement
It is the total length covered by object during motion.	It is the shortest length between initial and final position.
It is always positive and cannot be zero or negative.	It can be positive, zero or negative.
It depends on the nature of path travelled.	It is independent of the path travelled.

Note Displacement is always less than or equal to distance for the same motion of an object i.e., displacement ≤ distance.

Uniform Motion and Non-Uniform Motion

- **Uniform Motion** When an object travels equal distances in equal intervals of time, the motion of the object is said to be uniform.
  e.g. Suppose a car covers 60 km in first hour, another 60 km in second hour and so on.
- **Non-Uniform Motion** When an object travels unequal distances in equal intervals of time, the motion of the object is said to be non-uniform.
  e.g. Motion of car on a crowded street, a person is jogging in a park etc.

Speed

- The distance covered by the body in a unit time is called speed of the body.

$$\text{Speed} = \frac{\text{Total Distance travelled}}{\text{Total Time taken}}$$

- It is a scalar quantity and its SI unit is m/s. Speed of body is always positive.

Types of Speed

1. **Uniform Speed** When a body covers equal distances in equal intervals of time, the speed of the body is said to be uniform.
2. **Non-Uniform or Variable Speed** When a body covers unequal distances in equal intervals of time, the speed of the body is said to be non-uniform or variable speed.
3. **Average Speed** The average speed of a body is obtained by dividing the total distance travelled by the total time taken i.e.,

$$\text{Average speed} = \frac{\text{Total distance travelled}}{\text{Total time taken}}$$

   If an object travels s distance in t time, then its speed is, $v = \frac{s}{t}$

4. **Instantaneous Speed** The speed of an object at a particular moment (instant) in time is called Instantaneous speed.

Velocity

- The displacement of an object or the distance covered by an object in a particular direction in unit interval of time, is called the velocity.

$$\text{Velocity} = \frac{\text{Distance covered in given direction}}{\text{Time taken}}$$

or $\text{Velocity} = \frac{\text{Displacement}}{\text{Time}}$

i.e., $v = \frac{s}{t}$

- The unit of velocity is metre/second or ms^{-1}. It is a vector quantity.

Types of Velocity

1. **Uniform Velocity or Constant Velocity** If an object covers equal displacement in equal intervals of time, then it is said to be moving with a uniform velocity or constant velocity.
2. **Non-uniform or Variable Velocity** If an object covers unequal displacement in equal intervals of time, then it is said to be moving with a non-uniform or variable velocity.
3. **Average Velocity** The ratio of the total displacement to the total time taken, is called average velocity.

$$\text{Average velocity} = \frac{\text{Total displacement}}{\text{Total time}}$$

The average velocity is given by the arithmetic mean of initial velocity and final velocity for a given period of time. i.e.,

$$\text{Average velocity} = \frac{\text{Initial velocity} + \text{Final velocity}}{2}$$

Mathematically, $v_{av} = \frac{u+v}{2}$

where, v_{av} is the average velocity, u is the initial velocity and v is the final velocity of the object.

4. **Instantaneous Velocity** The velocity of an object at any instant of time is called instantaneous velocity.

Distinction between Speed and Velocity

Speed	Velocity
The measure of the rate of motion of the object is called speed.	The distance travelled by the body in a given direction in unit time is called velocity.
It is a scalar quantity.	It is a vector quantity.
Its magnitude can be zero or positive but not negative.	Its magnitude can be positive, zero or negative.
Average speed remains constant through the motion.	Average velocity changes with the time intervals and it can also be zero.

Acceleration

- The rate of change of velocity of the body with time is called acceleration of that body. i.e.,

$$\text{Acceleration} = \frac{\text{Change in velocity}}{\text{Time taken}}$$

- If the velocity of an object changes from an initial value u to the final value v in time t, then the acceleration a is, $a = \frac{v-u}{t}$
- Acceleration is a vector quantity. Its SI unit is ms^{-2}.
- If the motion is along a straight line and the velocity of the body is increasing with time, the acceleration is in the direction of velocity. The motion is said to be accelerated motion. e.g. The motion of a freely falling body.
- The negative acceleration is called **retardation**. It's direction is opposite to the direction of velocity of the body. e.g. when a body is thrown vertically upwards, its acceleration is negative due to opposing gravity.

Types of Acceleration

1. **Uniform Acceleration** If the velocity changes uniformly at equal intervals of time, then the acceleration of the object is said to be uniform.

   e.g. Motion of freely falling body under the action of gravity (g).
2. **Non-Uniform Acceleration** When the velocity of an object changes at a non-uniform rate, then the acceleration of the object is said to be non-uniform or variable. e.g. Motion of a car on crowded street.
3. **Average Acceleration** The ratio of the total change in velocity of the object during motion to the total time.

$$\text{Average acceleration} = \frac{\text{Total change in velocity}}{\text{Total time taken}}$$

4. **Instantaneous Acceleration** The acceleration of the object of a given instant of time or at a given point during the motion, is called its instantaneous acceleration.

Equations of Motion for Uniformly Accelerated Body

- When an object moves along a straight line with uniform acceleration, it is possible to relate its velocity, acceleration during motion and the distance covered by it in a certain time interval by a set of equations, known as the equations of motion.
- These are :

1. $v = u + at$ 2. $s = ut + \frac{1}{2}at^2$ 3. $2as = v^2 - u^2$

where, u = initial velocity, v = final velocity,
a = acceleration, t = time, s = distance.

Note The displacement covered in t th second is given by

$$s = u + \frac{1}{2}a(2t - 1)$$

Equations of Motion Due to Action of Gravity

When the velocity of an object changes due to gravity, then the equations of motion are written as,

1. $v = u + gt$ 2. $h = ut + \frac{1}{2}gt^2$ 3. $v^2 = u^2 + 2gh$

where, g is acceleration due to gravity.

When the object is thrown vertically upwards, then value of acceleration due to gravity, $g = -g$.

Graphical Representation of Motion

To describe motion of an object, distance-time, velocity-time and acceleration-time graphs are drawn. From the nature of the graphs, nature of motion is studied.

1. Distance-Time Graphs

The change in the position of an object with time can be represented on the distance-time graph. In this graph, time is taken along X-axis and the distance is along Y-axis.

Distance-time graphs can be employed under conditions are explained below :

- **Case 1** When the body is at rest then, the s-t graph is a straight line in parallel to time axis.

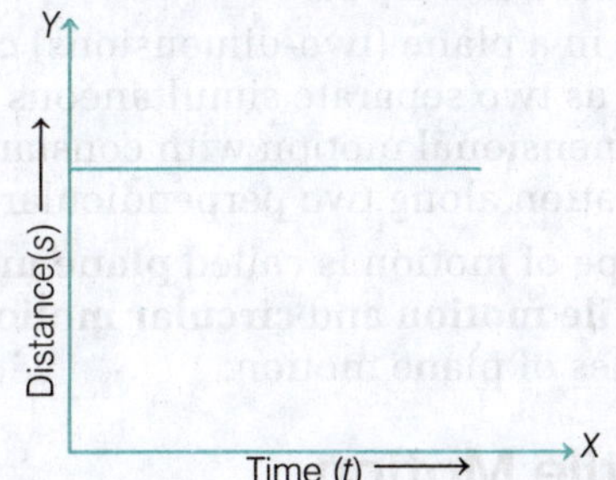

- **Case 2** When the body is in uniform motion. The graph for a body in uniform motion is a straight line, inclined at angle θ with X-axis, as shown

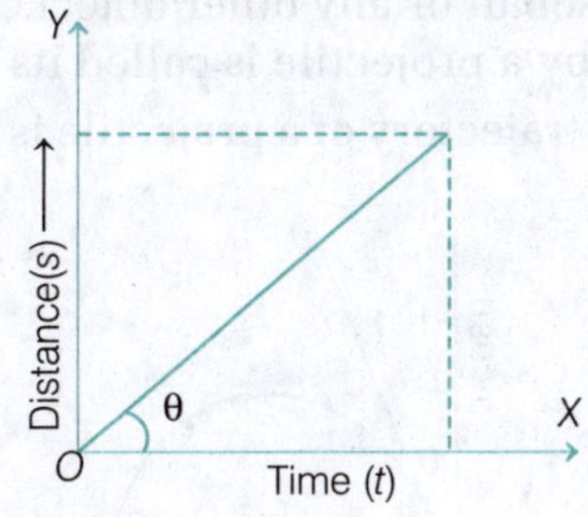

- **Case 3** When the body is in non-uniform motion or accelerated motion.
The distance-time graph in this case is a curved line.

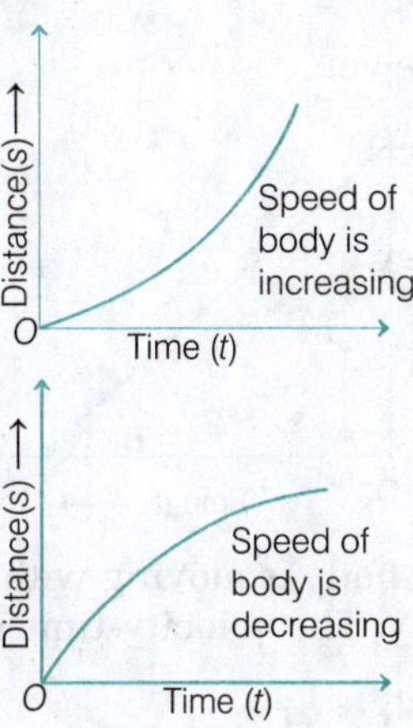

2. Velocity-Time Graph

- The variation in velocity with time for an object moving in a straight line can be represented by a velocity-time graph. In this graph, time is represented along the X-axis and the velocity is represented along Y-axis. Velocity time-graph under various conditions are explained as below :
- **Case 1** When the body is moving with a uniform velocity.
If the object moves at uniform velocity, the height of its velocity-time graph will not change with time.

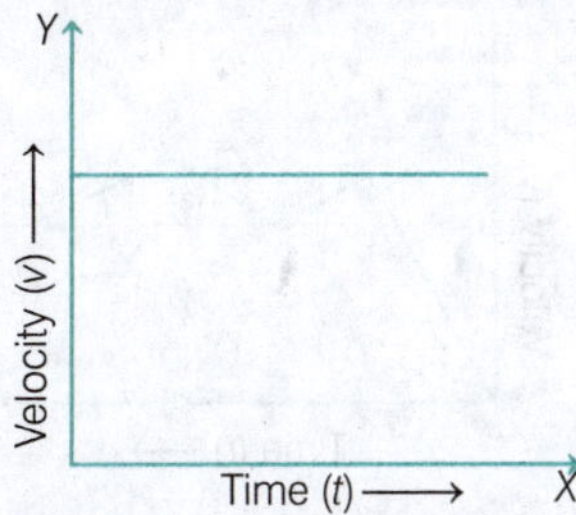

- **Case 2** When the body is moving with a positive uniform acceleration. If the velocity changes by equal amounts in equal intervals of time. Thus, for all uniformly accelerated motion, the velocity-time graph is a straight line.

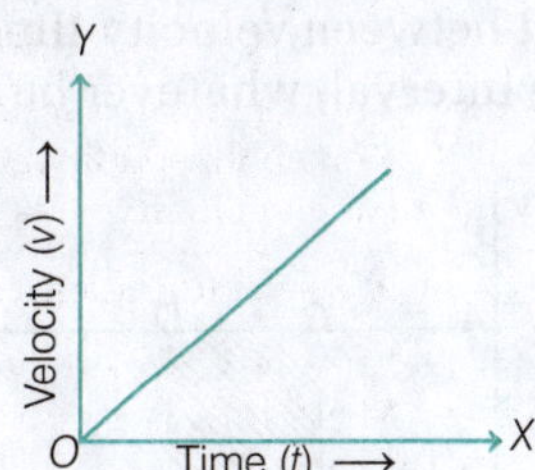

- **Case 3** When an object is moving with constant negative acceleration, then the graph is a straight line and slope is negative.

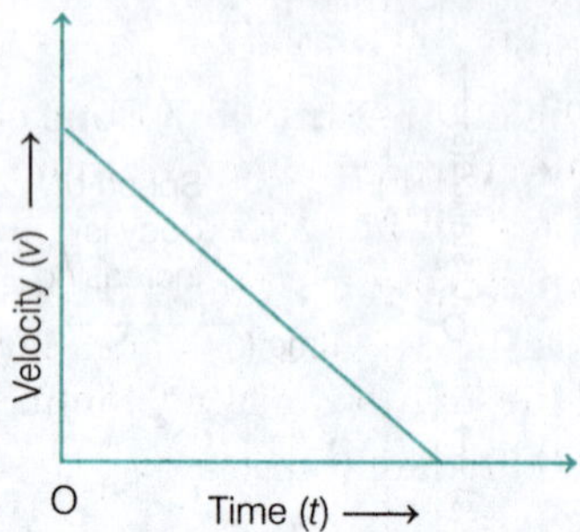

- **Case 4** When the body is moving with a non-uniform (variable) velocity. The velocity-time graph in this case is a curve line.

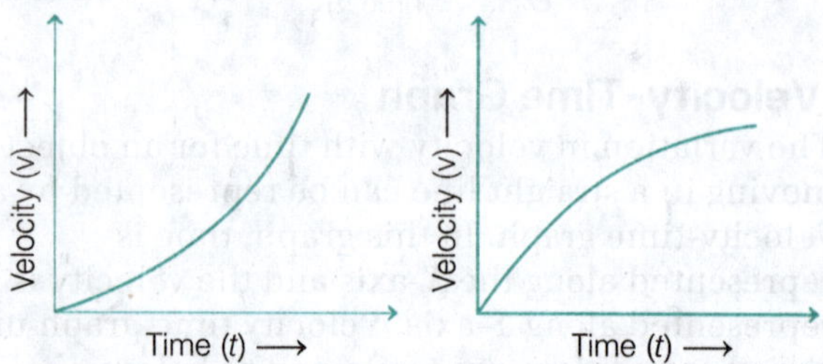

The area enclosed by the velocity-time graph gives the displacement or distance covered by the body.

For non-uniform accelerated motion, velocity-time graph can be *zig-zag* line.

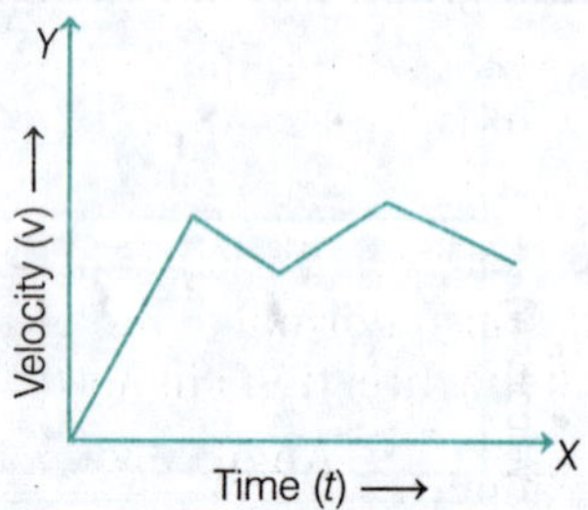

Note In the case of non-uniformaly accelerated motion, velocity-time graph can have any shape.

Determination of Displacement from Velocity-time Graph

- The displacement of an object in a time-interval is equal to the area enclosed between velocity-time graph and time axis for that time interval, whatever be the shape of the graph.

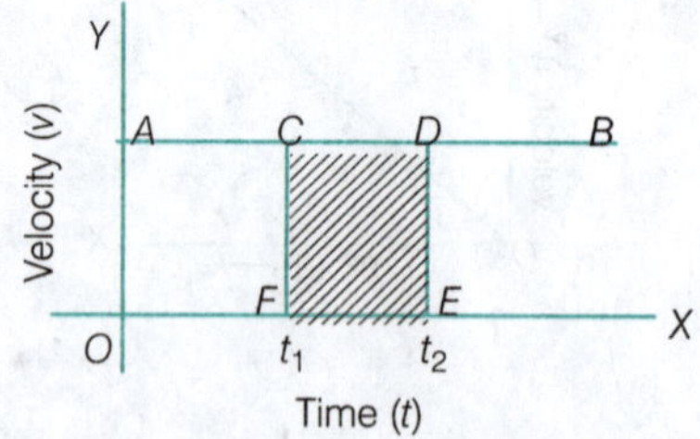

Here, in the below graph, time interval $= t_2 - t_1$
$= EF$

Velocity, $v = FC$

Determination of Displacement

Displacement of object = Velocity × Time interval

$$= v \times (t_2 - t_1)$$
$$= FC \times EF$$
$$= \text{Area of } CDEF$$

Therefore, displacement of object = Area enclosed between time interval velocity graph and time axis.

Relative Velocity

- The velocity of an object with respect to another is called relative velocity of that object.
- It is the time rate of change of relative position of one object with respect to another object.
  e.g. Consider two objects A and B moving with velocities v_A and v_B in same direction, then the velocity of object B with respect to A is
  $$v_{BA} = v_B - v_A$$
  and velocity of object A relative to B is,
  $$v_{AB} = v_A - v_B$$
  If the objects A and B move in opposite direction, then relative velocity is
  $$v_{AB} = v_A + v_B$$

Motion in a Plane

- Motion in a plane (two-dimensions) can be treated as two separate simultaneous one-dimensional motion with constant acceleration along two perpendicular directions.
- This type of motion is called **plane motion. Projectile motion** and **circular motion** are the examples of plane motion.

Projectile Motion

- An object that is in flight after being thrown or projected under the gravity, is called a **projectile.**
- Such a projectile might be a football, a cricket ball, a baseball or any other object. The path followed by a projectile is called its **trajectory**.
  Thus, the trajectory of a projectile is parabolic.

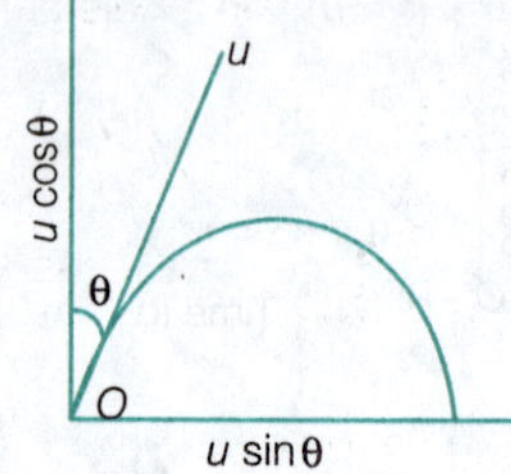

- It was Galileo who first stated this independency of the horizontal and the vertical components of projectile motion in his Dialogue on the great world systems (1632).

Formulae for Projectile Motion

- **Time of Flight** The time taken by a projectile to return to its initial elevation after projection is known as its time of flight (T). It is given by

$$T = \frac{2u \sin\theta}{g}$$

where, u = initial velocity
g = acceleration due to gravity
θ = angle

- **Horizontal Range of Projectile** The maximum horizontal distance between the point of projection and the point on the horizontal plane where, the projectile hits is called horizontal range.

It is given by $$R = \frac{u^2 \sin 2\theta}{g}$$

Note If $\theta = 45°$, then the projectile has maximum range, $R_{max} = \frac{u^2}{g}$

- **Maximum Height of Projectile** The maximum vertical distance travelled by the projectile during its journey is called maximum height attained by the projectile. It is given by,

$$H = \frac{u^2 \sin^2\theta}{2g}$$

Circular Motion

- When an object moves along the circumference of a circle or rotates along a circular path, then the motion of the object is said to be circular.
- When an object travels with uniform speed or velocity in a circular path, then the motion is said to be uniform circular motion.
- When a body takes one round of a circular path, then it travels a distance equal to its circumference which is $2\pi r$, where, r is the radius of the circular path.
- The speed of the body moving in a circular path is $v = \frac{2\pi r}{t}$.

Note Uniform circular motion is an accelerated motion.

Variables of Circular Motion

- **Time Period** Time taken by the particle to complete one revolution on circular path. It is denoted by T and its unit is second.
- **Frequency** The number of revolutions completed by an object on its circular path in a unit time. It is denoted by n and its unit is s^{-1} or hertz (Hz).
- **Angular Displacement** The angle traced out by the radius vector at the centre of the circular path in a given time is called the angular displacement.

It is expressed in radian (rad).

$$\text{Angular displacement, } \theta = \frac{\text{Arc}}{\text{Radius}}$$

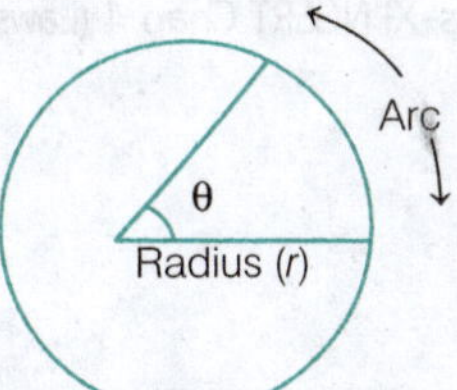

- **Angular Velocity** The time rate of change of its angular displacement in circular motion is called the angular velocity of the object.

It is denoted by ω and is measured in radian per second ($rad\,s^{-1}$).

$$\text{Angular velocity, } \omega = \frac{\text{Angular displacement } (\theta)}{\text{Time } (t)}$$

- **Angular Acceleration** The time rate of change of its angular velocity. It is denoted by α and its unit is radian/second^2.

It occurs due to change in direction of angular velocity. So, its direction is also normal to the plane of circle in accordance with the direction change of angular velocity.

$$\text{Angular acceleration, } \alpha = \frac{\text{Angular Velocity } (\omega)}{\text{Time } (t)}$$

- **Centripetal Acceleration** The acceleration of an object moving with speed in a circle and having radius is always directed towards the centre called centripetal acceleration.

$$\text{Centripetal acceleration, } a = \frac{v^2}{r}$$

where, v is the velocity and r is the radius of circular path.

03

Force and Newton's Laws of Motion

[SOURCES]

Class-VIII NCERT Chap 8 (Force and Pressure), Chap 9 (Friction), Class-IX NCERT Chap 8 (Force and Laws of Motion), Class-XI NCERT Chap 4 (Laws of Motion)

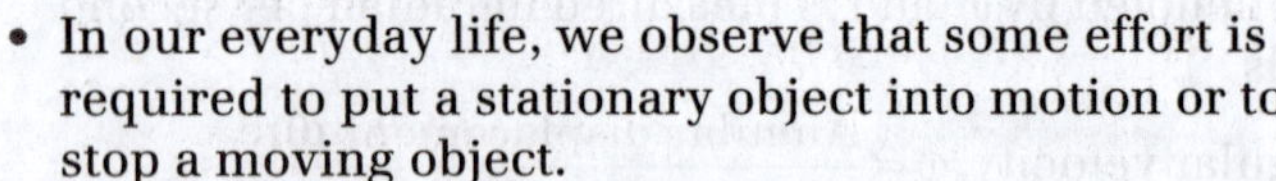

- In our everyday life, we observe that some effort is required to put a stationary object into motion or to stop a moving object.
- To move an object, it has to be pushed or pulled. The name of this pull or push is force.

Force

- The motion imparted to an object was due to the action of a force. It is an external effort in the form of pushing, pulling, stretching, compressing etc, which may move an object from rest or stop a moving object. It has a magnitude and a direction i.e., it is a **vector quantity**.
- The SI unit of force is newton (N) and CGS unit is dyne.

$$1 \text{ newton} = 1 \text{ kg-ms}^{-2}$$

Effect of Force

A force applied on an object can produce four types of effects such as :

- Force can start or stop a motion.
- Force can change the speed of an object, making it to move slower or faster.
- Force can change the direction of motion of an object.
- Force may bring about a change in the shape of an object.

Types of Forces

Forces are of following types :

Contact Forces

The force which arises due to the contact between two surfaces, is called a contact force. e.g. Muscular force, friction force etc.

1. **Muscular Force** Generally, to apply a force on an object, our body has to be in contact with the object. The force resulting due to the action of muscles is known as the muscular force.
   Animals also make use of muscular force to carry out their physical activities and other tasks.
2. **Friction Force** The force which oppose (impending or actual) relative motion between two surface in contact is called frictional force.

Non-Contact Forces

The force experienced by two objects without even touching each other, is called non-contact force. e.g. Magnetic force, electrostatic force, gravitational force etc.

1. **Magnetic Force** Like poles of two magnets repel each other and unlike poles attract each other. Attraction or repulsion between objects is an example of non-contact force. A magnet can exert a force on another magnet without being in contact with it.

2. **Electrostatic Force** The force exerted by a charged body on another charged or uncharged body is known as **electrostatic force**. This force comes into play even when the bodies are not in contact.
3. **Gravitational Force** Objects or things fall towards the earth because it pulls them. This force is called **gravity**. Every object in the universe, whether small or large, exerts a force on every other object. This force is known as the gravitational force. This is an attractive force. Water in rivers flows downward due to the force of gravity.

Nuclear Force

- The force that acts between the protons and neutrons of atom is called **nuclear force**.
- It is the fundamental force of nature that holds protons and neutrons together in the atomic nucleus. Nuclear force is the strongest force in nature.

Balanced Forces

- If a body is pulled from both side with equal force, the body will not move. Such forces are called **balanced force**. They do not change the state of rest or of motion of an object.
- For example, in a tug of war, when both the teams apply similar force from both sides, rope does not move either side, i.e., resultant force is zero. Hence, it is a balanced force.

Unbalanced Forces

- Two opposite forces of different magnitudes pull a body. In this case, the body would begin to move in the direction of the greater force. Thus, the two forces are not balanced. Such forces are called unbalanced force.
- An **unbalanced force** acting on an object brings it in motion. Thus, to accelerate the motion of an object, an unbalanced force is required.
- For example, in a tug of war, when one of the teams suddenly releases the rope, then an unbalanced force acts on the other team, due to which it falls backward.

Conservative and Non-Conservative Forces

- **Conservative Forces** A force is said to be conservative, if the work done by the force (or against the force) in moving a body depends only upon the initial and final position of the body. It is independent of the path followed between the initial and final positions.
  e.g. Electrostatic force, gravitational force, elastic force, magnetic force, etc and all the central forces are conservative in nature.
- **Non-conservative Forces** A force is said to be non-conservative, if the work done by the force (or against the force) in moving a body from one position to another, depends upon the path followed between the two positions.
  e.g. Frictional force, viscous force, air drag, etc.

Inertia

- The natural tendency of an object to resist a change in their state of rest or uniform motion along a straight line is called inertia of the object.
- It is the inherent property of all the objects. A moving body keeps moving not because of its inertia but only because of the absence of a force to slow it down, change its state or speed it up.

Inertia is divided into three types as given below :

1. Inertia of Rest

The tendency of a body to resist (oppose) any change in its state of rest is known as **inertia of rest**.

Examples

- A person standing in a bus falls backward when bus starts moving suddenly.
- This is because the fact of the person, which are in contact of the floor of the bus, starts moving but because of inertia, the upper part of the body tends to remain at rest. Hence, the person leans backwards.
- The carpet is beaten with a stick to remove the dust particle.
- By beating the carpet, it comes into the state of motion but the dust particles inside the carpet remains in the state of rest. As a result, they are fallen down.
- When a tree is vigorously shaken, then some of the leaves fall from the tree, this is because of the property of inertia of the leaves.
- Shaking of tree changes its state from rest to motion, but the leaves of the tree still remain in the state of rest. Hence, some leaves fall down from the tree.

2. Inertia of Motion

The tendency of a body to resist (oppose) any change in its state of uniform motion is known as **inertia of motion**.

Examples

- When a bus or train stops suddenly, a person sitting inside tends to fall forward. This is because lower part of his body comes to rest with the bus or train, but the upper part of his body tends to continue its motion, due to inertia of motion.

- A person jumping out of a speeding train may fall forward. This is because on jumping, his feet come to rest as they touch the ground. But his remaining body continues to move forward due to inertia of motion.
- A luggage is usually tied with a rope on the roof of a bus so that it doesn't fall down due to inertia of motion.

3. Inertia of Direction

The tendency of a body to oppose any change in its direction of motion is known as inertia of direction.

Examples

- When a car rounds a curve suddenly, a person sitting inside is thrown outwards. This is because when the car turns, the person tries to maintain his original direction of motion due to inertia of direction.
- When a vehicle passes through mud, the rotating wheels of the vehicle throw out mud due to directional inertia. The mud guards are used over the wheels for protecting the clothes of driver from the mud.
- A stone tied on string is whirling in a horizontal circle. If the string breaks, then the stone flies away tangentially. This is because once the stone is released, it continues to move along the direction it has been moving at that instant due to directional inertia.

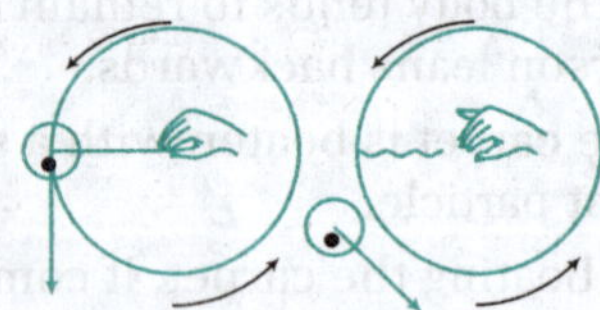

- When a knife is sharpened by pressing it against a grinding stone, the sparks fly off along the tangent to the grinding stone, on account of directional inertia.

Inertia and Mass

Inertia of an object is measured by its mass. It is directly proportional to the mass. It means that inertia increases with increase in mass and decreases with decrease in mass. A heavy object will have more inertia than the lighter one.

For example, it is easier to push an empty box than to push a box full of books. The box full of books has larger mass and hence, greater inertia as compared to the empty box.

Newton's Laws of Motion

Newton formulated three fundamental laws that govern the motion of objects, which are given below :

1. Newton's First Law of Motion

It states that, everybody continue to be in its state of rest or of uniform motion in a straight line unless compelled by some external force to act otherwise.

Note Newton's First Law of Motion is also known as the **Law of Inertia** or **Law of Galileo**.

Common Examples based on Newton's First Law of Motion

- Safety belts are worn to prevent injury that caused due to the impact or collision from the application of sudden brakes in vehicles.
- Only the carrom coin at the bottom of a pile is removed when a fast moving carrom coin (or striker) hits it.
- A card with a coin is placed on tumbler. When the card is flicked with the finger, the coin placed over it, falls in the tumbler.

Momentum

- The impact of motion produced by objects depends on their mass and velocity. Thus, the product of mass m of the object and velocity v of the object is called momentum p, i.e.,

$$p = m \times v$$

- Momentum is a vector quantity. Its direction is the same as the direction of velocity. The SI unit of momentum is kg-ms^{-1}.

Common Examples Based on Momentum

- Suppose a light weight vehicle (say, a car) and a heavy weight vehicle (say a truck) are parked on a horizontal road. We all know that a much greater force is required to push the truck than the car to bring them to the same speed in same time.
- Also, a greater opposing force is required to stop the truck than the car at the same time if they are moving with the same speed.
- If two stones, one is light and other is heavy, are dropped from the top of a building, a person on the ground will find it easier to catch the light stone than the heavy one. The mass of a body is thus, an important parameter that determines the effect of force on its motion.

2. Newton's Second Law of Motion

- According to this law, the rate of change of momentum of an object is proportional to the applied force and take place in the direction in which the force acts. i.e.,

$$F \propto \frac{\Delta p}{\Delta t}$$

where, Δp = change in momentum,
and Δt = change in time.

- If a body of mass m moving at initial velocity u accelerates uniformly with acceleration a for time t, so that its final velocity changes to v, then according to second law of motion,

$$F \propto \frac{\text{change in momentum}}{\text{time}}$$

$$F \propto \frac{mv - mu}{t} = \frac{m(v-u)}{t}$$

$$\Rightarrow \quad F = kma \qquad \left[\because \frac{v-u}{t} = a\right]$$

$$\therefore \quad F = ma \qquad [\because k = 1]$$

Hence, the force acting on the body is the product of mass and acceleration of the body.

Common Examples of Newton's Second Law of Motion

- **Hurting by a cricket ball not table tennis ball** During the game of table tennis if the ball hits a player, it does not hurt him. On the other hand, when a fast moving cricket ball hits a spectator, it may hurt him because the speed of cricket ball is higher due to which its acceleration is also higher.
- **Falling on Sand Bed in High Jump** In a high jump athletic event, the athletes are made to fall either on a cushioned bed or on a sand bed. This is to increase the time of the athlete's fall to stop after making the jump. This decreases the rate of change of momentum and hence the force.
- **Moving of hands backwards while catching a ball by a cricketer** A cricket player moves his hand backwards on catching a fast cricket ball, because the cricket player increases the time during which the high velocity of moving ball decreases to zero. Thus, the acceleration of the ball is decreased and therefore, the impact of catching the fast moving ball is also reduced.

  If the ball is stopped suddenly then its high velocity decreases to zero in a very short interval of time. Thus, the rate of change of momentum of the ball will be large. Therefore, a large force would have to be applied for holding the catch that may hurt the palm of the player.

Impulse

- The product of force and short time interval which is equal to change in momentum is called an impulse.

  Impulse = force × time duration = change in momentum
- According to Newton's second law, $F = ma$

$$F = \frac{m(v-u)}{t}$$

$$\Rightarrow \quad F = \frac{mv - mu}{t} \Rightarrow Ft = mv - mu$$

Impulse, $I = Ft = \Delta p$

or Impulse = Change in momentum of the body

The SI unit of impulse is N-s or kg-ms^{-1}.

Common Examples based on Impulse

- **Chinawares wrapped in Paper or Straw Pieces** Chinawares are wrapped in paper or straw pieces while packing. In the event of fall, impact will take a longer time to reach the glass/Chinawares through paper or straw.
- Due to reduce the force on the Chinawares if they fall. It also reduces their chances of breaking.
- **Use of Buffers in Bogies** Bogies of a train are provided with the buffers, due to which they avoid severe jerks during shunting of the train. The presence of buffer increases the time of impact, so force during jerks decreases, hence the chances of damage decrease.
- **Finishing of fast Race slowly by an athlete** An athlete is advised to come to stop slowly after finishing a fast race, so that time to stop increases and hence force experienced by him decreases.
- **Receiving Jerk and Shocks on Uneven Road** When a vehicle moves over an uneven road, it receives jerk or shock. So the vehicle receives the impulsive force. To minimise this impact shock absorbers are used because they increase the time of jerk, thereby reducing the impulsive force.

3. Newton's Third Law of Motion

- It states that, whenever one object exerts a force on another object, then the second object instantaneously exerts an equal and opposite force back on the first object, i.e., to every action, there is a equal and opposite reaction.

Note Force always occurs in pairs. Force on a body *A* by *B* is equal and opposite to the force on the body *B* by *A*.

Common Examples based on Newton's Third Law of Motion

- **Collision of Two Persons** When two persons walking or running in opposite direction collide with each other, then both feel hurt because they apply force to each other. Two opposing forces are in action and reaction pair.
- **Walking of a Person** A person is able to walk because of the Newton's third law of motion. During walking, a person pushes the ground in backward direction and in the reaction, the ground also pushes the person with equal magnitude of force but in opposite direction. This enables him to move in forward direction against the push.
- **Recoil of Gun** When bullet is fired from a gun, then the bullet also pushes the gun in opposite direction with equal magnitude of force. Since, the gun has a greater mass than bullet, acceleration of the gun is much less than the acceleration of the bullet.

- **Propulsion of a Boat in Forward Direction** Sailor pushes water with oar in backward direction resulting water to push the oar in forward direction. Consequently, the boat is pushed in forward direction. Forces applied by oar and water are of equal magnitude but in opposite directions.
- **Rocket Propulsion** The propulsion of rocket is based on the principle of action and reaction. The rapid burning fuel rush out from the nozzle at the rear end at a very high speed. The equal and opposite reaction force moves the rocket upward at a great speed.

Law of Conservation of Linear Momentum

- According to this law, the total momentum of a system of objects remains conserved before and after their interaction or collision provided no other external unbalanced force acting on them.
- Consider a system of two objects of masses m_A and m_B moving with initial velocities u_A and u_B, respectively in the same direction. After collision, they move with velocities v_A and v_B respectively. Then, according to law of conservation of momentum,

  Total momentum before collision
  = Total momentum after collision

  $$m_A u_A + m_B u_B = m_A v_A + m_B v_B$$

  Thus, the total momentum of two objects is unchanged or conserved before and after the collision.

Common Examples Based on Law of Conservation of Linear Momentum

- **Hold the gun tight while firing** While firing a bullet, the gun should be held tight to the shoulder, due to recoil of the gun.
- **Jumping to the shore from a boat** When a man jumps out of a boat to the shore, then the boat slightly moves away from the shore to conserve the momentum.
- **Rocket propulsion** It is an example of conservation of momentum in which large backward momentum of the injected gases gives an equal forward momentum to the rocket. Due to decrease in mass of fuel, the acceleration of the rocket increases.
- **Showing of object in opposite direction by an astronaut** An astronaut in open space, who wants to return to the spaceship, throws some object in the direction opposite to the direction of motion of the spaceship.

Friction

A force which opposes (impending or actual) relative motion between two surfaces in contact. This opposing force is called friction. It is the component of the contact force along the common tangent to the surface in contact.

Reasons of Friction

There are two reasons of friction as follows :

1. First Reason : Irregularities of Planes

- Friction is caused by the irregularities on the two surfaces in contact. Even those surfaces which appear very smooth have a large number of minute irregularities on them. Irregularities on the two surfaces lock into one another.
- When we attempt to move any surface, we have to apply a force to overcome interlocking. On rough surfaces, there are a larger number of irregularities. So, the force of friction is greater if a rough surface is involved.

Limitations of First Reason

According to this reason :

- Larger the area of contact between the surfaces, greater should be the force of friction between them. However, experiments show that force of friction between any two surfaces in contact is independent of the actual area of contact between them.
- When surfaces in contact are extra smooth, force of friction between them should almost vanish. However, it is found that force of friction increases when surfaces in contact are extra smooth.

2. Second Reason : Molecular Forces

- It arises on account of strong atomic or molecular forces of attraction between the two surfaces at the points of actual contact.
- When an object A is placed over another object B then due to irregularities in their surfaces actual contact takes place only at few points.
- These areas are roughly in the ratio $1:10^4$. At the contact points, the molecules of the two surfaces are so close together that they exert very strong intermolecular forces of adhesion on one another.
- As actual area of contact is very small, therefore, the adhesive pressure (force per unit area) at the points of contact becomes too large, that many of the contact points may deform plastically and become 'Cold welded' together.
- When one body tries to move over the other, it involves rupturing of thousands of such tiny cold welds. This gives rise to opposing force of friction.

Note That the tiny cold welds reform continuously as chance of contacts are made.

Limitations of the Reason

According to this reason :

- Frictional force will be independent of the area of contact.
- This is because with increase in area of contact, force of adhesion also increases (in the same ratio), but the adhesive pressure (i.e. force per unit area) responsible for friction, remains the same.
- When the surfaces in contact are extra smooth, distance between the molecules of the surfaces in contact decrease, increasing that adhesive force between them. Therefore, the adhesive pressure and the force of friction increase.

Types of Friction

According to the state of motion of object, friction is divided into three types :

1. **Static Friction** Static friction is a self-adjusting force because it comes into play when the body is lying over the surface of another body without any motion.
2. **Limiting Friction** Maximum force of static friction which comes into play when a body just starts moving over the surface of another body is called limiting friction. If we have not applied any force on a body to move the body, the frictional force also becomes zero. If we start applying force, the frictional force also starts increasing.

   This happens until the applied force is less than the limiting frictional force.
3. **Kinetic or Dynamic Friction** When a body moves over the other body, then the force of friction acting between two surfaces in contact in relative motion is called kinetic friction.

   Kinetic friction is of two types :

   (i) **Sliding Friction** The force of friction that acts between two sliding bodies is called sliding friction.

   For example, a child sliding down through a slide in a park, the frame and the edge of the door sliding against one another etc. In most cases sliding, friction is less than static friction.

   (ii) **Rolling Friction** When one body rolls over the surface of another body, the resistance to its motion is called rolling friction. Rolling reduces friction.

   It is always easier to roll than to slide a body over another. That's why rolling friction is always less than the static friction.

Advantages of Friction

- Friction helps in walking, turning and stopping, without friction it is difficult to walk. Friction provides a force in backward direction that helps in moving forward.
- A nail is fixed in the wall due to friction.
- If there is no friction between the tyres of the automobiles and the road, they could not be started or stopped or turned to change the direction of motion.
- Wearing of cap, ring and belt is only possible because of friction.
- We can write using pens because of the friction between the nib of the pen and paper.

Disadvantages of Friction

- Friction wears out the materials whether they are screws, ball bearings or soles of shoes.
- Friction produces unwanted heat in machines, and hence, reduces the overall efficiency of the machines. It opposes the motion of objects, hence more energy is needed to overcome friction.

Methods of Reducing Friction

There are different methods to reduce friction as follows :

- **By Polishing** A rough surface have a large number of irregularities which increase the friction, so by polishing the surface, we can reduce the value of friction.
- **By Lubricants** When oil, grease or graphite between the moving parts of a machine, a thin layer is formed there and moving surfaces do not directly rub against each other. These substances act as a lubricant in reducing friction.
- **By Using Suitable Materials** Friction acts between the two surfaces, so it depends on the nature of material of the two surfaces. Hence, by using suitable materials, we can reduce the friction. For example, friction between rubber and concrete is less, that's why tyres are made up of rubber.
- **By Using Ball Bearing** Use of ball bearing between two moving parts of a machine. Since, the rolling friction between ball bearing and the surface in contact is very small, power dissipation is reduced.

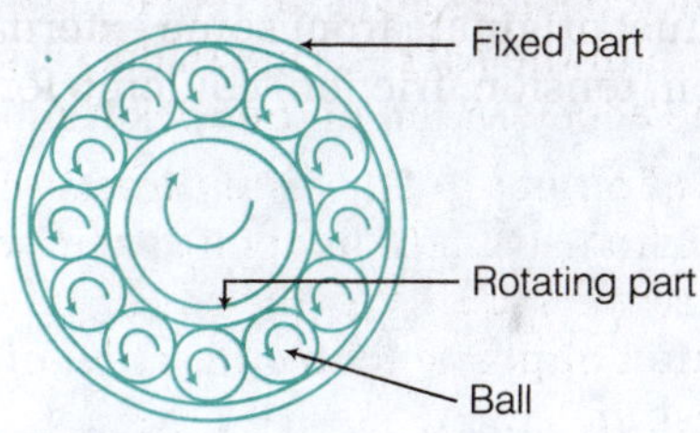

Fluid Friction

- The common name of gases and liquids is fluids, so the force of friction that is exerted by fluids is called fluid friction or drag. The fluid friction depends on the speed of object with respect to the fluid and also depends on the shape and nature of the object.
- When objects move through fluids, they have to overcome friction acting on them, in this process they lose energy. Therefore, the objects are given special shapes. Hence, all vehicles are designed to have shapes which reduce fluid friction.

Methods of Increasing Friction

There are different methods to increase friction as follows :

- **By Making the Surface Rough** To increase friction, surface have to be made rough by increasing the surface irregularities. For example, soles of shoes are grooved for increasing friction. Similarly, the treaded tyres of cars, trucks and bulldozers provide better grip with the ground.
- **By Pressing Harder** When the two surfaces in contact are pressed harder, the value of friction increases.
  For example, when brake lever is pressed, the pads arrest the motion of the rim due to friction and the wheel stops moving.
- **By Use of Adhesive Materials** Use of adhesive materials that stick surfaces, also increases friction between them.
  For example, kabaddi players rub their hands with soil for a better grip of their opponents and gymnasts apply some coarse substance on their hands to increase friction for better grip.

Centripetal Force

Acceleration of a body moving in a circular path of radius R with uniform speed v is $\frac{v^2}{R}$ which is directed towards the centre. According to the second law, the force f_c providing this acceleration is

$$f_c = \frac{mv^2}{R} \quad \left[\because a = \frac{v^2}{R}, \text{centripetal acceleration} \right]$$

where, m is the mass of the body. This force directed forward the centre is called the centripetal force.

This force must originate from some external source such as gravitation, tension, friction, coulomb force etc.

Examples Based on Centripetal Force

Some examples based on centripetal force are as follows :

Motion on a Level Circular Road

- When a vehicle goes round a level curved path, it should be acted upon by a centripetal force. While negotiating the curved path, the wheels of the car have a tendency to leave the curved path and regain the straight line path. Frictional force between the tyres and the road opposes this tendency of the wheels.
- This frictional force acts towards the centre of the circular path and provides the necessary centripetal force. If this friction force cannot provide necessary centripetal force then the car skid or overturned.

Banking of Curved Roads and Tracks

- When a car goes round a level curve, the friction force provides the necessary centripetal force. If this force is not enough to necessary centripetal force, the car will skid.
- In order to avoid skidding, while going round a curved path the outer edge of the road is raised above the level of the inner edge. This is known as banking of curved roads or tracks.
  A cyclist has to bend slightly towards the centre of the circular track in order to take a safe turn without slipping.

Circular Motion in Nature

- The earth revolves around the sun in a circular motion, as we know that centripetal force is required for revolving of objects in a circular path.
- The necessary centripetal force is provided by gravitational pull of sun on the earth.
- Similarly, for the motion of moon around the earth, the necessary centripetal force is provided by gravitational pull of the earth on the moon.

Circular Motion in Atom

- In the atom, the charge of the nucleus is positive and the charge of the electron is negative. There exists an electrostatic force between the positive nucleus and negative electrons.
- This electrostatic force supplies the necessary centripetal force for revolving of electrons around the nucleus.

Centrifugal Force

- If an object is moving in a circular motion with uniform speed, it experiences an outward force, then this force is called the centrifugal force.
- In other words, we can say that centrifugal force is a pseudo force in a circular motion which acts along the radius and is directed away from the centre of the circle.
- It only comes into play when changing our reference frame from a ground/inertial to a rotating reference frame.

Apparatus Based on Centrifugal Force

Some apparatus based on centrifugal force are as follows:

Centrifuge

- Centrifuge is a device used to separate the particles of different masses present in a liquid. For example, when milk is churned, the cream is separated from it due to centrifugal force because this force acts in the outward direction and heavier particles in milk experience more force than the lighter particles.
- The heavier milk particles move towards the circumference. Hence, cream (lighter particles) is obtained from the inner part of the vessel and the milk from the outer part.
- Similarly, in blood test, the centrifuge spins the blood and separates the red blood cells, platelets and plasma because of their density difference.

Dryer of Washing Machine

- It is a long and perpendicular cylindrical drum, with holes in its walls.
- Wet cloths are placed inside this drum.
- The drum connected to a electrical motor, which rotates the drum with high speed.
- The principle behind this spinning drum of washing machine is centrifugal force.
- The fast spinning of the wet clothes in the drum creates a large centripetal force from the centre to the edge of the drum on the water molecules.
- The wet clothes are flung outwards to the drum edge and the water escapes through the drum holes.

04

Work, Energy and Power

[SOURCES]

Class-IX NCERT Chap 10 (Work and Energy), Class-X Old NCERT Chap 14 (Sources of Energy), Class-XI NCERT Chap 5 (Work, Energy and Power)

- In daily life, we generally use the terms work, energy and power.
- A farmer ploughing the field, a construction worker carrying bricks, a student studying for a competitive examination, all are said to be working.
- According to physics, work is said to be done by a force, when the body is displaced actually through some distance in the direction of the applied force.

Work

Work is said to be done, if on applying a force on an object, it is displaced from its position in the direction of force.

Scientific Conception of Work

- From the scientific point of view, the following two conditions need to be satisfied for work to be done :
  (i) A force should act on an object.
  (ii) The object must be displaced.
- If any one of the above conditions does not exist, then work is not done.

Work Done by a Constant Force

Work done by a force on an object is equal to the magnitude of the force multiplied by the distance moved in the direction of force i.e.,

Work done = Force × Displacement in the direction of force

or $W = F \times s$

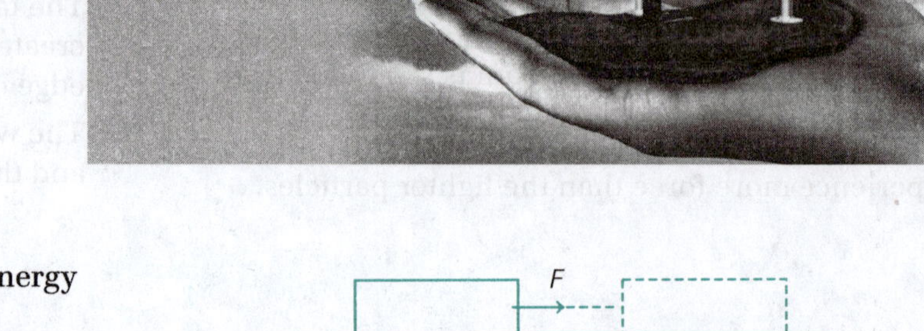

Displacement (s) in the direction of force

- If a force F acting on an object makes an angle θ with horizontal and displaces by s, then
  Work done $= \mathrm{F} \cdot \mathrm{s} = Fs\cos\theta$

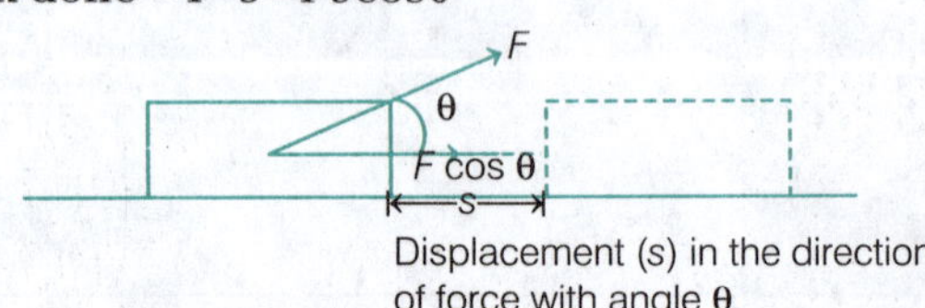

Displacement (s) in the direction of force with angle θ

Units of Work

- The SI unit of work is newton-metre (N-m) which is also called **joule** (J).
  $\because \quad W = F \times s$
  $\therefore \quad 1\ \mathrm{J} = 1\ \mathrm{N} \times 1\ \mathrm{m} = \mathrm{N\text{-}m}$
  Thus, 1 joule is the amount of work done on an object when a force of 1 N displaces it by 1 m along the line of action of the force.
- Work is a scalar quantity. The CGS unit of work is **erg**.

Alternative Units of Work/Energy in Joule

1 erg	10^{-7} J
1 electron volt (eV)	1.6×10^{-19} J
1 calorie	4.186 J
1 kilowatt hour (kWh)	3.6×10^{6} J

Types of Work

Depending on the values of the angle between force F and displacement s, there are three types of work :

1. Positive Work

If the angle between force and direction of displacement lies between 0° and 90°, then work done will be positive.

For example, when a load is lifted, then the lifting force and displacement act in the same direction. So, work done by the lifting force is positive.

2. Negative Work

If the angle between force and direction of displacement lies between 90° and 180°, then work done will be negative. For example, frictional force acts in the direction opposite to the direction of displacement, so work done by friction force will be negative.

3. Zero Work

- **When** $s = 0$, no work is done if the displacement is zero.

  For example, a weightlifter holds a heavy weight on his shoulder for a few seconds, then work done in this case is zero, since there is no displacement.
- **When** $F = 0$, no work is done if the force is zero.

  For example, an electron moving in empty space free of electromagnetic fields does no work as there is no force on it ($F = 0$).
- **When** $\theta = 90°$, the force and displacement are in perpendicular direction (angle between direction of force and displacement is 90°), work done is zero.

  For example, a coolie carrying load on his head. In this case, gravitational force is acting vertically downward (weight of load) and displacement is along horizontal direction, i.e. force and displacement are perpendicular to each other. So, in this case, work done by gravitational force is zero.

Energy

- The energy possessed by an object is thus measured in terms of its capacity of doing work. The unit of energy, is the same as that of work, that is joule (J). 1J is the energy required to do 1 joule of work.
- Sometimes a larger unit of energy called **kilojoule (kJ)** is used.
- 1kJ equals to 1000 J.

Various Forms of Energy

Some of the forms of energy are as follows :

- **Mechanical Energy** The sum of kinetic and potential energies is called as mechanical energy. Kinetic energy is due to motion while the potential energy is due to position or configuration.
- **Internal Energy** When the molecules of a body vibrate with respect to one another, the molecules possess potential energy due to their location against the intermolecular forces and possesses kinetic energy because of motion. The sum of these kinetic and potential energies of all the molecules constituting the body is called its internal energy.
- **Heat Energy** A body possesses heat energy due to the disorderly motion of its molecules. Heat energy is also related to the internal energy of the body. In winter, we generate heat by rubbing our hands against each other.
- **Chemical Energy** A stable chemical compound has lesser energy than its constituent atoms, the difference being in the arrangement and motion of electron in the compound. This difference is called chemical energy.

  If the total energy of the reactant is more than the product of the reaction, then heat is released and the reaction is said to be an **exothermic reaction.** If the reverse is true, then heat is absorbed and the reaction is **endothermic**.
- **Electrical Energy** Work is said to be done when electric charge moves from one point to another in an electric field or motion of a current carrying conductor inside a magnetic field. The energy is associated with an electric current. The flow of current causes bulbs to glow motor to run and electric heater to produce heat.
- **Nuclear Energy** When U^{235} nucleus breaks up into lighter nuclei on being bombarded by a slow neutron, a tremendous amount of energy is released. Thus, the energy so released is called nuclear energy and this phenomenon is known as **nuclear fission. Nuclear reactors** and **nuclear bombs** are the sources of nuclear energy.
- **Light Energy** The energy due to which things are clearly visible to us is known as light energy. e.g. Electric bulb, candle, etc.
- **Sound Energy** The energy possessed by vibrating objects and it produces the sensation of hearing is called sound energy.
- **Wind Energy** The energy possessed by the wind due to its high speed is called wind energy. This energy is used in wind mill, water pump, etc. Now a days, wind energy is used to generate electrical energy.
- **Hydro Energy** The form of energy obtained from running water is called hydro energy. This energy is used to generate electricity in hydroelectric power plants.

- **Bio-mass Energy** The energy obtained from the waste material of living things and dead plants and animals is called bio-mass energy. Methane gas is obtained from bio-mass energy.
- **Solar Energy** The energy radiated by the sun is called solar energy. Sun is the source of solar energy. Plants collect and store this energy to make food through photosynthesis.

Mass Energy Equivalence

- **Albert Einstein** discovered that mass can be converted into energy and *vice-versa*.
- He showed that mass and energy are equivalent and related by the relation

$$E = mc^2$$

where, c is the speed of light in vacuum, 3×10^8 m/s.

- According to Einstein's mass energy equivalence, the amount of energy associated with a kilogram of matter.

$$E = 1 \times (3 \times 10^8)^2 \text{ J or } E = 9 \times 10^{16} \text{ J}$$

This is equivalent to the annual electrical output of a large (3000 MW) power generating station.

Types of Mechanical Energy

Mechanical energy is of two types

1. Kinetic Energy

The energy which is possessed by an object due to its motion is called kinetic energy.

It is measured by the amount of work that the object can do against an opposing force before it comes to rest.

The kinetic energy possessed by an object of mass m, moving with a uniform velocity v is given by $E_K = \frac{1}{2}mv^2$

Its SI unit is joule (J) and it is always a positive quantity.

Examples of Kinetic Energy

- Due to kinetic energy, a bullet fired from a gun can pierce a target.
- The kinetic energy of a fast stream of water is used to run water mills.
- The kinetic energy of air is used to run wind mills.
- The kinetic energy of a hammer is used in driving a nail into a piece of wood.

2. Potential Energy

The energy possessed by a body due to its change in position or shape is called potential energy.

We can say that, the potential energy possessed by a body is the energy present in it by virtue of its position or configuration. Its SI unit is joule (J).

Examples of Potential Energy

- Water stored in dam has potential energy due to its position at the height.
- A stone lying on the roof of the building has potential energy due to its height.
- A wound spring of a watch has potential energy due to change of its shape.

Types of Potential Energy

Potential energy is mainly classified into the following types :

(i) **Gravitational Potential Energy** When an object is raised through a certain height above the ground, its energy increases. This is because work is done on it against gravity while it is being raised.

The energy present in such an object is the gravitational potential energy. The gravitational potential energy of an object at a point above the ground is defined as the work done in raising it from the ground to that point against gravity.

Gravitational potential energy, $U = mgh$

where, m = mass of the object

g = acceleration due to gravity

h = height of the object.

(ii) **Elastic Potential Energy** It is the potential energy associated with the state of compression or extension of an elastic or spring like object. The elastic potential energy is given by $U = \frac{1}{2}kx^2$ where, k is the spring constant and x is the displacement of the object.

Law of Conservation of Energy

- According to this law, energy can neither be created nor be destroyed, it can only be transformed from one form to another.
- The total energy before and after transformation, always remains constant. The law of conservation of energy is valid in all situations and for all kinds of transformation.

Transformation of Energy

One form of energy can be converted into other form of energy and this phenomenon is called transformation of energy. Its examples are as follows :

- **Preparation of Food by Green Plants** Green plants prepare their own food (stored in the form of chemical energy) by using solar energy through the process of photosynthesis.
- **Conversion of Muscular Energy into Kinetic energy** When we throw a ball, the muscular energy which is stored in our body; gets converted into kinetic energy of the ball.

- **Potential Energy in a Spring of Toy Car** The wound spring in the toy car possesses potential energy. As the spring is released its potential energy changes into kinetic energy due to which toy car moves.
- **Potential Energy in a Stretched Bow** In a stretched bow, potential energy is stored.
- As it is released, the potential energy of the stretched bow gets converted into the kinetic energy of arrow which moves in the forward direction with large velocity.

Some Energy Transformations

Instruments	Transformations
Electric motor	Electrical energy into mechanical energy
Electric generator	Mechanical energy into electrical energy
Steam engine	Heat energy into kinetic energy
Electric bulb	Electrical energy into light energy
Dry cell	Chemical energy into electrical energy
Solar cell	Light energy into electrical energy

Law of Conservation of Mechanical Energy

- The principle of conservation of mechanical energy states that if only the conservative forces are doing work on a body, then its total mechanical energy remains constant.
- Although, the kinetic energy and potential energy may change individually from one state of the system to another, but their sum or the total mechanical energy of the system remains constant under the conservative force.
- When an object is dropped from some height, its potential energy continuously converts into kinetic energy. When an object is thrown upwards, its kinetic energy continuously converts into potential energy.

Rate of Doing Work : Power

The rate of doing work or the rate at which energy is transferred or used or transformed to other form is called power. If work W is done in time t, then

$$\text{Power} = \frac{\text{Work}}{\text{Time}} \Rightarrow P = \frac{W}{t}$$

The unit of power is watt (W) in honour of James Watt. We express larger rate of energy transfer in kilowatt (kW).

$$1\ \text{W} = 1\ \text{Js}^{-1}$$

The bigger units of power are kilowatt (kW) and horse power (Hp).

$$1\ \text{kW} = 1000\ \text{W} = 1000\ \text{Js}^{-1} \Rightarrow 1\ \text{MW} = 10^6\ \text{W},$$

$$1\ \text{Hp (horse power)} = 746\ \text{W}$$

Commercial Unit of Energy

The unit joule is too small and hence, it is inconvenient to express large quantities of energy. Therefore, a bigger unit of energy is used. The commercial unit of electric energy is kilowatt-hour (kWh) or Board of Trade (BOT) unit. It is the amount of electric energy consumed by an appliance of power 1000 W in one hour.

$$1\ \text{kWh} = 1\ \text{kW} \times 1\ \text{h} = 1000\ \text{W} \times 3600\ \text{s}$$
$$= 1000\ \text{Js}^{-1} \times 3600\ \text{s}$$
$$1\ \text{kWh} = 3.6 \times 10^6\ \text{J}$$

The energy used in households, industries and commercial establishments is expressed in kilowatt-hour. The electrical energy used, is expressed in terms of units in our monthly bills.

Here, 1 unit = 1 kilowatt-hour.

Sources of Energy

Any system which is capable of providing energy in a convenient form at a steady rate over a long period of time is called source of energy.

Therefore, a good source of energy can be characterised by the following factors :

- It should do a large amount of work per unit volume or mass.
- It should be easily accessible.
- It should be easy to store and transport from the place of their production to consumers.
- It should be economical.

Conventional Sources of Energy

Conventional sources of energy are those sources of energy which have been accumulated in nature over a long time.

These sources cannot be quickly replaced and will be exhausted one day. These are also called **non-renewable sources of energy.**

For example, fossil fuels such as coal, petroleum, natural gas and fissionable materials.

Some important conventional sources are as follows :

Fossil Fuels

- There were remaining of prehistoric plants and animals which got buried deep inside the earth millions of years ago. They get changed into fuel due to excess of heat and high pressure inside the earth and hence, are known as fossil fuels.
- Coal, petroleum and natural gas are the most consumed fossil fuels.
  - **Coal** It is a naturally occurring material which is a mixture of carbon and compounds of carbon

containing hydrogen, nitrogen, oxygen and sulphur, It is used for heating purposes in home and industry.

- **Petroleum** It is a dark coloured, viscous and foul smelling crude oil. It is a mixture of several solid, liquid and gaseous hydrocarbons mixed with water, salt and earth particles. It is mainly used in vehicles.
- **Natural Gas** It is the cleanest burning fossil fuel as it gives off 50% of carbon dioxide released by coal and 25% less carbon dioxide than oil for the same amount of energy produced.

  It is lighter than air and is a mixture of methane (about 97%) and small quantities of ethane, propane and butane. It is used as domestic fuel and as fuel in thermal power plants to generate electricity.

  When natural gas in liquid form is subjected to high pressure, we get Compressed Natural Gas (CNG) which is used as fuel in vehicles like cars, buses and trucks.

Disadvantages of Fossil Fuels

- Burning of fossil fuels causes air pollution.
- Burning of fossil fuels releases acidic oxides which lead to acid rain which affects our water and soil resources.
- Greenhouse gases like CO_2 (carbon dioxide) are also released on burning of fossil fuels.
- Fossil fuels are not burnt completely. They leave ashes after burning.

Thermal Power Plant

- Large amount of fossil fuels are burnt everyday in power stations to heat up water to produce steam which further runs the turbine to generate electricity. The transmission of electricity is more efficient than transporting coal or petroleum over the same distance.
- Therefore, many thermal power plants are set up near coal or oil fields. The term 'thermal power plant' is used since fuel is burnt to produce heat energy which is converted into electrical energy.

Hydro Power Plants

- Another traditional source of energy is the kinetic energy of flowing water or the potential energy of water at a height.
- Hydro power plants convert the potential energy of falling water into electricity, which is known as hydroelectricity. Hydro power plants are associated with dams.

Principle of Generating Hydroelectricity

- In order to produce hydroelectricity, high-rise dams are constructed on the river to obstruct the flow of water and thereby collect water in larger reservoirs.
- The water level rises and in this process the kinetic energy of flowing water is converted into the potential energy of water stored behind the dam. The water from the high level in the dam is carried through pipes, to the turbine, at the bottom of the dam. This is connected to the electric generator.
- When the water turbine rotates, then the armature of generator also rotates rapidly and produces electricity.

Improvements in the Technology for using Conventional Sources of Energy

Technology can be improved by different uses of sources of energy.

Bio-mass

- The waste material of living things such as cattle dung and dead parts of plants which are used as a source of energy is called bio-mass. Wood and cow dung are popular bio-mass used in India.
- These fuels do not produce much heat on burning and produce a lot of smoke.
- Therefore, technological inputs are required to improve the efficiency of these fuels. Cow dung cakes are also used as fuels for domestic as well as industrial uses.

Charcoal

- It is obtained by heating the wood in the limited supply of air (destructive distillation of wood). During this process, water and volatile materials present in wood are removed and charcoal (a black mass) is left behind as the residue.
- Charcoal is a better fuel than wood because it burns without flames and is comparatively smokeless. It also has a higher heat generation efficiency.

Bio-gas

It is a mixture of methane (upto 75%), hydrogen sulphide, carbon dioxide and hydrogen.

It is produced by the decomposition of animal waste like animal dung or plant waste in the absence of oxygen. Since, the starting material is mainly cow dung, it is popularly known as **gobar gas**.

Bio-gas Plant

The set up used to produce bio-gas is known as bio-gas plant. This plant has a dome like structure built with bricks.

The main components of bio-gas plant are as follows :

- **Outlet chamber or overflow tank** It is an outlet to take out the left over slurry.
- This slurry is used as a manure as it is rich in nitrogenous compounds.
- **Mixing tank** In mixing tank, the mixture of animal dung and water is prepared called slurry. In mixing tank, it is fed into the digester.
- **Gas tank** Bio-gas is stored in this gas tank just above the digester tank from which it is drawn out through pipes for use.
- **Inlet chamber** It connects the mixing tank and the digester tank. It is having a slope to ensure smooth flow of slurry into the digester.
- **Digester tank** It is a sealed chamber in which there is no oxygen.
- Here, the anaerobic bacteria in the presence of water decompose or break down complex compounds of the cow dung slurry and bio-gas is formed. This process takes few days to complete.

Wind Energy

Moving air is called **wind.** The energy possessed by the wind is due to its high speed. The kinetic energy of wind is utilised for doing works like:

- Generating electricity.
- In water-lifting pump to pump out water from ground.
- Rotatory motion of wind mill is used to lift water from a well.

Note Denmark is called the country winds, more, then 25% of their electricity need are generated through wind mills has highest share in wind energy capacity.

Wind Mill

- It is a machine which works with the energy of blowing air or wind. It is a structure similar to a large electric fan that is erected at some height on a rigid support.
- When the blowing wind strikes across the blades of a wind mill. It exerts a force on them. Due to which the blades of the wind mill start rotating.
- This rotational motion of the blades can be used to drive a large number of machines like water pumps, flour mills and electric generators.
- Wind mill used for generating electricity is called **wind turbine** and the complete set up of generating electricity by using wind energy is called **wind generator.**

Wind Energy Farm

- For commercial purposes, a large number of wind mills are erected over a large area which is known as **wind energy farm.**
- The energy output of each wind mill in a farm is coupled together to get electricity on a commercial scale.

Non-Conventional Sources of Energy

With improved technological progress and increased demand, the conventional sources of energy are likely to be depleted soon. To cater the rising demand, keeping a balance with limited availability of conventional sources is important.

Non-conventional sources of energy are those sources of energy which are being produced continuously in nature and are inexhaustible.

These are also called **renewable** or **alternative source of energy.** e.g. Solar energy, wind energy, hydro energy, bio fuels (such as wood, bio-gas and alcohol), hydro energy from ocean (tidal energy, sea waves energy and ocean thermal energy).

Some non-conventional or alternative sources of energy are discussed below:

1. Solar Energy

- It is the energy obtained from the sun. The sun provides us heat and light. Only a small part of solar energy reaches the outer layer of the earth's atmosphere. Nearly half of it is absorbed, while passing through the atmosphere and rest reaches the earth's surface.
- It is estimated that during a year, India receives the energy equivalent to more than **5000 trillion kWh.** Here, the daily average varies from 4 to 7 kWh/m^2 under clear (cloudless) sky conditions.
- The advantages of solar energy are as given below :
  - It does not cause any pollution.
  - It is available in abundance in a hot country like ours.
  - Its harnessing cost is very less.
- The limitations of solar energy are as given below :
  - Energy reaching the surface is very much diffused, so direct utility is limited.
  - It is not available uniformly all the time and at all the places.
  - It is not available at night and on cloudy days.

Solar Constant

- The amount of solar energy received by the earth's surface of 1 m^2 area in one second is called solar constant.

Solar Energy Devices

- The various devices which are commonly used for harnessing sun's energy are called **solar energy devices**. e.g., Solar cooker, solar panel and solar cells.

Solar Cooker

- It is the device used to cook food by utilising the energy radiated by the sun. It consists of an insulated metal box or a wooden box which is painted black from inside. This is done so that it can absorb maximum solar radiations.
- The box has a thick glass sheet as a cover over the box. The reflector is a **plane mirror** which is attached to the box.
- Some solar cookers achieve a higher temperature by using concave mirrors to focus the rays of the Sun.

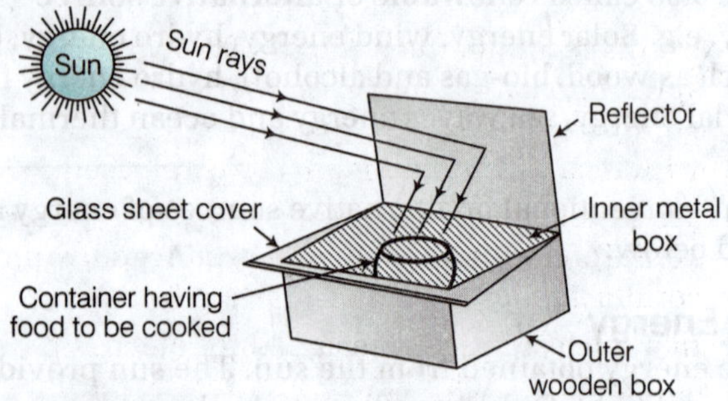

- The advantages of solar cooker are as follows :
  - It saves fuel.
  - It does not cause air pollution.
  - Since, the food is cooked slowly in the solar cooker, the nutrients do not get destroyed.
  - It can cook four food items at a time.
- The limitations of solar cooker are given below :
  - It cannot be used to cook food on cloudy days and during night.
  - It cannot be used to cook chappaties and for frying.
  - The direction of solar cooker has to be changed from time to time to enable it to keep facing the sun.

Solar Cell

- It is a device which converts **solar energy** into **electrical energy.**
- These cells are made of silicon. It has the advantage that it is environment friendly and is also available in abundance. But availability of special grade silicon for making solar cell is limited.
- Solar cells have no moving parts and requires little maintenance.
- They work without the use of any focussing device. This is main advantage of solar cells.
- These can be set up in remote and inaccessible places easily; where laying of power transmission is expensive and not commercially viable.
- The uses of solar cells are as follows :
  - It is used for many scientific and technological applications.
  - It provides electricity in artificial satellites and space probes like Mars orbiters.
  - It is used for street lighting, traffic signals, operating water pumps, etc.
  - It provides radio and TV transmission to remote areas.
  - Calculators and many toys are fitted with solar cells.

Solar Panel

- The arrangement where many solar cells are arranged side by side, connected with each other is called **solar cell panel.**
- They are arranged in such a way that the total potential difference and the total capacity to provide electric current is much increased.
- It provides a much higher power for many practical uses.
- The entire process of manufacturing is still very expensive. Silver used for interconnection of the cells in the panel further adds to the cost.

2. Energy from the Sea

Sea acts as a **renewable source** of energy. The energy from sea is available in different forms. These are explained as below :

Tidal Energy

- Due to the gravitational attraction between moon and earth, sea water level rises and falls. This phenomenon is called high and low tides and the difference in sea-levels gives us tidal energy.
- Energy possessed by rising and falling water tides is known as **tidal energy.**
- The tidal waves in the sea build up and recede (rise and fall) twice a day.
- The enormous movement of water between the high tides and low tides provides a very large source of energy in the coastal areas of the world.
- The tidal energy can be harnessed by constructing a **tidal dam** across a narrow opening to the sea.

Wave Energy

- The waves are generated by strong wind blowing across the sea. The kinetic energy possessed by huge waves near the sea-shore can be trapped to genetic electricity.
- Wave energy would be a viable preposition only, where waves are very strong. This energy, with the help of various devices can be used to rotate the turbine of generator and electricity is generated.

Ocean Thermal Energy

- The water at the surface of the sea or ocean is heated by the sun, while the water in deeper sections is relatively cold.
- This difference in temperature is exploited to obtain energy and is known as **Ocean thermal energy.**
- The devices used to harness this form of ocean energy are known as **Ocean Thermal Energy Conversion** (OTEC) power plants.
- These power plants can operate, if the temperature difference between the surface water and water at depths upto 2 km is 293K (20 °C) or more.
- The warm surface water is used to boil a volatile liquid like ammonia. The vapours of the liquid are then used to run the turbine of the generator.
- The cold water from the depths of the oceans is used to condense vapour again to liquid.
- The energy potential from the sea (tidal energy, wave energy and ocean thermal energy) is quite large, but efficient commercial exploitation is difficult.

3. Geothermal Energy

- The heat from interior of the earth can be utilised as a source of energy.
- This can be done under certain favourable conditions that are created by natural processes. This is known as **Geothermal energy.**
- Molten rocks formed in the deeper hot regions of the earth's crust are pushed upward and trapped in certain regions due to geological changes. These spots are called **hot spots.**
- When underground water comes in contact with these hot spots, gets converted into **steam** due to heat of **molten rocks** (magma).
- Sometimes hot water from that region finds outtels at the surface. Such outtels are known as hot springs. The steam trapped in rocks is routed through a pipe to a turbine and used to generate electricity.
- The cost of production would not be much but there are very few commercially viable sites, where such energy can be exploited.
- There are a number of operational power plants based on geothermal energy in New Zealand and United States of America.

4. Nuclear Energy

Energy contained in the nucleus of atom is called **nuclear energy.**

It is released during a nuclear reaction. A reaction in which composition of the reacting nuclei changes to form new elements with a simultaneous release of large amount of energy is called a **nuclear reaction.**

Nuclear reactions occur in the following two ways:

Nuclear Fission

- In this reaction, the nucleus of a heavy atom splits into two or more smaller nuclei. It is bombarded with low energy neutrons due to which large amount of energy is released.
- The fission of an atom of uranium, e.g. produces 10 million times, the energy produced by the combustion of an atom of carbon from coal.
- In a nuclear reactor designed for electric power generation, such nuclear fuel can be part of a self- sustaining fission chain reaction. They release energy at a controlled rate.

Energy Released in Fission Reactions

In all fission reactions, a small quantity of matter is lost. This lost matter gets converted into energy which is released in any nuclear fission reaction.

The energy E obtained due to loss of matter of mass Δm is given by the famous Einstein's equation in 1905,

$$E = \Delta mc^2$$

where, $c = \text{velocity of light} = 3 \times 10^8 \text{ m/s}$

Note Nuclear power reactors located at Tarapur (Maharashtra), Rana Pratap Sagar (Rajasthan), Kalpakkam (Tamil Nadu), Narora (UP), Kakrapar (Gujarat) and Kaiga (Karnataka) have the installed capacity of less than 3% of the total electricity generation capacity of our country. However, many industrialised countries are meeting more than 30% of their electrical power needs from nuclear reactors.

Nuclear Fusion

- A reaction in which two or more lighter nuclei fuse to form a heavy nucleus and large amount of energy is released is called **nuclear fusion reaction.**
- Conditions for fusion reaction to take place are as given below :
  - High temperature (~4-15 million kelvin)
  - High pressure (~1 million atmosphere)

As these reactions require a very high temperature, therefore, they are called **thermo nuclear reactions.**

Hydrogen Bomb

- The hydrogen bomb is based on **thermonuclear fusion reaction.**
- A nuclear bomb based on the fission of uranium or plutonium is placed at the core of the hydrogen bomb.
- This nuclear bomb is embedded in a substance which contains deuterium and lithium.
- When the nuclear bomb (based on fission) is detonated, then the temperature of this substance is raised to $\mathbf{10^7}$ **K** in a few microseconds.
- The high temperature generates sufficient energy for the light nuclei to fuse and a devastating amount of energy is released.

Environmental Consequences

- We have seen that the exploitation of any energy source causes harm to the environment and its balance. However, the degree of damage caused by the **non-conventional sources** of energy is very less as compared to **fossil fuels.**
- Hence, it becomes the moral responsibility of every common man on the earth to look upto the cleanest possible sources of energy.
- The environmental consequences of the increasing demand for energy are as follows :
  - The combustion of fossil fuels is producing acid rain and damaging plants (crops), soil and aquatic life.
  - The burning of fossil fuels is increasing the amount of greenhouse gas like carbon dioxide in the atmosphere.
  - The cutting down of trees from the forest (deforestation) for obtaining fire-wood is causing soil erosion and destroying wildlife.
  - The construction of hydro power plants is disturbing ecological balance.
  - Nuclear power plants are increasing radioactivity in the environment.

Gravitation

[SOURCES]

Class-IX NCERT Chap 9 (Gravitation),
Class-XI Old NCERT Chap 8 (Gravitation)

- When an object dropped from a height falls towards the earth. All the planets go around the sun. The moon go around the earth, in all these cases, the same force is acting on the objects, the planets and on the moon.
- Newton generalised this idea and said that not only the earth but every object in the universe attracts every other object.
- The force of attraction between any two bodies in the universe is called the **force of gravitation or gravitational force**.
- The force with which the earth pulls the objects towards its centre is called the **Gravitational force of the earth** or **Gravity of the earth.**

Universal Law of Gravitation

- According to this law, every object in the universe attracts every other object with a force which is proportional to the product of their masses and inversely proportional to the square of the distance between them.
- Consider two bodies A and B having masses m_1 and m_2 lie at a distance r from each other. Then, the gravitational force F is given by

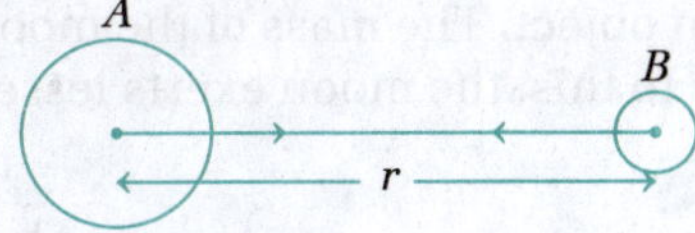

$$F \propto \frac{m_1 m_2}{r^2}$$

or $$F = \frac{G m_1 m_2}{r^2}$$

where, $G = 6.67 \times 10^{-11}$ N-m^2/kg^2 is the constant of proportionality and is called the universal gravitational constant.

The value of G does not depend on the medium between the two bodies and the masses of the bodies or the distance between them.

The SI unit of G is N-m^2/kg^2.

- The value of G was found out by **Henry Cavendish** (1731-1810) by using a sensitive balance.
- The universal gravitational constant defined as the gravitational force between two object of unit masses and separated by a unit distance from each other placed any where in space.
- If distance gets bigger by a factor of force becomes $\frac{1}{36}$th times smaller.

Importance of Universal Law of Gravitation

The universal law of gravitation successfully explained by several phenomena given as below :

- The force that binds us to the earth.

- The motion of the moon around the earth.
- The motion of planets around the sun.
- The occurrence tides is due to the gravitational force of attraction of moon.
- The flow of water in rivers is also due to gravitational force of the earth on water.

Gravity and Free Fall

- Gravity is the force of attraction between the earth and any object lying on or near earth surface and is also called **earth's gravitational pull.** For example, a body thrown up falls back on the surface of the earth due to earth's force of gravity.
- When objects fall towards the earth under the influence of earth's gravitational force alone, then these are called freely falling objects and such motion is called **free fall.**

Acceleration due to Gravity

- When a body is dropped down freely from a height, it begins to fall towards the earth under gravity and its velocity of fall continuously increases.
- The acceleration developed in its motion is called acceleration due to gravity. It is denoted by g. The value of g is 9.8 m/s^2.
- This value is taken at the sea level of the latitude of 45°.

Variation in Acceleration due to Gravity

As we know, the earth is not a perfect sphere. Therefore, value of g changes from place to place on the surface of earth.

These changes are as follows :

- **Effect of Shape of the earth on g** The earth is flattened at poles. Thus, radius of the earth is less at poles than at equator. The value of g is less at equator than at poles. Therefore, acceleration due to gravity is maximum at poles and minimum at equator.
- **Effect of Height above the Surface of earth on g** As we move above the surface of the earth, distance R from the centre of earth increases. As, $g = \frac{GM}{R^2}$, therefore, value of acceleration due to gravity decreases with height above the surface of earth.
- **Effect of Depth below the earth Surface on g** The value of g decreases, as we go down inside the earth and becomes zero at the centre of earth.

Relation between g and G

Let mass of the earth be M and of an object falling freely towards it be m. The distance between centres of the earth and the object is R.

From Newton's law of gravitation,

$$F = \frac{GMm}{R^2} \quad \text{...(i)}$$

Also, from second law of motion, force exerted on an object,

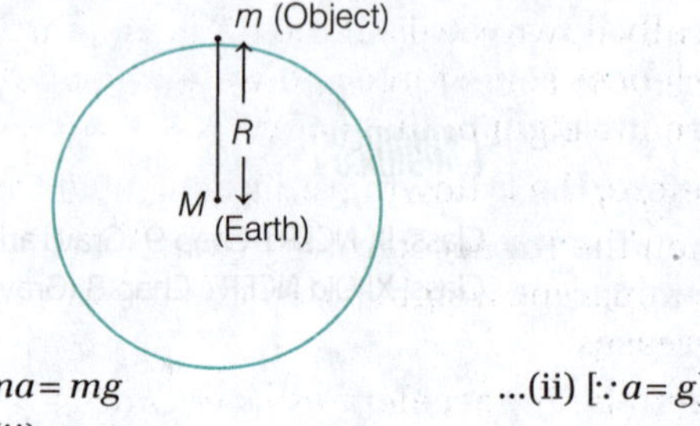

$$F = ma = mg \quad \text{...(ii)} \; [\because a = g]$$

From Eqs. (i) and (ii), we get

$$mg = \frac{GMm}{R^2} \quad \text{or} \quad g = \frac{GM}{R^2}$$

It is clear that, the value of g does not depend on the mass of falling object. It depends only on the mass of the earth.

The earth is not a perfect sphere. As the radius of the earth increases from the poles to the equator, the value of g becomes greater at the poles than at the equator.

Mass and Weight

- **Mass** Total substance of the body which measures the inertia of a body. It is a scalar quantity and its SI unit is kilogram (kg).

  Irrespective of the position of the body in the universe, mass always remains constant everywhere. The mass of the body cannot be zero.
- **Weight** The weight of an object is the force with which it is attracted towards the earth.

  Weight = Mass × Acceleration due to gravity

  $\Rightarrow \quad w = mg$
- It is a vector quantity and it acts in vertically downward direction. Its SI unit is Newton (N).
- As, mass of an object is always constant therefore, the weight of an object is directly proportional to the acceleration of gravity. Hence, the weight of the object changes as the g changes.

  Weight of 1 kg mass = 1 kg × 9.8 m/s^2

  1 kg-weight = 9.8 N

Weight of an Object on the Moon

The weight of an object on the moon is the force with which the moon attracts that object. The mass of the moon is less than that of the earth. Due to this, the moon exerts lesser force of attraction on objects.

The value of g at the surface of moon is one-sixth of the value of g at the surface of the earth.

Hence, weight of the object on the moon

$$= \frac{1}{6} \times \text{Its weight on the earth.}$$

Apparent Weight of a Body in a Lift

A body of mass m is placed on a weighing machine placed in a lift. The actual weight of the body is mg which acts vertically downwards. If the lift is moving, then the body experiences some force and weighing machine reads the apparent weight of that body.

Therefore, the following situations will arise :

- When the lift accelerates upwards with acceleration a, the apparent weight $[w = m(g + a)]$ of the body inside it, increases.
- When the lift accelerates downwards with acceleration a, the apparent weight $[w = m(g - a)]$ of the body inside it, decreases.
- When the lift is at rest or moving with uniform velocity v downward/upward, the apparent weight is equal to the actual weight ($w = mg$).
- When the lift falls freely, then the apparent weight of the body becomes zero ($w = 0$).

Gravitational Field

- The space around an object in which its gravitational force of attraction can be experienced is called its gravitational field.
- The force acting on a unit test mass at a point in gravitational field is known as **intensity of gravitational field** at that point. It is a vector quantity and is measured in Newton per kilogram (N/kg).
- The earth is surrounded by a gravitational field. Any body brought in this field experiences a force of attraction towards the centre of the earth.

Gravitational Potential Energy

- Gravitational potential energy of an object at a point is defined as the amount of work done in bringing the object from infinity to a that particular point against gravitational field of the other object.
- The gravitational potential energy is always negative. It is given by

$$U = -\frac{GMm}{r}$$

Weightlessness

Weight of an object is the force with which the earth attracts it. If somehow, the object does not feel his weight since there is no upward force on it, it is weightless and this phenomenon is called weightlessness.

A body can be in the state of weightlessness under the following circumstances :

- **In a Freely Falling Lift** The apparent weight of an object becomes zero because there are no forces of action reaction. Hence, the object is in a state of weightlessness.
- **Inside a Spacecraft** People inside spacecraft experiences no gravity. That is why, pictures of astronauts floating in a spacecraft show this fact.
- **In a Satellite which revolves in its Orbit around the earth** In this case, the acceleration of the person and that of the satellite revolving around the earth are equal (each is equal to acceleration due to gravity g), then acceleration of the person with respect to the satellite is zero. Therefore, person is weightless with respect to the satellite.

Escape Speed

- The minimum speed with which a body just escape the gravitational field of the earth, is called escape speed.
- It depends on the mass and radius of the planet from the surface of which the body is projected.
- The escape speed does not depend on the angle of projection and mass of the body projected.
- The escape speed for the earth is 11.2 kms^{-1} while for moon it is 2.3 kms^{-1}. If the root mean square velocity of the planet atmospheric molecules is less than escape speed, then the atmosphere of that planet will exist.

Planets

A celestial body that revolves in a well defined orbit around the sun is called planet.

Kepler's Laws of Planetary Motion

Johannes Kepler proposed three laws of planetary motion in 16th century. The three laws are given below :

1. Kepler's First Law (Law of Orbits)

- It states that the path of any planet in an orbit around the sun follows the shape of an ellipse with the sun at one of the foci.

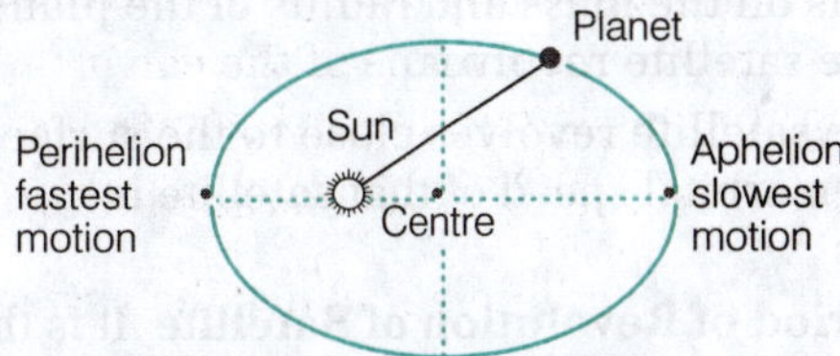

- The point in the orbit of a planet nearest to the sun is called **perihelion** and the point farthest from the sun is called **aphelion**.

2. Kepler's Second Law (Law of Areas)

- It states that an imaginary line from the sun to the planet sweeps out equal areas in equal intervals of time.
- Thus, if the time of travelling of a planet from A to B and from C to D is same, then the areas AOB and COD are equal.

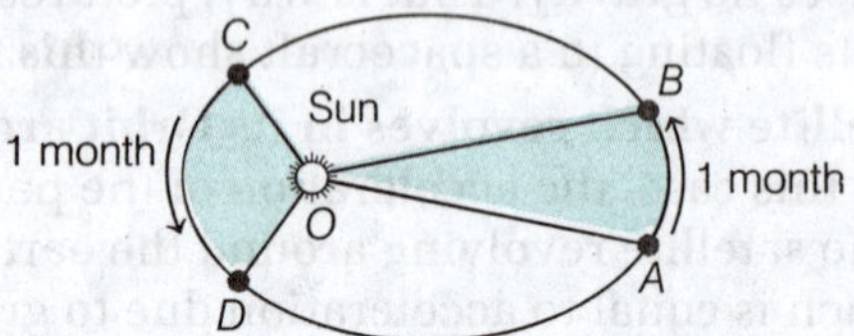

3. Kepler's Third Law (Law of Periods)

- It states that the cube of the mean distance of a planet from the sun is directly proportional to the square of its orbital period T. It is expressed as :

$$r^3 \propto T^2,\ r^3 = k \times T^2$$

$$k = \frac{r^3}{T^2}$$

- Kepler could not give a theory to explain the motion of planets. Newton showed that the cause of the planetary motion is the gravitational force that the sun exerts on them.
- He observed that, the gravitational force between the sun and the planet is inversely proportional to the square of the distance between their centres.

Satellites

A body which continuously revolves in an orbit around a comparatively much larger body is called a satellite. For example, the moon is a natural satellite of the earth.

- **Orbital Speed of a Satellite** The speed required to put the satellite into its orbit around the earth is called orbital speed of that satellite.
- The orbital speed of a satellite is independent of the mass of the satellite.
- It decreases with increase in the radius of the orbit and with increase in the height of the satellite.
- It depends on the mass and radius of the planet about which the satellite revolves.
- When the satellite revolves close to the surface of the earth, then orbital speed of that satellite is 7.92 km s^{-1}.
- **Time Period of Revolution of Satellite** It is the time taken by a satellite to complete one revolution around the body. It depends on the height of the satellite from the surface of the planet or body, as the height of satellite increases, its time period will also increase.
- **Total Energy of a Satellite** When a satellite revolves around a planet, it possesses kinetic energy due to its motion and potential energy due to its position. So, the total energy of a satellite is calculated as the sum of the kinetic energy and the potential energy possessed by the satellite.

When a satellite revolves around a planet of mass M and radius R, if the mass of satellite is m, then the potential energy of satellite is given by

$$U = -\frac{GMm}{r}$$

$$\Rightarrow \quad U = -\frac{GMm}{(r+h)}$$

If the orbital speed of satellite is v_0, then its kinetic energy is given by :

$$K = \frac{1}{2} mv^2$$

$$\Rightarrow \quad v_0 = \sqrt{\frac{GM}{(r+h)}}$$

$$\because \quad K = \frac{1}{2} m \left(\frac{GM}{m} \right) = \frac{GMm}{2(r+h)}$$

Total energy of satellite

$$E = U + K = \frac{-GMm}{r+h} + \frac{1}{2} \frac{GMm}{(r+h)}$$

$$\Rightarrow \quad E = -\frac{1}{2} \frac{GMm}{(r+h)}$$

Thus, the total energy of the satellite is negative. It indicates that the satellite is bound to the earth.

- **Binding Energy of a Satellite** The energy required by a satellite to leave its orbit around the earth and escape to infinity is called its binding energy. Binding energy of a satellite is $\frac{GMm}{2r}$.

Artificial Satellite

A manmade satellite is called an artificial satellite.

Geostationary Satellite

A satellite which revolves from West to East with a time period of 24 hours in a circular orbit concentric and coplanar with the equatorial plane of the earth is called geostationary satellite. Such a satellite is also known as **synchronous satellite** because its angular speed is same as that of the earth about its own axis.

Some Properties of Geostationary or Synchronous Satellite

- Its rotation is same as that of the earth i.e., from West to East. Its period of revolution is exactly same as that of earth rotation about its own axis i.e., 24 h.
- It revolves at a height of nearly 35830 km above the earth's surface and the radius of orbit is 42200 km.
- Three uniformly spaced satellites placed in a geostationary orbit can be used to provide line of sight communication between two points on the earth.
- It is used to reflect TV signals and telecast TV programs from one part of the world to another part of the world.
- They are used in studying upper regions of the atmosphere, weather forecasting, meteorites, solar radiations and cosmic rays.

Polar Satellites

- A satellite that revolves in a polar orbit is called a polar satellite.
- These are low altitude satellites whose orbit is about 500 to 800 km above the surface of earth.

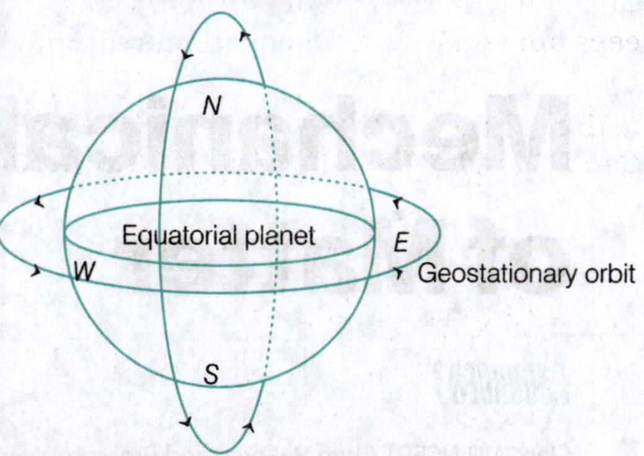

Some Properties of Polar Satellites

- They revolve around the earth in a North-South direction.
- Its time period is approximately 100 min, so it crosses any altitude many times a day.
- These satellites can view polar and equatorial regions at close distances with good resolution.
- They are very useful for remote sensing, meteorology as well as environmental studies of the earth.
- They provide more reliable information than geostationary satellites because their orbits are closed to the earth.

06

Mechanical Properties of Matter

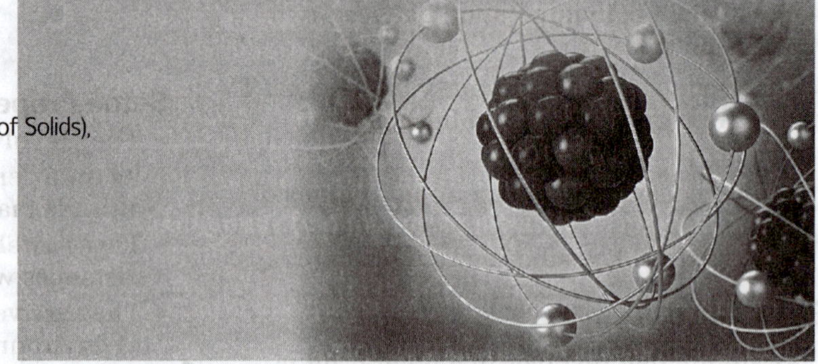

[SOURCES]

Class-VIII NCERT Chap 8 (Force and Pressure), Class-IX NCERT Chap 9 (Gravitation), Class-XI NCERT Chap 8 (Mechanical Properties of Solids), Chap 9 (Mechanical Properties of Fluids) Tamil Nadu Board (Class-IX), NIOS

- Matter is anything that has mass and occupies space. It exists in three different states which are **solid, liquid** and **gas.**
- In solids, strong intermolecular force exists, that's why they have definite shape and volume. In order to change the shape or size of a solid body, an external force is required, as they have a tendency to regain their shape.
- Liquids and gases are called as **fluids**. They do not have a definite shape, they take up the shape of the container in which they are kept. Gases possess high compressibility as compared to solids and liquids due to weak intermolecular forces.
- Solids and liquids have a fixed volume, whereas a gas fills the entire volume of its container.

Elasticity

The property of a body by virtue of which it regains its original size and shape when the deforming forces have been removed, is known as elasticity. e.g. Spring, rubber band etc. The deformation caused is known as **elastic deformation**.

Plasticity

- The property of a body by virtue of which it fails to regain its original shape even after the removal of deforming force, is known as plasticity and the bodies which get permanently deformed are called **plastic bodies**. e.g. Putty, mud, wax, etc.

Deforming Force

- A force which changes the size or shape of a body is called a deforming force.

Stress

- When a body is subjected to a deforming force, a restoring force is developed in the body. This restoring force is equal in magnitude but opposite in direction to the applied force.
- The restoring force per unit area is known as stress.

$$\text{Stress } (\sigma) = \frac{\text{Force applied } (F)}{\text{Area of cross-section } (A)}$$

- The SI unit of stress is **Nm^{-2}** or **pascal** (Pa).
- Its dimensional formula is $[ML^{-1}T^{-2}]$.

Following are the types of stress :

- **Tensile Stress** When an object is stretched by two equal forces applied normal to its cross-sectional area. The restoring force per unit area in this case is called tensile stress.
- **Compressive Stress** If an object is compressed under the action of applied forces, the restoring force per unit area is known as compressed stress.
- **Tangential or Shearing Stress** If two equal and opposite deforming forces are applied parallel to the cross-sectional area of the object, the restoring force per unit area developed due to the applied tangential force is known as tangential or shearing stress.

- **Hydraulic Stress** The body develops internal restoring forces that are equal and opposite to the forces applied by the fluid (the body restores its original shape and size when taken out from the fluid).
- The internal restoring force per unit area due to forces applied by the fluid is known as hydraulic stress.

Strain

- When a deforming force acts on a body, then body undergoes a change in its shape or size. The ratio of the change in dimension produced in the body to the original dimension is called strain. Strain is the ratio of two like quantities, it has no units or dimensional formula.
- The change in length due to deforming force per unit original length is **longitudinal strain**.

$$\text{Longitudinal strain} = \frac{\text{Change in length } (\Delta L)}{\text{Total length } (L)}$$

- The change in volume due to deforming force per unit original volume is **volumetric strain**.

$$\text{Volume strain} = \frac{\Delta V}{V}$$

- If the deforming force produces a change in the shape of the body without changing its volume, then strain is called **shearing strain**.

$$\text{Shearing strain} = \frac{\Delta x}{\tau} = \tan\theta$$

Here, θ is the angular displacement of the object from the vertical.

Elastic Limit

The maximum stress within which the body regains its original size and shape after the removal of deforming force is called elastic limit.

Hooke's Law

It states that for small deformations the stress and strain are proportional to each other.

Thus, $\text{Stress} \propto \text{Strain}$

$\text{Stress} = k \times \text{Strain}$

where, k is the proportionality constant and is known as **modulus of elasticity**.

Modulus of Elasticity

The ratio of stress and strain is called modulus of elasticity.

It is the characteristic property of material.

1. Young's Modulus

- Within the elastic limit, the ratio of longitudinal stress to the longitudinal strain is called Young's modulus. It is given by

$$\text{Young's modulus } (Y) = \frac{\text{Longitudinal stress}}{\text{Longitudinal strain}} = \frac{\sigma}{\varepsilon}$$

$$Y = \frac{FL}{A\Delta L}$$

where, L = initial length

A = area of cross-section,

ΔL = change in length and

F = deforming force

- The unit of Young's modulus is Nm^{-2} or pascal (Pa). For metals, Young's moduli are large. Therefore, these materials require a large force to produce small change in length.
- Steel is more elastic than copper, brass and aluminium, that's why it is preferred in heavy duty machines and in structural designs.
- Wood, bone, concrete and glass have rather small Young's moduli.

2. Bulk Modulus

Within the elastic limit, the ratio of hydraulic stress to the corresponding hydraulic strain is called bulk modulus.

$$\text{Bulk modulus } (B) = \frac{\text{Hydraulic stress}}{\text{Volumetric strain}}$$

$$B = -\frac{FV}{A\Delta V} = -\frac{PV}{\Delta V}$$

where, V = initial volume

ΔV = change in volume

Its unit is Nm^{-2} or pascal (Pa).

- The reciprocal of bulk modulus is called compressibility and is denoted by k. It's SI unit is m^2/N.
- Bulk moduli for solids are much larger than liquids and gases. Thus, solids are least compressible whereas gases are most compressible.

3. Shear Modulus

- Within the elastic limit, the ratio of tangential stress to shearing strain is called shear modulus of the material or modulus of rigidity.

$$\text{Modulus of rigidity } (G) = \frac{\text{Tangential stress}}{\text{Shearing strain}}$$

$$G = \frac{F/A}{\theta}$$

where, θ is shear strain.

- The unit of modulus of rigidity is Nm^{-2} or pascal (Pa).

Poisson's Ratio

When a wire is loaded, its length increases but its diameter decreases. The strain produced in the direction of applied force is called longitudinal strain and that produced in the perpendicular direction is called **lateral strain.**

Within the elastic limit, the ratio of lateral strain to the longitudinal strain is called Poisson's ratio.

$$\text{Poisson's ratio } (\sigma) = \frac{\text{Lateral strain}}{\text{Longitudinal strain}}$$

- **Elastic Potential Energy in a Stretched wire** When a wire is put under a tensile stress, work is done against the inter-atomic forces. This work is stored in the wire in the form of energy, this stored energy is called elastic potential Energy.

$$W = \frac{1}{2} \times \text{Young's modulus} \times \text{Strain}^2 \times \text{Volume of the wire}$$

$$W = \frac{1}{2} \times \text{Stress} \times \text{Strain} \times \text{Volume of the wire.}$$

The elastic potential energy per unit volume of the wire,

$$U = \frac{1}{2}\sigma\,\varepsilon$$

Thrust and Pressure

- **Thrust** is the force acting on an object perpendicular to its surface. The effect of thrust depends on the area on which it acts.

  The unit of thrust is the same as that of force, i.e. the SI unit of thrust is **newton** (N). It is a vector quantity.
- **Pressure** is the force acting perpendicularly on a unit area of an object.

$$\text{Pressure } (p) = \frac{\text{Force } (F)}{\text{Area } (A)} = \frac{\text{Thrust}}{\text{Area}}$$

- The SI unit of pressure is Nm^{-2}, which is also called **pascal** (Pa) named after the scientist **Blaise Pascal.** It is a scalar quantity.

$$1 \text{ Pa} = 1 \text{ Nm}^{-2}$$

- From the formula of pressure, it is clear that the same force can produce different pressures depending on the area over which it acts. A force acting on a smaller area exerts a large pressure, while the same force acting on a larger area exerts small pressure.

Density

- The density of a substance is defined as mass per unit volume.

$$\text{Density} = \frac{\text{Mass of the substance}}{\text{Volume of the substance}} \text{ or } \rho = \frac{m}{V}$$

- The SI unit of density is kilogram per metre cube (kg/m^3). It is a scalar quantity. The density of a substance under specified conditions always remains same. Hence, the density of a substance is one of its characteristic properties.
- It can help us to determine the substance purity. It is different for different substances. The lightness and the heaviness of different substances can be described by using the word density.
- Objects having less density than that of a liquid, they will float on the liquid. Objects having greater density than that of liquid, they will sink in the liquid.
- It decreases with increase in the temperature.

Note The object having density equal to that of liquid will float on the liquid in such a way that it is totally submerged in the liquid and no part of it remains above the surface of the liquid.

Relative Density

- The relative density of a substance is the ratio of its density to that of water.

$$\text{Relative density of a substance} = \frac{\text{Density of the substance}}{\text{Density of water at } 4^\circ\text{C}}$$

- In other words, we can say that,

  Relative density of a substance

$$= \frac{\text{Mass of the substance}}{\text{Volume of the substance}} \times \frac{\text{Volume of water}}{\text{Mass of water}}$$

$$\left[\because \text{Density} = \frac{\text{Mass}}{\text{Volume}}\right]$$

- Since, relative density is the ratio of similar quantities, it has no unit.

Pressure in Fluids

- All liquids and gases are fluids. A solid exerts pressure on a surface due to its weight. Similarly, fluids have weight and they also exert pressure on the base and walls of the container in which they are enclosed.
- Pressure exerted in any confined mass of fluid is transmitted undiminished in all directions.

Pressure in Liquid

The force exerted by the liquid on the submerged object on its surface is called pressure in liquid. This force is always normal to the object's surface. The pressure in liquid can be calculated using the following relation :

$$p = \rho g h$$

where, ρ is the density of liquid, g is acceleration due to gravity and h is height/depth of the liquid.

Laws of Liquid Pressure

- Liquid pressure is same in all directions about a point in a liquid.

- In a stationary liquid, the pressure is the same at all points on a horizontal plane.
- Pressure at a point inside the liquid increases with depth from the free surface. Pressure of fluid is directly proportional to the density of liquid.
- Pressure at the same depth is different in different liquids. It increases with an increase in the density of the liquid. A liquid seeks its own level.

Examples of Liquid Pressure

- **Divers Wear Special Diving Suits** As the depth of the sea increases, the pressure increases. So, the pressure exerted by water deep under the sea is much greater than at the sea level. Hence, the deep sea divers wear special suits which protect them from extreme pressure of water. These suits are called diving suits.
- **Walls of Sams Made Thicker at the Bottom** Dams hold back bodies of water and water pressure increases with the depth of the body of water. So, the pressure from water pushing horizontally on the dam is greater at the bottom than at the top. Hence, the walls of dams are made thicker at the bottom to bear the large pressure.

Some Practical Applications of Pressure

- The handles of bags, suitcases, etc., are made broad, so that less pressure is exerted on the hand.
- Buildings are provided with broad foundations, so that the pressure exerted on the ground becomes less.
- Railway tracks are laid on cement or iron sleepers, so that the pressure exerted by train could spread over the larger area and thus pressure decreases.
- Pins, needles and nails are provided with sharp pointed ends to reduce the area and hence to increase the pressure.
- Cutting tools have sharp edges to reduce the area, so that with lesser force, more pressure could be exerted.
- Pressure on ground is more when a man is walking than when he is standing because in case of walking, the effective area is less.
- Depression is much more when a man stands on the cushion than when he lies down on it because in standing case, area is lesser than in case of lying.
- The tractors have broad tyres, to create less pressure on the ground, so that tyres do not sink into comparatively soft ground in the field.

Hydrostatic Paradox

- According to the phenomenon of hydrostatic paradox, the pressure exerted by a liquid column depends only on the height of the liquid column and not on the shape of the containing vessel.
- The liquid pressure is the same at all points at the same horizontal level.

Atmospheric Pressure

- The gaseous envelope surrounding the earth is called **atmosphere**. The pressure exerted by the atmospheric air is called atmospheric pressure.
- The force exerted by air column of air on a unit area of the earth's surface is equal to the atmospheric pressure. The atmospheric pressure at sea level is 1.013×10^5 Nm^{-2} or Pa.

- Various units for measuring pressure are as follows :
  - SI unit of pressure = Nm^{-2} or pascal (Pa)
  - CGS unit of pressure = dyne cm^{-2},
  - 1 Pa = 10 dyne cm^{-2}
  - Atmosphere (atm),
    $1 \text{ atm} = 1.013 \times 10^5 \text{ Pa} = 10^6 \text{ dyne cm}^{-2}$
  - In meteorology, atmospheric pressure is measured in bar.
    $1 \text{ bar} = 10^5 \text{ Pa} = 10^6 \text{ dyne cm}^{-2}$
  - Atmospheric pressure is also measured in torr.
    1 torr = 1 mm of Hg
    1 atm = 1.013 bar = 760 torr = 101.3 kPa

Factors Affecting the Atmospheric Pressure

Some factors affecting the atmospheric pressure are as follows :

- **Temperature** When the temperature of a place increases, the atmospheric pressure decreases. This happens because, warm air expands and the molecules of the warm air becomes less dense and hence exert less pressure.
- **Altitude** Atmospheric pressure decreases with an increase in the altitude. As the gravity of the earth pulls the molecules and gases towards the ground, the lowest layer of the air becomes densest and exerts the greatest pressure.
- **Effect of Water Vapour** The density of air decreases by presence of water vapour in atmosphere. Therefore, atmospheric pressure decreases. In rainy day, atmospheric pressure decreases due to high vapour content.

Barometer

- The measurement of atmospheric pressure is carried out by barometer. It is also called **Fortin's barometer**. Barometers are also used for weather forecasting.
- If the barometric height falls suddenly, it indicates the coming of a storm. A gradual fall and rise in barometric height indicate the possibility of rain and fair weather respectively.

Note The pressure inside a human body equals to the atmospheric pressure. Due to this balance, human body does not crushes under the force of gravity.

Pascal's Law

Pascal's law states that, the pressure in a fluid at rest is same at all points. Which are at the same height. A change in pressure applied to an enclosed fluid is transmitted undiminished to every point of the fluid and the walls of the containing vessel.

Applications of Pascal's Law

- **Hydraulic Lift** It is used to lift heavy loads such as cars at a service station. It is based on the simple principle that when a small force is applied over a piston of small cross-sectional area, then due to transmission of the pressure, a large force appears over a piston of large cross-sectional area. This force is used to support and lift heavy weights.
- **Hydraulic Brakes** These are also based on the principle of transmission of the pressure in a liquid. When the driver of the vehicle puts pressure on the brake pedal, the lever system moves a piston into a cylinder containing brake oil.

  When the brake pedal is pressed, the increase in pressure is transmitted to the pistons through the brake oil. The pistons move outwards and press the brake shoes against the rim of the wheel, thus retarding the motion of the wheel.

Buoyancy

- The tendency of a liquid to exert an upward force on an object immersed in it is called buoyancy. Gases also exhibit this property of buoyancy.
- **Buoyant Force** is an upward force which acts on an object when it is immersed in a liquid. It is also called **upthrust**.
- It is the buoyant force due to which a heavy object seems to be lighter in water. As we lower an object into a liquid, the liquid underneath it, provides an upward force.
- For example, a piece of cork is held below the surface of water. When we apply a force by our thumb, the cork immediately rises to the surface. This is due to the fact that every liquid exerts an upward force on the objects immersed in it.

Factors Affecting Buoyant Force

The magnitude of buoyant force depends on the following factors :

- **Density of the Fluid** The liquid having higher density exerts more upward buoyant force on an object than another liquid of lower density. This is the reason why it is easier to swim in sea water in comparison to normal water.
- The sea water has higher density and hence exerts a greater buoyant force on the swimmer than the fresh water having lower density.
- **Volume of Object Immersed in the Liquid** As the volume of solid object immersed inside the liquid increases, the upward buoyant force also increases. The magnitude of buoyant force acting on a solid object does not depend on the nature of the solid object. It depends only on its volume.
- For example, when two balls made of different metals having different weights but equal volume are fully immersed in a liquid, they will experience an equal upward buoyant force. It is because both the balls displace equal amount of the liquid due to their equal volume.

Archimedes' Principle

According to this principle, when an object is fully or **partially in a fluid**, it experiences an upward force that is equal to the weight of the fluid displaced by the object.

Applications of Archimedes' Principle

Archimedes' principle is used in the following :

- Designing ships and submarines.
- Lactometer
  (a device used to determine the purity of milk).
- Hydrometer (a device used for determining the density of liquid).
- Relative density of a substance.

Floating or Sinking of Objects in Liquid

Whether an object will float or sink in a liquid, depends on the weight of the object and Buoyant force which acts on the object in opposite directions. There are three conditions of floating and sinking objects as follows :

- If the buoyant force or upthrust exerted by the liquid is less than the weight of the object, then **object will sink** in the liquid.
- If the buoyant force is equal to the weight of the object, then object will **float** in the liquid.
- If the buoyant force is more than the weight of the object, then object will rise in the liquid and then float.

Example of Laws of Floatation

- **Iron nail sinks in pure water, while ship made of iron floats on water** Iron nail sink in pure water because weight of iron nail is more than weight of water displaced by it.
- While shape of iron ship is made in such a way that it displaces more weight of water than its weight. Hence, ship floats on water.

- **It is easier to swim in sea water than in river water** Sea water contains dissolved salts which makes its density more than river water. Therefore, a person has to remove less volume of water to swim in the sea.
- **Life Preserver** This is a very big hollow tube, in which air can be filled. Its size becomes very big when air is filled. When a person jumps in water wearing it, its weight along with the person remains less than the weight of the water removed by it.

Flow of Liquids

The flow of liquids is mainly classified into two categories which are as follows :

- **Streamline Flow** When a liquid flows such that each particle of the liquid passing a given point moves along the same path and has the same velocity as its predecessor, the flow is called streamline flow or steady flow.
- The **critical velocity** of a liquid is that limiting value of its velocity of flow upto which the flow is streamlined and above which the flow becomes turbulent.

  Some properties of streamline flow are :

  – In a steady flow, no two streamlines can cross each other. If they do so the fluid particle at the point of will have two directions of flow.
  This will disturb the steady nature of the fluid flow.

  – The tangent at any point on the streamline gives the direction of velocity of fluid particle at that point.

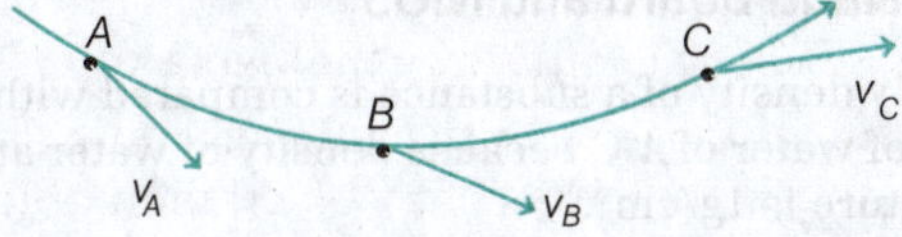

  – At narrower portions where the stream lines are closely spaced, velocity increases and its *vice-versa*.

  – Fluid velocity remains constant at any point of a streamline, but it may be different at different points of the same streamline.

  – When the velocity of the flow of a liquid is less than its critical velocity, the liquid flows steadily. Each layer of the liquid slides over the other. Such a flow is called **laminar flow.**

- **Turbulent Flow** When the liquid velocity exceeds critical velocity, then the liquid flow becomes *zig-zag*.
- The path and the velocity of a liquid particle changes continuously in irregular manner, then this flow is called turbulent flow.

Equation of Continuity

It states that during the streamline flow of the non-viscous and incompressible fluid through a pipe of varying cross-section, the product of area of cross-section (A) and the normal fluid velocity (v) remains constant throughout the flow, i.e., $A \times v =$ constant

Bernoulli's Principle

This theorem states that for the streamline flow of an ideal liquid, the total energy (the sum of pressure energy, potential energy and kinetic energy) per unit volume of the liquid remains constant at every cross-section throughout the liquid flow.

It is based on the law of conservation of energy.

Some applications based on Bernoulli's principle are :

- The venturimeter
- Atomizer or sprayer
- Blood flow and heart attack
- Curved path of a spinning ball: Magnus effect
- Lift of an aircraft wing

Viscosity

- When a solid body slides over another solid body, then a frictional force begins to act between them. This force opposes the relative motion of the bodies.
- When a layer of a liquid slides over another layer of the same liquid, then a frictional force acts between them which opposes the relative motion between the layers. This force is called **internal friction force** or **viscous force** and the property of the liquid is called viscosity.
- Therefore, the property of the liquid by virtue of which it opposes the relative motion between its adjacent layer is known as viscosity. The SI unit of viscosity is **Poiseuille** (Pl). Its other units are N-s m^{-2} or Pa-s.
- Viscosity is like friction and converts kinetic energy into heat energy. Generally, thin liquids like water, alcohol, etc., are less viscous than thick liquids like coal tar, blood, honey, glycerine, etc.

Stoke's Law

According to Stoke's law, the viscous drag force F acting on a small spherical body of radius r moving with uniform velocity v through fluid of viscosity η is given by

$$F = 6\pi\eta r v$$

Terminal Velocity

- When a body falls through a viscous fluid, it produces relative motion between its different layers. As the velocity of the body increases, the viscous force also increases.
- A stage is reached, when the weight of the body becomes just equal to the sum of the upthrust and viscous force. Then, no net force acts on the body and it begins to move with a constant velocity.

- The maximum constant velocity acquired by a body while falling through a viscous medium is called its terminal velocity.

Terminal velocity $(v_t) = \frac{2a^2(\rho - \sigma)g}{9\eta}$

Where, ρ and σ are mass densities of sphere and the fluid, respectively. η is viscosity and *a* is radius of sphere.
e.g. A rain drop falls through air with a terminal velocity.

Intermolecular Forces

Intermolecular forces are the forces of attraction or repulsion which act between neighbouring particles (atoms, molecules or ions).

They are classified into two categories as follows :

- **Cohesive Forces** It is the force of attraction between the molecules of the same substance.

  e.g. Solids have definite shape and size due to strong forces of cohesion amongst their molecules.
  It is due to the cohesive force that two drops of a liquid when brought in mutual contact coalesce into one.

Cold Welding

When a very high pressure is applied on two metal pieces in contact such that distance between them is reduced to less than 10^{-9}m, then metal pieces get stick together due to cohesive force. This is known as cold welding.

- **Adhesive Forces** It is the force of attraction between the molecules of two different substances.

  e.g. Ink sticks to paper while writing is due to force of adhesion. Writing on blackboard by chalk is also possible due to adhesive force.
  Water wets the walls of its glass container because the force of adhesion between water and glass is greater than the force of cohesion between the water molecules.

Surface Tension

- Surface tension is the property by virtue of which the free surface of a liquid at rest behaves like an elastic stretched membrane tending to contract so as to occupy minimum surface area.
- Surface tension is measured as the force acting per unit length of imaginary line drawn on the free surface of liquid.
- If *l* is the length of this imaginary line and *F* is the total force on either side of the line, then
  Surface tension, $T = \frac{\text{Force}(F)}{\text{Length}(l)}$
- Hence, surface tension is measured as the force acting per unit length of an imaginary line drawn on the liquid surface, the direction of force being perpendicular to this line and tangential to the liquid surface. Its SI unit is Nm^{-1}.

Factors Affecting Surface Tension

- **Temperature** The surface tension of liquid decreases with rise in temperature and *vice-versa.*
- The surface tension of a liquid becomes zero at a particular temperature, called **critical temperature** of that liquid.
- **Addition of Impurities** The surface tension of liquids changes appreciably with addition of impurities.
  - A highly soluble substance, like sodium chloride increases the surface tension of water.
  - A sparingly soluble substance, like phenol or soap reduces the surface tension of water.

Some Phenomena based on Surface Tension

- Needle supported on water surface.
- Raindrops are generally spherical in shapes.
- Small mercury droplets are spherical and larger ones tend to flattened.
- Oil rises up a cotton wick, inspite of gravity.

Extra Facts From Tamil Nadu Board and NIOS

- Generally density of a substance is compared with the density of water of 4°C because density of water at that temperature is $1g/cm^3$.
- Relative density can be measured using pycnometer (density bottle).
- **Hydrometer** is a direct instrument used for measuring the density or relative density of the liquid.
- One form of hydrometer is a lactometer, an instrument used to check the purity of milk. The lactometer works on the principle of gravity of milk.
- Salt water provides more buoyant force than fresh water, because buoyant force depends as much on the density of fluids as on the volume displaced.
- Cartesian diver is an experiment that demonstrates the principle of buoyancy.

07

Heat and Thermodynamics

[SOURCES]

Class-VII NCERT Chap 3 (Heat), Class-XI NCERT Chap 10 (Thermal Properties of Matter), Chap 11 (Thermodynamics), Chap 12 (Kinetic Theory) Tamil Nadu Board (Class-IX,X), NIOS

Temperature is a measure of 'hotness' of a body. A kettle with a boiling water is hotter than a box containing ice.

Temperature and Heat

- **Temperature** is a relative measure, or indication of hotness or coldness of a body. The measurement of temperature of a body is a relative measure.
- Consider, there are two bodies with temperatures T_1 and T_2 where $T_1 > T_2$, then the body with T_1 is called **hotter one** with respect to another one which is known as **colder body**.
- **Heat** is the form of energy which flows from hotter body to colder body by virtue of temperature difference.
- The process of transfer of heat is a non-mechanical process i.e., there is no mechanical work involved in the process of heat transfer.

Measurement of Heat

- The amount of heat is measured in joule (SI unit). Another widely used unit for the heat is calorie (in CGS), where 1 joule equals 4.2 calorie (cal).
- 1 calorie is equal to the amount of heat energy required to raise the temperature of 1 gram of water through 1°C (from 14.5°C to 15.5°C)

Note When a body is heated, the changes can take place in the body such as it may expand or its physical state may be changed.

Thermometer

- A device which is used to measure temperature is called a thermometer. Many physical properties of materials change sufficiently with temperature, such properties are used as the basis for constructing thermometers.
- The commonly used property is variation of the volume of a liquid with temperature. For example, a common thermometer (the liquid-in-glass type) uses mercury and alcohol as the liquids.
- The thermometers are caliberated so that a numerical value may be assigned to a given temperature in an appropriate scale.
- It measures the temperature of the body in the unit as kelvin (K), degree centigrade (°C), degree fahrenheit (°F), etc., among which kelvin (K) is taken as the SI unit of temperature.
- Different types of thermometers are used for different purposes.
- The maximum and minimum temperatures of the previous day, reported in weather reports, are measured by a thermometer called the maximum-minimum thermometer.

Liquid Thermometer

- It is a contact type thermometer which measures temperature from changes in the volume of liquid.

- It consists of a sealed glass tube with a small internal diameter (like a lumen) connected to a reservoir. A scale on the tube and the location of the expanded fluid indicate the temperature. It is of two types as follows :
  - **Alcohol Thermometer** It is a thermometer which utilises the expansion and contraction of alcohol in response to temperature changes to measure the temperature. Since, the melting and boiling point of alcohol is very low (for ethanol, –114°C and 78°C respectively), so they are used in very cold places to measure the temperature.
  - **Mercury Thermometer** It uses mercury as the expansion liquid to measure the temperature, as mercury is the only metal that is in liquid state at room temperature. The boiling point of mercury is very high, which makes mercury thermometer more suitable for measurement. It is also known as **'clinical thermometer'**. It reads temperature from 35°C to 42°C. Doctors use this thermometer for medical purpose.

Gas Thermometer

- It is a thermometer that measures temperature by the variation in volume or pressure of a gas. It can measure temperature ranging from –200°C to 800° C.

Platinum Resistance Thermometer (PRT)

- It is a piece of platinum wire which determines the temperature by measuring its electrical resistance. It is referred to as a temperature.
- It is referred to as a temperature sensor and can measure temperature ranging from –200° C to 1200°C. It is used both for precision measurements of the highest accuracy and for routine industrial work.

Total Radiation Pyrometer

- It is a type of pyrometer in which radiation or total heat emitted from the hot body or temperature source is focussed on the radiation sensing element.
- It is non-contact type of thermometer which measures high range temperature (> 800°C). It is used to measure temperature of hot objects in furnace.

Different Scales of Temperature

- As we know, two reference points are needed to define any standard scale. In case of water, these points are ice point and steam point at which the pure water freezes and boils respectively under standard pressure.
- The ice and steam point of water are 32°F and 212°F, respectively on the Fahrenheit scale and 0°C and 100°C on Celsius scale. On the Celsius scale, there are 100 equal intervals between two reference points (i.e. ice and steam point) while on the Fahrenheit scale, there are 180.
- One division on the scale is known as a degree, which is used as the unit for measuring temperature. The **Celsius**, **Fahrenheit**, **Reaumur** and **Kelvin** scale are related as,

$$\frac{C}{5} = \frac{F-32}{9} = \frac{R}{4} = \frac{K-273.15}{5}$$

- At –40°, the Celsius and the Fahrenheit scale shows same temperature. The normal temperature for human body is 36.9° C or 98.6° F or 310 K.

Different Scales to Measure the Temperature

Scale	Unit	Freezing or ice point (Lower fixed point)	Boiling or steam point (Upper fixed point)
Celsius scale	Degree centigrade (°C)	0°C	100°C
Fahrenheit scale	Degree Fahrenheit (°F)	32°F	212°F
Reaumur scale	Degree Reaumur (°R)	0° R	80°R
Kelvin scale	Kelvin (K)	273.15 K	373.15 K

Absolute Zero Temperature

- The lowest temperature of –273.15°C at which gas is supposed to have zero volume (or zero pressure) and at which entire molecular motion stops, is called **absolute zero** of temperature.
- The absolute zero temperature is regarded as 0 K or –273.15°C.
- This implies 273.15 K = 0°C.
- The temperature measured in Kelvin scale is known as **absolute temperature** and the scale itself is known as **absolute scale**.

Thermal Expansion

- It is generally observed that sealed bottles with metallic lids are so tightly screwed that it has to put the lid in hot water to open the lid.
- It would allow the metallic cover to expand and thereby loosening it to unscrew easily. So, when heat is supplied to material, its dimensions (length, area and volume) can be changed due to change in its temperature.
- The phenomenon of change in dimensions of an object due to heat supplied is known as **Thermal expansion.**

Types of Thermal Expansion

There are three types of thermal expansion :

Linear Expansion

- The expansion in length of a body due to increase in its temperature is called the linear expansion. It depends on the initial length and increase in temperature of solid.
- For example, due to thermal expansion in cable wires, they become loose in summer days.
  Linear expansion coefficient
  $$(\alpha) = \frac{\text{Increase in length } (\Delta L)}{\text{Original length } (L) \times \text{Rise in temperature } (\Delta T)}$$
- Hence, the coefficient of linear expansion of a material of a solid rod is defined as increase in length per unit original length per degree rise in temperature. Its unit is $^\circ C^{-1}$ or K^{-1}.

Superficial (Areal) Expansion

- The expansion in the area of a surface due to increase in its temperature is called superficial expansion.
  $$\beta = \frac{\text{Increase in surface area } (\Delta A)}{\text{Original surface area } (A) \times \text{ Rise in temperature } (\Delta T)}$$
- Hence, coefficient of areal expansion of metal sheet is defined as the increase in its surface area per unit original surface area per degree rise in its temperature. Its unit is $^\circ C^{-1}$ or K^{-1}.

Volume Expansion

- The expansion in the volume of an object due to increase in its temperature is known as volume expansion. For example, on heating an iron ball its volume expands.
  Coefficient of volume expansion
  $$(\gamma) = \frac{\text{Increase in volume } (\Delta V)}{\text{Original volume } (V) \times \text{Increase in temperature } (\Delta T)}$$
- Hence, the coefficient of volume (cubical) expansion of a substance is defined as the increase in volume per unit original volume per degree rise in its temperature. Its unit is $^\circ C^{-1}$ or K^{-1}.

Relation among the Coefficients of Expansion

Linear expansion coefficient

$$(\alpha) = \frac{\text{Area expansion coefficient } (\beta)}{2}$$

Linear expansion coefficient

$$(\alpha) = \frac{\text{Volume expansion coefficient } (\gamma)}{3}$$

$\therefore \quad \alpha : \beta : \gamma = 1 : 2 : 3$

Applications of Thermal Expansion in Daily Life

Some of the applications of thermal expansion in our daily life are discussed below :

- **Iron Tyre on Wooden Wheel** The iron tyre on the wooden wheel of a bullock cart or horse cart is placed after heating it. The reason is that on heating the iron tyre, it expands and it gets easily placed over the wooden wheel. When it cools, the iron tyre contracts and it firmly gets attached with the wheel.
- **Cap in Railway Tracks** While laying the railway track, some gap is left between the two rails in succession so that in summer when they increase in length due to rise in temperature, they may not overlap each other otherwise the train may derail.
- **Construction of an Iron Bridge** In construction of an iron bridge, some space is left between the ends of two girders and their ends are not rigidly fixed on pillars, but they are placed on solid rollers so that they can freely expand in summer.
- **Iron Rods in Coal Stone** In a coal stone, the ends of the iron rods are left free so that they may expand on being heated otherwise they will bend.
- **Electricity and Telephone Wire** The telephone wire between the two poles are not kept tight in summer, otherwise in winter when they contract, they may break. This is why it is preferred to put the telephone wires tight in winter.
- **Joining of Iron Plates** To join the two iron plates of boiler of an engine, holes are made in them and then red hot rivets are inserted in these holes. The rivets are then hammered. On cooling, the rivets contract so that the plates are firmly joined with each other.
- **Taking Out Cork from Bottle** To take out the cork from the mouth of a bottle, its mouth is slightly heated from outside so that it expands and the cork can easily be taken out.
- **Use of Pyrex Glass and Silica as Utensils** The coefficients of linear expansion of pyrex glass and silica are very small hence, when they are suddenly heated or cooled, there are little chances of them to crack. This is why precious utensils in kitchen, windows of ovens, laboratory beakers, flasks, crucibles etc., are made of pyrex glass or silica.
- **Bimetallic Strips in Bimetal there no Water** A bimetallic strip consists of two thin strips of different metals such as brass and iron joined together. On heating the strip, brass expands more than iron. This unequal expansion causes the bending of the strip. They are used in bimetal thermometers to measure

temperature in furnaces and ovens. They are also used in thermostats which is used to control the temperature of heater coil in an electric iron.

Anomalous Expansion of Water

- Generally, matter expands on heating and contracts on cooling. In case of water, it expands on heating if its temperature is greater than 4°C. In the range 0°C to 4°C, water contracts on heating and expands on cooling.
- This behaviour of water in the range from 0°C to 4°C is called anomalous expansion. At 4°C, density of water is maximum while its specific volume is minimum.

Examples of Anomalous Expansion of Water in Daily Life

- **Water Helps in Preserving Aquatic life during Extreme Cold Weather** In winters, when atmospheric temperature falls to 0°C or below it, the surface water of lakes or other water bodies turns into ice.
  When the temperature of water at the surface falls below 4°C, water contracts and its density increases. Therefore, it sticks to the bottom.
  Thus, the layer of water at 4°C will settle down at bottom followed by 3°C to 0° C. Top layer of water is at 0°C, in the form of ice and this layer doesn't allow further exchange in temperature. So, the water below the ice layer does not freeze and marine animals remain alive and move freely near the bottom.
- **Water Pipes in Colder Countries often Burst in Winter** In winter nights, as the temperature starts falling below 4°C, water in pipe lines expands and it exerts large pressure on the pipes, causing them to burst.
- **Farmers Fill their Fields with Water to Protect the Crops from Frost** Plants died up due to expansion of the frozen water in capillary tube of plants. Due to this crops are destroyed. In order to protect plants against it, farmers filled their fields with water.

Heat Capacity

- To change the temperature of substance, a given quantity of heat is absorbed or rejected by it, which is characterised by a quantity is known as **heat capacity**.
- The heat capacity is defined as amount of heat needed to change the temperature by unity i.e. 1° C, it is denoted by S and having SI unit JK^{-1}.

  Heat capacity, $S = \dfrac{\Delta Q}{\Delta T}$

  where, ΔQ = heat absorbed or rejected by body and
  ΔT = change in temperature.

Note Mass of water having the same heat capacity as a given body is called **water equivalent** of the body. The unit of water equivalent is gram.

Specific Heat Capacity

- The amount of heat absorbed or given off by any substance depends on its mass m, the change in temperature ΔT and the nature of substance which is being warmed.

  ⇒ Specific heat capacity,

  $$s = \frac{1}{m}\frac{\Delta Q}{\Delta T} = \frac{S}{m}$$

  where, m = mass of given substance,
  ΔQ = heat absorbed or rejected by body
  ΔT = change in temperature
  and S = Heat capacity.

  The amount of heat needed to raise the temperature of unit mass of a substance by unity is known as the **specific heat capacity** or **specific heat**. It is denoted by s and its SI unit is $Jkg^{-1}K^{-1}$.

  then $$Q \propto m\,\Delta T$$
  $$Q = m \times S \times \Delta T$$

  Water has the highest specific heat capacity ($4.18 \times 10^3\ J\ g^{-1}\ {}^\circ K^{-1}$) compared to other substances.
- Following are some applications of higher specific heat of water :
  - Hot water bottles are used for fomentation purposes.
  - Water is used as a coolant in automobile radiators.
  - In summer, the temperature of land away from the sea increases quickly by taking heat from the sun, while the temperature of sea water rises very slowly, as a result of which the air coming from sea is cold.

Principle of Calorimetry

- The principle of measurement of heat is based on the law of conservation of energy. When a hot body is kept in contact with a cold body, heat energy passes from the hot body to the cold body, till both the bodies attain the same temperature.
- A system is said to be isolated if no exchange or transfer of heat occurs between the system and its surroundings. i.e, if the system is fully insulated then, heat lost by the hot body = Heat gained by the cold body.
  This is called the principle of calorimetry.

Change of State

Matter normally exists in three states: solid, liquid and gas. A transition from one of these states to another is called a change of state. These changes can occurs when exchange of heat takes place between the substance and its surroundings.

Terms Related to Change of State

There are some important terms related to change of state as given below :

- **Melting and Melting Point** The process of change of state from solid to liquid is called **melting.** The temperature at which solid starts to liquefy is known as the **melting point** of that solid.
- **Fusion and Freezing Point** The process of change of state from liquid to solid is called **fusion.** The temperature at which liquid starts to freeze is known as the **freezing point** of the liquid.
- **Vaporisation and Boiling Point** The process of change of state from liquid to vapour (or gas) is called **vaporisation.** During the change of state (completely), the temperature remains constant which implies both liquid and vapour states of the substance co-exist in thermal equilibrium.

  The temperature at which the liquid and the vapour states of the substance co-exist is called the **boiling point** of the liquid.
- **Liquefaction or Condensation** The process of change of state from vapour (or gas) to liquid is called liquefaction or condensation. It is the reverse of vaporisation.
- **Sublimation** The process of change of state directly from solid to vapour (or gas) is known as **sublimation.** There is no matter of liquid state of substance. The reverse process of sublimation is not possible e.g. camphor, nephthalene balls, etc.
- **Regelation** The phenomenon of melting of a substance under high pressure and refreezing when the pressure is reduced is called regelation.

  For example, skating is possible on snow due to the formation of water below skates which is formed due to the increase of pressure and it acts as a lubricant.

Humidity

Water vapour in the atmosphere is referred to as humidity. Humidity capacity refers to the capacity of the air of certain volume at certain temperature to retain maximum of moisture content.

There are two types of humidity:

Relative Humidity

- The ratio of the mass of water vapour actually present in a given volume of air to the mass of water required to saturate the same volume at the same temperature is called the relative humidity.

  Relative humidity is measured with an instrument called the **hygrometer.**
- The examples of relative humidity are :
  - Clothes get dry earlier in winter than in comparison to rainy season but the temperature of air quite high in rainy season than in winter. This is due to the fact that in rainy season relative humidity increases and rate of vaporisation decreases.

Absolute Humidity

The amount of water vapour present in a unit volume of air, is called the absolute humidity of air. It is denoted by g/m^3.

Air Conditioning

The climate of any place on the earth's surface is determined by various parameters like temperature relative humidity, the wind flowing direction etc. Usually for a hygienic and comfortable climate the following conditions should be fulfilled :

- The temperature should lie between 23°C to 25°C.
- The relative humidity should lie between 60% to 65%.
- The speed of wind should lie between 0.70 m/min to 2.5 m/min.

Such climate usually does not exist naturally specially in the urban areas. Thus, it is prepared artificially and on this principle of air conditioning operates.

Evaporation

- From the outer surface at any liquid at any temperature slowly and steadily the transformation of liquid into vapour is called evaporation.
- In this process, the liquid absorbs heat from itself or from its surroundings so, the liquid and its surroundings get cooled.
- The evaporation depends on various factors given below :
  - **Pressure** When the pressure is high, the rate of evaporation decreases.
  - **An increase of surface area** If the surface area is increased, the rate of evaporation increases.
  - **An increase of temperature** With the increase of temperature, more number of particles get enough kinetic energy to go into the vapour state.
  - **Humidity** It is the amount of water vapour present in the air, if the amount of water in air is low, the rate of evaporation increases and *vice-versa*.
  - **Wind speed** It is a common observation that clothes dry faster on a windy day.

    With the increase in wind speed, the particles of water vapour move away with the wind, decreasing the amount of water vapour in the surrounding.

Applications of Evaporation

- When the perfume or spray bottle is kept open, the perfume evaporates consequently, the bottle becomes cool.
- In summer, *surahi* (water container made of ceramic) by the evaporation process lowers the temperature and water becomes cool.
- The air of cooler is cold due of evaporation.
- For the evaporation of sweat from the body the heat is taken out from the skin, which helps to keep the body cool.

Latent Heat

The amount of heat transferred per unit mass during the change of state of a substance without any change in its temperature is called latent heat of the substance for particular change.

Thus, if a mass m of a substance undergoes a change from one state to the other, then the quantity of heat required is given by $Q = mL$ i.e. Latent heat, $L = Q/m$

where, L is the latent heat. Latent heat is also called as **heat of transformation.** Its SI unit is J/kg.

Types of Latent Heat

There are two types of latent heat of materials as discussed below :

- **Latent Heat of Fusion** The latent heat of fusion of a substance is the quantity of heat required to change unit mass of the solid substance from solid state to liquid state, while temperature remaining constant.

  In case of ice, the latent heat of fusion of ice is 80 cal/g or 3.33×10^5 J/kg.
- **Latent Heat of Vaporisation** The latent heat of vaporisation of a substance is the quantity of heat required to change unit mass of liquid substance into vapour state while temperature remaining constant.

  In case of water, the latent heat of vaporisation is 536 cal/g or 22.6×10^5 J/kg.

Some Practical Applications of Latent Heat

- **Snow on mountains does not melt all at once** The reason is that ice has a high specific latent heat of fusion (equal to 336000 J $^{-1}$). It is due to this fact that it changes into water slowly as it gets heat energy from the Sun. If latent heat would have been low, all the snow would have melted in a short time on getting heat from the Sun and there would have been flood in the rivers.
- **In cold countries water in lakes and ponds does not freeze all at once** The reason is that the specific latent heat of fusion of ice is sufficiently high (336000 J/kg). The water in lakes and ponds will have to liberate a large quantity of heat to the surrounding before freezing. The layer of ice is formed on water, being a poor conductor of heat, will also prevent the loss of heat from water of lake, hence, it does not freeze all at one.
- **When ice in a frozen lake starts melting, its surrounding becomes very cold** The reason is that quite a large amount of heat energy is required for melting the frozen lake which is absorbed from the surrounding atmosphere. As a result, the temperature of the surrounding falls and it becomes very cold.
- **It is generally more cold after a hail storm (when ice melts) than during or before the hail storm.** The reason is that after the hail storm, ice absorbs the heat energy required for its melting from the surroundings. So, the temperature of the surroundings falls further down and we feel more cold.
- **Ice cream is much more colder than ice cooled water as 0°C.** When ice cream melts, it takes sufficient heat from the teeth. So, the sensation of coldness felt by teeth from ice cream is much more than ice cooled water at 0°C.
- The latent heat of steam is more than of water. This is why burns from the team are more serious than those from boiling water.

Heat Transfer

Heat is the form of energy which can flow from one body to another due to their temperature difference in the form of radiations, molecular vibrations, molecular displacement, etc. These processes of heat flow are collectively known as **heat transfer**.

There are three modes of heat transfer namely:

- Conduction
- Convection
- Radiation

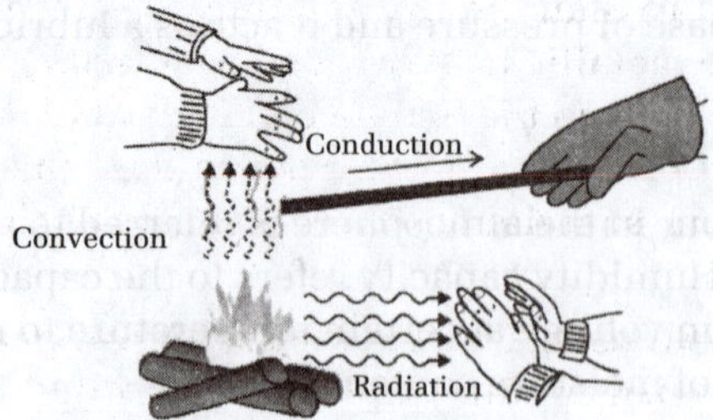

Heating by conduction, convection and radiation

Conduction

The transfer of heat taking place due to molecular vibrations (i.e. molecular collisions) is known as **heat conduction**. In this process, there is no change in average position of the molecule and hence, there is no mass movement of matter.

- Generally in solids, heat is transferred by the process of conduction.
- Conduction requires medium for heat transfer. It is a slow process.

Thermal Conductivity

The ability of material to conduct the heat through it is known as **thermal conductivity**. Thus, heat conduction is defined as the time rate of heat flow in a material for a given temperature difference.

Consider a metallic rod of length L and uniform cross-section A with its two ends maintained at different temperature. Then, rate of heat transfer through conduction is

$$H = \frac{Q}{t} = kA\frac{\Delta T}{L}$$

where, k is known as coefficient of thermal conductivity of rod. The greater value of k implies that the material will conduct the heat more rapidly. The SI unit of k is

$^{-1}$ or .

According to the process of conduction, materials are divided into two main categories as follows :

- **Conductors** The materials which allows heat to pass through them easily are conductors of heat. For example, aluminium, iron, copper, etc.
- **Insulators** The materials which do not allow heat to pass through them easily are poor conductors of heat and known as insulators. For example, plastic, wood, water, air, etc.

Applications of Thermal Conduction in Daily Life

Some applications of conductivity in daily life are as follows :

- **In winter, a metallic handle appears colder than the wooden door** In winter, the human body is at a higher temperature than the surrounding objects. As we touch the metallic handle (good conductor), heat flows from our body to the handle and feels cold. But no heat flows from our body to the wooden door (bad conductor), so it does not feel that cold as the metallic handle.
- **Cooking utensils are provided with wooden handles** Wood is a bad conductor of heat. A wooden handle does not allow heat to be conducted from the hot utensils to the hand. So, we can easily hold the hot utensils with the help of wooden handles.
- **Birds swell their feather in winter** By doing so the birds enclose air between their feathers and the body. Air is poor conductor of heat. It prevents the loss of heat from the bodies of the birds to the surroundings and as such they do not feel cold in winter.
- **Ice is packed in saw dust** Air trapped inside saw dust are poor conductors of heat. This prevents the conduction of heat from the surroundings to the ice which may otherwise melt the ice.
- **When a wire gauge is placed over the burning Bunsen's burner, the flame does not go beyond the gauge** Copper is a very good conductor of heat. The copper gauge absorbs most of the heat.
- Therefore, the temperature of the gas above the gauge is not high enough to ignite the gas.
- **A refrigerator is provided with insulated walls** Generally, fibre glass is used as an insulating material. This is done to minimise the chances of heat flowing into the refrigerator from outside.

Convection

Convection is the process in which heat is transferred from one point to another by the actual motion of matter from a region of high temperature to a region of lower temperature. This process of heat transfer takes place only in liquids.

There are two types of convections:

- **Forced Convection** In forced convection, material is forced to move by a pump or by some physical means. The heat transfer in human body is an example of forced convection.
- **Natural or Free Convection** In this process of convection, if the heated material moves due to difference in density. This process of heat transfer is called natural or free convection such as heat transfer in water.

Applications of Convection in Daily Life

Some applications of convection in daily life are as follows:

- **In Regulating the Temperature of Human Body** In the human body, the heart acts as the pump that circulates blood through different parts of the body, transferring heat by forced convection and maintaining it at a uniform temperature.
- **In Maintaining Comfortable Room Temperature in Cold Countries** In cold countries during winter, the outside temperature is much below than 0°C while the inside temperature of room is maintained around 20°C.

  Thus, heat is continuously transferred from the room to the outside by convection and this heat loss is compensated by the heating system provided in the room.
- **Use of High Chimneys in Big Factories** In big factories, high chimneys are used to produce the

convection currents. Smoke and hot air being lighter due to less density rise up and escape out of the chimney.

The suction effect of the chimney depends on the difference in temperature of inner hot air and outer cold air. Higher the chimney, more is the difference in temperature and so more will be the suction effect. This is why the chimneys are made high.

- **In a Refrigerator, the Freezer Chest is Kept at the Top** By doing so, the remaining space underneath the freezer chest remains cool by the convection currents. The reason is that the hot air from its bottom, being lighter, rises up and gets cooled on striking with the freezer chest.

  The upper cold air, being heavier, comes down and cools the drinks, water bottles, vegetables etc. placed in the space inside the refrigerator.

- **Land and Sea Breezes** During the day, the land heats up faster than the sea. This occurs because the water has greater specific heat and because mixing currents disperse the absorbed heat throughout the great volume of water.

  The hot air above the land expands and becoming less dense and hence, the warmer air rises and colder air from the sea takes its place. The warmer air from the land moves towards the sea to complete the cycle. This creates a breeze from the sea to the land which is called a sea breeze.

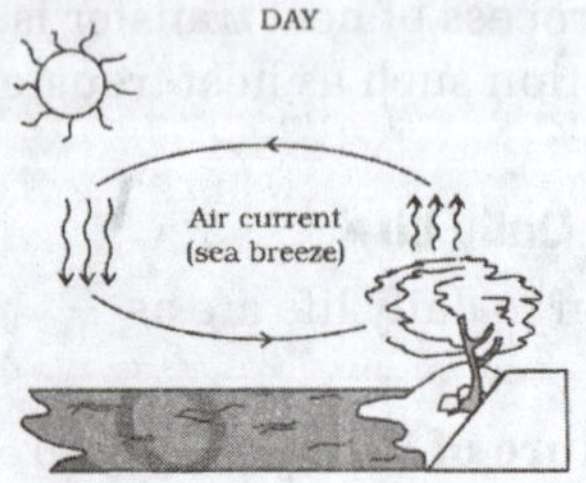

Land warmer than water

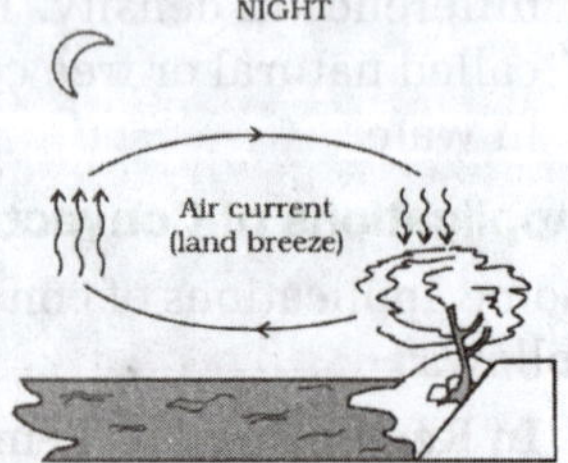

Water warmer than land

Convection Cycles

During the night, the opposite happens. The land cools faster than sea. The warm air above the sea rises. This warm air is replaced by colder air from the land creating a land breeze.

- **Formation of Trade Winds** Winds are convection currents on a large scale in nature. At the equator, where the surface of earth is hottest, warm air rises vertically upwards while cooler air from the North and the South latitudes moves to take place of the warm air. These large-scale movements of air form **trade winds** which blow all the year round. Owing to the rotation of earth, the trade winds do not blow from North and South, but from North-East and South-East.

Radiation

- It is a mode of heat transfer from one place to another needs no medium. The heat is transferred by the mean of thermal radiations, radiant energy or simply radiation. Here, the term radiation is used in two meanings.
- The first is the process by which the energy is emitted by a body, is transmitted in space and falls on another body. The second one is the energy itself is being transmitted in space.
- The heat from the Sun reaches to the Earth by radiation. These are travelling millions of kilometres of empty space (i.e. without any material medium).

Thermal Radiation

The electromagnetic radiation emitted by a body, by virtue of its temperature like the radiation by a red hot iron or light from filament lamp is called thermal radiation. Characteristics of thermal radiation are :

- These are electromagnetic waves having wavelength ranges from 1 μm to 100 μm. These are also called **infrared waves.**
- Like light, thermal radiations travel in a straight line.
- They show the phenomena of interference, diffraction and polarisation.
- Thermal radiations produce heat when they are absorbed by a body.

Colour of a Body

When thermal radiation falls on some other body, it may partly reflected and partly absorbed. The amount of heat that a body absorbed by radiation depends on the colour of the body.

Applications of Thermal Radiation in Daily Life

- **Light coloured clothes are preferred in summers while dark coloured clothes are preferred in winter** This is because in summer, light coloured clothes are poor absorbers and good reflectors of heat. They keep the body cool.

  On the other hand,, dark coloured clothes are preferred in winter because they absorb most of the heat from the Sun and keep the body warm.

- **Outer surface of tea pots are made radiant** The radiant surface neither absorbs heat from outside nor it allows heat to flow outside. Thus, tea remains hot for a long time.
- **Surface of cooking utensils are blackened and rough** Black and rough surfaces are good absorbers and emitters of heat. Therefore, black and rough surface of utensils can receive more heat from the fire place as a

result the vegetable inside the utensils receive more heat and hence food cooks fast.

- **Deserts are hot in day and cold in night** Sand is a good absorber and good emitter of heat, therefore in day hours it absorbs heat from the sun light. In night it re-emit the heat and gets cool.
- **Cloudy nights are more warmer than clear sky nights** The earth becomes warmer in day sunlight and gets cool in night by radiating radiation .When the sky remains clear then heat travels from the Earth towards the Sun by radiation.

  When clouds (bad absorber of heat or good reflector) appear in sky then heat moving towards the sky gets reflected from the clouds and more towards the Earth which result in warming the Earth.
- **Thermos flask** It is a device to minimise heat transfer between the contents of the bottle and outside.

  It consists of a double-walled glass vessel with the inner and outer walls coated with silver.

  Radiation from the inner wall is reflected back into the content of the bottle. The outer wall, similarly, reflects back any incoming radiation. The space between the walls is evacuated to reduce conduction and convection losses and the flask is supported on an insulator like cork.

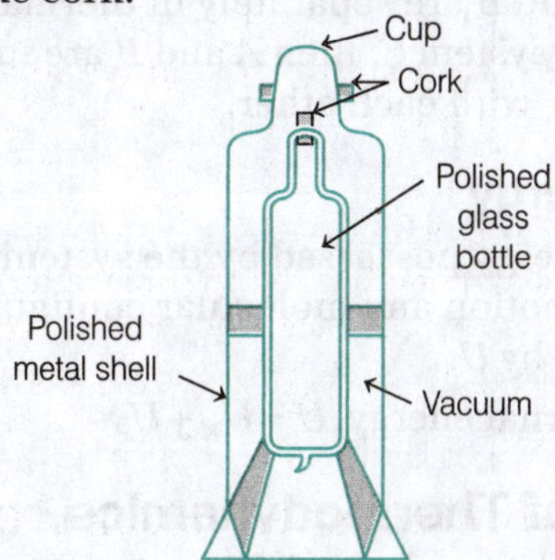

Absorptive and Emissive Powers

- **Absorptive Power** The ratio of the amount of thermal radiation absorbed by a body in a given time to the total amount of thermal radiations incident on it in the same time is known as absorptance (*a*) or absorptive power of the body.

$$\text{Absorptive power} = \frac{\text{Energy absorbed}}{\text{Total incident energy}}$$

- **Emissive Power** The total amount of radiant energy emitted per unit area of a surface per second is called the emissive power.

$$\text{Emissive power, } (e) = \frac{\text{Radiant energy}}{\text{Area of surface} \times \text{time}}$$

Black Body

- A body that absorbs all the radiations falling on it is known as a black body. It emits the radiations at the fastest rate. The radiations emitted by a black body is known as **black body radiation**. The black body is also called the **ideal radiator**.
- A perfect body absorbs 100% of radiations falling on it, is only an ideal concept because within the universe there is no existence of black body.

  For example, lamp black is close to a black body because, it reflects only 1% of radiation falling on it. It is not essential that a perfectly black body should appear black.

Kirchhoff's Law

It is the ratio of emissive power to the absorptive power of all substances is same and it is equal to the emissive power of a perfectly black body.

i.e., $\frac{e_\lambda}{a_\lambda} = E_\lambda$ (at any temperature)

where, e_λ = emissive power of the body

a_λ = absorptive power of the body

and E_λ = constant.

Wien's Displacement Law

- The wavelength (λ_m) corresponding to which the energy emitted by a black body is maximum and is inversely proportional to its absolute temperature (T).

  Thus, $\lambda_m \propto \frac{1}{T}$ or $\lambda_m T = b =$ Constant

  where, $b =$ Wien's constant $= 2.9 \times 10^{-3}$ mK
- This law can be used to estimate the surface temperatures of the Moon, Sun and other Stars.

Stefan-Boltzmann Law

- The total energy emitted per second by a unit area (A) of a perfect black body is proportional to the fourth power of its absolute temperature (T). i.e. $E \propto AT^4$

  $\Rightarrow$ Total energy, $E = \sigma AT^4$

  where, σ is a universal constant called Stefan-Boltzmann constant.

  $$\sigma = 5.67 \times 10^{-8}\ \text{Wm}^{-2}\ \text{K}^{-4}.$$
- If the body is not a perfect black body and has emissivity ε, then above relations get modified as $E = \varepsilon\sigma T^4$

  where, ε = emissivity of that body

Newton's Law of Cooling

According to this law, the rate of loss of heat of the body is directly proportional to the difference of temperature of the body and the surroundings.

The two necessary conditions for this law are as follows :

- This law good only for small difference of temperatures.
- The loss of heat radiation depends upon the nature of the surface of the body and the area of the exposed surface.
- Hot water takes much less time in cooling from 100°C to 95°C than from 20°C to 15°C.

Greenhouse Effect

- It is defined as, a process of having a high temperature in the greenhouse although it receives fewer radiations than the outside. It occurs due to the high concentration of carbon dioxide and vapour content. The glass walls are also included under it. They allow the short wave radiations to enter the house.
- There is almost no dissipation of energy as the longer heat waves cannot penetrate through the carbon dioxide and vapour. It leads to the warmer dust and cloudy nights as compared to the dry nights.
- The gas such as carbon dioxide is known as the **greenhouse gas** as it is transparent to the solar radiations but have the ability to absorb infrared waves. These are also known as the **long waves.**
- The carbon dioxide concentration in the atmosphere has increased which may be attributed to the increase in the temperature of atmosphere. This effect is known as the **greenhouse effect**. It melts the ice and increases the sea level.
- The downward flux, of long wave radiations by the greenhouse gases, is called **greenhouse flux**. This plays a very significant role in keeping the Earth warm, at an average or mean temperature, around (nearly) 15°C.
- In the absence of this flux, the Earth mean temperature would drop to –18°C. At such a low temperature, water will freeze and most of life on Earth would not survive.

Thermodynamics

- Thermodynamics is the field of physics which deals heat and work transfer and the associated changes in the properties (such as pressure, volume, temperature, etc) of a working substance.
- It is a **macroscopic science** and involves few macroscopic variables of the system. The state of a gas in thermodynamics is specified by macroscopic variables such as pressure, volume, temperature, mass and composition of gas.

Work and Heat

- Work and Heat are two different forms of energy which can transformed into one another.
- Heat is a form of energy which is transferred from one body to another body due to temperature difference, while work does not depend on the temperature difference.

  For example, when a hot body is brought in contact with a cold body, then energy is transformed from the hot body to the cold body, till their temperatures do not become equal. This energy is heat.

  When a person stirs cold water taken in vessel, then energy is transferred from the person into the water and water becomes slightly hot, whatever be the initial temperature of the water. It this condition, transferred energy is the work done by the person.

Thermal Equilibrium

Two systems are said to be in thermal equilibrium with each other if they are at the same temperature.

Zeroth Law of Thermodynamics

- This law was formulated by **RH Fowler** in 1931.
- The zeroth law of thermodynamics states that if two systems A and B are separately in thermal equilibrium with a third system C, then A and B are in thermal equilibrium with each other.

Internal Energy

- The total energy possessed by the system due to molecular motion and molecular configuration. It is represented by U.

  Then, Internal energy, $U = U_K + U_P$

First Law of Thermodynamics

- First law of thermodynamics is a statement of conservation of energy applied to any system in which energy transfer from or to the surroundings is taken into account.
- It states that heat is given to a system used in doing external work and it increases the internal energy of the system.

  i.e. Heat supplied, $\Delta Q = \Delta U + \Delta W$

  where,

  ΔQ = Heat supplied to the system by the surroundings

  ΔW = Work done by the system on the surroundings

  ΔU = Change in internal energy of the system

  ΔU depends only on the initial and final states.

Thermodynamic Processes

When a state of a system changes or the state variables changes with time, then this process is known as thermodynamic process. Practical applications of thermodynamic processes are as follows :

- **Cyclic Process** When a system after passing through different states returns to its original state, then it is called a cyclic process. In this process, the heat given to system equals the net work done by the system.
- **Isothermal Process** When a thermodynamic system undergoes through a process in which its temperature remains constant throughout, then this process is said to be isothermal process. *e.g.,* boiling process is also an isothermal process.
- **Adiabatic Process** When a thermodynamic system undergoes a process under the condition that no heat comes into or goes out of the system, then the process is said to be adiabatic. *e.g.,* sudden bursting of the tube of a bicycle tyre and propagation of sound waves in air and other gases.
- **Isobaric and Isochoric Process** When a process takes place at constant pressure, then the process is called isobaric process. *e.g,* heating of water in the boiler of a steam engine, formation of steam, superheating of steam, freezing of water, etc.

  While, a process taking place at constant volume, is called isochoric process an ideal gas is an example of isochoric process. The heat absorbed by the ideal gas is entirely used in the work done by gas.

Reversible and Irreversible Process

- **Reversible process** A process which could be reserved in such a way that the system and its surrounding returns exactly to their initial states with no other changes in the universe is known as reversible process.
- Some examples of reversible process are:
  - All isothermal and adiabatic changes are reversible if they are performed very slowly.
  - When a certain amount of heat is absorbed by ice, it melts. If the same amount of heat is removed from it, the water formed in the direct process will be converted into ice.
  - An extremely slow extension or contraction of a spring without setting up oscillations.
  - When a perfectly elastic ball falls from some height on a perfectly elastic horizontal plane, the ball rises to the initial height.
  - Very slow evaporation or condensation.

Note It should be remembered that the conditions mentioned for a reversible process can never be realised in practice. Hence, a reversible process is only an ideal concept. In actual process, there is always loss of heat due to friction, conduction and radiation, etc.

- **Irreversible Process** Any process which is not reversible exactly is an irreversible process. All natural processes such as conduction, radiation, radioactive decay etc., are irreversible processes. All practical processes such as free expansion, Joule-Thomson expansion, electrical heating of a wire are also irreversible.
- Some examples of irreversible processes are :
  - When a steel ball is allowed to fall on an inelastic lead sheet, its kinetic energy changes into heat energy by friction. The heat energy raises the temperature of lead sheet. No reverse transformation of heat energy occurs.
  - The sudden and fast stretching of a spring may produce vibrations in it. Now, a part of the energy is dissipated.
  - This is the case of irreversible process.
  - Sudden expansion or contraction and rapid evaporation or condensation are examples of irreversible processes.
  - The combustion reaction of a mixture of petrol and air ignited by a spark.
  - Heat transfer between bodies at different temperatures is also irreversible.
  - Joule-Thomson effect is irreversible because on reversing the flow of gas, a similar cooling or heating effect is not observed.

Heat Engine

Heat engine is a device by which a system is made to undergo a cyclic process that results in conversion of heat to work.

The essential parts of a heat engine are as follows :

- **Source of Heat** It is a reservoir of heat at high temperature and infinite thermal capacity. Any amount of heat can be extracted from it and its temperature remains unchanged.
- **Working Substance** A material which absorbs heat energy from the source and converts it into mechanical energy (useful work) by rejecting some of the heat to sink is called **working substance.** e.g. Steam, petrol, etc.
- **Sink** It is a reservoir of heat at low temperature and infinite thermal capacity. Any amount of heat can be given to the sink and its temperature remains unchanged.

  In this, the working substance absorbs heat q_1 from the source, does an amount of work W, rejects the remaining amount of heat to the sink then it comes back to its original state and there occurs no change in its internal energy.

By repeating the same cycle over and over again, work is continuously obtained.

Second Law of Thermodynamics

- The principle that put a restriction on the first law of thermodynamics is known as the **second law of thermodynamics.** The second law of thermodynamics gives a fundamental limitation to the efficiency of a heat engine and the coefficient of performance of a refrigerator.
- Two statements of Kelvin-Planck and Clausius put restrictions on the possibility of perfect heat engine and perfect refrigerator, respectively.
  - **Kelvin-Planck's Statement** No process is possible whose sole result is the absorption of heat from a reservoir and the complete conversion of the heat into work.
  - **Clausius Statement** No process is possible whose sole result is the transfer of heat from a colder object to a hotter object.

Carnot Engine

- Carnot engine is an ideal heat engine proposed by **Sadi Carnot** in 1824. The reversible engine which operates between two temperatures of source and sink is known as Carnot heat engine.
- The designed engine is a theoretical engine which is free from all the defects of a practical engine.
- The efficiency of Carnot engine will be 100%, if the temperature of the sink is 0K. As practically, we cannot attain a sink at 0K, so it is not possible to have 100% efficiency.

Refrigerator or Heat Pump

- A refrigerator or heat pump is basically a heat engine which runs in reverse directions. In this, the working substance takes heat from a sink (contents of refrigerator) at lower temperature.
- An amount of work W is done on it by some external agency (usually compressor of refrigerator) and gives out a larger amount of heat to a hot body at temperature (usually atmosphere). Thus, it transfers heat from a cold to a hot body at the expense of mechanical energy supplied to it by an external agent. The cold body is thus cooled more and more.

Molecular Nature of Matter

- Molecules which are made up of one or more atoms constitute matter.
- In solids, these atoms and molecules are rigidly fixed and space between them is very less and hence they cannot move, while in liquids, the atoms are not as rigidly fixed as in solids and can move around. This enables a liquid to flow.
- In gases atoms are free to travel without colliding for large distances such that if gases were not enclosed in an enclosure they would disappear.
- The average distance a molecule can travel without colliding is called the **mean free path.**
- In gases, the mean free path is of order of thousands of angstroms.

Physical Properties of Gases

Gases do not possess any definite volume or shape. They totally fill all the space accessible to them.

Some important properties of gases are discussed below :

- As intermolecular forces between molecules of a gas is minimum, hence they can be compressed easily.
- Gases exert pressure on the walls of the vessels in which they are kept and on its surroundings.
- Gases have no shape and size and always take the shape of the container.
- Gases expand indefinitely and uniformly to fill the available space and density of substance in gaseous state is very low.

Ideal gas

- A gas that satisfies exactly at all pressures and temperature is defined to an ideal gas.
- A ideal gas is a simple theoretical model of a gas.
- No real gas is truly ideal.
- The perfect gas or ideal gas equation can be written as,

$$pV = \mu RT$$

where, μ = Number of moles of that gas

R = Universal constant ($R = 8.314 \text{ J mol}^{-1} \text{K}^{-1}$)

T = Absolute temperature

p = Pressure

V = Volume

Gaseous Laws

Law	Description
Boyle's law	It states that for a given mass of a gas at constant temperature, the volume (V) of that mass of gas is inversely proportional to its pressure (p) i.e $V \propto \frac{1}{p}$ or pV = constant
Charle's law	It states that for a given mass of an ideal gas at constant pressure, volume (V) of a gas is directly proportional to its absolute temperature (T) i.e $V \propto T$ or $\frac{V}{T}$ = constant
Gay Lussac's law (or pressure law)	It states that for a given mass of an ideal gas at constant volume, the pressure (p) of that mass of gas is directly proportional to its absolute temperature (T) i.e $p \propto T$ or $\frac{p}{T}$ = constant
Dalton's law of partial pressure	It states that the total pressure of a mixture of non-interacting ideal gases is equal to the sum of partial pressures exerted by individual gases in the mixture i.e $p = p_1 + p_2 + p_3 \cdots\cdots$

Behaviour of Gases

- The study of gases shows that the volume, pressure and temperature of a given mass of a gas are inter-related to one another. If we fix the value of any two of them, then the value of the third cannot changed.

Extra Facts From Tamil Nadu Board and NIOS

- Higher the value of specific heat of a substance lower will be the rate at which it is heated or cooled as compared to the substance of lower specific heat under identical conditions.
- **Calorie** One calorie is defined as the amount of heat energy **to rise the temperature of 1 g of water through 1°C.**
- **Kilocalorie** One kilocalorie is defined as the amount of heat energy required to rise the temperature of 1 kg of water through 1°C.
- **Real Expansion** If a liquid is heated directly without using any container, then the expansion that you observe is termed as real expansion.
- **Apparent Expansion** The expansion of a liquid apparently observed without considering the expansion of the container is called apparent expansion.

Oscillations

[SOURCES]

Class-XI NCERT Chap 13 (Oscillations)

- In our daily life, we come across various kinds of motions. In some cases, the motion is repeated after a certain interval of time, i.e., it is periodic motion.
- The leaves and branches of a tree oscillating in breeze, boats bobbing at anchor and the surging pistons in the engines of cars, etc execute a periodic or to and fro motion.

Periodic Motion

- When a particle repeats its motion continuously on a definite path in a regular interval of time, then its motion is called periodic motion.
- The motion of any planet around the sun in an elliptical orbit, the motion of the hands of a clock are periodic motions.

Oscillatory or Vibratory Motion

- If a body moves back and forth (to and fro) repeatedly about its mean position, its motion is said to be oscillatory or vibratory motion. Such a motion repeats itself over and over again about a mean position, such that it remains confined within well-defined limits (known as extreme positions) on either side of the mean position.
- Every oscillatory motion is periodic, but every periodic motion need not be oscillatory. **Circular motion** is a periodic motion, but it is not oscillatory.

Examples of Oscillatory Motion

- The swinging motion of the pendulum of a wall clock.
- The oscillations of a mass suspended from a spring.
- The motion of the piston of an automobile engine.
- The vibrations of the string of a guitar.
- The motion of a freely suspended bar magnet.

Simple Harmonic Motion

- When oscillation is along a straight line, it is known as Simple Harmonic Motion (SHM).
- In this motion, acceleration of oscillating body is always towards a fixed point naming centre of oscillation.
- The magnitude of acceleration is directly proportional to the distance of object from the point of oscillation.
- Oscillations of a loaded spring, vibrations of a tuning fork, vibrations of the balance wheel of a watch, etc, are examples of SHM.

Conditions for Simple Harmonic Motion

Some necessary conditions for simple harmonic motion are as follows :

- The motion of particle should be to and fro about its mean position.

- The direction of restoring force should be towards the mean position.
- Restoring force (F) acting on the particle should always be proportional to its displacement (y) from the mean position,

i.e., $F \propto y$ or $F = -ky$

Here, k is a positive constant called **force constant** or **spring factor.**

The negative sign shows that the restoring force F always acts in the opposite direction of the displacement.

Note A simple harmonic motion can always be expressed in terms of a simple harmonic function of sine or cosine.

Definitions Related to SHM

- **Displacement** (x) The distance of the oscillating particle from its mean position at any instant is called its displacement. It is represented by

$$x = a \sin \omega t$$

- **Amplitude** (A) The maximum displacement of the oscillating particle on either side of its mean position is called its amplitude.
- **Time Period** (T) The time taken by a particle to complete one oscillation is called its time period or it is the smallest time interval after which the oscillatory motion repeats.
- **Frequency** (ν) It is defined as the number of oscillations completed per unit time by a particle. Frequency is equal to the reciprocal of time period i.e.,

$$\nu = \frac{1}{T}$$

The unit of frequency is $(\text{second})^{-1}$ or s^{-1}. It is also expressed as cycles per second (cps) or Hertz (Hz).

- **Phase** (ϕ) The phase of a vibrating particle at any instant gives the state of the particle as regards its position and the direction of motion at that instant.

Important Terms Related to Simple Harmonic Motion

- The **displacement** of a particle in simple harmonic motion at any instant t is given as,

$$y = A \sin \omega t \text{ and } x = A \cos \omega t$$

or $$y = A \sin \frac{2\pi t}{T}$$

and $$x = A \cos \frac{2\pi t}{T}$$

- The **velocity** of a particle in simple harmonic motion at any instant t is given as,

$$v = \omega\sqrt{A^2 - y^2}$$

- The **acceleration** of a particle in simple harmonic motion at any instant t is given as,

$$a = -\omega^2 y$$

- The **time period** of a particle executing simple harmonic motion is given as,

$$T = 2\pi\sqrt{\frac{\text{Displacement}}{\text{Acceleration}}} = 2\pi\sqrt{\frac{y}{a}}$$

- The **time period** of body attached by a **spring** is given as

$$T = 2\pi\sqrt{\frac{m}{k}}$$

where, m is the mass of the body and k is the force constant of spring.

Energy in Simple Harmonic Motion

When a body is displaced from its equilibrium position by doing work upon it, it acquires potential energy.

When the body is released, it begins to move back with a velocity, thus acquiring kinetic energy.

Hence, the body executing simple harmonic motion has kinetic and potential energies, both varying between the limits, zero and maximum.

- **Kinetic Energy** The kinetic energy of the particle at any displacement y is given by

$$K = \frac{1}{2}m\omega^2(A^2 - y^2)$$

or $$K = \frac{1}{2}k(A^2 - y^2)$$

When the particle is at mean position, its kinetic energy is maximum and when the particle is at its extreme position, the kinetic energy is zero because velocity at extreme position is zero.

- **Potential Energy** The potential energy of a particle at displacement y is given by

$$U = \frac{1}{2}m\omega^2 y^2$$

or $$U = \frac{1}{2}ky^2$$

The potential energy of particle is zero at the mean position and it is maximum at the extreme position.

- **Total Energy** The sum of kinetic energy and potential energy is total energy in simple harmonic motion.

$$E = U + K$$

or $$E = \frac{1}{2}m\omega^2 A^2$$

or $$E = \frac{1}{2}kA^2$$

Thus, the total mechanical energy of a particle in SHM is independent of time and displacement.

Simple Pendulum

It is said that Galileo measured the periods of a swinging chandelier in a church by his pulse beats. He observed that the motion of chandeliner was periodic. This kind of system called **pendulum**.

- A small metallic bob suspended by a light inextensible string from a rigid support, such that it is free to oscillate without friction about a point, is called a simple pendulum.
- In practice, a simple pendulum is obtained by suspending a small metal bob by a long and fine cotton thread from a rigid support.
- The bob is free to swing to and fro in the plane i.e., to the left and right of a vertical line through the pivot point or point of suspension as shown below :

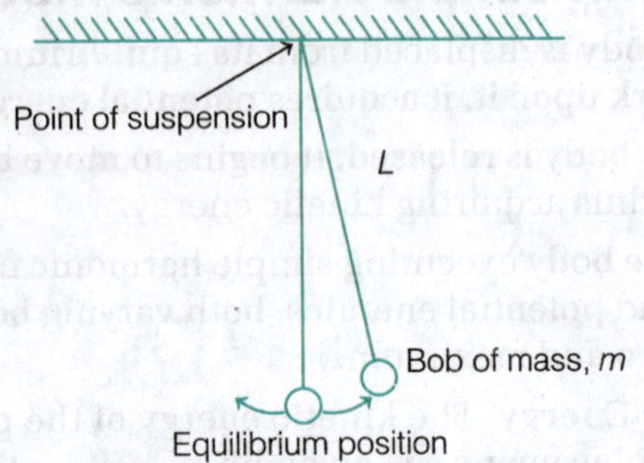

- If the bob is slightly displaced on either side and released, it begins to oscillate about the mean position. Its time period is given by

$$T = 2\pi\sqrt{\frac{l}{g}}$$

where, l is the length of pendulum and g is acceleration due to gravity.

- Conclusions from the above are :
  - The time period of simple pendulum is directly proportional to the square root of length of the pendulum. If the length of the pendulum be increased to four times, the time period of pendulum will become twice.
  - The time period is independent of the mass m of the bob.
  - As the acceleration due to gravity decreases, the time period of simple pendulum increases or *vice-versa*.
  - The motion of a simple pendulum swinging through small angles is approximately simple harmonic motion.
  - The time period of seconds pendulum is 2 s.
  - The time period of simple pendulum of infinite length is 84.6 minute.
  - When a pendulum clock is taken upto a hill or down in a mine, then due to decrease in the value of g, its periodic time increases (i.e. the clock is slowed down).
  - If the lift is going up with accelerated motion, then the time period of the pendulum is decreased because the acceleration due to gravity is increased. While the lift is coming down, then the periodic time of the pendulum is increased because the effective value of g is decreased from its actual value.
  - If the string of the lift breaks (i.e., the lift falling like a free body), then the periodic time of the pendulum becomes infinite because the effective value of g becomes zero.
  - The effective length of pendulum will increase with the rise of temperature due to which the time period will increase. But in winter season the effective length is contracted, thus time period is decreased and the clock based on pendulum becomes fast.
  - The time period of oscillation of the pendulum clock is increased on the Moon's surface because acceleration due to gravity is $g/6$ on the Moon surface, where g is the acceleration gravity on the earth. So, pendulum clock is slowed down.

Natural or Free Vibrations

- A body clamped at one point when disturbed slightly from its rest position, starts vibrating. The vibrations so produced are called natural or free vibrations of the body.
- The time period of the body is called its natural period and the frequency is called its natural frequency.

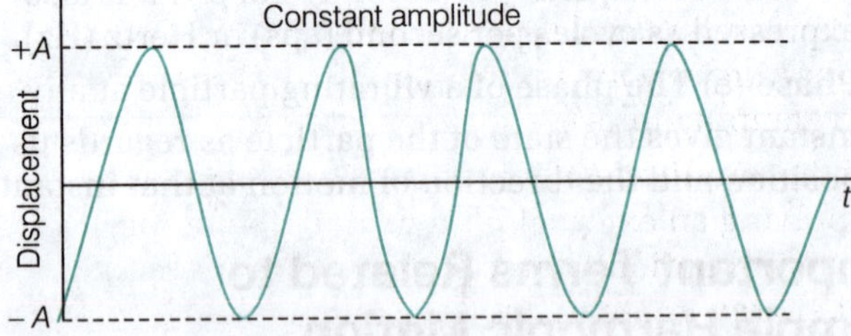

- The natural vibrations of a body occur only in vacuum because the presence of medium offers some resistance, due to which the amplitude of vibrations does not remain constant but it continuously decreases.

Examples of Natural (or Free) Vibrations

- If the bob of a simple pendulum is displaced slightly from its mean position, it starts vibrating with its natural frequency.
- When a tuning fork is struck against a hard rubber pad, it vibrates with its natural frequency.

- When we strike the keys of a piano, various strings are set in vibrations each at its natural frequency.
- When an air column in a flute is made to vibrate, it vibrates with its natural frequency which is inversely proportional to the length of air column.
- Different parts of building bridges, ships machines, etc, execute free oscillations.

Damped Vibrations

When a body is made to vibrate in a medium, the amplitude of the vibrating body continuously decreases with time and ultimately the body stops vibrating.

Thus, the periodic vibrations of a body of decreasing amplitude in presence of a resistive force are called the damped vibrations and the phenomenon is called **damping**.

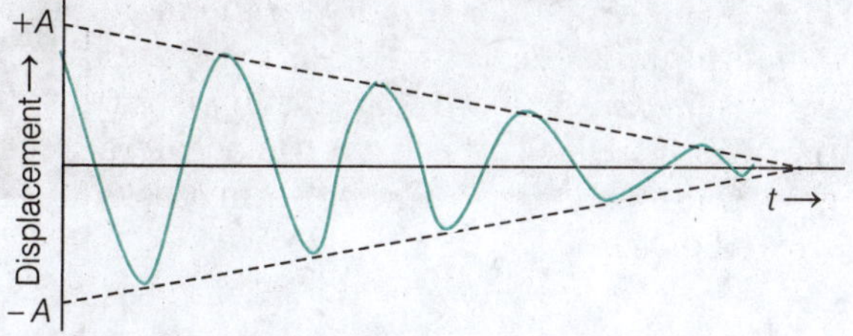

Examples of Damped Vibrations

- When a slim branch of a tree is pulled and then released, it makes the damped vibrations.
- A simple pendulum oscillating in air, (or any medium) executes damped vibrations.
- The vibrations of loaded spring in air.

Forced Vibrations

- The amplitude of natural vibrations of a body vibrating in a medium gradually decreases due to damping forces.
- If the amplitude of vibrations kept constant by applying an external periodic force, then the external periodic force compensates for the loss of energy in each vibrations due to the damping forces.
- The vibrations of the body, are called the forced vibrations.
- Thus, when a body being acted by an external periodic force, vibrates with the frequency of the force, then the vibrations of the body are called forced vibrations.

Examples of Forced Vibrations

- When the stem of a vibrating tuning fork is pressed against the top of a table, it forces the table to vibrate with its own frequencies. The vibrations produced in the table top are the forced vibrations.
- The vibrations produced in the diaphragm of a microphone sound box with frequencies corresponding to the speech of the speaker, are the forced vibrations.
- In a guitar, an artist applies the periodic force on the strings of the guitar to execute the forced vibrations in them.

Resonance

- Resonance is a special case of forced vibrations. When the frequency of the external force on a body is exactly equal to its natural frequency of the body, then the body readily begins to vibrate with an increased amplitude. This phenomenon is known as resonance.
- The vibrations of large amplitude are called the **resonant vibrations**.

Examples of Resonance

- When a troop crosses a suspension bridge, the soldiers are asked to break their steps. The reason is that, if the natural frequency of bridge becomes equal to the frequency of steps, then the bridge will vibrate with a large amplitude due to resonance and may collapse.
- The air column in a resonance tube produces a loud sound when its frequency matches the frequency of the tuning fork.
- Sometimes, in an earthquake, short and tall structures remain unaffected while the medium height structures fall down.
- This happens because the natural frequencies of the short structures happen to be higher and those of taller structures lower than the frequency of the seismic waves.
- Due to resonance, aircraft designers make sure that none of the natural frequencies at which a wing can oscillate match the frequency of the engines in flight.

09

Wave Motion

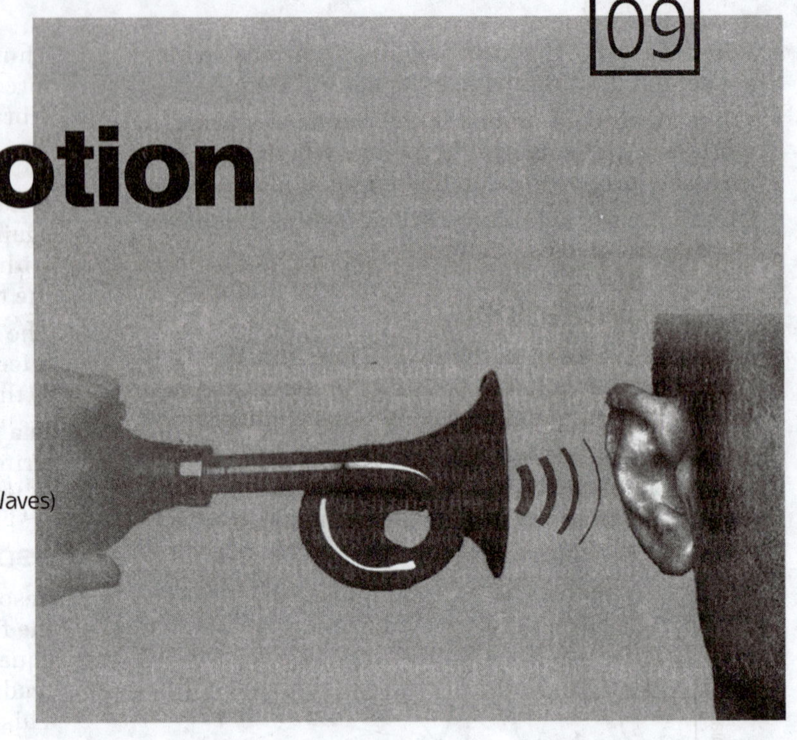

[SOURCES]

Class-VIII NCERT Chap 10 (Sound),
Class-IX NCERT Chap 11 (Sound),
Class-XI NCERT Chap 14 (Waves),
Class-XII NCERT Chap 8 (Electromagnetic Waves)
Tamil Nadu Board (Class-IX), NIOS

- In our daily life, we encounter different types of waves like light waves, sound waves etc. In a wave, information and energy propagate, in the form of signals from one point to another but no material object makes the journey.
- When we make a telephone call to a friend at a distant place, a sound wave carries the message from our vocal cords to the telephone.
- All types of waves do not require a medium for their propagation as some waves can also propagate without medium.

Waves

A wave is a disturbance produced in a material medium and advancing with a definite speed in the medium without changing its form. Waves involve the transport of energy without the transport of matter. Sound waves, radio waves, electromagnetic waves, etc, are the examples of waves.

Types of Waves

There are mainly two types of waves :

1. Mechanical or Elastic Waves

The waves which require a material medium for their propagation are called mechanical waves. Such waves are also called **elastic waves** because their propagation depends on the elastic properties of the medium.

These waves are governed by Newton's laws and can exist in a material medium, such as air, water, rock etc. e.g., water waves, sound waves, seismic waves, etc.

These waves are classified into two categories as follows :

Transverse Waves

- These are the waves in which the individual particles of the medium oscillate perpendicular to the direction of wave propagation.
- The waves produced by a moving one end of a long rope, up and down rapidly, whose one end is fixed, are transverse waves. Similarly, light wave is a transverse wave but it is not a mechanical wave.
- The points of maximum displacement in upward direction are called **crests** and the points of maximum displacement in downward direction are called **trough.**

  These waves involve changes in the shape of the medium. Transverse wave can be produced only in solid which have rigidity.
- Gases have no rigidity. Hence, transverse waves cannot be produced in gases. In liquids, transverse waves cannot be formed in the interior, they can be formed only on the surface of liquids.

  e.g. Waves in string, ripples on the surface of the water, movement of string of stringed musical instruments like sitar, guitar etc.

Longitudinal Waves

- These are the waves in which the individual particles of the medium oscillates along the direction of wave propagation.
- Sound waves produced in air are longitudinal waves.
- Longitudinal waves travel in the form of compressions and rarefactions. They involve changes in volume and density of the medium.
  - **Compression** is the part of a longitudinal wave in which the particles of the medium are closer to one another than normal state and it is the region of high pressure.
  - **Rarefaction** is the part of a longitudinal wave in which the particles of the medium are farther apart than normal state and it is the region of low pressure.
- Longitudinal waves can be produced in all three media such as solid, liquid and gas.

  e.g., waves in spring, sound waves, vibration of air column in organ pipe etc.

Note The waves in an ocean are a combination of both longitudinal and transverse waves.

Seismic Waves

Seismic waves are generated by the sudden movement of materials within the Earth during an earthquake. Volcanic eruptions, explosions, landslides, avalanches and even rushing rivers can also cause seismic waves.

These are three types of seismic waves i.e., *P*-Waves, *S*-Waves and *L*-Waves.

The nature of *P*-waves (Primary waves) is longitudinal. Therefore, they can travel through the solid and liquid both.

The nature of *S*-waves (Secondary waves) is transverse waves. Therefore, they can travel through the solid only.

2. Electromagnetic Waves

The waves which travel in the form of oscillating electric and magnetic fields are called electromagnetic waves. Such waves do not require any material medium for their propagation and are also called non-mechanical waves. For example, light waves, radio waves, *X*-rays, γ-rays etc.

Properties of Electromagnetic Waves

- The oscillations of electric field and magnetic field in EM waves are in same phase and are perpendicular to each other as well as perpendicular to the direction of propagation of the wave.
- They are transverse in nature.
- They travel with the speed of light in vacuum but with different speeds in any material medium.
- The amplitude ratio of the electric field to and magnetic field (Bo) is, $\frac{E_0}{B_0} = C$ (velocity of light).
- These waves are not affected by the electric and magnetic fields.
- These waves show the properties of reflection, refraction, interference, diffraction and polarisation.

Electromagnetic Spectrum

- Electromagnetic waves include visible light waves, *X*-rays, gamma-rays, radio waves, microwaves, ultraviolet and infrared waves.
- The orderly distribution of the electromagnetic waves according to their frequency or wavelength is called electromagnetic spectrum.
- The brief description of different types of electromagnetic waves in order of decreasing wavelength is as follows :

1. Radio Waves

Radio waves are produced by the accelerated motion of charges in conducting wires. These are the electromagnetic waves of longest wavelength and minimum frequency. They are generally in the frequency range from 500 kHz to about 1000 MHz.

Uses of radio waves are :

- These are used in AM (Amplitude Modulation) from 530 kHz to 1710 kHz. These are also used in ground wave propagation.
- These are used in TV (Television) waves ranging from 54 MHz to 890 MHz.
- These are used in FM (Frequency Modulation) ranging from 88 MHz to 108 MHz.
- UHF (Ultra High Frequency) waves are used in cellular phones.

2. Microwaves

Microwaves are short wavelength radio waves with frequencies (1 GHz to 300 GHz), are produced by special vacuum tubes.

Uses of microwaves are :

- These are used in radar systems for aircraft navigation.
- These are used in long-distance communication systems via geostationary satellites.
- These are used in microwave ovens for cooking purpose.
- These are used in study of atomic and molecular structures.

3. Infrared Waves

Infrared waves are produced by hot bodies and molecules. These radiations lie close to the low frequency or long wavelength end of the visible spectrum.

Infrared waves produce heating effect, so they are also referred as heat waves or thermal radiations. Their frequency range is from 3×10^{11} Hz to 4×10^{14} Hz.

- Uses of infrared waves are :
  - Infrared lamps are used in physical therapy.
  - Infrared radiation maintains average temperature of Earth through greenhouse effect.
  - Infrared detectors are used in Earth satellites, both for military purposes and to observe growth of crops.
  - Infrared waves are used in remote control switches of household electronic systems such as TV, video recorders and hifi systems.

4. Visible Rays

- Visible ray is that part of the electromagnetic spectrum that is detected by the human eye. It lies from frequency range of 4×10^{14} Hz to 7×10^{14} Hz.
- Uses of visible light are :
  - Visible light emitted or reflected from objects around us provides us information about the world.
  - It can cause chemical reactions.
- Visible rays are used by the optical organs of humans and animals for three primary purposes given below :
  - To see things, avoid bumping from them and escape danger.
  - To find stuff to eat.
  - To find other living things with which to consort so as to prolong the species.

5. Ultraviolet Rays

Ultraviolet (UV) radiation is produced by special lamps and very hot bodies. The Sun is an important source of UV light. But fortunately, most of it is absorbed in the ozone layer in the atmosphere. Their frequency range is from 10^{14} Hz to 10^{16} Hz.

Uses of Ultraviolet rays are :

- UV lamps are used to kill germs in water purifiers.
- UV radiations are used in LASIK (laser-assisted in situ keratomileusis) eye surgery because it can be focussed into very narrow beams for high precision.
- They are used in the study of molecular structure.
- UV light can be used in food preservation.
- They are used in the study of invisible writings, forged documents and finger prints.

6. X-Rays

X-rays region lies beyond the UV-region of the electromagnetic spectrum. They are generated when a metal target is bombarded by high energy electrons.

X-rays can pass through many forms of matter.

Their frequency range lies from 4×10^{16} Hz to 3×10^{21} Hz.

Uses of X-rays are :

- These are used in medical diagnosis because they can pass through flesh but not through bones.
- These are used in radiotherapy to cure untraceable skin diseases and malignant growths.
- These are used in detections of explosives, diamond, gold etc.
- These are used in engineering for detecting faults, cracks, flaws and holes in the metal products.
- These are used in the study of crystal structure because X-rays can be reflected and diffracted by crystals.

7. Gamma Rays

Gamma rays are high frequency radiations. They are produced in nuclear reactions and also emitted by radioactive nuclei.

These rays are most penetrating EM waves. Their frequency range lies from 3×10^{18} Hz to 5×10^{22} Hz. Uses of Gamma Rays are :

- These are used in radiotherapy for the treatment of tumors and to destroy cancer cells.
- These are used to initiate some nuclear reactions.
- These are used to study the structure of atomic nuclei.
- These are used to preserve food stuffs for a long time because soft γ-rays can kill micro-organisms.
- These are used in the manufacturing of polyethylene from ethylene.

Different Types of Electromagnetic Waves

Type	Wavelength range	Production	Detection
Radio waves	> 0.1 m	Rapid acceleration and deceleration of electrons in aerials	Receiver's aerials
Microwave	0.1 m to 1 mm	Klystron valve or magnetron valve	Point contact diodes
Infrared waves	1 mm to 700 nm	Vibration of atoms and molecules	Thermopiles Bolometer, Infrared photographic film
Light	700 nm to 400 nm	Electrons in atoms emit light when they move from one energy level to a lower energy level	The eye Photocells Photographic film
Ultraviolet rays	400 nm to 1 nm	Inner shell electrons in atoms moving from one energy level to a lower level	Photocells Photographic film
X-rays	1 nm to 10^{-3} nm	X-ray tubes or inner shell electrons	Photographic film, Geiger tubes, Ionisation chamber
Gamma rays	$< 10^{-3}$ nm	Radioactive decay of the nucleus	Photographic film, ionisation chamber

Microwave Oven

- The EM wave spectrum contains microwaves which have frequency and energy smaller than visible light and these radiations are used to cook food or warm it up.
- The basic principle of a microwave oven is to generate microwave radiation of appropriate frequency in the working space of the oven where food is kept.
- In the microwave oven, energy is directly delivered to water molecules which is shared by the entire food whereas the porcelain container is unaffected and cool because it cannot absorb microwaves.

Definitions Related to Waves

Some definitions related to waves are as follows :

- **Amplitude** The maximum displacement of the particles of the medium from their original mean positions on passing a wave through the medium is called amplitude of the wave. Even if the displacement of particle is negative, then the amplitude of wave is positive. Its SI unit is metre (m).

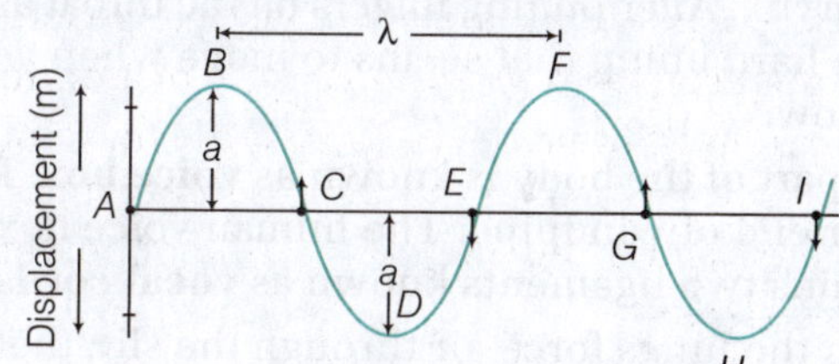

- **Time Period** The time taken by two consecutive compressions or rarefactions to cross a fixed point is called the time period of the wave.
  In other words, the time in which a particle of medium completes one vibration is called time period of the wave. It is denoted by symbol T. Its SI unit is second (s).
- **Frequency** The number of complete waves (or oscillations) produced in one second is called frequency of the wave. It is the number of vibrations that occur per second.
  Or the number of the compressions or rarefactions that cross a point per unit time.
  It is denoted by ν. Its SI unit is Hertz (Hz).
- **Wavelength** The distance covered by a wave during the time in which a particle of the medium completes one vibration about its mean position is called wavelength. It is denoted by λ.
- **Wave Number** The number of waves present in a unit distance of the medium is called wave number. It is denoted by $\bar{\nu}$. Its SI unit is metre^{-1}.
  Wave number, $\bar{\nu} = \frac{1}{\lambda}$ m^{-1}
- **Phase** The phase of a wave is a quantity that gives complete information of the wave at any time and at any position.
- **Phase Difference** The differences in phase of two waves is known as phase difference.
- **Path Difference** The path difference is the difference in the path traversed by the two waves.

Wave Velocity

The distance covered by a wave per unit time in its direction of propagation is called its wave velocity or phase velocity. It is denoted by v.

The relation between wave velocity (v), frequency (ν) and wavelength (λ) is given by $v = \nu \times \lambda$

Velocity of Transverse Waves

The velocity of transverse waves on a string is determined by two factors, which are as follows:

- The linear mass density or mass per unit length, (μ)
- The tension (T), Thus the velocity of transverse waves on a stretched string is given by

$$v = \sqrt{\frac{T}{\mu}}$$

It is independent of the frequency of the wave.

Velocity of Longitudinal Waves

In a longitudinal wave, the constituents of the medium oscillate forward and backward in the direction of propagation of the wave. These waves travel in all the three media—solid, liquid and gas.

- **In Fluids** The velocity of propagation of a longitudinal wave in a fluid depends only on the Bulk modulus (B) and the density (ρ) of the medium and it is given by $v = \sqrt{\frac{B}{\rho}}$
- **In Solid bar** The velocity of a longitudinal wave through a solid bar of Young's modulus (Y) and density (ρ) is given by $v = \sqrt{\frac{Y}{\rho}}$
- **In Ideal Gas** The velocity of a longitudinal wave of sound in an ideal gas is given by $v = \sqrt{\frac{p}{\rho}}$, where p is pressure exerted by the ideal gas. This relation is known as Newton's formula. Later on, this formula is modified by Laplace as $v = \sqrt{\frac{\gamma p}{\rho}}$
  This modification is referred as **Laplace correction.**
- **For Air,** $\gamma = \frac{7}{5}$ and then speed of sound in air at STP is estimated to 331.3 ms^{-1}.

Progressive and Stationary Waves

Progressive waves and stationary waves are given below :

Progressive Waves

The waves originating from a source and travelling forward in a medium are called progressive waves.

e.g. Waves formed at the surface of liquid are progressive waves.

Properties of Progressive Waves

- These waves move through the medium transferring energy in the direction of propagation.
- The amplitude of vibration of all particles of the medium is same in progressive waves.
- The phase of the vibrations vary continuously from one particle to another.
- In progressive waves, all the particles move with same velocity in the medium.

Stationary Waves

The wave produced by superposition of two progressive waves of equal amplitude and frequency, travelling with the same speed in opposite directions is called stationary wave. They remain in a constant position.

e.g. Waves produced in a plucked guitar string are stationary waves.

Properties of Stationary Waves

- The waveform in a stationary wave does not move forward in medium, therefore these waves do not transmit energy.
- These waves consist of two different points known as **nodes and anti-nodes.**
- The amplitudes of all particles are different.

Sound Waves

- Sound is a form of energy which produces a sensation of hearing in our ears. It is produced by vibrating objects.
- Vibration means a kind of rapid to and fro motion of an object.
- Since, sound requires a medium for its propagation, it is longitudinal in nature.

Propagation of Sound in Air

- Sound waves require a material medium like air, water steel etc. for its propagation. When an object vibrates, it sets the particles of the medium around it vibrating.
- A particle of the medium is first displaced from its position, then exerts a force on the adjacent particle. As a result of which, adjacent particle displaces from rest.
- After displacing adjacent particle, the first one comes back to its original position. This process continues in the medium till the sound reaches our ear.
- Air is the most common medium through sound travels. When a vibrating object moves forward, it pushes and compresses the air in front of it creating a region of high pressure called **compression** (C) and when the vibrating object moves backwards, it creates a region of low pressure called **rarefaction** (R).
- As the object moves back and forth rapidly, a series of compressions and rarefactions is created in air.
- Thus, propagation of sound can be visualised as propagation of density variations or pressure variations in the medium as pressure is related to the number of particles of a medium in a given volume.
- More density of the particles in the medium gives more pressure and *vice-versa.*

Sound Produced by Humans

- The sound in humans is produced by voice box or the larynx. After putting fingers on the throat and try to find a hard bump that seems to move when you swallow.
- This part of the body is known as **voice box**. It is the upper end of windpipe. The human voice box contains two ligaments known as **vocal cords.**
- When the lungs force air through the slit, the vocal cords vibrates, producing sound, muscles attached to the vocal cords can make the cords tight or loose. When the vocal cord are tight and thin, the type or quality of voice is different from that when they are loose and thick.

Characteristics of Sound

A sound has few characteristics. These are loudness, pitch and quality (or timbre).

Loudness

- It is the measure of the sound energy reaching the ear per second. Greater the sound energy reaching our ear per second, louder the sound will appear to be.

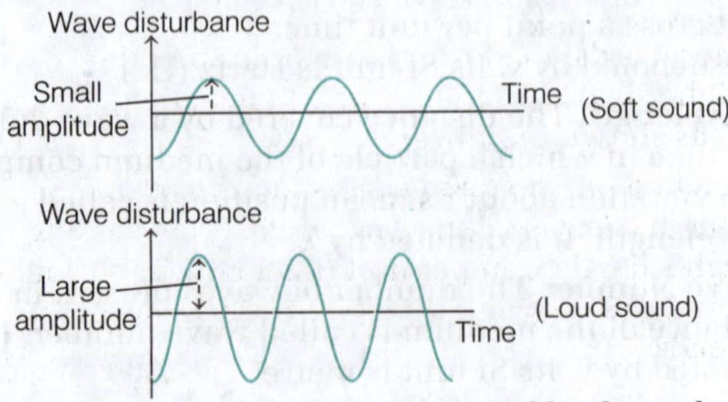

Soft sound has small amplitude and loud sound has large amplitude

- The loudness of sound depends on its amplitude. When the amplitude of vibration is large, the sound produced is loud. When the amplitude is small, the sound produced is feeble.
- Loudness of sound is proportional to the square of the amplitude of the vibration producing the sound.
- The loudness of sound is measured in **decibel** (dB). It depends on the sensitivity or the response of our ears.
- The following table gives some idea of the loudness of sound coming from various sources :

Normal breathing	10 dB
Soft whisper	30 dB
Normal conversation	60 dB
Busy traffic	70 dB
Average factory	180 dB

- Above 80 dB, the noise becomes physically painful.

Pitch or Shrillness

- It is that characteristic of sound by which we can distinguish between different sounds of the same loudness. Due to this characteristic, we can distinguish between a man's voice and woman's voice of the same loudness without seeing them.
- Pitch of a sound depends on the frequency of vibration. Greater the frequency of a sound, the higher will be its pitch.

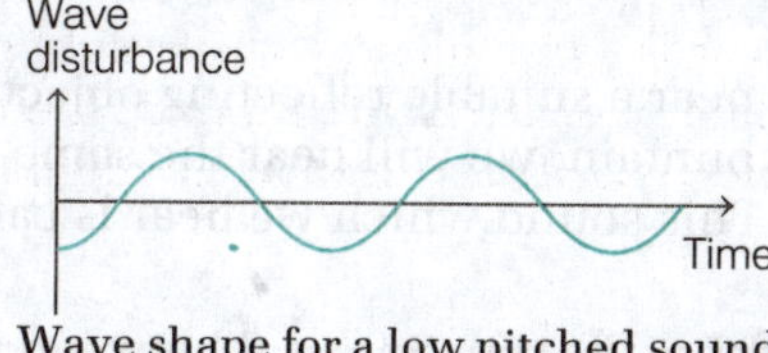

Wave shape for a low pitched sound

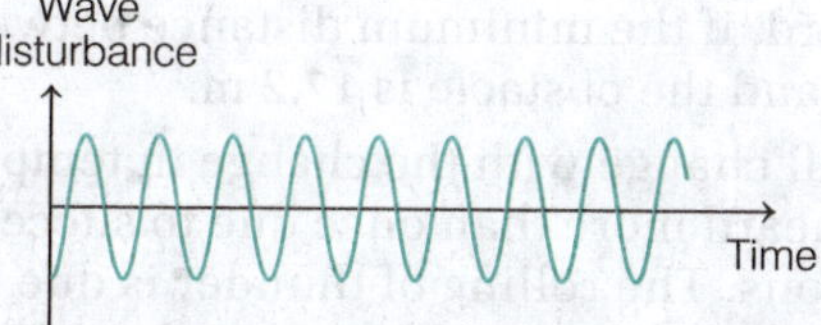

Wave shape for a high pitched sound

- In other words, the faster the vibration of the source, the higher is the frequency and hence higher is the pitch, as shown in figure.

Thus, a high pitch sound corresponds to more number of compressions and rarefactions passing through a fixed point per unit time. Low pitch sound has low frequency and high pitch sound has high frequency.

Quality or Timbre

- The quality or timbre of sound enables us to distinguish one sound from another having the same pitch and loudness.
- A sound of single frequency is called **a tone**. The sound produced by a mixture of several frequencies is called **a note** and is pleasant in listening too. Noise is unpleasant to ear. Music is pleasant to ear and it is of rich quality.

Audible and Inaudible Sounds

- Sounds of frequencies less than about 20 vibrations per second (20 Hz) cannot be detected by human ear. Such sounds are called **Inaudible**.
- One the higher side, sounds of frequencies higher than about 20,000 vibrations per second (20 kHz) are also not audible to the human ear.
- Thus, for human ear the range of audible frequencies is roughly from 20 to 20,000 Hz are called **Audible**.
- Some animals can hear sounds of frequencies higher than 20000 Hz. Dogs have this ability. The police use high frequency whistles, which dogs can hear but humans cannot.
- The ultrasound equipment, familiar to us for investigating and tracking many medical problems, works at frequencies higher than 20000 Hz.

Intensity of Sound

- The amount of sound energy passing each second through unit area is known as the intensity of sound.
- Loudness and intensity are not the same terms. Loudness is a measure of the response of the ear to the sound.
- Even when two sounds are of equal intensity, we may hear one as louder than the other, simply because our ear detects it in better way.
- The SI unit of intensity is **watt per square metre** (W/m^2).
- The intensity of a sound wave in air is proportional to the
  - square of the amplitude of vibrations
  - square of the frequency of vibrations
  - density air

Speed of Sound in Different Media

- Sound propagates through a medium at a finite speed. It travels with a speed which is much less than the speed of light.
- The speed of sound depends on the elasticity of medium through which it travels and the density of the medium.

- If the elasticity of medium is E and density is d, then the speed of sound is given by
$$v = \sqrt{E/d}$$
- The speed of sound decreases when we go from solid to gaseous state because solids are most elastic while gases least.
- The speed of sound in air is 331 ms^{-1} at 0°C and 344 ms^{-1} at 22°C.
- The sound of in water is 1450 m/s and in metal is 5000 m/s. The sound waves go from one medium to other medium. Its frequency does not change.

Speed of Sound in Different Media at 25°C

State	Substance	Speed in m/s
Solids	Aluminium	6420
	Nickel	6040
	Steel	5960
	Iron	5950
	Brass	4700
	Glass (flint)	3980
Liquids	Water (sea)	1531
	Water (distilled)	1498
	Ethanol	1207
	Methanol	1103
Gases	Hydrogen	1284
	Helium	965
	Air	346
	Oxygen	316
	Sulphur dioxide	213

Effect of Physical Parameters on Speed of Sound

Speed of sound is affected by the following physical parameters :

- **Effect of Temperature** The speed of sound in a gas is directly proportional to the square root of absolute temperature of the gas.

  i.e., $v \propto \sqrt{T}$

  So, velocity of sound in air increases roughly by 0.61 m/s per degree celsius rise in temperature.
- **Effect of Pressure** If temperature remains constant, then there is no effect of change in pressure on the velocity of sound.
- **Effect of Humidity** In humid air, velocity of sound increases as compared to that in the dry air.
- **Effect of Wind** If the wind is blowing, then the speed of sound changes. The speed of sound is increased if wind is blowing in the direction of propagation of sound waves.
- **Effect of Frequency** The speed of sound in air is independent of its frequency. Sound waves of different frequency travel with the same speed in air but their wavelengths in air are different.
- **Speed of Sound in gases** Speed of sound in gas is inversely proportional to the square root of density of gas. The speed of sound in hydrogen gas is maximum because hydrogen gas is lighter than other gases.

Mach Number

- Mach number is the ratio of the speed of a body to the speed of sound in the surrounding medium i.e.,
$$\text{Mach number} = \frac{\text{Speed of body in medium}}{\text{Speed of sound in medium}}$$

Reflection of Sound Wave

- The bouncing back of sound when it strikes a hard surface is known as **reflection** of sound.
- It can be reflected from any surface whether, it is smooth or rough. Sound is reflected in the same way as light and follows the same laws of reflection, which are as follows :
  - The incident sound wave, the reflected sound wave and the normal at the point of incidence, all three lie in the same plane.
  - The angle of incidence of sound is equal to the angle of reflection of sound.

Echo

- If we shout or clap near a suitable reflecting object such as a tall building or a mountain, we will hear the same sound again a little later. This sound which we hear is called an echo.
- To hear a distinct echo, the time interval between the original sound and the reflected one must be atleast 0.1 s. Echo will be heard, if the minimum distance between the source of sound and the obstacle is 17.2 m.
- This distance will change with the change in temperature. Echoes may be heard more than once due to successive multiple reflections. The rolling of thunder is due to successive reflections of sound from a number of reflecting surfaces, such as clouds and the land.

Reverberation

- A sound created in a big hall will persist by repeated reflection from the walls until it is reduced to a value, where it is no longer audible. The repeated reflection that results in this persistence of sound is called reverberation.
- A short reverberation is desirable in a concert hall, where music is being played, as it boosts the sound level. But excessive reverberation is highly undesirable because sound becomes blurred, distorted and confusing due to overlapping of different sounds.

- To reduce reverberation, the roof and walls of the auditorium are generally covered with sound absorbent materials like compressed fibre board, rough plaster or draperies.

Uses of Multiple Reflections of Sound

- **Megaphone and Horn** Musical instruments such as trumpets and shehanais are all designed to send sound in a particular direction without spreading it in all direction. In these instrument, a tube followed by a conical opening reflects sound successively to guide most of the sound waves from the source in the forward direction towards the audience.
- **Stethoscope** It is a medical instrument used by doctors to listen to the sound produced within the heart and the lungs in human body. The sound of heartbeats (or lungs) reaches the doctor's ears by the multiple reflections of sound waves through the stethoscope tube.
- **Sound Board** It is a concave board (curved board) placed behind the stage in big halls, so that sound after reflecting from sound board, spreads evenly across the width of the hall.

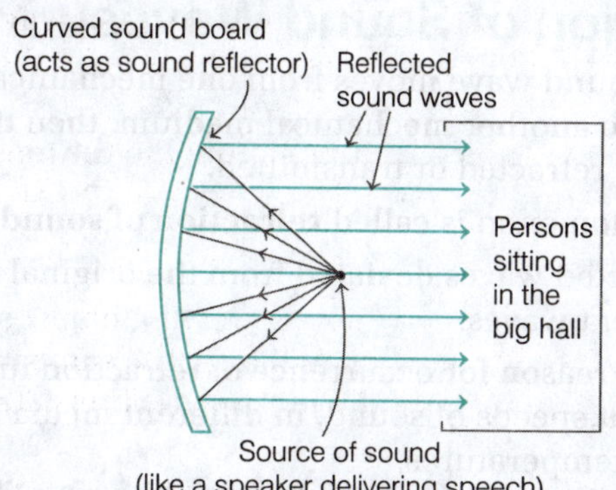

Curved sound board behind the speaker or the stage in big hall

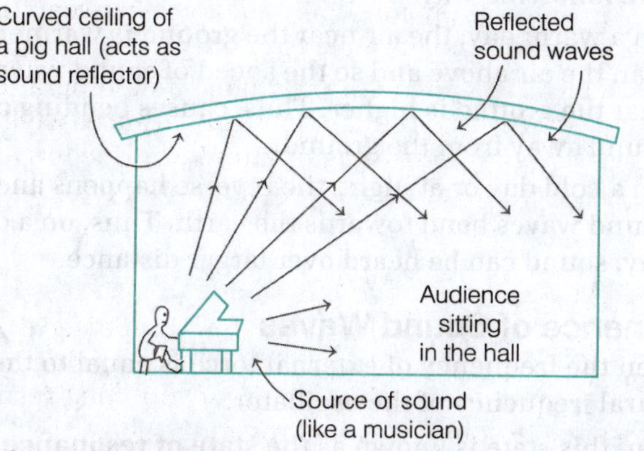

Curved sound board behind the speaker or the stage in big hall

Generally, the ceilings of the concert halls, conference halls and cinema halls are curved, so that sound after reflection reaches all corners of the hall.

Range of Hearing

- The average frequency range over which the human ear is sensitive is called **audible range**. The audible range of sound for human beings is from 20 Hz to 20000 Hz (20 kHz).
- Children under the age of five and some animals such as dogs can hear up to 25 kHz. As people grow older, their ears become less sensitive to higher and lower frequencies.

On the basis of range, sound waves can be classified in the following categories :

- **Audible Sound** Sound waves having frequencies lying between 20 Hz-20000 Hz are called audible sound.
- **Infrasonic Sound** The sound of frequencies lower than 20 Hz are known as infrasonic sounds or infrasound, which cannot be heard by human beings.
  - Earthquakes and some animals like whales, elephants and rhinoceroses produce infrasonic sound of frequency 5 Hz.
  - It is observed that some animals get disturbed and start running here and there just before the earthquakes occur.
  - This is because earthquakes produce low frequency infrasound before the main shock waves begin which possibly alert the animals and they get disturbed.
- **Ultrasonic Sound** The sounds of frequencies higher than 20000 Hz are called ultrasonic sounds or ultrasounds which cannot be heard by human beings. Dogs can hear ultrasonic sounds of frequency up to 50000 Hz. This is why dogs are used for detective work by the police. Bats, dolphins, and porpoises can produce ultrasonic sounds.

Ultrasound and Its Applications

Ultrasounds are high frequency waves. They travel in straight line without bending around the corners. They can penetrate into matter to a large extent.

Some of the important applications of ultrasound are given below :

- Ultrasound is used to clean parts located in hard-to-reach places.
- Ultrasounds can be used to detect cracks and flaws in metal blocks.
- Ultrasonic waves or ultrasound is also used for diagnosing heart diseases by scanning the heart from inside. This technique is called **echocardiography.**
- Ultrasound scanner is an instrument which uses ultrasonic waves for getting images of internal organs of human body like gall bladder, uterus, kidney etc. It helps the doctor to detect abnormalities, such as stones in the gall bladder and kidney or tumors in different organs.

- **Ultrasonography** is used for examination of the foetus during pregnancy to detect congenial defects and growth abnormalities.
- Ultrasound may be employed to break small stones formed in the kidneys into fine grains. These grains later get flushed out with urine.
- Bats, search out prey and fly in dark night by emitting and detecting reflections of ultrasonic waves. The high pitched ultrasonic squeaks of the bat are reflected from the obstacles or prey and returned to bat's ear.
- The nature of reflections tells the bat where the obstacle or prey is and what it is like. Porpoises also use ultrasound for navigation and location of food in the dark.

Hearing Aid

People with hearing loss may need a hearing aid. A hearing aid is an electronic, battery operated device. The hearing aid receives sound through a microphone. The microphone converts the sound waves to electrical signal. These electrical signals are amplified by an amplifier. The amplified electrical signals are given to a speaker of the hearing aid.

The speaker converts the **amplified electrical signals** to **sound** and then sends it to the ear for clear hearing.

Human Ear

The ears are the sense organs which help us in hearing sound. It allows us to convert pressure variations in air with audible frequencies into electric signals which travel to the brain *via* **auditory nerve**.

Structure and Working of Human Ear

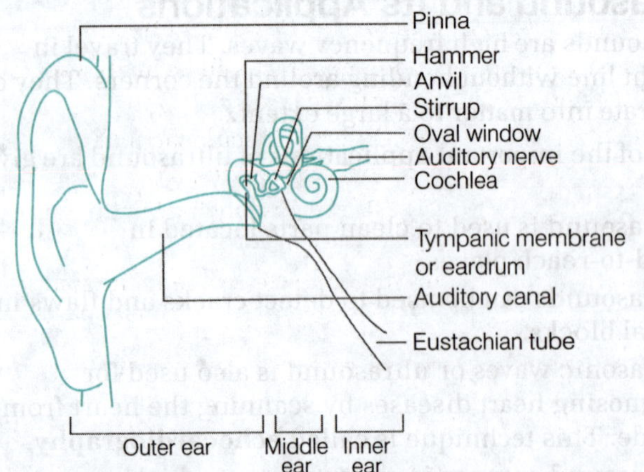

The ear consists of three compartments:

- **Outer Ear** The part of ear which we see outside the head is outer ear. It is called **pinna**. It collects the sound from the surroundings.

The collected sound passes through the auditory canal. At the end of the auditory canal, there is a thin membrane called the **eardrum or tympanic membrane.**

When a compression of the medium reaches the eardrum, the pressure on the outside of the membrane increases and forces the eardrum inward. Similarly, the eardrum moves outward when a rarefaction reaches it. In this way the eardrum vibrates.

- **Middle Ear** It contains three small bones hammer, anvil and stirrup, which are connected with each other. The vibrations are amplified several times by these three bones and these amplified pressure vibrations are received from the sound wave to the inner ear.
- **Inner Ear** It has a coiled tube, cochlea. One side of cochlea is connected to middle ear and other side to auditory nerve going into the brain.
- In inner ear, the pressure variations are turned into electrical signals by the cochlea. These electrical signals are sent to the brain via the auditory nerve and the brain interprets them as sound.

Refraction of Sound Waves

- When a sound wave moves from one mechanical medium to another mechanical medium, then the waves are refracted or transmitted.
- This phenomenon is called **refraction of sound.**
- The refracted waves deviated from the original path of the incident waves.
- The main reason for occurrence of refraction in sound is different speeds of sound, in different media at different temperatures.
- Range of sound and temperature depends on each other in the following ways :
  - On a warm day, the air near the ground is warmer than the air above and so the speed of sound waves near the ground is higher. Thus, causes bending of the sound away from the ground.
  - On a cold day or at night, the reverse happens and the sound waves bend towards the earth. Thus, on a cold day, sound can be heard over larger distance.

Resonance of Sound Waves

- When the frequency of external force is equal to the natural frequency of the oscillator.
- Then, this state is known as the **state of resonance.**
- When the frequency of sound Waves is equal to the natural frequency, then the amplitude of the Sound waves increases.
- This phenomenon is called **resonance of sound waves.**

Interference

- When two waves of same frequencies stand in the medium in the same direction, then the resultant intensity due to their superposition at a point, is different from the sum of intensities of two waves. This phenomenon is called **interference**.
- In interference, energy is neither created nor destroyed but is redistributed.
- Due to interference the result intensity of sound of a point is different from the sum of intensities due to each wave separately.
- When the waves meet a point with some phase constructive interference is obtained or that point.
- When the waves meet a point with opposite phase, destructive interference is obtained that point.

Diffraction of Sound Waves

- When sound waves are originated by a vibrating source, then they spread in the medium. If the medium is homogeneous, then these waves have spherical wavefronts from the point source.
- Far from the source, the wavefronts are nearly planes and the shape of the wavefronts is changed, when the sound waves meet an opening in its path.
- This leads to bending of sound waves around the edges. Such bending of sound waves from an opening is called **diffraction.**
- Since, the wavelength of the sound waves is approximately 1 m and of the same order as the doors and windows, etc., of our houses.
- Therefore, the sound waves diffracted broadly and one person easily hears the voice of the another person.

Extra Facts From Tamil Nadu Board and NIOS

- **Particle Velocity** The velocity with which the particles of the medium vibrate in order to transfer the energy in the form of a wave is called particle velocity.
- **Laws of Reflection**
  (i) The incident wave, the normal to the reflecting surface and the reflected wave at the point of incidence lies in the same plane.
  (ii) The angle of incidence ($< i$) is equal to the angle of reflection ($< r$).
- The minimum distance required to hear an echo is $\frac{1}{20}$ th part of the magnitude of the velocity of sound in air.
- **Sonic Boom**
  - When the speed of any object exceeds the speed of sound i.e., mach number is greater than 1, it is said to have supersonic speed. Many objects such as some aircrafts, bullets and rockets etc., travel at supersonic speeds.
  - When a sound producing source moves with a speed higher than that of sound, it produces shock wave in air, which carry a large amount of energy. The tremendous air pressure variations caused by the shock waves produce a loud burst of sound is known as sonic boom.
- **SONAR** The word SONAR stands for Sound Navigation and Ranging. SONAR is an apparatus that uses ultrasonic waves to measure the distance, direction and speed of under water objects.
- SONAR is used to determine the depth of the sea and to locate underwater wells, valleys, submarines, ice-bergs, Sunken ship, etc.
- **Electrocardiogram** The electrocardiogram is one of the simplest and oldest cardiac investigations available. It can provide a wealth of useful information and remains an essential part of the assessement of cardiac patients. In ECG, the sound variation produced by heart is converted into electrical signal.
- **Radar** Radar is an acronym for radio defection and ranging and is useful in many ways to us
  - Observation of atmospheric object and phenomena like clouds, cyclones rain drops, etc.
  - Air traffic control.
  - Ship navigation.
- A wave transfer energy from one point to the other without the medium particles moving from one point to the other. An electromagnetic wave result from acceleration of charge. It does not require a medium to travel.
- The apparent change in frequency heard by the observer due to relative motion between source and observer is known as **Doppler's effect.**
- **Doppler's effect** will be analysed under three cases :
  (i) Observer is stationary but the source is moving.
  (ii) Observer is moving but the source is stationary.
  (iii) Both the observer and the source are moving.

10

Electricity

(SOURCES)

Class-VI NCERT Chap 9 (Electricity and Circuits),
Class-VIII Old NCERT Chap 11 (Chemical Effects of Electric Current),
Class-X NCERT Chap 11 (Electricity),
Chap 12 (Magnetic Effects of Electric Current),
Class-XII NCERT Chap 1 (Electric Charges and Fields),
Chap 3 (Current Electricity), Chap 4 (Moving Charges and Magnetism)
Tamil Nadu Board (Class-X), NIOS

- When a glass rod is rubbed with silk, it acquires a power to attract light bodies such as, small pieces of paper.
- The objects which acquire the attracting power said to be electrified or charged.
- The flow of charge in metallic wire constitutes electric current.
- The electric current has various types of effect like magnetic effect, chemical effect, thermal effect etc.

Electric Charge

- Electric charge is a physical entity which is defined by excess or deficiency of electrons on a body. Due to the electric charges various objects exert strong electric forces of attraction or repulsion on each other.
- The SI unit of electric charge is coulomb (C).
- It is a **scalar quantity.**
- The total charge acquired by a body is an integral multiple of magnitude of charge on a single electron. This principle is called **quantisation of electric charge**. If system contains n number of electrons, then its total charge is

$$q = ne,$$

where, $n = 0, \pm 1, \pm 2, \ldots$

Types of Electric Charge

According to **Benjamin Franklin**, the convention of electric charges are of two types :

- **Positive charge** A body gets positively charged if it loses electrons. For example, the charge developed on a glass rod when rubbed with silk is called positive charge.
- **Negative charge** A body is said to be negatively charged if it gains electron. For example, the charge developed on a plastic rod when rubbed with wool is called negative charge.

  A charge carried by a proton is positive $(+e)$ while charge carried by an electron is negative $(-e)$, where $e = 1.6 \times 10^{-19}$C.

Basic Properties of Electric Charge

The electric charge has following three basic properties :

- **Attractive and Repulsive Property of Electric Charge** Unlike charges i.e, opposite charges always attract each other while like charges i.e, similar charges always repel each other.
- **Additivity of Electric Charge** When the total charge of a system is equal to the algebraic sum of all the individual charges located at different points inside

the system, then we can say that electric charge is additive in nature. If system contains electric charges $q_1, q_2, \ldots\ldots, q_n$, then its total charge is

$$q = q_1 + q_2 + \ldots + q_n$$

- **Conservation of Electric Charge** According to law of conservation of charges, the total charge of an isolated system remains constant and electric charges can neither be created nor destroyed, they can only be transferred from one body to another.

Coulomb's Law

According to this law, the force of attraction or repulsion between two stationary charges is directly proportional to the product of the magnitudes of the two charges and inversely proportional to the square of the distance between them. This force acts along the line joining the two charges.

If two point charges q_1 and q_2 are separated by distance r, then the electrostatic force between them is such that

$$F \propto \frac{q_1 q_2}{r^2}$$

$$\therefore \quad F = k\frac{q_1 q_2}{r^2}$$

where, $k = 9 \times 10^9 \text{Nm}^2\text{C}^{-2}$ is a constant of proportionality called electrostatic force constant.

Electric Field

The space surrounding on electric charge in which another charge experiences a force of attraction or repulsion is called the electric field of the charge.

Electric Lines of Force

Michael Faraday introduced the concept of lines of force to visualise the nature of electric charges. An electric line of force is that imaginary smooth curve drawn in an electric field along which a free isolated unit positive charge moves.

The tangent drawn at any point on the electric line of force gives the direction of the force acting on a positive charge placed at that point.

Properties of electric lines of force are :

- The lines of force are continuous smooth curves without any breaks.
- The lines of force start at positive charges and end at negative charges i.e., they cannot form closed loops. If there is a single charge, then the lines of force will start or end at infinity.
- The tangent to a line of force at any point gives the direction of electric field at that point.
- No two lines of force can cross each other.
- The relative closeness of the lines of force gives a measure of the strength of the electric field.
- The lines of force do not pass through a conductor because the electric field inside a charged conductor is zero. The lines of force are always normal to the surface of a conductor.

Intensity of Electric Field

- The electric field intensity at a point is defined as the force experienced by a unit positive test charge placed at that point, without disturbing the position of source charge.
- Suppose a test charge, q_0 experiences a force F at a point, then the electric field intensity at that point will be $E = \frac{F}{q_0}$
- It is a vector quantity. The SI unit of electric field intensity is **Newton per Coulomb** (NC^{-1}) which is equivalent to **volt per metre** (Vm^{-1}).

Equipotential Surface

Any surface that has same electric potential at every point on it is called an equipotential surface. Some important properties of equipotential surface are as follows :

- No work is done in moving a test charge over an equipotential surface.
- Electric field is always normal to the equipotential surface at every point.
- Equipotential surfaces are closer together in the regions of strong field and further apart in the regions of weak field.
- No two equipotential surfaces can intersect each other.

Capacitance

- The capacitance of a conductor is the measure of its ability to hold electric charge. When an insulated conductor is given some charge, it acquires a certain potential. If the charge on a conductor increases, its potential also increases.
- If a charge Q put on an insulated conductor increases its potential by V, then $Q \propto V$ or $Q = CV$ where, C is constant of proportionality called the capacitance of the conductor. Thus,

$$\text{Capacitance } (C) = \frac{\text{Charge } (Q)}{\text{Potential } (V)}$$

- The SI unit of capacitance is **Farad** (F) .

Capacitor

- A capacitor is an arrangement which can store sufficient quantity of charge.

Parallel Plate Capacitor

- A parallel plate capacitor consists of two large plane parallel conducting plates separated by a small distance. The two plates have charge Q and $-Q$.
- The direction of the electric field is from the positive to the negative plate and the field is uniform throughout. The capacitance of the parallel plate capacitor is

$$C = \frac{\varepsilon_0 A}{d}$$

where, A = area of each plate,

d = distance between the two plates

and ε_0 = permittivity of free space and its value is $8.854 \times 10^{-12} C^2 N^{-1} m^{-2}$.

- If the space between the plates of capacitor be filled with a dielectric materials of dielectric constant k, then the capacitance of capacitor is given by

$$C = \frac{k\varepsilon_0 A}{d}$$

Electric Current

- Electric current is expressed by the amount of charge flowing through a particular area in unit time. In other words, it is the rate of flow of electric charges.
- Conventionally, in an electric circuit the direction of electric current is taken as opposite to the direction of the flow of electrons, which are negative charges.
- If a net charge q flows across any cross-section of a conductor in time t, then the current i, through the cross-section is

$$i = \frac{q}{t}$$

- The SI unit of electric current is **Ampere** (A).
- It is a scalar quantity. 1 ampere is constituted by the flow of 1 coulomb of charge per second. Small quantities of current are expressed in **milliampere** (mA) and in **microampere** (μA).

$$1 \text{ mA} = 10^{-3} \text{A}$$

$$1 \mu\text{A} = 10^{-6} \text{A}$$

- An instrument called an **ammeter** measures the electric current in a circuit.
- It is always connected in series in a circuit through which the current is to be measured.

Electric Circuit and Electric Circuit Diagram

- A closed and continuous path through which electric current flows is known as electric circuit.
- It comprises a cell (or a battery), a plug key, electrical components and connecting wires. The circuit diagram is a schematic diagram which represents the relative positions and connections of various circuit components represented by their symbols.

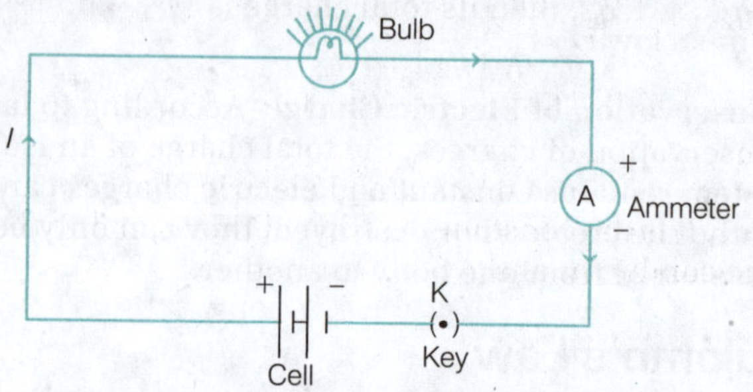

A schematic diagram of an electric circuit having cell, electric bulb, ammeter and plug key

Electric Potential

- The work done by an external agent in carrying a unit positive test charge from infinity to a point in the electric field is called the electric potential at that point.
- If work done in moving a positive charge q from infinity to a point is W, then electric potential V of that point is

$$V = \frac{W}{q}$$

- The SI unit of electric potential is volt (V). It is **scalar quantity**.

Electric Potential Difference

- The electric potential difference between two points in an electric circuit carrying some current as the workdone to move a unit charge from one point to the another.

Potential difference (ΔV) between two points

$$= \frac{\text{Work done } (W)}{\text{Charge } (q)}$$

- The SI unit of electric potential difference is volt (V), named after **Alessandro Volta** (1745-1827), an Italian physicist. 1 volt is the potential difference between two points in a current carrying conductor when 1 Joule of work is done to move a charge of 1 coulomb from one point to the another.
- The potential difference is measured by means of an instrument called the **voltmeter**. The voltmeter is always connected in parallel across the points between which the potential difference is to be measured.

Ohm's law

- According to this law, the electric current flowing through a conductor is directly proportional to the potential difference applied across its ends, providing the physical conditions remains unchanged.

- If V is the potential difference applied across the ends of a conductor through which current i flows, then according to Ohm's law $V \propto i$

$$\Rightarrow \quad \frac{V}{i} = R \text{ (constant)}$$

$$V = iR$$

where, R is the constant of proportionality called resistance of the conductor at a given temperature.

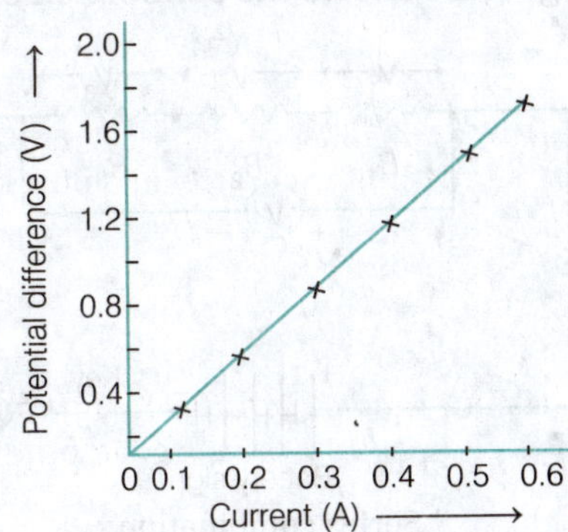

Note The conductors which obey Ohm's law are called Ohmic conductors while the conductors which do not obey Ohm's law are called non-ohmic conductors.

Electric Resistance

- Electric resistance is that property of a conductor by virtue of which it opposes or resists the flow of charges through it.
- Its SI unit is **ohm** and it is represented by Greek letter Ω.

  Resistance of a conductor is given by $R = \frac{V}{I}$

- If the potential difference across the two ends of a conductor is 1 V and the current through it is one ampere, then the resistance R, of the conductor is 1Ω.
- A component in an electric circuit which offers resistance to the flow of electrons constituting electric current is known as **resistor**.
- These are used to make those electrical devices, where high resistance is required. It reduces current in a circuit e.g, Alloys like nichrome, manganin and constantan.
- **Rheostat/variable resistance** is a variable resistor, which is used to control the flow of electric current by manually increasing or decreasing the resistance.
- A component of identical size that offers a higher resistance is poor conductor. An insulator of the same size offers even higher resistance.

Factors on which Resistance of a Conductor Depends

The electrical resistance of a conductor depends on the following factors:

- **Length of the conductor** The resistance of a conductor R is directly proportional to its length l

  i.e, $R \propto l$

  Therefore, when the length of a wire is doubled / halved, then its resistance will also get doubled / halved.

- **Area of cross-section of the conductor** The resistance of a conductor R is inversely proportional to **its area** of cross-section A.

  i.e, $R \propto \frac{1}{A}$

  Therefore, when the cross-sectional area is doubled, then its resistance gets halved or *vice-versa*.

Note When a conductor is stretched (increased its length), then its area of cross-section decreases accordingly but the volume (i.e, area × length) of the conductor remains the same.

- **Nature of the material of the conductor** The resistance of a conductor depends on the nature of the material of which it is made. Some materials have low resistance, whereas others have high resistance.

Specific Resistance

- Resistance of a conductor depends on its cross-sectional area A and length l as follows :

$$R \propto \frac{l}{A} \text{ or } R = \rho \frac{l}{A}$$

Where, ρ is the constant of proportionality and is called **resistivity** or **specific resistance** of the conductor.

$$\rho = \frac{RA}{l}$$

- It is defined as the resistance of a conductor of unit length and unit area of cross-section. Its SI unit is **ohm-metre** (Ω-m).

Resistivity or Specific Resistance of Various Materials

On the basis of resistivity, materials are divided in the following categories :

- **Good conductor** A material which offers low resistance or resistivity to the flow of electrons or electric current in an electric circuit is known as a good conductor.

  e.g., Silver, copper, aluminium, etc.

- **Insulator** A material which offers very high resistance or resistivity to the flow of electrons or electric current in an electric circuit is known as an insulator.

e.g., Rubber, dry wood, plastic, etc. Electric current does not flow through them.

- **Semiconductor** These have resistance or resistive it higher than conductor but lower than insulator. e.g., Germanium, silicon and carbon.

Temperature Dependence of Resistivity

The resistivity of a material does not depend on its length or thickness but depends on the nature of the substance and temperature. Resistivity is a characteristic property of the material and varies only if its temperature changes. It affects metals, semiconductors and insulators as follows :

- **Metals** The resistivity of a metal increases with the increase in temperature.
  The resistivity of an alloy is very high than that of its constituent metals.
  The resistivity of alloys also increases with increase in temperature, but this increase is less as compared to pure metal.
  Alloys do not oxidise (burn) readily at high temperatures. For this reason, they are commonly used in electrical heating devices like electric iron, toasters, etc.
- **Semiconductors and insulators** The resistivity decreases exponentially with increase in temperature in semiconductors and insulators.

Conductance and Conductivity

- **Conductance** The conductance of a conductor is equal to the reciprocal of its resistance. It is denoted by G. Thus,

$$\text{Conductance} = \frac{1}{\text{Resistance}} \quad \text{or} \quad G = \frac{1}{R}$$

The SI unit of conductance is $^{-1}$ or mho or siemens (S).

- **Conductivity** The reciprocal of the resistivity of a material is called its conductivity and is denoted by σ. Thus,

$$\text{Conductivity} = \frac{1}{\text{Resistivity}} \quad \text{or} \quad \sigma = \frac{1}{\rho}$$

The SI unit of conductivity is ohm^{-1} m^{-1} or mho m^{-1} or Sm^{-1}.

Superconductors

They are the materials which have zero resistance at a particular temperature, called the **critical temperature. Mercury** at 4.2 K and **copper** at 40 K are considered as superconductors.

Combination of Resistances

There are two methods of joining the resistances together which are as given below:

1. Series Combination

When two or more resistances are connected end to end to each other, then they are said to be connected in series. The following figure shows the connection of resistors in series.

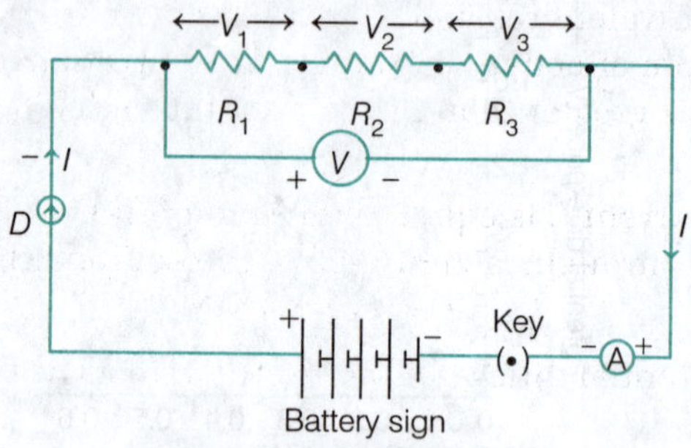

Series combination

The equivalent resistance, $R_s = R_1 + R_2 + R_3$

Some important points regarding series combination of resistors are as follows:

- The equivalent resistance is equal to the sum of the individual resistances.
- The equivalent resistance is also known as maximum effective resistance.
- The current through each resistor is same.
- The potential difference across each resistor is different.
- Total potential difference across a combination of resistors in series is equal to the sum of potential difference across the individual resistors, $V = V_1 + V_2 + V_3$

2. Parallel Combination

When two or more resistances are connected simultaneously between two points to each other, then they are said to be connected in parallel combination. The following figure shows the connection of resistors in parallel :

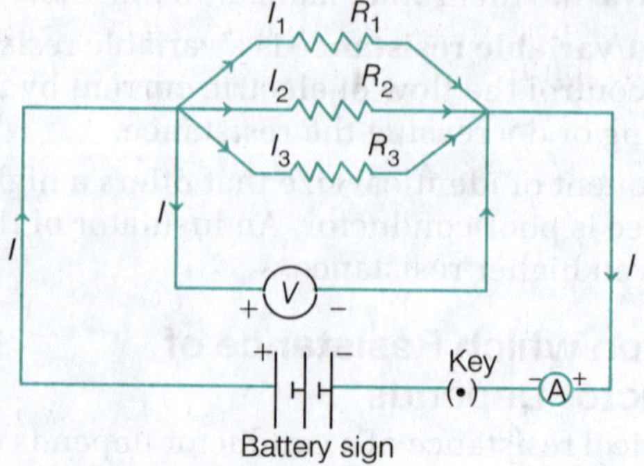

The reciprocal of equivalent resistance,

$$\frac{1}{R_p}=\frac{1}{R_1}+\frac{1}{R_2}+\frac{1}{R_3}$$

Some important points regarding parallel combination of resistors are as follows:

- The reciprocal of equivalent resistance is equal to the sum of the reciprocal of individual resistances.
- The equivalent resistance is also known as minimum effective resistance. The current from the source is greater than the current through either resistor.
- Total current I, is equal to the sum of the separate current through each branch of the combination.

$$I=I_1+I_2+I_3$$

- The potential difference across each resistor is same.

Electric Energy

- The total work done by a current in an electric circuit is called electric energy.

  If potential difference across the circuit is V, then work done in carrying a charge Q is given by

$$W=V\times Q$$

- This work done by current measures the electric energy.

  The SI unit of electric energy is joule (J)

  If the charge flows for time t, then

$$W=V\times it \qquad [\because Q=it]$$

or $$W=i^2Rt=\frac{V^2}{R}t$$

Heating Effect of Electric Current

- The heat produced in a resistor is (i) directly proportional to the square of current for a given resistance, (ii) directly proportional to the time for which the current flows through the resistor is known as Joule's law of heating.

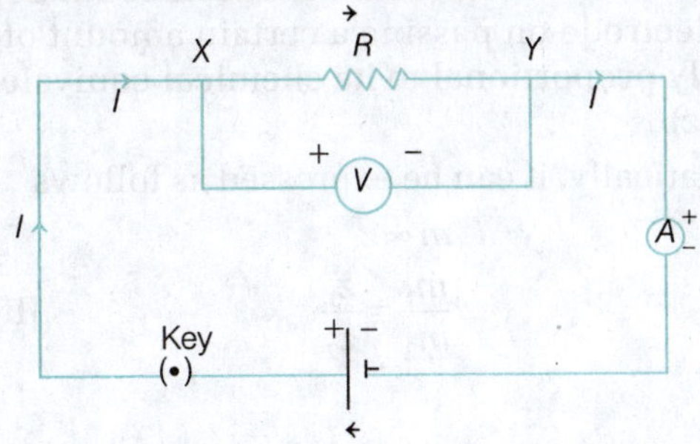

- Consider a current i flowing through a resistor of resistance R, then the amount of heat H produced in time t is

$$H=i^2Rt \text{ Joule}$$

or $$H=\frac{i^2Rt}{4.2}\text{ Calorie}$$

- The SI unit of H is **Joule** (J).

Practical Applications of Heating Effect of Current

Some useful applications of heating effect of current are given below :

1. Electric Bulb

- An electric bulb is used to provide light by heating its filament. The filament appears as heat, but a small part of it is in the form of light radiated.
- Tungsten (melting point 3380°C) is used for making filament of electric bulb. Most of the power consumed by the filament appears as heat, but a small part of it is in the form of light radiated.
- The filament is thermally isolated and the bulb is filled with chemically inactive nitrogen and argon gas to prolong the life of filament.

2. Electric Iron

- An insulator known as mica is placed in between the metal part and the coil in the iron. The coil gets heated up when an electric current is passed.
- It then gets transferred to the metallic part *via* mica. Lastly, the metal part gets heated up, which we use to iron our clothes.

3. Electric Heater

- A high resistance nichrome wire is used in the form of a coil in electric heater. Nichrome is an alloy of Ni : 60%, Cr : 12%, Mn : 2% and Fe : 26%, which has high resistivity and high melting point.
- This nichrome coil is then wound on the grooves that are made up from either a ceramic material or China clay. Whenever the current flows through the coil, it gets heated, which is in turn, used in heating the cooking vessels.

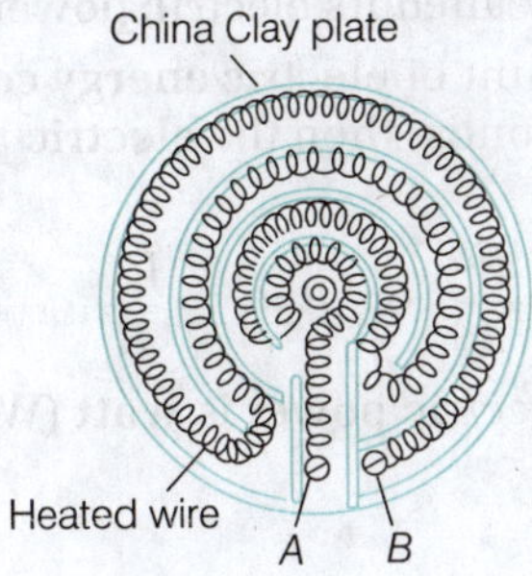

4. Electric Fuse

- It is used as a safety device in household circuits. It protects the circuits by stopping the flow of any unusual high electric current. It is connected in series with the mains supply. It consists of an alloy of lead (37%) and tin (63%) which has appropriate melting point.
- When the current flowing through the circuit exceeds the safe limit, the temperature of the fuse wire increases, the fuse wire melts and breaks the circuit. This helps to protect the other circuit elements from hazards caused by heavy current.
- Fuses are always rated for different current values such as 1A, 2A, 5A, 10A, 15A, etc.

Compact Fluorescent Lamps

- An incandescent light bulb waste a lot of electricity in the form of heat while no electric energy is wasted as heat in a fluorescent lamp. A CFL (Compact Fluorescent Lamp) is miniature fluorescent tube and works on the same principle.
- It is a 4 to 6 times more efficient than an incandescent bulb. That's why one can buy a 15 W fluorescent lamp that produces the same amount of light as a 60 W incandescent bulb.
- Although, initial cost for CFL is more but its lasting is 15 times longer than that of other bulbs. (Fluorescent lamp contains mercury which is a hazardous substance). In terms of light emission 40 W incandescent bulb = 10 W CFL,

  60 W incandescent bulb = 15 W CFL

  100 W incandescent bulb = 26 – 29 W CFL.

LED Lamp

- A LED lamp is light emitting diode product, which is assembled into a lamp or light bulb for the use in lighting fixture.
- LED lamps have longer life expectancy and higher efficiency than most other lighting. Also LED sources are compact which gives flexibility in designing lighting fixtures and good control over the distribution of illumination.

Electric Power

- The amount of electric energy consumed in a circuit per unit time is called its electric power.
- If W be the amount of electric energy consumed in a circuit in t seconds, then the electric power is given by

$$P = \frac{W}{t} \quad \text{or} \quad P = Vi = \frac{V^2}{R}$$

- The SI unit of electric power is **watt** (W).

Practical Units of Electric Energy

- The commercial unit of electric energy is called **kilowatt hour** (kWh) or **Board of Trade Unit** (BOTU). It is commonly known as Unit.

$$1\text{ kWh} = 1\text{ kW} \times 1\text{h} = 3.6 \times 10^6\text{ J}$$

Chemical Effects of Electric Current

- When an electric current flows through a conducting solution causes chemical reactions. This is called the chemical effect of electric current.
- Those solutions in which electric current can pass is called **electrolyte**. Thereby, whenever in any aqueous solution of salt, acid, an electric current is passed and if these solutions decompose into positive and negative ions, this phenomenon is called **electrolysis.**
- The equipment in which electric decomposition occurs is called **voltmeter**. Two metallic conductors which are kept at the entrance and exit of the voltmeter are called **electrodes**.
- The electrode through which electric current enters inside the voltmeter is called **anode**, while the electrode through which electric current comes out is called **cathode**.

Faraday's Laws of Electrolysis

In 1833, **Michael Faraday** explained the relationship between the substance deposited at electrode and the quantity of electric charge passed with the help of his two laws, which are as follows:

First Law

- This law states that the mass of a substance (m) deposited at any electrode is directly proportional to the amount of charge (q) passed.
- Mathematically, it can be expressed as,

$$m \propto q \quad \text{or} \quad m = zq$$

where, z is the proportionality constant which is called as **electrochemical equivalent.**

Its unit is **gram per Coulomb** (g/C).

Second Law

- This law states that the mass of substance m deposited at any electrode on passing a certain amount of charge is directly proportional to its chemical equivalent weight (z).

Mathematically, it can be expressed as follows

$$m \propto z$$

$$\therefore \quad \frac{m_1}{m_2} = \frac{z_1}{z_2} \qquad [\text{If } q_1 = q_2]$$

Faraday Constant

- The amount of electric charge carried by one mole of electrons. It is denoted by F and expressed in **Coulomb per mole** (C mol^{-1}).

$$1\ F = 9.65 \times 10^4\ C/mol$$

Electroplating

- The process of depositing a layer of any desired metal on another material by means of electricity is called electroplating.
- It is one of the most common applications of chemical effect of electric current.
- Electroplating is a very useful process. It is widely used in industry for coating metal objects with a thin layer of a different metal. The layer of metal deposited has some desired property, which the metal of the object lacks.

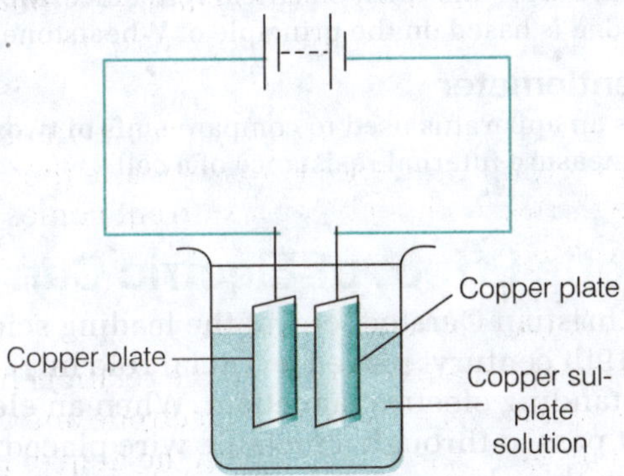

Process of Electroplating

- On the basis of the principle of electrolysis electroplating (then layer of any metal is coated on another metallic body) is done.
- The metallic body which is to be coated acts like an anode and the metal whose layer is to be coated on another acts like a cathode.
- Thus, an electrolysed cell is formed and the process of electrolysis occurs.
- When electric current flows through the electrolyte then the metal from the anode starts to dissolve in the solution and deposits on the cathode. Thereby after sometimes a thin layer is to be coated on the cathode and ultimately metal is coated.
- For example, if silver is to be coated on copper, then solution of silver nitrate is taken as electrolyte and copper is connected to cathode and silver to the anode. When current is passed, the electrolysis of silver nitrate takes place and silver ions gets deposited on copper.

Examples of Electroplating

- Chromium having shiny appearance, does not corrode and resists scratches. However, chromium is highly expensive and it may not be economical to make the whole object out of chromium.
- So, the object is made from a cheaper metal and only a coating of chromium over it is deposited.
- Jewellery makers electroplate silver and gold on less expensive metals. These ornaments have the appearance of silver or gold but are much less expensive.
- Tin cans used for storing food, are made by electroplating tin onto iron. Tin is less reactive than iron. Thus, food does not come into contact with iron and is protected from getting spoilt.
- Iron is used in bridges and automobiles to provide strength.
- However, iron tends to corrode and rust. So, a coating of zinc is deposited on iron to protect it from corrosion and formation of rust.

Electric Cell

- The electric cell is an equipment which maintains a potential difference between any two points of the conducting wire so that the flow of electric current is continuously sustained.
- In electric cells the chemical energy which is produced by various chemical reactions transforms into electrical energy.

Usually electric cells are of two types :

Primary cell

- In a primary cell chemical energy is directly converted into electrical energy and when all the chemical energy is exhausted (used up) the cell becomes dead.
- The voltaic cell, Leclanche's cell, dry cell, Daniel cell etc., are the examples of primary cell.

Secondary cell

- In a secondary cell first the electrical energy is converted into chemical energy. Then, this chemical energy is converted into electrical energy.
- The entire process is completed by charging and during its use it is discharged, then it is again charged and this is the process (way) of its functioning. That's why all the secondary cells are rechargeable.
- The process of recharging is done through an external source of electrical energy. The battery or cell attached in motor vehicle, motor bike, emergency light, etc. are the examples of secondary cell.

Types of Electrochemical Cells

There are two types of electrochemical cells as follows :

- **Galvanic cells** They are also known as voltaic cells. They convert chemical energy into electrical energy. In these electrochemical cells, the anode is negatively charged and cathode is positively charged.
- **Electrolytic cell** They transform electrical energy into chemical energy.
- These cells have a positively charged anode and negatively charged cathode.

Electromotive Force (EMF) of a Cell

- The work done by the cell in moving unit positive charge through the whole circuit (including the cell) is called the electromotive force (emf) of the cell.
- If during the flow of q coulomb of charge in an electric current the work done by the cell is W, then emf of the cell

$$E = \frac{W}{q}$$

Its unit is joule per coulomb (JC^{-1}) or volt (V)

Terminal Potential Difference

- Terminal potential difference of a cell is equal to the work done in moving a unit positive charge from one terminal to other terminal of the cell through external circuit. Its unit is **volt** (V).

$$V = E - iR$$

Internal Resistance

Internal resistance of a cell is defined as the resistance offered by the electrolyte of the cell to the flow of current through it.

It is denoted by R. Its unit is ohm (Ω).

Internal resistance of a cell depends on the following factors :

- It is directly proportional to the separation between the two plates (anode and cathode) of the cell.
- It is inversely proportional to area of plate dipped into the electrolyte.
- It depends on the nature, concentration and temperature of the electrolyte and increases with increase in concentration.

Automobile Battery

- The standard automotive battery is a 12 volt battery. Electrical energy in a battery is generated by a chemical reaction.
- In the case of a car battery, which is a lead acid battery, cathode is made up of PbO_2 while anode is made up of Pb and a mixture of sulphuric acid and water known as electrolyte, reacts with active material inside the battery.
- A battery's voltage depends on the concentration of sulphuric acid.
- As the battery is discharged, the concentration of sulphuric acid declines.

Kirchhoff's Laws

- Kirchhoff gave the following two rules to solve complicated electrical circuits :
- **Junction Law** This is based upon the conservation of charge.
- **Loop law** This is based upon the conservation of energy.
- **Wheatstone Bridge** It is an electric circuit used to measure an unknown electrical resistance. Metre Bridge is based on the principle of Wheatstone bridge.

Potentiometer

- It is an apparatus used to compare emfs of two cells or to measure internal resistance of a cell.

Magnetic Effect of Electric Current

- Hans Christian Oersted, one of the leading scientists of the 19th century, played a crucial role in understanding electromagnetism. When an electric current passed through a metallic wire placed nearby. Through this observation he found that electricity and magnetism were related phenomena.
- An electric current passes through any conductor, then a magnetic field is produced (generated) around the conductor. This phenomenon is called magnetic effect of current.

Intensity of Magnetic Field

- Intensity of magnetic field at a point is equal to the force acting on current carrying conductor of unit length having unit current placed perpendicular to the direction of magnetic field.
- It is a vector quantity and its SI unit is **tesla** or **weber/metre^2**.

Magnetic Field due to a Current Carrying Conductor

- When electric current flows through a conductor, a magnetic field is produced around it.
- The pattern of magnetic field produced by a current carrying conductor depends on its shape.

- Different magnetic field patterns are produced by current carrying conductors of different shapes.

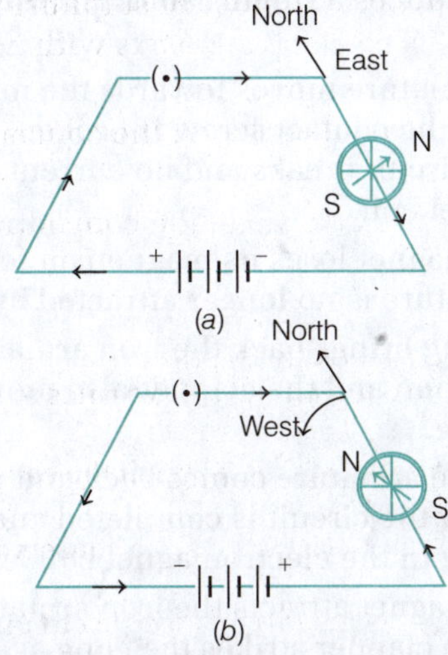

Magnetic Field due to a Current a Straight Conductor

- The magnetic field lines around a current carrying straight conductor are concentric circles whose centres lie on the wire.
- The magnitude of magnetic field B produced by a straight current carrying wire at a given point is
  - **Directly proportional** to the current I passing through the wire.
  - **Inversely proportional** to the distance r from the wire i.e., the magnetic field is stronger at a point which is nearer to the conductor and goes on decreasing on moving away from the conductor.
- If the direction of current in a straight wire is known, then the direction of magnetic field produced by it is obtained by **Maxwell's right hand thumb rule.**

Maxwell's Right Hand Thumb Rule

- It states that, if you hold the current carrying straight wire in the grip of your right hand in such a way that the stretched thumb points in the direction of current, then the direction of the curl of the fingers will give the direction of the magnetic field.
- This rule is also called **Maxwell's corkscrew rule.**

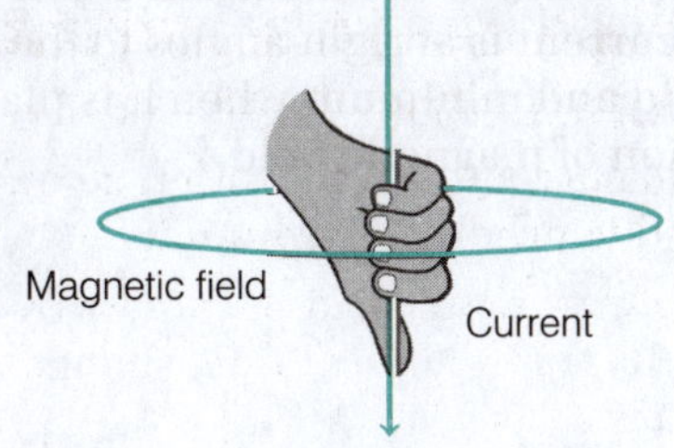

Magnetic Field due to a Current in a Circular Loop

- At every point on a current carrying circular loop, the magnetic field is in the form of concentric circles around it.

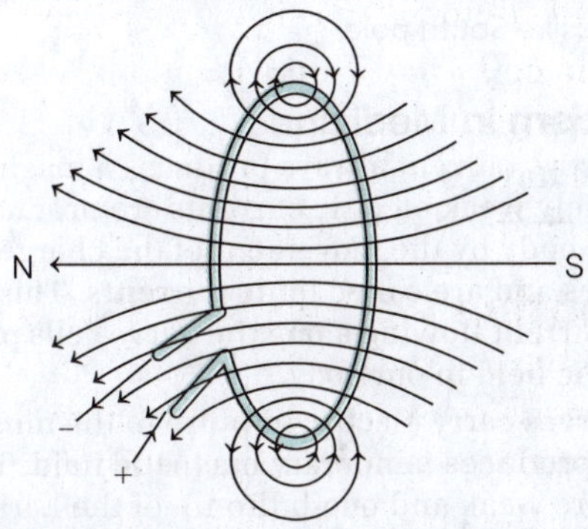

- As, we move away from it, the circles would become larger and larger.
- When we reach the centre of loop, the field appears to be a straight line.
- The magnetic field produced by current carrying circular wire at a given point is
  - **Directly proportional** to the amount of current flowing through it.
  - **Directly proportional** to the number of turns of the wire.
  - **Inversely proportional** to the radius of loop.
- Thus, the strength of magnetic field produced by a current carrying circular coil can be increased by :
  - increasing the number of turns of the coil.
  - increasing the current flowing through the coil.

Magnetic Field due to Current in a Solenoid

- A coil of many circular turns of insulated copper wire wrapped closely in the shape of a cylinder is called a solenoid.

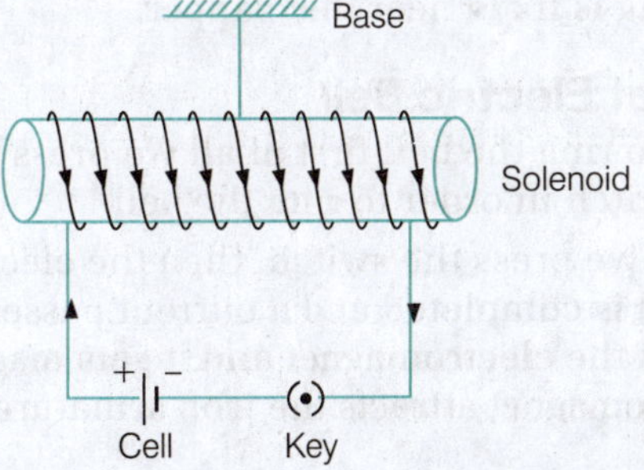

- The field lines around a current carrying solenoid are similar to that produced by a bar magnet. This means that a current carrying solenoid behaves as if it has North pole and South pole.

- The field lines inside the solenoid are parallel to each other. Thus, the strength of magnetic field is the same at all points inside a solenoid.

Note If the current in a circular loop (or coil) is in anti-clockwise direction, then it behaves like a North pole. If the current in a circular loop (or coil) is in clockwise direction, then it behaves like South pole.

Magnetism in Medicine

- An electric current always produces a magnetic field. Extremely weak electric currents are produced in human body by the movement of the charged particles and are called **ionic currents**. This weak ionic current flowing along the nerve cells produces magnetic field in our body.
- Our nerves carry electric impulse to the muscles which produces temporary magnetic field. These fields are weak and one-billionth of the Earth's magnetic field. The heart and the brain are the two main organs of human body, where magnetic field produced is significant.
- This magnetic field inside the body forms the basis of obtaining the images of different body parts and it is done by using a technique called **MRI** (Magnetic Resonance Imaging). Analysis of these images helps in medical diagnosis. Thus, magnetism has an important role in medicine.

Electric Bell

An electric bell works on the magnetic effect of current. It has an electromagnet in it.

Construction of Electric Bell

- The electric bell has a U-shaped electromagnet. There is a small iron bar called armature which is held in front of the poles of the electromagnet.
- The lower end of iron bar is attached to a flat spring and the flat spring is itself fixed to a metal bracket. The upper end of iron bar has a clapper attach to it. A metal gong is fixed near the clapper.

Working of Electric Bell

- In order to ring the bell first of all we press the push button switch in order to ring the bell.
- So, when we press the switch, then the electric circuit of the bell is completed and a current passes through the coil of the electromagnet and it gets magnetised. The electromagnet attracts the iron armature towards itself.
- So, as the armature moves towards the poles of the electromagnet, the clapper attached to it strikes the gong and produces a ringing sound. It implies that the bell rings.
- When the armature moves towards the magnet, its contact with the contact screw is broken. Due to this, the electric circuit breaks and no current flows in the electromagnet coil.
- The electromagnet loses its magnetism for a moment and the armature is no longer attracted by it.
- The flat spring brings back the iron armature to its original position and the clapper also moves away from the gong.
- As soon as the armature comes back and touches the contact screw the circuit is completed and current starts flowing in the electromagnet coil again.
- The electromagnet attracts the iron armature once again and the clapper strikes the gong again producing a ringing sound.
- This process of **make and break** of the electric circuit continues as long as we are pressing the switch.
- Due to this, the armature vibrates forwards and backwards rapidly each time making the clapper strike the gong.
- Thus, the clapper strikes the gong rapidly producing almost continuous sound.

Force on a Current Carrying Conductor in a Magnetic Field

When a current carrying conductor is placed in an external magnetic field, it experiences a force which is due to interaction between magnetic field produced by the current carrying conductor and external magnetic field in which the conductor is placed.

The direction of force on the conductor depends on

- **Direction of current** The direction of force on the conductor can be reversed by reversing the direction of current.
- **Direction of magnetic field** The direction of force on the conductor can be reversed by reversing the direction of magnetic field by interchanging the position of poles.

  Force on the conductor is maximum when the direction of current is at right angles to the direction of magnetic field and minimum when it is placed parallel to the direction of magnetic field.

Fleming's Left Hand Rule

- The direction of force which acts on a current carrying conductor placed in a magnetic field is given by Fleming's left hand rule.

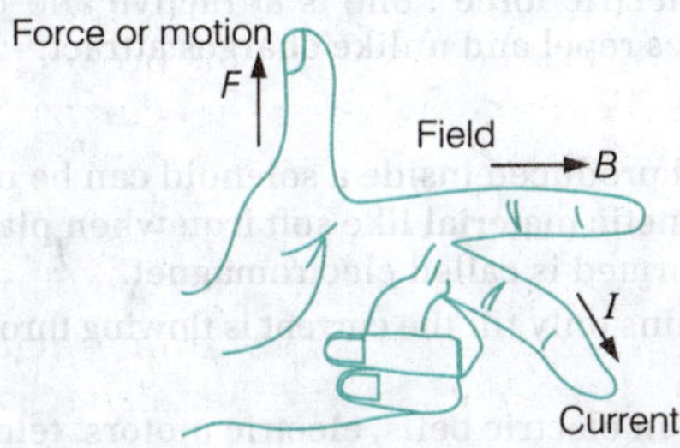

- It states that, if the forefinger, thumb and middle finger of left hand are stretched mutually perpendicular to each other, such that the forefinger points along the direction of external magnetic field, middle finger indicates the direction of current, then the thumb points towards the direction of force acting on the conductor.

Cyclotron

- Cyclotron is a device used to accelerate charged particles like protons, deuterons, α-particles etc. to very high energies. It was invented by **EO Lawrence** and **MS Livingston** in 1934 at Berkeley, California University.
- The principle of cyclotron is that a charged particle can be accelerated to very high speed or energy when they pass through electric field a number of times. This can be done with the help of a perpendicular magnetic field.
- Uses of Cyclotron are :
  - High speed particles produced in cyclotron are used to bombard nuclei and hence, study the nuclear structure.
  - High speed particles are used to produce other high speed particles, such as neutrons which are used in atomic reactors.
  - It is used to produce radioactive isotopes which are used in hospitals for diagnosis and treatment.

Galvanometer

- It is an instrument that can detect the presence of current in a circuit. The pointer remains at zero (the centre of the scale) for zero current flowing through it.
- Depending upon the direction of current, it deflects either to the left or to the right of the zero mark.

Conversion of Galvanometer into an Ammeter

- An **ammeter** is a device used to measure current through a circuit element.
- A **galvanometer** is converted into an ammeter by connecting a low resistance in parallel with the galvanometer. This low resistance is called **shunt resistance.**
- The scale is now calibrated in ampere and the range of ammeter depends on the values of the shunt resistance.
- The resistance of an ideal ammeter is **zero**.

Conversion of Galvanometer in Voltmeter

- **Voltmeter** is an instrument used to measure potential difference across any two points in a circuit.
- A **galvanometer** can be converted into a voltmeter by connecting a high resistance in series connection within it.
- The scale is calibrated in volt and the value of resistance connected in series decides the range of the voltmeter. An ideal voltmeter should have infinite resistance.

Domestic Electric Circuits

- Electricity generated at power stations is brought to our homes by two good conducting wires.
- One of these is called **live wire** (in red insulation cover), which is at a potential of 220V with a frequency of 50Hz and the other is called **neutral wire** (in black insulation cover), which is at zero potential.
- These wires (live and neutral) pass into an **electricity meter** (connected in homes) through a main fuse. They are connected to the line wires in the home through a main switch.
- Usually, there are two separate circuits in a house, the **lighting circuit** with a 5A fuse (bulbs, fans, etc.) and the **power circuit** with a 15A fuse (geysers, air coolers, etc.).
- Each **distribution circuit** is provided with a separate fuse. If a fault like short circuiting occurs in one circuit, its corresponding fuse blows off but the other circuit remains unaffected.
- Various distribution circuits are connected in parallel.
- All the electrical appliances like bulbs, fans and sockets, etc., are connected in parallel across the live wire and neutral wire.

Faults and Safety Measures in Domestic Electric Circuit

- **Earth Wire** To avoid risk of electrical shock, the metal body of appliances is earthed. The metal case of the appliance is connected to the earth (i.e. zero potential) by means of a metal wire called **earth wire** (in green insulation cover).

One end of the metal wire is buried in the earth. The appliances are connected to the earth by using the top pin of a 3-pin plug. Earthing saves us from electrical shocks.

- **Fuse** It is a safety device. It is a thin wire made of **tin** and **lead** alloy having low melting point around 200°C.
  It is used to prevent the possible damage caused by overloading and short circuiting.
- **Short Circuiting** If the live wire and neutral wire come in contact either directly or *via* conducting wire, then it is called short circuiting. In this case, the resistance of the circuit is almost zero which results in the flow of a large current.
- This heats up the wire dangerously and may lead to fire.
- **Overloading** If many electrical appliances of high power rating are switched on at the same time, then they draw a large current from the circuit. This is called overloading.
- The large amount of current flowing through the wire excessively heats up the wire and may lead to fire.

Extra Facts From
Tamil Nadu Board and NIOS

Electric Force

- The force existing between the charges is called as **electric force.**
- There are two types of electric force : one is attractive and the other is repulsive. The like charges repel and unlike charges attract.

Electromagnet

- The strong magnetic field produced inside a solenoid can be used to magnetise a piece of magnetic material like soft iron when placed inside the coil. The magnet so formed is called electromagnet.
- The magnetic effect remains only till the current is flowing through the solenoid.
- An electromagnet is used in electric bells, electric motors, telephone diaphragms, loudspeakers and for sorting scrap metal.
- Steel is a favourable substance for making permanent magnet. Electromagnet cannot be made by steel.

Advantages of Electromagnet over Permanent Magnet

An electromagnet is a temporary form of magnet because its magnetism is only for the duration of current flowing in its coil.

Actually, an electromagnet is better than a permanent magnet in many respects. There are some of the advantages of the electromagnets over the permanent magnets which are stated as follows:

- The magnetism of an electromagnet can be switched ON or switched OFF as desired. While it is not possible with a permanent magnet.
- By increasing the number of turns in the coil and by increasing the current passing through the coil an electromagnet can be made very strong. On the other hand, a permanent magnet cannot be made so strong.

11

Magnetism and Electromagnetic Induction

(SOURCES)

Class-VI NCERT Chap 10 (Fun with Magnets), Class-X NCERT Chap 12 (Magnetic Effects of Electric Current), Class-XII NCERT Chap 4 (Moving Charges and Magnetism), Old NCERT Chap 5 (Magnetism and Matter), Old NCERT Chap 6 (Electromagnetic induction), Chap 7 (Alternating Current)
Tamil Nadu Board (Class-IX), NIOS

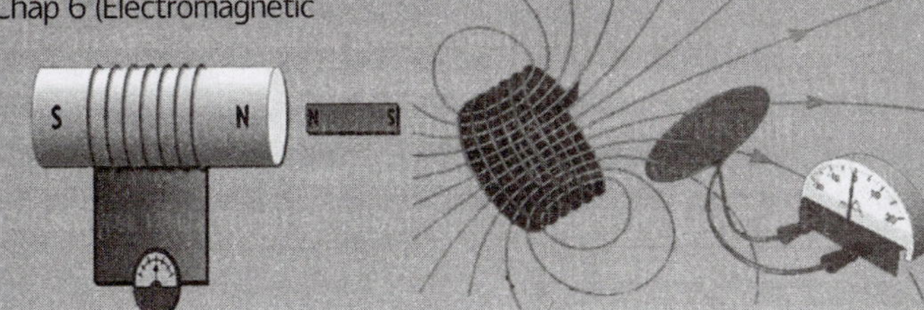

Magnet

- A magnet is a material that has both attractive and repulsive properties. It attracts small pieces of iron, nickel, cobalt, etc. This property attraction is called **magnetism.**
- A magnet is a material or an object that produces a magnetic field. The magnetic field is invisible but is responsible for most notable property of a magnet.
- Magnets are of the following two types:
  - **Natural magnets** A natural magnet is an ore of iron (Fe_3O_4). They are generally irregular in shape and weak in strength. Natural magnets are also known as lodestone.
  - **Artificial magnets** These magnets have desired shape and strength. They are stronger than natural magnets. e.g, A bar magnet, a horse shoe magnet, compass needle, etc.

General Properties of Magnet

- **Attractive property** A magnet attracts small pieces of iron, cobalt, nickel, etc. When a magnet is brought near a heap of iron filings, at the ends of magnet attraction is greatest. The ends where magnetic attraction is maximum, are called **poles of the magnet.** Thus, every magnet has two poles (North and South).
- **Directive property** When a bar magnet is suspended freely, it points in the North-South direction. The tip of the magnet which points to the geographic North is called **North pole.** The tip which points to the geographic South is called the **South pole** of the magnet.
- **Like poles repel and unlike poles attract** When North poles (or South poles) of two magnets are brought close together, there is a repulsive force between them. Conversely, if two opposite poles brought close to each other, then there is attractive force between them.
- **Magnetic poles always exists in pairs** If a single magnet is break into many pieces, then each pair has two poles (North and South) and acts as a magnet. Thus, every magnet exists as a dipole, magnetic monopoles do not exist.
- **Magnetisation of other material** It is possible to make magnets with iron and its alloys. When a piece of a substance, such as soft iron, steel, cobalt, nickel etc is placed near a magnet, it acquires magnetism and acts as a magnet.

Magnetic and Non-Magnetic Materials

- The materials which get attracted towards a magnet are magnetic. e.g., –Iron, nickel, cobalt, etc.
- The materials which are not attracted towards a magnet are non-magnetic. e.g.,–Glass, wood, plastics, etc.

Magnetic Field

- The space in the surroundings of a magnet in which its magnetic influence can be experienced i.e, its force can be detected is called magnetic field.
- It is a vector quantity. The SI unit of magnetic field is **Tesla** (T) or **weber/metre^2** (Wbm^{-2}), named after the American Engineer **Nikola Tesla**. The smallest unit of magnetic field is **gauss** (G).

$$1 \text{ Tesla} = 10^4 \text{ gauss}$$

Magnetic Field Lines

- The magnetic field lines in a magnetic field are those imaginary lines which continuously represent the direction of the magnetic field.

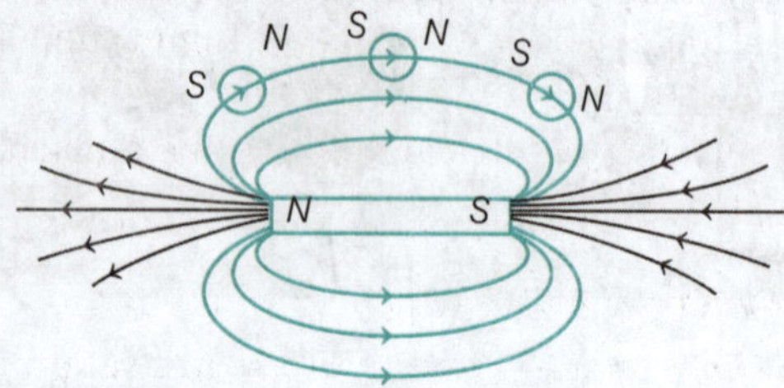

Magnetic Dipole

- An arrangement of two magnetic poles of equal and opposite strength separated by a small distance is called a magnetic dipole.
- Every bar magnet is a magnetic dipole. A current carrying loop behaves as a magnetic dipole.
- An atom acts as a magnetic dipole due to the circulatory motion of electrons around its nucleus.

Pole Strength

The strength of a magnetic pole to attract magnetic materials towards itself is called its pole strength.

It is a scalar quantity and its SI unit is **ampere-metre** (A-m). The strength of North and South pole of a magnet is always equal and opposite in nature.

Earth's Magnetism

- The earth is a natural source of magnetic field where the magnetic field is present everywhere near the source of the earth.
- A freely suspended magnet always points in the North-South direction even in the absence of any other magnet.
- This suggests that the Earth itself behaves as a large magnet which causes a freely suspended magnet to point always in a particular direction (South and North).
- The Earth's magnetic field resembles that of a bar magnet of length one-fifth of the earth's diameter buried at its centre.
- The South pole of the Earth's magnet is towards the Earth's North, while the North pole of the Earth's South. Thus, there is a magnetic South-pole near the geographical North and a magnetic North pole near the geographical South. The Earth has its own magnetic field and it resembles that of a magnetic dipole located at the centre of the earth.
- The pole near the geographic north of the earth, is called the **magnetic North pole.** Similarly, the pole near the geographic south pole, is called the **magnetic South pole**. This dipole is aligned making a small angle with the rotation axis of the Earth.
- The vertical plane passing through the geographic North and South poles is called **geographic meridian**.
- The vertical plane which passes through the imaginary line joining the magnetic North and the South pole is called **magnetic meridian.**

Elements of Earth's Magnetic Field

The magnetic field of Earth at a place can be completely described by three parameters which are called elements of Earth's magnetic field. These are :

- **Magnetic Declination** The angle between the geographical meridian and the magnetic meridian at a place is called the magnetic declination or angle of declination at that place. The declination is greater at higher latitudes and smaller near the equator.
- **Angle of Dip** The angle made by the total magnetic field $\vec{\mathbf{B}}$ of the earth with the horizontal direction in the magnetic meridian is called angle of dip (δ) or **inclination.** It is zero at the magnetic equator and 90° at the magnetic poles.
- **Horizontal Component of Earth's Magnetic Field** The direction of the earth's magnetic field at the magnetic poles is normal to the earth's surface (i.e. in vertical direction) and at magnetic equator, it is parallel to the earth's surface, called horizontal component of earth's magnetic field.

i.e., $Be = \sqrt{H^2 + V^2}$ and $\tan\theta = \dfrac{V}{H}$

where, H = Horizontal component
V = Vertical component

Some Terms used for Magnetic Properties of Materials

- **Magnetising field** When a magnetic material is placed in a magnetic field, a magnetism is induced in it. The magnetic field that induces magnetism is called magnetising field.

- **Magnetic intensity** The ability of a magnetising field to magnetise a material medium is called magnetic intensity (H).
- **Intensity of magnetisation** The intensity of magnetisation (I) shows the degree to which the substance is magnetised

$$I = \frac{M \text{ (Magnetic moment)}}{V \text{ (Volume)}}$$

It is a vector quantity and its SI unit is Am^{-1}.

- **Magnetic permeability** It is the ratio of magnetic induction B to the magnetic intensity H.

$$\mu = \frac{B}{H} \text{ Tesla (ampere metre)}^{-1}$$

- **Relative permeability** It is defined as the ratio of the permeability of the medium to the permeability of free space.

$$\mu_r = \frac{\mu}{\mu_0} \quad \text{(For vacuum, } \mu_r = 1\text{)}$$

- **Magnetic susceptibility** It measures the ability of a substance to take up magnetisation when placed in a magnetic field.

The magnetic susceptibility of a magnetic substance is defined as the ratio of the intensity of magnetisation (I) to the magnetic intensity (H).

$$\text{i.e., } X_m = \frac{I}{H}$$

Classification of Magnetic Materials

On the basis of their behaviour in external magnetic fields, materials are classified into three categories :

- **Diamagnetic Substances** Diamagnetic substances are those which have tendency to move from stronger to the weaker part of the external magnetic field. In other words, unlike the way a magnet attracts metals like iron, it would repel a diamagnetic substance.
  e.g., Bismuth, copper, lead, silicon, nitrogen (at STP), water and sodium chloride are diamagnetic materials. The most exotic diamagnetic materials are superconductors.
- **Paramagnetic Substances** Paramagnetic substances are those which get weakly magnetised when placed in an external magnetic field. They have tendency to move from a region of weak magnetic field to strong magnetic field i.e., they get weakly attracted to a magnet.
  e.g., Aluminium, sodium, calcium, oxygen (at STP) and copper chloride are paramagnetic materials.
- **Ferromagnetic Substances** Ferromagnetic substances are those which get strongly magnetised when placed in an external magnetic field.
- They have strong tendency to move from a region of weak magnetic field to strong magnetic field i.e., they get strongly attracted to a magnet.
  e.g., Iron, cobalt, nickel, gadolinium are ferromagnetic materials.
  The temperature of transition from ferromagnetic to paramagnetism is called **curie temperature.**

Electromagnet

- An electromagnet is a temporary **strong magnet made** from a piece of soft iron, when current flows in the coil wound around it. It is an artificial magnet.
- It can be easily demagnetised by switching off the current.
- Magnetic field of an electromagnet is very strong and its strength can be changed according to the value of current and number of turns in coil.
- They are used in electrical devices like electric bell, loudspeakers, electric fan, telegraph, etc.

Permanent Magnet

- Substances which at room temperature retain their ferromagnetic property for a long period of time are called permanent magnet.
- A permanent magnet is a naturally occuring magnet which is made from steel.
- Once the steel is magnetised, it does not lose its magnetism easily (since steel has more magnetic retentivity than soft iron) so it becomes a permanent magnet.
- These magnets are used in electric metres, in magnetic compasses, etc.

Magnetic Flux

The magnetic flux through any surface placed in magnetic field is the total number of magnetic field lines crossing this surface normally. Mathematically, it is expressed as

$$\phi = BA = BA\cos\theta$$

where, B = magnetic field
and A = area of cross-section

It is a scalar quantity and its SI unit is **Weber** (Wb) or Tm^2.

Electromagnetic Induction

An electric current produced in a closed circuit by a changing magnetic field is called an **induced current.** This phenomenon is called electromagnetic induction. This was discovered by **Michael Faraday.**

In other words, we can say that the phenomenon of production of induced emf (and hence induced current) due to a change of magnetic flux linked with a closed circuit is called electromagnetic induction.

Faraday's Laws of Electromagnetic Induction

Faraday gives two laws which governs the phenomenon of the electromagnetic induction, which are stated as :

- **First Law** Whenever the magnetic flux linked with closed circuit changes, an emf is induced in it which lasts so long there is a change in magnetic flux linked with it.
- **Second Law** The magnitude of the induced emf is equal to the rate of change of magnetic flux linked with the closed circuit.

$$e = \frac{-d\phi}{dt} \text{ or } \frac{-Nd\phi}{dt}$$

where, N = number of turns in a coil.

Lenz's Law

This law states that the direction of induced current is such that it opposes the cause which produces it i.e, it opposes the change in magnetic flux.

Types of Electromagnetic Induction

- **Self-Induction** The phenomenon of production of induced emf in a coil when a changing current passes through it, is called self-induction. Some phenomena associated with self-induction are sparking, non-inductive winding and electromagnetic damping.
- **Mutual Induction** The phenomenon of production of induced emf in one coil due to a change of current in the neighbouring coil, is called mutual induction.

Eddy Current

Whenever the magnetic flux linked with a metal sheet or block changes, the induced current are produced in it. The flow of these current look like swirling eddies or whirl-pools in water and, so they are known as eddy currents.

Applications of Eddy Current

Eddy currents have certain applications like :

- **Magnetic braking in trains** Strong electromagnets are situated above the rails in some electrically powered trains. When the electromagnets are activated, the eddy currents induced in the rails oppose the motion of the train. As there are no mechanical linkages, the braking effect is smooth.
- **Electromagnetic damping** Certain galvanometers have a fixed core made of non-magnetic metallic material. When the coil oscillates, the eddy currents generated in the core oppose the motion and bring the coil to rest quickly.
- **Induction furnace** Induction furnace can be used to produce high temperatures and can be utilised to prepare alloys, by melting the constituent metals.

  A high frequency alternating current is passed through a coil which surrounds the metals to be melted. The eddy currents generated in the metals produce high temperatures sufficient to melt it.
- **Electric power meters** The shiny metal disc in the electric power meter (analogue type) rotates due to the eddy currents.

  Electric currents are induced in the disc by magnetic fields produced by sinusoidally varying currents in a coil.

Direct Current (DC) and Alternating Current (AC)

- **Direct Current** (DC) An electric current whose magnitude is either constant or variable but the direction remains the same is called direct current. It is denoted by DC. Sources of DC are voltaic cell, a dry cell, battery, DC generator, etc.
- **Alternating Current** (AC) An electric current whose magnitude changes with time and direction reverses periodically is called alternating current. It is denoted by AC. Sources of AC are hydro-electric generators, thermal power generators and nuclear power generators, etc.
  - The number of cycles completed by the AC in one second is called the **frequency of AC**. The frequency of AC in India is 50 Hz which means that AC changes its direction after $\frac{1}{100}$ second.
  - The major difference between AC and DC is that DC always flows in one direction, while AC reverses its direction periodically.

Advantages of AC over DC

- AC generation is easy and economical.
- It can be easily converted into DC, with the help of rectifier.
- In AC, energy loss is minimum, so it can be transmitted over large distances.

Disadvantages of AC over DC

- AC shock is attractive, while DC shock is repulsive. So, 220V AC is more dangerous than 220V DC.
- AC cannot be used in electroplating process because here constant current with constant polarity is needed which is given by DC.

Electric Motor

- Electric motor is a rotating device that converts electrical energy into mechanical energy. It is based on the principle that when a rectangular coil is placed in a magnetic field and current is passed through it, two equal and opposite forces act on the coil which rotates it continuously.

- A commercial electric motor uses:
  - An electromagnet in the place of permanent magnet.
  - A large number of turns of conducting wire in the current carrying coil.
  - A soft iron core on which the coil is wound. The combination of soft iron core and coil is called **armature**. It enhances the power of motor.
- Electric motor is used in electric fans, refrigerators, mixers, washing machine, computers, MP3 player, etc.

Electric Generator

It is a device used to convert mechanical energy to electrical energy. An electric generator is based on the principle of electromagnetic induction. It is also known as **dynamo**. Electric generator is of two types:

AC Generator

- It generates alternating current.
- AC generator is based on the principle that whenever in a closed circuit, the magnetic field lines change, an induced current is produced.

Construction

- An AC generator consists of a rectangular armature coil placed in a region of strong magnetic field (between the two poles of a permanent magnet).
- It experiences the torque, due to the forces acting on the coil and produces a current in it (and hence, in external circuit having load or resistance R).
- The two slip rings (R_1 and R_2) maintain contact of the coil with the load resistor through brushes, brushes B_1 and B_2 without resistor being moved.

DC Generator

It generates direct current. The principle of DC generator is same as that of AC generator.

Construction

- Construction of DC dynamo is same as that of AC generator, except that in place of slip-ring commutator. Slip-ring type commutator is used.
- With this arrangement, one brush is at all times in contact with the arm moving up in the field, while the other is in contact with the arm moving down.

Transformer

- Transformer is a device which is used to increase or decrease the alternating voltage. It is based on the **principle of mutual induction**.
- If the transformer increases the input voltage, is called **step up transformer** and if it decreases the input voltage, it is called **step down transformer**.

Construction

- A transformer consists of two sets of coils, insulated from each other.
- They are wound on a soft-iron core, either one on top of the other (shell type arrangement) or on separate limbs (core type arrangement) of the core as shown.

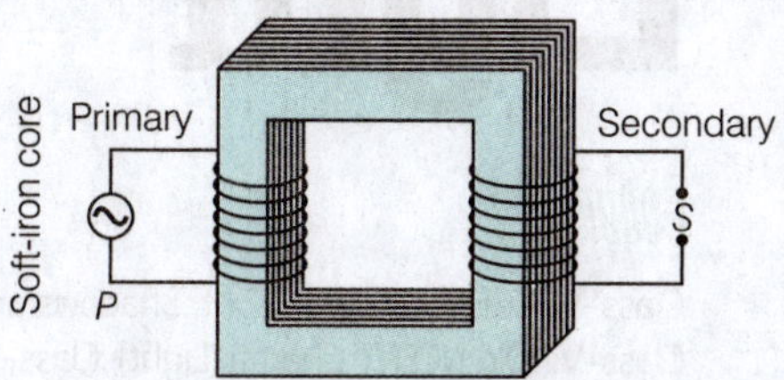

- One of the coils called the **primary coil** has N_p turns and the other coil is called **secondary coil** has N_s turns. The primary coil is the input coil and the secondary coil is the output coil of the transformer.

Working

When an alternating voltage is applied to the primary, the resulting current produces an alternating magnetic flux which links the secondary and induces an emf in it.
The value of this emf depends on the number of turns in the secondary. In step up transformer, $N_s > N_p$ and in step down transformer $N_s < N_p$.

Uses

- Small transformers are used in radio receivers, telephones, loudspeakers, etc.
- Transformers are used in stabilised power supplies.
- A step down transformer is used for obtaining large current for electric welding and in induction furnace for melting metals.
- A step up transformer is used for production of X-rays.
- Transformers are used in the transmission of electric energy from the generating stations to the consumers.

Extra Facts From Tamil Nadu Board and NIOS

Properties of Magnetic Lines of Forces

- Magnetic lines of force are closed, continuous curves, extending through the body of the magnet.
- Magnetic lines of force start from the North pole and end at the South pole.
- Magnetic lines of force never intersect.
- They will be maximum at the poles than at the equator.

Connection between Electricity and Magnetism

When there is current, the magnetic field is produced and the current carrying conductor behaves like a magnet. The magnetic property arises due to the motion of electrons in the lodestone. In the circuit, the electrons flow from negative of the battery to positive of the battery and constitute current. As a result, it produces magnetic field.

Light

(SOURCES)

Class-VI NCERT Chap 8 (Light, Shadows and Reflections), Class-VII Old NCERT Chap 11 (Light), Class-VIII Old NCERT Chap 13 (Light), Class-X NCERT Chap 9 (Light, Reflection and Refraction), Chap 10 (The Human Eye and the Colourful World), Class-XII Old NCERT Chap 9 (Ray Optics and Optical Instruments), Old NCERT Chap 10 (Wave Optics) Tamil Nadu Board (Class-IX), NIOS

12

- We see a variety of objects in the world around us. However, we are unable to see anything in a dark room. On lighting up the room, things became visible. During the day, the sunlight helps us to see objects.
- There are a number of common wonderful phenomena associated with light such as image formation, twinkling of stars, rainbow, bending of light in a medium and so on. A study of the properties of light helps us to explore them.

Light

- Light is a form of energy that enables us to see all the objects around us. An object reflects the light rays that fall on it.
- These reflected light rays, when received by our eyes, make the object visible to us.

Light Sources

A source of light is an object from which light is given out. Some sources of light are natural like the sun, stars and some are man made like oil lamp, a candle, an electric bulb, etc.

The sources of light are of two kinds:

- **Self-luminous Sources** The sources that emit light of their own are called self-luminous. e.g., The sun, the stars, electric lamps, candles, etc.
- **Non-luminous Sources** The sources that does not emit light of their own are called non-luminous. They receive light from an external source and scatter it to the surroundings. e.g., The moon, glass, book, etc.

Properties of Light

- Light is a form of energy that gives us the sensation of sight.
- Light travels in a straight line and the straight line path along which light travels is called **ray of light**.
- It does not need any material medium for propagation.
- The speed of light in a vacuum or in air is 3×10^8 m/s. It does not need any material medium for propagation.
- Light travels in the form of electromagnetic radiations, so it does not require any medium to travel.

Optical Medium

The medium through which a light propagates is called optical medium. They are classified into three categories as follows :

- **Transparent** It is a medium through which light propagates easily. e.g., Air, water, glass, etc.
- **Translucent** It is a medium through which light propagates partially. e.g., Ground, glass, paper, etc.
- **Opaque** It is a medium through which light cannot propagate. e.g., Wood, metals, etc.

Rectilinear Propagation of Light

- In an isotropical materialistic medium, the rays of light move in a straight line. This is called the rectilinear propagation of light.
- The formation of various types of shadows, the formation of image through a pinhole camera, occurrence of solar and lunar eclipses etc., are the examples of rectilinear propagation of light.

Umbra and Penumbra

- When an opaque body is placed infront of a source of light, then behind the opaque body a black or dark region appears which is called **shadow**.
- The formation of shadows depends on the types of source of light. If the source of light is a point source, then the shadow formed is called **umbra**, while an extended source of light is called **penumbra**.

Reflection of Light

The phenomenon of bouncing back of light rays in the same medium on striking a smooth surface is called reflection of light.

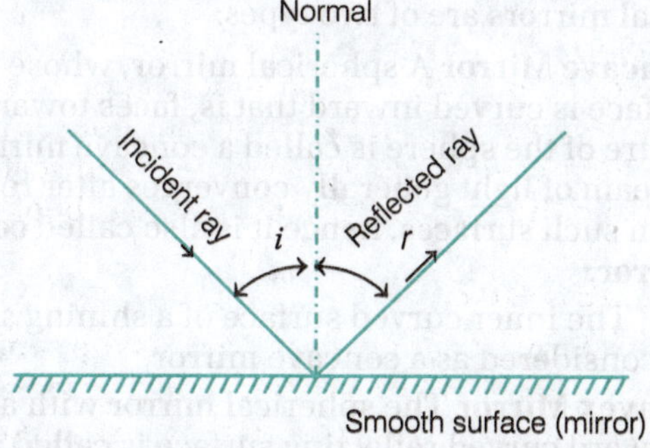

- The light ray, which strikes any surface, is called the **incident ray**.
- The ray that comes back from the surface after reflection is known as the **reflected ray**.
- A line making an angle of 90° to the line representing the shiny surface (mirror) at the point, where the incident ray strikes the mirror. This line is known as the **normal to the reflecting surface** at that point.
- The angle between the normal and incident ray is called **angle of incident** ($\angle i$).
- The angle between the normal and the reflected ray is known as the **angle of reflection** ($\angle r$).

Laws of Reflection

- There are two laws of reflection as follows :
  - Angle of incidence is always equal to the angle of reflection (i.e, $\angle i = \angle r$).
  - The incident ray, the reflected ray and the normal at the point of incidence, all lie in the same plane.
- These laws of reflection are applicable to all types of reflecting surfaces.

Types of Reflection

Reflection of light occurs in two different types, which are as follows :

- **Regular Reflection** When parallel rays falling on a smooth and polished reflecting surface then after reflection, reflected rays are going in one particular direction. This reflection is called regular reflection.

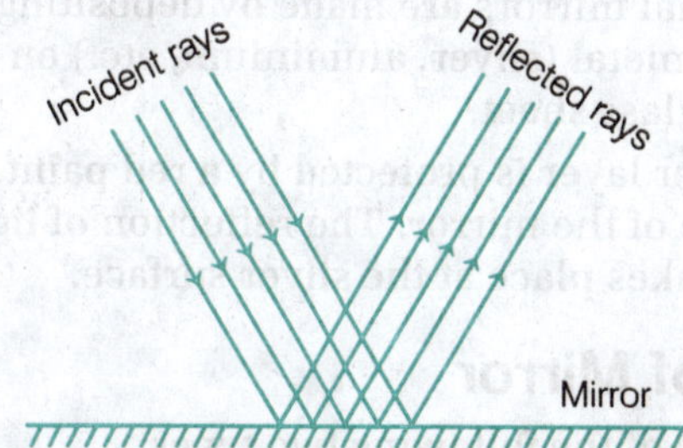

- **Irregular or Diffused Reflection** When parallel rays are falling on a rough and unpolished surface then after reflection, the reflected rays go in different directions. This is called irregular or diffused reflection.

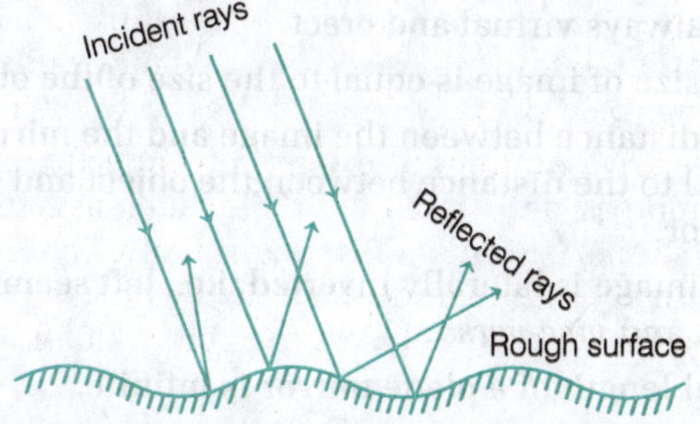

Diffused reflection has the following uses in daily life :

- The rough glass in the window of the room reflects the sunlight, which prevents excessive glare.
- Newspapers are printed on rough and cheap paper, so that the light falling on it can be reflected back and its small letters can be read easily.

Image

If light rays coming from a point after reflection meet at another point or appear to meet at another point, then the second point is called the image of the first point. Images are of two types:

- **Real Image** If the light rays coming from a point actually, meet after reflection, then the image formed is called a real image. They can be obtained on screen.

- **Virtual Image** If the light rays coming from a point, after reflection does not meet actually, but appear to meet at another point, then the image formed is called a virtual image. These images cannot be obtained on the screen.

Mirror

- Mirror is the smooth and polished surface which reflects almost all the light incident on it. Silver metal is one of the best reflectors of light.
- So, normal mirrors are made by depositing a thin layer of shiny metal (silver, aluminium, etc.) on one side of a plane glass sheet.
- The silver layer is protected by a red paint on the backside of the mirror. The reflection of light in a mirror takes place at the silver surface.

Types of Mirror

Mirrors are of the following two types:

1. Plane Mirror

If the reflecting surface of a mirror is plane, then the mirror is called a plane mirror.

Image formed by a plane mirror has following properties:

- It is always virtual and erect.
- The size of image is equal to the size of the object.
- The distance between the image and the mirror is equal to the distance between the object and the mirror.
- The image is laterally inverted, i.e., left seems to be right and *vice-versa*.
- Focal length of a plane mirror is infinite.
- To see the full size of image, the height of plane mirror should be atleast half the size of object.
- The image formed in a plane mirror is laterally inverted. So, the word AMBULANCE is written as ƎƆNA⅃UBMA. When a driver of a vehicle ahead of an ambulance look in rear view mirror, then he can read AMBULANCE written on it and give way to it.
- If a person moves with a velocity u towards or away from the mirror, then his image appears to move with a velocity $20u$ towards or away from the mirror to him, but if a stationary observer observes the image, then it appears to move with a velocity u.
- When two plane mirrors are kept facing each other at angle θ and an object is placed between them, a number of images are formed due to multiple reflection. The number of images is given by $n\left(=\dfrac{360°}{\theta°}-1\right)$.
- Plane mirrors are commonly used as looking glass, in making periscopes, kaleidoscopes, etc.

Notes An image formed by a mirror the left of the object appears on the right and the right appears on the left. This is known as lateral inversion.

Periscope

- In periscope, two plane mirrors are attached to each other at 45° in such a way that the reflecting surfaces are oppositely directed.
- Light ray first incidents on the reflecting surface of the **first** (upward) mirror and reflected from beam now incidents upon the **second** (downward) mirror, so that after reflection it enters the eye.
- That's why during war time the arms use periscope to defeat the enemies who are hidden in bunkers. Also in submarines periscopes are frequently used today.

2. Spherical Mirror

If the reflecting surface of the mirror is curved inwards or outwards, then the mirror is called a spherical mirror.

Types of Spherical Mirror

Spherical mirrors are of two types:

(a) **Concave Mirror** A spherical mirror, whose reflecting surface is curved inward that is, faces towards the centre of the sphere is called a concave mirror. A beam of light generally converges after reflection from such surfaces, hence it is also called **convergent mirror.**

e.g., The inner curved surface of a shining spoon can be considered as a concave mirror.

(b) **Convex Mirror** The spherical mirror with an outward curved reflecting surface is called a convex mirror. A beam of light generally diverges after reflection from this surface, hence, it is also called **divergent mirror.**

e.g., The outer curved surface of a shining spoon can be treated or considered as convex mirror.

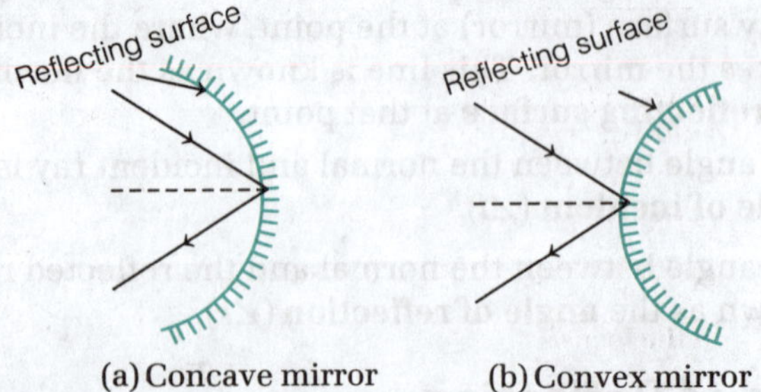

(a) Concave mirror (b) Convex mirror

Some Definitions Related to Spherical Mirrors

- **Centre of Curvature** Centre of curvature of a spherical mirror is the centre of the imaginary sphere of which the mirror is a part.

It is shown by C.

- In case of concave mirror, the centre of curvature lies in front of it, while in case of convex mirror, the centre of curvature lies behind it.
- **Radius of Curvature** Radius of curvature of a spherical mirror is the radius of imaginary sphere of which, mirror is a part. It is shown by R.
- **Pole** Pole of the spherical mirror is the centre of its reflecting surface. It is shown by P.
- **Principal Axis** The principal axis of a spherical mirror is the line joining the pole and centre of curvature.

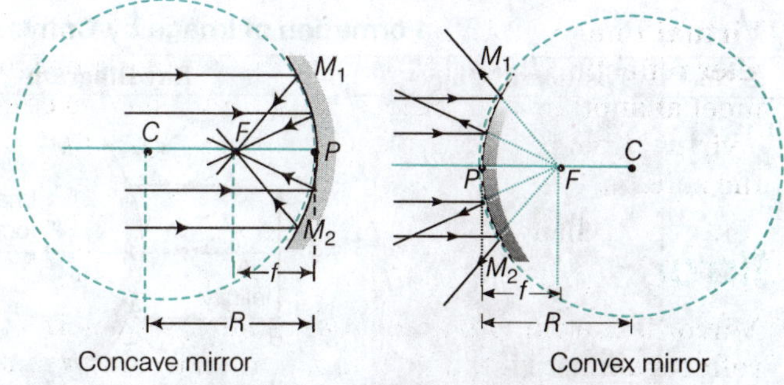

Concave mirror Convex mirror

- **Principal Focus of a Spherical Mirror** It is a point on the principal axis of the mirror at which the light rays coming parallel to principal axis, after reflection actually meet. It is represented by F.
- For a concave mirror, the focus is in front of the mirror, while for a convex mirror, the focus is behind the mirror.
- The focus of a concave mirror is real, while the focus of a convex mirror is virtual.
- **Aperture** The diameter of the reflecting surface of a spherical mirror is called its aperture. It is that part of the reflecting surface of a mirror which is exposed to the incident light. It is equal to the straight line distance between two ends of the mirror. M_1M_2 is the aperture of mirror.
- **Focal Length** The distance between pole and principal focus of a spherical mirror is called its focal length. It is represented by f. If the aperture of the mirror is small, then $f = R/2$.

Formation of Image by Concave Mirror for Different Positions of Object

S.No.	Position of Object	Ray Diagram	Position of Image	Nature and Size of Image
1.	At infinity		At focus or in the focal plane	Real, inverted, extremely diminished in size
2.	Beyond the centre of curvature but at finite distance from mirror		Between focus and the centre of curvature	Real, inverted and diminished
3.	At the centre of curvature		At the centre of curvature	Real, inverted and same size as that of object
4.	Between focus and centre of curvature		Beyond the centre of curvature	Real, inverted and magnified
5.	At the focus		At infinity	Real, inverted and extremely magnified
6.	Between the pole and focus		Behind the mirror	Virtual, erect and magnified

Formation of Image by Convex Mirror for Different Positions of Object

S.No.	Position of Object	Ray Diagram	Position of Image	Nature and Size of Image
1.	At infinity		At the principal focus, behind the mirror	Virtual, erect and extremely diminished
2.	Between infinity and the pole (i.e. at finite distance)		Between the principal focus and the pole, behind the mirror	Virtual, erect and diminished

Sign Convention for Reflection by Spherical Mirrors

While dealing with the reflection of light by spherical mirrors, we shall follow a set of sign convention called the new Cartesian sign convention based on Cartesian coordinates.

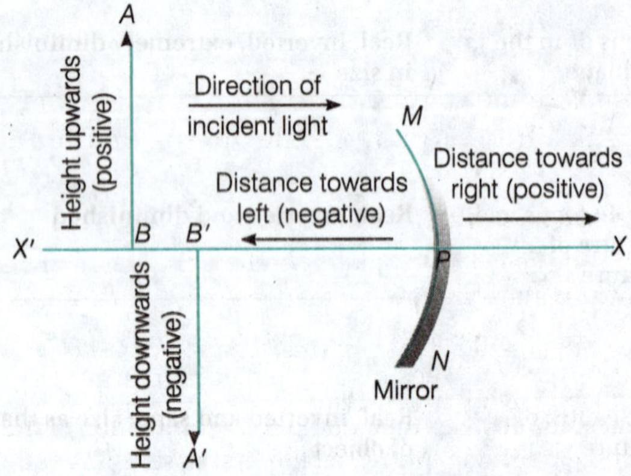

The conventions are as follows :

- The object is always placed to the left of the mirror.
- All distances parallel to principal axis (X-axis) are measured from the pole of the mirror.
- Distances to the left of pole (– ve X-axis) are **negative**. Distances to the right of pole (+ ve X-axis) are **positive**.
- Distances measured perpendicularly above the principal axis (along $+Y$-axis) are taken as **positive**.
- Distances measured perpendicularly below the principal axis (along $-Y$-axis) are taken as **negative**.

Also, focal length of convex mirror is taken as **positive**, whereas focal length of concave mirror is taken as **negative**.

Mirror Formula

- In a spherical mirror, the distance of the object from its pole is called the **object distance** (u). The distance of the image from the pole of the mirror is called the **image distance** (v).
- The distance of the principal focus from the pole is called **focal length** (f). The relation between quantities u, v and f is called mirror formula.

  It is expressed as $\frac{1}{v}+\frac{1}{u}=\frac{1}{f}$

Magnification by Spherical Mirror

Magnification produced by a spherical mirror gives the relative extent to which the image of an object is magnified with respect to the object size.

It is represented by letter m.

$$\text{Magnification, } (m) = -\frac{\text{Height of image } (h_i)}{\text{Height of object } (h_o)}$$

$$m = \frac{\text{Image distance } (v)}{\text{Object distance } (u)} = \frac{-v}{u}$$

Uses of Concave Mirrors

- Concave mirrors are commonly used in torches, search lights and vehicles, headlights to get powerful parallel beams of light.
- Concave mirrors are used as shaving mirrors to see larger image of the face.
- Dentists use concave mirrors to see large images of the teeth of patients.
- Large concave mirrors are used to converge sunrays on a point to produce large amount of concentrated heat in a solar furnace.

Uses of Convex Mirrors

- Convex mirrors are commonly used as rear view mirrors in vehicles because they always give an erect image and have wider field of view as they are curved outward.
- Big convex mirrors are used as shop security mirrors. The shop owner can keep an eye on the customers to look for thieves and shoplifters among them.

Refraction of Light

- The change in path of a light ray as it passes from one medium to another medium is called refraction of light.

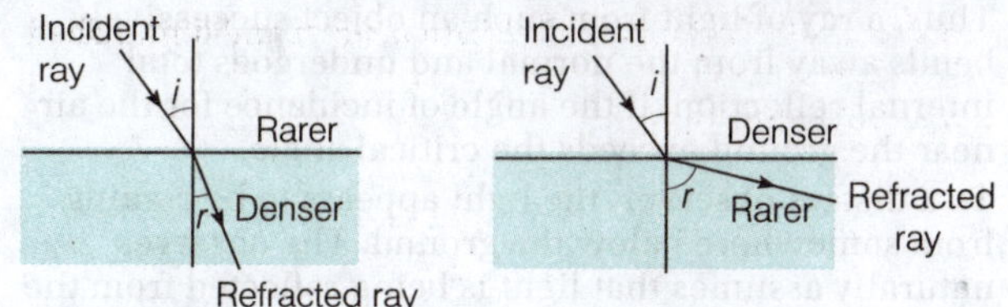

- When light travels from a rarer medium to a denser one, it bends towards the normal and when travels from a denser medium to a rarer one, it bends away from the normal.

Causes of Refraction

- Speed of light is different in different media, i.e. more in rarer medium and comparatively less in denser medium.
- So, when light enters a denser medium, its speed reduces and it bends towards the normal and when it enters rarer medium, its speed increases and it bends away from the normal.

Note The refraction of light caused by earth's layers of different densities is called atmospheric refraction.

Refraction through a Rectangular Glass Slab

- When a light ray enters in a glass slab, then the emergent ray is parallel to the incident ray but it is shifted sideward slightly.

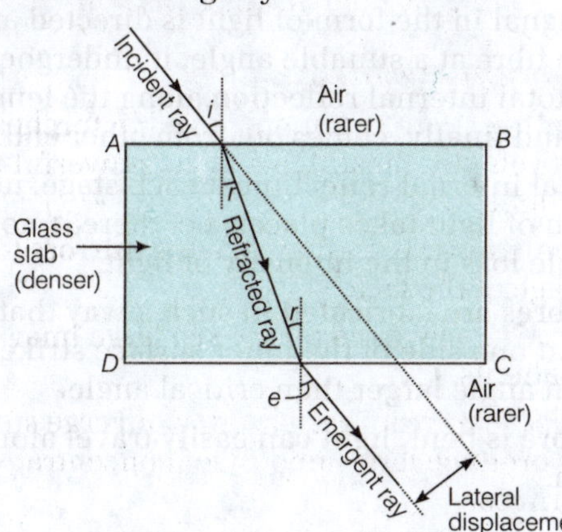

- In this case, refraction takes place twice, first when ray enters glass slab from air and second when exits from glass slab to air.
- **Lateral Displacement** Lateral displacement is the perpendicular distance between the emergent ray and incident ray when the light passes out of a glass slab.

Note Angle of incidence = Angle of emergence, i.e. $\angle i = \angle e$.
If the incident ray falls normally to the surface of glass slab, then there is no bending of the ray of light, it goes straight without any deviation.

Laws of Refraction

- The incident ray, the refracted ray and the normal to the interface of two transparent media at the point of incidence, all lie in the same plane.
- The ratio of sine of angle of incidence to the sine of angle of refraction for light of given colour is constant for a given pair of media **(Snell's law)**. It is expressed as

$$\frac{\sin i}{\sin r} = \mu = \text{constant } (\mu \text{ or } n)$$

This constant is known as **refractive index (μ)**.

- If one medium is represented by 1 and another medium is represented by 2, then the refractive index of the medium 2 relative to medium 1 will represented by ${}_1\mu_2$.

So, $${}_1\mu_2 = \frac{\mu_2}{\mu_1} = \frac{\sin i}{\sin r}$$

The refractive index of a medium with respect to vacuum is called **absolute refractive index of the medium.**

Refractive Index and Speed of Light

If c is the speed of light in air and v is the speed of light in medium, then the refractive index of the medium is

$$\mu = \frac{\text{Speed of light in vacuum / air}}{\text{Speed of light in medium}} = \frac{c}{v}$$

Hence, for any two media, the refractive index of the second medium with respect to first medium is equal to the ratio of the velocities of light in the mediums.

Examples of Refraction of Light

- The bottom of a tank or pond containing water appears to be raised due to refraction of light which takes place when light rays pass from the pool of water into the air.
- The letters appear to be raised when viewed through a glass slab placed over the document because of refraction of light.
- A pencil partially immersed in water appears to be bent because of the refraction of light coming from the part of pencil that is under water. A lemon kept in water in a glass tumbler appears to be bigger than its actual size, when viewed from the sides.

- The twinkling of stars is due to atmospheric refraction of starlight. As the light from the stars enters the earth's atmosphere, it undergoes refraction due to varying optical densities of air at various altitudes.
- The continuously changing atmosphere refracts the light by different amounts. In this way, the starlight reaching our eyes increases and decreases continuously and the star appears to be twinkle at night.
- The sun is visible to us about two minutes before the actual sunrise and about two minutes after the actual sunset. This is because of atmospheric refraction.

Total Internal Reflection (TIR)

- The critical angle for two given media is the angle of incidence in the denser medium for which the angle of refraction in the rarer medium is 90°.
- When a ray of light travelling from denser medium to rarer medium, is incident at the interface of two media at an angle greater than the critical angle for the two media, the ray is totally reflected back to denser medium. This phenomenon is called Total Internal Reflection (TIR).
- Necessary conditions for total internal reflection to take place are as follows :
  - The ray incident on the interface of two media should travel in the denser medium.
  - The angle of incidence should be greater than critical angle for the two media.

Some Practical Applications of Total Internal Reflection

Some phenomena related to the total internal reflection are given below :

- **The Cracked Part of Glass Appears to be Brighten** The cracked part of glass contains air, which acts like a rarer medium with respect to it.

  When light rays enter through the glass (cracked) to air then they refract in which the angle of incidence becomes greater than the critical angle, and the phenomenon of total internal reflection takes place. That's why cracked part of glass appears to be brightened.
- **Brighten Test Tube** Test tube filled with water appear to be brighten due to the total internal reflection.
- **In Sparkling of Diamond** Brilliancy of diamonds is mainly due to total internal reflection of light inside them.
- The critical angle for diamond-air interface is very small, therefore once light enters a diamond, it is very likely to undergo total internal reflection.

  Brilliancy of diamond depends on its cutting.

Mirage in Deserts

- It is an optical illusion occurring in deserts and on roads on a hot summer day. Some tall objects such as trees, appear to be inverted. Due to mirage, the persons get the wrong impression of water. On hot summer days, the air near the ground becomes hotter than the air at higher levels. The refractive index of air increases with its density. Hotter air is less dense and has smaller refractive index than the cooler air.
- If the air currents are small, i.e. the air is still, the optical density at different layers of air increases with height. As a result, light from a tall object such as a tree passes through a medium whose refractive index decreases towards the ground.
- Thus, a ray of light from such an object successively bends away from the normal and undergoes total internal reflection, if the angle of incidence for the air near the ground exceeds the critical angle.
- To a distant observer, the light appears to be coming from somewhere below the ground. The observer naturally assumes that light is being reflected from the ground say, by a pool of water near the tall object.

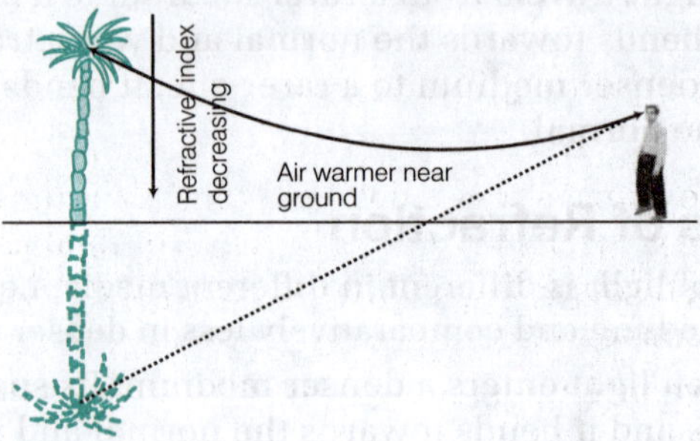

Optical Fibres

- An optical fibre is a thin tube of transparent material that allows light to pass through, without being refracted into the air or another external medium. Optical fibres are based upon the total internal reflection.
- Optical fibres are fabricated with high quality composite glass/quartz fibres. The refractive index of core is higher than that of the cladding.
- When a signal in the form of light is directed at one end of the fibre at a suitable angle, it undergoes repeated total internal reflection along the length of the fibre and finally, comes out from other end.
- Due to total internal reflection at each stage, no absorption of light takes places, i.e. there is no appreciable loss in the intensity of light.
- Optical fibres are fabricated in such a way that light reflected at one side of the inner surface strikes the other at an angle larger than critical angle.
- Even if fibre is bent, light can easily travel along the length.

Uses of Optical Fibres

- In transmitting electrical and optical signals.
- In visual examination of internal organs like esophagus, stomach and intestine.
- In decorative lamps.

Lens

Lens is a transparent material bound by two surfaces, of which one or both surfaces are spherical.

Lenses are of two types:

- **Convex or Converging Lens** A lens which is thicker at the centre and thinner at its ends is called convex lens. Convex lenses are of three types as shown below:

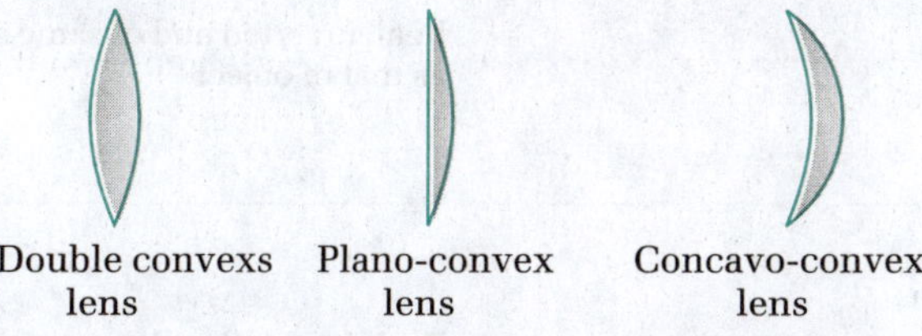

  A convex lens is also known as converging lens because it converges a parallel beam of light rays passing through it. A double convex lens is simply called **convex lens.**

- **Concave or Diverging Lens** A lens which is thinner at the centre and thicker at its ends is called a concave lens. Concave lenses are of three types as shown below:

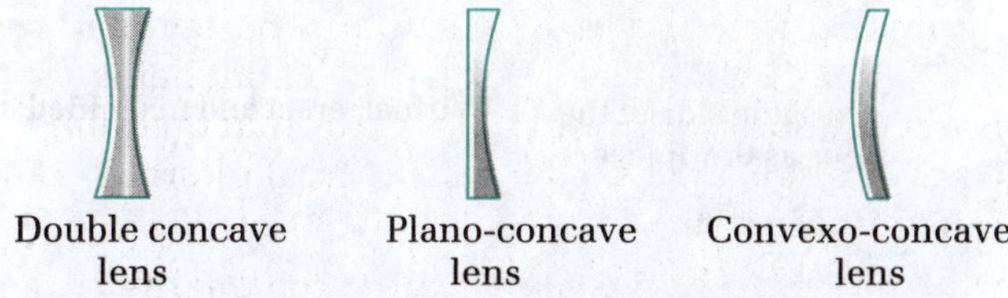

- A concave lens is also known as **diverging lens** because it diverges a parallel beam of light rays passing through it. A double concave lens is simply called concave lens.

Some Definitions Related to Lenses

- **Optical Centre** The centre point of a lens is known as its optical centre.
- It is represented by *O*. The optical centre is a point of the lens, directed to which incident rays refract without any deviation in the path.
- **Centre of Curvature** Centre of curvature of the spherical refracting surface is the centre of the sphere of which this is a part. It is represented by *C*. A lens has two centres of curvature with respect to its two curved surfaces.
- **Radius of Curvature** Radius of the sphere of which the spherical refracting surface is a part called radius of curvature. A lens has two radii of curvature. These may or may not be equal.
- **Principal Axis** The imaginary line joining the two centres of curvature is called principal axis of a lens. Principal axis also passes through the optical centre.
- **Principal Focus** Lens has two principal **foci:**
  - **First Principal Focus** It is a point on the principal axis of lens, the rays starting from or directed to which, become parallel to principal axis after refraction.

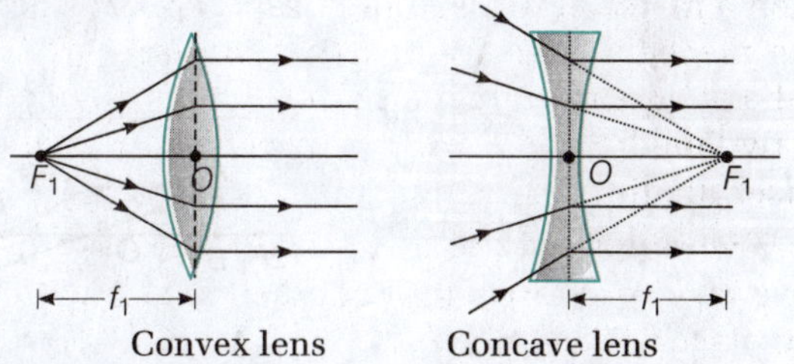

  - **Second Principal Focus** It is the point on the principal axis at which the rays coming parallel to the principal axis, converge on the other side of lens (convex) or appear to meet on the same side of lens (concave), after refraction from the lens.

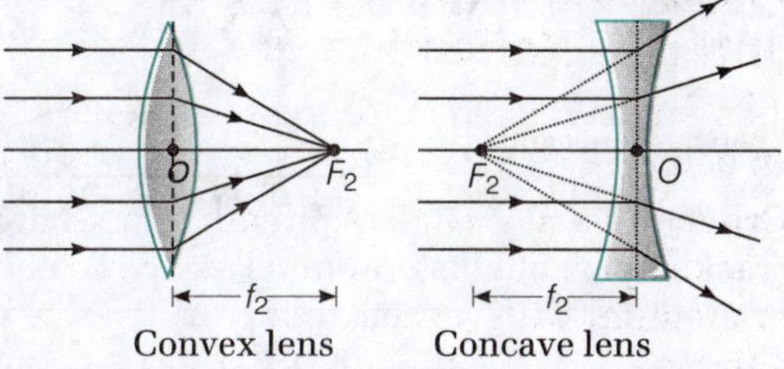

  Both the foci of convex lens are real while that of concave lens are virtual.

- **Focal Length of Lens** The distance between focus and optical centre of lens is called focal length of lens.
- **Focal Plane** The plane passing through the focus and perpendicular to the principal axis is called focal plane.
- **Aperture** The effective diameter of the circular outline of a spherical lens is called its aperture.

Formation of Image by Convex Lens for Different Positions of Object

S. No.	Position of Object	Ray Diagram	Position of Image	Nature and Size of Image
1.	At infinity	2F1 F1 O F2 2F2	At F_2	Real, inverted and extremely diminished
2.	Beyond $2F_1$ (At finite distance)	A B 2F1 F1 O F2 B′ 2F2 A′	Between F_2 and $2F_2$	Real, inverted and diminished
3.	At $2F_1$	A B 2F1 F1 O F2 2F2 B′ A′	At $2F_2$	Real, inverted and of same size as that of object
4.	Between F_1 and $2F_1$	A 2F1 B F1 O F2 2F2 B′ A′	Beyond $2F_2$	Real, inverted and magnified
5.	At F_1	A F1 2F1 B O F2 2F2 To infinity	At infinity	Real, inverted and highly magnified
6.	Between lens and F_1	A′ A 2F1 B′ F1 B O F2 2F2	On same side of the lens as the object	Virtual, erect and magnified

Formation of Image by Concave Lens for Different Positions of Object

S. No.	Position of Object	Ray Diagram	Position of Image	Nature and Size of Image
1.	At infinity	2F1 F1 O	At focus on same side of lens as object	Virtual, erect and highly diminished
2.	At finite distance	A A′ 2F1 B F1 B′ O F2 2F2	Between focus and optical centre, on the same side of lens as object	Virtual, erect and diminished

Lens Formula

This formula gives the relationship between object distance (u), image distance (v) and the focal length (f).

The lens formula is expressed as

$$\frac{1}{v}-\frac{1}{u}=\frac{1}{f}$$

The lens formula is general and is valid in all situations for any spherical lens.

Magnification by Lenses

The ratio of height of image (h_i) and the height of object (h_o) is called magnification (m).

Magnification $(m)=\frac{h_i}{h_o}$

or $m=\frac{v}{u}$

Power of a Lens

The ability of a lens to converge or diverge light rays is called power of the lens.

It is defined as the reciprocal of focal length.

i.e. $P=1/f$ (in metre)

$$\text{Power}=\frac{100}{f\text{(in cm)}}$$

Its SI unit is dioptre (D) ($1\text{ D}=1\text{ m}^{-1}$).

For concave lens, power and focal length are **negative**.

For convex lens, power and focal length are **positive**.

Power of Combination of Lenses

When two or more thin lenses are used in combination, the equivalent focal length (f) and power of the combination (P) can be calculated as

$$\frac{1}{f}=\frac{1}{f_1}+\frac{1}{f_2}+\ldots$$

and $P=P_1+P_2+\ldots$

Uses of Lenses

- Convex lenses are used as a magnifying glass.
- In the manufacturing of spectacles, camera, microscope, telescope and binoculars, convex lenses are used.
- In order to see the image of the person standing outside, concave lenses are used in the peep holes in the door of hotel rooms. Concave lenses are used in making spectacles.

Prism

Prism is a transparent refracting medium bounded by at least two lateral surfaces, inclined to each other at a certain angle. It has two triangular bases and three rectangular lateral surfaces. The angle between two lateral surfaces is called **angle of prism** (A).

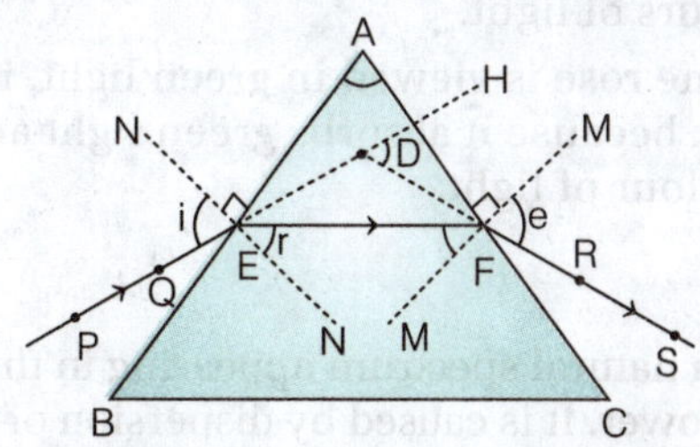

PE - Incident ray
EF - Refracted ray
FS - Emergent ray
∠A - Angle of the prism
∠1 - Angle of incidence
∠r - Angle of refraction
∠e - Angle of emergence
∠D - Angle of deviation

Dispersion of White Light by a Glass Prism

- The phenomenon of splitting of white light into its constituent colours, when it passes through a prism is called **dispersion**.
- The white light is split into a band of colours. This band of seven colours so obtained, the VIBGYOR is called **spectrum**.
- The acronym **VIBGYOR** stands for Violet, Indigo, Blue, Green, Yellow, Orange and Red.

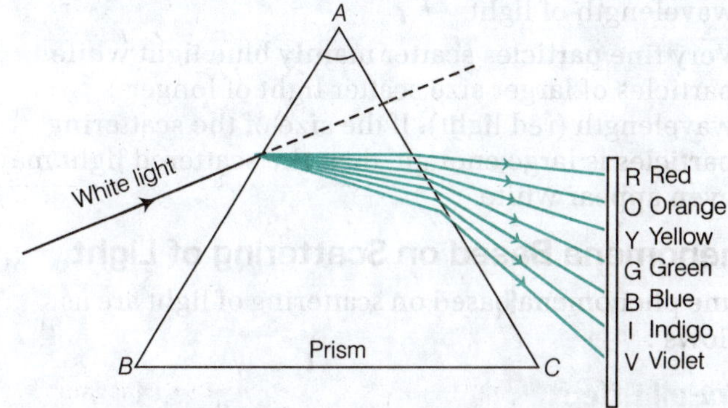

- Light rays of different colours, travel with the same speed in vacuum and air but in any other medium, they travel with different speeds and bend through different angles, which leads to the dispersion of light.
- **Red light** has the maximum wavelength and **Violet light** has the minimum wavelength. So in any medium, red light travels fastest and deviates least, while violet light travels slowest and deviates maximum.

Colour of Objects

- When light is incident on an object, it reflects only a part of it. The reflected light gives the colour to the objects.
- A rose appears red when white light is incident on it and it reflects only red colour of light and absorbs other all colours of light.
- When the same rose is viewed in green light, it appears black because it absorbs green light and reflects no colour of light.

Rainbow

- A rainbow is a natural spectrum appearing in the sky after a rain shower. It is caused by dispersion of sunlight by tiny water droplets present in the atmosphere.
- A rainbow is always formed in a direction opposite to that of the Sun. The water droplets act like small prisms.
- They refract and disperse the incident sunlight, then reflect it internally. Finally, they refract it again when it comes out of the raindrop.
- Due to the **dispersion of light** and **internal reflection**, different colours reach the observer's eye.

Scattering of Light

- The reflection of light from an object in all directions is called scattering of light. The colour of scattered light depends on the size of scattering particles and wavelength of light.
- Very fine particles scatter mainly blue light while particles of larger size scatter light of longer wavelength (red light). If the size of the scattering particles is large enough, then the scattered light may even appear white.

Phenomena Based on Scattering of Light

Some phenomena based on scattering of light are as follows :

Tyndall Effect

- The phenomenon of scattering of light by the colloidal particle is called Tyndall effect.
- The earth's atmosphere is a heterogeneous mixture of minute particles of smoke, tiny water droplets, suspended particles of dust and molecules of air which becomes visible due to scattering of light.

The Colour of Clear Sky is Blue

- During the day time, sky appears blue. This is because the size of the particles in the atmosphere is smaller than the wavelength of visible light, so they scatter the blue light of shorter wavelengths.
- The scattered blue light enters our eye. It should be noted that the sky appears black to the passengers flying at higher altitudes because scattering of light is not prominent at such height due to the absence of particles.

Colour of Sun at Sunrise and Sunset

- At sunrise and sunset, the sun and the sky appear red. Light from the sun near the horizon passes through thicker layers of air and covers larger distance in the atmosphere before reaching our eyes.
- Near the horizon, most of the blue light and shorter wavelengths are scattered away by the particles. Therefore, the light that reaches our eyes is of longer wavelengths. This gives rise to the reddish appearance of the sun and the sky.
- However at the noon, the light from the sun overhead would travel relatively shorter distance. So, it appears white as only a little of the blue and violet colours are scattered.

Red Light is Used in Danger Signals

- This is because there is a little scattering of red light passing through the atmosphere and hence, the signal is seen distinctly from quite large distance.
- That's why the banner used to stop the train, the cricket ball, the cross painted on ambulance are all red in colour.

Interference of Light

- When two light waves of same frequency and constant phase difference travelling in same direction, superimpose (overlap) on each other, then the intensity of resultant wave is not uniform.
- The intensity in the region of superposition gets redistributed, it becomes maximum at some points and minimum at some other points. This phenomenon is called interference of light.
- At the points, where the resultant intensity of light is maximum, interference is said to be constructive and at the points where the resultant intensity is minimum, the interference is said to be destructive.

Examples of Interference of Light in Daily life

- The soap bubbles have a brilliant colour in the Sunlight due to interference of the light.
- The kerosene oil spread on the water surface seems to be in decent colour due to interference of the light.
- The anti-reflective coating present on the surface of lenses of the spectacles, camera etc. is one of the prime applications of interference of light. The main purpose of this coating is to reduce the intensity of light falling on the surface of the object.

- Hologram technology makes use of interference of light radiations to produce a three-dimensional image of objects in real life.

Diffraction of Light

- The phenomenon of bending of light around the sharp corners and the spreading of light within the geometrical shadow of the opaque obstacles is called diffraction of light. Thus, the light deviates from its linear path.
- The deviation becomes much more pronounced, when the dimensions of the aperture or the obstacle are comparable to the wavelength of light.

Polarisation of Light

- Light is an electromagnetic wave in which **electric** and **magnetic field vectors** are perpendicular to each other as well as perpendicular to the direction of propagation of light.
- In an ordinary or unpolarised light the vibrations of electric vector occur symmetrically in all possible directions in a plane perpendicular to the direction of propagation of light.
- The phenomenon of restricting the vibrations of light electric vector in a particular direction, perpendicular to the direction of wave motion is called polarisation of light. Polarisation of light takes place with transverse wave only.
- **Plane of vibration** is the plane containing the direction of vibration of the electric vector and the direction of propagation of light is called the plane of vibration.
- **Plane of polarisation** is the plane containing the direction of propagation of light and perpendicular to the plane of vibrations is called the plane of polarisation.

Polaroids

- Polaroids is a cheap commercial method to produce plane polarised light. **Tourmaline** is a natural polarising material. A polaroid on which unpolarised light is incident is called **polariser** and on which polarised light is incident is called **analyser**.

Uses of Polaroids

- Polaroids are used in sun glasses. Such goggles are more efficient than those made of coloured glasses. They protect the eyes from the glare.
- The wind shield of an automobile is made of polaroid. Such a wind shield protects the eyes of the driver of the automobile from the dazzling light of the approaching vehicles.
- For the same reasons, the covers of head lights are made of polaroids.
- The polaroids are used in window panes of a train and especially of an aeroplane. They help to control the light entering through the windows.

Human Eye

- The human eye is one of the most valuable and sensitive sense organs in the human body. It enables us to see the wonderful world and colours around us.
- The human eye is like a camera.
- Its lens system forms an image on a light-sensitive screen called the **retina**. The eye lens is a convex lens made of a transparent soft and flexible material like a jelly made of proteins.
- Light enters the eye through a thin membrane called **cornea**. It forms the transparent bulge on the front surface of the **eyeball**.
- The eyeball is approximately spherical in shape with a diameter of about 2.3 cm.
- Most of the refraction for the light rays entering the eye occurs at the outer surface of the cornea.
- The **crystalline lens** merely provides the finer adjustment of focal length required to focus objects at different distances on the retina.
- **Iris** is a dark muscular diaphragm that controls the size of the pupil.
- The **pupil** regulates and controls the amount of light entering the eye.
- The **eye lens** forms an inverted real image of the object on the retina.
- The retina is a delicate membrane having enormous number of light-sensitive cells. The light sensitive cells get activated upon illumination and generate electrical signals.
- These signals are sent to the brain *via* the optic nerves.
- The brain interprets these signals and finally processes the information, so that we perceive objects as they are.

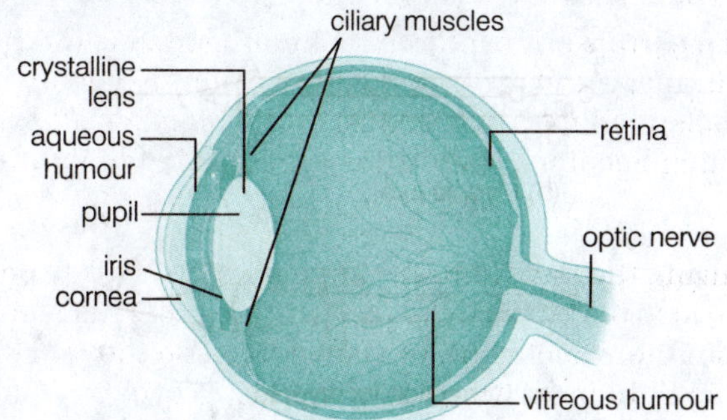

Power of Accommodation of Human Eye

- The ability of the eye to adjust its focal length to see object at various distances is called power of accommodation.
- Our eye has the property of being able to form on the retina clear image nearby as well as distant objects.
- While viewing nearly objects, the ciliary muscles are relaxed the lens becomes thin and its focal length is increased.
- This enables us to see distant objects clearly, muscles contract.
- So, the lens becomes thicker and its focal length decreases.
- **Far point of the eye** is the farthest point from the eye at which one object can be seen clearly by the eye is called the far point of the eye. For a normal eye, the far point is at infinity.
- **Near point of eye lens** is the minimum distance at which objects can be seen without strain. It is also called the **least distance of distinct vision** or near point of the eye. For a young adult, near point is about 25 cm.

Defects of Vision and their Correction

There are mainly three common refractive defects of vision as follows :

1. Myopia

- Myopia is also known as **near-sightedness.** A person with myopia can see nearby objects clearly but cannot see distant objects distinctly.
- A person with this defect has the far point nearer than infinity. This defect arises due to the decrease in focal length of the lens because of :
  - excessive curvature of eye lens.
  - elongation of the eyeball.

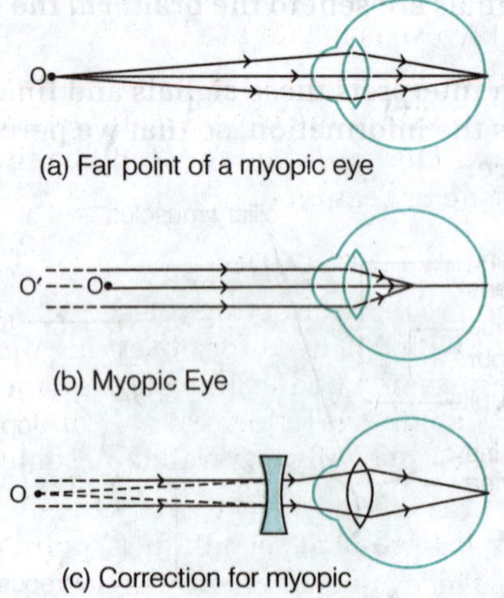

(a) Far point of a myopic eye

(b) Myopic Eye

(c) Correction for myopic

- As a result, the image is formed before retina. This defect can be corrected by using a concave lens of suitable power.

2. Hypermetropia

- Hypermetropia is also known as **far-sightedness.** A person with hypermetropia can see distant objects clearly but cannot see nearby objects distinctly.
- The near point, for the person, is Farther away from the normal near point (25 cm). This is because the light rays from a closeby object are focussed at a point behind the retina. In this case, the image is formed beyond retina.
- This defect arises either because :
  - the focal length of the eye is too long.
  - the eyeball has become too small.
- This defect can be corrected by using a convex lens of appropriate power.

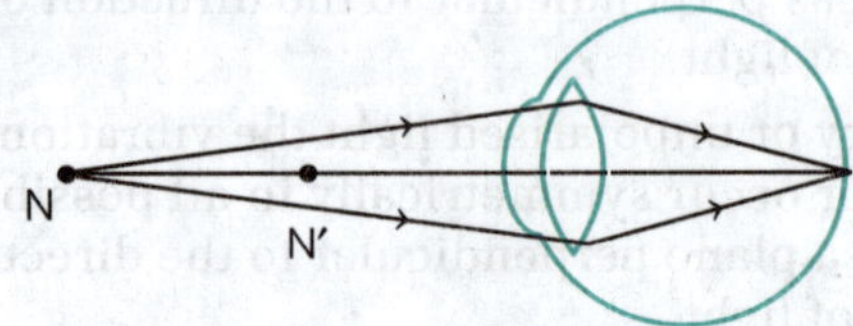

(a) Near point of a Hypermetropic eye

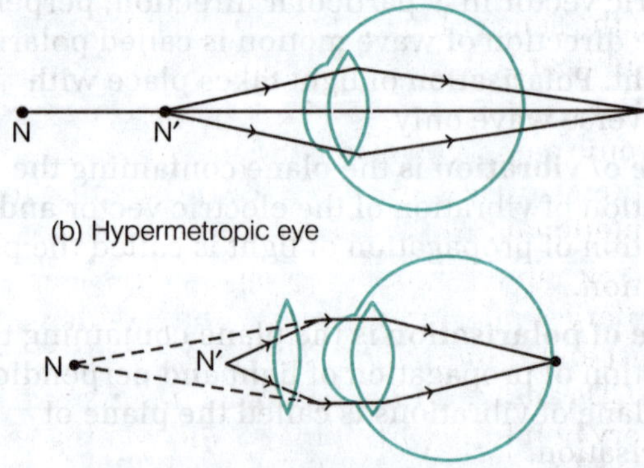

(b) Hypermetropic eye

(c) Correction for Hypermetropic eye

3. Presbyopia

- The power of accommodation of the eye usually decreases with ageing. For most people, the near point gradually recedes away. They find it difficult to see nearby objects comfortably and distinctly without corrective eye-glasses. This defect is called presbyopia.
- It arises due to the gradual weakening of the ciliary muscles and diminishing flexibility of the eye lens.
- People suffering from presbyopia require bi-focal lenses to correct this defect.
- Bi-focal lenses consists of both concave and convex lenses at upper portion and lower portion respectively.

Eye Properties of Different Animals

- Eyes of a crab are quite small but they enable the crab to look all around. So, the crab can sense even if the enemy approaches from behind.
- Butterflies have large eyes that seem to be made up of thousands of litter eyes. They can see not only in the front and the sides but the back as well.
- A night bird (owl) can see very well in the night but not during the day. On the other hand, day light birds (kite, eagle) can see well during the day but not in the night. The owl has a large cornea and a large pupil to allow more light in its eye. Its retina has a large number of rods and only a few cones while the day birds have more cones and fewer rods.

Visually Challenged

Some person are visually impaired. Some of them cannot see at all since, birth while some persons may lose their eyesight because of disease or an injury. Such persons try to identify things by touching and listening to voices more carefully.

Non-optical and Optical Aids for Visually Impaired

- Non-optical aids include visual aids, tactual aids (using the sense of touch), auditory aids (using the sense of hearing) and electronic aids.
- Recorders, talking books and other such devices. Electronic aids, such as talking calculators and computers, are also available for performing many computational tasks.
- Closed circuit television, also an electronic aid, enlarges printed material with suitable contrast and illumination. Now-a-days, use of audio CDs and voice boxes with computers are also very helpful for listening to and writing the desired text.
- Optical aids include bi-focal lenses, contact lenses, tinted lenses, magnifiers and telescopic aids.
- While the lens combinations are used to rectify visual limitations, telescopic aids are available to view chalkboard and class demonstrations.

Braille System

- **Louis Braille** developed a system for visually challenged person. There is Braille code for common languages, Mathematics and scientific notations. This Braille system has **63 dot patterns** or characters.
- Each character represents a letter, a combination of letters, a common word or a grammatical sign.
- Dots are arranged in cells of two vertical rows of three dots each. These patterns when embossed on Braille sheets, help visually challenged persons to recognised words by touching. To make them easier to touch, the dots are raised slightly.

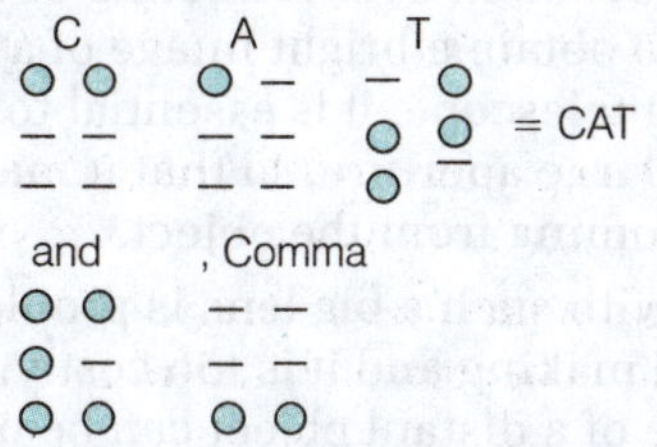

Example of dot patterns used in Braille system

Optical Instruments

Using the reflecting and refracting properties of mirror, lenses and prisms, many optical instruments have been designed like microscopes and telescopes. Our eye is a natural optical device.

Simple Microscope

- Simple microscope is an optical instrument which forms large image of close and minute objects. A simple microscope is a converging lens of small focal length.
- When an object is at a distance less than the focal length of the lens, the image obtained is virtual, erect and magnified and when the object is at a distance equal to the focal length of the lens, the image is formed at infinity.
- The simple microscope is used by watch-makers and jewellers to have magnified view of tiny components of watches and fine work of jewellery.
- It is also used to examine fingerprints and plane lines and by the students to read **vernier scales**, etc.

Compound Microscope

- The compound microscope consists of two coaxial convex lenses, one is called **objective** near to which object is located and the other is called **eye piece** near to which the eye is located.
- The aperture and the focal length of the objective is smaller than that of the eye piece in the compound microscope. They are used for studying the structure of cell, tissue or section of organ.

Astronomical Telescope

- An astronomical or refracting telescope is an optical instrument which is used for observing distinct images of heavenly bodies like stars, planets etc., When the final image is formed at infinity. It has two convex lenses coaxially separated by some distance.
- Light from the distant object enters the objective and real image is formed at second focal point of objective. The eye piece magnifies this image producing a final inverted image.

Reflecting Telescope

- It is an improvement over refracting or astronomical telescope. To obtain a bright image of a distant star by refracting telescope, it is essential to have an objective of large aperture, so that it may collect more light coming from the object.
- But to deal with such a big lens is problem in terms of using and making and it is too costly. The same bright image of a distant object can be obtained by using a concave mirror of large aperture in place of objective.

Kaleidoscope

- In Kaleidoscope, three rectangular plane mirror of equal length and equal breadth or attached to each other in such a way that the angle between two mirrors is of 60°.
- The reflecting surfaces of all these mirrors are inwardly confined and in the space confined by the mirror, the pieces of colour glass are kept. These mirrors are kept inside a thick long pipe.
- The spherical piece of glass is attached to the first end of the pipe and at another end the piece of rubbed glass is attached.
- When we look inside the pipe through the transparent glass end, then on rotating the pipe new colour images are seen which have been formed due to the multiple reflections of the plane mirror.
- On moving the pipe, location of the pieces of the colour glasses and colour of images are changed.

Extra Facts From Tamil Nadu Board and NIOS

- **Astigmatism** It is due to imperfect spherical nature of eye lens. The focal length of eye is in two orthogonal directions simultaneously. This defect in direction can be removed by using cylindrical lens in particular direction.
- The wavelength of visible light is from 4000 Å to 7000 Å.

Type of Scattering

1. **Elastic Scattering** If the energy of incident beam light and scattered beam of light are same, then it is called 'elastic scattering'.
2. **Inelastic Scattering** If the energy of the incident beam of light and the scattered beam of light are not same, then it is called 'inelastic scattering'. The nature and size of the scatterer results in different types of scattering.

   They are

   - **Rayleigh Scattering** The scattering of sunlight by the atoms or molecules of the gases in the Earth's atmosphere. Scattering is proportional $\frac{1}{\lambda^4}$. This is called Rayleigh scattering.
   - **Mie Scattering** Mie scattering (sometimes reffered to as a non-molecular scattering) takes place when the diameter of the scatterer is similar to or larger than the wavelength of the incident light.
   - **Tyndall Scattering** The scattering of light by the colloidal particle in the colloidal solution.
   - **Raman Scattering** The interaction of light ray with the particles of pure liquids or transparent solids, which leads to a change in wavelength or frequency.

13

Dual Nature of Radiation and Matter

[SOURCES]

Class-XII Old NCERT Chap 11 (Dual Nature of Radiation and Matter).

- Light behaves sometimes as a wave and sometimes as a particle. This behaviour of light is known as its **dual nature**. Phenomena of interference, diffraction, polarisation, colour of thin films, etc., can be explained on the basis of wave nature of light.
- However, the particle nature of light explains phenomena such as **photoelectric effect, Raman effect** and **Compton effect**.

Electron Emission

- In metals, the electrons in the outer shells (valence electrons) are loosely bound to the atoms, hence they are free to move easily within the metal surface but cannot leave it. Such electrons are called **free electrons**.
- These free electrons can be emitted from the metals, if they have sufficient energy to overcome the attractive pull of metal surface. The phenomenon of emission of electrons from the surface of metal is called electron emission.
- The minimum energy required by an electron to escape from the metal surface is called the **work function of that metal**.
- It is generally denoted by ϕ_0 or W_o and measured in **electron volt** (eV). 1 electron volt is the energy gained by an electron when it has been accelerated by a potential difference of 1volt.

$$1\text{eV} = 1.602 \times 10^{-19} \text{ J}$$

- It depends on the properties of the metal and the nature of its surface. It decreases with the increase in temperature.

Types of Electron Emission

The minimum required energy for the electron emission from the metal surface can be supplied to the free electrons by any of the following physical process :

- **Thermionic emission** The process in which energy is supplied as heat to emit electron from metal surface, is called thermionic emission.
- The emitted electrons are called **thermions** or **thermal electrons**. The number of thermions emitted depends on the temperature of the metal surface.
- **Field emission or cold cathode emission** The process in which energy is supplied by applying an electric field to accelerate the electrons, is called field emission. One such example is emission in spark plug.
- **Photoelectric emission** The process in which energy is supplied as light to emit the electrons is called photoelectric emission.
- The number of electrons emitted depends on the intensity of the incident light.

Photoelectric Effect

- The phenomenon of emission of electrons from the surface of metal, when radiations of suitable frequency fall on it, is called photoelectric effect. The emitted electrons are called **photoelectrons**.

- Alkali metals like lithium, sodium, etc, show photoelectric effect with visible light, whereas the metals like zinc, cadmium, etc., are sensitive only to Ultraviolet (UV) light.

Photoelectric Current

- In photoelectric effect, the current produced due to the emission of electrons is called photoelectric current.
- The photocurrent is directly proportional to the number of photoelectrons emitted per second. This implies that the number of photoelectrons emitted per second is directly proportional to the intensity of incident radiation.
- **Threshold Frequency** The minimum frequency of light which can emit photoelectrons from a material is called **threshold frequency** or cut-off **frequency** of that material. It is a characteristic property of material.

Laws of Photoelectric Emission

- For a given material and a given frequency of incident radiation, the photoelectric current or number of photoelectrons ejected per second is directly proportional to the intensity of the incident light.
- For a given material and frequency of incident radiation, saturation current is found to be proportional to the intensity of incident radiation, whereas the stopping potential is independent of its intensity.
- For a given material, there exists a certain minimum frequency of the incident radiation below which no emission of photoelectrons takes place. This frequency is called **threshold frequency.**
- Above the threshold frequency, the maximum kinetic energy of the emitted photoelectrons or equivalent stopping potential is independent of the intensity of the incident light. It depends upon only the frequency (or wavelength) of the incident light.

Einstein's Photoelectric Equation

- In 1905, **Einstein** explained photoelectric effect on the basis of **Planck's quantum theory**. According to which, a light radiation travels in the form of discrete packets called **quanta of energy of radiation.**
- Each quantum of radiant energy has energy $E = h\nu$ where, h is Planck's constant and ν is the frequency of light radiation.
- In photoelectric effect, an electron absorbs a quantum of energy ($h\nu$) of radiation. If this quantum of energy absorbed exceeds the minimum energy needed for the electron to escape from the metal surface (work function ϕ_0), the electron is emitted with maximum kinetic energy.

$$K_{max} = h\nu - \phi_0$$

This equation is called **Einstein's photoelectric equation.**

Photon : Particle Nature of Light

- Photoelectric effect gave an evidence that light consists of packets of energy.
- These packets of energy were called light **quantum** that are associated with particles named as **photons.**

Characteristic Properties of Photons

- In interaction of radiation with matter, radiation behaves as if it is made up of particles called photons.
- A photon travels at a speed of light c in vacuum (i.e, 3×10^8 m/s).
- Each photon has energy $E(= h\nu)$ and momentum $p = \left(\frac{h\nu}{c}\right)$.
- Photons are not deflected by electric and magnetic fields. This shows that photons are electrically neutral.
- In a photon particle collision (such as photoelectron collision), the total energy and momentum are conserved.

Wave Nature of Matter

- The French scientist, **Louis Victor de-Broglie** suggested that the particles like electrons, protons, neutrons, etc., have dual nature. i.e., they can have particle as well as wave nature.
- According to de-Broglie, the wave associated with moving particle is called matter wave or de-Broglie wave. These waves can travel in vacuum hence, they are not mechanical waves.
- The wavelength of these waves is given as

$$\lambda = \frac{h}{p} = \frac{h}{mv}$$

where, p is momentum of that particle.
The wave nature of electron was verified by **Davisson** and **Germer.**

Photocell

- It is a device which converts light energy into electrical energy. As, the photoelectric current sets up in the photoelectric cell corresponding to incident light, it provides the information about the objects.
- Some applications of photocell are given below :
  - Used in television camera for telecasting scenes and in photo telegraphy.
  - Reproduction of sound in cinema film.
  - Used in counting devices.
  - Used in burglar alarm and fire alarm.
  - To measure the temperature of stars.
  - Used for the determination of Planck's constant.

14

Semiconductor Electronics

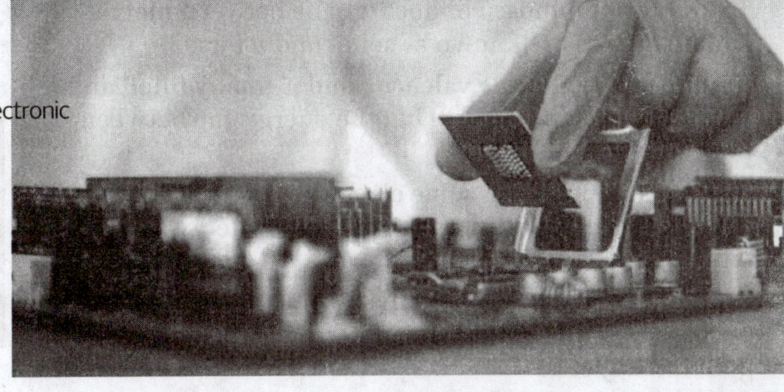

[SOURCES]

Class-XII Old NCERT Chap 14 (Semiconductor, electronic Material, Device and Simple Circuits).

- Devices in which a controlled flow of electrons can be obtained are the basic building blocks of all the electronic circuits. The supply and flow of charge carriers in these devices are within the solid itself, no vacuum or external heating is required.
- So, these devices are small in size, consume low power, operate at low voltage and have long life and high reliability.

Solid and Energy Band

- The particles are closely packed in solids and they do not change shape or volume. **A solid object** has the tendency of maintaining a defined shape and volume due to strong **intermolecular force**.
- According to **Bohr's atomic model** and concept of electronic configuration in an isolated atom, the electrons have certain definite discrete amounts of energy corresponding to different shells and subshells, i.e., there are well-defined energy levels of electrons in an isolated atom.
- Inside the crystal due to interatomic interaction, valence electrons are shared by more than one atom. Due to this, splitting of energy levels takes place. The collection of these closely spaced energy levels is called an **energy band**.
- These bands are formed due to the continuous energy variation in different levels because inside the crystal, each electron has a unique position and no two electrons is exactly at the same pattern of surrounding charges.
- The energy band, which includes the energy levels of the valence electrons is called **valence band**. This band may be partially or completely filled with electrons but is never empty.
- The energy band above the valence band is called **conduction band**. At room temperature, this band is either empty or partially filled with electrons. Electrons can gain energy from external field and jump from valence band to conduction band and contribute to the electric current.
- The minimum energy required for shifting electrons from valence band to conduction band is called **Energy band gap**. It can be zero, small or large depending upon the material.

Types of Solids on the Basis of Energy Bands

On the basis of Energy bands, types of solids are as follows:

Conductor

The substance in which the electrons can easily flow, is called the conductor. In conductor, either there is no energy gap between the conduction band and valence band or both conduction band and valence band overlap each other. e.g., Silver, gold, copper, etc.

Insulator

- Those substance in which electrical conduction is not possible is called the insulator. In insulators, valence band is completely filled and conduction band is completely empty.
- In this, energy gap is quite large (> 3*e*) and even energy from any other source cannot help electrons to overcome it. e.g., Rubber, ebonite, glass, etc.

Semiconductor

- The materials whose conductivity lie between metals and insulators are known as semiconductors.
- In semiconductor, the valence band is totally filled and conduction band is empty but the energy gap between them is very small (< 3*e*).
- At room temperature, some electrons from valence band can acquire enough energy to cross the energy gap and enter the conduction band.
- Thus, acquire small conductivity. At low temperature, pure semiconductors are insulators. e.g., Silicon, germanium, etc.

Types of Semiconductors

On the basis of purity, semiconductors are of two types as follows :

- **Intrinsic semiconductor** This type of semiconductor is also called an undoped semiconductor or *i*-type semiconductor.
- It is a pure semiconductor without any significant presence of dopant species.
  Pure germanium, silicon in their natural state are intrinsic semiconductors. In intrinsic semiconductors, the number of excited electrons is equal to number of holes.
  At a temperature of 0 K, the intrinsic semiconductor behaves like an insulator.
- **Extrinsic Semiconductor** When a small amount, say, a few parts per million (ppm), of a suitable impurity is added to the pure semiconductor, the conductivity of semiconductor is increased.
  - Such materials are known as extrinsic semiconductors or impurity semiconductors.
  - When some desirable impurity is added to intrinsic semiconductors deliberately, then this process is called **doping** and the impurity atoms are called **dopants.**
  - Such a material is also called a **doped semiconductor**.
  - Extrinsic semiconductors are basically of two types :
    (a) *n* - type (b) *p* - type
- ***n*-type Semiconductors** If pentavalent impurity atom (such as antimony, arsenic, phosphorus etc) is added to the pure germanium or silicon crystal, the crystal so obtained is called the *n*-type semiconductors. For such a material, the electrons are majority carriers and holes are minority carriers.
- ***p*-type semiconductors** If trivalent impurity atom (such as aluminium, boron, indium, gallium etc) is added with pure germanium or silicon crystal, the crystal so obtained is called *p*-type semiconductor.
- For such materials, the holes are majority carriers and electrons are minority carriers.

p-n Junction

It is a single crystal of Ge or Si doped in such a manner that one half-portion of it acts as *p* - type semiconductor and the other half as *n* - type semiconductor. Here, the term junction implies the boundary or region of transition between *n*-type and *p*-type semiconductor materials.
p -*n* junction used in many semiconductor devices like diodes, LED, solar cell, transistors.

Semiconductor Diode

- A semiconductor diode is basically a *p* - *n* junction with metallic contacts provided at the ends for the application of an external voltage. It is a two terminals device.

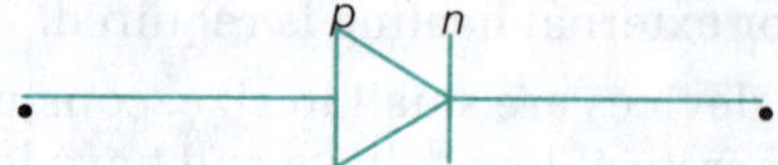

- A junction diode is said to be **forward biased** when the positive terminal of the external battery is connected to the *p*-side and negative terminal to the *n*-side of the diode.
- A junction diode is said to be **reverse biased** when the positive terminal of the external battery is connected to the *n*-side and negative terminal to the *p*-side of the diode.

Diode as a Rectifier

- A *p-n* junction diode allows current to pass only when it is forward biased. So, if an alternating voltage is applied across a diode the current flows only in that part of the cycle when the diode is forward biased.
- This property is used to rectify alternating voltages and the circuit used for this purpose is called a **rectifier**. With the help of rectifier AC is converted into DC.

Zener Diode

- It is a special purpose semiconductor diode, named after its inventor **C. Zener**.
- It is designed to operate under reverse bias in the breakdown region and used as a voltage regulator.
- **Photodiode** is a special type of junction diode used for detecting optical signals.
- A photodiode fabricated with a transparent cover to allow light to fall on the diode and operated under reverse bias.
- When the photodiode is illuminated with light (photons), which have energy greater than the energy gap of the semiconductor, then electron-hole pairs are generated due to the absorption of photons.
- These are used in photo detectors, camera and optical switch, etc.

Light Emitting Diode (LED)

- It is a heavily doped *p-n* junction which under forward bias emits spontaneous radiation.
- The diode is covered with a transparent cover so that emitted light can come out. It converts electrical energy into light energy.
- LEDs have the following advantages over conventional incandescent low power lamps:
  - Low operational voltage and less power consumed
  - Fast action and no warm-up time required
  - The bandwidth of emitted light is 100Å to 500Å or nearly (but not exactly) monochromatic.
  - Long life and ruggedness
  - Fast on off switching capability

Solar Cell

- A solar cell is basically a p - n junction which generates emf when solar radiations falls on the p - n junction.
- It works on the same principle (photovoltaic effect) as the photodiode. Uses of solar cells are :
  - Solar cells are used in space vehicles for charging batteries in day time.
  - Solar cells are used in photometers.
  - Solar cells are used in electronic devices like calculator, wrist watches.

15

Stars and Solar System

[SOURCES]

Class-VIII Old NCERT Chap 17 (Stars and Solar System)

- The solar system is a vast place, with lots of empty space between planets. There are comets, asteroids and rocky, frozen objects (including dwarf planets) yet to be discovered in the space. Stars are found in huge groups called **galaxies**.
- In 1929, American astronomer **Edwin P Hubble**, stated that galaxies are not stationary. They are continuously moving away from each other.
- The sun and its solar system including the earth are part of the **Milky Way Galaxy**. There are billions of galaxies in the universe.
- Astronomy is a branch of science that studies celestial bodies and the associated phenomena.

Celestial Bodies

Celestial bodies are the bodies that are found in the universe. These include planets, moons, satellites, meteoroids, stars, galaxies etc.

Moon

- The moon is a natural satellite of the earth. It revolves around the earth on a regular path. The gravitational attraction between the earth and the natural satellite holds it in its orbit even as the moon revolves around the earth.
- The moon completes one rotation on its axis as it completes one revolution around the earth.

Surface of Moon

- The Moon's surface is covered by rocks and loose dirt which is known as **lunar soil**.
- It is pockmarked with craters of different sizes because of meteorites that hit its surface.
- It is about one-fourth the size of earth. It also has a large number of steep and high mountains.
- Some of these are high as the highest mountains on the earth. The moon has no atmosphere and no water.

Phases of the Moon

- The moon does not produce its own light, whereas the sun and other stars do.
- The moon is visible because the sunlight falling on it gets reflected towards us. We, therefore, see only that part of the moon, from which the light of the sun is reflected towards us.

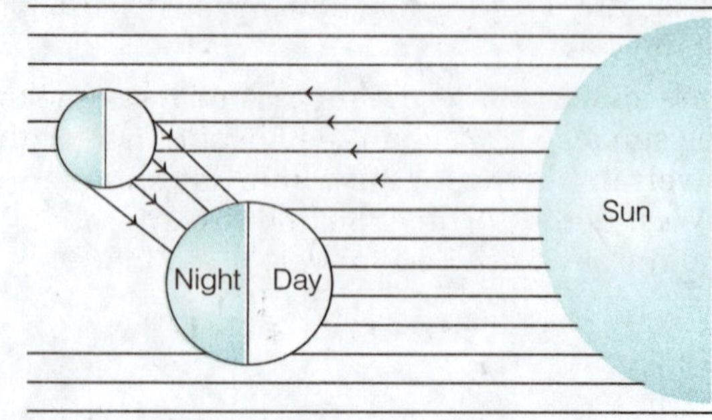

- The day on which the whole disc of the moon is visible is known as the **full moon day**. Thereafter, every night the size of the bright part of the moon appears to become thinner and thinner.
- On the fifteenth day the moon is not visible. This day is known as the **new moon day**. The next day, only a small portion of the moon appears in the sky. This is known as the **crescent moon**.
- Then, again the moon grows larger every day. On the fifteenth day once again we get a full view of the moon.
- The various shapes of the bright part of the moon as seen during a month are called **phases of the moon**.

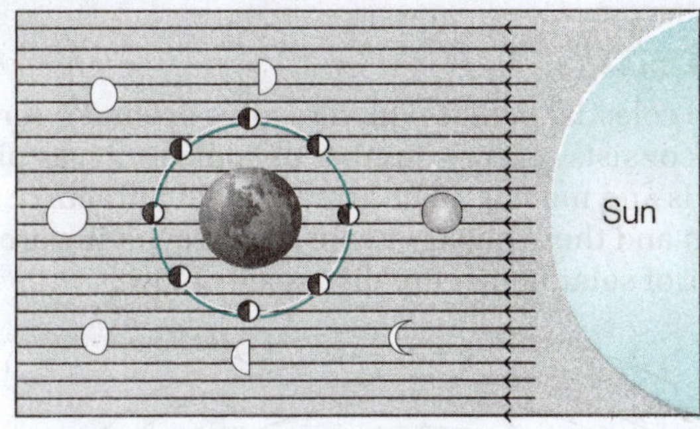

Note The time period between one full moon to the next full moon is slightly longer than 29 days. In many calendars, this period is called a **month**.

The Stars

- There is a large number of stars in the sky. These are those celestial objects that are extremely hot and have light of their own. Stars emit heat and light continuously.
- The stars are much bigger as compared to the size of the earth and many of the stars are even bigger than the sun. The stars appear to be small because they are very far away from us.
- The sun is also a star which is nearest to the earth. The sun appears much bigger and brighter because it is much nearer to us than any other star.
- We can see the stars only at night. Though, the stars are present in the sky even during the day time but we cannot see them during day time because of the bright light of the sun.
- The stars appear to move from East to West due to this, the sun also rises up in the East in the morning and travels in the sky for the whole day and then sets in the West in the evening. So, the sun appears to move in the sky from East to West direction.
- This apparent motion of the stars and the sun in the sky from East to West is due to the rotation of the earth from West to East on its axis.
- So, when the earth moves (rotates) on its own axis from West to East, then the stars in the sky seem to move in the opposite direction, i.e., East to West. For example, if we stand in the centre of a room and start rotating, then we will see that the objects in the room seem to move in the direction opposite to the direction of our motion.
- Only one star which does not appear to move in the sky is called **Pole star** or **Dhruva tara**. This star remains fixed at the same place in the sky in the North direction.
- It appears to be at rest because it lies on the axis of rotation of the earth and the axis of the earth is fixed and does not vary with time.

Unit of Measuring Distance in the Universe

- The sun is nearly 150,000,000 km (150 million km) away from the earth.
- The next nearest star is Proxima centauri which is about 40 billion km away from earth.
- Such large distances are expressed in another unit known as **light year**. It is the distance travelled by light in one year. One light year = 9.46×10^{15} m.
- The speed of light is about 3×10^8 m/s. Thus, the distance of the sun from the earth may be said to be about 8 light minutes. The distance of alpha centauri is about 4.3 light years.

Constellations

- The stars forming a group that has a recognisable shape of animals, human beings or other objects is called a constellations. Each constellation is signified by an animal, a human being or some other object which it appears to resemble.
- These constellations seem to move in the sky from East to West. The shape of all constellations seen in the sky always remains the same.

Some Important Constellations

Some of the famous constellations are :

- **Ursa Major** (Saptarshi) It is one of the most famous constellations which can be seen during summer time in the early part of the night. It is also known as the **Big Dipper**, the **Great Bear** or the **Saptarshi**.

There are seven prominent stars in this constellation. It appears like a big ladle or a question mark. There are three stars in the handle of the ladle and four in its bowl.

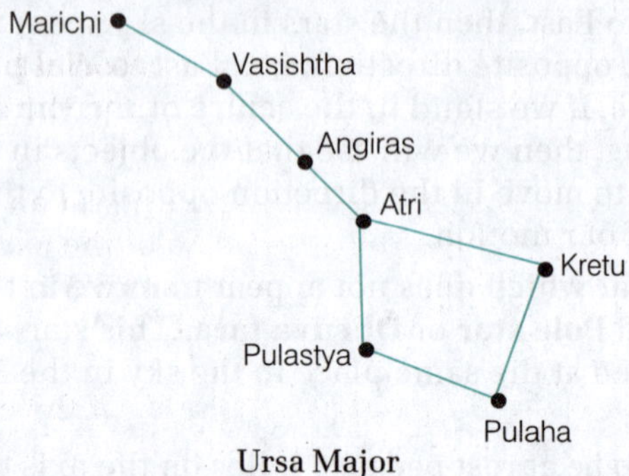

Ursa Major

- **Orion** It is a well-known constellation that can be seen during winter in the late evenings. It is one of the most magnificent constellations in the sky. It also has seven or eight bright stars.
  Orion is also called the **Hunter**. The three middle stars represent the belt of the hunter. The four or five bright stars appear to be arranged in the form of a quadrilateral.
  The star Sirius, which is the brightest star in the sky, is located close to Orion.

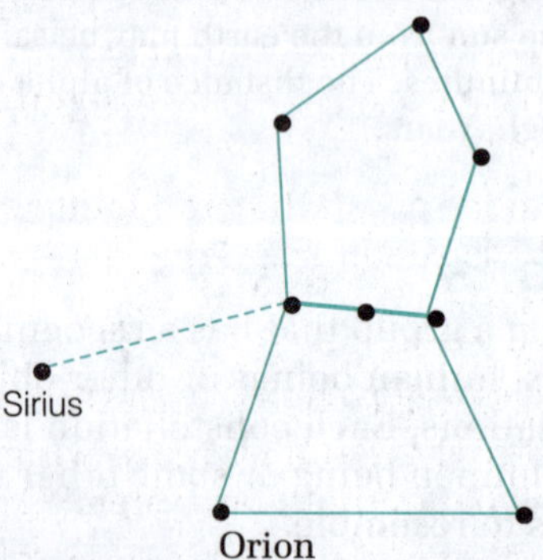

Orion

- **Cassiopeia** It is another prominent constellation in the northern sky. It is visible during winter in the early part of the night. It looks like a distorted letter *W* or *M*.

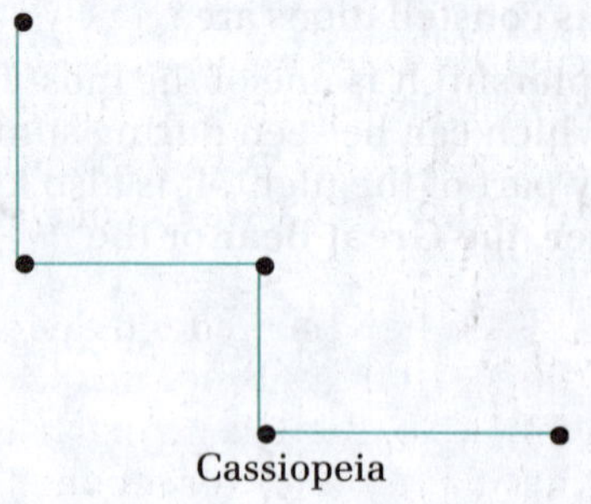
Cassiopeia

- **Leo Major** The constellation in the Northen sky which consists of nine main stars is known as **Leo Major Constellation**. Leo means lion, so the arrangement of stars in the Leo Major Constellation form the outline of a big lion. This constellation is visible during summer in the early part of the night.

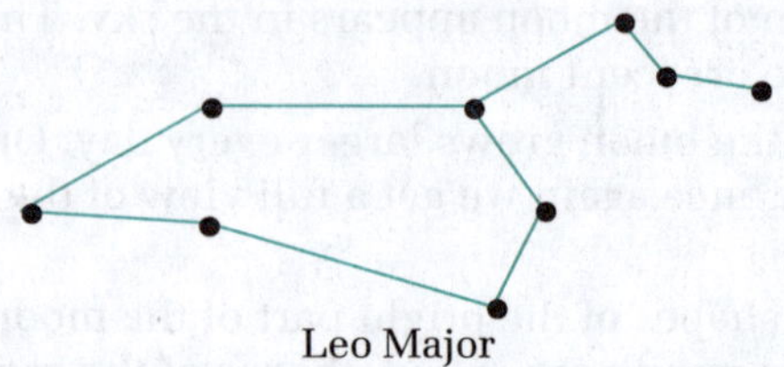
Leo Major

Solar System

The sun and the celestial bodies which revolve around it form the solar system. It consists of large number of bodies such as planets, comets, asteroids and meteors. The gravitational attraction between the sun and these objects keeps them revolving around it. The members of solar family are discussed below:

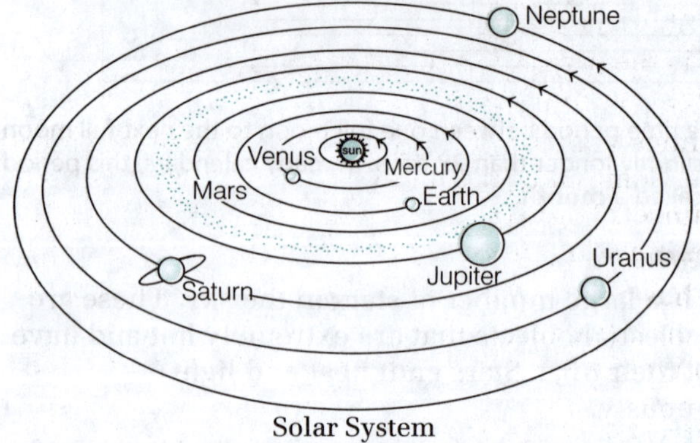

Solar System

Sun

- The sun is the nearest star from us. It is continuously emitting huge amounts of heat and light.
- The sun is the source of almost all energy on the Earth. In fact, the sun is the main source of heat and light for all the planets.

Planets

- A planet is a celestial body that revolves around the sun. They are non-luminous. They reflect the light that falls on them. The simplest method of identifying planets from stars is that stars twinkle, whereas planet do not.
- A planet has a definite path in which it revolves around the sun.
- This path is called an **orbit**. The time taken by a planet to complete one revolution is called its **period of revolution**.
- The period of revolution increases as the distance of the planet increases from the sun.

- Besides revolving around the sun, planet also rotate on its own axis like a top. The time taken by a planet to complete one rotation is called its **period of rotation.**
- The eight planets in their order of distance from the sun are : Mercury, Venus, Earth, Mars, Jupiter, Saturn, Uranus and Neptune.

Note Till 2006, there are nine planets in the solar system. Pluto was the farthest planet from the sun. In 2006, the **International Astronomical Union** (IAU) adopted a new definition of a planet. Pluto does not fit this definition. It is no longer a planet of the solar system.

Mercury (Budh)

- The planet Mercury is nearest to the sun. It is the smallest planet of our solar system. As Mercury is very close to the sun, it is very difficult to observe it because it is hidden in the glare of the sun.
- However, it can be observed just before sunrise or just after sunset, near the horizon. So, it is visible only at places where trees or buildings do not obstruct the view of the horizon. Mercury has no satellite of its own.

Venus (Shukra)

- Venus is the earth's nearest planetary neighbour. It is the brightest planet in the night sky.
- Sometimes Venus appears in the Eastern sky before sunrise. Sometimes it appears in the Western sky just after sunset. Therefore, it is often called a **morning** or an **evening star**, although it is not a star.
- Venus has no moon or satellite of its own. Rotation of Venus on its axis is somewhat unusual. It rotates from East to West while the earth rotates from West to East.

The Earth (Prithvi)

- The earth is the only planet in the solar system on which life is known **to exist**. Some special environmental conditions are responsible for the existence and continuation of life on the earth.
- These include just the right distance from the sun, so that it has the right temperature range, the presence of water and suitable atmosphere and a blanket of ozone.

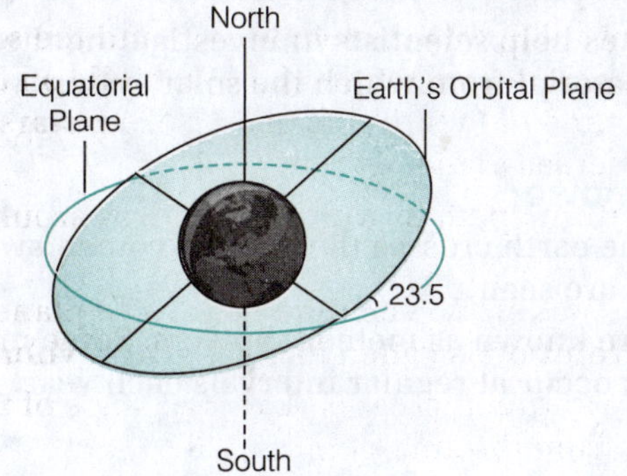

- From space, the earth appears blue-green due to the reflection of light from water and landmass on its surface. The axis of rotation of the earth is not perpendicular to the plane of its orbit. The tilt is responsible for the change of seasons on the earth. The earth has only one moon.
- The plane of the equator is called the **equatorial plane.** The plane in which the earth revolves round the sun is called the **orbital plane of the earth.**
- These two planes are inclined to each other at an angle of 23.5°. This means that the axis of the earth is inclined to its orbital plane at an angle of 66.5°.

Mars (Mangal)

- The next planet, the first outside the orbit of the earth is Mars. It appears slightly reddish and, therefore, it is also called the **red planet**. Mars has two small natural satellites which are named as **Phobos** and **Deimos.**
- Mars is a rocky planet, also known as **terrestrial planet.** Its solid surface has been altered by volcanoes, impacts, crustal movement and atmospheric effect such as dust storms. Mars has thin atmosphere made up mostly of carbon dioxide, nitrogen and argon.

Jupiter (Brihaspati)

- Jupiter is the largest planet of the solar system. It is so large that about 1300 earths can be placed inside this giant planet. However, the mass of Jupiter is about 318 times that of our earth. It rotates very rapidly on its axis. Jupiter is a gas-giant planet whose atmosphere is made up mostly of **hydrogen** and **helium**, so it does not support life.
- It has a large number of satellite and faint rings around it. Jupiter has a total of 67 moons.

Saturn (Shani)

- The Saturn appears yellowish in colour.
- The sixth planet from the sun is saturn which is the second biggest planet of the solar system. One interesting thing about Saturn is that it is the least dense among all the planets of the solar system.
- The density of Saturn is even less than that of water. As Saturn is lighter than water, so if we imagine it in a large pool of water, then it will float on water. It will not sink in water.
- The system of colourful rings which surround it, is the most distinguishing feature of saturn. Three distinct sets of rings around saturn are visible from the earth. Saturn is the only planet with a system of well-developed rings encircling it.
- The rings of saturn can be observed only with the help of a telescope. Being far off from the sun, saturn is an extremely cold planet. So, there is no existence of life on the Saturn. It has 62 satellites (or moons).

Uranus (Indra)

- Uranus is the seventh planet from the sun. It can be seen only with the help of a large telescope. It is almost four times that of the earth, so it appears as a small disc through a telescope.
- Uranus rotates on its axis from East to West. It is made up mainly of hydrogen and helium. Uranus is an extremely cold planet. It is surrounded by an atmosphere of poisonous gases. Due to these reasons, no life can exist on the planet Uranus.
- Uranus has 27 satellites (or moons). It has also some rings around it.

Neptune (Varun)

- Neptune is the eighth planet from the sun. It is the most distant planet from the sun. Neptune is made up mainly of liquid and frozen hydrogen and helium gases. It is an extremely cold planet. So, no life can exist on this planet.
- Neptune has 14 satellites (or moons). It also has some rings around it.

Pluto

- Till 2006 there were nine planets in the solar system.
- Pluto was the farthest planet from the sun till 2006.
- But In 2006, the International Astronomical Union (IAU) adopted a new definition of a planet and Pluto does not fit in this definition. It is no longer a planet of the solar system.

Inner and Outer Planets

- The first four planets, Mercury, Venus, Earth and Mars are much nearer the sun than the other four planets. They are called the inner planets. The inner planets have very few moons.
- The planets outside the orbit of Mars, namely Jupiter, Saturn, Uranus and Neptune are much farther off than the inner planets.
- They are called the outer planets. They have a ring system around them. The outer planets have large number of moons.

Some Other Members of the Solar System

There are some other bodies which revolve around the sun. They are also members of the solar system. Some information about them is discussed below :

Asteroids

- There is a large gap in between the orbits of Mars and Jupiter. This gap is occupied by a large number of small objects that revolve around the sun.
- These are called asteroids. Asteroids can only be seen through large telescopes.

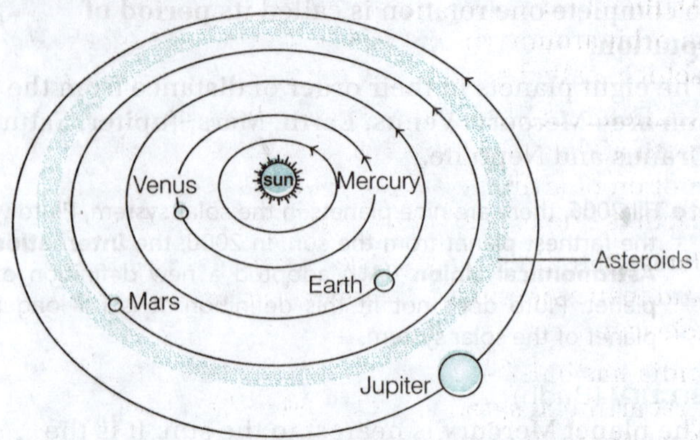

Comets

- Comets are also members of our solar system. They revolve around the sun in highly elliptical orbits. However, their period of revolution round the sun is usually very long.
- A comet appears generally as a bright head with a long tail. The length of the tail grows in size as it approaches the sun. The tail of a comet is always directed away from the sun.
- Many comets are known to appear periodically. One such comet is **Halley's comet**, which appears after nearly every 76 years. It was last seen in 1986.

Meteors and Meteorites

- At night when the sky is clear and the moon is not there, sometimes bright streaks of light in the sky are seen. These are commonly known as **shooting stars**, although they are not stars. They are called **meteors**.
- A meteor is usually a small object that occasionally enters the earth's atmosphere. At that time it has a very high speed.
- The friction due to the atmosphere heats it up. It glows and evaporates quickly. That is why, the bright steak lasts for a very short time.
- Some meteors are large and so they can reach the earth before they evaporate completely. The body that reaches the earth is called a **meteorite**.
- Meteorites help scientists in investigating the nature of the material from which the solar system was formed.

Meteor Shower

- When the earth crosses the tail of a comet, swarms of meteors are seen.
- These are known as meteor showers. Some meteor showers occur at regular intervals each year.

Artificial Satellites

- Artificial satellite is a man-made spacecraft placed in orbit around the earth with the help of a launch vehicle called **rocket**.
- Artificial satellites move in an orbit around the earth at the height of few hundred kilometres. The motion of artificial satellite into its orbit around the earth is due to gravitational pull of the earth.
- These satellites carry a large variety of equipment and instruments like cameras, infrared sensors, telescope, etc.
- India has built and launched many satellites. The first artificial satellite launched by India was **Aryabhata**. It was launched in 1975.
- Some other Indian satellites are Bhaskara, INSAT (Indian National Satellite), IRS (Indian Remote Sensing Satellite), Rohini, Kalpana-1 and EDUSAT Education Satellite.
- The agency responsible for the development of space science programmes in our country is **Indian Space Research Organisation** (ISRO).
- There are some important uses of artificial satellites in the form of their practical applications which are as given below:
  - Information is usually collected about other planets, stars, galaxies, etc with the help of artificial satellite.
  - These kinds of satellites are used for communication purpose such as long distance transmission of television programmes, telephone calls and internet.
  - These are used for surveying the natural resources of the earth like minerals, potential fishing zone, agriculture crops, etc.
  - These are used for weather forecasting such as rainfall, snowfall, etc and also for giving advance warning of cyclones and floods.

Extra Facts From Tamil Nadu Board and NIOS

- Scientists think that the universe began with start of massive explosion called the **Big Bang**.
- Galaxies, immediately after the Big Bang, clouds of gases began to compares under gravity to form the building blocks of galaxies.
- A galaxy is a massive collection of gas, dust and billions of stars and their solar systems.
- **Time Period of a Satellite** Time taken by a satellite to complete one revolution round the earth is called time period.

$$T = \frac{2\pi(R+h)}{\sqrt{\frac{GM}{(R+h)}}}$$

- **International Space Station** ISS is a large space craft which can house of astronauts.
- It goes in lower or earth orbit at approximately 400 km distance.
- **Benefit of ISS**
  - Supporting water-purification
  - Eye tracking technology
  - Robotic arms in surgeries

ISS and International Cooperation

- A great as the ISS' scientific achievements are, no less in accomplishment is the international cooperation which result in the construction of the ISS.
- An international collaboration of five different space agencies of 16 countries provides, maintains and operates the ISS.
- They are : NASA (USA), Roskosmos (Russia), ESA (Europe), JAXA (Japan), and CSA (Canada), Belgium, Brazil, Denmark, France, Germany, Italy, Holland, Norway, Spain, Sweden, Switzerland and the United Kingdom are also parts of the consortium.

01

Chemisty

Atomic Structure & Radioactivity

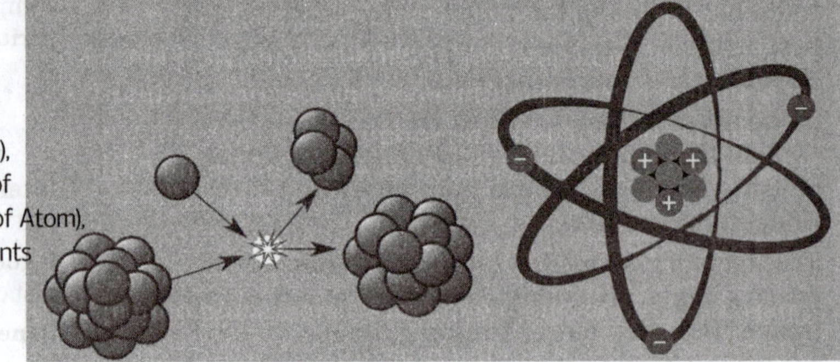

(SOURCES)

Class-IX NCERT Chap 3 (Atoms and Molecules), Class-IX NCERT Chap 4 (Structure of the Atom), Class-XI NCERT Chap 1 (Some Basic Concepts of Chemistry), Class-XI NCERT Chap 2 (Structure of Atom), Class-XI NCERT Chap 3 (Classification of Elements and Periodicity in Properties)
Tamil Nadu Board (Class-IX), NIOS

- The idea of divisibility of matter was considered long back in India, around 500 BC. An Indian Philosopher **Maharishi Kanad** talked about the indivisible particles and named it as *Parmanu*.
- Another Greek Philosopher, **Democritus** called these indivisible particles atoms.
- The word atom originated from the Greek word 'a-tomio' which means 'non-divisible'.
- By the end of 18th century, scientists had found out the difference between elements and compounds.
- They became interested in finding how and why elements combine and what happens when they combine.

Dalton's Atomic Theory

In the year 1808, **John Dalton** presented the atomic theory of matter, which is called Dalton's Atomic Theory. According to this theory, all matter whether an element, a compound or a mixture is composed of small particles called **atoms**.

The main postulates of Dalton's Atomic theory are as follows:

- Every matter is made up of very small particles called the atoms, which undergo chemical reactions.
- Atoms are indivisible particles, which can neither be created nor be destroyed in a chemical reaction.
- Atoms of a given element are identical in masses as well as in chemical properties.
- Atoms of different elements have different masses and chemical properties.
- Atoms combine in the ratio of small whole numbers to form compounds.
- The relative numbers and kinds of atoms are constant in a given compound.

Subatomic Particles

In the starting of 20th century, it was proved through the experiments of research workers like **J.J. Thomson** (1897), **Rutherford, Neils Bohr, J. Chadwick (1932)** etc., that an atom is made up of three fundamental particles called **electron, proton** and **neutron**.

Discovery of Electron (e^-)

- In 1850s many scientists mainly **Faraday** began to study electrical discharge in partially evacuated tubes, known as **cathode ray discharge tubes.**
- In this experiment, when sufficiently high voltage and low pressure is maintained, a stream of particle is originated from negative electrode (cathode) to positive electrode (anode).
- These originated particle were called **cathode rays or cathode ray particles.**

- These rays themselves are not visible but their behaviour can be observed with the help of **fluorescent or phosphorescent** materials which glow when hit by them.
- In the absence of electrical or magnetic field, these rays travel in straight lines.
- In the presence of electrical or magnetic field, these rays behaves same as the negatively charged particles, suggesting that the cathode rays consist of negatively charged particles, called **electrons**.
- In 1897, British physicist J.J. Thomson identified the electron as one of the sub-atomic particles.

Charge on Electron

- The charge on electron is -1.602×10^{-19} C which was determined by R.A. **Millikan** through **oil-drop method.**
- Mass of electron is 9.11×10^{-31} kg (was determined by **J.J. Thomson**).
- The mass of an electron is considered to be negligible and its charge is minus one.
- Charge to mass ratio (e/m_e) is 1.76×10^{8} C/g, which is independent of the nature of gas and electrode used.

Discovery of Protons (^1_1p)

- Before the discovery of electrons, **E. Goldstein** in 1886 discovered the presence of new radiations known as **canal rays.**
- These rays were positively charged radiations which ultimately led to the discovery of another sub-atomic particle.
- These sub-atomic particles had a charge, equal in magnitude but opposite in sign to that of the electron. It was given the name proton by **Rutherford** in 1919.
- These also travel in straight line and get deflected in electrical and magnetic field.
  - Mass of proton is 1.67×10^{-27} kg and its charge is $+1.602\times10^{-19}$ C.
  - Their charge to mass ratio depends upon the nature of gas, taken in discharge tube.

Discovery of Neutrons (^1_0n)

- When fast moving α-particles collides on beryllium sheet, electrically neutral particles are emitted, whose mass is slightly greater than the mass of protons, these are named as **neutrons.**
- **Chadwick** discovered these particles in the year 1932.

Characteristics of Fundamental Particles of an Atom

Particle	Electron	Proton	Neutron
Symbol	e	p	n
Charge/SI (Coulombs)	-1.602×10^{-19}	$+1.602\times10^{-19}$	0
Amount of charge	-1	$+1$	0
Mass/SI (kg)	9.109382×10^{-31}	1.6726216×10^{-27}	1.674927×10^{-27}
u (Atomic mass)	0.00054	1.00727	1.00867
Founder	J.J. Thomson	E. Rutherford	James Chadwick
Presence	Outside the nucleus	Inside the nucleus	Inside the nucleus

Characteristics of Temporary Fundamental Particles Present in an Atom

Particle/Symbol/ Nature	Charge (esu) $\times10^{-10}$	Mass (in u)	Founders
Positron ($e^+, {}_1e^0, \beta^+$) +	+ 4.8029	0.0005486	Carl David Anderson (1932)
Neutrinos (ν) (–)	0	< 0.00002	Pauli
Antiproton (p^-) (–)	4.8029	1.00787	Owen Chamberlain and Emilio Segre (1955)
Photon ($h\nu$) (0)	0	0	Planck
Graviton (G) (0)	0	0	—
Positively charged Mu meson (μ^+) (+)	+ 4.8029	0.1152	Yukawa (1935)
Negatively charged Mu meson (μ^-) (–)	– 4.8029	0.1152	Yukawa (1935)
Positively charged meson (π^+) (+)	+ 4.8029	0.1514	—
Negatively charged meson (π^-) (–)	– 4.8029	0.1514	Cecil Powell (1947)
Neutral (π^0) (0)	0	0.1454	—

Atomic Models

Following atomic models were proposed to explain the distribution of charged particles in an atom :

Thomson Model

- It was proposed by **J.J. Thomson** in 1898. This model was similar to Christmas pudding or water melon model.
- In this model, atom is considered as sphere, in which positively charged particles are uniformly distributed and negatively charged particles are embedded in them.
- Mass of atom is assumed to be uniformly distributed through out the atom.

Limitations of Thomson Model

- It could not explain the stability of an atom.
- It could not explain the experiment results of other scientists such as Rutherford, as there is no nucleus in the atomic model proposed by Thomson.

Rutherford's Model

- It was proposed by **Ernest Rutherford** and his students (**Hans Geiger** and **Ernest Marsden**).
- This model was based on α-particle (doubly-charged helium ions having a mass of 4 u) scattering experiment on thin foil of gold metal (1000 atoms thick).
- On the basis of his experiment, Rutherford put forward the **nuclear** model of an atom, having following features :
  - There is a positively charged, highly densed centre in an atom, called **nucleus**. Nearly, the whole mass of an atom resides in the nucleus.
  - Electrons revolve around the nucleus with very high speed in circular paths called **orbits**.
  - Electrons and the nucleus are held together by **electrostatic forces** of attraction.
  - Size of nucleus is very small as compared to the size of the atom.

Limitations of Rutherford's Model

- It could not explain the stability of an atom, when charged electrons are moving under the attractive force of positively charged nucleus.
- During acceleration, charged particles would radiate energy. Thus, the revolving electron would lose energy and finally fall into the nucleus.

Bohr's Model of an Atom

To overcome objections raised against Rutherford's model of the atom, **Niels Bohr** put forward the following postulates about the model of an atom :

- Electrons can only revolve in certain special orbits, which are called **discrete orbits of electron.**
- When electrons revolve in these discrete orbits, the energy is not radiated. These orbits or shells are called **energy levels.**
- These orbits or shells are represented by *K, L, M, N* or by the number$(n) = 1, 2, 3, 4 \ldots$.

Characteristics of an Atom

Atomic Number (Z)

It is defined as, the number of protons present in the nucleus of an atom.

It is denoted by '*Z*'. The number of electrons is equal to the number of protons in an atom to maintain electrical neutrality of an atom.

Atomic number (*Z*) = Number of protons in the nucleus
= Number of electrons in an atom

Mass Number (A)

The sum of total number of protons and neutrons or total number of **nucleons** present in the nucleus of an atom is termed as **mass number** (*A*).

Mass number (*A*)
= Number of protons (*p*) + Number of neutrons (*n*)
= Atomic number (*Z*) + Number of neutrons (*n*)

In the notation for an atom, the atomic number, mass number and symbol of the element are to be written as:

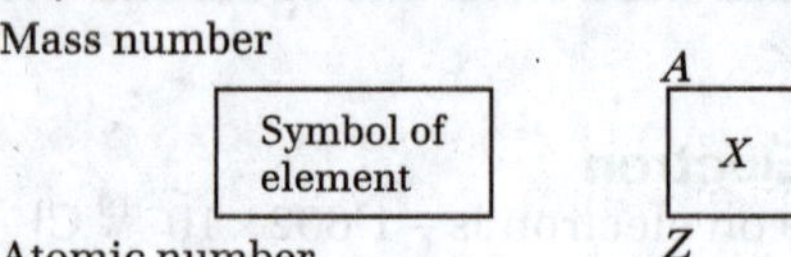

e.g., nitrogen is written as ${}^{14}_{7}N$.

Types of Atomic Species

The following are the types of atomic species :

- **Isotopes** Atoms of the same elements having the same atomic number (*Z*) but different mass number (*A*) are called isotopes.
  e.g., Hydrogen has three isotopes i.e., ${}^{1}_{1}H$, ${}^{2}_{1}H$, ${}^{3}_{1}H$.
- **Isobars** Atoms of different elements which have the same mass number (*A*) but different atomic number (*Z*) are called isobars.
  e.g., ${}^{40}_{18}Ar$, ${}^{40}_{20}Ca$.
- **Isotones** Atoms which have different atomic number and mass number but same number of neutrons are called isotones.
  e.g., ${}^{3}_{1}H$ and ${}^{4}_{2}He$ contain 2 neutrons.
- **Isoelectronic species** Atoms or ions which have the same number of electrons are called isoelectronic species.
  e.g., F^-, Ne, $Na^{\oplus}$ and Mg^{2+} each have 10 electrons species.

Structural Features of the Atom

The structural features of the atom are as follows :

Shells and Subshells

- The circular paths in which electrons move with different and definite energies are called **shells.**
- Each shell or the orbit is made up of one or more sub shells. The symbols *K, L, M, N*, etc are used to denote different shells. Each subshell consists of one or more orbitals, which are denoted by *s, p, d, f*.

Number of Shells, their Subshells, Orbitals and Electrons

Shells	Subshells	Orbitals	Total number of electrons
K-shell ($n=1$)	1 (s-)	1	2
L-shell ($n=2$)	2 (s and p)	$1+3=4$	8
M-shell ($n=3$)	3 (s, p and d)	$1+3+5=9$	18
N-shell ($n=4$)	4 (s, p, d and f)	$1+3+5+7=16$	32
O-shell ($n=5$)	5 (s, p, d and f)	$1+3+5+7=16$	32
P-shell ($n=6$)	6 (s, p and d)	$1+3+5=9$	18
Q-shell ($n=7$)	7 (s and p)	$1+3=4$	8

Orbitals

An orbital is a region in space around the nucleus where the probability of finding the electron is maximum.

Distribution of Electrons in Different Orbits (Shells)

The distribution of electrons into different orbits of an atom was suggested by **Bohr** and **Bury**, which is known as **Bohr-Bury Model.** For writing the number of electrons in different energy levels or shells, some rules are followed. These are :

- The maximum number of electrons present in a shell is given by the formula $2n^2$, where n is the orbit number or energy level index, 1,2,3, ...

  Therefore, the maximum number of electrons in different shells are as follows :

  First orbit or K-shell $= 2 \times (1)^2 = 2$

  Second orbit or L-shell $= 2 \times (2)^2 = 8$

  Third orbit or M-shell $= 2 \times (3)^2 = 18$

  Fourth orbit or N-shell $= 2 \times (4)^2 = 32$ and so on.
- The maximum number of electrons that can be accommodated in the outermost orbit is 8.
- Electrons are not accommodated in a given shell, unless the inner shells are filled. (i.e., the shells are filled in a step-wise manner).

nl^x Type Scheme

It is written as 2, 8, 8, 18, 32, or as nl^x (where, n indicates the principal quantum number, l indicates the azimuthal quantum number, or subshell and x is the number of electrons). e.g., $2s^2$ means that two electrons are present in the s-subshell of second energy level.

Valency

- The electrons present in the outermost shell of an atom are known as the **valence electrons.**
- An outermost shell which had 8 electrons is called an **octet.**
- The number of electrons lost or gained or shared by an atom to become stable or to achieve an octet in the outermost shell is known as **valency of that element.**

Quantum Numbers

- The quantum numbers are the set of four numbers that give complete information about :
  (i) the position or energy (i.e., orbit number or shell),
  (ii) subshell,
  (iii) orientation (i.e., orbitals of the subshell) and
  (iv) spinning (i.e., direction of rotation in the orbital) of an electron.
- Quantum numbers are of four types as follows :

Principal Quantum Number (n)

- It is a positive integer with value of $n = 1, 2, 3, \ldots$.
- It identifies the shell or orbit number of an electron.
- It also determines the size and energy of the orbital.
- As, the value of 'n' increases, energy of orbital increases.

Azimuthal Quantum Number (l)

- It is also called as orbital quantum number or orbital angular momentum or subsidiary quantum number.
- It is used to describe subshell or angular momentum of the revolving electron.
- In other words, it defines the three-dimensional shape of the orbital.

  If, $l = 0, 1, 2, 3, 4, \ldots (n-1)$

  Subshell $= s, p, d, f, g, \ldots$

For principal quantum number n, l has the values from 0 to $(n-1)$.

Magnetic Orbital Quantum Number (m_l)

- It determines the spatial orientation of the orbital with respect to standard set of co-ordinate axis. Its value depends upon the value of l.
- Its values vary from $-l, \ldots, 0, \ldots, +l$.
- Total values of $m_l = (2l+1) =$ Number of orbitals in a subshell (l).

Electron Spin Quantum Number (m_S)

- It represents the spin of an electron in an orbital. Mechanically, two types of spins are possible for an electron, i.e., clockwise or anti-clockwise. The value of m_s may be $+\frac{1}{2}$ or $-\frac{1}{2}$.
- Two spin states of the electron are normally represented by two arrows, ↑ (spin up) and ↓ (spin down).

Rules for Filling Electrons in the Orbitals

Filling of electrons in different orbitals is governed by the following three rules :

Aufbau Principle

- Electrons in the orbitals of different atoms are filled according to the Aufbau principle.
- The Aufbau's principle is based on the Pauli exclusion principle, Hund's rule of maximum multiplicity and the relative energies of the orbitals. The principle states that in the ground state of the atoms, the orbitals are filled in the order of their increasing energies.
- Orbitals of lower energy are filled first and when it is filled up completely, the remaining electrons enter in the orbital of next higher energy.

  The order of energies of the orbitals :

  $1s < 2s < 2p < 3s < 3p < 4s < 3d < 4p < 5s < 4d < 5p < 6s < 4f < 5d < 6p < 7s < 5f < 6d < \ldots$

Pauli Exclusion Principle

- This principle states that, 'No two electrons in an atom can have the same set of four quantum numbers'.
- Only two electrons may exist in the same orbital and these electrons must have opposite spin.
- It means that, if two electrons have same values of n, l and m (three quantum numbers), then they must differ in the value of s.

Hund's Rule of Maximum Multiplicity

- According to this law, "Pairing of electrons in the orbitals belonging to the same subshell (p, d or f) does not take place until each orbital of subshell are singly occupied."
- For half filled and fully filled degenerate set of orbitals, spin multiplicity or stability is maximum but energy is minimum.

Molecular Mass

- It is the sum of atomic masses of all the elements present in a molecule. It is therefore, the relative mass of a molecule expressed in atomic mass units (u).
- It is obtained by multiplying the atomic mass of each element by the number of its atoms and adding them together.
- Molecular mass of water ($= 2 \times$ Atomic mass of hydrogen $+ 1 \times$ Atomic mass of oxygen

  $= (2 \times 1.008) + (1 \times 16) = 18016$

Formula Unit Mass

- The formula unit mass of a substance is the sum of the atomic masses of all the atoms in a formula unit of a compound.
- Formula unit mass of sodium chloride (NaCl) can be calculated as :

  $=$ Atomic mass of sodium $+$ Atomic mass of chlorine

  $= 1 \times 23$ u $+ 1 \times 35.5$ u $= 58.5$ u

Mole Concept

- In 1896, **Wilhelm Ostwald** introduced the word 'mole' which means 'heap' or pile.
- One mole of any species (atoms, molecules, ions or particles) is that quantity in number having a mass equal to its atomic or molecular mass in grams.
- The number of particles present in 1 mole of any substance is same and fixed, which is equal to $6.02214076 \times 10^{23}$.
- It is known as **Avogadro constant** and denoted by N_A in honour of **Amedeo Avogadro**.
- The atomic mass of an element gives us the mass of one atom of that element in atomic mass units (u).
- To get the mass of 1 mole of an atom of that element, we have to take the same numerical value but change the units from 'u' to 'g'.
- Molar mass of atoms is also known as **gram atomic mass.**

  e.g., Mass of hydrogen atom = 1u

  So, gram atomic mass of hydrogen = 1 g
- In 1u hydrogen, only 1 hydrogen atom is present and in 1g hydrogen, 1 mole atoms of hydrogen are present i.e., 6.022×10^{23} H-atoms are present.

Radioactivity

- Henri Becqueral observed that there are certain elements which emit radiation on their own and named this phenomenon as **radioactivity** and the elements known as **radioactive elements.**
- Later on other scientists Marie Curie, Piere Curie, Rutherford and fredrick soddy observed three kinds of rays i.e., α, β and γ-rays are emitted.

Rutherford Conclusion About α, β- and γ-rays

- α-rays consists of high energy particles carrying two units of positive charge and four unit of atomic mass.
- He concluded that α-particles are helium nuclei as when α-particles combined with two electrons yielded helium gas.
- β-rays are negatively charged particles similar to electrons.
- γ-rays are high energy radiations like X-rays, are neutral in nature and do not consist of particles.
- According to the penetrating power, α-particles are the least, followed by β-rays (100 times that of α–particles) and γ-rays (1000 times that of α-particles).

Properties of α, β and γ rays

Properties	α rays	β rays	γ rays
Nature	Helium nucleus ($_2$) consisting of two protons and two neutrons.	They are electrons ($_{-1}e^0$), basic elementary particle in all atoms.	They are electromagnetic waves consisting of photons.
Charge	Positively charged particles. Charge of each alpha particle = + 2e	Negatively charged particles. Charge of each beta particle = – e	Neutral particles. Charge of each gamma particle = zero
Ionising power	100 time greater than β rays and 10,000 times greater than γ rays.	Comparatively low	Very less ionisation power
Penetrating	Low penetrating power (even stopped by a thick paper)	Penetrating power is greater than that of α rays. They can penetrate through a thin metal foil.	They have a very high penetrating power greater than that of β rays. They can penetrate through thick metal blocks.
Effect of electric and magnetic field	Deflected by both the fields. (in accordance with Fleming's left hand rule)	Deflected by both the fields; but the direction of deflection is opposite to that for alpha rays. (In accordance with Fleming's left hand rule)	They are not deflected by both the fields.
Speed	Their speed ranges from 1/10 to 1/20 times the speed of light.	Their speed can go up to 9/10 times the speed of light.	They travel with the speed of light.
Effect on photographic plate	Turns black	Turns black	Turns black
Effect on ZnS plate	Gives fluorescence	Gives fluorescence	Gives fluorescence

Extra Facts From
Tamil Nadu Board and NIOS

- The mass of an atom can be converted into energy using formula ($E = mc^2$).
- **Relative atomic mass** of an element is the ratio between the average mass of its isotopes to 12th part of the mass of a carbon-12 atom. It is denoted as Ar. Also known as **Standard Atomic Weight.**
- $$(A_r) = \frac{\text{Average mass of the isotopes of the element}}{\frac{1}{12^{th}} \text{ of the mass of one carbon -12 atom}}$$
- **Average Atomic Mass** is the weighted average of the masses of element naturally occurring isotopes.
- Average atomic mass = (Mass of 1st isotope × % abundance of 1st isotope) + (Mass of 2nd isotope × % abundance of 2nd isotope)
- **Atomicity** the number of atoms present in the molecule.
- **Homoatomic Molecules** are made up of similar kind of atoms.
- **Heteroatomic molecules** are made up of atoms of different elements.
- **Polyatomic Molecule** contains more than three atoms.

Table-Classification of molecules

Atomicity	No. of atoms present	Name
1	1	Monoatomic
2	2	Diatomic
3	3	Triatomic
> 3	> 3	Polyatomic

- **Relative Molecular Mass** is the ratio between the mass of one molecule of the substance to $\frac{1}{12^{th}}$ mass of an atom of carbon -12.
- **Molar volume** One mole of any gas occupies 22.4 L or 22400 mL at STP.
- Calculation of number of moles by different modes;

Number of moles

= Mass/Atomic mass

= Mass/Molecular mass

= Number of atoms/6.023 × 10^{23}

= Number of molecules / 6.023 × 10^{23}

- Mass % of an element

$$= \frac{\text{Mass of that element in the compound}}{\text{Molecular mass of the compound}} \times 100$$

- **Avogadro's law** states that "equal volumes of all gases under similar conditions of temperature and pressure contain equal number of molecules".

Physical & Chemical Changes of Substances and Their Separation

[SOURCES]

Class-VI NCERT Chap 3 (Separation of Substances), Class-VII NCERT Chap 5 (Physical and Chemical Changes), Class-IX NCERT Chap 1 (Matter in Our Surroundings), Class-IX NCERT Chap 2 (Is Matter Around us Pure), Class-XI NCERT Chap 1 (Some Basic Concepts of Chemistry), Chap 8 (Organic Chemistry-Some Basic Principles and Techniques), Class-XII NCERT Chap 1 (Solutions)

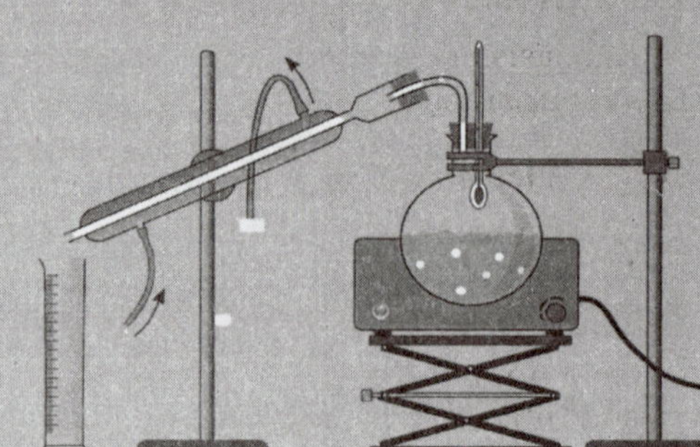

Changes

- In everyday life, we see many changes around us that are due to the involvement of one or more substances.
- Making a solution of sugar is one change. Similarly, setting curd from milk is another change. Sometimes, milk turn sour, so souring of milk is a change. A pulled rubber band also indicates a change.
- Mainly, these changes are of the following two types :
  (i) Physical changes (ii) Chemical changes

Physical Changes

- The properties that we can observe and describe are called physical properties.
  For example, colour, hardness, firmness, fluidity, density, melting point, boiling point, etc., are physical properties. The change in these physical properties of matter is called a physical change.
- Interconversion of states involves a physical change because these changes occur without any change in the composition of substance and their chemical nature also does not change.
  For example, the change of water into ice is a physical change because chemically both ice and water are similar. Although, ice water and vapour appear different and show different physical properties but chemically, these are similar.
- **Crystallisation** is the process of separating solid compounds from the solution in the form of crystals. This method is mainly used for the separation of a solid in pure form from the solution. It is an example of physical change.

Chemical Changes

- When chemical composition is changed by the action of one substance with another, it is a chemical change.
- A chemical change brings about a change in the chemical properties of a substance from which we get a new substance.
- The reactions taking place at the time of chemical changes are known as chemical reactions.
- The ripening of fruits, sunlight from the Sun, burning of iron, curdling etc are examples of chemical changes.
- **Galvanisation** is the process in which a layer of metal like chromium or zinc is deposited to prevent iron from rusting. It is an example of chemical change.

Comparative Study of Physical and Chemical Change

Physical Change	Chemical Change
Only the physical properties of matter changes.	The chemical properties also changes.
No new substance is formed.	One or more new substances are formed.
Change does not usually accompany energy change.	During these transformations there is usually a change of energy.
E.g., melting of ice, cutting of paper, melting of wax, etc.	E.g., combustion of coal, formation of curd through milk, etc.

Note Both physical and chemical changes takes place during the burning of candle.

Matter

- Anything which has mass, occupy volume, can have physical resistance, inertia and can be realised by the sense organs is known as matter.
- Early Indian philosophers classified matter in the form of five basic elements i.e., the *Pancha Tatva*—air, earth, fire, sky and water. According to them everything, living or non-living, was made up of these five basic elements.

Classification of Matter

On the basis of chemical composition or purity, matter can be classified as follows :

Pure Substances

- A substance that consists of only a single type of constituent particles is called **pure substance**, e.g., gold, water, baking soda etc.
- Based upon the nature of the constituent particles, a pure substance is of two types :
  (i) **Elements** In 1661, **Robert Boyle** was the first scientist to use the term element. Antoine laurent Lavoisier, a French chemist, was the first to establish an experimentally useful definition of an element. He defined the element as, "pure matter which can't be divided into two or more simpler substances by physical or chemical methods and cannot be made from them, is called an element". This shows that all atoms of the same element have the same atomic number. In fact, elements are the basic substances of nature.
  e.g., iron, chlorine, sulphur, gold, bromine etc.
  (ii) **Compounds** A compound is a substance composed of two or more elements, chemically combined with one another in a fixed proportion.
  For example, water (H_2O) is a compound because it contains two constituent elements. The ratio of mass of hydrogen and oxygen is always 1 : 8.
  According to **Dalton's Atomic Theory**, a compound is a substance from which the molecules are formed by the combination of different types of atoms in definite proportions.

Impure Substances/Mixtures

- These substances are formed by mixing two or more different types of substances in any proportion. The components of impure substances or mixtures, can be separated by simple physical methods.
  e.g., mixture of sugar and water, mixture of salt and water, syrup, alloy, gunpowder, etc.
  The properties of a mixture are the mixed properties of its components.
- Mixtures are of the following two types :
  (i) **Homogeneous Mixture** A mixture in which the constituents are uniformly distributed throughout, is called homogeneous mixture. e.g., a mixture of salt or sugar in water.
  (ii) **Heterogeneous Mixture** A mixture that does not have uniform composition, is called heterogeneous mixture. e.g., a suspension of chalk or sand in water.

Solution

- A homogeneous mixture of two or more substances is called a solution.
- Lemonade, soda water, salt solution etc., all are the examples of solutions.
- In a solution, there is homogeneity at the particle level. For eg., lemonade tastes same throughout.
- There are two main components of a solution which are as follows :
  (i) **Solvent** (Dissolving Phase) The component (usually present in larger amount) of the solution that dissolves the other component in it, is called the solvent.
  (ii) **Solute** (Dissolved Phase) The component (usually present in lesser quantity) of the solution that is dissolved in the solvent is called the solute.
- Some common examples of solution, solute and solvent are :
  (i) In sugar solution, sugar is the solute and water is the solvent.
  (ii) In solution of soda and water, soda is solute and water is solvent.

Properties of a Solution

- A solution is a homogeneous mixture, in which the particle size of the solute and the solvent are almost same.
- The particle size of solute in solution are smaller than 1 nm (10^{-9} m) in diameter. Therefore, they cannot be seen by naked eyes.
- Due to very small particle size, they do not scatter a beam of light passing through the solution. So, the path of light is not visible in a solution.
- A solution is stable, i.e., the solute particles do not settle down, when left undisturbed. The solute particles cannot be separated from the solution by the filtration technique.

Types of Solution

Broadly, solution can be categorised on the basis of physical phase and concentration.

(i) On the Basis of Physical Phase

Nine types of solutions can be prepared on the basis of physical phase of solute and solvent.

When solute is in solid state

- Mixing of solid in solid. e.g., brass is an alloy of zinc (30%) and copper (60%).
- Solution of a solid into a liquid. e.g., solution of salt in water.
- Solution of solid in a gas. e.g., smoke, it is the solution of carbon in air.

When solute is in liquid state

- Solution of a liquid into a solid. e.g., jelly
- Solution of a liquid in a liquid. e.g., liquor, ethyl alcohol solution in water.
- Solution of liquid in gas. e.g., water vapour in the air.

When solute is in gaseous state

- Solution of gas into solid. e.g., homogeneous mixture of hydrogen gas and palladium metal.
- Solution of gas into liquid. e.g., soda water.
- Solution of gas in gas. e.g., air, it is mainly a mixture of two components, oxygen (21%) and nitrogen (78%).

(ii) On the Basis of Concentration

On the basis of concentration, the solutions can be of the following types :

- **Dilute Solution** The solution in which the amount of solvent is much more than that of the solute is called dilute solution.
- **Concentrated Solution** The solution in which the amount of solvent is less or almost equal to that of the solute is called concentrated solution.
- **Saturated Solution** The solution in which no more solute can be dissolved at constant temperature is called saturated solution.

Note At a given temperature, the amount of solute dissolved in a saturated solution is called its **solubility**.

- **Unsaturated Solution** If the amount of solute in a solution is less than the amount required for the saturation, then that solution is called unsaturated solution.
- **Supersaturated Solution** When a saturated solution is heated, the ability to dissolve the solute in it increases, such a solution is called a supersaturated solution. This solution cannot be produced at normal temperature.

Concentration of a Solution

- The **concentration of a solution** is the amount of solute present in a given amount (mass or volume) of solution or the amount of solute dissolved in a given mass or volume of solution at a given temperature.
  Concentration of solution
  $$= \frac{\text{Mass of solute}}{\text{Mass or volume of solution}}$$
- The concentration of solution can be expressed in three of the following simplest ways
  (i) Mass by mass percentage of a solution
  $$= \frac{\text{Mass of solute}}{\text{Mass of solution}} \times 100$$
  (ii) Mass by volume percentage of a solution
  $$= \frac{\text{Mass of solute}}{\text{Volume of solution}} \times 100$$
  (iii) Volume by volume percentage of a solution
  $$= \frac{\text{Volume of solute}}{\text{Volume of solution}} \times 100$$

Suspension

- A suspension is a heterogeneous mixture in which the solute particles do not dissolve, but remain suspended throughout the bulk of the medium, the size of the dispersed particles is 10^{-8} and 10^{-4} or more.
- For example, a mixture of sand in water, dirty water of river, smoke coming out of a chimney of a factory, paint etc.
- Some important properties of suspension are as follows:
  - It is a heterogeneous mixture.
  - Suspension particles can be seen by naked eyes.
  - Suspension particles scatter a beam of light passing through it and makes its path visible.
  - The solute particles settle down when a suspension is left undisturbed, that means **suspension is unstable** and can be separated from the mixture by filtration process.

Colloidal Solution

- A colloid (or colloidal solution) is a mixture that is actually heterogeneous but appears to be homogeneous as the particles are uniformly spread throughout the solution.
- The size of the dispersed particles is between 10^{-5} to 10^{-7} cm. For example, milk, blood, ink, etc.
- Colloidal solution consists of the following two phases:

(i) **Dispersed Phase** The phase in which matter is dispersed or distributed in the form of colloidal particles is called dispersed phase. e.g., solute.

(ii) **Dispersion Medium** The continuous phase in which the particles of other matter are dispersed is called dispersion medium. e.g., solvent.

Classification of Colloidal Solutions

On the basis of dispersion medium and dispersed phase, colloidal solutions can be of the following eight types.

Types of Colloidal Solutions

Dispersed phase	Dispersing medium	Type	Examples
Liquid	Gas	Aerosol	Fog, clouds, mist
Solid	Gas	Aerosol	Smoke, automobile, exhaust
Gas	Liquid	Foam	Shaving cream
Liquid	Liquid	Emulsion	Milk, face cream
Solid	Liquid	Sol	Milk of magnesia, mud
Gas	Solid	Foam	Foam, rubber, sponge, pumice
Liquid	Solid	Gel	Jelly, cheese, butter
Solid	Solid	Solid sol	Coloured gemstone, milky glass

- The names of colloidal solutions are based on the name of the dispersed phase and the dispersion medium. A few common examples are in the table given above.
- Following are the important properties of a colloidal solution :
  - A colloid is a heterogeneous mixture.
  - The size of particles of a colloid is too small to be individually seen by naked eyes.
  - Colloids are big enough to scatter a beam of light passing through it and make its path visible.
  - The colloids are quite stable. Particles do not settle down, when a colloid is left undisturbed.
  - Particles of colloid can pass through filter paper, therefore a colloidal particle cannot be separated by filtration. However, they can be separated by a special technique called **centrifugation**.

Note The gases mix completely with each other, so their mixture is always homogeneous and hence, they do not form a colloidal solution.

Tyndall Effect

The scattering of light by colloidal particles is known as Tyndall effect. In a true solution, the size of the solute particles are so small, that they cannot scatter light falling on them. In a colloidal solution, the particles are big enough to scatter light.

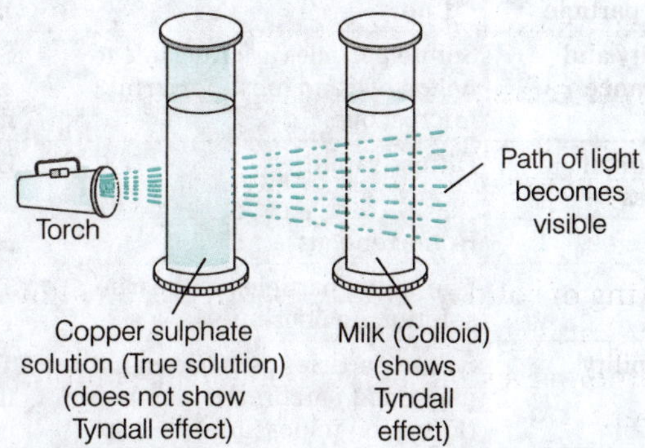

Tyndall effect can also be observed in the following situations :

- When a fine beam of light enters a room through a small hole (due to scattering of beam of light by the particles of dust and smoke in air).
- When sunlight passes through the canopy of a dense forest.
- There are small water droplets in the fog of the forest, which behaves like colloid particles.

Emulsions

- These are liquid colloidal systems in which there is a dispersion of finely divided liquid droplets dispersed in another liquid.
- When a mixture of two immiscible or partially miscible liquids is stirred, an emulsion is obtained.
- The process of turning a liquid mixture into an emulsion is called emulsification.
- Milk, butter, cream, egg yolk, paints cough syrups, facial creams, pesticides, etc are examples of emulsions.
- It also shows Brownian motion and Tyndall effect.
- They can be broken down into constituent liquids by heating, cooling or centrifugation.

Types of Emulsion

These are of following two types :

- **Dispersion of oil in water** e.g., milk, vanishing cream, etc.
- **Dispersion of water in oil** e.g., butter, cream, etc.
- The main property of emulsion is the dispersion of finely divided liquid drops into another liquid.

Comparison of True Solution, Colloidal Solution and Suspension

Property	True Solution	Colloidal solution	Suspension
Size of particle	< 1 nm.	1 nm to 100 nm.	> 100 nm.
Visibility and appearance	Solute particles are invisible to naked eye and most powerful microscope.	Solute particles are invisible to naked eye and their scattering effect can be seen by microscope.	Solute particles are visible to naked eye and can be seen by microscope.
Diffusion of particles	Diffuse rapidly	Diffuse slowly	Do not diffuse
Nature	Homogeneous	Heterogeneous	Heterogeneous
Setting	The solute particles of the true solution do not settle.	The solute particles settle by centrifugation.	The solute particles settle under gravity.
Filterability	Solute particles pass through filter paper and parchment membrane (Filtration impossible).	The solute particles pass through ordinary filter paper but not through parchment membrane (Filtration impossible).	The solute particles cannot pass through filter paper or parchment membrane (Filtration possible).
Tyndall effect	Do not show Tyndall effect.	Show Tyndall effect.	Shows Tyndall
Brownian motion	No Brownian movement.	Show Brownian movement.	Do not show Brownian movement.

Separation of Substances

Before using any substance, we need to separate harmful and unusable substances mixed in it.

The particles of the substance to be separated may have different sizes or masses. These can be any of the three states of matter such as solid, liquid and gas.

Some common methods of separation of substances are as follows :

- **Handpicking** This method can be used for separating slightly larger sized impurities like the pieces of dirt, soil, stone, husk and straw from wheat, rice or pulses. The quantity of such impurities is usually not very large. In such situations, handpicking is a convenient method for separating substances.
- **Threshing** This process is usually used to separate grain from stalks etc. In this process, the stalks are beaten to free the grain seeds.
- **Winnowing** This method is used to separate heavier and lighter components of a mixture by wind or by blowing air. Generally, farmers use this method to separate light straw from heavy grain.
- **Sieving** This method is used to separate two components of a mixture which have different sizes. Sieving allows the fine flour particles to pass through the holes of the sieve while the bigger impurities remain on the sieve.
- **Sedimentation** When the heavier component in a mixture settle down after water is added to it, then the process is called sedimentation.
- **Decantation** After sedimentation, when the water (along with the dust) is removed, the process is called decantation. The same principle is used for separating mixture of two liquids that do not mix with each other. e.g, oil and water from their mixture can be separated by this process.
- **Filtration** The process in which solid particles in a liquid or gaseous fluid are removed by the use of a filter medium that permits the fluid to pass through, but retains the solid particles. e.g., soft white cheese (*paneer*) is prepared at homes by this method.
- **Condensation** The process of conversion of water vapour into its liquid form is called condensation.

Separating the Components of a Mixture

- Most of the natural substances are not chemically pure. Different methods of separation are used to get individual components from a mixture.
- In order to separate components of a mixture, single or a combination of methods are used. Selection of method depends upon the nature of the components present in the mixture.
- **Heterogeneous mixtures** can be separated into their respective constituents by simple physical methods like handpicking, sieving, filtration, etc., that we use in our day-to-day life.
- Sometimes, special techniques are adopted for the separation of components of a mixture. Some of these are

1. Evaporation

- The process of conversion of a substance from a liquid state to a gaseous state is called **evaporation** and the substance is said to be **volatile**.
- This method can be used to separate a volatile component (solvent) from a non-volatile component (solute) of a mixture.
- On heating the mixture, the volatile component evaporates leaving behind the non-volatile component. e.g., common salt from sea water can be separated by this method.

- The heat of Sun gradually evaporates water in the shallow lakes and common salt is left behind as a solid.

Note Separation of dye (ink) from water is done via evaporation. Direct heating of ink is avoided because the blue or the black dye may decompose on direct heating.

2. Centrifugation

- Two components having difference in densities can be separated by centrifugation. This method is based on the principle that, the denser particles are forced to the bottom and the lighter particles stay at the top, when spin rapidly.
- A device used to separate liquids from solids by spinning is called **centrifuge**. Centrifugal machines are commonly used for this method.
- Following are the major applications of this technique :
  - In diagnostic laboratories for blood and urine tests.
  - In dairies and home to separate butter from cream.
  - In washing machines to squeeze out water from wet clothes.

3. Separation by using Separating Funnel/ Solvent Extraction

- This method is used to separate a mixture of two immiscible liquids.
- This method is based upon the principle that immiscible liquids separate out in layers depending on their densities or difference in solubility of two immisible liquids.
- Separating funnel is used in the following situations:
  - Separation of mixture of oil and water.
  - Solvent extraction method is used in pharmaceutical and petroleum industries.

4. Sublimation

- Some solids have a tendency to sublime on heating, i.e., they convert directly from solid to gaseous/vapour phase on heating without passing through the liquid phase.
- A mixture containing such solid with any other (normal) solid can be separated by sublimation.
- Examples of solids that sublime are camphor, ammonium chloride, naphthalene, iodine, anthracene, etc.
- Hence, sublimation is used to separate such mixtures that contain a sublimable volatile component from a non-sublimable impurity, e.g., a mixture of common salt and ammonium chloride can be separated by sublimation.

5. Chromatography

- The term chromatography is based on Greek word, **kroma** means **colour**.
- This technique was first used for the separation of colour that's why, it is named as Chromatography.
- This technique is used for the separation of those solutes that dissolve in the same solvent.
- The separation of different components of a mixture is depend upon their different solubility in the same solvent. e.g., separation of dyes present in ink by paper chromatography.
- The ink that we use, has water, as the solvent and the dye is soluble in it. As, the water rises on the filter paper, it takes along with the dye particles.
- Usually, a dye is a mixture of two or more colours. The coloured component that is more soluble in water, rises faster and in this way the colours get separated.
- Chromatography is used to separate the following :
  - Drugs from blood
  - Pigments from natural colours
  - Colours in a dye

6. Simple Distillation

- If liquids in a mixture are miscible, boil without decomposition and possess different boiling points, then they can be separated by distillation.
- This process involves the conversion of a liquid into vapour followed by the condensation of vapour back into the liquid.
- It is used only if, the liquids have a difference in boiling points of more than 25 K.

7. Fractional Distillation

- To separate a mixture of two or more miscible liquids for which the differences in boiling points is less than 25 K, fractional distillation process is used. e.g., separation of different gases from air, different fraction from petroleum products, etc.
- The apparatus used in this method is similar to that for simple distillation, except that a fractionating column is fitted in between the distillation flask and the condenser.
- A simple fractionating column is a tube packed with glass beads. The beads provide surface for the vapour to cool and condense repeatedly.

Separation of Different Gases Present in Air

- Air is a homogeneous mixture and can be separated into its components by fractional distillation.
- For this purpose, the air is compressed by increasing the pressure and cooled to a very low temperature. Thus, liquid air is obtained.
- This liquid air is allowed to warm up slowly in a fractional distillation column, where gases get separated at different heights depending upon their boiling points.

Chemical Reaction, Bonds and Chemical Equations

(SOURCES)

Class-X NCERT Chap 1 (Chemical Reactions and Equations), Chap 2 (Acids, Bases and Salts), Chap 4 (Carbon and Its Compounds), Class-XI NCERT Chap 6 (Equilibrium), Chap 7 (Redox Reactions)

Chemical Reaction

- A chemical reaction is a change in which one or more substances or reactants reacts to form new substances or products with entirely different physical and chemical properties.
- It involves breaking of the old bonds and formation of new bonds.

  For example, magnesium ribbon burns in the presence of air to form white powder of magnesium oxide, whose physical and chemical properties are different from magnesium metal.

Identification of Chemical Reaction

A chemical reaction can be identified by either of the following observations:

(i) Change in state
(ii) Change in colour
(iii) Evolution of a gas
(iv) Change in temperature
(v) Formation of a precipitate

Chemical Equation

- A chemical equation is the symbolic representation of a chemical reaction.
- The simplest way to write a chemical reaction is in the form of a word equation.

The word equation can be written as follows

$$\underset{\text{(Reactants)}}{\text{Magnesium} + \text{Oxygen}} \rightarrow \underset{\text{(Product)}}{\text{Magnesium oxide}}$$

- The substances or compounds which takes part in a chemical reaction are called **reactants**. These are written on the left hand side (LHS) of the equation. with a (+) sign between them.
- The substances or compounds formed in the course of chemical reaction are called **products**. These are written on the right hand side (RHS) of the equation with a (+) sign between them.
- A **chemical equation** shows a change of reactants to products through an arrow (→) placed between them.

Writing a Chemical Equation

- Chemical equations can be made more concise and useful if we use chemical formulae instead of words.
- A chemical equation represents a chemical reaction.
- The reaction between magnesium (Mg) and oxygen (O_2) resulting into the formation of magnesium oxide can be written as:

$$\underset{\text{(Reactants)}}{Mg + O_2} \longrightarrow \underset{\text{(Product)}}{MgO}$$

- In the above equation, number of magnesium and oxygen atoms are not same on both sides of an equation. Such an unbalanced equation is called **skeletal chemical equation**.

Balanced Chemical Equations

- A balanced chemical equation is that in which the total number of atoms of each element are equal on both sides of the equation.
- The balancing of a chemical equation is based on law of conservation of mass.
- According to the **law of conservation of mass**, "mass can neither be created nor be destroyed during a chemical reaction."
- In the same way, the number of atoms of each element remains the same, before and after a chemical reaction.

Balancing of a Chemical Equation

- **Hit and trial method** can be used to balance a chemical equation.
- Several steps are involved in balancing a chemical equation. These steps are as follows:

Step (*a*) Writing unbalanced equation and enclosing the formulae in brackets.

$$\underset{\text{Sodium}}{Na} + \underset{\text{Water}}{H_2O} \longrightarrow \underset{\text{Sodium hydroxide}}{NaOH} + \underset{\text{Hydrogen}}{H_2}$$

Step (*b*) Making list of number of atoms of different elements present in unbalanced equation.

Element	Number of Atoms in Reactants (LHS)	Number of Atoms in Products (RHS)
Na	1	1
H	2	3
O	1	1

Step (*c*) **Balancing First Element** It is often convenient to start balancing with the compound that contains maximum number of atoms. From the table shown above, it is clear that, only the hydrogen atoms which has two atoms of the LHS and three atoms on RHS. So, firstly we try to balance it.

Atoms of H	In Reactants	In Products
Initial	2 (in H_2O)	3 (1 in NaOH and 2 in H_2)
To balance	2×2	2×1 in NaOH, 2 in H_2 = 4 H atoms

Thus, the equation now becomes

$$(Na) + 2(H_2O) \longrightarrow 2(NaOH) + (H_2)$$

Step (*d*) **Balancing Second Element** We examine the obtained equation and select another element which is still unbalanced. In the above equation, Na is still unbalanced.

To balance the number of Na atoms :

Atoms of Na	In Reactants	In Products
Initially	1 (in Na)	2 (in NaOH)
To balance	2×1	2

Thus, after balancing Na and removing the brackets, we get the equation:

$$2Na + 2H_2O \longrightarrow 2NaOH + H_2$$

Step (*e*) **Balancing Other Elements** If we further examine the reaction, no element is found to be unbalanced. This method of balancing chemical equation is called **hit and trial method.**

Step (*f*) **Checking the correctness of equation** To check the correctness of the equation, we further tabulate the number of atoms of each element separately.

Element	Number of Atoms in Reactants	Number of Atoms in Products
Na	2	2
H	4	4
O	2	2

The above table clearly reveals that the obtained equation is a balanced chemical equation.

Making a Chemical Equation More Informative

- The physical states of the reactants and products can be represented by using the symbols, (*s*) for solid, (*l*) for liquid, (*g*) for gas and (*aq*) for aqueous solution, along with their respective formulae.
- The word aqueous (*aq*) is written, if the reactant or product is present as a solution in water.

$$2Na(s) + 2H_2O(l) \longrightarrow 2NaOH\,(aq) + H_2(g)$$

- Precipitate can also be represented by using an arrow pointing downwards (↓) instead of using symbol (*s*).
- In the same way, the gaseous state of an evolved gas can be represented by using an arrow pointing upward direction (↑) instead of using symbol (*g*), e.g., magnesium reacting with dilute sulphuric acid is represented by the chemical equation;

$$\underset{\text{Magnesium}}{Mg(s)} + \underset{\text{Sulphuric acid}}{H_2SO_4\,(aq)} \longrightarrow \underset{\text{Magnesium sulphate}}{MgSO_4\,(aq)} + \underset{\text{Hydrogen}}{H_2\uparrow}$$

- The specific conditions of the reaction like temperature, pressure, catalyst, etc., are written above or below the arrow in the chemical equation.

$$\underset{\text{Carbon monoxide}}{CO(g)} + \underset{\text{Hydrogen}}{2H_2(g)} \xrightarrow{340\text{ atm}} \underset{\text{Methanol}}{CH_3OH(l)}$$

- Evolution of heat or absorption of heat can be indicated by writing [+Heat] on the right hand side or left hand side of the equation, respectively
  e.g., Burning of carbon in the presence of air.

$$\underset{\text{Carbon}}{C(s)} + \underset{\text{Oxygen}}{O_2(g)} \longrightarrow \underset{\text{Carbon dioxide}}{CO_2(g)} + \text{Heat}$$

- To indicate the strength of acid or base, dil. for dilute or conc. for concentrated is written before the formula of acid or base.

$$Cu(s) + 2\,\text{dil.}HCl(aq) \longrightarrow CuCl_2(aq) + H_2(g)$$

Types of Chemical Reactions

The chemical reactions are classified into different types depending upon the chemical changes taking place.

1. Combination Reaction

- A reaction in which two or more reactants combine to form a single product, is called combination reaction. Such reaction may occur in between the elements or compounds.
  e.g., Calcium oxide reacts vigorously with water to form calcium hydroxide.

$$\underset{\substack{\text{Calcium oxide}\\\text{(Quick lime)}}}{CaO(s)} + H_2O(l) \longrightarrow \underset{\substack{\text{Calcium hydroxide}\\\text{(Slaked lime)}}}{Ca(OH)_2(aq)} + \text{Heat}$$

- Solution of calcium hydroxide is used for white washing walls.
- Calcium hydroxide reacts slowly with carbon dioxide in air to form a thin layer of calcium carbonate on the walls, which gives a shiny appearance to the walls.

$$\underset{\substack{\text{Calcium}\\\text{hydroxide}}}{Ca(OH)_2(aq)} + CO_2(g) \longrightarrow \underset{\substack{\text{Calcium}\\\text{carbonate}}}{CaCO_3(s)} + H_2O(l)$$

- Other examples of combination reactions are :
  (i) Burning of coal $C(s) + O_2(g) \longrightarrow CO_2(g)$
  (ii) Formation of water from $H_2(g)$ and $O_2(g)$

$$2H_2(g) + O_2(g) \longrightarrow 2H_2O(l)$$

2. Decomposition Reaction

- A reaction in which a single reactant breaks down to form two or more products, is known as decomposition reaction.
- On the basis of the form of energy required for the reaction, these reactions are of three types :
  (i) **Thermal Decomposition** These reactions use the energy in the form of heat for decomposition of the reactant.
  e.g., Decomposition of lead nitrate and calcium carbonate is given as

$$\underset{\text{Lead nitrate}}{2Pb(NO_3)_2(s)} \xrightarrow{\text{Heat}} \underset{\text{Lead oxide}}{2PbO(s)} + \underset{\substack{\text{Nitrogen}\\\text{dioxide}}}{4NO_2(g)} + \underset{\text{Oxygen}}{O_2(g)}$$

$$\underset{\substack{\text{Calcium}\\\text{carbonate}}}{CaCO_3(s)} \xrightarrow{\text{Heat}} \underset{\text{Quick lime}}{CaO(s)} + \underset{\text{Carbon dioxide}}{CO_2(g)}$$

  (ii) **Electrolysis** These reactions involve the use of electrical energy for the decomposition of the reactant molecules. In this process, positive charge accumulate at cathode and negative charge accumulate at anode.

$$\text{e.g., } \underset{\text{Water}}{2H_2O(l)} \xrightarrow{\text{Electric current}} \underset{\text{Hydrogen}}{2H_2(g)} + \underset{\text{Oxygen}}{O_2(g)}$$

  (iii) **Photolysis** These reactions involve the use of light energy for the purpose of decomposition.
  e.g., Decomposition of silver halide.

$$\underset{\text{Silver chloride}}{2AgCl(s)} \xrightarrow{\text{Sunlight}} \underset{\text{Silver}}{2Ag(s)} + \underset{\text{Chlorine}}{Cl_2(g)}$$

$$\underset{\text{Silver Bromide}}{2AgBr(s)} \xrightarrow{h\nu} \underset{\text{Silver}}{2Ag(s)} + \underset{\text{Bromine}}{Br_2(g)}$$

  Above reaction is used in black and white photography.

3. Displacement Reaction

- A reaction in which more reactive element displaces less reactive element from its compound present in dissolved state, is called a displacement reaction.
- For example, iron being more reactive than copper displaces copper from the aqueous solution of its compound.

$$\underset{\text{Iron}}{Fe(s)} + \underset{\text{Copper sulphate}}{CuSO_4(aq)} \longrightarrow \underset{\text{Ferrous sulphate}}{FeSO_4(aq)} + \underset{\text{Copper}}{Cu(s)}$$

4. Double Displacement Reaction

- The reaction in which two different ions or group of atoms in the reactant molecules exchange ions between each other is called **double displacement reaction.**
- The reaction that produces a precipitate is known as **precipitation reaction.**
- Reaction between Na_2SO_4 and $BaCl_2$ is a double decomposition reaction which forms $BaSO_4$ precipitate along with NaCl solution.

$$\text{e.g., } \underset{\text{Sodium sulphate}}{Na_2SO_4(aq)} + \underset{\text{Barium chloride}}{BaCl_2(aq)} \longrightarrow \underset{\text{Barium sulphate}}{BaSO_4(s)\downarrow} + \underset{\text{Sodium chloride}}{2NaCl(aq)}$$

5. Neutralisation Reaction

The reaction in which acid react with base to form salt and water are called neutralisation reactions.

$$\text{e.g., } \underset{\substack{\text{Sodium}\\\text{hydroxide}}}{2NaOH} + \underset{\substack{\text{Sulphuric}\\\text{acid}}}{H_2SO_4} \longrightarrow \underset{\text{Sodium sulphate}}{Na_2SO_4} + \underset{\text{Water}}{2H_2O}$$

6. Reversible and Irreversible Reaction

- A chemical reaction which proceeds in both directions is called a reversible reaction.

e.g., $\underset{\text{Nitrogen}}{N_2} + \underset{\text{Hydrogen}}{H_2} \xrightleftharpoons{\text{Fe, Mo}} \underset{\text{Ammonia}}{2NH_3}$

- A chemical reaction which proceeds only in one direction, is called an irreversible reaction.

e.g., $\underset{\text{Sodium hydroxide}}{2NaOH} + \underset{\text{Sulphuric acid}}{H_2SO_4} \longrightarrow \underset{\text{Sodium sulphate}}{Na_2SO_4} + \underset{\text{Water}}{2H_2O}$

7. Exothermic and Endothermic Reaction

- Reactions occurring with the evolution of heat energy are called exothermic reactions. e.g., Respiration, decomposition, burning of natural gas, etc.
- Reactions which occur by the absorption of heat energy are called endothermic reactions. e.g., Photosynthesis, decomposition, etc.

8. Isomerisation or Rearrangement Reaction

- A chemical reaction in which the atoms of the molecule of a compound undergo rearrangement is called an isomerisation or rearrangement reaction. It is generally seen in case of organic compounds.

e.g., $\underset{\text{Ammonium cyanate}}{NH_4CNO} \xrightarrow{\Delta} \underset{\text{Urea}}{NH_2CONH_2}$

9. Hydrolysis Reaction

- It is the reaction between salts of weak acid or weak base with water. Due to high dielectric constant, water has a very strong hydrating tendency.
- It dissolves many ionic compounds. However, certain covalent and some ionic compounds are hydrolysed in water.

e.g.,

$\underset{\text{Sodium acetate}}{CH_3COONa} + H_2O \longrightarrow \underset{\text{Acetic acid}}{CH_3COOH} + \underset{\text{Sodium hydroxide}}{NaOH}$

10. Photochemical Reaction

- These chemical reactions take place in the presence of sunlight.

e.g., $6CO_2 + 12H_2O \xrightarrow[\text{Photosynthesis}]{\text{Sunlight}} C_6H_{12}O_6 + 6H_2O + 6O_2$

- The rate of a photochemical reaction is affected by the intensity of light.
- Photosensitizer is a substance which brings about a reaction without undergoing any chemical change itself.
- In the process of photosynthesis, chlorophyll acts as a photosensitizer.

Oxidation and Reduction

- **Oxidation** refers to a chemical reaction in which a substance gains oxygen or any other electronegative element.

  It is also defined as loss of hydrogen or electrons. It shows increase in oxidation number.

  e.g., $2Cu + O_2 \xrightarrow{\text{Heat}} 2CuO$

  (Copper is oxidised to CuO)

  - Combustion is an example of oxidation reaction in which, the reactants burns in the presence of oxygen to give carbon dioxide, heat and light.

    e.g. $CH_4 + 2O_2 \longrightarrow CO_2 + 2H_2O$ + heat and light

- **Reduction** refers to a chemical reaction in which a substance gains hydrogen or electrons or electropositive element.

  - It is also defined as loss of oxygen or electronegative element. It shows decrease in oxidation number.

    e.g., $CuO + H_2 \xrightarrow{\text{Heat}} Cu + H_2O$

    (Copper oxide is reduced to Cu)

Oxidising and Reducing Agent

- A substance which is oxidised or oxidation number is increased acts as a **reducing agent.** It also acts as electron donor.
- A substance which is reduced or oxidation number is decreased acts as an **oxidising agent**. It also acts as electron acceptor.
- Reactions in which oxidation and reduction takes place simultaneously are called **redox reactions.**

e.g.,

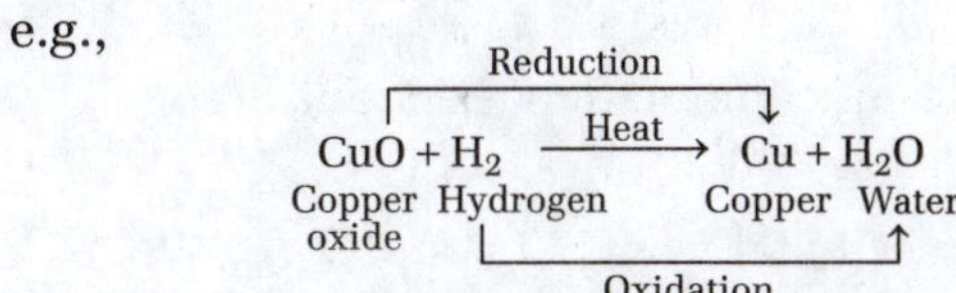

Oxidation State and Oxidation Number

- The real or imaginary charge which an atom appears to have in its combined state is known as **oxidation state** or **oxidation number** of an atom.
- Rules for the calculation of oxidation number are :
  - The oxidation number of an atom in its elemental (free) state is zero. e.g., Oxidation number of H in H_2, S in S_8 and P in P_4 is zero.
  - The oxidation number of F is always –1 in all of its compounds. Other halogens also have an oxidation number of –1, when they occur as halide ions in their compounds.

- The oxidation number of O is always –2 except peroxides (–1), superoxides $\left(-\frac{1}{2}\right)$ and oxygen fluorides (+2 or +1).
- The oxidation number of H in metallic hydrides is –1 while in rest of the compounds, it has +1 oxidation number.
- The oxidation number of an ion is equal to the charge present on it.
- The sum of the oxidation number of all the atoms present in a compound is zero.

  For example, oxidation state of O in OF_2 is calculated as

$$x + (-1)2 = 0 \Rightarrow x = +2$$

  Similarly, in H_2O

$$2 \times 1 + x = 0 \Rightarrow x = -2$$

Effect of Oxidation Reactions in Daily Life

Following are the effects of oxidation reactions in daily life :

Corrosion

- It is the process of oxidative deterioration of a metal surface by the action of substances present in environment (air, water and chemicals).
- In this process, a metal is oxidised by the loss of electrons to oxygen and form oxide.
- The rusting of iron, tarnishing of silver and formation of green coating on copper or bronze are some examples of corrosion.
- Iron acquires a coating of brown flaky substance, when exposed to moist air for a long time. This coating is known as rust.
- Surface of copper acquires a green coating of basic copper carbonate in moist air.
- The rusting of iron can be prevented by painting, oiling and greasing, galvanising, chrome plating etc.
- Galvanising is a process of coating iron objects with zinc.

Rancidity

- This process involves oxidation of food items containing oils and fats, when exposed to air or oxygen due to which the food becomes stale and its colour and smell changes.
- Following methods can be used to prevent rancidity :
  - By keeping food materials in air-tight container.
  - By packing food items like potato wafers etc, in packets containing nitrogen gas instead of air.
  - Refrigeration of cooked food at low temperature.
  - By adding antioxidants like BHT (Butylated Hydroxytoluene), BHA (Butylated Hydroxyanisole) and N_2 (Dinitrogen).

04

Periodic Classification of Elements

[SOURCES]

Class-X Old NCERT Chap 5 (Periodic Classification of Elements), Class-XI NCERT Chap 3 (Classification of Elements and Periodicity in Properties)

- Periodic table of elements is a tabular arrangement of the chemical elements, arranged by atomic number, electronic configuration and recurring chemical properties, whose structure shows periodic trends. At present, **118 elements** are known. Out of these, only 94 are naturally occuring.
- Initially, only few elements were known. So, it was quite easy to study and remember the properties of those elements and their compounds individually.
- Later on, to study the properties of large number of elements classification was required. So, all the elements have been divided into groups in such a way that elements in the same group have similar properties.

Development of Periodic Table

Some major attempts made for classification of elements are as follows:

Dobereiner's Triads (1829)

- In the year 1829, **Johann Dobereiner** has made an attempt to arrange the elements with similar properties into groups having three elements each. He called these groups as **triads**.
- Dobereiner showed that, when three elements in a triad were arranged in the order of increasing atomic masses, the atomic mass of the middle element was roughly the average of the atomic masses of the other two elements.

Example,	Elements	Li	Na	K
	Atomic mass	7	23	39

Average atomic mass of the first and third elements

$$= \frac{7 + 39}{2} = 23$$

- Dobereiner could identify only three triads from the elements known at that time.

Newland's Law of Octaves (1865)

- In 1865, **John Alexander Newlands**, an English Chemist arranged the known elements in the order of increasing atomic masses and found that every eighth element had properties similar to that of the first.
- He compared this pattern to the octaves found in music i.e., sa, re, ga, ma, pa, da, ni.
- Therefore, he called it the **Law of Octaves**. This is known as Newland's Law of Octaves.

Newland's Octaves

Notes of Music						
sa (do)	**re (re)**	**ga (mi)**	**ma (fa)**	**pa (so)**	**da (la)**	**ni(ti)**
H	Li	Be	B	C	N	O
F	Na	Mg	Al	Si	P	S
Cl	K	Ca	Cr	Ti	Mn	Fe
Co and Ni	Cu	Zn	Y	In	As	Se
Br	Rb	Sr	Ce and La	Zr	–	–

- In order to fit elements into his table, Newlands adjusted two elements in the same slot and also put some unlike elements under the same column.
- Cobalt and nickel are in the same slot and these are placed in the same column as fluorine, chlorine and bromine which have very different properties than these elements.
- Iron, which resembles cobalt and nickel in properties, has been placed far away from these elements. Hence, Newlands' law of octaves worked well with lighter elements only.

Limitations of Newland's Law of Octaves

- This law was applicable only upto calcium. After calcium, every eighth element did not possess the same properties similar to that of the first.
- Newland assumed that there were only 56 elements existed in nature and no more elements would be discovered in the future. But later on, several new elements were discovered, whose properties did not fit into the law of octaves.

Atomic Volume Curve

In 1830-1907, **Lothar Meyer's** plotted a graph between atomic weight and atomic volume known as **Atomic Volume Curve**. He found that elements with similar properties occupied the similar position on the graph.

Mendeleev's Periodic Table (1869)

- **Dmitri Mendeleev** was the most important contributor for the early development of a periodic table of elements. Only 63 elements were known at his time.
- According to Mendeleev's periodic law, "The physical and chemical properties of the elements are a periodic function of their atomic mass."

Features of Mendeleev's Periodic Table

- This table contains 8 vertical columns, called **groups** and 7 horizontal rows, called **periods.**
- **Discovery of new elements** In his table, Mendeleev's left gaps for the elements not discovered at that time. He predicted the atomic masses and properties of several elements that were not known and named such elements by prefixing a Sanskrit numeral Eka (one), divi (two), tri (three), etc., to the name of the preceding similar (analogous) element in the same group. e.g., as Eka-Boron, Eka-Aluminium, Eka-Silicon, which after their discovery were named as scandium, gallium and germanium, respectively.

Mendeleev's Predictions for the Elements Eka-aluminium (Gallium) and Eka-silicon (Germanium)

Property	Eka-aluminium (Predicted)	Gallium (found)	Eka-silicon (predicted)	Germanium (found)
Atomic weight	68	70	72	72.6
Density/ (g/cm^3)	5.9	5.94	5.5	5.36
Melting point/K	Low	302.93	High	1231
Formula of oxide	E_2O_3	Ga_2O_3	EO_2	GeO_2
Formula of chloride	ECl_3	$GaCl_3$	ECl_4	$GeCl_4$

- **Systematic Study of the Properties of Elements** In order to group the elements having similar properties together at some places, Mendeleev had to place an element with a slightly greater atomic mass before an element with a slightly lower atomic mass.
- **Noble gases** Like helium (He), neon (Ne), argon (Ar) etc., were discovered very late because they are very inert and present in extremely low concentrations in our atmosphere. One of the strength of **Mendeleev's periodic table** was that, when these gases were discovered, they could be placed in a new group without disturbing the existing order.

Periodic System of the Elements in Groups and Series

S.No.	Groups of Elements								
	0	I	II	III	IV	V	VI	VII	VIII
1.	-	Hydrogen H 1.008	-	-					
2.	Helium He 4.0	Lithium Li 7.03	Beryllium Be 9.1	Boron B 11.0	Carbon C 12.0	Nitrogen N 14.04	Oxygen O 16.00	Fluorine F 19.0	
3.	Neon Ne 19.9	Sodium Na 23.5	Magnesium Mg 24.3	Aluminium Al 27.0	Silicon Si 28.4	Phosphorus P 31.0	Sulphur S 32.06	Chlorine Cl 35.45	
4.	Argon Ar 38	Potassium K 39.1	Calcium Ca 40.1	Scandium Sc 44.1	Titanium Ti 48.1	Vanadium V 51.4	Chromium Cr 52.1	Manganese Mn 55.0	Iron Fe 55.9, Cobalt Co 59, Nickel Ni 59 (Cu)
5.		Copper Cu 63.6	Zinc Zn 65.4	Gallium Ga 70.0	Germanium Ge 72.3	Arsenic As 75	Selenium Se 79	Bromine Br 79.95	
6.	Krypton Kr 81.8	Rubidium Rb 85.4	Strontium Sr 87.6	Yttrium Y 89.0	Zirconium Zr 90.6	Niobium Nb 94.0	Molybdenum Mo 96.0		Ruthenium Ru 101.7, Rhodium Rh 103.0, Palladium Pd 106.5 (Ag)
7.		Silver Ag 107.9	Cadmium Cd 112.4	Indium In 114.0	Tin Sn 119.0	Antimony Sb 120.0	Tellurium Te 127.6	Iodine I 126.9	
8.	Xenon Xe 128	Caesium Cs 132.9	Barium Ba 137.4	Lanthanum La 139	Cerium Ce 140	-	-	-	
9.		-	-	-	-	-	-	-	
10.	-	-		Ytterbium Yb 173	-	Tantalum Ta 183	Tungsten W 184	-	Osmium Os 191, Iridium Ir 193, Platinum Pt 194.9 (Au)
11.		Gold Au 197.2	Mercury Hg 200.0	Thallium Tl 204.1	Lead Pb 206.9	Bismuth Bi 208	-	-	
12.	-	-	Radium Ra 224	-	Thorium Th 232	-	Uranium U 239		
					Higher Saline Oxides				
	R	R_2O	RO	R_2O_3	RO_2	R_2O_5	RO_3	R_2O_7	RO_4
					Higher Gaseous Hydrogen Compounds				
					RH_4	RH_3	RH_2	RH	

Mendeleev's Periodic Table

Limitations of Mendeleev's Periodic Table

- **Position of Hydrogen** The electronic configuration of hydrogen resembles with alkali metals. Moreover, it combines with halogen, oxygen and sulphur to give similar type of compounds as given by alkali metals, e.g., (HCl, NaCl), (H_2O, Na_2O) and (H_2S, Na_2S).

  But just like halogen, it exists in diatomic form and combines with metals and non-metals to form covalent compounds. Thus, its position was not fixed in the Mendeleev's periodic table but it was kept with alkali metals.
- **Position of Isotopes** Isotopes of an elements have similar chemical properties but different atomic masses. In Mendeleev's periodic table, no place was given to these elements.

  For example, the element chlorine has two isotopes, Cl-35 and Cl-37, having atomic masses of 35 and 37, respectively. The placing of these two isotopes of chlorine (having different atomic masses) in the same group of periodic table could not be explained by Mendeleev's periodic law.
- **Uncertainty in Atomic Masses** Another problem was that the atomic masses do not increase in a regular manner in going from one element to the next.

  So, it was not possible to predict, how many elements could be discovered between two elements especially, when we consider the heavier elements.
- **Placing of Heavier Element Before the Lighter One** Few elements, those possess higher atomic mass were placed before elements having a lower atomic mass. For example argon (39.9) was placed before potassium (39.1), cobalt (58.9) before nickel (58.7), tellurium (127.60) before iodine (126.9).

Modern Periodic Table

- In 1913, **Henry Moseley** showed that the atomic number of an element is a more fundamental property.
- On the basis of this, he modified Mendeleev's periodic law as "Physical and chemical properties of the elements are a periodic function of their atomic number". This is called **Modern Periodic Law.**
- When the elements were arranged in the increasing order of their atomic number, the obtained table is called **Modern Periodic Table.**

Features of Modern Periodic Table

This table has 18 vertical columns, known as **groups** and 7 horizontal rows, known as **periods.**

Features of Groups

A few important features of the elements present in groups are as follows:

- The groups are not divided into sub-groups.
- The elements present in a group have the same number of valence electrons.
- The elements present in a group have the same valency.
- The number of shells increases, as we go down the group.
- The elements present in a group have identical chemical properties.
- The physical properties of the elements such as melting point, boiling point, density in a group vary gradually.

Features of Periods

The important features of the elements in a period are as follows :

- Elements of a period do not have the same number of valence electrons but they contain the same number of shells.
- The number of valence shell electrons increases by one unit, as the atomic number increases by one unit on moving from left to right in a period. Therefore, the atoms of different elements with same number of shells are placed in the same period.
- As, the number of valence shell electrons change, the chemical properties of the elements also change.
- Different periods have different number of electrons which can be explained on the basis of filling of electrons into various shells.
- Maximum number of electrons that can be accommodated in a shell is given by the formula, $2n^2$. where, n = number of given shell from the nucleus. Examples,
  - *K*-shell — $2\times(1)^2 = 2$, hence, the first period has 2 elements and is called **very short period.**
  - *L*-shell — $2\times(2)^2 = 8$, hence, the second period has 8 elements and is called **short period.**
  - *M*-shell — $2\times(3)^2 = 18$ but the outermost shell can have only 8 electrons, so the third period also has only 8 elements thus, it is also called **short period.** Fourth and fifth periods have 18 elements and are called **long periods.**
- Sixth and seventh periods have 32 elements and are also called **long periods.**

Types of Elements

The electronic configuration of atoms provides a theoretical foundation for the periodic classification. Elements of a group exhibit similar chemical properties because they have same electronic configuration of their outermost shell. Depending upon the type of orbital receiving the valence electron, the elements can be classified into following four blocks :

-Block Elements

- In these elements, valence electrons enter in *s*-orbital.
- Group-1 and 2 (IA and IIA) of the periodic table belong to this block.
- Group-1 (IA) of the periodic table is collectively called as **alkali metals**. Group-2 (IIA) of the periodic table is collectively called as **alkaline earth metals.**
- The general electronic configuration of *s*-block elements is ns^1 for alkali metals and ns^2 for alkaline earth metals.
- These elements are soft metals, electropositive and form basic oxides.

p-Block Elements

- In *p*-block elements, valence electron(s) enters in *p*-orbital. Valence shell electronic configuration is ns^2 np^{1-6}.
- Group-13 to 18 (IIIA to VIIIA) are *p*-block elements in the periodic table. It is the only block which contains **metals, non-metals** and **metalloids.**
- Heavier members of this block show inert pair effect, i.e., their lower valency becomes more stable. e.g., +2 valency is more stable for Pb as compared to its +4 valency.
- Similarly, +1 valency is more stable for Tl as compared to its +3 valency.

d-Block Elements

- These elements are called **transition elements** (except zinc, cadmium and mercury).
- In *d*-block elements, valence electrons enter in *d*-orbital.
- General outer electronic configuration is $(n-1)\, d^{1-10} ns^{0-2}$.
- This block contains the elements of group-3 to 12 of the periodic table.
- The three series of transition metals are known **3*d* series** (Sc to Zn), **4*d* series** (Y to Cd) and **5*d* series** (La to Hg, excluding Ce to Lu).

Modern Periodic Table

Metals | Metalloids | Non-metals

The *zig-zag* line separates the metals from the non-metals.

PERIODS	1	2	3	4	5	6	7	8	9	10	11	12	13	14	15	16	17	18
1	1 H Hydrogen 1.0																	2 He Helium 4.0
2	3 Li Lithium 6.9	4 Be Beryllium 9.0											5 B Boron 10.8	6 C Carbon 12.0	7 N Nitrogen 14.0	8 O Oxygen 16.0	9 F Fluorine 19.0	10 Ne Neon 20.2
3	11 Na Sodium 23.0	12 Mg Magnesium 24.3											13 Al Aluminium 27.0	14 Si Silicon 28.1	15 P Phosphorus 31.0	16 S Sulphur 32.1	17 Cl Chlorine 35.5	18 Ar Argon 39.9
4	19 K Potassium 39.1	20 Ca Calcium 40.1	21 Sc Scandium 45.0	22 Ti Titanium 47.8	23 V Vanadium 50.9	24 Cr Chromium 52.0	25 Mn Manganese 54.9	26 Fe Iron 55.9	27 Co Cobalt 58.9	28 Ni Nickel 58.7	29 Cu Copper 63.5	30 Zn Zinc 65.4	31 Ga Gallium 69.7	32 Ge Germanium 72.6	33 As Arsenic 74.9	34 Se Selenium 79.0	35 Br Bromine 79.9	36 Kr Krypton 83.8
5	37 Rb Rubidium 85.5	38 Sr Strontium 87.6	39 Y Yttrium 88.9	40 Zr Zirconium 91.2	41 Nb Niobium 92.9	42 Mo Molybdenum 95.9	43 Tc Technetium (99)	44 Ru Ruthenium 101.1	45 Rh Rhodium 102.3	46 Pd Palladium 106.4	47 Ag Silver 107.9	48 Cd Cadmium 112.4	49 In Indium 114.8	50 Sn Tin 118.7	51 Sb Antimony 121.8	52 Te Tellurium 127.6	53 I Iodine 126.9	54 Xe Xenon 131.3
6	55 Cs Caesium 132.9	56 Ba Barium 137.3	57 La* Lanthanum 138.9	72 Hf Hafnium 178.5	73 Ta Tantalum 181.0	74 W Tungsten 183.9	75 Re Rhenium 186.2	76 Os Osmium 190.2	77 Ir Iridium 192. 2	78 Pt Platinum 195.1	79 Au Gold 197.0	80 Hg Mercury 200.6	81 Tl Thallium 204.4	82 Pb Lead 207.2	83 Bi Bismuth 209.0	84 Po Polonium (210)	85 At Astatine (210)	86 Rn Radon (222)
7	87 Fr Francium (223)	88 Ra Radium (226)	89 Ac** Actinium (227)	104 Rf Rutherfordium (267)	105 Db Dubnium (268)	106 Sg Seaborgium (271)	107 Bh Bohrium (272)	108 Hs Hassium (277)	109 Mt Meitnerium (276)	110 Ds Darmstadtium (281)	111 Rg Roentgenium (280)	112 Cn Copernicium (285)	113 Nh Nihonium (286)	114 Fl Flerovium (289)	115 Mc Moscovium (290)	116 Lv Livermorium (291)	117 Ts Tennessine (294)	118 Og Oganesson (294)

f-block or inner-transition elements

* Lanthanoids	58 Ce Cerium 140.1	59 Pr Praseodymium 140.9	60 Nd Neodymium 144.2	61 Pm Promethium (145)	62 Sm Samarium 150.4	63 Eu Europium 152.0	64 Gd Gadolinium 157.3	65 Tb Terbium 158.9	66 Dy Dysprosium 162.5	67 Ho Holmium 164.9	68 Er Erbium 167.3	69 Tm Thulium 168.9	70 Yb Ytterbium 173.0	71 Lu Lutetium 175.5
** Actinoids	90 Th Thorium 232.0	91 Pa Protactinium (231)	92 U Uranium 238.1	93 Np Neptunium (237)	94 Pu Plutonium (242)	95 Am Americium (243)	96 Cm Curium (247)	97 Bk Berkelium (245)	98 Cf Californium (251)	99 Es Einsteinium (254)	100 Fm Fermium (253)	101 Md Mendelevium (256)	102 No Nobelium (254)	103 Lr Lawrencium (257)

f-Block Elements

- The f-block consists of two series **lanthanoids** (fourteen elements following lanthanum) and **actinoids** (fourteen elements following actinium) of the periodic table.
- The outermost electronic configuration of f-block elements is $(n-2)f^{1-14}(n-1)d^{0-1}ns^2$.
- Electronic configuration of actinoids are irregular.
- Elements of this block are also called **inner-transition elements.**
- Elements beyond uranium (at. no. 92) are man-made elements i.e., synthesised by man artificially. So, these are called **transuranium or synthetic elements**.
- All these elements are radioactive in nature. e.g., neptunium (Np), plutonium (Pu), americium (Am), curium (Cm), berkelium (Bk), californium (Cf), einsteinium (Es), mendelevium (Md), etc.

Determining Atomic Number and Mass Number of an Element

- The atomic number is defined, as the total number of protons present in the nucleus of an atom.
- The mass number is defined, as the sum of the total number of protons and neutrons present in the nucleus.
- For s-block elements, atomic number = number of valence electrons.
- For p-block elements, atomic number = 10 + number of valence electrons.
- For d-block elements, atomic number = ns electrons + $(n-1)$ d electrons.

Trends in Modern Periodic Table

The properties which are repeated at regular intervals are known as periodic properties. These properties show a regular order along a group and period.

1. Valency

- It is the combining capacity of an element to acquire noble gas configuration. It depends upon the number of valence electrons present in the outermost shell of its atom.
- **Along a period**, it generally increases from 1 to 7 with respect to hydrogen but with respect to oxygen, it first increases from 1 to 4 and then decreases to 0.
- **In a group**, outer electronic configuration is same for all the elements, so all have the same number of valence electrons and the valency.

2. Atomic Size

- It refers to the radius of an atom. It may be visualised as the distance between the centre of the nucleus and the outermost shell of an isolated atom.
- Moving along one period from left to right, atomic radius decreases. This is due to an increase in nuclear charge which tends to pull the electrons closer to nucleus and reduces the size of the atom. Thus, size of alkali metals is largest and that of halogens is smallest in a period.
- On moving from top to bottom, atomic size increases. This is because, new shells are being added, as we go down the group. This increases the distance between the outermost electrons and the nucleus.
- As a result, the atomic size increases inspite of the increase in nuclear charge.

3. Metallic and Non-metallic Properties

- It is the tendency of an element to form cation by the loss of electrons.
- Across a period, as the effective nuclear charge acting on the valence shell electrons increases, the tendency to lose electrons will decrease. Hence, **metallic character** decreases along a period.
- Down the group, the effective nuclear charge experienced by valence electrons decreases because the outermost electrons are farther away from the nucleus. Therefore, they can be lost easily. Hence, metallic character increases down a group.

4. Nature of Oxides

- Oxides of the metals are of basic nature while those of non-metals are acidic. This means that along a period, the basic character of the oxides of the elements decreases while their acidic character increases.
- On going down in a group, the basic character of oxides increases and acidic character of oxides decreases.

5. Electronegativity

- It may be defined as the relative electron attracting tendency of an atom from a shared electron pair in a covalent bond with other atom.
- The electronegativity of the elements increases along a period and decreases down the group.

Highest/Lowest Qualities of Some Elements

Element	Highest/Lowest Quality	Element	Highest/Lowest Quality
Hydrogen	Lightest element	Fluorine	Reactive non-metal
Osmium	Heaviest element	Tungsten	Highest melting point
Mercury	Liquid metal	Helium	Highest ionisation enthalpy
Bromine	Liquid non-metal	Caesium	Lowest ionisation enthalpy
Silver	Good conductor (metal)	Sodium	Placed in kerosene oil
Graphite	Good conductor (non-metal)	Calcium	Present in bones and teeth
Caesium	Reactive metal	Arsenic	Highly poisonous metal

05

Acids, Bases and Salts

(SOURCES)

Class-VII NCERT Chap 4 (Acids, Bases and Salts),
Class-X NCERT Chap 2 (Acids, Bases and Salts),
Class-XI NCERT Chap 6 (Equilibrium)
Tamil Nadu Board (Class-IX), NIOS

- All the chemical compounds can be classified on the basis of their chemical properties as acids, bases and salts.
- They have certain definite properties which distinguish these compounds from each other.
- The sour and bitter tastes of food are due to acids and bases present in them respectively. Yogurt, lemon juice, orange juice and vinegar are sour in taste because they contain **acids**.

Acids

The word acid comes from the Latin word **'acere'** which means **sour.**

Some Naturally Occuring Acids and their Sources

Acid	Natural Source
Acetic acid	Vinegar
Citric acid	Orange, lemon
Ascorbic acid (vitamin C)	Amla, citrus fruits
Tartaric acid	Tamarind, grapes, unripe mangoes
Oxalic acid	Tomato, spinach
Lactic acid	Curd (sour milk)
Formic acid (methanoic acid)	Ant's sting, nettle's sting

- According to **Arrhenius theory**, those substances which dissociate in aqueous solution to give only hydrogen ion (H^+) and do not give any other cation other than H^+ ion are called **acids.** So, it is clear that, hydrogen element is present in all acids.
- Following are the **physical** properties of acids :
  - Acids are sour in taste and soluble in water.
  - Acids turn blue litmus paper red.
  - Acids are corrosive in nature. Their action destroys cloth, wood, paper, skin etc.
- The following are the **chemical** properties of acids :
  - **Reaction with metals** Acid react with metal to form salt and hydrogen gas.

    Acid + Metal $\longrightarrow$ Salt + Hydrogen gas
  - **Reaction with metal carbonate and metal hydrogen carbonate** Limestone, chalk and marble are different forms of calcium carbonate.

    Acid reacts with metal carbonates and metal hydrogen carbonates (bicarbonate) to produce their corresponding salts, carbon dioxide and water.

    Acid + Metal carbonate/Metal hydrogen carbonate $\longrightarrow$ Salt + Carbon dioxide gas + Water
  - **Reaction with metallic oxides** The reaction between metal oxides and acids form salt and water.

    Acid + Metal oxide $\longrightarrow$ Salt + Water

Types of Acids

On the basis of studies, acids are categorised as follows :

(i) **Strong acids** They ionise completely in water to produce large number of H^+ ions.
e.g. Hydrochloric acid (HCl), sulphuric acid (H_2SO_4), nitric acid (HNO_3) etc.

(ii) **Weak acids** They partially ionise in water to produce small number of H^+ ions.
e.g. Carbonic acid (H_2CO_3), acetic acid (CH_3COOH), phosphoric acid (H_3PO_4) etc.

Bases

- The chemical substances which are bitter in taste and soapy to touch are called bases.

Some Bases and their Sources

Source	Bases
Lime water	Calcium hydroxide
Antacid (Milk of magnesia)	Magnesium hydroxide
Soaps	Sodium hydroxide/Potassium hydroxide
Window cleaner	Ammonium hydroxide

- According to **Arrhenius theory**, those chemical substances which after ionisation dissociate in water to give only hydroxide ions [OH^-] in the form of negatively charged ions are called **bases**.

Note Those bases which are soluble in water are called alkalis. So, all alkalis are bases but all bases are not alkalis.

- Following are the main physical properties of bases :
  - Bases are soluble in water.
  - They are bitter and pungent in taste.
  - They turn red litmus paper blue.
  - Like acids, bases also tend to be corrosive. This tendency is less than that of strong acids.
- Following are the chemical properties of bases :
  - **Reaction with metal** Strong bases react with active metals to generate hydrogen gas. Therefore, bases should not be kept in metal containers (active metals).
    Base + Metal $\longrightarrow$ Salt + Hydrogen gas
  - **Reaction with non-metallic oxide** Base reacts with non-metal oxide (acidic oxide) to form salt and water.
    This reaction proves the acidic nature of non-metal oxides.
    Base + Non-metallic oxide $\longrightarrow$ Salt + Water
  - **Reaction with acid** Bases destroy its effect by reacting with acids and form salt and water (H_2O).

Types of Bases

On the basis of ionisation, bases can be classified into two types :

(i) **Strong bases** They completely dissociate in water and produce hydroxide (OH^-) ions.
e.g. sodium hydroxide (NaOH), barium hydroxide [$Ba(OH_2)$], potassium hydroxide (KOH) etc.

(ii) **Weak bases** They partially dissociates in water.
e.g. ammonium hydroxide (NH_4OH), aluminium hydroxide [$Al(OH)_3$] etc.

Reaction between Acid and Base

- Acid reacts with base to produce salt and water with the evolution of heat.

$$\text{Acid} + \text{Base} \longrightarrow \underset{\text{(Heat is evolved)}}{\text{Salt} + \text{Water}}$$

This reaction is known as **neutralisation reaction.**

- The process of dissolving an acid or a base in water is extremely exothermic. Extreme care should be taken when adding concentrated nitric acid or sulphuric acid to water.
- Acid should always be added slowly to water with constant stirring. If water is added to a concentrated acid, the heat generated can cause the mixture to splash out and cause burns.

Aqueous Solution of Acids or Bases

- In presence of water, acid gives H^+ ions but it can't exist in the free state. So, these ions exists as H_3O^+ (hydronium ion).
- The aqueous solution obtained after dissolving an acid or base in water, conducts electricity because free ions are present in it. Due to this, the aqueous solution of bases give OH^- ion.

e.g.,
$$HCl + H_2O \longrightarrow H_3O^+ + Cl^-$$
$$H^+ + H_2O \longrightarrow H_3O^+$$
$$NaOH(s) \xrightarrow{H_2O} Na^+(aq) + OH^-(aq)$$

- Therefore, acids and bases conduct electricity due to the presence of free ions in their aqueous solutions.

Note All bases are not soluble in water.

Effect of Dilution on an Acid or Base

- Mixing of an acid or base with water is called **dilution**. It results in decrease in the concentration of ions $\left[\frac{H_3O^+}{OH^-}\right]$ per unit volume and the acid or base is said to be **dilute**.
- The flow of electric current in acidic solution is done by these ions present in the acid.

- Acid contains cation i.e. H^+ and anions such as Cl^- in HCl, NO_3^- in HNO_3, CH_3COO^- in CH_3COOH and SO_4^{2-} in H_2SO_4 since, the acid produces hydrogen ion (H^+) in the solution, it shows that they are acidic in nature.

Indicators

- To test whether a substance is acidic or basic, a special type of substances are used which is known as **indicators**.
- Turmeric, litmus, hibiscus petals are some of the naturally occuring indicators.
- Litmus solution is a purple colored pigment, which is extracted from Lichen plant of **Thallophyta group**. It is the most commonly used indicator. Generally, it is available in the form of red and blue litmus paper.
- Many natural substances such as red cabbage leaves, turmeric, hydrangea, petunia and geranium like colored petals of many flowers indicate the presence of acids and bases in a solution. These are called **acid-base indicators**.
- The substances whose odour varies in acidic or basic medium are called **odorous indicators**.

pH Scale

- A scale which is used for measuring hydrogen ion concentration in solution is called **pH scale**.
- The *p* in pH stands for 'potenz' which means power in German. On the pH scale we can measure pH generally from 0 (very acidic) to 14 (very alkaline).
- pH is a number which indicates the acidity or basicity of a solution. Higher the concentration of hydronium ion, lower will be the value of pH.
- The pH of any neutral solution is 7. If the value of a solution is less than 7 in the pH scale, then it will be acidic solution and if the pH value increases from 7 to 14, it indicates an increase in the concentration of OH^- in the solution. Hence, the solution will be alkaline.

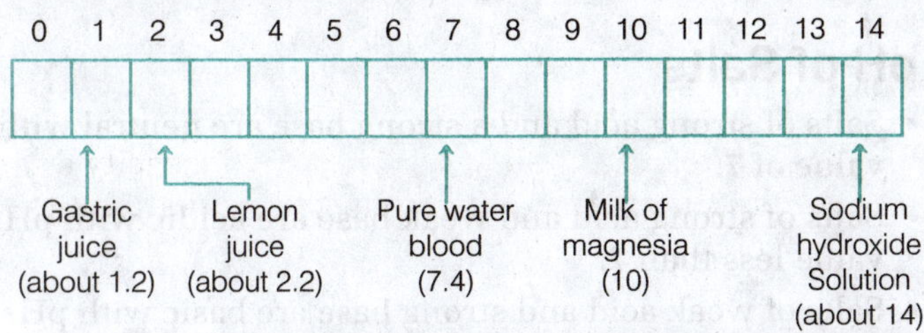

pH of some common substances shown on a pH paper

Importance of pH in Everyday Life

- Living organism can survive within a pH range of 7.0 to 7.8.
- When pH of rain water goes below 5.6, it is called **acid rain** which makes aquatic life difficult.
- Plants require a specific pH range for their healthy growth.

pH of Our Digestive System

- Our stomach produces hydrochloric acid. It helps in the digestion of food without harming the stomach.
- During indigestion the stomach produces too much acid and this causes pain and irritation.
- To get rid of this pain, people use bases called antacids such as magnesium hydroxide (milk of magnesia). These antacids neutralise the excess of acid.

pH Change Leads to Tooth Decay

- Decay of tooth enamel starts, when the pH of the mouth is lower than 5.5.
- Tooth enamel is made up of calcium phosphate and is the hardest substance in the body.
- The best way to prevent this is to clean the mouth after eating food.

Self-Defence by Animals and Plants Through Chemical Warfare

- Bee sting or ant bite leaves an acid into the skin which causes pain and irritation. Use of mild base like baking soda (sodium hydrogen carbonate) or calamine (zinc carbonate) on the stung area gives relief.
- Nettle is a herbaceous plant, which grows in forests. There are stinging hairs in its leaves which if accidentally touched, causes burning and pain, because these hairs release methanoic acid (HCOOH).
- Traditionally, it is treated by rubbing the leaves of the dock plant on the sting site.

Neutralisation in Everyday Life

When a basic solution is added to an acidic solution, both the solutions neutralise each other's effect. Following are the main examples of neutralisation in daily life :

- **Indigestion** When an ant bites, it pours acidic fluid into the skin. The effect of sting can be neutralised by adding moistened baking soda, sodium hydrogen carbonate ($NaHCO_3$) or calamine solution, which contains zinc carbonate.
- **Soil Treatment** To increase the fertility of soil, excessive acidic soil is treated with base like quick lime (calcium oxide) or slaked lime (calcium hydroxide). Excessive basic soil is treated with organic matter which releases acids. By this process, we can neutralises the nature of soil.
- **Factory Wastes** The wastes of factories contain acids which is neutralised by adding alkaline substances before discharging into water bodies and rivers.

Buffer Solutions

- The solution which resist the change in its pH value on addition of a small amount of acid or base are called buffer solutions.
- These solutions have a definite pH value.
- Acidic buffer solutions have pH value less than 7 i.e. equimolar mixture of acetic acid (CH_3COOH) and sodium acetate (CH_3COONa).
- Basic buffer solutions have pH value more than 7 i.e. equimolar mixture of ammonium hydroxide (NH_4OH) and ammonium chloride (NH_4Cl).
- pH of blood is maintained with the help of H_2CO_3/HCO_3^- buffer inspite of many acidic foods we eat.

Salts

- These are the compounds obtained by the reaction of acid and base, such reactions are called **neutralisation reaction.**
- Cation of the salt comes from a base while its anion comes from an acid.

$$NaOH + HCl \longrightarrow \underset{\text{Salt}}{NaCl} + H_2O$$

- If a normal salt is obtained from a weak acid and a strong base, the salt is called **alkaline salt,** as its aqueous solution turns red litmus blue.
  e.g. Na_2CO_3, CH_3COONa, $Na_2B_4O_7 \cdot 10H_2O$, etc.
- If the normal salt is obtained by the reaction of a strong acid with a strong base, the salt is called **neutral salt**, as its aqueous solution has no effect on litmus paper.
  e.g. NaCl, KCl, K_2SO_4, $NaNO_3$, $KClO_3$ etc.
- If the normal salt is obtained by the neutralisation of a strong acid and a weak base, the salt is called **acidic salt**, as its aqueous solution turns blue litmus red.
  e.g. $FeCl_3$, $ZnCl_2$, $HgSO_4$, $CuSO_4$, $FeSO_4$ etc.

Types of Salts

Different types of salts are as follows :

(i) **Common Salts** These are formed by the complete replacement of hydrogen atom from acid by a metal. e.g. KCl, NaCl, $FeSO_4$, KNO_3, K_2SO_4, $Ca_3(PO_4)_2$, Na_3BO_3 etc. The salts so obtained have no replaceable hydrogen atom.

(ii) **Acidic Salts** These are formed by the incomplete neutralisation of acids i.e. by the partial replacement of hydrogen $[H^+]$ atoms by base or metal. These salts still contain one or more replaceable hydrogen atoms in their molecules.
e.g. $NaHSO_4$, $NaHCO_3$, NaH_2PO_4 etc.

(iii) **Basic Salts** These are formed by the incomplete neutralisation of bases $[OH^-]$. These salts still contain one or more hydroxyl groups in their molecules.
e.g. Mg(OH)Cl, Zn(OH)Cl etc.

(iv) **Double Salt** It is the mixture of two salts and exists only in solid state. e.g. Potash alum $[K_2SO_4 \cdot Al_2(SO_4)_3 \cdot 24H_2O]$ and mohr salt $[FeSO_4 \cdot (NH_4)_2SO_4 \cdot 6H_2O]$ etc. Such salts give test of all the constituents present in their formula.

(v) **Complex Salts** These salts contain complex ion and also exist in solutions. A complex ion contains a central metal ion surrounded by a number of neutral or negative ions called the ligands. e.g. potassium ferrocyanide $K_4[Fe(CN)_6]$ contains a complex ion $[Fe(CN)_6]^{4-}$ and tetraamino cupric sulphate $[Cu(NH_3)_4]SO_4$ contains a complex ion $[Cu(NH_3)_4]^{2+}$.

(vi) **Mixed Salts** These salts give more than one cation or anion on dissolving in water. e.g. Bleaching powder ($CaOCl_2$), sodium potassium sulphate ($NaKSO_4$) and Rochelle's salt.

pH of Salts

- Salts of strong acid and a strong base are neutral with pH value of 7.
- Salts of strong acid and weak base are acidic with pH value less than 7.
- Salts of weak acid and strong base are basic with pH value more than 7.

Uses of Some Common Salts

Some of the salts are generally used in day to day life. Their description is as follows :

Sodium Chloride

- Sodium chloride (NaCl) is formed by the combination of hydrochloric acid and sodium hydroxide solution.

- It is obtained on large scale from sea water by separating other salts from it. It can also be obtained from rock salts.

Bleaching Powder

- Chlorine is formed by electrolysis of aqueous sodium chloride. This chloride gas is used for the production of bleaching powder.
- Bleaching Powder ($CaOCl_2$) is produced when dry slaked lime [$Ca(OH)_2$] is treated with chlorine.
- It undergoes auto-oxidation, if kept for longer time.
- The bleaching powder is used :
  - For bleaching clothes, cotton, wood pulp in laundry, in textile and paper industry.
  - As an oxidising agent in many chemical industries.
  - As a disinfectant for water.

Sodium Hydroxide

- Sodium hydroxide (NaOH) is produced, when electricity is passed through an aqueous solution of sodium chloride.
- This process is known as **chlor-alkali process** because of the products formed i.e. chlor for chlorine and alkali for sodium hydroxide.
- Chlorine gas is liberated at the anode and hydrogen gas is liberated at the cathode and sodium hydroxide solution is formed near the cathode.

Baking Soda

- The chemical name of the compound is sodium hydrogen carbonate ($NaHCO_3$). Sodium chloride is used as a basic substance in its preparation.
- Baking soda has been used in the manufacture of baking powder, which is a mixture of baking soda (Sodium hydrogen carbonate) and a mild edible acid such as a tartaric acid.
  It makes cake to rise, soft and spongy due to carbon dioxide produced, when mixed with water.
  $NaHCO_3 + H^+ \longrightarrow CO_2 + H_2O + \text{Sodium salt of any acid.}$
- Sodium hydrogen carbonate is also a component of antacids. Being alkaline, it provides relief by neutralising the excess acid in the stomach.
  It is used in soda-acid fire extinguishers and also acts as preservative for milk.

Washing Soda

- Washing Soda ($Na_2CO_3 \cdot 10H_2O$) is formed by recrystallisation of sodium carbonate which is obtained by heating baking soda.

$$\underset{\text{(Sodium carbonate)}}{Na_2CO_3} + 10H_2O \longrightarrow \underset{\text{(Washing soda)}}{Na_2CO_3 \cdot 10H_2O}$$

- It is white crystalline solid having alkaline nature.
- It is used in glass, soap and paper industries.
- It is used in manufacture of sodium compounds like borax.
- It also removes permanent hardness of water. It is used as a cleaning agent in houses and laundries.

Plaster of Paris (Calcium Sulphate Hemihydrate)

- Gypsum on heating gives up water molecules to form calcium sulphate hemihydrate at 373K. It is called Plaster of Paris $\left(CaSO_4 \cdot \frac{1}{2}H_2O\right)$.
- It is a white powder which further converted into gypsum providing a hard solid substance on mixing with water.
- Plaster of Paris has been used on the basis of the following points :
  - It is used to make toys.
  - It is used by doctors for joining fractured bones.
  - It is also used for making decorative pieces and for making design on ceilings.

Potassium Nitrate

- It is used in the production of gun powder, firecrackers, in glass industry, in production of fertilisers etc.

Copper Sulphate

- It is used as an insecticide, in electroplating, in colouration and printing and in the purification of copper.

Potash Alum

- It is used in the purification of water, blood clotting, in leather industry, in manufacturing drugs and as a colour bonding in colouration.

Extra Facts From Tamil Nadu Board and NIOS

- Sulphuric acid is called 'king of chemicals'.
- Citric acid is used in the preparation of effervescent salts and as a food preservative.
- Aqua-regia ($3HCl + HNO_3$) is used chiefly to dissolve metals such as gold and platinum.

06

Metals

[SOURCES]

Class-VIII Old NCERT Chap 4 (Materials : Metals and Non-metals), Class-X NCERT Chap 3 (Metals and Non-metals), Class-XII Old NCERT Chap 6 (General Principles and process of isolation of elements)

Element is the smallest entity by which a substance is made. To simplify the study of elements, they are categorised into three categories according to their physical and chemical properties :

(i) Metals (ii) Non-metals (iii) Metalloids

Metals

- Elements which forms positive ions by losing electrons are called **metals**. e.g., aluminium, copper, etc.
- In the periodic table, except the elements on the right corner, all other elements are metals.

Physical Properties of Metals

Physical properties of metals are as follows :

- **Physical State** Metals are generally hard, except some alkali metals like lithium, sodium, potassium, which are soft in nature. All metals (except mercury) exist as solid at room temperature.
- **Metallic Lusture** These have metallic lusture in their pure state. e.g., gold.
- **Ductility** These are generally ductile i.e., can be drawn into thin wires.
- **Malleability** Most of the metals are malleable i.e., can be beaten into thin sheets.
- **Electric and Thermal Conductivity** These are good conductor of heat and electricity.
- Silver and copper are the best conductors of heat. Lead and mercury are comparatively poor conductors of heat.
- **Melting and Boiling Point** Metals have high melting points. Gallium and caesium have low melting points. Tungsten has the highest melting point.
- **Sonority** Metals are sonorous.

Chemical Properties of Metals

Metals exhibit many chemical properties. Prominent ones among them are as follows

(i) Reaction of Metals with Oxygen

- Almost all metals combine with oxygen to form metal oxides.

$$\text{Metal} + \text{Oxygen} \longrightarrow \text{Metal oxide}$$

e.g., Aluminium and copper, when heated in air form aluminium oxide and copper oxide, respectively.

$$2Cu + O_2 \longrightarrow 2CuO$$
$$4Al + 3O_2 \longrightarrow 2Al_2O_3$$

- Metal oxides are basic in nature.
- The metal oxides which react with both acids as well as bases to produce salt and water are called **amphoteric oxides.** Some metal oxides such as aluminium oxide and zinc oxide are amphoteric.
- Metallic oxides are insoluble in water. Some of them dissolve in water to form hydroxides known as **alkali**.

(ii) Reaction of Metals with Water

- Metals react with water and produce a metal oxide and hydrogen gas.
- Further metal oxides react with water to form metal hydroxide.

$$\text{Metal} + \text{Water} \longrightarrow \text{Metal oxide} + \text{Hydrogen}$$

$$\text{Metal oxide} + \text{Water} \longrightarrow \text{Metal hydroxide}$$

- Potassium, sodium and calcium reacts violently with cold water to produce hydroxide and hydrogen gas with heat.
- The reaction of calcium with water is less violent. The heat evolved is not sufficient for the hydrogen to catch fire.

$$Ca(s) + 2H_2O(l) \longrightarrow Ca(OH)_2(aq) + H_2(g)$$

- Calcium floats over water because the bubbles of hydrogen gas formed stick on the surface of the metal.
- Aluminium, iron and zinc only reacts with steam to form metal oxide and hydrogen.
- Lead, copper, silver and gold do not react with water at all.

(iii) Reaction of Metals with Acids

- Reactive metals react with dilute sulphuric acid and hydrochloric acid to produce salt and hydrogen gas.
- Due to strong oxidising nature of nitric acid, it does not evolve hydrogen gas on reaction with metals.
- Dilute nitric acid oxidises the hydrogen produced to water and itself gets reduced to any of the nitrogen oxide (N_2O, NO, NO_2).
- Only magnesium and manganese react with very dilute nitric acid to evolve hydrogen gas.

(iv) Reaction of Metals with Solution of other Metal Salts

- More reactive metals can displace less reactive metals from their compounds in solution or molten form.

e.g., $Fe + CuSO_4(aq) \longrightarrow FeSO_4(aq) + Cu\downarrow$

Reactivity Series of Metals

The reactivity series is a list of metals arranged in the order of their decreasing activities.

On the basis of their relative tendency to lose electron and their reactive nature, metals are arranged in a series, this series is called **activity series or reactivity series of metals.**

Reactivity Series (Activity Series) of Metals

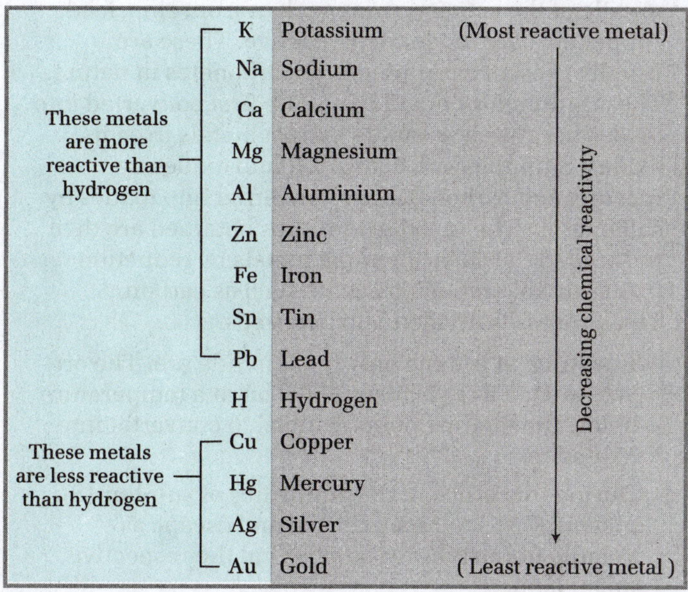

Occurrence of Metals

- The earth's crust is the major source of metals.
- Sea water also contains some soluble salts like sodium chloride, magnesium chloride etc.
- The elements or compounds which occur in earth's crust is known as **minerals.**
- Minerals from which metals can be extracted conveniently and profitably are known as **ores.**
- All ores are minerals but all minerals are not ores.
- Generally, metals occurs in the state of oxides, sulphides, carbonates, halides and sulphates.

Concentration of Ores

Removal of the unwanted materials (gangue or impurities) from ore is called **ore concentration**, dressing or benefaction.

Extraction of Metals from Ores Concentration

The process of obtaining pure metal from its ore is called extraction of metals or **metallurgy.**

This is a process of reduction of metal compound present in the ore. Thus, the various techniques used for extraction of metals based on their position in activity series. Hence, it is divided into three categories.

(i) **Metals of Low Reactivity** Metals low in activity series are very unreactive. The oxides of these metals can be reduced to metals by heating alone.

e.g. $\underset{\text{(Cinnabar)}}{2HgS(s)} + \underset{\text{(From air)}}{3O_2(g)} \xrightarrow{\Delta} \underset{\text{(Mercuric oxide) or Mercury (II) oxide}}{2HgO(s)} + 2SO_2(g)$

$$2HgO(s) \xrightarrow{\Delta} 2Hg(l) + O_2(g)$$

(ii) **Metal of Medium Reactivity** The metals in the middle of the activity series such as iron, zinc, lead, copper etc., are moderately reactive. These are usually present as sulphides or carbonates in nature. These sulphides or carbonates are first converted into oxides because it is easy to extract metals from its oxides. Sulphides are converted into oxides by roasting and carbonates are converted into oxides by calcination. The metal oxides thus obtained are then reduced to the corresponding metals by reduction using suitable reducing agents such as carbon. This process is divided into two steps.

(a) **Roasting** It is done only for sulphide ore. The ore is heated in a regular supply of air at a temperature below the melting point of metal to convert it into oxide ore.

During this process, the impurities of sulphur (S), arsenic (As), etc., get oxidised and escape as volatile impurities leaving behind the respective metal oxide.

e.g., $CuFeS_2 + 3O_2 \xrightarrow{\Delta} CuO + FeO + 2SO_2$

(b) **Calcination** It involves heating of ore with or without the presence of air. It is done in case of carbonate, hydroxide and oxide ores of metals. These substances get decomposed to respective oxides as major product.

e.g. $ZnCO_3(s) \xrightarrow{\text{Heat}} ZnO(s) + CO_2(g)$

(iii) **Metals of high Reactivity** The metals high up in the reactivity series are very reactive. They cannot be obtained by heating with carbon or any other reducing agent. It is due to their high affinity for oxygen than carbon. Therefore, electrolytic reduction is employed for metals like Na, Mg, Ca etc.

Reduction of Metal Oxide to Metal

- **Smelting** It is the process of heating an metal oxide ore above its melting point with suitable reducing agent like carbon in the form of coke. Metals in the middle of activity series are reduced by this process.

e.g., $PbO + CO \xrightarrow[\text{temperature}]{\text{High}} Pb(\text{molten lead}) + CO_2\uparrow$

Sometime displacement reactions can also be used to reduce metal oxides to metals. The highly reactive metals such as sodium, calcium, aluminium etc are used as reducing agents.

- Oxides of metals such as chromium and manganese are reduced by aluminium.

e.g., $Cr_2O_3 + 2Al \longrightarrow Al_2O_3 + 2Cr$

- **Auto-Reduction** It is used for metals low in the activity series. The oxides of these metals such as Cu, Hg, Pb can be reduced to metals by heating alone.
- **Electrolytic reduction Method** It is used for metals high in the activity series such as sodium, aluminium, calcium, etc. Their oxides are reduced to metals by this process. The salts of these metals like chloride in molten form are electrolysed. Metal is deposited at the cathode (the negative electrode) and chlorine is liberated at the anode (the positive electrode).

e.g.

These reactions are as follows

At cathode, $Na^+ + e^- \rightarrow Na$ (Reduction)

At anode, $2Cl^- \rightarrow Cl_2 + 2e^-$ (Oxidation)

- Sodium is obtained by electrolysis of sodium chloride.
- **Refining** A metal extracted by any method is usually contaminated with some impurities. The process of extraction of pure metals from their impure or crude form under suitable conditions, is called refining of metal.

It depends upon the nature of element (metal) as well as the nature of associated impurities.

For obtaining metals of high purity, several techniques are used as follows :

- **Distillation** Purification of Zn, Cd, Hg metals is done by this method as they are low boiling metals.
- **Liquation** Metals such as tin, mercury, lead are purified by this method as they have low melting point.
- **Electrolytic Refining** Metals such as copper, silver, gold, aluminium and lead are purified by this method.
- Impure metal acts as anode, pure metal acts as cathode and salt of metal acts as an electrolyte.
- **Zone Refining** This method is useful for producing semiconductor and other metals of very high purity. e.g., Germanium, silicon, boron, gallium and indium. It is based on the principle that impurities are soluble in the molten than in the solid state of metal.
- **Vapour Phase Refining** In this method, the metal is converted into its volatile compound and then it is decomposed to give pure metal.
- **Mond's Process** It is used for nickel (Ni).

$$\underset{\text{Impure}}{Ni} + 4CO \longrightarrow \underset{\text{Volatile and stable}}{Ni(CO)_4} \xrightarrow{\Delta} \underset{\text{Pure}}{Ni} + 4CO$$

- **Van Arkel Process** It is used for zirconium (Zr) and titanium (Ti).

$$\underset{\text{Impure}}{Ti} + 2I_2 \longrightarrow TiI_4 \xrightarrow[1600°C]{\Delta} \underset{\text{Pure}}{Ti} + 2I_2$$

- **Chromatographic Method** It is based on the principle that different components of mixture are differently absorbed.

Corrosion

- It is the process of oxidative deterioration of a metal surface by the action of environment to form unwanted corrosion products. e.g., conversion of iron into rust ($Fe_2O_3 \cdot xH_2O$), tarnishing of silver (due to the formation of Ag_2S), development of green coating of $Cu(OH)_2 \cdot CuCO_3$ (basic copper carbonate) on copper and bronze. It is basically an electrochemical process. Corrosion of iron is called **rusting**.
- It is accelerated by the presence of impurities, H^+, electrolytes such as NaCl and gases such as O_2, CO_2, SO_2, NO, NO_2 etc.

Alloy

- An **alloy** is a homogeneous mixture of two or more metals or a metal and a non-metal. It is prepared by mixing the metals in molten form and then cooling the mixture.
- **Pure gold** is very soft. It is called **24 carat gold.** To increase the strength and hardness of gold and to make it suitable for making jewellery, alloy of gold is made either with silver or copper.

  For example, 22 carat gold means 22 parts pure gold mixed with 2 parts of Cu or Ag.
- If an alloy contains mercury as one of its components, it is called **amalgam**. Silver amalgam is used in dental filling. The properties of an alloy is modified as compared to pure metals according to the purpose for with it can be used than that of pure metals, e.g., brass (an alloy of copper) and zinc (Cu and Zn).
- **Nichrome** (Ni-Cr) is an alloy of nickel (Ni), chromium (Cr) and iron (Fe). The coil of an electric heater is made of nichrome.

Components and Uses of Some Alloys

Name of Alloy	Components	Uses
Brass	Copper + Zinc	In making utensils and decorative materials.
Steel	Iron + Carbon	In buildings, infrastructure, tools, ships, automobiles, appliances and weapons.
Stainless Steel	Steel + Nickel + Chromium	In making utensils, surgical tools and medical equipment, in architect, automotive and aerospace applications etc.
Solder	Lead + Tin	Soldering is a process of joining two or more metals by heating
Bronze	Copper + Tin	In making bronze bearings, spark free tools, coins, medals, sculptures and musical instruments.
Duralumin (a hard, light alloy)	Aluminium + Copper + Magnesium + Manganese	Widely used in aircraft construction and in making cookwares.
German Silver	Copper + Nickel + Zinc	It is extensively used because of its hardness, toughness and resistance to corrosion for articles such as tableware, marine fittings and plumbing fixtures. Because of its high electrical resistance it is also used in heating coils.
Alnico	Iron + Aluminium + Nickel + Cobalt	Used to make permanent magnet.
Nichrome	Nickel + Iron + Chromium + Manganese	Used in heating elements.

Some Other Important Metals and Compounds

- **Tungsten** (W) it's melting point is 3500°C. It is produced from Degana mines located in Rajasthan. Bulb has a filament made up of tungsten. This filament is thermally isolated and the bulb is filled with chemically inactive nitrogen or argon gas to prolong the life of filament.
- **Titanium** (Ti) is used to make boats because it is not corroded by sea water.
- **Zirconium** (Zr) has the property of absorbing neutrons. Hence, it is used in nuclear furnace.
- **Chromium** (Cr) is used in magnetic recording products such as Audio cassettes and VHS tapes.
- **Francium** (Fr) is a radioactive liquid metal.
- **Stannous sulphide** (SnS_2) is also called mosaic gold.
- **Palladium** (Pd) is used in the manufacture of aircrafts.
- **Caesium** (Cs) is used in photoelectric cells.
- **Barium sulphate** ($BaSO_4$) (Barium-meal) is used as the helpful compound during X-ray testing of human stomach because barium is a good absorber of X-rays. Hence, it helps to show clearer pictures of the stomach than other areas.
- **Potassium bromide** (KBr) is used in photography, potassium nitrate (KNO_3) in gun powder and monopotassium tartarate in bakery.
- **Potassium carbonate** (K_2CO_3) is known as pearl ash.
- **Osmium** (Os) is the heaviest metal.

Non-Metals

(SOURCES)

Class-VIII Old NCERT Chap 4 (Materials : Metals and Non-metals),
Class-VIII NCERT Chap 3 (Coal and Petroleum),
Class-VIII NCERT Chap 4 (Combustion and Flame),
Class-X NCERT Chap 3 (Metals and Non-metals),
Class-X NCERT Chap 4 (Carbon and Its Compounds),
Class-XI Old NCERT Chap 9 (Hydrogen)

Those elements which form negative ions by gaining electrons are called **non-metals.** The non-metals are less in number than metals. e.g., Carbon, sulphur, iodine, oxygen, hydrogen etc.

The non-metals are either solids or gases except bromine, which is a liquid.

Physical Properties of Non-Metals

Physical properties of non-metals are as follows :

- **Lustre** Non-metals do not have lustre, i.e., shining surface. However, diamond, graphite (the allotropic forms of carbon) and iodine have lustre, even though they are non-metals.
- **Electrical and thermal conductivity** Non-metals are generally poor conductors of heat and electricity. Graphite, an allotrope of carbon, is a good conductor of electricity.
- **Brittleness** Non-metals are brittle in nature. For example, sulphur is a brittle solid. If it is hammered, it breaks into pieces.
- **Malleability and ductility** Non-metals are neither malleable nor ductile, i.e., they cannot be beaten into thin sheets or drawn into wires.
- **Physical state** Most of the non-metals are soft (if solid). Only diamond, an allotropic form of carbon is the hardest known substance.
- **Melting and boiling points** Generally, non-metals have low melting and boiling points. But non-metals that are solids have comparatively higher boiling points. e.g., B, Si, C etc.
- **Sonorous** Non-metals are generally non-sonorous. They do not produce a sound on striking a hard surface.
- **Solubility** Non-metals are generally highly soluble in many liquids. For example, S (sulphur) is soluble in CS_2 (carbon disulphide) and I_2 (iodine) is soluble in Cl_2 (chlorine).

Chemical Properties of Non-Metals

Non-metals also exhibit many chemical properties. Some of these are as follows :

- **Reaction of Non-metals with Oxygen** Non-metals react with oxygen to give oxides. These oxides are acidic in nature.

  $$C(s) + O_2(g) \longrightarrow CO_2(g) \text{ (Acidic)}$$

  Carbon and sulphur react with oxygen to form oxides; which on reaction with water gives respective acid.

  $$CO_2(g) + H_2O(aq) \longrightarrow \underset{\text{(Carbonic acid)}}{H_2CO_3(aq)}$$

- **Reaction of Non-metals with Water** Non-metals does not react with water.
- **Reaction of Non-metals with Acid** Non-metals does not react with dil. acids.

  The reason is that they act as an electron acceptor and cannot supply electrons to the H^+ ions of acids to reduce them to hydrogen gas. But on heating, readily form oxides or salts with conc. acids.

  e.g. $S(s) + 2H_2SO_4(\text{Conc.}) \xrightarrow{\text{Heat}} 3SO_2(g) + 2H_2O(l)$

  $S(s) + 6HNO_3(\text{Conc.}) \xrightarrow{\text{Heat}} H_2SO_4(aq) + \underset{\text{(Reddish brown vapour)}}{6NO_2(g)} + 2H_2O(aq)$

- **Reaction of Non-metals with Chlorine** Non-metals reacts with chlorine to form various chlorides.

  e.g. $\underset{\text{Phosphorus}}{P_4} + \underset{\text{Chlorine}}{6Cl_2} \longrightarrow \underset{\text{Phosphorus trichloride}}{4PCl_3(g)}$

- **Reaction of Non-metals with Hydrogen** Non-metals react with hydrogen to form corresponding hydrides.

  e.g. $\underset{\text{Nitrogen}}{N_2(g)} + \underset{\text{Hydrogen}}{3H_2} \longrightarrow \underset{\text{Ammonia}}{2NH_3(g)}$

  $\underset{\text{Carbon}}{C(s)} + \underset{\text{Hydrogen}}{2H_2(g)} \longrightarrow \underset{\text{Methane}}{CH_4(g)}$

Uses of Non-metals

- 'Oxygen' is very important for life. It is taken during respiration by all the living organisms.
- Nitrogen is used for the growth of plants.
- Chlorine is used during the purification of water.
- Iodine with violet blue colour is used as an antiseptic.
- Sulphur and phosphorus are also used in fire-crackers.

Carbon

- Carbon (C) is the **seventeenth most abundant element** by mass in earth's crust. Its atomic number is 6 and mass number is 12.
- It is widely distributed in nature in free as well as in combined state.
- In elemental state, it is available as **coal, graphite** and **diamond**. However in combined state, it is present as metal carbonates, proteins, carbohydrates, hydrocarbons, CO_2 (0.03%) in air and other complex compounds.
- Carbon is an element that react with another molecules (such as H_2, O_2, Cl_2, S etc) to form compounds that are used in medicines or formation of plastics.
- The chemistry of carbon is based on the compounds of carbon. It is important for living organisms.
- In nature, two isotopes of carbon are stable, i.e., ${}^{12}_{6}C$ and ${}^{13}_{6}C$. Another isotope, ${}^{14}_{6}C$ is also present.
- ${}^{14}_{6}C$ is a radioactive isotope (half-life 5770 years) and emits β-rays.
- ${}^{12}_{6}C$ is taken as an international standard of atomic weight, which is expressed in atomic mass units (amu).
- Carbon being the first element in the group shows different characteristics. It is due to small size, high electronegativity, high ionisation enthalpy and absence of *d*-orbitals.
- Carbon atoms link with one another through covalent bonds to form chains and rings. This property of self linking is called **catenation**.
- Due to the property of catenation, carbon is able to exist in allotropic forms.

Allotropes of Carbon

- Carbon exhibits many allotropic forms; both crystalline as well as amorphous.
- Diamond, graphite and fullerene are crystalline forms of carbon.
- While carbon black, coke, wood charcoal, coal, etc are its amorphous forms.
- **HW Kroto, E Smalley** and **RF Curl** in 1985 discover another allotrope known as **fullerene**.

Diamond

- It is a three-dimensional giant molecule of carbon in which C-atoms (sp^3-hybridised) are arranged tetrahedrally by utilising their sp^3 hybrid orbitals.
- The C—C bond distance is 154 pm.
- Each C-atom seems to lie at the centre of a regular tetrahedron and is linked to four surrounding C-atoms lying at the corners of the tetrahedron through strong covalent bonds.

Graphite

- Graphite possess layered structure.
- The sheet or layers are held together by relatively weak **van der Waals' forces**. The C—C bond distance is 141.5 pm.
- The distance between two successive layers is 340 pm.
- Its hybridisation is sp^2 having 3 covalent bonds with 3 other C-atoms in the same plane.

- The 4th electron of C does not participate in the bonding, remains free and is responsible for electrical conductivity of graphite.
- The bonding between layers involve only the van der Waals' forces (weak forces) hence, these layers can slide over each other. This gives softness, greasiness and lubricating character to graphite.

Fullerenes

- These are prepared by heating graphite in an electric arc in the presence of inert gases like He or Ar.
- The vapour on condensation give sooty material that mainly contains C_{60} with smaller quantity of C_{70} and traces of fullerenes have even number of carbon atoms upto 350 or above.
- The structure of fulleren is smooth without any dangling bonds.

Buckminster fullerene

- It is a type of fullerene with formula C_{60}.
- It has a cage-like fused ring structure that resemble a soccer ball, made of 20 hexagons and 12 pentagons, with a carbon atom at each vertex of each polygon, and a bond along each polygon edge.
- Six-membered rings are fused with both six membered as well as five membered rings while five membered rings are attached only with six-membered rings.
- Each carbon atom in the structure, forms three σ bonds with other three carbon atoms and the fourth electron remains free (i.e., sp^2 hybridised).

Uses of Carbon

- Light weight composites materials of the high strength are obtained by embedding graphite fibres in plastic material.
- These composites are used in products such as tennis rockets, fishing rods, aircrafts and canoes.
- **Activated charcoal** (because of its highly porous nature) is used to absorb poisonous gases.
- It removes organic contaminators from the filters and control odour in air conditioning system.
- **Carbon black** is used as a black pigment in black ink and as filler in automobile tyres. It is used in making electrodes because it is a good conductor of electricity due to the presence of free electrons.

Hydrogen

- It has the simplest atomic structure among all the elements around us in nature. In atomic form, it consists of only one proton and one electron but no neutron.
- However, in elemental form it exists as a **diatomic** (H_2) molecule and is generally called **dihydrogen**.

Position of Hydrogen in the Periodic Table

- It is the first element in the periodic table. Its electronic configuration is $1s^1$.
- It resembles with alkali metals as well as with halogens in some properties. So, it is best placed separately in the periodic table.
- Just like alkali metals, hydrogen readily loses its one and only electron to form hydrogen ion (H^+). And like halogens, chalcogens, hydrogen requires only one electron to achieve the nearest inert or noble gas configuration.
- Like alkali metals, it combines with electronegative elements like halogens, oxygen, sulphur to form halides, oxides and sulphides.

Occurrence of Hydrogen

- **Dihydrogen** is the most abundant element in the universe (70% of the total mass of universe). It is the principal element in the solar atmosphere.
- The giant planets Jupiter, Saturn and stars consist mostly of hydrogen.
- However, due to its light nature, it is much less abundant in the Earth's atmosphere.
- It constitutes about 15.4% of the Earth's crust and the oceans.
- Besides water, it is also present in plant and animal tissues, carbohydrates, proteins, hydrides including hydrocarbons, coal, petroleum and many other compounds.

Isotopes of Hydrogen

- There are three isotopes of hydrogen: protium (^1_1H), deuterium (^2_1H) and tritium (^3_1H).
- **Protium** has atomic number and mass number equal to 1. It is stable form without any neutron.
- **Deuterium** is also known as **heavy hydrogen** which has atomic number = 1 and mass number = 2. It has one neutron.
- **Tritium** is radioactive in nature. It has atomic number and mass number 1 and 3, respectively. Its half life period is 12.4 years.

Compounds of Hydrogen

The compounds of hydrogen are discussed as follows :

Water

- A major part of all living organisms is made up of water.
- Human body has 65% (about) and some plants have as much as 95% water.

- 97% part of the entire water is assumed to be confined in oceans while rest is present in pure form. **Rain water** is the purest form of water.

Properties of Water

- It is colourless and tasteless liquid. In pure form, it is neutral. Its pH is 7.
- Due to the presence of extensive H-bonding between water molecules, it has high freezing point, high boiling point, high heat of vaporisation, high heat of fusion in comparison to H_2S and H_2Se and exists in liquid state.
- In comparison to other liquids, water has a higher specific heat, thermal conductivity, surface tension, dipole moment and dielectric constant, etc.
- Due to its high specific heat, it is a good coolant and is used to cool the engines of cars, buses, trucks, etc.
- Due to its high dielectric constant, it is an excellent solvent for the transportation of ions and molecules required for plant and animal metabolism.
- Due to H-bonding with polar molecules, even covalent compounds like alcohols and carbohydrates (glucose, sugar) dissolve in water.
- Crystalline form of water is **ice**. At room temperature crystallisation of ice forms hexagonal lattice but at very low temperature, it condenses to given cubic form.
- Density of ice is lesser than water. As a result, it floats on water.
- In winters, the layer of ice on water provides thermal insulation to the aquatic animals.

Soft and Hard Water

- The water free from soluble salts of calcium and magnesium, is called **soft water.** It gives lather with soap.
- Presence of calcium and magnesium salts (mainly) and iron salt in the form of hydrogen carbonate, chloride and sulphate in water makes water hard.
- The **hard water** cannot be used for washing clothes with soap because it contains Ca^{2+} and Mg^{2+} ions, which react with soap (i.e., sodium stearate, $C_{17}H_{35}COONa$ or, other sodium or potassium salt of higher fatty acids) to form scum or precipitate of Ca/Mg stearate.
- Hard water is also harmful for boilers as the salts present in hard water get deposited in the form of scale and thus reduce the efficiency of the boilers.

Temporary Hardness

This type of hardness occurs due to presence of magnesium and calcium hydrogen carbonates. The methods used to remove temporary hardness are as follows :

- **By boiling** During boiling, the soluble $Mg(HCO_3)$ is converted into insoluble $Mg(OH)_2$ and $Ca(HCO_3)$ changed to insoluble $CaCO_3$. These precipitates can be removed by filtration.
- **Clark's method** (or calcium hydroxide method) In this method calculated amount of lime is added to hard water. It precipitates out calcium carbonate and magnesium hydroxide which can be filtered off.

Permanent Hardness

It is because of the presence of chlorides and sulphates of calcium and magnesium in the water. It is called permanent hardness as it cannot be removed by simple boiling.

Following methods can be employed to remove this type of hardness :

- **By using washing soda (Sodium carbonate)** When hard water is treated with washing soda, the soluble chlorides and sulphates of calcium and magnesium get converted into their insoluble carbonates, which can be filtered off.
- **Calgon's method (Sequestration)** Sodium hexametaphosphate ($Na_6P_6O_{18}$), commercially called Calgon or Graham's salt, when added to hard water, the following reacting take place.

$$Na_6P_6O_{18} \longrightarrow 2Na^+ + Na_4P_6O_{18}^{2-}$$

$$M^{2+} + Na_4P_6O_{18}^{2-} \longrightarrow [Na_2MP_6O_{18}]^{2-} + 2Na^+$$

(where, $M = $ Mg, Ca)

- **Ion exchange method or zeolite or permutit method** Hydrated sodium aluminium silicate ($NaAlSiO_4$) is also known as **permutit or zeolite.** However, for the sake of simplicity, it can also be represented as NaZ (where, $Z = Al_2Si_2O_8 \cdot xH_2O$).

$$2NaZ(s) + M^{2+}(aq) \longrightarrow MZ_2(s) + 2Na^+(aq)$$

(where, $M = $ Mg, Ca)

- When all the sodium of the permutit is used up, the permutit is called **exhausted.** It can be regenerated by passing 10% solution of sodium chloride through it.

$$\underset{\text{Exhausted zeolite}}{MZ_2(s)} + 2NaCl(aq) \longrightarrow \underset{\text{Regenerated zeolite}}{2NaZ(s)} + MCl_2(aq)$$

(where, $M = $ Ca or Mg and $Z = Al_2Si_2O_8$)

- **Synthetic resins method** This method is superior than permutit method as all types of cations (Na^+, Ca^{2+}, Mg^{2+}etc.) and anions (Cl^-, SO_4^{2-}, HCO_3^- etc.) can be removed by this method.
- These resins contain large organic molecules with reactive acidic group such as R—SO_3H or

R—COOH group and are water insoluble. (Here, R = giant hydrocarbon framework).

$$2M\text{Na}(s) + M^{2+}(aq) \longrightarrow R_2M(s) + 2\text{Na}^+(aq)$$

- When hard water is treated with cation exchange resins, the Na^+, Ca^{2+}, Mg^{2+} and other cations present in the hard water get exchanged with H^+. Consequently protons are released which makes the water acidic.

$$2R\text{—H}(s) + M^{2+}(aq) \longrightarrow MR_2(s) + 2\text{H}^+(aq)$$

(where, M = Ca or Mg)

- During anion exchange process, OH^- ions are generated which neutralise the H^+ions obtained during cation exchange.

$$R\text{NH}_2(s) + \text{H}_2\text{O}(l) \longrightarrow R\text{NH}_3^+ \cdot \text{OH}^-(s)$$

$$\underset{\text{Anion exchange resins}}{R\text{NH}_3^+ \cdot \text{OH}^-(s)} + \underset{\text{From hard water}}{X^-(aq)} \longrightarrow R\text{NH}_3^+ \cdot X^-(s) + \text{OH}^-(aq)$$

- The exhausted cation and anion exchange resins are regenerated by treating them with dilute acids and alkalies, respectively.

Heavy Water (D_2O)

- It is generally obtained by exhaustive (or multistage) electrolysis of ordinary water as shown by **Washburn** and **Urey**.
- Used as a moderator in nuclear reactors as it slows down the fast moving neutrons and thus helpful in controlling the nuclear reactions.
- It is used for the preparation by deuterium (by electrolysis) or deuterium compounds by exchange reactions.

Hydrogen Peroxide (H_2O_2)

- It is very important to control environmental pollution. It is used as effluents.
- It is light blue in pure anhydrous form, odourless syrupy liquid (due to H-bonding), produces blister on skin and soluble in water, alcohol and ether has bitter taste.
- Preparation of H_2O_2 is important due to its industrial use. Some of its uses are :
  - It is used in hair bleach and as a mild disinfectant. It has germicidal and antiseptic properties, so it is used for washing cuts, wounds, ears etc., and in gargles under the name perhydrol (30% solution of H_2O_2).
  - Many important chemicals like sodium perborate and percarbonate that are used in high quality detergents are obtained from hydrogen peroxide.
  - Certain compounds like hydroquinone, tartaric acid etc. and certain food products and pharmaceuticals like cephalosporin are synthesised from hydrogen peroxide.

Nitrogen

- Molecular nitrogen comprises of 78% by volume of the atmosphere.
- In the earth's crust, it occurs as **Chile saltpetre** (sodium nitrate) and **Indian saltpetre** (potassium nitrate).
- In plants and animals, it is found as proteins. Plants take it from the soil in the form of nitrates. It is the main component of urea (46% N).
- Liquid N_2 is used a refrigerant to preserve biological materials, food items.

Compounds of Nitrogen

- **Ammonia** (NH_3) It has a pungent smell and is a colourless gas.
  It is highly soluble in water. It is used to manufacture various compound (NH_4NO_3, urea, ammonium phosphate and ammonium sulphate).
- **Nitric acid** (HNO_3) It is used for the preparation of explosives such as nitroglycerin (dynamite), trinitrotoluene (TNT), trinitrophenol (TNP), etc., and other organic compounds.
  It is used in the pickling of stainless steel and etching of metals.

Sulphur

- It is the **sixteenth most abundant element** and constitutes 0.03-0.1% by mass of the earth's crust.
- It occurs in the combined form as sulphide ores as galena (PbS), zinc blende (ZnS), copper pyrites ($CuFeS_2$) and sulphate ores, such as gypsum ($CaSO_4 \cdot 2H_2O$), epsom salt ($MgSO_4 \cdot 7H_2O$), baryte ($BaSO_4$).
- It is also present as H_2S in natural gas and crude oil and organosulphur compounds in oil shales and coal.
- Some organic materials such as eggs, proteins, garlic, onion, mustard, hair and wool also contain sulphur.

Compounds of Sulphur

Sulphur dioxide (SO_2)

- It is used in refining petroleum and sugar. It acts an antichlor, disinfectant and preservative.
- It is used in bleaching wool and silk.
- Liquid SO_2 used as a solvent.
- It is used in the preparation of industrial chemicals like H_2SO_4, $NaHSO_3$, $CaHSO_3$, etc.

Sulphuric acid (H_2SO_4)

- It is used as an important industrial chemical for the manufacture of hundreds of other compounds.
- It is used in heavy amount (e.g., ammonium sulphate, superphosphate etc.) in the manufacture of fertilisers.

Uses of Sulphur

Some of the important uses of sulphur are as follows :

- As a laboratory reagent.
- In petroleum refining and manufacture of paints, pigments and dyestuff intermediates.
- In detergent industry and metallurgical applications like electroplating, galvanising, etc.
- In storage batteries.
- In the manufacturing of nitrocellulose membrane.

Halogen

- Fluorine, chlorine, bromine, iodine and astatine belong to group 17 and are collectively known as **halogens**. Greek word '*halo*' means 'salt' and 'genes' means 'born', i.e., salt producers. These are highly reactive non-metallic elements.
- The elements of group 17 show more similarity amongst themselves.
- There is a regular gradation in their physical and chemical properties found in this group. Astatine is a radioactive element.
- Fluorine and chlorine are fairly abundant while bromine and iodine are less.
- Fluorine is present mainly as insoluble **fluorides** [fluorspar (CaF_2), cryolite (Na_3AlF_6) and **fluoroapatite** [$3Ca_3(PO_4)_2 \cdot CaF_2$]. It is present in small quantities in soil, river water plants bones and teeth of animals.
- Sea water contains chlorides, bromides and iodides of sodium, potassium, magnesium and calcium but is mainly sodium chloride solution (2.5% by mass).
- The deposits of dried up seas and beds of inland lakes contain sodium chloride and carnallite ($KCl \cdot MgCl_2 \cdot 6H_2O$) and calcium chloride ($CaCl_2$).

Noble Gases

- Group 18 consists of six elements i.e. helium, neon, argon, krypton, xenon and radon. All these are gases and chemically unreactive. They form very few compounds, that's why, these are termed as **noble gases**.
- All the noble gases except radon occur in the atmosphere. Their atmospheric abundance in day air is nearly 1% by volume; of which argon (0.93%) is the major constituent.
- Helium is also present in natural gas to the extent of 2 to 7%.
- He and sometimes Ne are found in minerals of radioactive origin. e.g., pitch blende monazite, cleveite. **Xenon** and **radon** are the rarest elements of this group.
- Uses of noble gases are as follows :
  - **Helium (He)** It is used in filling balloons for meteorological observations as it is a non-inflammable and light gas. It also used in gas-cooled nuclear reactors and as diluent for oxygen in modern diving apparatus because of its very low solubility in blood. Liquid helium is used as a cryogenic agent for carrying out various experiments at low temperatures.
  - **Neon (Ne)** It is used in discharge tubes and fluorescent bulbs for display in advertisement. Its bulbs are used in botanical gardens and in greenhouses. It is used in voltage regulators and indicators.
  - **Argon (Ar)** It is used to provide an inert atmosphere in high temperature metallurgical process (arc welding of metals or alloys) and for filling electric bulbs. it is used in rectifier and in valves.
  - **Krypton (Kr)** It is used in high-efficiency miners' cap lamps.

Extra Facts From Tamil Nadu Board and NIOS

- Graphite is the only non-metal which is a good conductor of electricity but poor conductor of heat.
- Diamond is a better conductor of heat than copper but poor conductor of electricity.

08

Carbon Compounds

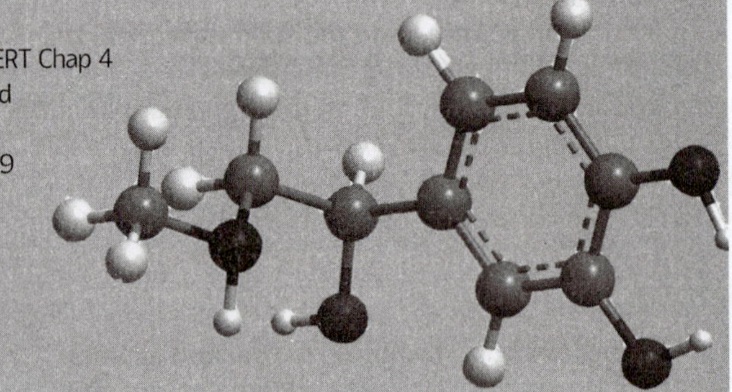

[SOURCES]

Class-VIII NCERT Chap 3 (Coal and Petroleum), Class VIII NCERT Chap 4 (Combustion and Flame), Class-X NCERT Chap 4 (Carbon and its Compounds), Class-XI NCERT Chap 8 (Organic Chemistry some basic Principle and Techniques). Class XI NCERT Chap 9 (Hydrocarbons), Class-XII NCERT Chap 6 (Haloalkanes and Haloarenes), Chap 7 (Alcohols, Phenols and Ethers), Chap 8 (Aldehydes, Ketones and Carboxylic acids) Tamil Nadu Board (Class-IX), NIOS

- Hydrocarbons and their derivatives i.e. carbon compounds with the exception of CO, CO_2, carbonates and bicarbonates are called **organic compounds.**
- A Swedish chemist **Berzelius,** proposed that a vital force was responsible for the formation of organic compounds **(Vital Force Theory).**
- In 1828, **Wöhler** synthesised the first organic compound 'urea' accidentally, when he was trying to prepare ammonium cyanate from the inorganic compounds ammonium sulphate and potassium cyanate.

Petroleum : Source of Organic Compounds

The mixture of hydrocarbons mainly aliphatic with lesser amounts of aromatic hydrocarbons is called petroleum. It also contains a small amount of organic compounds of sulphur and nitrogen.

Various Constituents of Petroleum and their Uses

Constituents of Petroleum	Uses
Petroleum gas in liquid form (LPG)	Fuel for home and industry
Petrol	Motor fuel, aviation fuel, solvent for dry cleaning
Kerosene	Fuel for stoves, lamps and for jet aircrafts
Diesel	Fuel for heavy motor vehicles, electric generators
Lubricating oil	Lubrication
Greases, vaseline, petroleum jelly	Pharmaceutical preparations
Paraffin wax	Ointments, candles, waxed papers
Asphalt or tar (bitumen)	Paints, road surfacing

Petrochemicals

- Many useful substances are obtained from petroleum and natural gas. These are known as 'petrochemicals'.
- Some petrochemicals are **saturated hydrocarbons** (methane, ethane, propane etc.) **unsaturated hydrocarbons** (ethylene, propylene, butylene, etc), **aromatic hydrocarbons** (benzene, toluene), alcohols, formaldehyde, acetone, acetic acid, vaseline etc.
- Petrochemicals are used in the manufacture of detergents, fibres, polythene and other man-made plastics.
- Hydrogen gas obtained from natural gas is used in the production of fertilisers (urea). Due to its commercial importance, it is also called **black gold.**

Calorific Values of Different Fuels

Name of the Fuel	Calorific Value (kJ/g)
Charcoal	33
Coal	25-33
Wood	17-22
Cow dung cake	6-8
Kerosene	45
Fuel oil	48
Ethyl alcohol	30
Hydrogen	150
Methane	55
Butane	55
Biogas	35-40

Classification of Organic Compounds

Organic compounds can be classified in the following manner :

- **Acyclic or Open Chain Compounds** These compounds are also called aliphatic compounds. They consist of straight or branched open chains.
- **Alicyclic or Closed Chain Compounds** They contain carbon atoms joined in the form of a ring (homocyclic).
- Sometimes, atoms other than carbon are also present in the ring (heterocyclic).
- **Aromatic Compounds** This word was taken from the word 'aroma' which means smell. These compounds include benzene (six carbon ring compound with alternate single and double bonds) and other related ring compounds (benzenoid).
- Like alicyclic compounds, aromatic compounds may also have hetero atom in the ring (heterocyclic aromatic compounds).

Homologous Series

- The group of compounds in which the same functional group substitutes for hydrogen in a carbon chain are called homologous series.
- Members of a homologous series are called **homologues.** For example methane (CH_4), ethane (C_2H_6), propane (C_3H_8), butane (C_4H_{10}) belong to straight chain alkanes.
- Similarly, methyl alcohol (CH_3OH), ethyl alcohol (C_2H_5OH), propyl alcohol (C_3H_7OH), butyl alcohol (C_4H_9OH) and amyl alcohol ($C_5H_{11}OH$) are the homologues of alcohol series. This phenomenon is called **homology**.

Isomerism

Organic compounds with identical molecular formula but different configuration or properties are called **isomers** and this phenomenon is called **isomerism.**

There are two types of isomerism :

(i) Structural Isomerism

This isomerism is exhibited by the compounds having the same molecular formula but different structures i.e. **structural isomers.** e.g. *n*-pentane, *iso*-pentane and *neo*-pentane have same molecular formula C_5H_{12} but they have different structures.

n-pentane → $H_3C-CH_2-CH_2-CH_2-CH_3$

iso-pentane → $H_3C-CH(CH_3)-CH_2-CH_3$

neo-pentane → $H_3C-C(CH_3)_2-CH_3$

(ii) Stereoisomerism

This isomerism is due to the difference in relative position of their atoms or molecules in space. Stereoisomerism is of two types; geometrical and optical isomerism.

Hydrocarbons

The term 'hydrocarbon' means **compounds of hydrogen** and **carbon only**.

Their natural source is petroleum or crude oil. Hydrocarbons are of different types.

Depending upon the types of carbon-carbon bonds present, they can be classified into three main categories :

1. Saturated Hydrocarbons

They contain carbon-carbon and carbon-hydrogen single bonds. These are of two types :

(i) **Alkanes or Paraffin** The word paraffin is derived from a latin word meaning less affinity, thus these are chemically inert (or unreactive) towards most of the chemicals.

In these compounds, different carbon atoms are joined together to form open chain of carbon atoms with single bonds. General formula for alkanes is C_nH_{2n+2} (where, $n = 1, 2, 3...$). Methane is the first member of this family.

Other members of this family with increasing order of molecular mass is ethane (C_2H_6) < propane (C_3H_8) < butane (C_4H_{10}) < pentane(C_5H_{12}) < hexane (C_6H_{14}) < heptane (C_7H_{16}).

Methods or Marsh Gas (CH_4)

- It is generally released through the septic tank. Wet and marshy land is also a major source of methane. Decomposition of vegetable generates methane.
- In laboratory, it is prepared by heating the mixture of sodium acetate and soda lime. Commercially, it is prepared by the reaction of aluminium carbide on water.
- Its mixture with air is explosive and sometimes, it is responsible for explosion in coal mines.
- Its shape is tetrahedral with 109°28′ angle and it is black in colour.
- It is mainly used as a fuel to produce light and energy, in the preparation of important organic compounds like methyl alcohol, chloroform etc., carbon black (printing ink), hydrogen (at industrial level) and in making motor tyre.

(ii) **Cycloalkanes** In cycloalkanes, carbon atoms form a closed chain or a ring. General formula for cycloalkanes is $C_n H_{2n}$. Cyclopropane (C_3H_6) is the first member of this family.

Distance between two carbon atoms bonded through a single bond is always larger than that present between two carbon atoms joined together through multiple bonds (double or triple bond). Thus, C—C bond length in ethane is greater than that of ethyne, ethene and benzyne.

2. Unsaturated Hydrocarbons

They contain carbon-carbon multiple bonds i.e. double bonds, triple bonds or both.

These are of two types :

(i) **Alkenes** They contain atleast one carbon-carbon double bond. These are also known as **olefins** (oil forming). General formula for alkenes is C_nH_{2n}.

The first member of alkene is **ethylene** or **ethene** (C_2H_4) was found to form an oily liquid on reaction with chlorine.

- **Ethylene** (C_2H_4) is prepared by heating ethyl alcohol with conc. H_2SO_4 at 170°C. It is used in making mustard gas, in ripening fruits artificially, in oxyethylene flame, in fruit preservation and as an anaesthesia. Trichloroethylene is also used for dry cleaning purposes.
- **Butene** ($CH_3CH_2CH=CH_2$) is a constituent of liquefied petroleum gas and used as a fuel.

(ii) **Alkynes or Acetylenic Hydrocarbon** They contain atleast one carbon-carbon triple bond. Their general formula is C_nH_{2n-2}. Ethyne (C_2H_2 **acetylene**) is the first member of this family. Reaction of acetylene with silver nitrate shows its acidic property.

- **Acetylene** (C_2H_2) It was prepared for the first time by American scientist **Wilson**. It is prepared by the reaction of calcium carbide on water.

It is used in the synthesis of benzene, in oxy-acetylene welding and cutting (flame temperature –3200°C) as a raw material for plastics, in making camphor, in making neoprene (artificial rubber) and in the form of anaesthesia.

3. Aromatic Hydrocarbons

These hydrocarbons are also known as **arenes.** Most of them possess pleasant odour (Greek word aroma means pleasant smelling).

Most of these compounds contain benzene ring.
e.g. **Benzene, toluene, naphthalene, anthracene** etc.
General formula for arenes is $C_n H_{2n-6}$.

- **Benzene** (C_6H_6) was first isolated by **Michael Faraday** in 1825 from the cylinders of compressed illuminating gas obtained by the pyrolysis of whale oil. **Hofmann** obtained benzene by fractional distillation of coaltar.

  It was first synthesised by **Berthelot** by passing acetylene through red hot tube. It is used in the production of various organic compounds, manufacturing of explosives, dry cleaning of clothes (woollen), as a solvent and fuel in motor vehicle when mixed with petrol.

- **Toluene** ($C_6H_5CH_3$) was first extracted from **tolu balsam**, a resin.

  It is used in the manufacturing of trinitrotoluene (TNT) explosives, as antifreezer, as solvent, in making chloramine-T drug and in artificial sweetener saccharin.

Organic Compounds Containing Carbon, Hydrogen and Oxygen

These are alcohols, phenols, ethers, aldehydes, ketones, carboxylic acids, acid anhydrides and esters.

Alcohols

- These are formed when a hydrogen atom of aliphatic hydrocarbon is replaced by —OH group (alcoholic group).
- General formula for alcohol is $C_nH_{2n+1}OH$. Alcohols may be classified as mono, di, tri or polyhydric compounds depending on whether they contain one, two, three or more hydroxyl groups, respectively.
  e.g., **Monohydric alcohol**—methanol, ethanol etc.
  Dihydric alcohol — glycol
  Trihydric alcohol — glycerol
- Presence of this group is identified by esterification test.
- Formation of pleasant smelling compound with carboxylic acid shows the presence of alcohol.

Methyl Alcohol or Methanol (CH_3OH)

- It is produced by the destructive distillation of wood, that's why also called **wood spirit**. It is also obtained by heating formaldehyde with potassium or sodium hydroxide. Sodium or potassium formate is also formed during the reaction.
- It is a colourless poisonous liquid with wine like odour.
- Its ingestion in small amount causes blindness (because it affects optic nerve) and in large amount causes death.
- In liver, methanol is oxidised to methanal which reacts rapidly with the cells. It causes coagulation of protoplasm.
- It is used as a solvent, in paints varnishes and in the production of artificial colours, formaldehyde and denatured alcohol as a fuel by mixing petrol in it.

Ethyl Alcohol or Ethanol (C_2H_5OH)

- Industrially, it is prepared by the fermentation of molasses (by product of sugar industry) or starched food grains. It is also prepared by treating ethene with water (steam) in the presence of phosphoric acid.

$$\underset{\text{Ethene}}{CH_2 = CH_2} + H_2O \xrightarrow{H_3PO_4} \underset{\text{Ethanol}}{CH_3CH_2OH}$$

- It is a colourless volatile liquid. It is used as a solvent in varnishes, paints etc. It is used in making transparent soaps, perfumes, iodine tincture, polish, in the production of wine and a number of carbon compounds. It is also used as fuel in spirit lamp, stones and for cleaning wound.
- When ethanol is ingested in large quantities, it slows down the metabolic processes and depresses the central nervous system. The individual may feel relaxed but does not realise that his sense of judgement, timing and muscular coordination have been seriously impaired.

Ethylene Glycol ($CH_2OH—CH_2OH$)

- It is a dihydric alcohol with sweet taste and used as antifreezer (to depress the freezing point of water and petrol) in radiator of cars in cold regions.

Glycerol or Glycerine ($CH_2OHCHOHCH_2OH$)

- It is an extremely hygroscopic substance which is used in making explosives such as trinitroglycerine by the treatment with conc. HNO_3 in the presence of concentrated sulphuric acid and dynamite etc.
- It is also used in making stamp ink, shoe polish, medicines, cosmetics, lubricants, antifreezer wine, transparent soaps etc. Parts of watches are cleaned by it. It also acts as fruit preservator.
- Glycerol is found in fats and vegetable oils in the form of esters. In the free state, it is found in fermented sugar solution and in human blood.

Phenols (C_6H_5OH)

- These are formed, when a hydrogen atom in an aromatic hydrocarbon is replaced by —OH group (alcoholic group).
- Phenol is the simplest hydroxy derivative of benzene. Ferric chloride test is used to indicate presence of phenols.
- It is commonly known as **carbolic acid** and was prepared by **FF Runge** in 1834. It is used to prepare many compounds like salol, bakelite, phenolphthalein, aspirin, salicylic acid, phenyl (a household germicide) and in explosives like picric acid.

Ethers

- These are formed when a hydrogen atom in a hydrocarbon is replaced by alkoxy or aryloxy (R—O/Ar—O) group. e.g. dimethyl ether, diethyl ether, ethyl methyl ether etc.
- General formula for ethers is $C_nH_{2n+2}O$.
- Diethyl Ether ($C_2H_5OC_2H_5$) is commonly called ether also. It is obtained by heating ethanol with Conc. H_2SO_4 at 140°C. Other method for its synthesis is Williamson synthesis. It is used as an anaesthesia as it is better than chloroform.

Aldehydes

- These organic compounds contain —CHO functional group (aldehyde group). General formula for aldehydes is $C_nH_{2n}O$. e.g., formaldehyde (HCHO), acetaldehyde (CH_3CHO), etc. These are identified by **Tollen's reagent, Fehling solution and Schiff's reagent.**
- **Formaldehyde** (HCHO) It is used as a tissue fixative and embalming agent. It is used as a disinfectant and its 40% aqueous solution (solution in water,) called **formalin**, is used as preservative for biological specimens i.e. in embalming biological materials.

Ketones

- These organic compounds contain $> C{=}O$ functional group (ketonic group).
- General formula for ketones is $C_nH_{2n}O$ or $(C_nH_{2n+1})_2CO$. e.g. acetone or dimethyl ketone, ethyl methyl ketone, etc.

Carboxylic Acids

- Carbon compounds containing a —COOH functional group (carboxyl group) are called carboxylic acids.
- General formula for carboxylic acid is $C_nH_{2n}O_2$. e.g. formic acid (HCOOH), acetic acid (CH_3COOH) etc.

Formic Acid (HCOOH)

- It was prepared firstly by the distillation of water with red ants so named as formic acid (In Latin formica means ants).
- It is used in rubber, leather textile, dyeing and electroplating industry, in the production of medicines of arthritis and various compounds.
- It is also used as insecticide and fruit juice preservative.

Acetic Acid (CH_3COOH)

- On commercial scale, it is obtained from pyroligneous acid.
- It is a common laboratory reagent and is used to form various organic compounds like alcohol, acid as a solvent and as vinegar in food.
- Its 4-6% aqueous solution is called vinegar. It is also used in making photographic film, rayon (as cellulose acetate) and jelly.

Oxalic Acid ($C_2H_2O_4$)

- It is a dicarboxylic acid which is present in the family of plants as oxalis and rumex, in the form of potassium-hydrogen salt.
- It is used in metallurgy, in colouration and printing of clothes.
- It is used in cleaning the spot of ink (10% solution) and bleaching of leather.
- It is also used in photography in the form of ferrous oxalate. It is also used for making ink and coaltar for colouring and printing clothes.

Lactic Acid [$CH_3CH(OH)COOH$]

- It is a monohydroxy carboxylic acid.
- It is present in milk and provides it sour taste.
- It is also produced in muscles during exercise. So, human beings feel tired due to its accumulation.
- It is more soluble in water as compared to organic solvents is because of the formation of hydrogen bonding. It is used in food products to produce yogurts.
- It is also used in detergents, pharmaceutical and cosmetic industries.

Salicylic Acid [$C_6H_4(OH)COOH$]

It is a white crystalline aromatic acid used in the medicines (pain killers and skin ointment).

Citric Acid

It is a monohydroxy tricarboxylic acid. It occurs in all citrus fruits such as lemon, orange etc.

Esters

- These organic compounds contain —COO*R* functional group and have fruity smell.
- General formula of this class is $C_nH_{2n}O_2$ or $C_nH_{2n+1}COOR$. e.g., methyl formate ($HCOOCH_3$), methyl acetate (CH_3COOCH_3), ethyl acetate ($C_2H_5COOCH_3$) etc.
- Ethyl acetate is used for making artificial perfumes, scented colour, dyes, etc.

Some Other Important Organic Compounds

- **Chloroform** ($CHCl_3$) It was discovered by **Liebig** in 1831. It is stored in closed dark coloured bottles completely filled because it is oxidised in air slowly to produce a poisonous gas, phosgene (carbonyl chloride).

  It was used as anaesthesia for the first time by Simpson who later used it in surgical operations.
- **Iodoform** (CHI_3) It is a yellow crystalline sublimative substance with specific odour. It is prepared in the haloform reaction by the reaction of iodine, NaOH and ethanol.

  It is insoluble in water and soluble in alcohol and ether. It was used earlier as an antiseptic, the antiseptic properties are due to the liberation of free iodine not due to iodoform itself. It is a bactericidal substance.
- **Chlorofluorocarbons (CFCs) (Freons)** These are extremely stable, unreactive, non-toxic, non-corrosive and easily liquefiable gases. Freon-12 is one of the most common freons in industrial use. These are used in refrigeration and air conditioning purposes and in aerosol propellants. They play a significant role in ozone layer depletion.
- **Aniline** ($C_6H_5NH_2$) (Aminobenzene) It is an amine derivative and took its name from a Portuguese word 'anil' means 'indigo'. **Otto Unverdorben** synthesised it for the first time by the distillation of lime water and indigo in 1826.

  Ferdinand Runge obtained it from coaltar and **Fritsche** by heating indigo with conc. alkali. It is used in the preparation of various compounds like sulphonilic acid, nitroaniline and in explosives. It is used in the preparation of drugs, coloured dye and Zwitter ion. It is also used in rubber industry.

  Methyl Isocyanide (CH_3NC) It is used in the production of rubbers, adhesives and in pesticides. Leakage of this gas from union carbide company of USA in 1984 led the Bhopal Gas Tragedy in which thousands of people were killed.
- **Gammaxene or Benzene Hexachloride (BHC) or Lindane** It is prepared by reaction of benzene and chlorine in presence of sunlight. It is used as an insecticide and in pharmaceutical industries.

- **Naphthalene** ($C_{10}H_8$) It is a polynuclear hydrocarbon. Its major source is coaltar. It is used as an germicide and moth repellent.
- **Chlorobenzene** (C_6H_5Cl) It is prepared by treating benzene with chlorine in the presence of iron as catalyst.

$$\underset{\text{Benzene}}{C_6H_6} + \underset{\text{Chlorine}}{Cl_2} \xrightarrow[\text{Dark}]{\text{Fe}} \underset{\text{Chlorobenzene}}{C_6H_5Cl} + \underset{\text{Hydrochloric acid}}{HCl}$$

Industrially, it is prepared by **Raschig process.**

It is used in manufacturing of phenol, aniline, etc.

- **Dichloromethane** (CH_2Cl_2) It is used as solvent for paint remover, propellant in aerosols, in metal cleaning etc.
- **Dichloro Diphenyl Trichloroethane** (DDT) It is used as an insecticide for mosquito and lice, and have many industrial applications.
- **Urea** (NH_2CONH_2) It was the first organic compound synthesised in laboratory. It was extracted for the first time from urine in 1773. It is a colourless, odourless substance that is soluble in water. It is a polyhalogen compound.

  In it, the nitrogen content is 46%. That's why it is used as fertiliser and for the production of baronial medicines, formaldehyde-urea, plastics etc.

Explosive Substances

These are the substances which on combustion produce extreme heat and energy with a strong cracking sound. They consist of pure compound like TNT or a mixture of fuel and an oxidiser. Explosives can be classified as primary explosives, secondary explosives and tertiary explosives.

- **Trinitroglycerine** (TNG) It is also called **Noble's oil** and prepared by mixing C and Conc. HNO_3 in glycerine. So, it is an ester. It is a colourless oily liquid used in making dynamite, invented in 1846.
- **Trinitrotoluene** (TNT) It is prepared by the reaction of toluene with nitrating mixture (Conc. H_2SO_4 and Conc. HNO_3). It is frequently used as an explosive. It was firstly invented in 1863 but commercially used for the first time by UK.
- **Research and Development Explosive** (RDX) Chemically, it is cyclotrimethylene trinitramine. It is also known as **cyclonite** (in USA), **hexogen** (in Germany) and **T4** (in Italy). It was firstly invented by Henning in 1899. It is also called **plastic exploder**. It is a very powerful explosive and can be used in plastic explosives.
- When plastic substance like polybutenic acrylic acid is added to RDX, it is called **Plastic Bonded Explosive** (PBE). The explosion energy in normal RDX is nearly 1510 kcal. When some aluminium powder is added to RDX, explosive C-4 is obtained which is deadly destructor (cracker).
- **Trinitrophenol** (TNP) It is prepared by the reaction of phenol with Conc. H_2SO_4 and Conc. HNO_3. It is also called **picric acid.** It is ultra exploder explosive.
- **Dynamite** It was invented by Swedish chemist and engineer **Alfred Nobel** in 1863. It consists of three parts; nitroglycerin, one part diatomaceous earth (Kieselguhr) and a small mixture of sodium carbonate. It is used in blast purposes in mines.

Extra Facts From Tamil Nadu Board and NIOS

- Rectified spirit contains 95.5% of ethanol and 4.5% of water.
- Methylated spirit contains 95% of ethanol and 5% of methanol.
- Power alcohol is a mixture of petrol and ethanol.
- Denaturated spirit is a mixture of ethanol with pyridine.
- TFM (Total Fatty Matter) is one of the important factors to be considered to assess the quality of soap. Soap with higher TFM is considered a good bathing soap.

Food Preservatives and Biomolecules

[SOURCES]

Class-XII NCERT Chap 10 (Biomolecules),
Old NCERT Chap 16 (Chemistry in Everyday life)

- Living systems are made up of various non-living complexes, named as biomolecules, like carbohydrates, proteins, nucleic acids, lipids, etc. **Carbohydrates** and **proteins** are essential constituents of our food.
- These biomolecules interact with each other and form molecular logic of life processes.
- In addition, some simple molecules such as **vitamins** and **minerals** also play an important role in the functioning of living organisms.

Carbohydrates

- According to modern definition, carbohydrates are optically active polyhydroxy aldehydes or ketones or the compounds producing these molecules, when subjected to hydrolysis.
- General formula of the carbohydrates is $C_x(H_2O)_y$.
  e.g., Glucose [$C_6H_{12}O_6$ or $C_6(H_2O)_6$], fructose, sucrose, etc.
- These are primarily produced by plants. Cereals (wheat, maize, rice), potato, turnip, beet root, banana, etc. are the major sources of carbohydrates.

Classification of Carbohydrates

On the basis of their behaviour on hydrolysis, carbohydrates are divided into following three groups :

(i) **Monosaccharides** These are most simple form of carbohydrate, which further cannot be hydrolysed. e.g., Triose (glyceraldehyde), tetrose (erythrose), pentose (ribose), hexose (glucose, fructose), etc.

(ii) **Oligosaccharides** They give 2 to 10 monosaccharide units upon hydrolysis. e.g., sucrose (sugarcane), maltose, lactose, etc all give two molecules of monosaccharides on hydrolysis, so these are also called **disaccharides**.
On hydrolysis, sucrose gives two molecules each of glucose and fructose whereas maltose gives two molecules of glucose.

(iii) **Polysaccharides** They yield a large number of monosaccharide units upon hydrolysis. e.g., starch, cellulose, gums, glycogen, etc. These are usually, insoluble in water and extracted from plants.

- On the basis of physical properties, they are classified as :

(i) **Sugars** It is the class of carbohydrates, which are sweet in taste. e.g., Sucrose, lactosemilk sugar etc.

(ii) **Non-sugars** They refer to the carbohydrates, which are not sweet in taste. e.g., all polysaccharides.

- On the basis of their reducing properties, classification is as follows :
  (i) **Reducing carbohydrate** They reduce Tollen's reagent into silver mirror and Fehling's solution into red precipitate.
  e.g., all monosaccharides and common disaccharides (except sucrose).
  (ii) **Non-reducing carbohydrates** They are unable to reduce Tollen's reagent and Fehling's solution.
  e.g., Sucrose and all the other higher saccharides.

Some Common Carbohydrates

- **Glucose** ($C_6H_{12}O_6$) is also known as **dextrose**. It is present in sweet fruits, ripe grapes and honey. It is commercially obtained from starch upon hydrolysis. It is the main sugar which is metabolised by the body for energy. It's concentration in blood stream ranges between 70-115 mg/100 mL. It provides instantaneous energy to the human body.
- **Fructose** ($C_6H_{12}O_6$) is also known **as fruit sugar**. It is present in honey, other fruits and high fructose corn syrup. Natural fructose is also called **leavulose**. It is used in medicinal syrup, toffies etc.
- **Sucrose** ($C_{12}H_{22}O_{11}$) is obtained from sugarcane and is also known as cane sugar. On hydrolysis, it gives glucose and fructose in equal amounts and the product is called **invert sugar**. It is an excellent preservative which is present in many jarred foods like jams.
- **Maltose** ($C_{12}H_{22}O_{11}$) is composed of two unit of glucose. It is also known as **malt sugar** and used in alcohol production.
- **Lactose** ($C_{12}H_{22}O_{11}$) is found in milk of mammals. i.e., 4-6% in cow's milk and 5-8% in human milk. So, it is called milk sugar and composed of galactose and glucose.
- **Starch** $(C_6H_{10}O_5)_n$ is found in cereals, roots, tubers and some vegetables. It gives maltose on digestion which further decomposes to glucose. It is a polymer of glucose and it consists of two components i.e., **amylose** (water soluble) and **amylopectin** (water insoluble).
- **Cellulose** $(C_6H_{10}O_5)_n$ occurs exclusively in plants and is predominant constituent of cell wall of plant cells. It is a straight chain polysaccharide of glucose. It is used for making shatterproof glass.
- **Glycogen** In animal body, carbohydrates are stored as glycogen, so it is also known as animal starch which is present in liver, muscles and brain.

Protein

- These are the most abundant biomolecules in the living world. Its main sources are milk, cheese, pulses, peanuts, fish and meat, etc.
- They are present in every part of the body and form the fundamental basis of structure and functions of life.
- It is also necessary for growth and maintenance of the body. The word protein is derived from the Greek word, **proteios** which means **primary** or of prime **importance**. All proteins are polymers of α-amino acids.

Amino Acids

- The acids which contain amino (—NH_2) and carboxyl (—COOH) functional groups is known as amino acid.
- These acids can be classified into α, β, γ, δ and so on depending on the relative positions of the amino group with respect to the carboxyl group. They are obtained by hydrolysis of proteins.
- All α-amino acids have some particular names that indicate the properties or sources of these compounds.
- Each amino acid is usually represented by a three letter symbol.

Structure of Proteins

- Proteins are polymers of α-amino acids. These are held together by **peptide bonds**. Chemically, a peptide bond is a amide formed between the —COOH group and the —NH_2 group.
- It is formed, when the reaction occur between the molecules of the same or different amino group of one molecule and carboxyl group of another molecule. As a result, a water molecule is liberated and a peptide bond —CO—NH— is formed. Since, the product is formed by two amino acids, hence it is called **dipeptide**. e.g., When the carboxyl group of glycine combines with the amino group of alanine, we get a dipeptide i.e. glycylalanine. If a third amino acid combines with a dipeptide, the product is called a **tripeptide**.

It consists of three amino acids that are held together by two peptide bonds.

- Similarly when four, five or six amino acids combine, the resulting products are called **tetrapeptides, pentapeptides or hexapeptides**.
- When the number of amino acids is more than ten, the products are called **polypeptides.**
- A polypeptide containing more than 100 amino acid residues and whose molecular mass is more than 10,000 u is called a **protein.**

Classification of Proteins

On the basis of molecular shape, proteins are classified as follows :

(i) **Fibrous protein** in which polypeptide chains run parallel and held together by hydrogen and disulphide bonds. These type of proteins are generally insoluble in water. e.g., myosin, keratin etc.

(ii) **Globular protein** in which polypeptide chains coil around to give a spherical shape.

These type of proteins are soluble in water e.g., insulin, albumin etc.

Denaturation of Proteins

- When protein is subjected to physical change such as change in temperature or chemical change (change in pH), then chaos arises in hydrogen bonds. Due to which the globule opens and the helix becomes uncoiled. As a result, protein loses its biological activity. This is called the denaturation of proteins.
- During denaturation, the **secondary** and **tertiary** structures are destroyed but primary structure remains unaffected.
- The **coagulation** of egg on boiling is a common example of denaturation.
- Another example is **curdling**, which is caused due to the production of lactic acid by the bacteria present in milk.

10

Chemistry in Everyday Life

[SOURCES]

Class-VIII Old NCERT Chap 3 (Synthesised Fibres and Plastics), Class-XII Old NCERT Chap 16 (Chemistry in Everyday Life)
Class-XII NCERT Chap 10 (Biomolecule)

- Basic principles of chemistry influence almost every aspect of human life. They are used for the benefit of mankind.
- Explosives, fuels, rockets, propellants, building materials, electrical equipment etc are used in day-to-day life.
- Chemistry has affected our lives so much that we do not even realise that all our activities are conducted by chemicals.

Following chemicals are used in daily life :

Fibres

These are long thread-like structures. Fabrics (cloths) are made from fibres.

These are of following three types :

(i) **Natural Fibres** These are obtained from plants or animals. These are biodegradable. Plant fibres consist of cellulose therefore these are used in the manufacture of paper and textile. e.g. cotton, hemp, jute flax etc.

Animal fibres consist of proteins. e.g. silkworm silk, spider silk, wool etc.

(ii) **Semisynthetic Fibres** These are obtained by treated natural fibres with some chemicals. For example, rayon is obtained by the chemical treatment of wood pulp (cellulose a natural fibre). Cellulose is first treated with cold sodium hydroxide and then carbon disulphide to obtain viscose. That's why rayon is sometime called **viscose rayon**.

(iii) **Synthetic Fibres** These are obtained from chemicals in laboratories or industries.

These are of various types like carbon fibre, nylon, polyester, metallic fibre, silicon carbide fibre, etc.

Some Synthetic Fibres, their Monomers and Uses

Fibre	Monomers	Uses
Nylon	Hexamethylenediamine $NH_2(CH_2)_6NH_2$ and adipic acid $HOOC-(CH_2)_4-COOH$	In making tooth brushes, parachute, net of fish trapping, garments, etc.
Polyester (dacron/ terylene)	Ethylene glycol $H_2COH-CH_2OH$ and terephthalic acid $HOOC-C_6H_4-COOH$	In making cloths, hose pipes of fire extinguisher.
Carbon fibres	Carbon	In making the parts of space vehicles and sports items.
Orlon (synthetic wool)	Acrylonitrile $CH_2=CH-CN$	As a substitute of wool for making blankets etc.

Drugs

Chemicals of low molecular masses are called drugs.

Some drugs which are used in diagnosis, prevention and treatment of diseases are called **medicines**.

On the basis of therapeutic action, drugs are classified as follows :

- **Antipyretics** 'Anti' means *against* and 'pyretics' means *pertaining to fever*. These drugs are used to reduce fever i.e. they bring down body temperature at the time of high fever.

  The drugs used as antipyretics are aspirin, crocin, ibuprofen, paracetamol, phenacetin, analgin, novalgin, etc.
- **Analgesics** These are used to reduce pain without causing impairment of consciousness, mental confusion or some other disturbances of nervous system. e.g. aspirin, paracetamol, morphine (which is an opium alkaloid obtained from poppy plant) etc.
- **Antibiotics** These are the chemicals that inhibit the growth or even kill the microorganisms. These are obtained from microorganisms and used to destroy the other microorganisms.

  Penicillin was the first natural antibiotics discovered by **Alexander Fleming** in 1929. Penicillin (which is obtained from fungus), amino glycosides and ofloxacin are bactericidal (killing) antibiotics. Erythromycin, tetracycline (obtained from bacterium) and chloramphenicol are bacteriostatic (inhibitory) antibiotics.
- **Antiseptic** They prevent the growth of microorganisms or kill them but are not harmful to living tissues. e.g. furacin, soframycin.

  These are not ingested like antibiotics. Other antiseptics are dettol, bithionol, tincture iodine, boric acid, iodoform and 0.2% solution of phenol.
- **Disinfectants** These are applied to inanimate objects such as floors, drainage system, instruments etc. e.g. phenyl, 1% solution of phenol.
- **Sulpha Drugs** These drugs contain sulphur and nitrogen also. Sulfapyridine, sulfadiazine, sulfaguanidine and sulfathiazole are some important sulpha drugs.

  These are effective against bacterial infection. **Sulfanilamide** was first sulpha drug prepared in 1932.
- **Anaesthesia** These drugs cease the sense organs and thus are given during the major surgical operations.

  The first anaesthesia diethyl ether was used by **William Morten** in 1846. Chloroform was once used as a general anaesthetic in surgery by **James Sampson** but has been replaced by less toxic, safer anaesthetic, such as ether.

  Other examples of compounds used as anaesthesia are cocaine, diazepam, halothane, nitrous oxide, pentothal sodium, etc.
- **Antacids** These drugs reduce or neutralise the acidity in stomach. Metal hydroxides such as aluminium and magnesium hydroxide do not increase the pH above neutrality, so these are better antacids than sodium hydrogen carbonate.
- **Histamine** is a potent vasodilator. It is responsible for the nasal congestion associated with common cold and allergic response to pollen.
- **Equanil** is used in controlling depression and hypertension.

Soaps and Detergents

These are used as cleansing agents. They help in removal of fats which bind other materials to the fabric or skin.

Soaps

- These are the sodium or potassium salts of long chain fatty acids (*R*COONa). e.g. stearic acid ($C_{17}H_{35}COOH$), oleic acid ($C_{17}H_{33}COOH$) and palmitic acid ($C_{15}H_{31}COOH$).
- These are obtained from petroleum products. Soaps are used to improve the cleansing properties of water. These are biodegradable compounds.

Types of Soaps

(i) **Toilet Soaps** These are prepared by using better grades of fats and oils and are free from excess alkali. Colour and perfumes are also added to them.

(ii) **Floating Soaps** These are made by beating tiny air bubbles before their hardening.

(iii) **Transparent Soaps** These are made by dissolving soap in ethanol and then evaporating.

(iv) **Medicated Soaps** They have substances of medicinal value.

Soaps do not work in hard water

- Soaps react with calcium and magnesium ions present in hard water and form insoluble precipitate which separate as scum in water and also adhere to clothes as gummy mass. Hair washed with hard water looks dull due to this sticky precipitate.
- Generally, potassium soaps are soft to the skin than sodium soaps.
- In acidic medium, soaps are hydrolysed to give corresponding insoluble long chain fatty acids and thus, they lose their cleansing effect.

Detergents

- They have all the properties of soaps but actually do not contain any soap.
- They can be used both in soft and hard water because their calcium and magnesium salts are soluble in water thus scum formation does not occur. Thus, they have relatively stronger cleansing property as compared to soaps.
- Detergents are chemically alkyl sulphate or sulphonate or ammonium salt of long chain fatty acids (having 12-18 carbon atoms).
  e.g. sodium lauryl sulphate, sodium *p*-dodecylbenzenesulphonate. These are generally obtained from vegetable oils.

Classification of Synthetic Detergents

These are mainly classified into three categories :

(i) **Anionic Detergents** These are sodium salts of sulphonated long chain alcohols or hydrocarbons.
e.g. sodium lauryl sulphate, sodium *p*-dodecylbenzenesulphonate. Anionic part of these detergents is involved in the cleansing action.
These are used for household work and also used in tooth pastes.

(ii) **Cationic Detergents** These are quaternary ammonium salts of amines with acetates, chlorides or bromides as anions.
e.g. cetyltrimethylammonium bromide which has germicidal properties. It is used in hair conditioners.

(iii) **Non-ionic Detergents** They do not contain any ion in their constitution.
e.g., partially esterified compound like pentaerythritol monostearate. These are used as liquid dishwashing detergents.

Dyes

These are coloured substances used to impart permanent colour to fabric, food stuffs etc.

Chromophore group such as nitro, azo etc is responsible for colour of a substance.

It absorbs certain radiations from white light and reflects complementary coloured light.

Classification of Dyes

These are classified on the basis of application and chemical composition.

On the Basis of Applications

- **Acid Dyes** These are used as their sodium salts which are freely soluble in water. These are used to dye wool, silk and nylon directly but these are not used to dye cotton. e.g. methyl orange, methyl red, congo red, orange-I, orange-II.
- **Basic Dyes** These are used to dye modified nylons and polyesters. e.g. aniline yellow, malachite green.
- **Direct Dyes** These can be directly applied to fabrics from their aqueous solutions.
  e.g. martius yellow, congo red.
- **Disperse Dyes** These are applied in the form of dispersion. e.g. celliton fast pink B.
- **Fibre Reactive Dyes** They get attached to the fibre by a chemical reaction. e.g. procion cibacron.
- **Vat Dyes** These are mainly used to dye cotton fibres. e.g. indigo.
- **Mordant Dyes** These dyes need a binding agent between fibre and dye. Depending upon the binding agent, the same dye can give different colours. e.g. alizarin gives bright red colour with aluminium and blue colour with barium.

On the Basis of Chemical Composition

- **Azo Dyes** e.g. methyl orange, congo red etc.
- **Phthalein Dyes** e.g. phenolphthalein and mercurochrome.
- **Indigoid Dyes** e.g. indigo and tyrian purple.
- **Anthraquinone Dyes** e.g. alizarin (a natural dye).
- **Triphenyl Methane Dyes** e.g. malachite green.

Glass

- It was first prepared in Egypt. Chemically, it is a homogeneous mixture of silicates of various alkaline metals of non-crystallised and transparent or non-transparent chemicals.
- The ordinary glass (soda glass or window glass) has approximately the composition $Na_2O \cdot CaO \cdot 6SiO_2$.
- It is prepared by melting sand (silica), sodium carbonate (soda) and calcium carbonate (limestone) in proper proportions at moderate temperature.
- Some scrap glass (cullet) is also added to the mixture as flux which makes the mixture fusible.

Types of Glasses, Their Properties and Uses

Types of Glasses	Properties	Uses
Soda glass or soft glass	Contains sodium carbonate, calcium carbonate and silica; brittle; cheapest	Window glass, bottles, dishes, tubelights, domestic utensils etc
Potash glass or hard glass	Contains carbonate of K and Ca and silica, high temperature resistant	Hard boiling glass test tubes, beakers etc
Photochromatic glass	Turns dark in sharp shining UV light because of the presence of embedded microcrystalline silver compound (silver chloride) in glass	Eye lenses and goggles
Pyrex glass (borosilicate glass)	Contains borax and silica, withstand sudden alterations in temperature	Laboratory equipment
Flint glass	Contains sodium, potassium and lead silicate, have high refractive index	Optical instruments like lens of camera, prisms, microscopes, telescope and in electric bulbs
Crown glass	Contains oxides of potassium, barium and silicon, have high refractive index	Optical instruments
Jena glass (best form of glass)	Soft, strong and more resistant to acids and alkalies, contains zinc and barium borosilicate	Bottles for keeping acids and alkalies in laboratory
Crook's glass	Contains cerium oxide (CeO_2) and silica, thus, absorbs UV rays	Eye lenses used in different eye defects
Lead crystal glass	Contains potassium carbonate, lead oxide and silica, shows optical phenomenon of total internal reflection	Various ornamental items, costly glass containers
Quartz glass or silica glass	Ultraviolet rays emerge out through it	In making bulb of ultraviolet lamp, laboratory equipment

- Water glass is basically a compound of sodium meta silicate (Na_2SiO_3) and prepared by heating sodium carbonate with silica. It is soluble in water.
- Safety glass has a transparent plastic layer of vinyl acetate resin in between two glass layers.

Annealing of Glass

- In this process, glass utensils are allowed to cool slowly, steadily and moderately.
- If glass is cooled very slowly, it becomes opaque and if it is cooled very rapidly, it becomes brittle and fragile.

Coloured Glass

- These are obtained by mixing colour supplying substances in the molten or fused state of glass. Such substances are tabulated below :

Substances	Colour	Substances	Colour
Carbon	Brownish black	Nickel and manganese monoxide	Black
Cadmium sulphide	Yellow (lemon)	Manganese dioxide	Pink
Cobalt oxide	Deep blue	Ferric salt or sodium diuranate	Fluorescent yellow
Cuprous oxide	Glitter red	Potassium dichromate	Green and green yellow
Cupric oxide	Metalic black	Gold chloride or purple of cassius	Ruby red
Selenium oxide	White	Sodium chromate or ferrous oxide	Green
Ferric oxide	Brown		

Glass Wool

- It is an insulating material obtained from fibre glass arranged into a texture similar to wool.
- It is produced in rolls or in slabs with different thermal and mechanical properties. Its tensile strength is greater than that of steel.
- It is actually fireproof and is used to prepare fire glass. Fibre glass is used for making glass reinforced plastic.

Cement

- It is an important building material, first introduced in England in 1824 by **Joseph Aspdin**.
- It is also called Portland cement because it resembles with natural limestone quarried in the **Isle of Portland**, England.
- It is a grey coloured powder. Chemically, it is calcium aluminium silicate.
- Cement has a specific property of handing when comes in contact of water as silicate and aluminate present in it react with water and form a colloidal solution which is solidified.

Fertilizers

Fertilizers increase the fertility of soil by supplying nitrogen, phosphorus, potassium and other nutrients. These are used to ensure good vegetative growth giving rise to healthy plants.

Types of Fertilizers

Fertilizers are of following types :

Nitrogenous Fertilizers

These are obtained from ammonia and its derivatives. e.g. ammonium sulphate, calcium ammonium nitrate, basic calcium nitrate, calcium cyanamide (nitrolim), urea, etc.

- **Ammonium sulphate** $(NH_4)_2SO_4$ contains 25% ammonia which is transformed into the nitrate by denitrifying bacteria present in the alkaline soil.
  - The nitrates are easily absorbed by crop plants. It is produced on a large scale at Sindri, Jharkhand in India.
- In **calcium ammonium nitrate** $[Ca(NO_3)_2NH_4NO_3]$, the amount of nitrogen is about 20% which is directly absorbed by plants.
  - Because of its higher solubility, it has no adverse effect on the soil. It is manufactured at Nangal in Punjab.
- **Urea** (NH_2CONH_2) contains nearly 46% nitrogen and it does not affect the pH of the soil. It is the extensively used nitrogenous fertilizer.
  - Urea is prepared by heating carbon dioxide with ammonia at 125–150°C and 8.5 atmospheric pressure.
  - This fertilizer is never brought in direct contact of seed.
  - After using this fertilizer, water is supplied 3-4 days later.

Phosphatic Fertilizers

- These are superphosphate of lime, triple superphosphate (obtained from bone ash) and Thomas slag or phosphatic slag.
- Potassium chloride, potassium nitrate and potassium sulphate etc are also included in this category. **Superphosphate of lime** is a mixture of calcium dihydrogen phosphate and gypsum.
- In this fertilizer, 16-20% P_2O_5 exists. **Thomas slag** contains 14-18% of P_2O_5. It is a by-product of steel industry because of its higher solubility, it is easily assimilated by plants.

Potash Fertilizers

- Potassium chloride, potassium nitrate and potassium sulphate are examples of potash fertilizers.

Nitrogen-Phosphorus (NP) Fertilizers

- They supply nitrogen and phosphorus to the soil. These are obtained by mixing nitrogen and phosphate fertilizers in proper quantity.
- Examples of NP fertilizers include calcium superphosphate nitrate, ammoniated phosphate, sulphate and dihydrogen ammoniated phosphate.

Nitrogen-Phosphorus & Potassium (NPK) Fertilizers

- They supply three main nutrients i.e. nitrogen, phosphorus and potassium to the soil. That's why these are also called compound fertilizers or complete fertilizers.
- These are obtained by mixing all three types of fertilizers (nitrogenous, phosphate and potash fertilizers) in proper quantity.

Chemicals in Food

Chemicals are added to food for following purpose :

(i) Artificial Sweetening Agents

- These are the chemical substances which provide sweetness to the food without increasing the calories of body.
- They act as substitutes for sugar in foods and beverages.
- Some examples includes saccharin, aspartame, sucralose, alitame etc.
- Natural sweeteners like sucrose add to calorie intake and therefore many people mainly diabetic prefer to use artificial sweeteners.
- Some commonly marketed artificial sweeteners are as follows :
  - **Saccharin** It is *ortho*-sulphobenzimide. It is first popular artificial sweetening agent. It is about 550 times as sweet as cane sugar. It is excreted from the body in the form of urine.
    It appears to be entirely inert and harmless, when taken.
  - **Aspartame** It is the most successful and widely used artificial sweetener. It is 100 times as sweet as cane sugar. Its use is limited to cold foods and soft drinks because it is unstable at cooking temperature.
  - **Alitame** It is high potency sweetener. It is about 2000 times as sweet as cane sugar.
  - **Sucralose** It is trichloro derivative of sucrose. Its appearance, color and taste are like sugar. It is 600 times sweeter than sucrose. It is used in hot foods because it is stable at cooking temperature.

(ii) Food Preservatives

- They prevent spoilage of food due to the microbial growth. The most commonly used preservatives include table salt, sugar, vegetable oils, sodium metabisulphite and sodium benzoate.
- **Salts of sorbic acid** and **propanoic acid** are also used as preservatives.
- Refrigeration also helps in food preservation because it provides low temperature and reduces the rate of biochemical reaction (i.e., reactions occuring in living organisms). Due to which bacterial (microbes) activities are reduced greatly, i.e., they cannot reproduce or eat food.

(iii) Antioxidants

- They inhibit the oxidation of other molecules.
- Chemically it is used to prevent oxidation of fats in processed food like potato, chips etc.
- It is found in dietary supplements.
- Unsaturated oils and fats containing food materials, when stored, undergo deterioration because of the oxidation by atmospheric oxygen.
- To avoid their oxidation and to prevent their spoilage, certain chemicals which are able to prevent their oxidation are added. These chemicals are known as antioxidants.
- Therefore, the chemicals which retard the action of oxygen on the food material and thereby help in its preservation are called antioxidants.
- BHA (Butylated *p*-hydroxyanisole), BHT (Butylated *p*-hydroxytoluene), esters of gallic acid and lecithin are some examples of antioxidants.

Sources of Some Antioxidants

Antioxidants	Food Materials Containing Antioxidants
Vitamin-C (ascorbic acid)	Fruits and vegetsables
Vitamin-E (tocopherols)	Vegetable oils
Carotenoids	Fruits and vegetables
Polyphenol	Tea, coffee, soyabean, chocolate, etc.

Fats and Oils

- Fats mainly contain saturated esters while oils mainly contain unsaturated esters derived from the single alcohol glycerol. These are also called **triglycerides**.
- Thus, these are esters of glycerol with higher fatty acids such as palmitic acid ($C_{15}H_{31}COOH$), oleic acid ($C_{17}H_{33}COOH$), stearic acid ($C_{17}H_{35}COOH$), etc.
- Like carbohydrates, these are also composed of carbon, hydrogen and oxygen but oxygen content is much lesser as compared to carbohydrates.
- These are insoluble in water but soluble in organic solvents like benzene, carbon tetrachloride, petroleum, etc.
- These are the major food reserve of organisms and are responsible for several functions.
- **Phospholipids** are an important group of phosphorus containing fats.
- Further, glycerides having melting point below 20°C are oils while glycerides having melting point above 20°C are fats.
- At room temperature, fats are in solid state. Unsaturation of any fat or oil is determined by its **iodine value**.

11

Environmental Chemistry

[SOURCES]

Class-XI Old NCERT Chap 14 (Environmental Chemistry)

- The composition of the physical and biological conditions in which we live is called an **environment**.
- The changes may originate from either a natural source or human activity. The **living (biotic)** and **non-living (abiotic)** components that are affected adversely are called **receptors or targets**.
- The increase in toxicity due to action of pollutants is termed as **synergism**.

Environmental Pollution

- The effect of undesirable changes in our surroundings which have adverse effects on plants, animals and human beings is termed as **environmental pollution.** Substances responsible for causing pollution, are called **pollutants.**
- An average human being needs about 12-15 times more air than the food. So, even a small amount of pollutants in the air become significant compared to similar level present in food. Pollutants can be classified into following two categories :
  - **Biodegradable Pollutants** The substances that get degraded by microorganisms such as bacteria into simpler substances which rapidly break down by natural processes are called biodegradable pollutants. e.g. discarded vegetables, wastes sludges etc.
  - **Non-Biodegradable Pollutants** The substances that degrade slowly and remain in the environment in an unchanged form for many decades are called non-biodegradable pollutants.

    Since, such pollutants cannot be degraded by natural phenomenon, so they are harmful for living organisms, e.g., DDT (dichlorodiphenyl Trichloro ethane), heavy metals, nuclear wastes, plastic materials etc.

Global Warming

- It is the increase in the average temperature of earth's atmosphere and oceans, i.e., air and sea on earth's surface. Since late 19th century, this temperature increase has to occured due to the increase in concentration in the atmosphere.
- The main causes of global warming are burning of fossil fuels like coal, oil and natural gas for energy, increasing greenhouse gases, burning forests to create pastures, plantation and carbon accumulation.
- Earth temperature has increased by 0.6°C in last three decades. This causes changes in precipitation patterns.
- Scientists have proposed that rise in temperature causes deleterious changes in the environment resulting in odd climatic changes (e.g., El Nino effect.).

Greenhouse Effect

It is a process by which thermal radiation from a plantary surface is absorbed by atmospheric greenhouse gases and is re-radiated in all directions. It mainly results in the elevation of the average surface temperature.

The four major greenhouse gases are as follows

- **Carbon dioxide** (CO_2) Its present level in atmosphere is 380 ppm (parts per million). Its atmospheric life time is 5-200 year. Concentration of CO_2 increases due to fossil fuel's burning, deforestation, etc. Its high concentration may cause harmful effects on both plant and animal life.
- **Methane** (CH_4) Its present level in atmosphere is 1750 ppb (parts per billion). Methanogen bacteria increase greenhouse effect by producing methane. Its major sources are fresh water wetlands, enteric fermentation in cattle, flooded rice fields along with biomass burning, etc.
- **Nitrous Oxide** (N_2O) Its present atmospheric concentration is 316 ppb (parts per billion). Its major sources are biomass burning, nylon industries, nitrogen rich fertilisers and fuels.
- **Chlorofluorocarbons** (CFCs) Its present atmospheric concentration is 282 ppt (parts per trillion). Its atmospheric life time is 45-260 year. Its major sources include leaking from air conditioners, refrigeration units, evaporation of industrial solvents, production of plastic foams and propellants in aerosol, spraycans, etc.

Acid Rain

- The pH of rain water drops below 5.6 because of the presence of certain acids, called **acid rain.**
- Oxides of nitrogen, carbon and sulphur, released into the atmosphere from thermal power plants, industries automobiles etc are the main sources of acid rain.
- These oxides on oxidation followed by hydrolysis (i.e., reaction with water) sulphuric acid (H_2SO_4) and nitric acid (HNO_3) that alongwith HCl are responsible for the acidity of rain. The oxidation reaction is catalysed by particulate matter present in the polluted atmosphere.
- Acid rain shows the ways through which acids from the atmosphere get deposited on the earth's surface. Wind also carries oxides of nitrogen and sulphur along with solid particles in the atmosphere.
- These oxides finally settle down either on ground in the form of dry deposition or in water, fog and snow in the form of wet deposition.

Stratospheric Pollution

- **Ozone layer** present in stratosphere absorbs UV radiations of the Sun which are harmful to living organism. UV radiations cause skin cancer and cataracts in human and reduction of planktons in ocean water and depletion of plants.
- Freon is a dangerous chlorofluoro carbon is used in refrigerator, air conditioner and in making foams for sofa seats. The compound persist in the atmosphere for years and enters its upper layers which further decomposed by powerful UV rays. The decomposition products reacts with ozone to form chloro monoxide which further reacts with oxygen and produces chlorine atoms.

Smog

It is a serious air pollutant in many cities throughout the world. Actually, the word 'smog' is obtained by combining two words, **smoke** and **fog.**

Depending upon the nature of constituents forming smog, it is mainly of two types :

(i) **Classical Smog** It appears, when climate is cool and humid and carbon soot particles (smoke) react with gaseous oxides of sulphur (fog) present in the atmosphere.
Due to the presence of carbon particles and SO_2, it is **reducing in nature,** therefore it is also called as **reducing smog.**

(ii) **Photochemical Smog** It appears in warm, dry and sunny climate, generally during the day time from its components, which are obtained by the action of sunlight on unsaturated hydrocarbons and nitrogen oxides (produced by automobiles and factories).
Because of the presence of high concentration of oxidising agents, this smog is **oxidising in nature** and also called **oxidising smog.**

Effects and Control of Photochemical Smog

- Photochemical smog due to the presence of ozone, PAN (Peroxyacetyl nitrate) and nitric oxide, irritates eyes, nose, throat, lungs, causes headache, chest pain, cough, difficulty in breathing etc.
- It also leads to the cracking of rubber and extensive harm to plant life.
- It corrodes metals, stones and even painted surfaces.
- Its formation can be prevented by controlling the formation and release of primary precursors such as oxides of nitrogen, hydrocarbons etc., by their usual methods (like using catalytic converters in the automobiles).

- Other method of its prevention is plantation of certain plants such as pyrus, pinus, juniparus and vitis that have an ability to metabolise nitrogen oxide.
- **Bhopal Gas Tragedy** took place in Bhopal on 2nd December, 1984. It was a case of serious air pollution in which MIC (Methyl Isocyanate) gas released form a pesticide manufacturing plant of union carbide.
- It took the life of nearly 3200 peoples. MIC causes various lung diseases, irritation to eyes followed by blindness and other harmful effect which are passes to many generations.

Water Pollution

- The contamination of water by foreign substances such as solid particles, soluble salts, sewage, algae etc. which make it injurious for living organisms and unfit for domestic, agricultural and industrial use, is called **water pollution** and the foreign substances are called **water pollutants.**
- The sources from which these pollutants are obtained and released, are of two types.
  - **Point Sources** These are easily identifiable sources or places of pollution. These discharge pollutants directly into the water source. e.g., municipal and industrial discharge pipes.
  - **Non-point Sources** Such sources cannot be easily identified. These sources are usually scattered and are difficult to monitor, regulate and treat. These sources include run off from field lawns, construction sites, acid rain, storm water drainage (from streets and parking lots) etc.
- **Biochemical Oxygen Demand (BOD)** is defined as the total amount of oxygen (in milligram) required by microbes to decompose the organic matter present in 1L of water sample.
  - For clean water, the BOD value is less than 5 ppm while highly polluted water could have a BOD value of 17 ppm or more.
  - Water being an excellent solvent, dissolves most of the inorganic and organic chemicals that make it contaminated (or polluted).
  - For example, heavy metals such as Cd, Hg, Ni, etc., are important pollutants. All these metals are harmful for us because our body is unable to excrete them.
  - Sulphuric acid is present in mine drainage and a mixture of sodium chloride and calcium chloride is used to melt snow and ice in the colder climates. The acid and salt being water soluble dissolve in water and made it polluted.
  - **Petroleum product or oils** mainly pollute sea water, spilled accidently or intentionally into it. **Oil may** form a thin layer on the surface of water, called oil spill or a thick layer on the surface of sea water, called **oil slick**.
  - When pesticides (such as DDT) are mixed with water, they pollute it and cause several problems such as cerebral haemorrhage, hypertension, softening of brain.
  - Polychlorinated Biphenyls (PCBs), a cleansing solvent, detergents, (like alkyl benzene sulphonates) and fertilisers also increases the problem of water pollution. PCBs being carcinogenic is most harmful.
- **Fertilisers** contain phosphates and nitrates. When they are added to crop fields, a part of these fertilisers passed down to water bodies by rain water through surface run off. The contaminated water becomes rich in these nutrients.
  - It increases the growth of algae and other aquatic plants, i.e., causes eutrophication which leads to organic loading, lack of dissolved oxygen, death of animals and unpleasent odour of water.

Eutrophication

The process in which nutrient enriched water bodies support a dense plant population, which kills animals life by depriving it of oxygen and results in subsequent loss of biodiversity is known as eutrophication. The water containing nitrate is unfit for drinking purposes.

Concentration of General Metals in Potable Water

Metal	Maximum Concentration (ppm/mg dm^{-3})
Fe	0.2
Mn	0.05
Al	0.2
Cu	3.0
Zn	5.0
Cd	0.005

Oil Zapper

- It is a new technique developed by TERI (The Energy and Resource Institute, Government of India) to clean the oil spill by using a bacteria. This process is used for bioremediation process.
- In August 2010 it was used to clean the oil spill at Mumbai shore. It occurred due to the collision between a cargo and merchant ship resulting in 400 tonnes of oil leaked in the sea.
- The Maharashtra pollution board uses the service of TERI to clean oil sludge near the coast of Mumbai. There are five different bacterial strains that are immobilised and mixed with carrier

materials with powdered corncob. This mixture of bacteria is called oil zapper.

- Oil zapper reacts with hydrocarbon materials present in the oil sludge (A hazardous waste produced by oil refinery companies like Bharat Petroleum or ONGC) converts them into harmless CO_2 and water.

Green Chemistry

- In green chemistry, the reactions are generally carried out in the presence of mild and environment-friendly reagents such as ultraviolet light (photochemistry), sound waves (sonic chemistry), enzymes and microwaves so that harmful chemicals are neither used up nor released.
- This is the branch of chemistry in which chemicals of daily needs are produced by using such reactions or processes that neither use toxic chemicals nor emit such chemicals into the atmosphere.
- It is a way of thinking and is about utilising the existing knowledge and principles of chemistry and other sciences to reduce the adverse effect on the environment.
- Generally, a reaction, in which the reactants are converted completely into useful environment- friendly products in an environment-friendly medium, introduces no pollutant in the environment.
- Thus, such reactants should be chosen that can be converted into end products with 100% yield.
- Water has high specific heat and low volatility. It is cost effective, non-inflammable solvent that is non-carcinogenic. All the given properties of water makes it a good medium to carry out several synthetic reactions.

Green Chemistry in Day-to-Day Life

Some of the examples of green chemistry in day-to-day life are as follows

- **Dry Cleaning of Clothes** Earlier tetrachloroethene ($Cl_2C{=}CCl_2$) was used for dry cleaning purposes. This chemical contaminates the ground water and is also a suspected carcinogen.

  So, it is replaced by liquefied CO_2, which is much less harmful as compared to $Cl_2C{=}CCl_2$.
- **Bleaching of Paper** Earlier, the paper was bleached by using chlorine. But because of its harmful effects, now it has been replaced by hydrogen peroxide which works better in the presence of a suitable catalyst.
- **Synthesis of Chemicals** Ethanal is prepared from ethene by its one step oxidation in the presence of an ionic catalyst in aqueous medium. The yield of the reaction is 90%.

$$\underset{\text{ethene}}{CH_2{=}CH_2} + O_2 \xrightarrow[\text{Pd (II), Cu (II) (in water)}]{\text{Catalyst}} \underset{\text{ethanal}}{CH_3CHO}\ (90\%)$$

01

Biology

Introduction to Biology and Classification of Living Beings

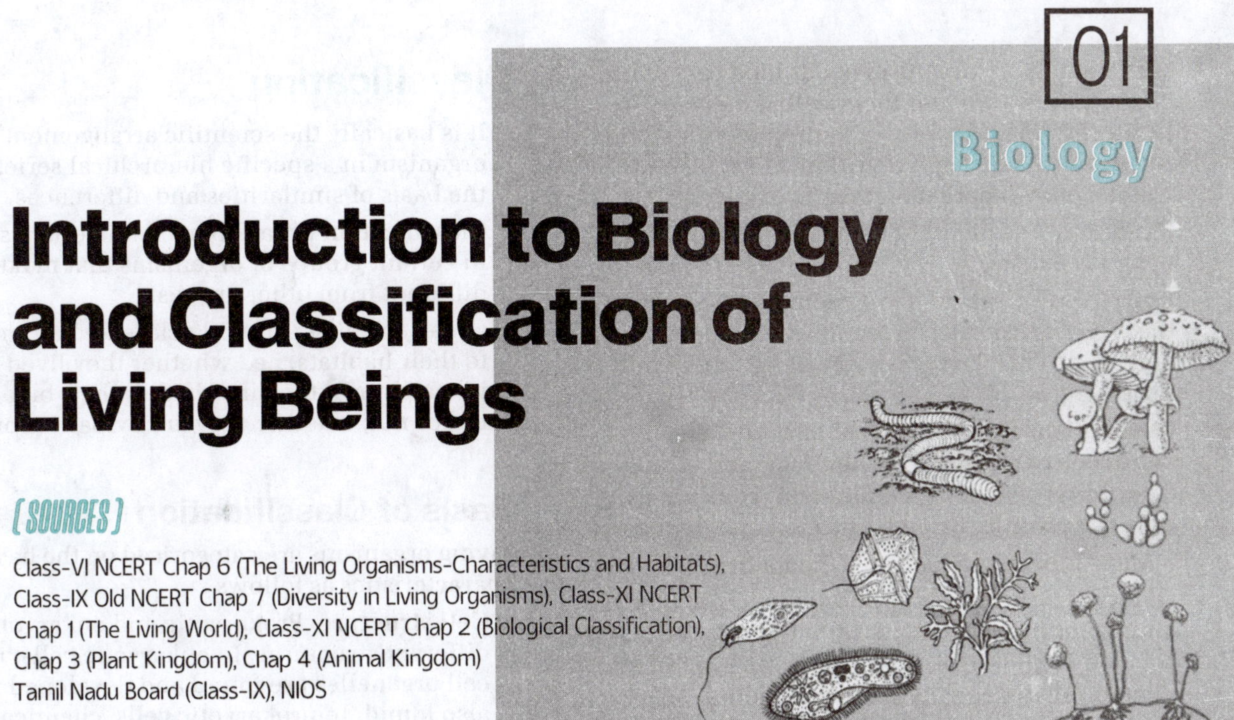

(SOURCES)

Class-VI NCERT Chap 6 (The Living Organisms-Characteristics and Habitats), Class-IX Old NCERT Chap 7 (Diversity in Living Organisms), Class-XI NCERT Chap 1 (The Living World), Class-XI NCERT Chap 2 (Biological Classification), Chap 3 (Plant Kingdom), Chap 4 (Animal Kingdom) Tamil Nadu Board (Class-IX), NIOS

Introduction to Biology

- Biology (*Bios*-life, *logos*-study) is the science of study of living organisms on the Earth. All living organisms are linked to one another by the sharing of the common genetic material, but to varying degrees.
- Living organisms vary in their form, structure and mode of life, but still they have similarities. Study of animals is called **Zoology**, whereas that of plants is called **Botany**. Both are categorised under **Biology**.
- In 384-322 BC, **Aristotle** was the earliest to attempt a scientific basis of classification using morphological characters, behaviour and reproduction.
- Thus, he is called **Father of Science of Biology** and **Zoology**. In his book *Historia Animalium*, he had discussed about 500 animals.
- **Theophrastus** is considered as the **Father of Botany** since, he was the first to conduct researches on plants in 370-287 BC.
- In his book *Historia Plantarum*, he has discussed about age and size of about 500 plants.
- Characteristics of living organisms include growth, reproduction, metabolism, cellular organisation, consciousness, respiration and excretion.
- **Protoplasm** is found in all living organisms. All biological processes take place in it.
- The diversity or the number and type of living organisms present on the Earth is called **biodiversity**.

Branches of Biology

There are different branches of biology as follows :

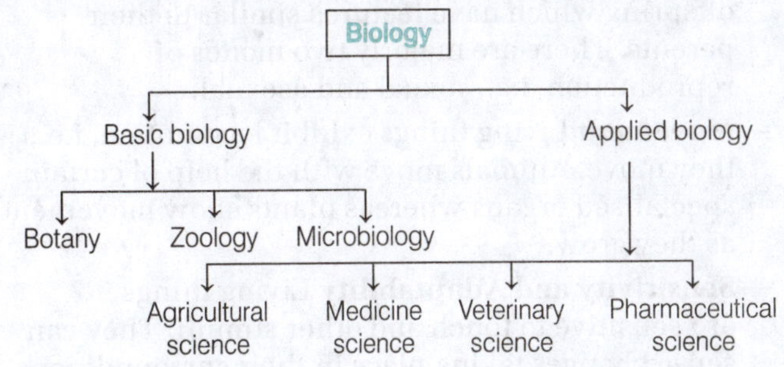

Living World

In the living world, two types of things are found, i.e., living and non-living. The things that growth, develop, react and show other features of life are called **living things**.

Features of living organisms are as follows :

- **Protoplasm** It is the physical basis of all living organisms. All biological activities take place here.
- **Cell structure** Cell is the structural and functional unit of all living beings. Organisms can be unicellular (single celled) or multicellular (more than one cell).

- **Nutrition** Every organism needs food in order to grow, as food provides them with the energy to fulfill certain tasks. They acquire their nutritional requirements through nutrition and digestion. Autotrophs prepare their own food.
- **Excretion** The digested food is eliminated from the body *via* excretion.
- **Cellular respiration** It is a chemical reaction that occurs inside a cell to release energy *via* digestion. This energy is utilised for other bodily purposes.
- **Metabolism** The sum total of anabolic or constructive reactions (**anabolism**) and catabolic or destructive reactions (**catabolism**) continuously occurring inside the body is called metabolism.

  Metabolism = Anabolism + Catabolism
- **Growth** Living things grow with increase in mass and increase in number of individuals or cells. In **multicellular organisms**, growth occurs by cell division or increase in number of cells.

  This growth occurs continuously in plants throughout their lifespan, whereas in animals, it occurs only upto a certain age. However, growth and replacement of lost cells occur throughout the life.
- **Reproduction** It is the process of producing offspring which have features similar to their parents. There are majorly two modes of reproduction, i.e., sexual and asexual.
- **Movement** Living things exhibit locomotion, i.e., they move. Animals move with the help of certain specialised organs whereas plants show movement as they grow.
- **Sensitivity and Adaptability** Living things are sensitive to touch and other stimuli. They can sense changes taking place in their surroundings.

Biodiversity

- It is the biological variety and variability that exist on Earth. It is a measure of variation at genetic, species and ecosystem level.
- The term biodiversity was coined by **Walter G Rosen** in 1985. Biodiversity plays a major role in establishing the balance in nature.
- Biodiversity holds ecological and economic importance as it provides us with nourishment, housing, fuel and other resources.
- Regions lying between Tropic of Cancer and Tropic of Capricorn are called **Megadiverse regions** since, they exhibit maximum biodiversity. e.g., India, Australia, China, Mexico, etc.

Classification

- It is basically the scientific arrangement of an organism in a specific hierarchical series of groups on the basis of similarities and differences.
- Classification is based on characteristics which occur in certain groups of organisms that make them different from other groups.
- Greek scientist, Aristotle classified animals according to their habitats, i.e., whether they lived on land, in water or in the air; whether their blood colour is red or not; whether they are oviparous or viviparous, etc.

Basis of Classification

Living organisms are categorised on the basis of certain characteristics as follows :

- **Cell structure** Prokaryotic and eukaryotic cells have different structures. In eukaryotic cells, membranous cell organelles are found and developed nucleus is also found. In prokaryotic cells, chemical processes are also different.
- **Body structure** In both unicellular and multicellular organisms, body structure is different. Cells that are found in groups have capacity to form any organism. They show division of labour. They make an organism by forming tissues and organs. This feature is absent in unicellular organism.
- **Nutrition** On the basis of nutrition, organisms are classified as follows :
  - **Autotrophs** They make their food by the process of photosynthesis.
  - **Heterotrophs** They obtain their food from autotrophs.
- **Body organisation** Plants and animals have different body organisations. Their cells are also different.
- **Functional organisation** Like body organisation, functional organisation is also different in different organisms. For example, *Amoeba* uses pseudopodia for locomotion and human beings use hindlimbs for movement.

Taxonomical Series

- Each unit of classification represents a rank and is termed as a **taxon**.
- The **taxonomic hierarchy** is the system of arranging taxonomic categories in a descending order. It was first introduced by **Carolus Linnaeus** (1751) and hence, it is also known as **Linnaean hierarchy**.
- Groups represent **category** and category further denotes **rank**. Each rank or taxon represents a unit of classification.

- These taxonomic groups/categories are distinct biological entities and not merely morphological aggregates.

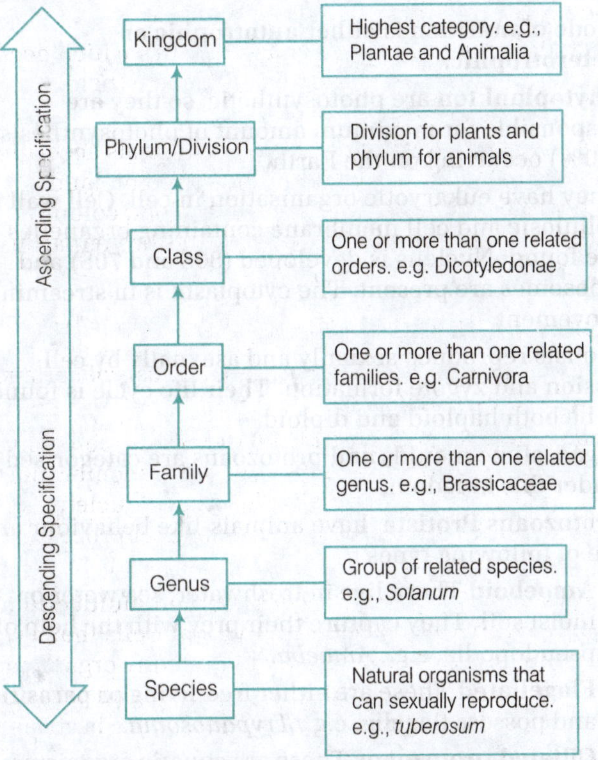

Taxonomic categories showing hierarchical arrangement in ascending order

Nomenclature

- Binomial nomenclature was proposed by Father of Taxonomy **Carolus Linnaeus** in his book *Systema Naturae.*
- It is a system of giving scientific names to plants and animals. Since, the name of every organism is composed of two components **genus** (generic) and **species** (specific), so this kind of naming is termed as **binomial nomenclature.**

  For example, the scientific name of human species is *Homo sapiens* where *Homo* is a generic name and *sapiens* is a specific name.
- Binomial nomenclature is therefore, guided by a set of rules stated in the **International Code of Binomial Nomenclature.**

  Certain conventions are followed while writing the scientific names as follows :
  - The name of the genus begins with a capital letter.
  - The name of the species begins with a small letter.
  - When printed, the scientific name is given in italics.
  - When written by hand, the genus and the species names have to be underlined separately.

Organisms with Their Taxonomic Categories

Common Name	Man	Housefly	Mango	Wheat
Biological Name	*Homo sapiens*	*Musca domestica*	*Mangifera indica*	*Triticum aestivum*
Genus	*Homo*	*Musca*	*Mangifera*	*Triticum*
Family	Hominidae	Muscidae	Anacardiaceae	Poaceae
Order	Primata	Diptera	Sapindales	Poales
Class	Mammalia	Insecta	Dicotyledonae	Monocotyledonae
Phylum/ Division	Chordata	Arthropoda	Angiospermae	Angiospermae

Classification of Living Organisms

- **RH Whittaker** (1969) proposed a five kingdom classification system based on certain criteria like cell structure, mode of nutrition, reproduction. He divided living organism into five kingdoms, as below :

1. Monera

- These organisms are **unicellular prokaryotes.** They do not have well-defined nucleus and membrane bound cell organelles like mitochondria, Golgi apparatus, plastids, lysosomes, etc., as found in eukaryotes.
- Mode of nutrition is either **autotrophic** (as in blue-green algae and some bacteria) or **heterotrophic** (mycoplasma and most bacteria).
- Based on the development, there are two types of bacteria, i.e., **Archaebacteria** and **Eubacteria.**

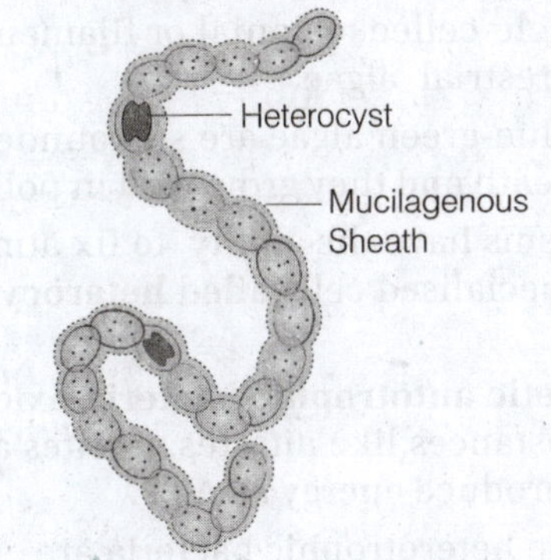

A filamentous blue-green algae-*Nostoc*

Archaebacteria

- These are a group of prokaryotes and are also known as **living fossils.**
- These are special bacteria which live in some of the most harsh habitats like extreme salinity, high temperature, acidic as well as hot springs and marshy areas.

- These are also found in gut of ruminants (e.g., cow) and help in digestion of cellulose and produce gases like methane.

Eubacteria

- They are called **true bacteria** and are characterised by the presence of a rigid cell wall. If they are motile, they have flagellum.
- It was discovered by **Leeuwenhoek** in 1676 and was named as bacteria in 1928 by **Ehrenberg**.
- **Louis Pasteur** worked on fermentation and is known as **Father of Microbiology**.

General Characters of Eubacteria

- These are the most simple and primitive organisms.
- These lack cell organelles like mitochondria, Golgi apparatus, etc. However, ribosomes are present.
- These have rigid cell wall made of peptidoglycan and an inner membrane made up of proteins and phospholipids.
- Usually, they lack chlorophyll and thus, depend upon other sources for food. Certain bacteria possess chlorophyll (e.g., cyanobacteria) and thus, have autotrophic mode of nutrition.
- They reproduce asexually by binary fission. Sometimes under unfavourable conditions, they produce spores.

Cyanobacteria

- They are also known as **blue-green algae**.
- They contain **chlorophyll-*a***, which is also a constituent of plant cell, thus making them photosynthetic autotrophs.
- These are single-celled, colonial or filamentous, marine or terrestrial algae.
- Colonies of blue-green algae are surrounded by a gelatinous sheath and they grow well in polluted water.
- These organisms have the ability to fix atmospheric nitrogen in specialised cell called **heterocysts**. e.g., *Nostoc*.
- **Chemosynthetic autotrophic bacteria** oxidise inorganic substances like nitrates, nitrites and ammonia to produce energy as ATP.
- Majority of the heterotrophic bacteria are decomposers, which are helpful in daily activities like curd formation.
- There are certain harmful bacteria which cause diseases like **typhoid**, **tetanus**, **cholera**, etc.

2. Protista

- This group consists of **unicellular eukaryotes**.
- Membrane bound cell organelles like mitochondria, plastids and sap-vacuoles are also present.
- Some protists use appendages, such as hair-like cilia or whip-like flagella for movement. In some protists like *Amoeba*, movement takes place by pseudopodia (false feet).
- Mode of nutrition is either **autotrophic** or **heterotrophic**.
- **Phytoplankton** are photosynthetic, so they are responsible for maximum amount of photosynthesis (80%) occurring on the Earth.
- They have eukaryotic organisation in cell. Cell wall is cellulosic and cell membrane containing organelles are found. Nucleus is developed (80S and 70S) and ribosomes are present. The cytoplasm is in streaming movement.
- Protists reproduce sexually and asexually by cell fission and zygote formation. Their life cycle is found to be both haploid and diploid.
- Algae, slime moulds and protozoans are categorised under this kingdom.
- **Protozoans Protista** have animals-like behaviour and are of following types :
  - **Amoeboid** These live in freshwater, sea water or moist soil. They capture their prey with the help of pseudopodia. e.g., *Amoeba*.
  - **Flagellated** These are either free-living or parasitic and possess flagella. e.g., *Trypanosoma*.
  - **Ciliated protozoans** These are aquatic organisms and have thousands of cilia. e.g., *Paramecium*.
  - **Sporozoans** These have infectious spore-like stage in their life cycle. e.g., *Plasmodium*.

3. Fungi

- These are eukaryotic non-green (lacking chlorophyll) organisms.
- They are heterotrophic in nutrition and obtain food from decaying organic matter and so are called saprophytes.
- Many become multicellular organisms at certain stages in their lives.
- They have cell wall made up of a tough complex sugar called **chitin**.
- Reserved food in fungi is in the form of **glycogen** and **oil**.
- Fungi are cosmopolitan, i.e., can be found in air, water, soil on plants and animals.
- Fungi are filamentous. Their body consists of long, slender, thread-like structures (**hyphae**) which form a network, called **mycelium**.
- Mycelium is septate and branched. e.g., *Trichoderma*.
- Its examples are yeast, *Agaricus* (mushroom), *Aspergillus*, *Penicillium*.

Fungi are divided into three main groups :

(i) **Sexual** This involves conjugation of two gametes or nuclei.

(ii) **Asexual** This types of reproduction occurs with the help of spores. e.g., *Mucor*.

(iii) **Vegetative** This type of reproduction occurs by fission.

4. Plantae

- These are **multicellular eukaryotes** with cellulosic cell walls.
- They are **autotrophs** and use chlorophyll (present in chloroplasts) for photosynthesis.
- All plants are included in this group forming visible forms of biodiversity.
- The first level of classification among plants depends on whether the plant body has well differentiated, distinct components (like root, stem, leaf, etc.).
- They can reproduce *via* sexual, asexual and vegetative means.
- The next level of classification is based on whether the differentiated plant body has vascular tissues for the transport of water and other substances within it.
- Further classification is based on the ability to bear seeds and whether the seeds are enclosed within fruits.

Classification of Kingdom-Plantae

- First level of classification in plant kingdom is based on the fact that the components of the plants body are developed or not.
- Next level classification is based on the presence or absence of certain specialised tissues for transport of water and other substances.
- Plants are also classified on the basis of the ability to hold seed.
- Based on above criteria, plants are divided as :

(i) Cryptogamae

The **thallophytes, bryophytes** and **pteridophytes** do not have external flower or seeds and have naked embryos called **spores**.

These plants are therefore also called **Cryptogamae** (meaning hidden reproductive organs) because their reproductive organs are not clearly visible.

(a) Thallophyta

- These include plants that do not have well differentiated body design.
- The plants in this group are commonly called as **algae**.
- These plants are predominantly aquatic.
- Algae are green thallophytes (autotrophic) that contain chlorophyll.
- These have **cellulosic cell wall**.
- Food is reserved as **starch**.
- Vascular tissues are absent in thallophytes.
- Most of these reproduce by asexual reproduction. Sexual reproduction takes place through the fusion of gametes.
- Fusion of male and female gametes lead to zygote, but embryo formation does not occur.
- Zygote formed by the fusion of gametes directly gives rise to offsprings plant by meiosis.
- Its examples are *Spirogyra, Ulothrix, Cladophora and Chara*.

(b) Bryophyta

- They are the first plants to live on land and need water for reproduction and are therefore called the **amphibians of the plant kingdom**.
- These are more developed when compared to thallophytes. The plant body is differentiated to form stem and leaf like structures.
- They have **rhizoids** in place of roots.
- There is no specialised tissue for the conduction of water and other substances from one part of the plant body to another.
- These are autotrophs and usually occur in damp, humid and shaded localities.
- Plant body is gametophytic, but sporophyte is attached to it in order to derive nutrition.
- They are divided into **liverworts** and **mosses**. Its examples are moss (*Funaria*) and liverworts (*Riccia, Marchantia*).

(c) Pteridophyta

- Plants belonging to Pteridophyta group are also called **botanical snakes**.
- They are the first land plants having vascular tissues.
- The plant body is differentiated into roots, stem and leaves.
- They are mostly found in cool, damp, shady places.
- They have specialised tissue for the conduction of water and other substances from one part of the plant body to another.
- These plants are mainly terrestrial and sporophytic.
- Flowers and seeds are not formed in these plants.
- Gametophytes in these plants is highly developed in structure and is very small.
- Fertilised eggs give rise to embryos.
- Its examples are *Marsilea*, ferns and horse tails.

(ii) Phanerogamae

- Plants which make seeds and have well-differentiated reproductive tissues are called **phanerogams.**
- In these plants, seeds consist of embryo along with stored food.
- The stored food serves the purpose of initial growth of the embryo during germination.
- Seeds result from reproductive process in plants.
- On the basis of whether the seeds are naked or enclosed in fruits, these are divided into two groups:

(a) Gymnosperms

- These are naked seeded plants, i.e., seeds are not enclosed within a fruit.
- The plants of this group are usually **perennial, evergreen** and **woody.**
- The flowers are represented by unisexual cones, both present on the same plant. e.g., *Pinus* (Pine).
- These plants have cones instead of inflorescence in which special leaves called **sporophylls** are attached in groups.
- Male and female cones are present in separate trees. These have highly developed vascular tissues, but their xylem lacks vessels and phloem lacks sieve tubes and adjacent cells.
- They do not form true fruits and are pollinated by wind.

(b) Angiosperms

- These are also called **flowering plants.** Their seeds develop inside an organ called **ovule.** It modifies to become a fruit.
- They may be **annual, biennial** or **perennial.**
- Flowers are differentiated and may be unisexual or bisexual.
- Ovary is present which gives rise to fruit.
- These flowers can be pollinated by various means like air, insects, animals, wind, etc.
- Seeds are always enclosed in fruits.
- Plant embryo in seeds have structures called **cotyledons.**
- Cotyledons are called **'seed leaves'** because they emerge and become green when the seed germinates.
- Angiosperms are divided into two groups on the basis of the number of cotyledons present in the seed :
  (i) **Monocotyledonous or Monocots** They are the plants with seeds having a single cotyledon. e.g., maize, wheat, rice, etc.
  (ii) **Dicotyledonous or Dicots** They are plants with seeds having two cotyledons. e.g., pea, gram, bean, etc.

5. Animalia

- These are multicellular eukaryotes without cell walls.
- They lack cell wall. They have stored food reserves in the form of glycogen or fat.
- They have a definite growth pattern, a definite shape and size.
- Most of them undergo sexual reproduction.
- They are heterotrophic in their mode of nutrition.
- Kingdom-Animalia or animals are further classified on the basis of the extent and type of the body design, differentiation.

Classification of Kingdom-Animalia

Animals are classified on the basis of certain characteristics. Animals from phylum-Porifera to Echinodermata are placed under Non-chordata and these along with hemichordates are invertebrates.

(i) Phylum-Porifera

These organisms were named **Zoophyta** by **Lamarck** (1801) and Porifera by **Robert Grant** (1825). They are branched but still. They show following features :

- They are the simplest multicellular animals and mostly marine except *Spongilla* (freshwater sponge).
- They are non-motile animals attached to some solid support.
- They are mostly aquatic, (found in seas and water bodies) and bisexual.
- They have cellular level of organisation, thus, they lack organs and tissues.
- Sponges have a canal system, which helps in various processes.
- The sponges are 'pore-bearing' animals with canal system.
- The characteristic canal system of the body helps in circulating water throughout the body to bring in food and oxygen.
- Choanocytes or collar cells line the spongocoel and canals.
- They have intracellular digestion.
- **Ostia** are minute pores for transportation of water.
- Fertilisation is internal and development is indirect with a larval stage.

- The animals are covered with a hard outside layer or skeleton.
- The body design involves minimal differentiation and division into tissues.
- These organisms are acoelomate (body cavity absent) with cellular level of body organisation. e.g., *Sycon* (scypha), *Spongilla* (freshwater sponge), etc.

(ii) Phylum-Coelenterata (Cnidaria)

The name Cnidaria is derived from cnidocytes present on the body. 'Cnidae' was quoted by **Aristotle**.

Following are the features of coelenterates :

- These are multicellular and are found in seas and water bodies.
- These animals live in water and show more body design differentiation.
- Coelenterates are also referred to as cnidarians.
- The body is made up of two layers of cells–one makes up cells on the outside of the body and the other makes the inner lining of the body and are called **diploblastic**.
- They exhibit tissue level of organisation.
- These also exhibit **radial symmetry**. Alternation of generation is found.
- Cnidarians exhibit two basic body forms—**polyp** and **medusa**.
- There is only one hole. It acts as mouth part as well as anus. There occur maximum chances of **regeneration**.
- Both sexual and asexual reproduction can be seen in these. e.g., anemone, jellyfish, etc.
- These animals live in water and show more body design differentiation.
- Colelenterates are also referred to as cnidarians.
- The body is made up of two layers of cells-one makes up cells on the outside of the body and the other makes the living of the body.
- Some of these species live in colonies (corals), while others have a solitary lifespan (*Hydra*).
- These are the first multicellular animals, which possess tissue level of organisation with a distinct division of labour.

  e.g., *Hydra*, *Aurelia* (jellyfish), *Adamsia* (sea-anemone), *Obelia*, etc.

(iii) Phylum-Platyhelminthes (Flatworms)

This is a group of soft bodied, flattened invertebrates having the following characteristics :

- They are mostly parasitic animals (living in the bodies of other animals) like liverflukes and some are free-living like *Planaria*.
- They are the first simplest **triploblastic animals**, i.e., having three layers of cells from which differentiated tissues can be made.
- The body is bilaterally symmetrical, meaning that the left and the right halves of the body have the same design. Body cavity or **coelom** is absent (**acoelomate**), with organ level of organisation.
- The body is dorsoventrally flattened, so they are called **flatworms**.
- Adhesive structures like **hooks**, **spines**, **suckers** are commonly found.
- Some members of the phylum have **pseudometamerism** (external body segments and every segment is independent of the other).
- Real head is not found in any member of the phylum. However, this phylum shows differentiation of head.
- Body of such organisms has a covering made of cuticle, which is resistant to any acid, base or enzyme.
- Digestive system is branched and incomplete without anus. However, respiratory, skeletal and circulatory systems are present.
- These have **flame cells** for excretion and fertilisation is internal. e.g., tapeworm.

(iv) Phylum-Nematoda (Thread or Roundworm)

These are free-living or may be parasitic and show the following characteristics :

- Their body is unsegmented and lined with **cuticle**.
- Mouth is found in frontal part and anus is found in posterior part.
- These are parasitic worms causing diseases such as elephantiasis (filarial worms) or the worms in the intestines (roundworm). The nematode body is bilaterally symmetrical and triploblastic.
- Body is elongated, narrow and cylindrical.
- Body do not have true coelom, it is called **pseudocoelom**.
- These are the first animals to have a complete and straight alimentary canal.
- Respiratory and circulatory system is absent in such organisms, whereas nervous system is developed.
- They have separate sexes and also show sexual dimorphism.

  e.g., *Ascaris* (roundworm), *Wuchereria* (filarial worm), etc.

(v) Phylum-Annelida (Segmented Worms)

- These animals are found in a variety of habitats freshwater, marine water as well as land.
- They are bilaterally symmetrical, triploblastic animals with organ level of organisation.

- Annelids are the first animals with true body cavity.
- Their body is covered by extra skin.
- Movement is facilitated by **parapodia, seta** or **suckers** and excretion is done by **nephridia**.
- Circulatory system is closed type, i.e., blood vessel and heart like organ is found carrying respiratory pigment (haemoglobin) in it.
- Nervous system is highly developed. They can be monosexual or bisexual and show either direct or indirect development as shown by earthworm.
- They have **metameric segmentation** with extensive organ differentiation. The segments of the body are lined up one after the other from head to tail.

 e.g., *Pheretima* (earthworm), *Hirudinaria* (leech), *Nereis*.

(vi) Phylum-Arthropoda (Animals with Jointed Legs)

This phylum includes the crabs, prawns, insects, spiders, mites, millipedes, etc.

They possess the following features :

- Arthropoda is the **largest group** of animals.
- They have segmented body which is divided into three regions-head, thorax and abdomen.
- The body is bilaterally symmetrical. They have modified **jointed appendages** that are specified for certain functions.
- The body wall consists of a thick **chitinous** exoskeleton.
- These are organisms which do not possess **cilia**.
- They have a complete digestive system.
- Respiration generally occurs by specialised organs, like **gills, trachea** or **book-lungs**.
- Body cavity contains blood and is called **haemocoel**.
- Circulatory system is generally **open type**.
- The excretory system may possess **green glands**, which directly open to the exterior or **Malpighian tubules** that open in gut.
- These have highly developed nervous system in which there is presence of nerve ring. Sense organs are found.
- These develop by two ways, i.e., development is either direct or indirect.
- Sexes are separate in such organisms and fertilisation is internal in most cases.
- They are found everywhere on the Earth-on land, in soil, in water and as parasites on plants and other animals.
- They show advancements over annelids in **having distinct heads, jointed appendages and developed sense organs.**
- e.g., *Palaemon* (prawn), scorpion, spider, butterfly, *Periplaneta* (cockroach), *Musca* (housefly), *Apis* (honeybee), *Anopheles* (mosquito), *Bombyx* (silkmoth).

(vii) Phylum-Mollusca (Soft Bodied Animals)

This is the **second largest** animal phylum and includes oysters, snails and cuttlefishes.

These have the following characteristics :

- They are **triploblastic and coelomate** animals.
- Body is covered by a **calcareous** shell and is unsegmented with a distinct head, muscular foot and visceral hump.
- They are usually soft bodied animals which have a thin layer of **mantle.** It is covered or surrounded by hard covering of calcium carbonate in the form of shell.
- Sexes are usually separate and fertilisation is either external or internal.
- They are mostly aquatic, living in sea water, some occur in freshwater.
- Bilateral symmetry is present.
- Their digestive tract is complete. Anus opens into a mantle cavity.
- The circulatory system is usually open. Blood has a blue-coloured respiratory pigment **haemocyanin.**
- The coelomic cavity is reduced and there is little segmentation.
- The body is divided into an anterior head, a ventral muscular foot and a dorsal visceral mass.
- Locomotion is brought about by muscular foot.

 e.g., *Chiton, Octopus, Pila, Unio, Sepia, Loligo.*

(viii) Phylum-Echinodermata (Spiny-Skinned Animals)

The members of this phylum have an endoskeleton of calcareous ossicles and have the following characteristics :

- They are exclusively free-living marine animals.
- Body is **triploblastic** and has a **coelomic** cavity.
- They have a peculiar water driven tube system that they use for moving around. It is called **water vascular system.**
- They have hard calcium carbonate structures that they use as a skeleton. Their digestive system is complete.
- Fertilisation is generally external.
- Symmetry is radial (Pentamerous radial symmetry) in adults but bilateral in larvae.

 e.g., *Asterias* (starfish), *Echinus* (sea urchin).

(ix) Protochordata
(Proto-first, Chordata-notochord)

They were initially considered sub-phylum under phylum-Chordata. Now, it is considered as separate phylum.

These are also called **half Chordata** or **Hemichordata** and have the following characteristics :

- They are exclusively **marine**, **triploblastic** and **coelomate**.
- A long rod-like support structure called **notochord** is present at some stage of life.
- These are worm-like animals and lack locomotory appendages.
- Excretory organ is **proboscis gland**. Sexes are separate and fertilisation is external.
  e.g., *Balanoglossus*.

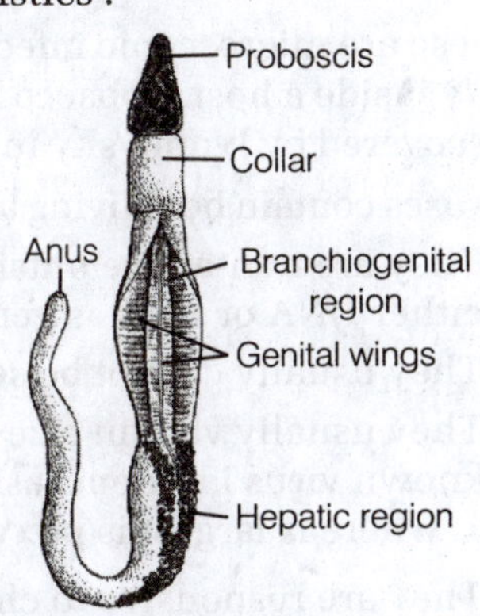

Balanoglossus

(x) Phylum-Chordata (Vertebrata)

- It comprises of all animals species including mammals, birds, reptiles, amphibians and fishes.
  Diagnostic characters of chordates are as follows :
  - **Notochord** It is a solid, unjointed, flexible rod, which is located between alimentary canal and nerve cord of the embryo. It persists throughout the life in lower chordates, but is partially or wholly replaced by a backbone.
  - **Dorsal hollow nerve cord** It forms nervous system in animals. It is located above the notochord front end. Dorsal hollow nerve cord forms brain and the remaining part forms spinal cord.
  - **Pharyngeal gill slits** These are paired openings which are retained throughout life in lower organisms, but are modified for other functions like hearing in higher animals.
- These animals have a true vertebral column and internal skeleton.
- Vertebrates are bilaterally symmetrical, segmented with complex differentiation of body tissues and organs.
- Vertebrates are grouped into one superclass and five classes, i.e., **Pisces, Amphibia, Reptilia, Aves** and **Mammalia.**

Classification of Phylum-Chordata

Phylum-Chordata is divided into following super classes :

(i) Superclass-Pisces

- These are fishes and exclusively live in water (aquatic).
- The body is covered with scales/plates.
- Body is streamlined and fins are present but limbs are absent.
- Respiration is through gills. They lay eggs.
- They are cold-blooded.
- Their heart is **two-chambered** having one auricle and one ventricle.
- Fertilisation is internal.
- Fishes are of two types based on the nature of their skeleton :
  - **Cartilaginous fish** Some with the skeleton made entirely of cartilage such as sharks, rays, etc. They are found in deep oceans.
  - **Bony fish** Some with skeleton made up of bones such as *Labeo rohita* (Rohu), *Catla, Hilsa, Exocoetus* (flying fish), *Hippocampus* (seahorse), etc. They are found in freshwater, but may be a part of marine water.

(ii) Superclass-Tetrapoda

It is classified into four groups :

(a) Class-Amphibia

- The amphibians are the first land vertebrates, but they are found both in water and land.
- Larval stages are found in water. They have moist skin without scales.
- Respiration is through gills lungs and skin.
- Heart is **three-chambered** and they lay eggs.
- Head and trunk is distinct, neck and tail may or may not be present.
- e.g., frogs (*Rana tigrina*), toads and salamanders.

(b) Class-Reptilia

- This class consists of creeping animals. They are also called **first true terrestrial animals.**
- They are first terrestrial animals living in warmer regions.
- They are cold-blooded animals.
- Their body is covered by dry and cornified skin.
- These are **poikilotherms** and they undergo internal fertilisation.
- Body is covered with epidermal scales.
- Most of them have **three-chambered** heart, while crocodiles have **four-chambered** heart.
- Skin is rough and dry. An exoskeleton of epidermal scales is present. However, it is sloughed off periodically.
- They lay eggs with thick covering on land.
  e.g., snakes, lizards, turtles and crocodiles.

(c) Class-Aves (Birds)

Since, the birds developed from reptiles, they are also called **glorified reptiles.**

They have the following characters :

- They are warm-blooded animals and their heart is **four-chambered.**

- They lay eggs, i.e., oviparous and their body is covered with a feathery endoskeleton.
- The two forelimbs are modified into wings for flight.
- They breathe through lungs.
- Endoskeleton is light with the bones having air cavities.
- Jaws are modified to form a strong beak. They do not have external ears.
- They are homoiothermic organisms.

 e.g., ostrich, pigeon, sparrow, crow, duck, owl, peacock, parrot, etc.

(d) Class-Mammalia

Mammals are the members of the vertebrate group of animals in which the young ones are nourished from the mammary glands.

They also include animals that possess hair and other features are as follows :

- They are found in diverse habitats ranging from deserts, polar ice caps, oceans, mountains, forests and grasslands.
- They are warm-blooded animals. Heart is four-chambered with two auricles and two ventricles.
- They have mammary glands for the production of milk to nourish their young ones.
- The skin of mammals has hair as well as sweat, mammary and oil glands. Milk glands are the characteristic feature. Hairs present on our body help in regulation of body temperature.
- They give birth to living young ones and are called as **viviparous**, except some like platypus and echidna lay eggs and some like kangaroo give birth to very poorly developed young ones.
- Respiration occurs through lungs.
- Their body is divided into head, neck, trunk and tail.
- Body shapes are variable, forelimbs and hindlimbs are present.
- Their mouth is small with rigid lips, teeth and jaws.
- They have 7 cervical vertebrae present in neck.
- Brain has large cerebrum and cerebellum. Nervous system is advanced type.
- Sense organs are highly developed with specific functions.
- They have an endoskeleton made up of bones.
- Excretory system is highly developed. Main excretory organ is kidney, which is present in pair.
- Sexes can be easily distinguished and fertilisation is internal.
- They are endothermic and can regulate temperature of the body (homoiothermous).

 e.g., humans, whales, cat, rat, bat, monkey, elephant, tiger, etc.

Viruses

These are microscopic infectious particles which replicate only inside a host. Tobacco Mosaic Virus (TMV) was first discovered by **Ivanovsky** in 1892.

Viruses contain both living and non-living characteristics :

- They are non-active outside the host. These contain either DNA or RNA as genetic material.
- They usually cannot be seen with normal microscope.
- They usually vary in size from 10-300 μm. Smallest known virus is **Adeno-associated Virus** (AAV) about 20 μ, whereas largest is **poxvirus** of 300 μm.
- They are responsive to chemicals, radiations and high temperature.
- Virus have protein coating that protects the nucleic acid. It is called **capsid**.

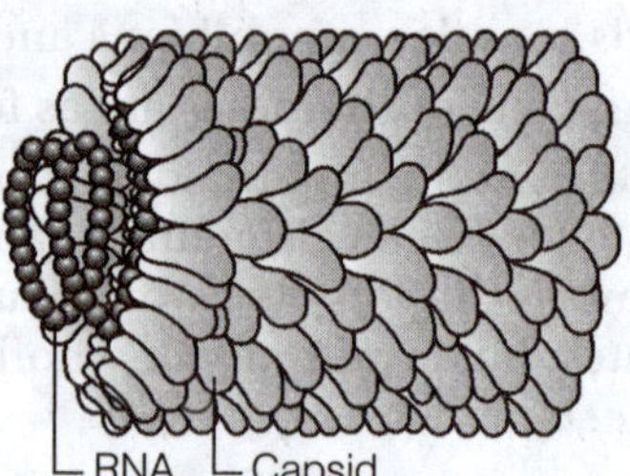

Tabacco Mosaic Virus (TMV)

Viroids

- These are infectious agents which affect only plants.
- These are smaller than viruses and have circular strands of RNA without protein coating.
- Viroids were discovered by **TO Diener** in 1971. It was first examined in potato spindle tuber, viroid that caused a huge loss to potato industry.
- Since, these attack only plants, they are also called **plant pathogens**.

Extra Facts From Tamil Nadu Board and NIOS

- Flatworms are hermaphrodite having both male and female reproductive organs in a single individual.
- Exoskeleton is made of **chitin** and is shed periodically as the animal grows. The casting off and regrowing of exoskeleton is called **moulting**.
- In aves, hindlimbs are adapted for walking, perching or swimming.

Cell

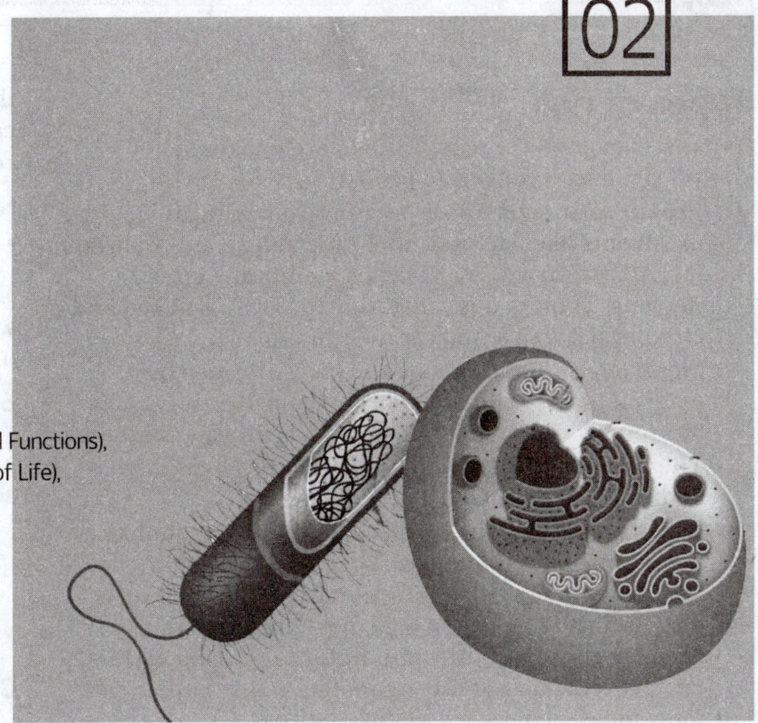

02

[SOURCES]

Class-VIII Old NCERT Chap 8 (Cell : Structure and Functions), Class-IX NCERT Chap 5 (The Fundamental Unit of Life), Class-XI NCERT Chap 8 (Cell : The Unit of Life), Chap 10 (Cell Cycle and Cell Division)

- **Robert Hooke** in 1665 observed honeycomb structure from a thin slice of cork through a self-designed microscope. He found that these cells consists of many little compartments or boxes whom he called **cells**.
- **Leeuwenhoek** in 1674 discovered the free-living cells in pond water for the first time with the help of improved microscope.
- **Robert Brown** in 1831 discovered the nucleus in the cell.
- **Purkinje** in 1839 coined the term **'protoplasm'** for the fluid substance of the cell.

Cell Theory

- Cell theory was given by two biologists **Schleiden** (1838) and **Schwann** (1839).
- According to this theory, all the plants and animals are composed of cells. The cell is the basic unit of life.
- The cell theory was further expanded by **Virchow** (1855) by suggesting that all cells arise from pre-existing cells.
- The discovery of electron microscope in 1940 made it possible to observe and understand the complex structure of the cell and its various organelles.
- Based on the number of cells, an organism may be **unicellular** or **multicellular**.
- The organisms such as *Amoeba, Chlamydomonas, Paramecium* and bacteria are made up of single cell and are called **unicellular organisms**.
- In many **multicellular organisms** such as some fungi, plants and animals, many cells group together in a single body and assume different functions in it to form various body parts.

Shape and Size of Cells

- Some cells have fixed shape (e.g., most plant and animal cells), while some cells like WBCs and *Amoeba* keep changing their shapes and are pleomorphic.
- Fixed shaped cells may be of various types like **elliptical** (e.g., fat cell), **spherical** (e.g., ovum), **spindle-shaped** (e.g., smooth muscle cell), **knobbed thread** (e.g., sperm), **discoidal** (e.g., RBC), **elongated** (e.g., nerve cells), etc.

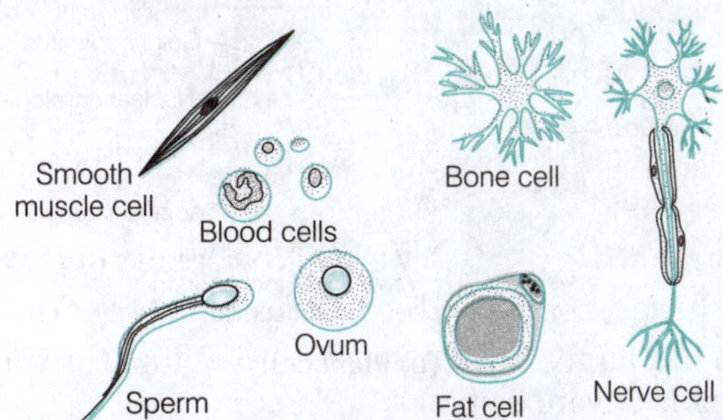

Various cells from the human body

- The size of cell varies significantly from the smallest cell of **mycoplasma** 0.3 μm to very large egg cells of the **ostrich** 18 cm. Longest cells of human body are the **nerve cells**, which may reach up to a length of 90 cm.

Types of Cell

Cells are categorised on the basis of organisation, complexity and variety as follows :

(i) **Prokaryotic cells** These are represented by unicellular organisms like bacteria, blue-green algae, mycoplasma, etc. All prokaryotic cells lack a membrane bound nucleus. Their genetic material i.e., DNA is naked and circular without a nuclear membrane.
Mesosomes (membranous structures formed by extensions of plasma membrane) and 70S ribosomes 50S+30S which are sites of protein synthesis are found. These lack membrane bound organelles like Golgi bodies, chloroplast, etc.

(ii) **Eukaryotic cells** These cells contain a true, double membrane bound nucleus. They possess membrane bound organelles like mitochondria. Cytoskeleton is present inside the cytoplasm and consists of micro filaments, microtubules and fibres to provide perfect shape to cell anchor the organelles and stimulate cell movement.

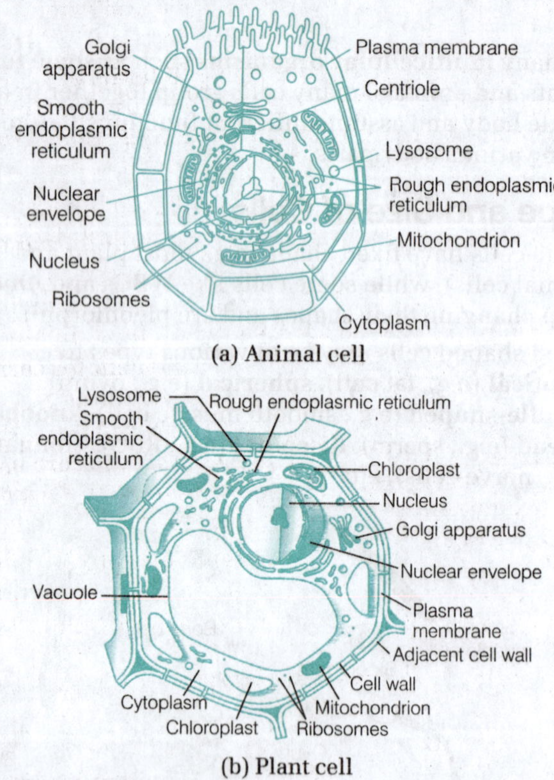

(a) Animal cell

(b) Plant cell

Structural Organisation of a Cell

Each cell has got certain specific compartments within it known as **cell organelles**. A cell is able to live and perform all its functions because of these organelles. These organelles together constitute the basic unit called the **cell**. The components of a cell can be broadly categorised under following three categories :

- Outer covering–cell wall, cell membrane.
- Protoplasm–fluid content of cell.
- Cell organelles–chloroplast, mitochondria, etc.

1. Outer Covering

- This includes cell wall and cell membrane. It is outermost, rigid and non-living covering of a cell.

Plasma Membrane

- The plasma membrane is flexible and is made up of organic molecules called **lipids** and **proteins**.
- The flexibility of the cell membrane enables the cell to engulf in food and other material from its external environment. Such processes are known as **endocytosis** like *Amoeba* which acquire its food through this process.

Cell Wall

- It is outer rigid covering present in plant cells, fungal cells and bacteria.
- Cell wall in plants is mainly composed of cellulose whereas, fungal cell wall contains **chitin** whereas. bacterial cell wall is made up of **peptidoglycan**.
- Cellulose is a complex substance and provides structural strength to plants.
- It is also responsible for a proper shape of the cell.
- When a living plant cell loses water through osmosis there is shrinkage of the contents of the cell away from the cell wall. This phenomenon is known as **plasmolysis**.
  (i) **Hypotonic solution** The medium or solution surrounding the cell has high water concentration as compared to inside of the cell (or the outside solution is very dilute). The cell gain water and swells up *via* **endosmosis**.
  (ii) **Isotonic solution** The medium surrounding a cell has same concentration of water as that present inside the cell.
  Thus, water crosses the cell membrane in both directions, but amount moving in remains the same as the amount moving out.
  (iii) **Hypertonic solution** The medium surrounding a cell has a lower concentration of water than the cell (i.e., outside solution is very concentrated). Water moves out of the cell and as a result, the cell protoplasm gets shrinked (**exosmosis**).
- Cell walls permits the cells of plants, fungi and bacteria to withstand very dilute (hypotonic) external media without bursting.

2. Protoplasm

- It is the complex fluid part of the cell that is viscous and colourless.
- It is living part of the cell, i.e., is capable of performing all the vital activities.
- **Thomas Huxley** (1869) referred protoplasm as the '**physical basis of life**' and considered that the property of life is a result of distribution of molecules within this substance.
- **Cytoplasm** (fluid content inside plasma membrane) and **nucleoplasm** (fluid content inside nucleus), together constitute **protoplasm**.
- Protoplasm of two adjacent cells are linked together by plasmodesmata present in the cell wall or cell membrane and help in exchange of materials.

3. Nucleus

- Since, it is the control center of metabolic activities occurring inside a cell, it is popularly called as the **brain of cell**.
- It is a double membrane bound dense body that has a control over all cellular metabolism and encloses the genetic information of the cell.
- **Robert Brown** is credited with the **discovery of nucleus** in the year 1831.
- Cells are usually stained with safranin, methylene blue, iodine solution in order to observe nucleus.

Following are the components of nucleus

(i) **Nuclear membrane** It is also called **nuclear envelope** and is bilayered, i.e., it consists of outer and inner membranes. These are separated by means of **perinuclear space** and contain **nuclear pores** for exchange of material.

(ii) **Chromatin** These are fine fibres comprising of DNA, some proteins (histone proteins) and transcribing RNA. During cell division, the chromatin condenses to form thick specialised structures called **chromosomes.**

(iii) **Nucleolus** It is a spherical membraneless body found within the nucleus and consists of DNA, RNA and proteins. It is formed from specific sites on chromosomes and is a site of ribosome synthesis.

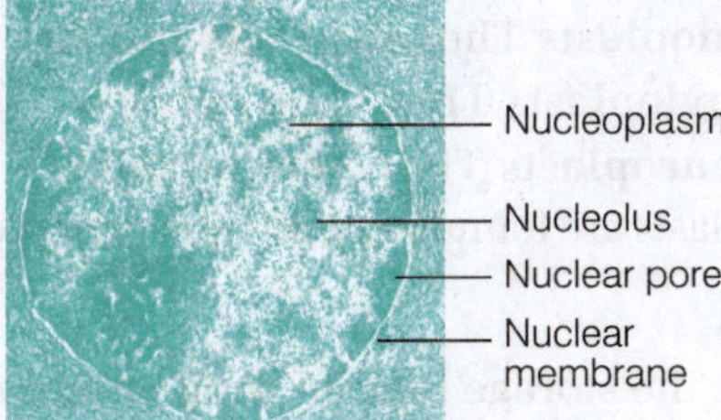

Structure of nucleus

4. Cell Organelles

- Many type of metabolic functions and processes take place in a cell collectively. These are done by cell organelles as they have a unique characteristics of **division of labour**, i.e., cells or organelles perform a specific function.
- Large and complex cells, including cells from multicellular organisms, need a lot of chemical activities to support their complicated structure and function.
- Cell organelles are membrane bound structures in the cell that perform specialised functions within themselves.

Endoplasmic Reticulum (ER)

- It is a large network of membrane bound tubes and sheets. It extends from outer nuclear membrane into the cytoplasm. It looks like long tubules, round and oblong bags (vesicles).
- The ER membrane is similar in structure to the plasma membrane. It occurs in three forms, i.e., cisternae, vesicles and tubules.

Depending upon the nature of its membrane, ER is of two types namely :

Rough Endoplasmic Reticulum (RER)

It has particles called **ribosomes** attached to its surface. These ribosomes are the sites of **protein synthesis**.

Smooth Endoplasmic Reticulum (SER)

It helps in manufacture of fat molecules or lipids. It is formed of vesicles and tubules. SER plays a crucial role in detoxifying many poisons and drugs.

- ER appears in varying forms in different cells. It always form a network system of vesicles and tubules and forms cytoskeleton in cytoplasm.
- ER functions as channels for the transport of materials (especially proteins) between various regions of the cytoplasm or between the cytoplasm and the nucleus.

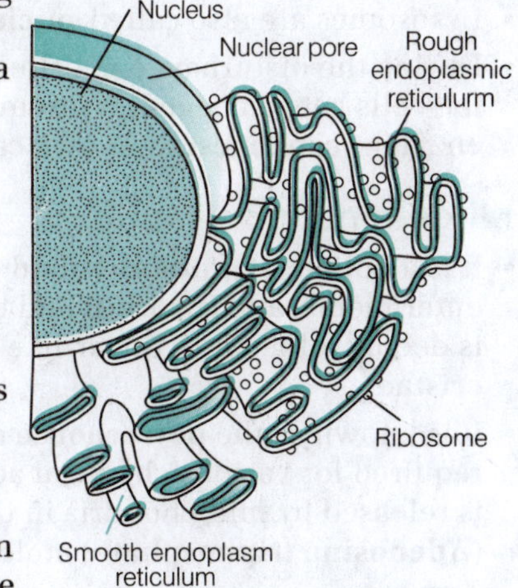

Endoplasmic reticulum

Ribosomes

- These are dense granules which do not have any membrane.

- These are found in all cells which synthesise proteins.
- These may be of 70S or 80S type (**S is Svedberg's unit**).

Golgi Apparatus
(Traffic Police of Cell)

- It was first described by **Camillo Golgi** and consists of a system of membrane bound vesicles arranged approximately parallel to each other in stacks called **cisternae**.
- These membranes often have connections with the membranes of ER, therefore material synthesised near the ER is packaged and dispatched to various targets inside and outside the cell through Golgi apparatus.
- Golgi apparatus is involved in formation of **lysosomes, plasma membrane, cell wall and complex sugars** from simpler ones.

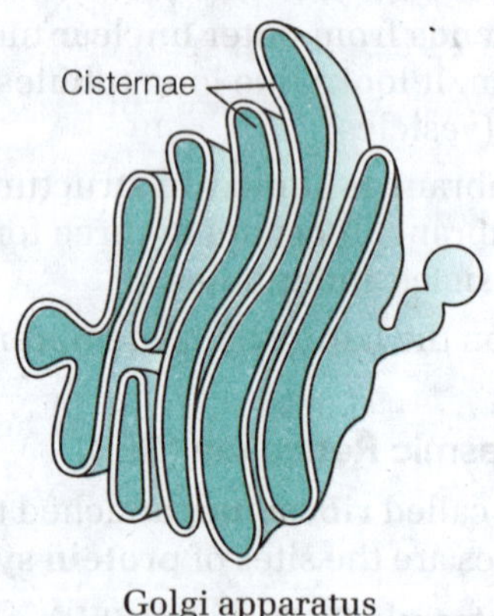

Golgi apparatus

Lysosomes

- These are membrane bound sacs, filled with digestive enzymes, which are made by RER.
- Lysosomes are also called **suicidal bags**.
- During the disturbance in cellular metabolism or when the cells gets damaged, lysosomes may burst and the enzymes can digest their own cell.

Mitochondria

- It is a double membrane bound cell organelle. The outer membrane is porous and the inner membrane is deeply folded into finger-like projections called **cristae**.
- It is known as the **powerhouse of the cell.** The energy required for various chemical activities needed for life is released by mitochondria in the form of ATP (**Adenosine triphosphate**) molecules.
- ATP is known as **energy currency** of the cell.
- Mitochondria is **self-replicating** (semi-autonomous) **organelle**. Which has its own protein synthesising machinery. 70S type ribosomes are found in mitochondria.
- **Mitochondria** F_1-particles are found in the mitochondria matrix and performs a major role in the formation ATP molecules. F_1-particles are also called **oxysomes**.

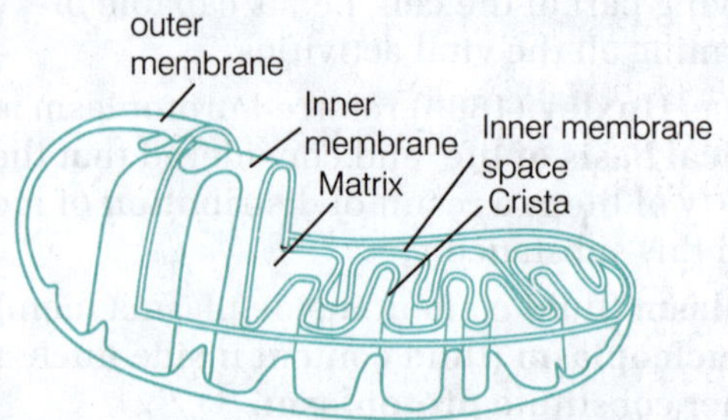

Structure of mitochondrion (Longitudinal section)

Plastids

- These are double membrane bound organelles found only in plant cells and have their own DNA and ribosomes like mitochondria.
- The internal organisation of the plastids consists of numerous membrane layers embedded in a material called the **stroma**.

Plastids can be categorised as :

(a) **Chromoplasts** These are variously coloured plastids, majorly yellow or reddish in colour, due to the presence of carotenoid pigments. These are found in coloured parts of a plant like flower, fruits, etc.

(b) **Chloroplast** These are green coloured plastids which contain chlorophyll as the major pigment, apart from carotenoid. It takes part in **photosynthesis**. Chloroplasts of algae other than green ones are called **chromatophores.**

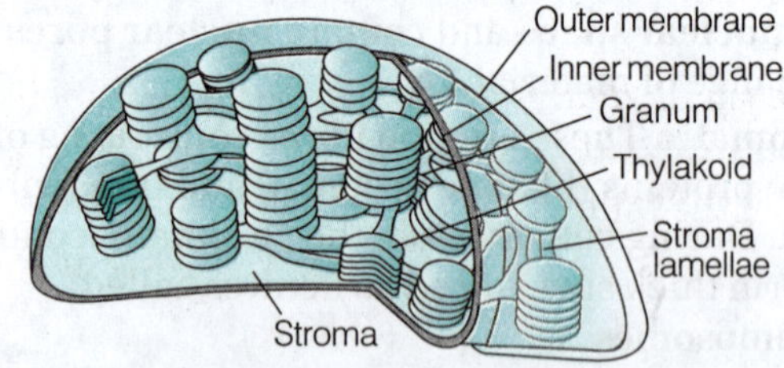

Sectional view of chloroplast

(c) **Leucoplasts** These are colourless plastids which are used for storage purposes.
These are of the following types :
- **Elaioplasts** They store oils and fats.
- **Amyloplasts** They store starch.
- **Aleuroplasts** They store proteins.

Leucoplasts are found in roots, underground stems, etc.

Vacuoles

- These are the storage sacs for solid or liquid contents.
- Vacuoles are small sized in animal cells while plant cells have a very large vacuole.

- The vacuole is bounded by a membrane called as **tonoplast**.
- The central vacuole is 50-90% of cell volume.
- In plant cells vacuoles are full of cell sap and provide turgidity and rigidity to the cell.
- Vacuoles helps to store amino acids, sugars, various organic acids and some proteins. They are thus called **dustbin of cell.**

Cytoskeleton

- It is a *criss-cross* network of interconnected filaments and tubules, called cytoskeleton.
- It extends from nucleus to plasma membrane and supports the shape of the cell. It also helps in anchoring cells organelles to fixed locations.

Centrosome and Centriole

- These are specialised structures of animal cells, lower plants and primitive flagellates only.
- A centrosome is made up of two cylindrical, rod-shaped structures, called **centrioles**, which are oriented at right angles to each other.
- A centriole can be differentiated into two regions **central** and **peripheral.**
- The latter contains fibrils of tubulin proteins which further possess **triplet fibril.**
- Adjacent triplet fibrils are interconnected and the central part (hub) consists of one or two longitudinally arranged strands.
- Centriole takes part in the formation of **cilia, flagella** and **spindle** fibres during cell division.

Microbodies

These are small, many-membrane bound organelles associated with oxidative reactions.

They are of the following types :

(a) Peroxisomes (b) Glyoxysomes

Difference between Plant and Animal Cells

Characters	Animal Cells	Plant Cells
Cell wall	Absent	Present (formed of cellulose)
Shape	Round (irregular shape)	Rectangular (fixed shape)
Centrioles	Present in all animal cells	Only present in lower plant forms
Vacuole	One or more small vacuoles (much smaller than plant cells)	One, large central vacuole taking up 90% of cell volume
Lysosomes	Lysosomes occur in cytoplasm	Lysosomes are usually not evident

Cell Cycle

- It is a sequential event by which a cell duplicates its genome, synthesise new cell constituents, undergoes growth and divides into two daughter cells.
- Duration of cell cycle varies with the organism. It may last up to 20 minutes (e.g., microbes), 90 minutes (e.g., yeast) and 24 hours (e.g., humans).
- Cell cycle occurs in the following two phases :

1. Interphase

- It represents the phase between two successive M-phases.
- It is the resting phase of the cell in which the cell does not divide, but prepares itself for division.
- It occurs in the following three phases :

(i) **G_1-phase or First gap phase** It represents the time between mitosis and initiation of DNA replication DNA content remains same in this phase.

(ii) **S-phase or Synthesis phase** In this phase, DNA replication occurs and DNA content doubles from 2C to 4C.

(iii) **G_2-phase or Second gap phase** It is the preparatory phase for cell division, protein and RNA synthesis.

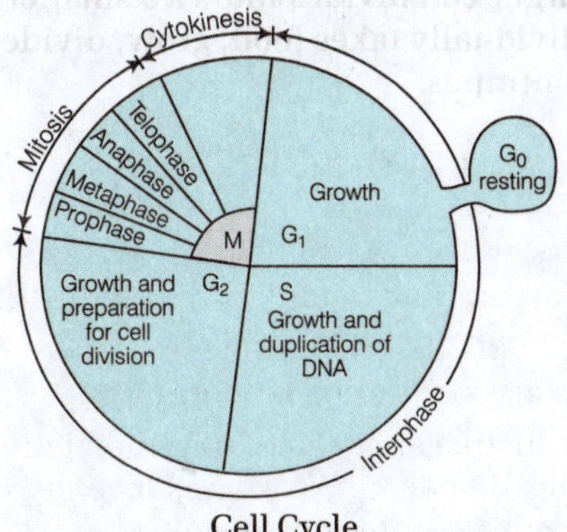

Cell Cycle

2. M-Phase (Dividing Phase)

- It is the phase of cell division in which already duplicated chromosomes get distributed into two daughter nuclei.
- It starts with division of nucleus (**karyokinesis**) and ends at division of cytoplasm (**cytokinesis**).
- Cell division is an important phase which lasts for about 1 hour in human beings.

Cell division is of two types :

Mitosis (Equational Division)

- It is a continuous process that gives rise to two identical cells, but the number of chromosomes in them remains the same.

- It helps in the growth and development of multicellular organisms, in healing and repair of wounds and in maintaining chromosome number (for asexual reproduction occurring in *Amoeba*).
- Since, it occurs during asexual reproduction, there are less or majorly no chances of genetic variations.
- Various phases in which mitosis occurs are :
  - **Prophase** It is first and the longest phase of cell division. It continues for about 50 minutes. It involves the condensation of chromosomal material.
  - **Metaphase** It is short and simple phase that lasts for only 2-10 minutes. In this phase, chromosome move towards the equatorial plane of the spindle.
  - **Anaphase** It continues for about 2-3 minutes only. As each chromosome moves away from the equatorial plate, the centromeres of each chromosome splits and the sister chromatids separates to move towards the opposite poles.
  - **Telophase** The chromosomes that have reached their respective poles start to decondense and lose their individuality. Cell organelles like nucleolus, Golgi complex and ER are reformed again.
- At the end of mitosis, division of cytoplasm and equal distribution of cell organelles in two daughter cells occurs by the process of **cytokinesis**. During this process, the original larger cell divides into two smaller identical cells, which individually takes food, grow, divide and the process continues.

Meiosis

- It is restricted to only reproductive cells due to which gametes are produced.
- As meiosis results in the reduction of chromosome number, by half it is called **reductional division.**
- Meiosis involves **crossing over** and hence leads to variation. It consists of two stages of division which occur successively.

Extra Facts From Tamil Nadu Board and NIOS

- **Plasma membrane** is the outer covering of the cells that separates the contents of the cells from its external environment.
- The plasma membrane allows or permits the entry and exit of some materials in and out of the cells. It also prevents the movement of some other materials. The cell membrane, therefore is called a selectively permeable membrane.
- **Cell wall** of plant, fungi and bacteria withstand much greater changes in the surrounding medium than animal cells.
- **Vacuole** helps the cells to perform functions like respiration, obtaining nutrition and clearing of waste material, or forming new proteins.

Tissues

03

(SOURCES)

Class-IX NCERT Chap 6 (Tissues), Class-XI NCERT Chap 7 (Structural Organisation in Animals) Tamil Nadu Board (Class-IX), NIOS

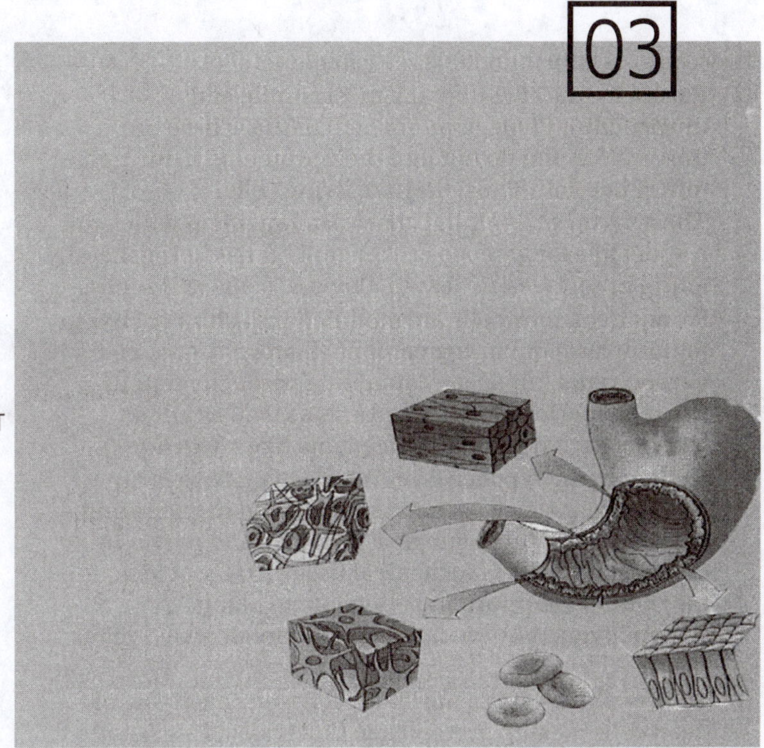

- A tissue is a group of cells that are structurally similar and carry out a specific function.
- In multicellular organisms, different group of cells perform different functions. This is called **division of labour**.
- Tissues further form organs and organ systems.
- The branch of biology that deals with the study of tissues called **Histology**.
- Tissues are broadly classified as **plant tissues** and **animal tissues.**

Plant Tissues

- Most of the tissues of the plants are dead and provide mechanical support to them.
- Based on the ability of a cell to divide, plant tissues are categorised as meristematic and permanent tissues :

1. Meristematic Tissue

- The tissues in which cells always remain in a continuous state of division, i.e., actively divide throughout their life are **meristematic tissue.**
- These are further classified into three parts based on their position in the plant body :

(i) **Apical meristem** These are found at the apices (growing tips) of main and lateral shoots and roots. The tissue is responsible for growth (in length) of roots and shoots, i.e., **primary growth.**

(ii) **Intercalary meristem** They lie at the base of leaves or on internodes. They are also found in between the permanent tissues. These help in **longitudinal growth** of plant by adding primary tissue.

(iii) **Lateral meristem** These are secondary meristems, responsible for **secondary growth.** The meristem is present along the lateral sides of stems and roots and lie especially in the mature regions of roots and shoots. e.g., cambium.

2. Permanent Tissues (Mature Tissues)

- These are made up of mature cells which have lost their ability of cell division. These are formed as a result of division and **differentiation** in meristematic tissues.
- These may be dead or living in nature. Cellular walls may or may not be thick.

On the basis of types of cells, these are of the two types :

(I) Simple Permanent Tissues

These are composed of similar types of cells and coordinate with each other to perform similar functions.

These are classified under three categories :

(a) **Parenchyma** These are the most simple and unspecialised type of permanent tissue. These are thin-walled and do not lose their protoplasm during differentiation. Thus, they are living cells.
These have intercellular spaces among them which are responsible for gaseous exchange. This tissue is generally found in roots, stem, leaves, flowers, fruits and seeds.
Parenchymatous cells are modified into **chlorenchyma** (chloroplast containing parenchymatous tissue) and **aerenchyma** (air space containing parenchymatous tissue) to perform photosynthesis as well as allow gaseous exchange in aquatic plants like *Hydrilla*.

(b) **Collenchyma** It consists of living cells. There is no intercellular space as they are elongated in shape and have irregular thickenings of cellulose and pectin in cellular walls. It is mechanical tissue that provides **mechanical support** and **elasticity** to plants.
Collenchyma tissue is not found in monocotyledonous plants.

(c) **Sclerenchyma** It is a mechanical tissue consisting of dead cells lacking protoplasm. Cell walls of such cells are greatly thickened due to the deposition of **lignin** or **cellulose** (or both).
These lack intercellular spaces and are of two types :
- **Sclerenchyma fibres** They occur in parts requiring mechanical strength.
  - **Sclereids or Stone cells** These are found in the hard parts of the plant.

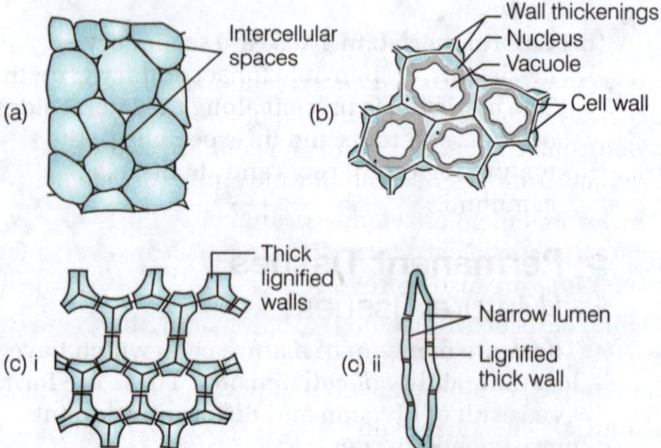

Various types of simple tissues : (a) Parenchyma (b) Collenchyma (c) Sclerenchyma (i) transverse section, (ii) longitudinal section

(ii) Complex Permanent Tissue

These are another type of permanent tissue which comprise of more than one type of cells. However, they perform different functions. They constitute the conducting tissues of the plants as follows :

(a) Xylem

- It is the chief conducting tissue of vascular plants. It is responsible for the conduction of water and inorganic solutes (minerals) from roots to apical parts of the plants.
- It also provides mechanical strength and rigidity to plants. It exists in the vascular pores of roots, stem and leaves of the plant.
- It has four main components, namely :
  - **Tracheids** These are dead, long, tubular structures with tapering ends which transport water and minerals vertically. They have varied lignin thickenings.
  - **Vessels** These are dead, long, tube-like structures formed by a row of cells, placed end-to-end. Cell wall is more lignified. They also help in conduction of water.
  - **Xylem parenchyma** These are living cells which help in radial conduction of water. Their cell walls are made up of cellulose. They store food material and tannins.
  - **Xylem fibres** These are dead, elongated cells having tapering ends. They have thick lignified walls. The lumen of xylem fibres is highly reduced. They provide mechanical support to the plant.

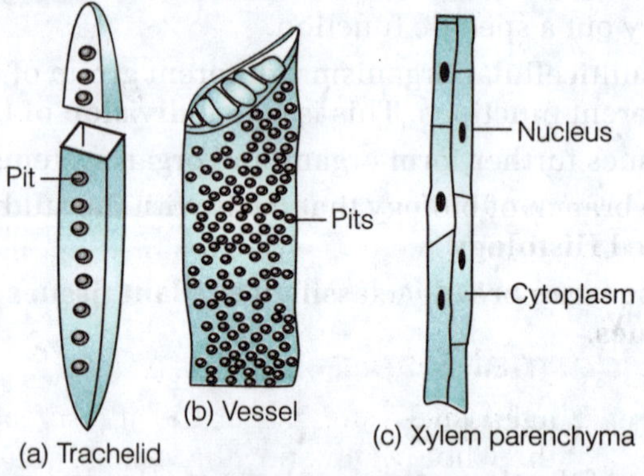

Types of xylem

(b) Phloem

- It is the chief conducting tissue of vascular plants responsible for the **bi-directional** conduction of organic solutes.
- Phloem is made up of the following four kinds of elements, namely :
  - **Sieve tubes** These are tubular cells arranged one above the other in longitudinal rows. Cell walls of sieve tube elements are thin and cellulosic. End walls of sieve tube elements are perforated. These are called **sieve plates** and possess many **sieve pores**. They are absent in **pteridophytes** and **gymnosperms**.

- **Companion cells** These are small, elongated cells having thin walls which are not perforated and have active cytoplasm. These are found to be attached to the lateral sides of sieve tubes. Companion cells are living and are found in angiosperms only. These control the functions of sieve tube elements.
- **Phloem fibres** They are known as **bast fibres**. These are thick walled sclerenchymatous cells which provide mechanical strength to the tissue.
- **Phloem parenchyma** These are the living cells of phloem tissue. These are thin walled cells which help in storage and show lateral conduction of food.

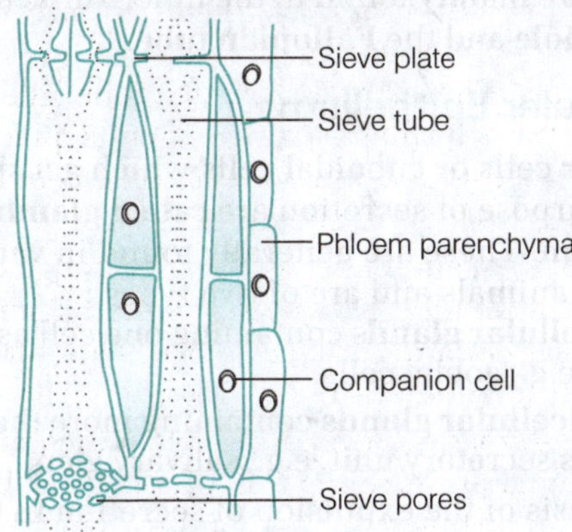

Phloem tissue

Plant Tissue System

- Tissue which perform similar functions, irrespective of their position constitute a tissue system.
- It is based on the type of cells present in a plant.
- On the basis of their structure and location, there are three types of tissue system, namely :

1. Epidermal Tissue System

The epidermal tissue system forms the outermost covering of the whole plant body. Its various components are epidermal cells, stomata and the epidermal appendages, i.e., trichomes.

- **Epidermis** The epidermis (Gk. *Epi*–upon; *derma* –skin) is the outermost layer of the main plant body. The epidermal cells are elongated and compactly arranged to form a continuous layer. This layer is interrupted by stomata.
- **Stomata** The stomata (sing. stoma) are openings in the epidermis of most of the aerial parts of the plants, especially the leaves. Each stoma is composed of two bean-shaped cells called as **guard cells,** which enclose stomatal pore. In some species, the guard cells are surrounded by **subsidiary cells** or **accessory cells** which differ morphologically from the other epidermal cells.
- **Epidermal appendages** (Outgrowths) The epidermis of most plants often bears outgrowth known as **epidermal appendages** or **epidermal outgrowths.** The epidermal hairs present on the stem are called trichomes.

2. Ground Tissue System

All tissues, except epidermis and vascular bundles constitute the **ground tissue system**. It mainly forms the bulk of the plant body.

It consists of simple permanent tissues. It's various components are hypodermis, cortex, endodermis, pericycle, medullary rays and pith.

In leaves, the ground tissue consists of thin-walled chloroplast containing cells called **mesophyll.**

- **Hypodermis** This is the region situated just below the epidermis and as an outer region of cortex.
- **Cortex** The cortex lies between epidermis and pericycle. It consists of parenchyma, collenchyma and sclerenchyma tissues. The cells of cortex contain starch grains, oil, tannins and crystals. Sometimes, cortical cells may develop chloroplasts become photosynthetic and are called **chlorenchyma.**
- **Endodermis** This is the innermost layer of the cortex. It is single-layered, barrel-shaped and arranged without intercellular spaces. The cells are parenchymatous. The presence of bands of suberin on the radial and transverse wall is the characteristic feature. These bands are called **Casparian strips.**

3. Vascular Tissue System

A **vascular bundle** is a strand of conducting tissue, which is generally composed of xylem and phloem in monocots and xylem, phloem and cambium in dicots. These tissues originate from the procambium and apical meristems.

The arrangement of xylem and phloem is the characteristic to particular plant organs. However, a few exceptions are also there.

On the basis of arrangement of xylem and phloem in the vascular bundles, there are three types of bundles, i.e., **radial, conjoint** and **concentric.**

- **Radial** The xylem and phloem alternate with each other separated by parenchymatous cells. This type of vascular bundles is called radial and is found mainly in roots.

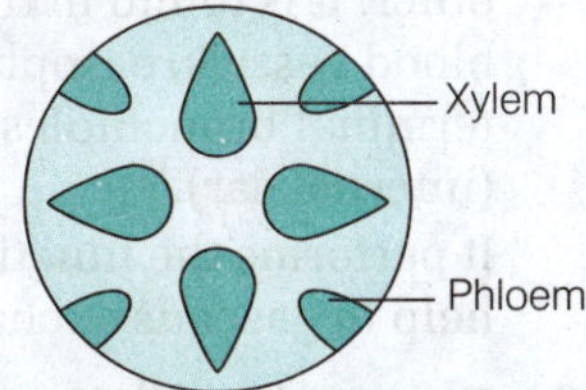

Radial vascular bundle

- **Conjoint** The xylem and phloem are present together in the same bundle on the same radius. Conjoint bundles are of two types, i.e., collateral and bicollateral.

- **Concentric** A vascular bundle in which one tissue is completely surrounded by the other is called concentric.

Animal Tissues

- These have organised layers of structurally similar cells and have same function.
- In comparison to plants, animals are more complex and show movement as they go in search of food or shelter, etc.
- These organisms show more adaptability to their environment than plants and thus, have more energy requirements. For this reason, most of the tissues are alive.
- All complex animals, consist of four types of tissues :

1. Epithelial Tissues

- They comprise of one or more layers of closely packed cells covering the external surface and internal lining of body organs.
- The lining of the skin, mouth, alimentary canal, etc. are formed of epithelial tissue.
- Epithelial cells are devoid of blood vessels.
- Epithelial tissues form a continuous sheet due to tightly packed cells, i.e., they lack intercellular spaces.
- These tissues help to protect organisms from invading microorganisms, injury to internal organs and fluid loss.

Epithelial tissues are classified as follows :

(i) Simple Epithelial Tissue

It is formed from a single layer of cells, resting on the basement membrane. Such tissues are mainly found on the secretory and absorptive surface. On the basis of layers of cells and cell shape, simple epithelial tissues are categorised as :

(a) **Squamous epithelium** It is also called **stratified squamous epithelial.** It is composed of a single layer of flat, thin, disc-like cells having irregular boundaries. The cells are closely attached to each other. It is found in the skin, lining of the mouth, blood vessels, oesophagus, alveoli of lungs, terminal bronchioles, membranous labyrinth (internal ear), etc.
It performs the function of diffusion and osmosis and help in gaseous exchange, also it provides protection.

(b) **Cuboidal epithelium** It consists of tall, wide, cube-shaped cells located in the centre of cells, near nucleus. They can be found in pancreatic ducts, thyroid vesicles and distal convoluted tubules of the nephrons of kidney.
These cells help in the **protection, secretion** and **absorption**.

(c) **Columnar epitheliam** It possess elongated cells placed side by side like a tall column. The nuclei are somewhat elongated and lie near the base of the cells. These contain **microvilli**. These tissues line the inner surface of the stomach, intestine, gall bladder and bile duct and play a major role in **protection, secretion** and **absorption**.
If the columnar or cuboidal cells possess cilia on their surface, they are known as **ciliated epithelial tissues**. These are mainly found in the inner surface of the **bronchiole** and the **Fallopian tube.**

(ii) Glandular Epithelium

- Columnar cells or cuboidal cells which get specialised for the purpose of secretion are called **glandular epithelium**. These are generally found in various glands of animals and are of two types :
  (a) **Unicellular glands** containing one cell as secretory unit. e.g., goblet cells.
  (b) **Multicellular glands** containing more than one cell as secretory unit. e.g., salivary gland.
- On the basis of the expulsion of secretion in the cell, glands can be **exocrine** or **endocrine**.
  - **Exocrine glands** release their secretions at specific sites *via* **ducts**. e.g., mucous, saliva, oil, enzymes, etc.
  - **Endocrine glands** or **ductless** glands as they pour their secretions directly into the blood. e.g., hormones.

(iii) Compound Epithelium (Multilayered Epithelia)

- It consists of a few to several layers of cell.
- They are thicker and stronger than simple epithelia and have a major role in providing protection to under lying tissues against odds like thermal, mechanical or osmotic stress.

It is further of two types :

- **Stratified epithelium** These consist of many layers of epithelial cells. The deepest layer is made up of **loose columnar** or **cuboidal cells**, but the outer surface may vary in nature.
- **Transitional Epithelium** It has few layers of cells. The cells of basal layer are columnar or cuboidal whereas cells of surface layer are large and umbrella-shaped. These are found in ureter, urinary bladder, renel pelvis and part of the urethra.

2. Connective Tissue

- These are the most abundant and widely distributed in the body of complex animals.

- They are named so because of their special function of **linking** and **supporting** other tissues or organs of the body.
- The cells of connective tissue are loosely packed, living and embedded in a jelly-like, intercellular matrix.

On the basis of structure, there are three types of **connective tissue** :

(i) Proper Connective Tissue

The cells of connective tissue are loosely packed, living and embedded in an intercellular matrix that may be jelly-like, fluid, dense or rigid in nature.

They are of the following types :

(a) **Loose connective tissue** It consists of cells and fibres loosely arranged in a matrix. Matrix contains **white collagen** and **yellow elastic fibres**. It provides strength, elasticity and support between organs. It is present beneath the skin, in between and around muscles, nerves and blood vessels and bone marrow. Loose connective tissue is of the following two types :
  - **Areolar Connective Tissue**
  - **Adipose Connective Tissue**

(b) **Dense connective tissue** It consists of fibres and fibroblast cells which are compactly packed in the matrix. They are mainly of two types :
  - **White fibrous connective tissue** This forms tendon.
  - **Yellow fibrous connective tissue** This forms ligament.

(ii) Skeletal Connective Tissues

This tissue forms the endoskeleton of the vertebrates and are of two types :

(a) **Cartilage** It is a soft, vascular tissue containing chondrocytes, chondrin (matrix) and core protein. It is a solid and pliable connective tissue which provides support and flexibility to the body parts.

(b) **Bone** In this, bone cells are embedded in a solid base of calcium phosphate. This tissue form the framework of the body by forming the skeleton. It also provides protection to the soft organs of the body along with RBCs and WBCs in the marrow.

(iii) Vascular Connective Tissue

- Cells are found floating in this tissue, since the base material is liquid.
- This tissue performs an important function of transporting substances between different parts of the body and is of two types, i.e., **lymph** and **blood.**

Lymph

It is a colourless or yellowish fluid present in the lymph vessels. It contains very small amounts of nutrients, protein and oxygen, but is abundant in carbon dioxide.

Blood

- It is a red-coloured, alkaline (pH = 7.3-7.5) motile connective tissue which consists of ground substance.
- It acts as the chief transport system of our body, transporting nutrients, hormones, etc. and has an important role in providing defence against disease.
- It also helps in regulating body temperature.

Following are the two major components of blood :

(i) **Plasma** It is a yellow transparent colloidal mixture that forms 55-60% of blood. Plasma contains 90-92% of water with inorganic and organic salts, majorly, albumins, globulins, fibrinogen, etc.

(ii) **Blood cells** These constitute about 45% of **blood** within the body.

These are of three types :

Red Blood Cells (RBCs) or Erythrocytes

- These are roughly circular and non-nucleated cells (i.e., lack nucleus).
- Their count is about 50-55 lakhs per cubic mm.
- Birth place of RBCs is **bone marrow,** i.e., RBCs originate from there.
- The average lifespan of human RBCs is about 120 days, after which they are destroyed in **spleen** (graveyard of RBCs).
- **Haemoglobin** is a reddish respiratory pigment present in RBCs. It acts as $O_2 - CO_2$ carrier.

White Blood Cells (WBCs) or Leucocytes

- These are colourless, nucleated and motile cells of blood. Their normal count is 6000-8000 cells/mm^3 and can last only upto a week.
- These aid in protecting the body against diseases, by producing antibodies.

These are majorly of two types :

(a) **Granulocytes** Eosinophil, neutrophil and basophil.

(b) **Agranulocytes** Monocyte and lymphocyte.

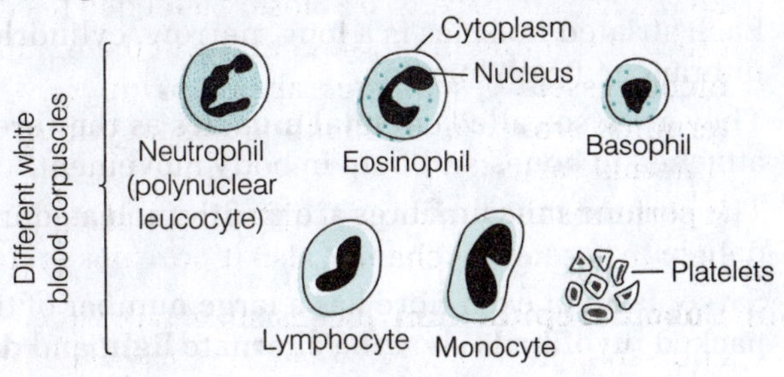

Different WBCs

Platelets or Thrombocytes

- These are the characteristic feature of mammals.
- Their count varies from 1.5 to 4.5 lakh per mm^3 of blood.
- The formation of these cells occur from certain large cells of bone marrow, called **megakaryocytes**.
- These help in **clotting** of **blood**.

Types of Leucocytes with their Composition and Functions

Type of Leucocytes	Composition	Functions
Neutrophils	60-65%	Phagocytic
Basophils	0.5-1%	Inflammatory reaction secretes histamine, serotonin, etc.
Eosinophils	2-3%	Resist infection, involved in allergic reaction.
Monocytes	6-8%	Phagocytic, include macrophages and dendritic cells.
Lymphocytes	20-25%	Immune response through B and T- lymphocytes.

3. Muscular Tissue

- The muscle tissue is composed of cells, called **mycocytes**.
- It comprises of many long cylindrical muscle cells or group of fibres (muscle fibre) arranged parallel to each other.
- Muscle fibres are made up of many smaller proteinaceous units, called **myofibrils**.
- This tissue is responsible for all kinds of movements of the body along with their contractions and relaxations.
- It is about 40-50 per cent of the body weight of a human adult is contributed by muscles.
- There are three types of muscular tissue :

Striated Muscles

- Each striated muscles is a long, narrow, cylindrical unbranched cell, forming.
- They are also called **skeletal muscles** as they are attached to bones and help in body movement.
- The striated muscle fibres are multi-nucleated in nature.
- Sarcoplasm of each fibre has a large number of tightly packed **myofibrils** showing alternate **light** and **dark** bands.
- These muscles are found in body walls, limbs, tongue, pharynx, etc.
- Since, the contraction of striated muscle is under the control of a person's will, they are called **voluntary muscles**.

Non-striated (Smooth) Muscle

- The cells of non-striated muscles are thin, long and spindle shaped, having single nucleus.
- These are found in the posterior part of oesophagus, stomach, intestine, lungs, iris, dermis of skin, ciliary body of eye, blood vessels, etc.
- These are **involuntary muscles**, i.e., their movement is not under the control of one's will.
- Unlike striated muscles, these are devoid of the alternate **dark** and **light** bands. Thus, they are called **non-striated muscles**.

Cardiac Muscles

- These are contractile tissues present only in the heart.
- These are cylindrical, branched and uninucleated muscles which possess stripes. Hence, are **striated muscles**.
- These generate their own wave of excitation, i.e., are **myogenic** and never experience fatigue.
- Muscle cells which make up cardiac muscle are interconnected by **intercalated disc**. This disc helps them to act as single functional organ.
- Their contraction is not under the control of a person's will.
- Thus, they are involuntary in nature and are rhythmic.

4. Nervous Tissue

- This tissue is specialised to receive stimuli and conducts impulses for controlling and coordinating body functions.
- This tissue makes up **brain** and the **spinal cord**.
- Neurons are the basic unit of neural tissue which show conductivity.

There are three parts of neurons, namely :

(i) **Cyton** (Cell body) It is a large part of the fibre of a nerve or neuron that regulates the metabolism of neuron and contains **Nissl's granules**.

(ii) **Axon** It is a tube-like structure that carries electrical impulses from cell body to axon terminals which further passes the impulse to another neuron.

(iii) **Dendrites** Branch-like structures which receive messages from adjacent neurons and transmit them to the cyton are called dendrites.

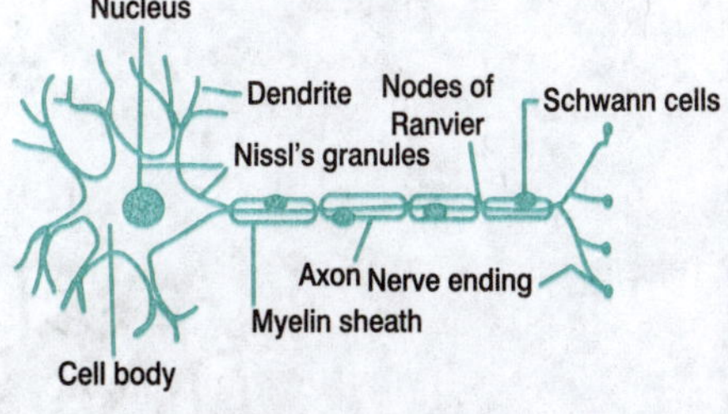

Structure of a neuron

- **Synaptic knob** It is a bulb-like structure present at the terminal positions of axon.
- It contains **neurotransmitters** and helps in transmission of impulses from one neuron to another.

Extra Facts From Tamil Nadu Board and NIOS

Permanent Tissue

- The term 'meristem' is derived from the Greek word '*Meristos*' which means divisible or having cell division activity. Parenchyma may store water in many succulent and xerophytic plants. It also serves the functions of storage of food reserves, absorption, buoyancy, secretion, etc.
- **Sclerenchyma** fibers are elongated cells with usually pointed ends. Their walls are lignified. These fibres are abundantly found in many plants. The average length of fibres is 1 to 3 mm, however in plants like *Linum usitatissimum* (flax), *Cannabis sativa* (hemp) and *Corchorus capsularis* (jute), fibres are extensively longer, ranging from 20 mm to 550 mm.
- **Complex tissues** consist of parenchyma and sclerenchyma cells. However, collenchymatous cells are not present in such tissues.
- The main function of sieve tubes is translocation of food, from leaves to the storage organs of the points.

Areolar Connective Tissue

- It has cells and fibres loosely arranged in a semi-fluid ground substance called **matrix.** It joins skin to muscles, fills space inside organs and is found around muscles, blood vessels and nerves.
- **Adipose or fatty connective tissue** It is the aggregation of fat cells or adipocytes, spherical or oval in shape. It serves as fat reservoir. They act as shock absorbers and regulate the body temperature.
- **Tendon** are cord-like, strong structures that join skeletal muscles to bones. They have great strength and limited flexibility.
- **Ligaments** are highly elastic structures and have great strength which connect bones to bones. They strengthen the joints and allow normal movement.

04

Genetics

[SOURCES]

Class-X NCERT Chap 8 (Heredity), Class-XII NCERT Chap 4 (Principles of Inheritance and Variation), Chap 5 (Molecular Basis of Inheritance)

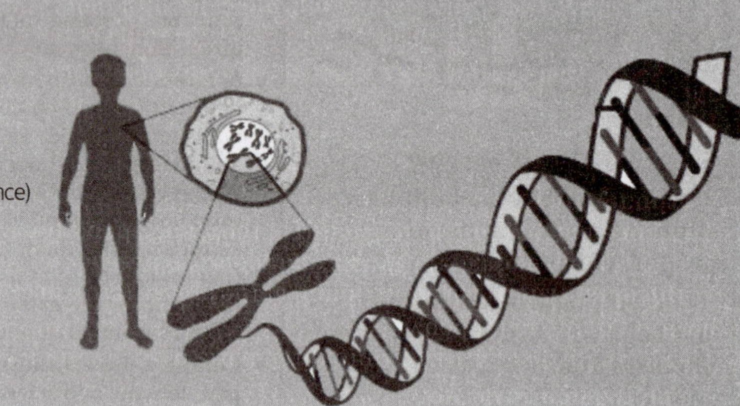

- **Heredity** is the process of passing the traits and characteristics from parents to their offspring.
- Traits or characteristics, which are passed on from parents to their offspring generation to generation are called **hereditary characters.** These are controlled by genes.
- A **gene** is a unit of DNA which governs the synthesis of one protein that constitutes a specific character of the organism.
- **Genetics** is the branch of biology that studies the genes, genetic variation and heredity in living organisms.

Rules of Inheritance

- **Gregor Johann Mendel** conducted immense research on garden pea *(Pisum sativum)* for 9 years (1856-1863) and proposed the **laws of inheritance** in living organisms.
- He is also known as **Father of Genetics.**
- According to Mendel, each genetic trait in an organism is controlled by factor. This factor also controls their inheritance.
- These factors were later called **genes** by Danish botanist **Wihelm Johansen** (1909).
- **Hugo de Vries, Carl Correns** and **Erich von Tschermak** rediscovered Mendel's laws in the year 1900.

Mendel's Work

- Mendel observed 7 contrasting characters in pea plant, i.e., height of plant, colour of flower, seed shape, seed colour, flower position, pod shape and pod colour.
- But he observed one trait at a time and performed monohybrid cross.
- He observed that first (F_1) generation showed character of only one of the parent.
- On hybridisation of plants belonging to F_1-generation both the parental characters were observed in the ratio 3 : 1 in second (F_2) generation.
- Mendel also found identical results in dihybrid cross as in monohybrid cross.

Seven Different Characters Studied by Mendel

Characters	Chromosomal Location	Dominant	Recessive
Length of stem	4	Tall	Dwarf
Shape of seed	7	Round	Wrinkled
Colour of seed	1	Yellow	Green
Shape of pod	4	Inflated	Constricted
Colour of pod	5	Green	Yellow
Position of flower	4	Axial	Terminal
Colour of flower	1	Red	White

Mendel's Laws of Inheritance

Mendel's work on pea plant is summarised under the following laws :

1. Law of Dominance

- Characters are controlled by discrete units called **factors** (now called **genes**).
- Factors occur in pairs. Out of two dissimilar pair of factors/contrasting alleles, only one is able to express its effects in the individual/hybrid is called **dominant**.
- While the other allele/factor which does not show its effect in the hybrid/heterozygous individual is called **recessive**.
- For example, when a homozygous tall plant (TT) is crossed with a homozygous recessive (tt), the F_1 progeny obtained is tall plant with (Tt) genotype.

2. Law of Segregation

- This law states that though the parents contain two alleles during gamete formation, factors or alleles of a pair segregate from each other such that a gamete receives only one out of the two factors.
- Thus, alleles do not show any blending and both characters are recovered as such in F_2-generation.
- This can be understood by the following cross :

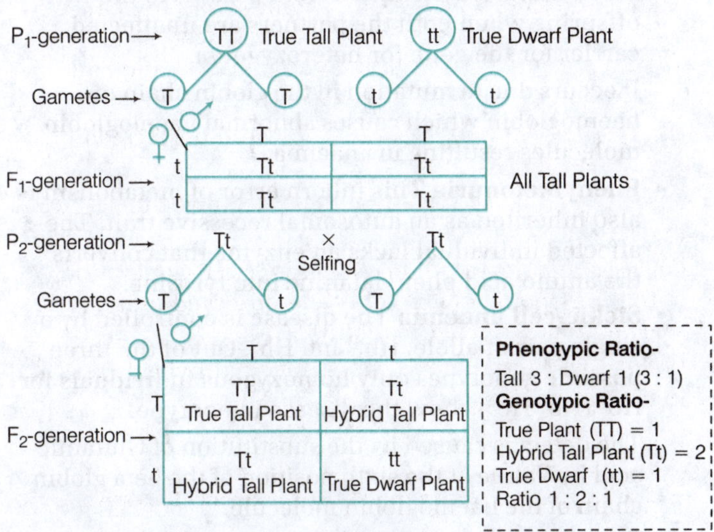

Law of segregation

3. Law of Independent Assortment

- The distribution of one pair of allele for contrasting character into the gametes is independent of the distribution of the other pair of alleles for another contrasting character. It is called law of **independent assortment**.

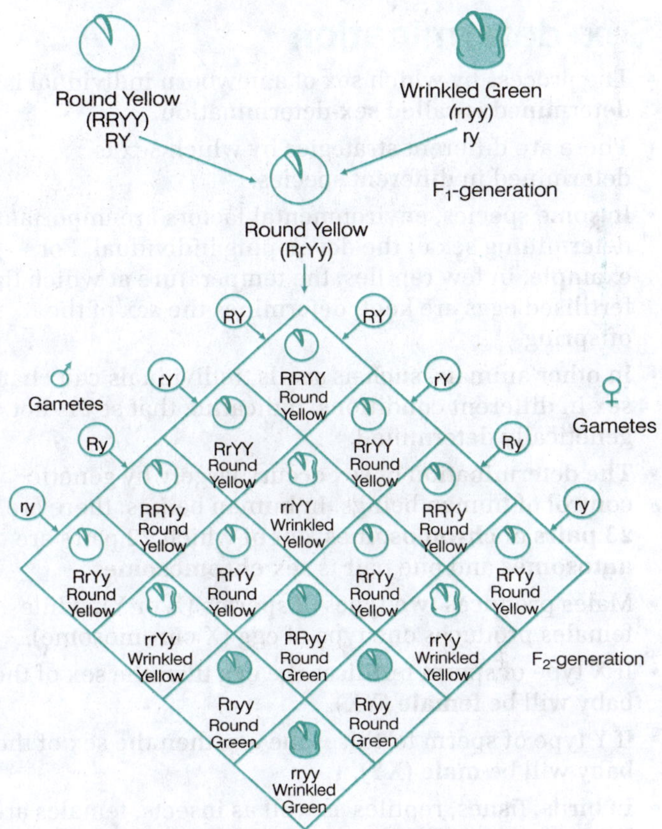

Phenotypic Ratio = Round Yellow : Round Green : Wrinkled Yellow : Wrinkled Green (9 : 3 : 3 : 1)

= 1 : 2 : 2 : 4 : 1 : 2 : 1 : 2 : 1

Law of independent assortment

Exceptions to Mendelism

Incomplete dominance and codominance are the exceptions to Mendelism :

- **Incomplete dominance** It is a form of gene interaction wherein both alleles of a gene at a locus are unable to express themselves completely, resulting in an intermediate phenotype.
- **Codominance** It is a form of inheritance in which the alleles of a pair of genes in a heterozygote are fully expressed. Thus, making the phenotype of offspring, a combination of the phenotype of parents.

Chromosomal Theory of Inheritance

- Chromosomes are thread-like structures of nucleic acids and proteins located within the nucleus of living cells and are involved in carrying genetic information in the form genes.
- Chromosomal theory of inheritance was given by **Boveri and Sutton** in the year 1902.

Sex-determination

- The process by which sex of a newborn individual is determined is called sex-determination.
- There are different strategies by which sex is determined in different species.
- In some species, environmental factors are important in determining sex of the developing individual. For example, in few reptiles, the temperature at which the fertilised eggs are kept, determines the sex of the offspring.
- In other animals, such as snails, individuals can change sex in different conditions, indicating that sex is not genetically determined.
- The determination of sex occurs largely by genetic control of human beings. In human beings, there are **23 pairs of chromosomes,** out of which 22 pairs are **autosomes** and one pair is **sex chromosomes**.
- Males produces two types of sperms (X or Y), while females produces one type of egg (X chromosome).
- If X type of sperm fertilises the egg then the sex of the baby will be **female** (XX).
- If Y type of sperm fertilises the egg then the sex of the baby will be **male** (XY).
- In birds, fishes, reptiles as well as insects, females are **heterozygous** (ZW) and males are **homozygous** (ZZ).

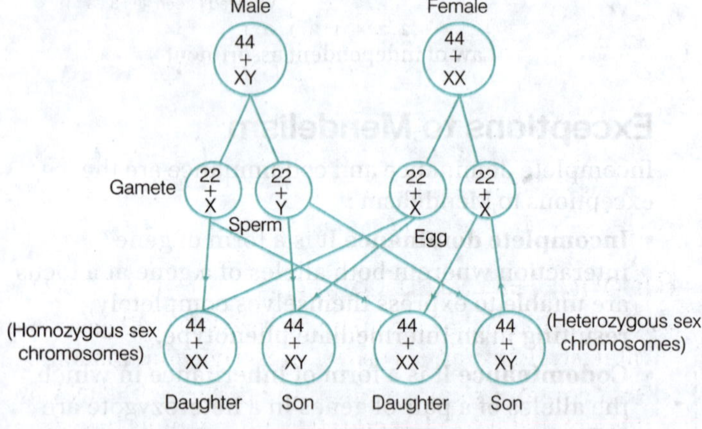

Sex-determination

Mutation

- Mutation is a change in DNA sequence due to which there is change in genotype and phenotype of an organism.
- They result from errors during DNA or viral replication, mitosis or meiosis or any other damage to DNA and also from insertion or deletion of DNA segments.
- Any physical and chemical agent that causes mutations is called **mutagen**. e.g., UV rays, X-rays, mustard gas, etc.

Genetic Disorders

Morphological, physiological, cytological and behaviouristic differences amongst the individuals of the same species or offspring of same parents are called **variations**. Variations can occur due to mutation, in the genes or due to change in the number of autosomes and sex chromosomes. These variation in human causes several genetic disorders as follows :

- **Haemophilia** also called **bleeder's disease** or **Royal disease** because it was first observed in British Royal family. It is caused by defect in a gene that determines the formation of factors responsible for blood clotting. It is genes are located on the X-chromosome, making haemophilia an X-linked recessive disease. Thus, haemophilia is a hereditary bleeding disorder caused by the lack of blood clotting factor VIII, thus bleeding to death of the person due to lack of blood.
- **Colour blindness** It is also an X-linked recessive disorder. In this, the patient is unable to distinguish between red and green colour due to problem in the development of one or more of the three sets of colour sensing cones in the eye.

  Males are more likely to be colourblind than females as the genes responsible for the most common forms of colour blindness are on the X-chromosome.
- **Thalassemia** It is an autosome linked recessive blood disease transmitted from parents to the offspring when both the partners are unaffected carrier for the gene (or heterozygous).

  It occurs due to mutation in the globin chain of haemoglobin which causes abnormal haemoglobin molecules resulting in anaemia.
- **Phenylketonuria** This inborn error of metabolism is also inherited as an autosomal recessive trait. The affected individual lacks an enzyme that converts the amino acid phenylalanine into tyrosine.
- **Sickle-cell anaemia** The disease is controlled by a single pair of allele, Hb^A and Hb^S. Out of the three possible genotypes only homozygous individuals for Hb^S ($Hb^S Hb^S$) show the disease phenotype.

  The defect is caused by the substitution of Glutamic acid by Valine at the sixth position of the beta globin chain of the haemoglobin molecule.
- **Down's syndrome** It is a genetic disorder which occur due to presence of an additional copy of the chromosome number 21 (trisomy of 21).
- **Klinefelter syndrome** This genetic disorder is caused due to an additional copy of X-chromosome resulting in karyotype 47, XXY.
- **Turner's syndrome** Such a disorder is caused due to the absence of one of the X-chromosome, i.e., 45 with XO. Such females are sterile with rudimentary ovaries.

Genetic Material

- **Friedrich Miescher** was the first to discover genetic material in the form of nucleic acids in 1869.
- **Frederick Griffith** declared the presence of genetic material in 1928 by a transformation experiment on *Streptococcus pneumoniae.*
- **Oswald Avery, MacLeod** and **McCarty** (1933-44) worked to determine the biochemical nature of transforming principle in **Griffith experiment**.
- The proof that DNA is the genetic material came from **A Hershey** and **M Chase** (1952).

Deoxyribonucleic Acid (DNA)

- It acts as the genetic material in most of the living organisms.
- It is a long polymer of deoxyribonucleotides. Thus, making itself a double stranded polynucleotide chain bound together *via* hydrogen bonds.
- Each nucleotide unit of DNA comprises of a **pentose sugar** (deoxyribose sugar), a **nitrogenous base** and a **phosphate group.**
- Nitrogenous bases in DNA are **adenine, guanine, thymine** and **cytosine.** Former two are **purines** and latter ones are **pyrimidines.**
- Adenine always pairs with thymine and cytosine with guanine.
- Pentose sugar and nitrogenous base together form **nucleoside.** These further add on with phosphate group to form **nucleotides.**
- In 1953 **James Watson** and **Francis Crick** proposed a very simple **double helix model** of DNA structure or based on X-ray diffraction.
- Each DNA strand is made up of two coiled polynucleotide complexes. Both these chains are coiled clockwise in a circular order. The diameter of this is 20Å.
- Two chains of DNA have **anti parallel** polarity, i.e., 5′ – 3′ and 3′ – 5′ and the C_1 of every sugar strands perpendicular to nitrogenous bases.

DNA Duplication/DNA Replication

- It is the process by which a DNA molecule produces exact copies of its own structure. Semi-conservative method of DNA replication was proposed by **Watson** and **Crick.**
- In this method, one strand of the DNA molecule serves as a template for the synthesis of a new complementary chain. This method is universally accepted and is experimentally proved by **Meselson** and **Stahl.**

Enzymes Involved in DNA Replication

Enzymes	Functions
DNA polymerases	DNA synthesis
Polymerase I	Repair, removes primer and fills gaps
Polymerase II	Repair
Polymerase III	Replication
Primase	Primer synthesis
Helicase	DNA unwinding
Gyrase	Swivel action
DNA ligase	Seals nicks
Endonuclease	Induces nicks
SSB proteins	Stabilise single-strand of DNA

DNA Packaging

- Organisation of DNA is much more complex in **eukaryotes** and is done by histone proteins.
- During packaging, eight histone proteins form a **histone octamer** around which negatively charged DNA is wrapped around. This organisation is called **nucleosome.**
- One nucleosome contains 200 base pairs and gives itself a beads on string appearance.

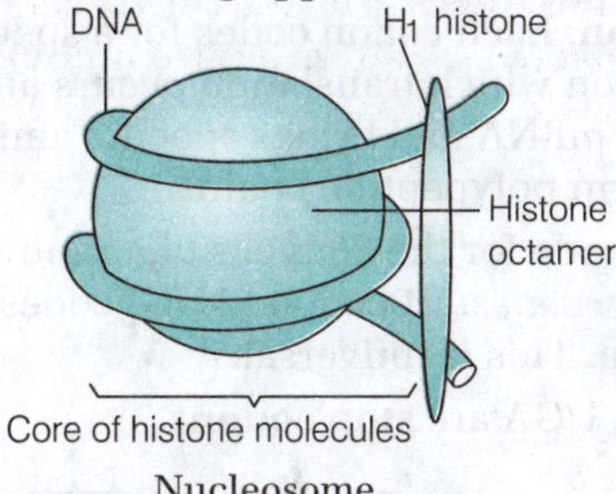

Nucleosome

Ribonucleic Acid (RNA)

- RNA used to act as a genetic material as well as a catalyst. However, it was very reactive and unstable.
- RNA contains **pentose sugar** and differs with DNA in the fact that it has **Uracil** (U) as nitrogenous base in place of **Thymine** (T) (as in DNA).

It is of following three types :

- *r***RNA** It refers to **ribosomal RNA** and makes up 80% of the total RNA. It is found in ribosomes and helps in protein synthesis.
- *t***RNA** It refers to **transfer RNA.** During translation, it transfers specific amino acids which correspond to *m*RNA sequence into the growing polypeptide chain.
- *m***RNA** It is also called **messenger RNA.** It carries the genetic information from DNA in a form that can be recognised to form proteins.

Central Dogma of Molecular Biology

Central dogma of molecular biology states that there is unidirectional flow of information from DNA to RNA (transcription) and from RNA to protein (translation).

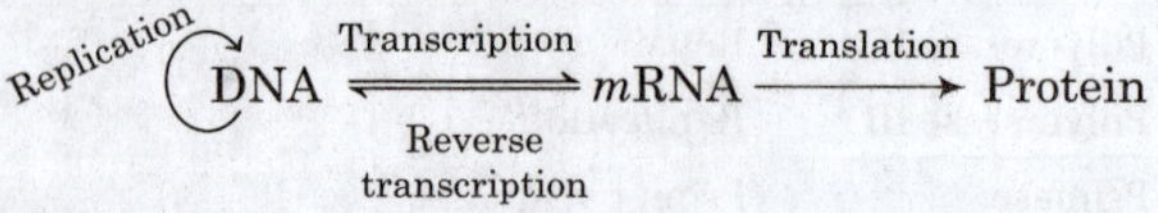

This principle was propounded by **Francis Crick** in 1958.

Gene Expression and Transcription

- Gene expression results in the **formation of a polypeptide** by joining amino acids as directed by DNA.
- Transfer of information from DNA strand to RNA is termed as **transcription**. It requires the enzyme, RNA polymerase.
- The RNA thus transcribed is known as **primary transcript** which functions directly as *m*RNA in prokaryotes while it undergoes various modifications in case of eukaryotes to be used further for polypeptide synthesis.

Genetic Code

- These are triplets of nucleotides present on *m*RNA, called **codon**. Each codon codes for a specific amino acid based on which translation occurs and *t*RNA, reads the code of *m*RNA and brings specific amino acid to *r*RNA to form polypeptide chains.
- 61 codons code for the 20 types of amino acids present in our body. e.g., start codon (AUG) codes for **methionine**. This is universal.
- UAG, UAA, UGA are **stop codons**.

Human Genome Project (HGP)

- This was a mega project of 13 years that was launched in the year 1990 by collaborative research work and completed in 2003.
- It was coordinated by US department of **Energy and the National Institute of Health**.
- Its main aim was to do complete mapping and decoding of all the genes (or genome) of human beings.
- The human genome project was in close association with new and the rapid developing era of biotechnology known as **bioinformatics**.
- The HGP revealed that there are probably about 20,000-25,000 human genes. This ultimately helps in getting the knowledge about the structure, organisation and function of the complete set of human genes.
- The **International Human Genome Sequence** was published in journal Nature, in February 2001. The full sequence was completed and published in April 2003.

DNA Fingerprinting

- It is also known as **DNA typing** or **genetic fingerprinting** and **DNA profiling**. This technique is mainly used to identify a person on the basis of person's DNA specificity. This technique was firstly reported by **Sir Alec Jeffreys** (in 1984).
- About 99.9% of human DNA sequences are same in every individual and the remaining amount (i.e., 0.1%) of DNA is enough to distinguish one individual from another unless they are monozygotic twins.
- Every individual has some specific sequences of nucleotide that do not carry any information for protein synthesis.
- These specific sequences are repeated many times and are found at many places within the genome. These loci are known as the **Variable Number Tandem Repeats** (VNTRs) **or minisatellites**.
- These VNTRs are used as genetic markers, which individuals inherit from their parents. These VNTRs are similar in twins only.
- For the process of genetic fingerprinting sample of blood, saliva, semen, hair or any other liquid or fluid from personal items such as razor, toothbrush are collected.
- DNA may also be collected from stored samples such as banked sperm, biopsy tissue, etc. in order to create one's DNA profile, which is then matched or compared against another sample to determine whether there is a genetic similarity or not.

Extra Facts From
Tamil Nadu Board and NIOS

- Mendel chose the pea plant as it was self-pollinating, short lifespan, easy to cross-pollinate, deeply defined contrasting characters and are bisexual flower.
- Parental generation are pure breeding tall plant and a pure breeding dwarf plant.
- External expression of a particular trait is known as **phenotype**.
- Two factors making up a pair of contrasting characters are called **alleles**.
- The dihybrid ratio of each phenotype of seeds in the F_2-generation is 9 : 3 : 3 : 1.
- Adenine (A) links Thymine (T) with two hydrogen bonds (A = T).
- Cytosine (C) links Guanine (G) with three hydrogen bonds (C ≡ G).
- Each turn of the double helix is 34Å (3.4 nm). There are ten base pairs in a complete turn.
- Nucleoside = Nitrogen base + Sugar.
  Nucleotide = Nucleoside + Phosphate.

05

Evolution

(SOURCES)

Class-X NCERT Chap 8 (Heredity), Class-XII NCERT Chap 6 (Evolution)

Origin of Life

- The universe have evolved around 2000 crore or 20 billion years ago.
- The sequence of gradual changes from simple life forms to complex life forms is called **evolution**. Since, the evolution involves the living organisms, so it is called **organic evolution**.
- The origin of life is considered a unique event in the history of universe.
- The study of history of life forms on earth is **evolutionary biology.**
- Universe is made up of huge group of many galaxies, stars and clouds of gases and dust.
- In the context of origin of universe, as per the **Big Bang Theory**, the universe originated due to great explosion, it expanded and its temperature declined and gases like hydrogen and helium came into existence.
- Due to the gravity of these gases, galaxies were formed.
- Earth originated in our galaxy **Milky Way** around 4.5 billion years ago. Initially, the earth lacked atmosphere.
- Gases like methane, carbon dioxide, ammonia, etc. and water vapour liberated from the molten mass of surface.
- UV radiations of sun broke down water into oxygen and hydrogen.
- After ozone formation, when the earth's atmosphere cooled a little bit, water precipitated down to earth as water vapour and gave rise to saline oceans.
- Origin of life is believed to be about 4 billion years ago.
- As per the **cosmozoic theory**, life originated at other planet and then moved in the form of units called **spores**.
- According to the **theory of spontaneous generation**, life originated from dead and decaying matter.
- This theory was discarded by **Louis Pasteur** in the year 1859.
- He conducted an experiment by taking S-shaped flasks and succeeded in establishing **biogenesis** as a **solid theory**.
- Another theory was given by **Oparin** and **Haldane** called **theory of chemical evolution**.
- They proposed that first form of life, originated from pre-existing non-living organic molecules.
- The formation of organic molecules from inorganic molecules is chemical evolution.
- **Stanley L. Miller** and **Harold C. Urey** (in 1953) gave an experimental support to Haldane theory of origin of life.

- They created an atmosphere similar to that which existed on early earth (containing hydrogen, ammonia, methane, hydrogen sulphide and water vapour, but not oxygen) over water in an air-tight apparatus. Their theory is known as **naturalistic theory or theory of chemical evolution**.
- Another famous theory of evolution was given by **Charles Robert Darwin** (1809-1882).
- He gave the theory of **natural selection**. It is based on certain facts such as rapid multiplication of organisms, limited natural resources (food and space), competition for resources due to which some survive and grow at the cost of other.

Organic Evolution

- **Evolution** is defined as the sequence of gradual changes from simple life forms to complex life forms, i.e. from primitive organisms that existed over million of years to new organisms that exists today.
- Evolution is all about changes, improvement and modification from simple life forms.
- **Organic evolution** is a biological process, that occurs in an individual organism, but counted in groups (populations).
- The time it takes for a living population to evolve depends on the reproduction time of the organism.
- Some microbes (one celled organisms like bacteria) take only about 30 minutes to double in number. Populations of microbes can evolve in about a week's time. Other organisms may take thousands, even millions of years.

Evidences of Organic Evolution

Evidences of organic evolution are as follows :

Fossils

- These are preserved traces of living organisms that lived millions of years ago and were not decomposed. e.g. dead insects carried in hot mud.
- The fossil *Archaeopteryx* is a connecting link between birds and reptiles.
- It has feathered wings and beak like birds, but teeth and tail like those of reptiles.

Types of Fossils

- **Petrified Fossils**, e.g. teeth, bones, etc.
- **Mould Fossils**, e.g. leaves, jelly fishes, etc.
- **Unaltered Fossils**, e.g. mammoths, hippopotamus
- **Compressed Fossils**, e.g. plant fossils
- **Print Fossils**, e.g. mollusc shells

Morphology and Comparative Anatomy

- **Homologous Organs** Such organs have same embryonic origin and basic structure, but have different functions, e.g. forelimbs of frog, bird and human.
- **Analogous Organs** Such organs have similar function, but different embryonic origin and basic structure, e.g. wings of insects and birds.
- **Vestigial Organs** These are non-functional organs in animals. These were functional in their ancestors, e.g. underdeveloped limbs of snakes, feathers of kiwi, human skin and hair, vermiform appendix, etc.
- **Atavism** It is the reappearance of certain ancestral characters which had either disappeared or were reduced, e.g. power of moving pinna in humans.

Theories of Organic Evolution

Various concepts explain the process of evolution, but the important concepts or theories that explain the scientific basis of organic evolution are Lamarckism, Darwinism, Neo-Darwinism and mutation theory.

(i) Lamarckism

- The first theory of evolution was proposed by **Jean Baptiste de Lamarck** (1744-1829), a French biologist. His famous book '*Philosophie Zoologique*' was published in 1809, in which he discussed his theory in detail.
- Lamarck coined the term '**invertebrates**' and **Annelida**. The term 'Biology' was given by **Lamarck** and **Treviranus** in 1802. Lamarckism includes four factors :
  - Internal vital force
  - Effect of environment
  - Use and disuse of organs
  - Inheritance of acquired characters.
- According to Lamarckism, organisms are striving to meet the demands of their environments acquire adaptations and pass them by heredity to their offspring.

(ii) Neo-Lamarckism

- The theory stresses on the direct effect of changed environment on the organism.
- Normally, only those modifications are transferred to next generation, which influence germ cells.

(iii) Darwinism

- The most impressive study on evolution was made by **Charles Darwin** (1809-1882).
- His principles were published, in his book '*The Origin of Species by Natural Selection*' in 1859. His ideas about the theory of natural selection is popularly known as **Darwinism**.

- In 1813, Darwin travelled to **Galapagos Islands** and found closely related species of finches known as **Darwin's finches**.
- From this he took an idea of **natural selection** and **branching descent**. According to Darwin, as a result of struggle for existence, only those organisms could survive which have favourable variations to adapt with the environmental conditions.
- Darwinism is based on the following facts :
  - **Enormous fertility in organisms** All living organisms are blessed with the ability to reproduce due to which their number increases rapidly.
  - **Struggle for existence** Organisms require basic needs like food, shelter and light. It has become a reason for their competition and they struggle to survive.
  - **Variations and their inheritance** Variation can be found in every organism. The organism are able to gain adaptability and learn to evolve and survive even in odd conditions.
  - Organisms which undergo these changes are in coordination with the changing environment while others fail to survive.
  - **Survival of the fittest** Organisms that are adapted to the environment are able to survive. They make themselves adaptable with the changing environment. Organisms which fail to adapt do not survive. This is called **survival** of the **fittest**, i.e fit organisms (those adapted to changing conditions), survive while others are eliminated.
  - **Theory of natural selection** It is mechanism of evolution. According to this theory, organisms that are more adapted to their environment have more chances of survival and pass on genes to next generation.

(iv) Neo-Darwinism

- According to Neo-Darwinism, there are dissimilarities among offspring of sexually reproducing organisms, which occur by mutation. Nature select only useful characters.
- Sexual differentiation occurs due to differences in the time period of reproductive activities in different species, resulting in the evolution of new species.

(v) Mutation Theory of Hugo de Vries

In 1901, Hugo de Vries found that mutation occurred in evening primrose *(Oenothera lamarckiana)* and gave **mutation theory**.

He proposed that the new species arise not by the accumulation of minor and continuous variations, but by sudden appearance of saltatory variations.

Main postulates of this theory are as follows :

- Mutations are large, heritable changes that occur in organisms.
- The origin of new species occurs by sudden appearance of certain characters (**saltatory variations**).
- Mutations are variable. They may appear in any special organ or in all organs suddenly, which results into the sudden appearance or disappearance of organs.
- Such new organisms are so different and special in comparison to their parents as these may be called as **new species**.

Speciation

It is the development of one or more species and existing species. It occurs when two populations are isolated (both geographically and reproductively), so that no gene flow occur between these two populations.

Factors Causing Speciation

Speciation may occur by the following means :

- **Gene Flow** It occurs when inbreeding continues within the isolated populations, producing more generations.
- **Genetic Drift** Random change in the frequency of genes in a population over successive generations. It may occur due to change in chromosome number, mutation, etc.
- **Natural Selection** Nature selects the better adapted individuals who possess favourable variations, to survive in a given environment, while eliminating the unfit ones.

  e.g. in a territory of one sub-population, crow may get eliminated by eagles.

Human Evolution

Humans show a great diversity in forms and features across the planet. Various tools used to study human evolution are time dating, excavating, studying fossils and determining DNA sequences.

Man originated through several stages are as follows :

- *Dryopithecus* and *Ramapithecus* is the earliest known **ancestor** of **man** found in some parts of Africa, Asia and Europe. They were the starting point of evolution. They were hairy and walked like gorillas and chimpanzees, i.e. were ape-like.
- *Australopithecus africans* lived in East Africans grasslands. They hunted with stone weapons but ate fruits. Since, they were the first human like being, thus called *Homo habilis*.

- The brain capacity was 650-800 cc and did not eat meat. They were succeeded by *Homo erectus*.
- *Homo erectus* had large brain, around 900 cc (cranial capacity).
- They ate meat and were more evolved. They had a prominent speech.
- *Homo sapiens neanderthalensis* had a cranial capacity of 1400cc.
- They lived near East and central Asia and used hides to protect their body.
- *Homo sapiens sapiens* are the first skeletal remains of *Homo sapiens sapiens* were found in Europe and were named **Cro-Magnon**.
  - In the *Homo sapiens sapiens,* there is final reduction of the jaws, the appearance of modern man's chin and of the rounded skull.
  - Mean cranial capacity was about 1350 cc. Modern man is very closely related to Cro-Magnon. Their culture which dates back to 35000 years is also called upper **palaeolithic culture**.
  - The modern *Homo sapiens* have four races, i.e. negroids, caucasoids, mongoloids and australoids.

Extra Facts From Tamil Nadu Board and NIOS

- The Big Bang theory explains the origin of Universe.
- Somatic variation are the variations which affect the body cells of the organisms. They are not heritable. They occur due to environmental factors.
- Germinal variations are produced in germ cells of an organism. They are inherited. They may be present in ancestors or may occur suddenly.
- The age of fossils is determined by radioactive elements present in it. They may be Carbon, Uranium, Lead or Potassium.
- Radiocarbon dating method was discovered by WF Libby (1946).
- Ethnobotany is the study of a region's plants and their practical uses through the traditional knowledge of the local culture of people.
- Astrobiology deals with the origin evolution and distribution of life in the universe and to investigate the possibility of life in the other world.
- Kaspar Maria von Sternberg is known as the 'Father of Paleobotany' (1761-1838).
- Birbal Sahni is the 'Father of Indian Paleobotany' (1891-1949).
- Goldilocks Zone for life is the orbit at just the right distance from its star that it allows liquid water to exist. Thus, the distance need to be neither too hot or not too cold.
- In our solar system 'Earth' is the only planet in the Goldilocks Zone.

Plant Morphology and Physiology

[SOURCES]

Class-VI NCERT Chap 4 (Getting to Know Plants), Class-VII NCERT Chap 1 (Nutrition in Plants), Chap 6 (Respiration in Organisms), Chap 7 (Transportation in Animals and Plants), Chap 8 (Reproduction in Plants), Class-X NCERT Chap 5 (Life Processes), Class-XI NCERT Chap 2 (Biological Classification), Chap 5 (Morphology of Flowering Plants), Chap 6 (Control and Coordination), Chap 7 (How do Organisms Reproduce?) Old NCERT Chap 11 (Transport in Plants), Old NCERT Chap 12 (Mineral Nutrition), Chap 11 (Photosynthesis in Higher Plants), Chap 12 (Respiration in Plants), Chap 13 (Plant Growth and Development), Class-XII Old NCERT Chap 1 (Reproduction in Organisms), Chap 1 (Sexual Reproduction in Flowering Plants), Tamil Nadu Board (Class-IX, X), NIOS

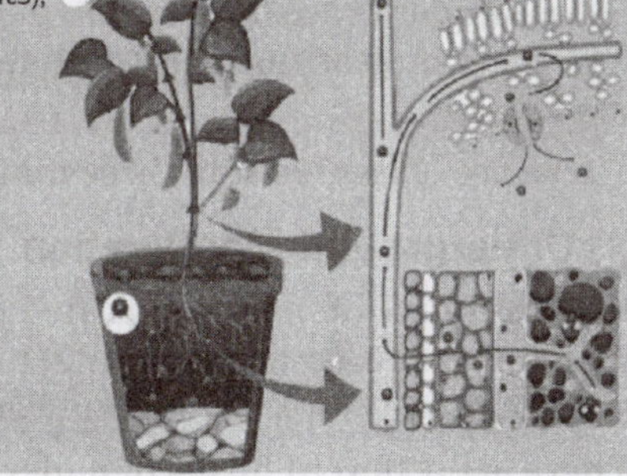

Plant Morphology

Morphology is the combination of two words *Morph* means **form** and *logos* means **study**. It deals with the study of outer forms and features of different plant organs like roots, stem, leaves, fruits, flowers, etc.

Plants are divided majorly into the following parts :

1. Root

- These are descending portion of plant axis which develop from **radicle** and grows down into the earth.
- Most of the roots are **positively geotropic**, i.e. they always show movement towards the direction of gravity.
- Roots of certain plants like sweet potato also contain **buds.**
- It helps in vegetative propagation and absorbs minerals and nutrients from soil.

Characteristics of Roots

- Photosynthesis does not occur in roots.
- The root apex is sub-apical and usually protected by a **root cap**. They have **root hairs** (unicellular) that help roots for the absorption of water by increasing surface area.
- Roots are not divided into **nodes or internodes**.

Types of Roots

Roots are of three types, i.e. **adventitious**, **fibrous root** and **tap roots.**

(i) **Adventitious Root** It develops from anywhere except the radicle. This is usually found in monocot plants.

(ii) **Fibrous Root** Originate from the base of stem, usually found in monocotyledonous plants.

(iii) **Tap Root** It develops from radicle and is usually found in dicot plants.

Functions of Root

- It keeps the plant in a static form, i.e. provides fixation to the plants with soil. It absorbs and helps transportation of water and mineral salts from the soil.
- It stores food for the use of other plants and animals.

2. Stem

This is the ascending organ of a plant that develops from the plumule of the embryo of a germinating seed. In flowering plants, it bears leaves, flowers, branches and fruits.

Characteristics of Stem

- It is usually erect, aerial and grows away from the soil towards light.
- It has a terminal bud for growing in length.
- In flowering plants, stem show distinction into nodes (attach leaves to stem) and internodes (portion of stem between the two nodes).
- The young stem is green and has ability to photosynthesis.

Types of Stem

On the basis of the position of the soil, stems are of the following three types :

(i) **Aerial Stem** When stem grows above the soil, e.g. lemons, roses, etc.

(ii) **Sub-aerial Stem** When aerial stem in some plants trails or creeps on the ground, e.g. water plant, grass root, etc.

(iii) **Underground Stem** When stem grows inside the soil, e.g. banana, potato, etc.

Modifications of Stem

Stems of plants are modified to perform different functions such as nutrition, vegetative propagation, food storage, etc.

These are classified into three main types :

(i) Underground Modification

Underground stems are modified plant structures which exist under the soil surface and functions as storage tissues for food and nutrients.

There are different forms of underground stems :

- **Sucker** e.g. banana.
- **Rhizome** e.g. *Alocasia indica*, ginger (*Zingiber officinale*), turmeric (*Curcuma domestica*), *Saccharum,* etc.
- **Corm** e.g. elephant foot (kachalu), *Fressia* (saffron), *Alocasia,* banana, etc.
- **Tuber** e.g. rose, stem tuber (potato).
- **Bulb** e.g. onion, tulip, nargis, etc.

(ii) Sub-aerial Modification

The sub-aerial stems are weak and do not stand erect. They may be partial subterranean. They are mainly used for the purpose of vegetative propagation. Various types of modifications found in such types of stem are :

- **Runner** e.g. grass, strawberry, etc.
- **Stolon** e.g. mint, jasmine, etc.
- **Offset** e.g. water hyacinth, *Pistia,* etc.
- **Sucker** e.g. banana, pineapple, etc.

(iii) Aerial Modification

Aerial stems are modified to carry out certain functions.

There are various types of aerial modifications found :

- **Stem Tendrils** for support and climbing, e.g. ghia, tori, *Cucurbita* (kaddoo), grape vine, etc.
- **Stem Thorns** for protection and reducing transpiration, e.g. *Citrus, Duranta, Boungainvillea,* pomegranate, etc.
- **Phylloclade** for photosynthesis in xerophytic conditions, e.g. *Cactus, Opuntia*, etc.
- **Bulbils** for storage of food and vegetative reproduction, e.g. *Dioscorea bulbifera.*
- **Cladodes/Cladophylls** for photosynthesis, e.g. *Asparagus*, etc.

Functions of Stem

- It bears leaves and hold them in such a manner so that they can get maximum sunlight.
- The stem conducts water and mineral nutrients from the roots to the leaves, flower and fruits.
- It also bears flower in suitable position so that pollination and fertilisation takes place. Stem branches help in providing support to its various parts.

3. Leaf

Leaf is green, flat, thin and expanded lateral appendage born on the stem. It emerges at a **node** and bears a **bud** in its **axil**.

The mode of arrangement of leaves on the stem and its branches is known as **phyllotaxy**, while distribution pattern of the **vein** and **veinlets** in the **lamina** of a leaf is called **venation**. Monocots have parallel venation, while dicots have reticulate venation.

Characteristics of Leaf

- There is always an axillary bud in the axil of a leaf.
- The growth of leaf is always limited.
- It has three distinct parts **leaf base, petiole** and **lamina.**

Modifications of Leaf

Leaves of plants are modified to perform different functions in addition to their main function, i.e. photosynthesis. Modifications of leaf are as follows :

- **Leaf Tendrils** These are thread-like sensitive structure which can coil around a support to help the plant in climbing, e.g. wild pea, sweet pea, lentils etc.
- **Leaf Spines** The leaf parts modified into spines in order to protect the plant from grazing animals and reduce transpiration, e.g. *Aloe,* cacti etc.
- **Phyllodes** It is a green, short and flattened petiole, which is modified for the purpose of photosynthesis. e.g. Australian *Acacia.*
- **Leaf Bladders** They occur in the aquatic carnivorous plants, which modify their leaf segments to form small bladders in order to trap insects present in the water. e.g., Bladderwort.
- **Leaf Pitcher** The leaf of the pitcher plant get modified into tube-like structures with hairs to trap insects. The base is expanded to carryout photosynthesis while the

leaf apex is modified into a lid. e.g., pitcher plant, Venus flytrap etc.

- **Succulent Leaves** These leaves are fleshy or swollen. They store water, food, etc. e.g., *Aloe, Agave, Bryophyllum*, etc.
- **Scale Leaves** These are specialised leaves or bract that gets modified in order to protect a bud and other soft organs. It is small having a colourless membrane such as on rhizome or forming part of a bulb. e.g., garlic, onion, etc.
- **Coloured Leaves or Bract** In this type of modifications, leaves get modified and become brightly coloured in order to fascinate insects towards themselves. e.g., *poinsettia*.

Functions of Leaf

- Its important function is to perform photosynthesis.
- It acts as a site of transpiration.
- It stores food as in the leaf base of onion.

4. The Flower

- Flower is the reproductive unit in the angiosperms, meant for sexual reproduction.
- Morphologically, it is considered as a condensed shoot bearing nodes and modified floral leaves.
- A flower arises in the axil of a leaf structure called **bract** and is attached to the main axis of shoot by a stalk. This is called **inflorescence.**

Parts of the Flower

A typical flower consists of four distinct parts, i.e. **calyx, corolla, androecium** and **gynoecium.**

These are described as follows

Calyx

- It is the outermost whorl of a flower made up of units like **sepals.**
- Sepals are generally green, leaf-like and protect the flower in the bud stage.
- They may be united together (gamosepalous condition) or free (polysepalous condition).

Corolla

- It lies inner to calyx and is comprised of **petals.** It is brightly coloured to attract insects for pollination.
- It may be tubular, bell-shaped or funnel-shaped.
- Like calyx, corolla may also be **gamopetalous** (petals united) or **polypetalous** (petals free).

Note Aestivation is the arrangement of sepals or petals in a floral bud, in relation to one another. It is of the following types—**valvate, twisted, imbricate, vexillary**.

Androecium

- It represents the **male reproductive** part of a flower which is composed of **stamens.**
- Each stamen consists of a stalk or filament and an anther.
- A typical angiosperm anther is bilobed with each lobe having two **theca** (dithecous).

Gynoecium

- It represents the female reproductive part of the flower which is made up of one or more **carpels.**
- A carpel comprises of three parts

(i) **Stigma** It is the receptive surface of pollen grains.

(ii) **Style** It is the elongated stalk that connects stigma to ovary.

(iii) **Ovary** It is the enlarged basal part in which the egg is formed.

Inflorescence

- The arrangement and distribution of flowers on the floral axis is called inflorescence.
- It is of two types, namely

(i) **Racemose Inflorescence** In this, the main axis continues to grow. Older flowers will be found towards the base as in acropetal arrangement.

(ii) **Cymose Inflorescence** In this, the tip of the main axis terminates in a flower. Further growth continues by lateral branches which will be one or more in number. Younger flowers may occupy **basal position** (basipetal arrangement).

5. Seed

A seed is a ripened ovule which contains an embryo or a future plant with sufficient food reserve for the development of embryo.

A typical seed consists of the following parts

- **Seed Coat** It is the outermost hard covering of seed which protects the embryo inside from extreme weather conditions.

  It is composed of two layers :

  – Outer covering which is hard and leathery is called **testa.**

  – Inner thin membranous layer is called **tegmen.**
- **Seed Leaves or Cotyledons** These absorb the food from the parent plant and store it for the embryo. They protect embryo. Some plants have two seed leaves like gram, pea, etc. These are called **dicot** or **dicotyledons.** Some seeds which have only one seed leaf are called monocot or **monocotyledons.**
- **Embryo** It develops into a new plant. It gives rise to a baby shoot (plumule) and root (radicle).

6. Fruit

- It is a mature or ripened ovary, developed after fertilisation.
- **True fruits** develop from ovary, whereas **false fruits** develop from other floral parts along with the ovary. The thalamus grows along with the ovary to form a false fruit, e.g. apple.
- The development of fruit can even take place without fertilisation (parthenocarpy). Fruits formed without fertilisation are known as **parthenocarpic fruits**. Such fruits lack seed.

Plant Physiology

Plants carryout several physico-chemical activities. The study of functioning of these activities is known as plant physiology.

It includes processes like transportation, mineral nutrition, photosynthesis, respiration, etc., which ultimately lead to growth, development and reproduction of plants.

Transport in Plants

- In plants, transport may start from roots or from leaves.
- Substances like water, mineral nutrients, organic nutrients, growth regulators, food manufactured by leaves, all need to be transported from one part of the plant to the other. This process is termed as **transportation**.
- **Xylem** and **phloem** carry substances from one part of the plant to another.
- Every substance has to pass through the **cell membrane** to reach the cell.
- Cell membrane is **selectively permeable**, i.e. allows certain substances to pass through itself.
- Following are the most common means of transport found in plants to establish the plant-water relations :
  - **Diffusion** It is the physical process in which different solvent molecules or solute ions get transported without any expenditure of energy.

  During diffusion, substances move from the region of higher concentration to region of lower concentration. The movement continues until an equilibrium is set up.
  - **Imbibition** It is the special phenomenon of water absorption by the solid particle of an adsorbent without forming a solution.

  e.g. dry piece of wood when placed in water swells and increases in volume. In plant systems, absorption of water by cell wall, swelling and rupture of seed coats during germination, etc.
  - **Osmosis** The movement of water molecules from high water concentration to low concentration through a Semi-Permeable Membrane (SPM) is called osmosis, e.g. absorption of water by plant roots. The movement of water across the SPM is also affected by the amount of substance dissolved in water.
  - **Plasmolysis** It is the phenomenon used to define the shrinkage of plant cell when water is lost from it due to exosmosis. And when the same plasmolysed (shrinked) cells are transferred back to distil water or hypotonic solution, they swell up again. This condition is referred to as **deplasmolysis.**

Transport of Water

- Plants absorb water from the roots and transport it to the tips of the growing stem in a very specific manner. The uptake of water involves processes like **diffusion, osmosis** and **potential gradient** for absorption to occur at short distances, i.e. from cell to cell, across membrane.
- For the water uptake to occur at long distances, movements involve complex processes such as **root pressure** and **transpirational pull.**

Transpiration and guttation are the processes through which loss of water takes place from the aerial parts of the plant.

(i) **Transpiration** Plants do not utilise the total amount of water absorbed by them. Only 5-10% is absorbed and rest 90-95% of water is lost from plants through aerial parts (mainly from leaves) in the form of water vapours.

Thus, transpiration is the evaporative loss of water by the plants. The process of transpiration is carried out by the special structure found in leaves of plants called **stomata.**

These are tiny pores in leaves present on its both or either surface which allows diffusion of water vapour and gaseous exchange of O_2 and CO_2 from atmosphere. The opening and closing of these pores are regulated by a pair of guard cells.

(ii) **Guttation** When the amount of root pressure is high and rate of transpiration is low, many herbaceous plants tend to loose small quantities of water or liquid in the form of drops.

These are present on the margins of the leaves or where the main vein ends. These are also present near the tips of blade of some vascular plants like grasses and small herbaceous plants (rose, strawberry, tomato, etc).

This phenomenon of water loss in its liquid phase is called **guttation**. It takes place usually in early morning. The water that oozes out contains organic and inorganic substances.

Transport of Minerals

- The mineral elements present in soil are absorbed by roots and transported in upward direction through xylem along with water. In rooted plants, the transport of inorganic nutrients is multidirectional.
- The major regions where mineral elements reach are the growing regions of the plant like the apical and the lateral meristems, young leaves, developing flowers, fruits, seeds and also the storage organs.
- Remobilisation of many minerals takes place inside the plants particularly from old parts to the young leaves.

Translocation of Organic Solutes

- The organic compounds are mainly synthesised during photosynthesis in leaves and young growing apices of roots and shoots.
- These compounds are transported by phloem to all parts of the plants in the form of starch solution.
- It is a multidirectional transfer process of food material.

Mineral Nutrition in Plants

- In addition to **carbon**, **hydrogen** and **oxygen**, plants required other essential element from the soil.
- Elements which are important for the growth and development of plants are called **mineral** nutrients. These elements are absorbed by the plants.
- On the basis of requirement, mineral nutrients are classified as **micronutrients** and **macronutrients.**
  - **Micronutrients** are required in a very small amount, e.g. iron, copper, zinc, chlorine, etc.
  - **Macronutrients** are required in more amounts in the plant body in order to facilitate proper growth and development.

  e.g., carbon (C), oxygen (O), sulfur (S), phosphorus (P), etc. These are major sources of minerals and their deficiency may lead to stunted growth or any disease.

Classification of Plants Based on Nutrition

On the basis of the type of nutrition, plants can be :

(i) **Autotrophic** These plants synthesise their own food in the form of glucose, e.g. green plants.

(ii) **Heterotrophic** Such plants are unable to prepare their own food and thus, depend on autotrophs for food. These are further divided as :

- **Parasitic** These plants depend on other plants for their nutritional requirements, e.g. *Cuscuta*.
- **Saprophytic** Such plants grow on dead and decaying matter, e.g. moulds.

Photosynthesis in Plants

- Plants possess **autotrophic mode of nutrition**. It is the process of obtaining food by themselves. The process of synthesis of food is known as **photosynthesis.**
- Photosynthesis can be defined as the synthesis of organic food in the form of carbohydrates from carbon dioxide and water in the presence of sunlight and chlorophyll.

$$\underset{\text{Carbon dioxide}}{6CO_2} + \underset{\text{Water}}{12H_2O} \xrightarrow[\text{Chlorophyll}]{\text{Sunlight}} \underset{\text{Carbohydrate}}{C_6H_{12}O_6} + \underset{\text{Oxygen}}{6O_2} + \underset{\text{Water}}{6H_2O}$$

- The carbohydrate formed is not used immediately but stored in the form of starch.
- Major events occurring in photosynthesis are
  - Absorption of light energy by chlorophyll.
  - Conversion of light energy into chemical energy.
  - Splitting of water molecules into hydrogen and oxygen.
  - Reduction of carbon dioxide to carbohydrates.
- Cells in leaves of green plants have some structures known as **chloroplasts** (containing chlorophyll) which are main site for the process of photosynthesis to occur.
- In leaf, some other structures are also present such as stomata (tiny pores present on the surface of the leaf) that participate in gaseous exchange during photosynthesis, but it is also responsible for large amount of water loss.
- These pores close when there is no need of carbon dioxide for photosynthesis. **Guard cells** are the bean-shaped cells that frame the stomatal openings.
- Each pair of guard cells is meant to control the opening of the stomata and hence control the rate of diffusion of gases and water vapour into and out of the leaf.
- Plants require some raw materials other than water like nitrogen, phosphorus, iron and magnesium that are taken up from the soil.
- Nitrogen is an essential component for synthesis of proteins and other compounds. It is mainly taken up in the form of inorganic nitrates or nitrites or in organic form (prepared from N_2).

Respiration in Plants

- Respiration is the process of biochemical oxidation of nutrients (occurring in cytoplasm of the cell) in the presence of specific enzymes at optimum temperature in the cells to release energy for metabolic activities.
- It is a catabolic process in which exchange of gases, i.e. oxygen and carbon dioxide takes place between the body and the outside environment.

- Respiration occurs in three steps

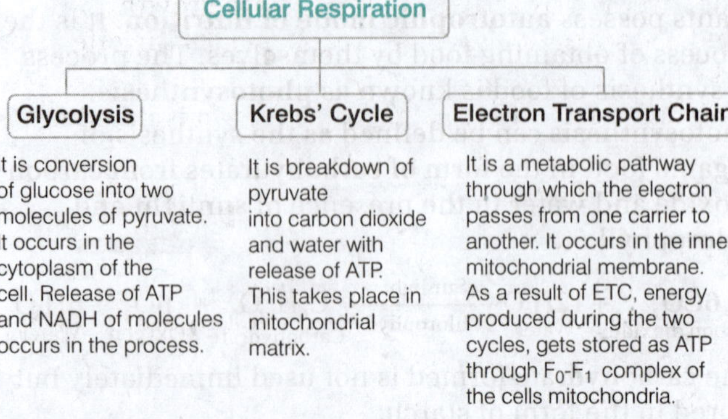

- Plants exchange gases through stomata and large intercellular spaces.
- Root, stem and leaf of a plant are the parts involved in respiration. It is rapid in meristematic tissue and slower in mature regions.
- In roots of a plant, exchange of gases takes place by the process of **diffusion**.
- In woody plants, gaseous exchange occurs through the small pores in the stems called **Lenticels**.
- In leaves, respiration takes place by diffusion of oxygen through stomata into the cells of the leaf from where carbon dioxide is released into the atmosphere.
- Based on oxygen requirement, respiration is categorised as
  - **Aerobic respiration** This type of respiration occurs in the presence of oxygen. Overall reaction can be represented as :

$$\underset{\text{Glucose}}{C_6H_{12}O_6} + \underset{\text{Oxygen}}{6O_2} \longrightarrow \underset{\text{Carbon dioxide}}{6CO_2} + \underset{\text{Water}}{6H_2O} + \underset{\text{(Energy)}}{38\ \text{ATP}}$$

  - **Anaerobic respiration** This type of respiration occurs in conditions which lack oxygen. Overall reaction is represented as :

$$\underset{\text{Glucose}}{C_6H_{12}O_6} \longrightarrow \underset{\text{Ethanol}}{2C_2H_5OH} + \underset{\text{Carbon dioxide}}{2CO_2} + 2\ \text{ATP (Energy)}$$

Excretion in Plants

- Plants give off gaseous wastes like carbon dioxide and oxygen through stomata and lenticels during **respiration** and **photosynthesis**.
- Plants also get rid of excess of water by the process of **transpiration** and can also store waste substances in old xylem such as resins and gums.
- Some plants store waste substances in the **cell vacuoles** and get rid of them by dropping their leaves. e.g., deciduous plants.
- While, other plants also excrete some solid waste substances into the soil around them.
- However, some plants like oak, store their excretory products as **tannins, essential oils, gums**, etc.

Coordination in Plants

- Plants do not have nervous system or muscle tissue like animals. However, they still show **movement** and **response**.
- They use chemical means to convey information from one cell to another.
- Plants respond to light, touch, gravitational force and other stimuli.
- The movement of a plant either towards stimulus or away from it is called **directional** or **tropic movement**.
- These responses are generally slow and occur due to the sensitivity of protoplasm.

These can be categorised as :

- **Immediate Response to Stimulus** All parts of the plant exhibit this response.
- **Increase in Growth** Plants shows response to a stimulus by exhibiting a directional growth.

Types of Tropic Movement

- **Phototropism** Response towards **light**. Here, light acts as the stimulus. Stem is **positively phototropic**.
- **Geotropism** Response to **gravity**, e.g. roots show **positive geotropism**, i.e. grow towards the earth.
- **Hydrotropism** Here, water act as a stimulus to bring about movement. Hydrotropic plants exhibit response of roots towards regions of water.
- **Thigmotropism** Response to contact with some physical object. Tendrils are modified leaves or stems which enable the plant to climb the object they come in contact with due to thigmotropism, e.g. tendrils coil in the direction of an object that it touches.
- **Chemotropism** It is the growth of organisms stimulated by chemicals, e.g. stigma of a flower secretes a type of sugar into the style and the pollen grain responds by growing a pollen tube downward into the style for the purpose of fertilisation.

Nastic and Thigmonastic Movement

- In some plants, movement is neither towards nor away from the stimulus. Such movements are called **nastic movements**, e.g. leaves of touch-me-not plant bend and drop when plant is touched.
- Some cells change their shape by changing the amount of water in them. This happens due to swelling or shrinking of cell.
- Similarly, **thigmonastic movement** is the nastic response of a plant or fungus to tactile stimuli. Such, movements are seen in carnivorous plants in response to the touch of an insect.

Plant Hormones

- The hormones (chemical messengers) present in plant which causes control and coordination in them are called plant hormones or **phytohormones**.
- These are small, simple organic molecules of diverse chemical composition.
- The term 'hormone' was first used by **Ernest Starling** in 1905.
- These are generally secreted from the root or stem (top part) of the plant.
- These hormones are responsible for the functioning of the plant system and also regulate their growth and development.

Classification of Plant Hormones

Some plant hormones are given below

1. Auxin

- The real plant auxin is chemically known as **Indole 3-Acetic Acid** (IAA).
- It is also known as **natural auxin**. Apart from this, Naphthalene Acetic Acid (NAA) and 2, 4 dichloro phenoxyacetic acid (2,4D) are known as **synthetic auxins.**

Functions of Auxin

- It promotes cell elongation and longitudinal growth.
- It leads to promotion of root growth and root initiation.
- It prevents early abscission of fruit and leaves but promote, i.e. shedding of mature leaves from stem or ripe fruits from the stem.
- It induces parthenocarpy, i.e. formation of seedless fruits without fertilisation.
- It generally promote flowering, e.g. in pineapple.

2. Gibberellin

- It was discovered by **Kurosawa** in 1926. These are generally known as **weakly acidic growth hormones.**
- Out of more than 100 different gibberellins being reported, GA_3 is the most important gibberellic acid. It was first to be discovered and was most extensively studied.

Functions of Gibberellin

- It promotes elongation of stem.
- It promotes seed germination in lettuce, cereals.
- It controls growth and development of fruits. It delay senescence (ageing) in fruits like citrus fruits, apples, etc.

3. Cytokinin

- It was invented by **Miller** in 1955. These growth hormones are basic in nature and have specific effects on cytokinesis.
- **Zeatin** is the naturally occurring cytokinin isolated from maize grains.

Functions of Cytokinin

- It acts on cell division but have little or no effect on growth. Breaks the dormancy of many seeds.
- It stimulates the growth of lateral buds and thus suppress apical dominance.
- It delay leaf **senescence** (ageing).

4. Ethylene

It is a simple gaseous plant hormone.

Functions of Ethylene

- It promotes senescence and abscission and helps in fruit growth and ripening.
- Flowering in pineapple, mango and various other plants is induced by the application of ethylene.
- It stimulates root initiation, growth of lateral roots and root hairs.
- It breaks the dormancy of buds and seeds.

5. Abscisic Acid

It is slightly acidic growth hormone that functions as a growth inhibitor with other mentioned growth hormones.

Functions of Abscisic acid

- It inhibits growth and metabolism.
- It inhibits seed development and germination.
- Reduce transpiration by closing stomata.
- It maintains dormancy in many seeds.
- It induces bud dormancy in a number of buds.
- It promotes abscission of leaves, fruits and flowers.

Reproduction in Plants

- The production of new individuals from their parents is known as **reproduction**.
- Most plants have roots, stems and leaves. These are called **vegetative** parts of a plant. After a certain period of growth, most plants bear flowers.
- Flowers perform the function of reproduction in plants and are known as the reproductive parts of plants.

Types of Reproduction in Plants

- There are several ways by which plants produce their offspring. These are categorised into two types :
  (i) Asexual Reproduction
  (ii) Sexual Reproduction

Asexual Reproduction in Plants

- The production of offspring by single parent without formation of gametes is called **asexual reproduction.**
- Offspring produced in asexual reproduction are genetically similar to their parents and do not show variations.
- Vegetative propagation is a type of asexual reproduction in which new plants are produced from **roots, stems, leaves** and **buds** which are the **vegetative parts** of the plant.
- Some plants like sugarcane, rose, etc. are vegetatively propagated as they do not require seeds and can also be obtained in less time.
- The vegetative propagation is mainly of two types

Natural Vegetative Propagation

- This type of vegetative propagation occurs naturally in plants.
- Vegetative reproduction occurs in potato (tuber), onion (bulb), ginger (rhizome) and *Colocasia* (corm) etc. by underground stem.
- Vegetative reproduction occurs in *Bryophyllum* by leaf buds.

Artificial Vegetative Propagation

- The process of artificially made vegetative propagules in plants is called **artificial vegetative reproduction**, e.g. **cutting, grafting,** etc.
- During **cutting**, a small piece of any plant part (i.e., root, stem or leaf) is used for propagation. e.g. rose, grapes, etc.
- In **grafting**, a small part of stem from one plant without roots (scion) is attached to the part with root (stock) of another plant, e.g. apples, mango, lemon, etc.

Tissue Culture

- Tissue culture is another artificial reproduction technique in plants. In this new plants are grown using tissues (like flower buds, stems, growing tips, leaves, etc.) *in vitro* in an artificial culture medium.
- The medium is rich in inorganic compounds, i.e. some vitamins and plant hormone.
- Using this technique, a large number of plants can be developed from a single parent.
- Disease free plants can be cultivated from diseased parents using meristem culture (such as root and shoot tips).
- Also, plants used for decorative purposes can be grown within less time using this technique.

Sexual Reproduction in Flowering Plants

- It involves the formation and fusion of the male and female gametes, produced either by same or different individuals of different sex.
- Higher plants like angiosperms, have special structures (flowers) to carry out sexual reproduction.

Following are the four stages of sexual reproduction in plants

Microsporogenesis and Gametogenesis

- It is the process of formation of haploid microspores from **Microspore Mother cell** (MMC) in males.
- Formation of male cells (male gametes) is called **male gametogenesis** whereas that of female cells (egg cells) is **female gametogensis** or **oogenesis.**

Following two processes take place under this

Formation of Male Gametophyte or Pollen Grain

- Each stamen comprises of anther and filament.
- A typical angiospermic anther is bilobed. It is a four sides structure consisting of four **microsporangia** located at the corners of the two theca.
- When the anther is young, sporogenous tissue (MMC) gives rise to several thousands of pollen grains or microspores forming **microspore tetrad.**
- These microspores, on undergoing meiosis form male gametophyte or pollen grains which remain scattered in the anther.

Structure of Pollen Grain

- A typical pollen grain has a two layered wall-outer hard layer—**exine** (made up of sporopollenin) and inner layer **intine** (composed of pectin and cellulose).
- Exine has **germ pores.** These areas lack sporopollenin.
- Each mature pollen grain in angiosperms, has two cells, the **generative** and the **vegetative cell.**
- Generative cell is small and floats in the cytoplasm of vegetative cell. It divides to produce two male gametes (*via* mitotic division).
- Vegetative cell is larger and has abundant reserve food material.

Female Gametogenesis or Development of Female Gametophyte

- **Gynoecium** represents the female reproductive part of flower.
- The basal part of the gynoecium, i.e. ovary, contains ovules attached to a structure (placenta).
- An ovule generally has a single embryo sac also called **female gametophyte.**

Structure of Ovule

- Ovule is a structure present in the ovary of a flower.
- It develops into seed after fertilisation.
- It is joined to placenta by a stalk called **funiculus** (funicle).
- Junction between an ovule and funicle is called **hilum**.
- Each ovule has one or two protective envelops (integuments) which encircle the ovule.
- The integuments leave a narrow pore at one end of the ovule. It is called **micropyle**.
- **Chalaza** is the basal part of ovule.
- A mass of cells, **nucellus**, is enclosed within the integuments. Cells of nucellus are rich in food reserve.
- **Embryo sac** is located inside the ovule.
- The 2-nucleate embryo sac divides mitotically to form 4 and then 8-nucleate stages. These stages comprise of micropylar end and chalazal end with 3-nuclei at each end and remaining are centrally placed.
- Three cells present towards, the **micropylar end**, group together, constitute the egg apparatus (i.e. two synergids and one egg cell).
- Three cells of the chalazal end form **antipodal** cells.
- The large central cell has two polar nuclei.

1. Pollination

- The transfer of pollen grains from anther of the stamen to the receptive stigma of the pistil is called **pollination**.

  Pollination is of two types

(i) Self-Pollination

- It is the kind of pollination achieved within the same flower.
- In this, pollen grains are transferred from the anther of a flower to the stigma of the same flower, e.g. wheat.

(ii) Cross-Pollination

- It involves the transfer of pollen grains from anther of one plant to stigma of another plant.
- It is the only type of pollination that brings genetically different types of pollen grains to stigma, e.g. papaya, maize, etc.

Methods of Cross-Pollination

There are several methods by which cross-pollination occurs as

- **Entomophily** Pollination carried out by insect is also termed as entomophily. Insect pollinated flowers are large, colourful, fragrant and rich in nectar. The surface of their pollen grains is sticky in order to stick to insect body, e.g. *Amorphophalus*.
- **Hydrophily** The pollination that takes place by water is known as hydrophily. Following adaptations are associated with water-pollinated flowers
  - Small and inconspicuous flowers.
  - Flowers are odourless, nectarless and colourless.
  - Pollen grains are small, lightweight and non-sticky.
  - Pollen grains float on water surface to reach the female flowers and carry out fertilisation, e.g. *Hydrilla, Vallisneria*, etc.
- **Anemophily** The pollination that takes place by wind is called **anemophily**. It is the most common amongst abiotic pollination. Wind pollinated flowers are devoid of scent or nectar.

  Pollen grains are dry, light weight, small sized and non-sticky. Stigma may be large and feathery and must project out. e.g. grasses, etc.
- **Zoophily** Certain plants get pollinated by birds, bats, etc. This kind of pollination is termed as **zoophily**, e.g. *Bignonia*.

2. Fertilisation

- Soon after the completion of pollination, the process of fertilisation begins.
- Fertilisation is defined as the union of male and female gametes to produce zygote.
- Pollen tube enters ovule and releases the two male gametes into the cytoplasm of the synergid.
- One of the two male gametes, fuses with egg cell to form a diploid zygote. This is called **syngamy**.
- The second male gamete fuses with two polar nuclei ($2n$) to form **primary endosperm nucleus** ($3n$). This is called **triple fusion**.
- As both the fusions, syngamy and triple fusion, occur in embryo sac, the phenomenon is termed as **double fertilisation**.

3. Formation of Fruit and Seed

- A **fruit** is formed after fertilisation as a result of cell division and differentiation in ovary. Fruit derived from the ovary of a flower and not any non-carpellary part is **true fruit**, e.g. mango.
- Ovules found in the ovary, develop into future seeds.
- The **Primary Endosperm Nucleus** (PEN) cell formed as a result of triple fusion, divides mitotically to form **endosperm**.
- Based on the presence or absence of endosperm, seeds are classified as
  - **Endospermic or Albuminous Seeds** These seeds have the endosperm as it is not used up completely, e.g. coconut, wheat, etc.
  - **Non-endospermic or Non-albuminous Seeds** Such seeds are devoid of endosperm, e.g. groundnut, pea, etc.

- Along with the development of endosperm and embryo, the integuments dry up and become hard. Thus, these make the seed coat. Nucellus is lost but, in some cases, is retained as a thin layer (perisperm).
- The process by which a seed gives rise to a new plant is called **seed germination.**
- Seeds germinate only under favourable conditions of availability of water, oxygen and proper temperature and sunlight (in some cases).
- At maturity, the funicle falls off, leaving a scar, called **hilum.**

Embryo

- It is the infant plant located inside the seed.
- It is formed as a result of fertilisation of egg.
- Embryo consists of two parts :
  - **Cotyledons** They are also called **seed leaves.** Their main function is to store food items. There is single cotyledon in a monocot plant and two in a dicot plant.
  - **Embryonal axis** It is the main axis of the seed or embryo. Cotyledons are attached to this axis.

Extra Facts From Tamil Nadu Board and NIOS

- The reactions that make up the process of photosynthesis can be divided into light-dependent reactions, which take place in the thylakoids and the light independent reaction (also known as dark reaction or Calvin cycle), which take place in the stroma of chloroplast.
- Melvin Calvin, an American biochemist discovered a chemical pathway for photosynthesis. The cycle was named as Calvin cycle. He was awarded with Nobel Prize in the year 1961 for his discovery.
- Indian scientist CNR Rao, conferred with Bharat Ratna (2013) is working on technology similar to the artificial photosynthesis to produce hydrogen fuel (renewable energy).
- Respiratory quotient is the ratio of volume of carbon dioxide liberated and the volume of oxygen consumed during respiration. It is expressed as

$$RQ = \frac{\text{Volume of } CO_2 \text{ liberated}}{\text{Volume of } O_2 \text{ consumed}}$$

07

Animal Physiology

(SOURCES)

Class-VII NCERT Chap 2 (Nutrition in Animals), Chap 6 (Respiration in Organisms), Chap 7 (Transportation in Animals), Class-VIII NCERT Chap 6 (Reproduction in Animals), Chap 7 (Reaching the Age of Adolescence), Class-X NCERT Chap 5 (Life Processes), Chap 6 (Control and Coordination), Chap 7 (How do Organisms Reproduce?), Class-XI Old NCERT Chap 16 (Digestion and Absorption)
Chap 14 (Breathing and Exchange of Gases),
Chap 15 (Body Fluids and Circulations)
Chap 16 (Excretory Products and Their Elimination),
Chap 17 (Locomotion and Movement),
Chap 18 (Neural Control and Coordination),
Chap 19 (Chemical Coordination and Integration),
Class-XII NCERT Chap 2 (Human Reproduction),
Chap 3 (Reproductive Health)
Tamil Nadu Board (Class-IX), NIOS

- **Animal physiology** is the scientific study of the life supporting properties, functions and processes of animals or their parts.
- Physiological mechanisms are the smaller physical and chemical events that makeup a large physiological process.
- The basic physiological process of life are growth, reproduction, digestion, respiration, excretion, transportation, movements, control and coordination. These are the basic life processes in **human**.

Integumentary System

- It is the set of organs which form the outermost layer of the body of an animal. It comprises of **skin** and its appendages.
- Skin acts as a physical barrier that protects the animal body from its outside environment.

Skin

- It is one of the largest organ of the body accounting for 12 to 15% of total body weight. The skin is made up of two layers of tissue- **epidermis** and the **dermis**.

Epidermis

- It is the superficial layer that acts as a first line of defence against **microorganisms**.
- Human epidermis comprises of **stratified squamous epithelial cells.**

The epidermis is subdivided into the following layers:

(i) **Stratum Corneum** It is 20-30 cell layers. It is the uppermost layer, made up of keratin and horny scales made up of dead keratinocytes, known as anucleate squamous cells.

(ii) **Stratum Lucidum** It is 2-3 cell layers. It is present in thicker skin found in the palms and soles, is a thin clear layer consisting of eleidin which is a transformation product of keratohyalin.

(iii) **Stratum Granulosum** It is 3-5 cell layers. It contains diamond-shaped cells with keratohyalin granules and lamellar granules. **Keratohyalin granules** contain keratin precursors that eventually aggregate, crosslink and form bundles. The **lamellar granules** contain the glycolipids that get secreted to the surface of the cells and function as a glue, keeping the cells stuck together.

(iv) **Stratum Basale** It is also known as stratum germinativum. It is the deepest layer, separated from the dermis by the basement membrane (basal lamina) and attached to the basement membrane by hemidesmosomes. This layer also contains melanocytes.

(v) **Stratum Spinosum** It is 8-10 cell layers. It also known as the prickle cell layer contains irregular, polyhedral cells with cytoplasmic processes, sometimes called 'spines', that extend outward and contact neighboring cells by desmosomes. Dendritic cells can be found in this layer.

Dermis

- The dermis is a connective tissue layer sandwiched between the epidermis and subcutaneous tissue. The dermis is a fibrous structure composed of collagen, elastic tissue, and other extracellular components that includes vasculature, nerve endings, hair follicles, and glands.
- The role of the dermis is to support and protect the skin and deeper layers, assist in thermoregulation and aid in sensation. Fibroblasts are the primary cells within the dermis, but histiocytes, mast cells and adipocytes also play important roles in maintaining the normal structure and function of the dermis.
- The dermis is divided into two layers, i.e. the papillary dermis and the reticular dermis.
- The **papillary dermis** is the superficial layer, lying deep in to the epidermis. The papillary dermis is composed of loose connective tissue that is highly vascular. The **reticular layer** is the deep layer, forming a thick layer of dense connective tissue that constitutes the bulk of the dermis.

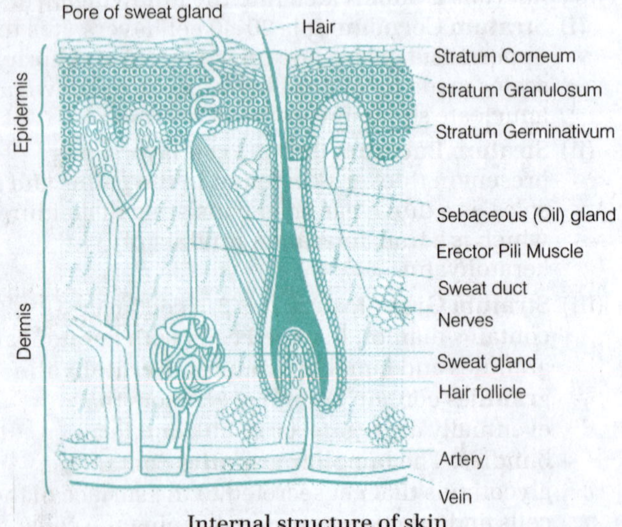

Internal structure of skin

Derivatives of Skin

Derivatives of skin are given as follows :

Hair and Hair Follicle

- A hair consists of **hair shaft, hair root** and **hair bulb**.
- Hair shaft is the part which projects from skin and extends below the epidermis.
- Hair root is embedded within the dermis
- Hair bulb forms base of hair follicle.
- Hair follicle encloses the hair root.
- Hair follicles contain pigment cells which produce **melanin**.
- Hair bulb are connected to **Erector Pili Muscle**. During fear and cold, these muscles contract due to which **goosebumps** occur.

Glands of the Skin

- **Sebaceous Glands** These are branched glands which open up into a hair follicle. They give out oily secretion (**sebum**) which makes the hair and the outer surface of the oily skin.
- **Sweat Glands** Each sweat glands is a simple coiled tube which runs upward to open surface. Outer openings of sweat glands are called **sweat pores**.
- **Mammary Glands** These are modified sweat glands, also called **milk glands**. Mammary glands are present in both males and females. However, in male they remain rudimentary (undeveloped). The activity of mammary glands is related to the reproductive hormones.
- **Ceruminous Glands** These are modified sebaceous glands. They are found in the auditory canal and secrete wax-like substance (ear wax).
- **Tear Glands** They are also known as **lacrimal glands**. They are located in the upper portion of the orbit and secrete tears.
- **Meibomian Glands** These are modified sebaceous glands. These open on the margins of the eyelids. Their secretion prevents overflow of tears.
- **Perineal Glands** These glands occur in pairs and are situated near the anus in some mammals.

Functions of the Skin

- **Protection from the environment** It is the most important function of skin. It keeps the pathogens away in order to prevent their entry into the body.
- **Prevention of water loss** Organisms with thick skins (e.g. humans) tend to lose less water as compared to those having thin skin.
- **Sensation** Skin acts as the main sensory organ which can sense heat, pressure, touch, pain and pleasure.
- **Regulation of temperature** Our skin perspires to lower down its temperature by losing body heat; thus, regulates body temperature.
- **Storage** The skin has the ability to store fats and water in its tissues, which provides an extra insulation to one's body.

Nutrients

The substances providing nourishment to living organisms are called **nutrients**, and are classified as **macronutrients** (proteins, lipids and carbohydrates) and **micronutrients** (vitamins and minerals).

In food products, many nutrients are found that keep human body healthy. Nutrients can be categorised as follows :

1. Organic Substances

In simple language, these substances are known as **biomolecules**. The organic substances found in the body of living organisms are as follows :

Carbohydrates

- These consists of carbon (C), hydrogen (H) and oxygen (O). The general formula of a carbohydrate is $C_n(H_2O)_n$.
- Its sources are potato, rice, wheat, maize, banana, sugar, jaggery etc. They are of following types :
  - **Monosaccharides** (simple sugar) include glucose, fructose, galactose (hexoses).
  - **Disaccharides** (monosaccharide units) include maltose, lactose (milk sugar), sucrose.
  - **Polysaccharides** are not soluble in water (union of large number of monosaccharides), e.g., starch, glycogen, cellulose. Cellulose is used in making shatter proof glass.

Functions of Carbohydrates

- They form a major portion of our food and supply energy to the body by the process of oxidation. They also form nucleic acid. Honey is used as an instant source of energy.
- These are used as storage molecules such as **starch** in plants and **glycogen** in animals.
- Cellulose in the form of wood is used in (build) furniture and clothes in the form of cotton fibres.

Proteins

- The term 'protein' is derived from the word 'proteios' means the 'prime importance'. This term was coined by **Muller** in 1838. These are the nitrogenous substances, i.e. have nitrogen along with C, H and O and called the **building blocks of the body**.
- All proteins are polymers of α-amino acids which are linked together through peptide linkage.
- Proteins make upto 15% by mass of our body. These are important components of most foods and are essential for nourishment purposes. Meat and eggs are their richest sources.
- In animals, 20 types of amino acid codes are found for the synthesis of proteins.
- Deficiency of protein leads to disorders like **Kwashiorkor** and **Marasmus**.

Functions of Proteins

- They act as an enzymes in plants and animals.
- These are the components of hair, muscles and skin.
- They act as hormones, e.g. insulin and vasopressin.
- They transport oxygen, fat and other substances required for metabolism.
- Proteins are vital for physiological growth and nourishment purposes. They help in the synthesis of cells, protoplasm and tissue culturing.
- They provide instantaneous energy only at the time of emergency when carbohydrates and fats are not available.

Fats

- These are made up of carbon, hydrogen and oxygen, but chemically different from carbohydrates.
- They are insoluble in water, but soluble in fat solvents such as acetone, chloroform, etc.

Functions of Fats

- They act as stored source of energy.
- These are stored up beneath the skin to provide resistive layer in the body.
- These are also stored in the form of shock resistive layer to protect various organs of the animals.

Vitamins

- These are the organic compounds required in small amounts in our diet. These are not required for providing energy, but essential for regulating the metabolism in human beings.
- Their deficiency causes specific diseases. Excess of vitamins is also harmful, therefore, vitamin pills should not be taken without the advice of doctor.
- Vitamins are represented by capital letters of English alphabets like A, B, C, D etc.
- Depending upon their solubility in water or fat, vitamins are classified as fat soluble and water soluble vitamins.

Fat Soluble Vitamins

- These are fat soluble vitamins-A, D, E and K. These are stored in liver and fat storing tissues.

Fat Soluble Vitamins

Name	Sources	Deficiency Symptoms
Vitamin-A (Retinol)	Carrot, tomato, papaya, mango, milk, eggs and cod-liver oil.	Night blindness (dim vision in the evening and at night), Xerophthalmia (hardening of cornea of eye), abnormal epithelial cell growth
Vitamin-D (Calciferol)	Cod liver oil, skin can synthesise vitamin-D in the presence of sunlight.	Rickets in children and osteomalacia in adults.
Vitamin-E (Tocopherol)	Wheat germ, green leafy vegetables, fats of vegetables	Reproductive failure, muscular dystrophy, increased haemolysis leading to macrocytic anaemia.
Vitamin-K	Leafy vegetables, wheat germ, vitamin-K is synthesised by bacteria of large intestine.	Faulty blood clotting.

Water Soluble Vitamins

- B group vitamins and vitamin-C are soluble in water.
- These vitamins must be supplied regularly in diet because they are readily excreted in urine, i.e. not stored in body (except vitamin-B_{12}).

Water Soluble Vitamins

Name	Sources	Deficiency Symptoms
Vitamin- B_1 (Thiamine)	Whole grain wheat germ, legumes, nuts, fish, dry chillies, uncleaned pulses.	Beri-beri disease, B_1 deficiency in alcoholics causes Wernicke-Korsakoff syndrome.
Vitamin- B_2 (Riboflavin)	Milk, cheese, meats, eggs, legumes, wheat germ, mushrooms and green leafy vegetables.	Cheilosis, cracks in skin, red eyes, cracks in tongue, etc.
Vitamin-B_{12}; Castle's Extrinsic Factor (Cyanocobalamin, Cobalamin)	It is reported in *Spirulina* (an algae), liver, meat, fish, eggs and milk.	Pernicious anaemia
Vitamin-C (Ascorbic acid)	Citrus fruits, amla, guava and tomato.	Its deficiency causes scurvy.

2. Inorganic Substances

Inorganic substances include the following :

(i) Minerals

- The inorganic elements required by living beings in a trace amounts are called **minerals**. These are essential components of our food. They are involved in various metabolic reaction of the cell and thus, helps in the growth and development of the cells.
- Calcium, magnesium and potassium are called **bulk minerals** because their daily intake is more than 200 mg per day.
- Copper, iron and zinc are called **trace minerals** because their requirement are less than 200 mg per day. These minerals are found in many foods, but can also be taken in dietary supplements.

Essential Minerals and Their Sources

Name	Sources	Functions	Deficiency Symptoms
Calcium (Ca)	Dairy products, eggs, wheat germ.	Useful for the formation of bones and teeth, helps in blood clotting, keeps muscles and nerve activity normal.	Rickets and muscular spasms, nervous disorders.
Iodine (I)	Iodised salt, sea food.	Constituent of thyroxine hormone, which is secreted by thyroid gland.	Goitre
Phosphorus/ Phosphate (P)	Dairy products, eggs, fish, meat, wheat germ.	Important for the formation of bones, teeth and biomembranes, keeps muscle and nerve activity normal. Synthesis of nucleic acids (DNA, RNA) and synthesis of ATP.	Loss of bone, minerals and many other metabolic disorders including cardiac muscle nerves disorders.
Iron (Fe)	Most meats, dried nuts, banana, honey, dates and green leafy vegetables.	Constituent of haemoglobin and myoglobin.	Anaemia

(ii) Water

- It is the main component of the body. Human body contains about 65% water and about 70% of this water is protoplasm. It controls the body temperature and acts as an important medium in the excretional activities.
- It regulates almost all biochemical reactions, which actually occur in aquatic environment (atmosphere).

Nutrition in Different Organisms

Unicellular organisms perform digestion by skin while multicellular organisms perform digestion with the help of digestive system.

Nutrition in *Amoeba*

- Nutrition in *Amoeba* occurs *via* phagocytosis.
- *Amoeba* does not have any specialised organs for nutrition. Thus, the entire process of nutrition is done *via* body surface.
- *Amoeba* pushes out the pseudopodia to encircle the food, engulfs it and a food vacuole is formed.
- The mode of nutrition in *Amoeba* is **holozoic nutrition**. It involves ingestion, digestion and egestion of food material.

Nutrition in Human Beings

- **Digestion** is a vital process in humans that involves breakdown of complex food molecules into simpler ones with the release of energy.
- Complete process of digestion occurs through a step wise process, which involves a systematic arrangement of various organs as described below :

Digestive System

- Digestion is a catabolic process where complex and large components of food are broken down into simpler forms with the help of hydrolytic enzymes which are absorbed by different parts of the body.

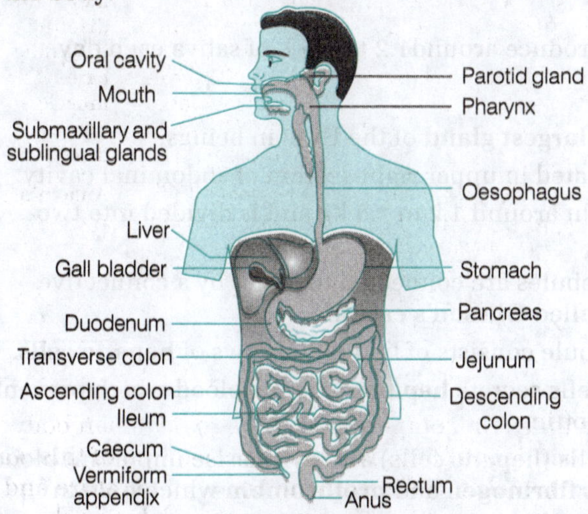

Human digestive system

- The digestive system of humans constitutes a long tubular alimentary canal and digestive glands.

1. Alimentary Canal

- It is a long tube (8-10 m) where the process of digestion takes place. It is an internal coiled tube, which runs from anterior **mouth** to the posterior **anus**.
- The complete process of ingestion, digestion, absorption, assimilation and egestion of food material is carried out within the alimentary canal itself. The major portions of alimentary canal are discussed below :

Mouth and Oral Cavity

- It acts as the first part of the digestive system from where the food enters into the alimentary canal. It opens into the oral cavity at the back. Mouth is mainly composed of tongue and teeth.
- The tongue is fleshy and present on the lower surface of the buccal cavity. It is independent on the front side.
- The cavity is surrounded by cheeks on each side. The roof of oral cavity (palate) separates the buccal cavity and the respiratory.

(a) Teeth

- Humans have 20 milk teeth and 32 permanent teeth. Four different types of teeth are incisors, canines, premolars and molars. These are as follows :
  - **Incisors** These are present at the front of mouth. These have sharp edges and are adapted for cutting food into small pieces or biting. They are eight in number.
  - **Canines** These are characteristically sharp and elongated. These are located in the upper and lower jaw (2 in each jaw). Thus, they are four in number. They are used for tearing the food.
  - **Premolars** They are located behind the canines. These have flat surface with ridges and are adapted for crushing and grinding of food. There are eight premolars, two on each side of the jaw.
  - **Molars** These are the largest and the strongest teeth. They are 12 in number and are adapted for grinding food.

Dental Formula

It expresses the arrangement of teeth in each half of the upper jaw and the lower jaw. It is represented as

Dental formula in human adult = (permanent teeth)

$$= \frac{I\,C\,P_m\,M}{I\,C\,P_m\,M}$$

Where I = Incisors, C = Canines, P_m Premolars, M = Molars

$$= \frac{2123}{2123} \times 2 = \frac{8}{8} \times 2 = 32$$

Dental formula for children (milk teeth)

$$\frac{I\,C\,P_m\,M}{I\,C\,P_m\,M} \times 2 = \frac{2102}{2102} \times 2 = \frac{5}{5} \times 2 = 20$$

(b) Tongue

- It is a fleshy structure present on the lower surface of the buccal cavity.
- It is attached on the back side but is independent or free on the front end.
- It makes voluntary movement.
- **Mucous** secreted by the tongue keeps it moist.
- The tongue consists of **taste buds** which help in determining the taste of the food.
- Front end of the tongue in humans, determines sweetness, while the sensation of bitterness are located at the base of the tongue.
- Taste buds for sourness are located on the two lateral sides and for salty taste, they are found at the anterior edges of the tongue.
- The tongue helps in chewing, swallowing food. It also secretes mucous that keeps the mouth wet.

Pharynx

- It is small and funnel-shaped tube located behind the oral cavity.
- It is 12-14 cm in length. It communicates with both oesophagus and trachea, inside the pharynx is large hole called **epiglottis** which covers the glottis and prevent the entry of food into **trachea.**

Oesophagus

- It is a thin, long muscular tube (23-27 cm) that leads into the stomach.
- Its opening is covered by leaf-like cartilaginous structure called **epiglottis.**
- It carries food from pharynx to stomach.

Stomach

- It is the most dilated J-shaped part of the alimentary canal. This serves as a storehouse of food where partial digestion takes place through the secretion of gastric glands.

Small Intestine

- It is the longest part of the alimentary canal about 6 m long. The surface of small intestine has **villi** and **microvilli** which helps in digestion and absorption of food as they provide a large surface area. The three major parts of small intestine are :
  - (i) **Duodenum** It is a U-shaped structure which is 4-4.5 cm in diameter. It is main digesting canal of the human alimentary canal. It lacks enzyme secreting glands but possess **Brunner's glands.**
  - (ii) **Jejunum** It is the middle part of the small intestine which is about 2.5 m long and coiled.
  - (iii) **Ileum** It is the longest portion of the small intestine which is highly coiled. It opens up into the large intestine.

  Secretions from liver and pancreas enter the intestine to help in the digestion process.

  Herbivores have longer small intestine as plants have cellulose that takes time to digest.

Large Intestine

- It is shorter than small intestine (in length) but is wider in diameter. Hence, it is called **large intestine.** It is about 1.5 m long and is divided into three main parts :
  - (i) **Caecum** It is a small pouch-like structure of about 6 cm. It also has an outgrowth known as **vermiform appendix**, which is slightly coiled tube of about 8 cm long.
  - (ii) **Colon** The caecum part leads into the colon. The colon is divided into four parts an ascending, transverse, descending part and a sigmoid curve.
  - (iii) **Rectum** The descending portion of colon leads into the rectum which is the last part of the intestine. Rectum is of about 20 cm in length and opens into the anus.
- The last part of rectum is called **anal canal** which opens outside *via* **anus** and help in exit of waste material.
- The absorption of water and nutrients and elimination of solid waste takes place mainly in large intestine.

2. Digestive Glands

Various types of digestive glands are present in mammals, namely :

Salivary Glands

- These digestive glands pour their secretions into the mouth.
- These produce around1.2 to 1.5 L of saliva each day.

Liver

- It is the **largest gland** of the Human beings.
- It is situated in upper right section of abdominal cavity.
- Its weight around 1.2 to 1.5 kg and is divided into two **lobes.**
- These lobules are connected together by a connective tissue called **Glisson's capsule.**
- Each lobule consists of two radial rows of **hepatic cells.**
- These cells secrete **heparin** into the blood which prevents blood clotting.
- Liver cells (hepatic cells) also synthesise important blood proteins **fibrinogen** and **prothrombin** which help in clotting.
- Excess amount of glucose gets converted into glycogen granules for storage. This is called **glycogenesis.**

Pancreas

- It is elongated, irregularly branched, flattened, digestive gland.
- It is a **mixed** gland since, it contains both endocrine and exocrine gland.
- **Islets of Langerhans** which contain α, β and δ cells, form an endocrine part of the pancreas.
- The exocrine part of pancreas secretes alkaline **pancreatic juice.**

Digestive Glands in Human Beings

Digestive Glands (Position)	Secretion	Enzymes	Digested Food
Salivary gland (oral cavity)	Saliva	Salivary amylase	Starch (converts starch into maltose)
Gastric glands (stomach)	Gastric juice	Pepsin, rennin and lipase	Protein, milk and lipids
Liver (above stomach)	Bile	None	Emulsify large fat droplets
Pancreas (behind stomach)	Pancreatic juice	Amylase, lipase, trypsinogen, chymotrypsi -nogen	Carbohydrate, fat, protein
Intestinal gland (small intestine)	Intestinal juice	Erepsin, maltase, lactase, sucrase, lipase	▪ Breakdown protein into amino acids ▪ Break maltose into 2 molecules of glucose. ▪ Breaks lactose into glucose and glactose. ▪ Breaks sucrose into glucose and fructose

Mechanism of Digestion of Food

Various steps involved in digestion of these nutrients are given below :

1. Ingestion

- It is the process of food intake by mouth. Food moistened by saliva, before swallowing is masticated into smaller particles by teeth.
- Different organisms have different ways of ingestion e.g., birds have beak, humans have mouth to intake food.

2. Digestion

- It takes place in alimentary canal in case of multicellular animals.
- The process of digestion occurs in two parts :
  (i) **Mechanical digestion** It involves chewing of food in the mouth. **Lysozyme** present in the saliva, kill all the microbes present in the food.

  After the food is chewed properly, it is brought down with the help of peristaltic movement in the alimentary canal.

  (ii) **Chemical digestion** After the absorption of certain juices secreted from glands, the enzymes breakdown complex molecules into simpler ones.

  Gastric juice Secreted by the gastric glands present in the wall of the stomach secretes, hydrochloric acid, pepsin, lipase, rennin and other enzymes which help in the process of digestion. HCl present in gastric juice, kills the microbes (bacteria) present in food.

3. Digestion in Small Intestine

- Chyme moves to duodenum where it gets mixed with bile (liver) to breakdown fats into smaller globules. It also makes the pH of food **alkaline.**
- Amylase converts starch into simple sugar.
- Lipase converts fats into fatty acids and glycerol.
- Food passes into ileum and mixes with intestinal juice.
- Maltase converts maltose into glucose.
- Lactase converts lactose into glucose and galactose.
- Sucrase converts sucrose into glucose and fructose.

4. Absorption of Food

The end products of digestion (monosaccharides, amino acids, nitrogenous bases, etc.) are absorbed in alimentary canal as :

- All the carbohydrates are absorbed in the blood capillaries.
- **Glucose** and **galactose** are absorbed by **active transport,** whereas fructose is absorbed by **facilitated diffusion.**
- Lipids are absorbed in lymph capillaries (lacteals) present within the villi.

5. Egestion

- It is the elimination of undigested remains of the food from the alimentary canal.
- It is carried out by **large intestine.**
- After the absorption of water in the blood, the chyle gets concentrated into **faeces.**
- This **faeces** is eliminated through anus.

Respiration

- Respiration is the process of biochemical oxidation of nutrients (occurring in cytoplasm of the cell) in the presence of specific enzymes at optimum temperature in the cells to release energy for metabolic activities.

- It is a catabolic process in which exchange of gases occur *viz.* oxygen (O_2) and carbon dioxide (CO_2) takes place between the body and the outside environment.
- In the cell, oxygen in the air helps in the breakdown of food with the release of energy called as **cellular respiration**.
- Cellular respiration takes place in the cells of all organisms.
- In the cell, the food (glucose) is broken down into and water using . When breakdown of glucose occurs with use of it is called **aerobic respiration**.
- Food can also be broken down, without using oxygen. This is called **anaerobic respiration**, like in yeast.
- Yeast can survive in the absence of oxygen, thus, are called **anaerobes**. Anaerobic respiration produces alcohol and carbon dioxide upon glucose breakdown.
- Human muscle cells also respire anaerobically during exercise when there is deficiency of oxygen in the cells. Here, glucose breakdown produces **lactic acid** and **energy**.
- The taking in of air rich in oxygen and giving out of air rich in carbon dioxide with the help of respiratory organs is called **breathing**.

Phases of Respiration

The process of respiration occurs in three stages.

(i) **External Respiration** In this, the exchange of CO_2 and O_2 occurs between the organism and the environment. Plants respire during day as well as during night. They take in CO_2 (during day) and release O_2 whereas the process is reversed during night time.

(ii) **Tissue Respiration** In this, respiration occurs between the tissue and the environment of the cell.

(iii) **Cellular Respiration** It is an enzyme controlled sequential chemical reaction in which glucose is oxidised in mitochondria, producing energy which is stored as ATP.

- Respiration is a biochemical oxidation process.
- This cycle is divided into the following three stages :
  (a) Glycolysis (b) Kreb's cycle
  (c) ETC

Respiration in Different Animals

- Organs involved in respiration are called **respiratory organs**. They form **respiratory system**.
- Respiratory organs for the exchange of gases vary in different organisms.
- In earthworm, the exchange of gases occurs through the moist skin. In fishes it takes place through gills and in insects through the trachea.

Respiratory Organs of Some Animals

Organs	Examples
Lungs	Humans, birds, frog, lizard, etc.
Skin	Frog, earthworm
Gills	Fishes and prawns
Trachea	Cockroach
General body surface	*Amoeba, Hydra*
Book lungs	Spider
Book gill	*Limulus*

Human Respiratory System

- In humans, the process of breathing is performed by lungs. Lungs are protected by ribcage. Lungs remain connected to the outside environment *via* **windpipe** and **nasal pipe**.
- The process which follows the intake of oxygen is known as **inspiration** and giving out of carbon dioxide known as **expiration.**

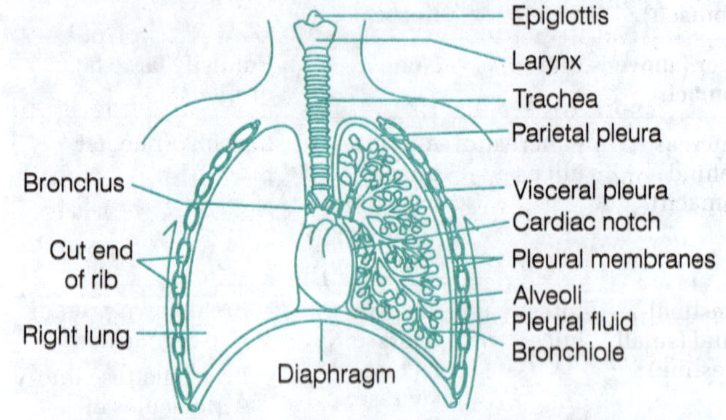

Diagrammatic view of human respiratory system

- Various parts and function of human respiratory system are as follows :

Respiratory Tract

Different components of respiratory tract are as follows :

(i) **Nostril** (nares) is one of the two channels of the nose, from the point where they bifurcate to the external opening. In birds and mammals, they contain branched bones or cartilages called **turbinates**, whose function is to warm air on inhalation and remove moisture on exhalation.

(ii) **Nasal cavity** is divided into two nasal chambers by the nasal septum. Each nasal chamber consists of three regions, i.e. vestibular, respiratory and olfactory regions. It produces mucus which filters, moistens and warms incoming air and acts as resonance chamber for speech.

(iii) **Pharynx** is a passageway that connects nasal cavity to larynx and oral cavity to oesophagus. It has three subdivisions namely, nasopharynx, oropharynx and laryngopharynx.

(iv) **Larynx** contains vocal cords, the sound producing elastic fibres called **voice box.** There is a little difference in the size of the larynx in man and woman, it grows larger and becomes prominent in man therefore, it is called **Adam's apple** in man. Human larynx consists of glottis, cartilages, hyoid bone, thyrohyoid membrane, vocal cords, laryngeal ligaments and muscles.

Glottis is an opening in the floor of pharynx leading to larynx. There are nine pieces of cartilages (3 are single and 3 are paired).

Epiglottis is a leaf-like structure that prevents the entry of food into respiratory tract during swallowing.

(v) **Trachea or Windpipe** is a continuation of the larynx, which is supported by incomplete (C-shaped) rings of hyaline cartilages. The mucosa of trachea is lined with a ciliated pseudostratified columnar-epithelium containing mucus secreting Goblet cells, which help in pushing mucus out.

(vi) **Bronchi** are one pair of small, thin-walled tubular structures formed by the division of trachea at the level of 5th thoracic vertebra.

(vii) **Bronchioles** are formed by the subdivision of the tertiary bronchi into smaller branches. After repeated branching one of the smaller bronchiole enters a lung lobule called **lobular bronchiole.**

Mechanism of Respiration in Humans

Mechanism of respiration in humans can be categorised as follows :

Inspiration

- Inspiration or inhalation is carried out mostly by the movement of diaphragm. During this, diaphragm straightens and lengthens the chest cavity. The abdominal muscles relax to accommodate the abdominal viscera.
- The external intercostal muscles contract to move ribs in upward and outward direction. Due to this movement of ribs, volume of thoracic cavity increases. As a result, negative pressure in the lungs develops and air rushes inside the lungs.

Expiration

- Expiration or exhalation involves relaxation of both phrenic (diaphragm) and external intercostal muscles. The diaphragm bends upwards, which reduces the vertical length of thoracic cavity.
- The relaxation of external intercostal muscles leads ribs and ribcage downwards and inwards, respectively.
- This induces thoracic volume in anteroposterior direction and creates positive pressure that results to exhalation.

Gaseous Exchange in Lungs

- It occurs by normal diffusion.
- Oxygen from the air present in the alveoli diffuse in capillaries and carbon dioxide from the blood capillaries diffuse out into the surroundings.

Transport of Oxygen

- Exercising can increase the respiratory rate upto 25 times per minute, i.e., the intake of oxygen is more as we breathe deeply.

Gaseous Exchange at Tissue Level

- CO_2 from the tissues diffuse out into the blood, whereas oxygen diffuses from blood into the tissues.
- The diffusion occurs across the concentration gradient.

Transport of Carbon dioxide

- About 7% CO_2 is carried in dissolved form through the plasma.
- About 70% of CO_2 is carried in the form of bicarbonates ions.

Respiratory Volumes and Capacities

The quantity of air lungs can receive, hold or expel under different conditions are called **respiratory** (or pulmonary) **volumes.** Combination of two or more pulmonary volumes are called **respiratory** (pulmonary) **capacities.**

The different volumes and capacities are as follows :

(i) **Tidal Volume** (TV) It is the volume of air inspired or expired during normal breathing in relaxed or resting position. It is about 500 mL.
It consists of 150 mL of dead space volume and 350 mL of alveolar volume. A healthy man can inspire or expire approximately 6000-8000 mL of air per minute.

(ii) **Inspiratory Reserve Volume** (IRV) It is the additional amount of air that can be inspired forcibly after a normal inspiration. It is about 2500-3000 mL of air.

(iii) **Expiratory Reserve Volume** (ERV) It is the additional volume of air that can be expired forcibly after a normal expiration. It is about 1000-1100 mL.

(iv) **Residual Volume** (RV) It is the volume of air remaining in the lungs even after a forcible expiration. It is about 1100-1200 mL. It cannot be measured by spirometry.

Various pulmonary capacities are derived from the above mentioned volumes. These help in the clinical diagnosis of functioning of lungs. These are as follows :

(i) **Inspiratory Capacity** (IC) It is the total volume of air a person can inspire after a normal expiration. It is about 2500-3000 mL. It includes **Tidal Volume** and **Inspiratory Reserve Volume**.

$$IC = TV + IRV$$

(ii) **Expiratory Capacity** (EC) It is the total volume of air a person can expire after a normal inspiration. It includes **Tidal Volume** and **Expiratory Reserve Volume.**

$$EC = TV + ERV$$

(iii) **Functional Residual Capacity** (FRC) It is the volume of air that will remain in the lungs after a normal expiration. It includes **Residual Volume** and **Expiratory Reserve Volume.**

$$FRC = RV + ERV$$

(iv) **Vital Capacity** (VC) It is the maximum volume of air a person can breathe in after a forced expiration or the maximum volume of air a person can breathe out after a forced inspiration.
This includes TV + IRV + ERV.

It varies from 3400-4800 mL depending upon age, sex and height of individual.

(v) **Total Lung Capacity** It is the total volume of air present in the lungs after a forced (maximum) inspiration. It includes
RV + ERV + TV + IRV or (VC+RV)

Respiratory Quotient (RQ)

It is the ratio of production of CO_2 to the consumption of O_2. The value of RQ varies for different substances, e.g. it is 1 for carbohydrates, 0.7 for fats.

$$RQ = \frac{\text{Rate of production of } CO_2}{\text{Rate of consumption of } O_2}$$

Circulatory System

- Circulation in human body occurs *via* means of blood, heart and blood vessels forming a network.
- This network supplies tissues in the body with oxygen and other nutrients, transport hormones and removes unnecessary waste products.
- The two basic types of circulatory system have evolved in animals such as :
  (i) **Open Circulatory System** It is the type in which blood is pumped by heart into an aorta, which branches off into a number of arteries that ultimately open into a series of spaces collectively called as **haemocoel**, e.g. most arthropods and some cephalopods.
  (ii) **Closed Circulatory System** It is the type in which blood stays in blood vessels. It does not come into direct contact with the body tissues. The only entry and exit to the system is through the walls of blood vessels, e.g., in annelids and chordates. This is considered to be the most advantageous method as it supplies blood to the deepest tissues of the body. Human circulatory system is of closed type and consists of blood vascular system and lymphatic system.

Structure of Circulatory System in Humans

Various components of circulatory system are described as follows :

Blood

- It is a red coloured fluid connective tissue that circulates in our body.
- It supplies nutrients and oxygen, to all living cells and collect waste products and carbon dioxide to be thrown out.
- It helps in regulation of pH and body temperature.
- Blood comprises of **plasma** (a straw coloured viscous fluid constituting 55% of blood volume) and **blood cells** or **corpuscles** (45% of the blood volume).
- Blood cells are suspended in the plasma. Blood cells include, **Red Blood Corpuscles** (RBCs), **White Blood Corpuscles** (WBCs) and **Platelets.**
- **RBCs** transport oxygen to all cells. **WBCs** helps to destroy foreign germs in the body. **Platelets** helps in blood clotting by forming mesh like structure at the site of injury.
- WBCs are of five types, i.e. eosinophils, basophils, neutrophils, lymphocytes and monocytes.
- Blood also possess antigens and antibodies which are immunological components of blood.
- Antigens are present on the surface of RBCs while antibody is present in the plasma.

Blood Groups

- Based on the presence and absence of antibodies and inherited antigenic substances, the blood is classified into various groups called **blood groups.**
- **Landsteiner** discovered three blood groups and two types of antigens (A and B).

- The antigen is a glycoprotein and is of two types, i.e. antigen A and B.
- In the absence of antigen, a special protein is found in plasma known as **antibodies a and b**.
- On the above basis, the different blood groups in human are :

Blood group	Antigen	Antibody
A	A	b
B	B	a
AB (Universal recipient)	A, B	—
O (Universal donor)	—	a, b

- Rh factor is a protein that may be present on the surface of red blood cells.
- Thus, on the basis of its presence or obsence the blood is **Rh-positive** and **Rh-negative**, respectively.

Lymph

- Apart from blood, lymph in our body is another type of fluid involved in transportation. This is also called **tissue fluid**.
- It is also meant to transport any digested and absorbed fat from intestine and drains excess fluid from extracellular space back into the blood.
- Lymph drains into lymphatic capillaries from the intercellular spaces, which join to form large lymph vessels that finally open into larger veins.

Heart

- The heart acts like a pumping machine in our body that pushes out the blood into the blood vessels.
- It is a muscular organ having size as big as our fist.
- The heart is situated between the lungs slightly towards the left side of the chest (thoracic cavity).
- It is surrounded by a protective covering called **pericardium** filled with **pericardial fluid**.

Structure of Heart

- Human heart is four-chambered (i.e. two upper atria and two lower ventricles).
- These different chambers are meant to prevent mixing of oxygenated (rich in oxygen) and deoxygenated (rich in carbon dioxide) blood.
- Oxygen rich blood from lungs comes to thin-walled upper chamber of the heart, left atrium which relaxes (while collecting this blood) and contracts and transfer blood to left ventricle then contracts and blood is pumped to the body parts.
- Deoxygenated blood enters in right atrium and when it contracts, it transfers blood to right ventricle, which again pumps blood to the lungs for oxygenation.
- Ventricles have thick walls than atrium because they have to pump blood into various organs.
- Both the atria are separated by **interatrial septum** and **interventricular sulcus** separates the ventricles.
- **Atrioventricular** (AV) nodes are present between the atria and the ventricles.
- These prevent the backflow of blood from ventricles to atrium.
- AV valves include **mitral valve** and **tricuspid valve.**
- Valves between the left atrium and ventricle is bicuspid and those between right atrium and right ventricle is **tricuspid.**

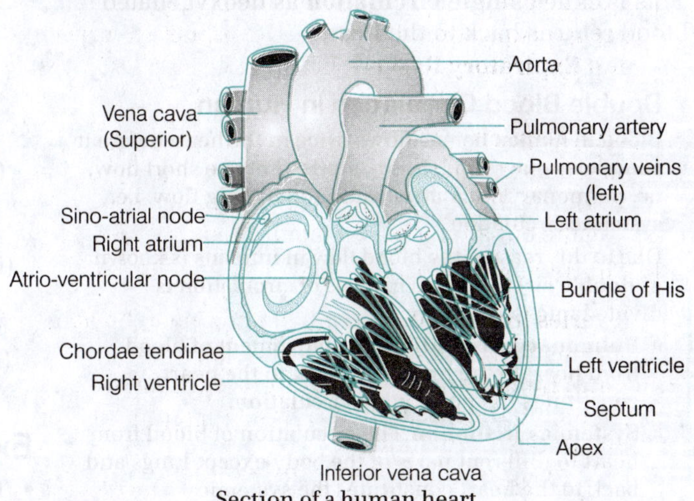

Section of a human heart

Blood Vessels

There are three types of vessels involved in blood circulation, i.e. arteries, veins and capillaries.

(i) **Arteries** The arteries have thick, muscular and elastic walls which carry blood at high pressure. They do not have valves. They carry blood away from the heart to various organs of the body.

(ii) **Veins** The veins have thin walls than arteries which carry blood at low pressure. They have valves to prevent the backflow of blood. They collect the blood from different organs and bring it back to the heart.

(iii) **Capillaries** They are formed when artery divides into smaller tubes. They have valves to prevent the backflow of blood.

The walls of capillaries are one cell thick. Exchange of material between blood and surrounding thick cells takes place across the thin walls of capillaries.

Blood Circulation in Animals

- In **amphibians** and **reptiles**, the heart is three-chambered or partially four-chambered (in reptiles).
- The oxygenated and deoxygenated blood gets mixed and are circulation jumped in the body of incomplete double circulation.

Note Crocodile has a four-chambered heart.

- In birds and mammals, heart is four-chambered and oxygenated blood remains separated from deoxygenated blood.
- In fishes, two-chambered heart (1-atrium), (1-ventricle) pumps blood to gills.
- There is no separation of pure and impure blood. This is called **single circulation** as deoxygenated blood returns back to the heart.

Double Blood Circulation in Human

Blood in human beings flows twice in the heart before it completes one round. It is comprised of one short flow, i.e. pulmonary circulation and another long flow, i.e. systemic circulation.

Due to this reason, the blood flow in humans is known as **double circulation**. This type of circulation is divided into two phases :

- **Pulmonary circulation** The movement of blood from heart to the lungs and back to the heart constitutes the pulmonary circulation.
- **Systemic circulation** The circulation of blood from heart to different parts of the body except lungs and back to the heart constitutes the systemic circulation.

Blood Pressure

- It is the pressure of circulating blood on the walls of blood vessels.
- Blood pressure is maximum during contraction of left ventricle and is known as **systolic pressure**. It is **120 mm Hg**.
- The **diastolic pressure** is specifically the minimum arterial pressure during relaxation and dilation of the ventricles. It is **80 mm Hg**.
- Blood pressure is measured by **sphygmomanometer**.
- The number of beats per minute is called the **pulse rate**.
- A resting person usually has a pulse rate between 72 and 80 beats per minute.
- A doctor feels your heartbeat with the help of an instrument called **stethoscope**. It is a device to amplify the sound of the heart.

Excretory System

- Excretion is the biological process by which an organism removes the metabolic wastes from the body.
- Organs which are involved in removal of such metabolic wastes are **excretory organs.**
- Unicellular organisms excrete waste by simple process like diffusion, whereas multicellular organisms use specialised organs for the removal of waste products.
- These specialised organs in multicellular organisms include flame cells in *Planaria*, nephridia in earthworm, etc.

Types of Excretion

Different organisms remove different type of metabolic waste or nitrogenous waste as follows :

(i) **Ammonotelic Animals** These animals secrete nitrogenous waste as ammonia, e.g., certain protozoans, polychaete annelids, crustacean, arthropods, molluscs, freshwater fishes, amphibian and crocodile.

(ii) **Ureotelic Animals** These animals secrete nitrogenous waste as urea, e.g., elasmobranch fishes, amphibian and mammals.

(iii) **Uricotelic Animals** Their main nitrogenous waste is uric acid, e.g., insects, some gastropods, lizards, snakes and birds.

(iv) **Uriotelism** There are certain organism which secrete waste as amino acid, e.g. Echinodermata.

Excretion in Human Beings

- The main organ involved in the human excretory system are a pair of **kidneys**, a pair of **ureters**, a **urinary bladder** and a **urethra**, Capsule and finally leads to collecting duct which collects the filtered urine.
- An adult human being normally passes about 1-1.8 L of urine in 24 hours. The urine consists of 95% water, 2.5% urea and 2.5% other waste products.
- The urine is acidic with pH 6.0
- Its pale yellow colour is due to the presence of pigment **urochrome** (urobilin).
- In some cases, excess waste crystalises as kidney stones (calcium oxalate). They grow and become painful that may require surgery or lithotripsy treatment.

Kidney

- Kidneys are reddish brown bean shaped organs situated in the abdomen, one on the either side of the backbone. These are about 10-12 cm long, 5-7 cm wide and 2-3 cm thick.
- The outer surface of each kidney is convex and the inner surface is concave and has a notch (hilum).

- Left kidney is placed a little higher than the right one due to the positioning of the liver.
- Kidneys remove excess of water from the body with nitrogenous wastes from blood as urine.
- They maintain constant concentration of blood plasma and regulate pH of blood.

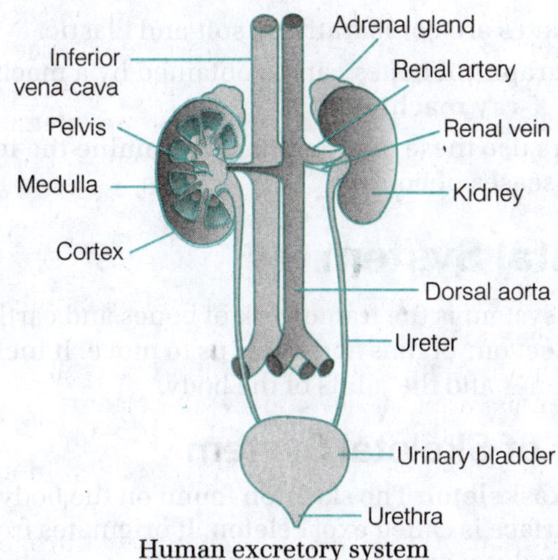

Human excretory system

- Nephrons are structural and functional units of kidney.
- Nephron has a cup-like capsule called **Bowman's capsule**, at its end and the lower end is tube-like and called **tubule**. Bowman's capsule and tubule together form a **nephron**.

  Each nephron has thousands of nephrons.

A. Malpighian Body

It is the composite structure of Bowman's capsule and glomerulus, found in the cortex region of kidney.

It consists of following parts :

(i) **Glomerulus**

- Tuft of capillaries formed by the afferent arteriole.
- It acts as a dialysing bag in the kidney.
- It facilitates the process of ultrafiltration.

(ii) **Bowman's Capsule**

- It is double-walled cup lined by thin flat cells called **podocytes**.
- It encloses the glomerulus.

B. Tubules

These are mainly associated with the process of reabsorption and secretion.

It consists of following four main regions :

(i) **Proximal Convoluted Tubule** (PCT)

- Highly coiled structure with numerous microvilli which increase the surface area for reabsorption.
- The process of reabsorption mainly takes place within PCT (i.e. nearly all essential nutrients, 70-80% of electrolytes and water).

(ii) **Henle's Loop**

- U-shaped tube, which plays a significant role in osmoregulation.
- It is long in mammals and birds, but short in other vertebrates like reptiles.
- It is divisible into the following regions :
  - **Descending Limb** Lined up by simple cuboidal epithelium with few cells and small microvilli. It is permeable to water and impermeable to electrolytes.
  - **Ascending Limb** Length of cells increases in this region and they are not brush-bordered. It is impermeable to water, but permeable to electrolytes and makes the filtrate dilute.

(iii) **Distal Convoluted Tubule** (DCT)

- Situated in the cortex region of kidney and connected to the collecting duct.
- Maintains the pH and sodium-potassium balance in blood.

(iv) **Collecting Duct**

- Long duct, extends from the cortex to the inner medulla of kidney.
- Several collecting tubes join to form the duct of Bellini.
- Large amount of water is reabsorbed here to produce a concentrated urine.
- Blood flows into tubules by blood capillaries called **glomerulus**. It is surrounded by Bowman's capsule.
- A long convoluted tubular structure follows the Bowman.

Mechanism of Urine Formation

Constituents of normal human urine include 95% water and 5% solid wastes. It is produced in the nephron, which is the structural and functional unit of the kidney. The mechanism of urine formation involves the following steps:

1. Glomerular Filtration

- Glomerular filtration occurs in the glomerulus where blood is filtered. This process occurs across the three layers-epithelium of Bowman's capsule, endothelium of glomerular blood vessels and a membrane between these two layers.
- Blood is filtered in such a way that all the constituents of the plasma reach the Bowman's capsule, except proteins. Therefore, this process is known as **ultrafiltration**.

2. Reabsorption

- Around 99% of the filtrate obtained is reabsorbed by the renal tubules. This is known as **reabsorption**. This is achieved by active and passive transport.
- The glomerulus filters water and small solutes out of the bloodstream.
- The resulting filtrate contains waste, but also other substances that the body needs essential ions, glucose, amino acids and smaller proteins.
- When the filtrate exits the glomerulus, it flows into a duct in the nephron called **renal tubule**. As it moves, the needed substances and some water are reabsorbed through the tube wall into adjacent capillaries.

3. Secretion

- The next step in urine formation is the tubular secretion.
- Waste ions and hydrogen ions pass from the capillaries into the renal tubule. This process is called **secretion**.
- The secreted ions combine with the remaining filtrate and become urine. Here, tubular cells secrete substances like hydrogen ion, potassium ion, etc. into the filtrate.
- By this process the ionic, acid-base and the balance of other body fluids are maintained.
- The secreted ions combine with the filtrate and form urine. The urine passes out of the nephron tubule into a collecting duct.

Haemodialysis

- Sometimes due to infections, injury or restricted blood flow to kidneys, reduces its normal activities. This leads to accumulation of poisonous wastes in the body, that can even lead to death.
- Kidney failures can be managed by **artificial kidney**, which is a device to remove nitrogenous waste from the blood through dialysis.
- Artificial kidney is different from natural kidney as the process of reabsorption does not occur in artificial kidney.

Movement in Humans

- The ability of organisms to change position by using their body parts is called **movement**.
- **Skeleton** is the internal structure in organisms, which helps bringing about movement.
- It forms a framework that gives the shape of the body and provides support to organisms.
- The skeleton is made up of bones. Different kinds of bones are joined to each other in a particular manner.
- These joints facilitate various types of movements.
- In higher animals, bones, muscles and cartilage together make the movement possible.
- There are about 650 muscles attached to the various bones in our body.
- The **bones** are hard and rigid.
- **Cartilages** are comparatively soft and elastic.
- Photographs of bones can be obtained by a machine called **X-ray machine**.
- Doctors use these photographs to examine the injuries and diseases of bones.

Skeletal System

Skeletal system is the framework of bones and cartilages that protect our organs and allow us to move. It includes all the bones and the joints of the body.

Types of Skeletal System

(i) **Exoskeleton** The skeleton found on the body surface is called exoskeleton. It originates from ectoderm or mesoderm, e.g., nails.

(ii) **Endoskeleton** The skeleton found inside the body is called endoskeleton. It originates from mesoderm, e.g., bones.

Human Skeleton

The skeleton in human body is made up of **206 bones** and few cartilages. On the basis of the position of the skeletal structures in the human body, the endoskeleton is divisible into two parts :

(i) **Axial Skeleton** It comprises of **80 bones**, which include skull, vertebral column, ribs and sternum.

(ii) **Appendicular Skeleton** It lies along the transverse (side) axis. It comprises of **126 bones**, which include pectoral and pelvic girdles and limb bones, i.e. bones of arms and legs.

The details of axial skeleton system are as follows :

Skull

It is the bony framework of the head. It is composed of two sets of bones (cranial and facial) that form total of 22 bones [bones of middle ear (6 bones) and hyoid bone (1) are also included in bones of skull].

Bones of skull are as follows :

- **Cranium** (8)

  They form the hard protective outer covering (cranium) for the brain.

Frontal–1	Parietal–2	Temporal–2
Occipital–1	Sphenoid–1	Ethmoid–1

- **Facial bones (14)**
  They form the front part of the skull.
  Maxillae–2 Palatine–2 Mandible–1
  Vomer–1 Nasal–2 Zygomatic–2
  Lacrimal–2 Inferior turbinate–2
- **Ear ossicles (6)**
  These three tiny bones belong to the middle ear.
  Malleus–2 Incus–2 Stapes–2
- **Hyoid** A U-shaped bone present at the base of buccal cavity. It is the only bone which is not in contact with any other bone. This is also called **tongue bone**.
  Human skull is **dicondylic,** the skull region articulates with vertebral column with the help of two **occipital condyles.**

Vertebral Column

- It is also called **backbone** or **spine.** It is dorsally placed, extending from the base of the skull and constitutes the main framework of the trunk.
- It is made up of **26** serially arranged units called **vertebrae.**
- It includes cervical (7), thoracic (12), lumbar (5), sacral (1-fused) and coccygeal (1-fused).

Sternum

It is a flat bone located on the ventral midline of thorax.

Ribs

- These are thin, flat curved bones that form a protective cage around the organs of upper body.
- The ribs are composed of **24 bones** arranged in **12 pairs**, connected dorsally to thoracic vertebrae and ventrally to sternum by **hyaline cartilage**.
- Ribs are mainly categorised into following types :
  - **True Ribs** The first seven ribs are attached directly with the sternum and are called **true ribs.**
  - **False Ribs** The 8th, 9th and 10th pairs of ribs join the seventh rib with the help of hyaline cartilage. They do not articulate directly with sternum. Hence, are called **vertebrochondral** (false) **ribs.**
  - **Floating Ribs** The last two (11th and 12th) pairs of ribs remain free anteriorly and are called **floating ribs.**

Pelvic (Hip) Girdle

- It is located in the lower part of the trunk. It consists of **two coxal** (hip) bones. Each coxal is also known as **ossa coxae** or **innominate bone.** This is formed by fusion of the following three bones :
  (i) Upper ilium (ii) Lower ischium
  (iii) Inner pubis
- The innominate at the middle of its lateral surface has a deep, cup-shaped **acetabulum**, where head of femur articulates. The two halves of the pelvic girdle meet ventrally to form **pubic symphysis** containing fibrous cartilage.

Appendicular Skeleton (Total bones 128)

Thorax	Pectoral girdle	Shoulder	Scapula (2)
			Clavicle (2)
Hip	Pelvic girdle		Innominate (2)
Forelimbs		Upper arm	Humerus (2)
		Forearm	Radius (2)
			Ulna (2)
		Wrist	Carpals (16)
		Palm	Metacarpals (10)
		Fingers	Phalanges (28)
Hindlimbs		Thigh	Femur (2)
		Shank	Tibia (2)
			Fibula (2)
		Knee	Patella (2)
		Ankle	Tarsals (14)
		Sole	Metatarsals (10)
		Fingers	Phalanges (28)

Pectoral (Shoulder) Girdle

It provides an attachment point for numerous muscles that allows shoulder and elbow joints to move.

It consists of following two bones, i.e., scapula and clavicle.

- **Scapula** (Shoulder blade) It consists of a sharp ridge- the **spine** and a triangular bone. The end of spine projects as a flattened and expanded portion called **acromion**. This articulates with the clavicle. **Glenoid cavity** is a depression below the acromion to which head of humerus articulates forming shoulder joint.
- **Clavicle** (Collar bone) Each clavicle is a long slender bone with two curvatures. The clavicle helps in articulation of the upper limb with axial skeleton.

Joints

The place of articulation between two or more bones or between a bone and a cartilage is called a **joint**. The study of joints is known as **arthrology**.

Classification of Joints

Classified as three major structural forms, i.e. fibrous, cartilaginous and synovial. The description of these joints is as follows :

Fibrous (Immovable Joints)

- The bones are held firmly by bundles of dense white fibrous tissue. So these joints do not allow any movement of bones.
- e.g., the **sutures** (joints between the bones of skull) and **syndesmosis** (joint between tibia and fibula).

Cartilaginous (Slightly Movable Joints)

- These bones are joined together by cartilage, so that slight movement of bones is possible.
- e.g., pubic symphysis of pubis, the joints between the adjacent vertebrae in the vertebral column.

Synovial (Freely Movable Joints)

- A considerable movement is allowed at all synovial joints.
- It is because there is present fluid-filled synovial cavity between articulating surface of bones.
- These are also surrounded by tubular articular capsule.
- The capsule consists of two layers, i.e., **outer fibrous capsule** and **inner synovial membrane** which 'secretes synovial fluid' that lubricates and is responsible for providing nourishment to articular cartilage.

Note In old age, stiffness of joints is due to decrease in synovial fluid in the synovial cavity.

Types of Synovial Joints

According to shape of bones and types of movement, the synovial joints are of following six types :

(i) **Ball and Socket Joint** In this type, a ball-like structure on one bone fits into a socket like structure in another bone.
e.g., shoulder joint (between pectoral girdle and head of humerus) and hip joint (between acetabulum and head of femur).

(ii) **Hinge** (Knee) **Joint** This joint allows the movement in one plane only, e.g. elbow, knee, ankle and interphalangeal joints.

(iii) **Pivot Joint** This joint is responsible for providing movement in one plane, e.g. joint between atlas and axis and radioulnar joint (between radius and ulna).

(iv) **Gliding Joint** This joint allows limited movement in all direction as the bones are closely packed together or held in place by ligaments, e.g. joints between the carpal bones and between the tarsal bones.

(v) **Saddle Joint** This type of joint is like ball and socket joint, but not developed fully, e.g. joint between carpal of hand and metacarpal of thumb.

Control and Coordination in Animals

In animals including humans, the nervous system and hormones control and coordinate the activities of the body.

Nervous System

- It is a special system found in animals.
- Nervous system functions in an integrated manner for control and coordination of various body functions.
- The system is **ectodermal** in origin.
- It conducts quick responses in the form of impulse against various environmental changes (stimuli).
- **Nerve cell** or **Neuron** is the main cell of the nervous system. Thus, it is called as the **structural** and **functional unit** of nervous system.

Types of Neurons

There are mainly three types of neurons :

(i) **Sensory Neurons** (Afferent neurons) They conduct impulses from receptors to central nervous system. The terminal ends of dendrites become modified to form receptor and acts as sensory.

(ii) **Inter Neurons** They act as a connectors and functions in connecting the sensory and motor neuron. It mainly carries stimuli in brain and spinal cord.

(iii) **Motor Neurons** They conduct impulses from central nervous system to the effectors, i.e. they mainly transmit impulse from brain and spinal cord to the muscle or gland, which will respond to the stimulus.

On the basis of number of dendrites and axons, neurons can be of other three types :

- **Multipolar** i.e. (with one axon and two or more dendrites),
- **Bipolar** i.e. (with one axon and one or more dendrites),
- **Unipolar** i.e. (with one axon only).

Generation and Conduction of Nerve Impulses

Nerve impulse can be defined as a wave of depolarisation of the nerve cell membrane travelling along a neuron and throughout the nervous system. The nerve impulse generation occurs in the following steps :

1. Resting Potential

- The axonal membrane is polarised and does not conduct impulse at this stage.
- Axoplasm inside the axon contain more K^+ and low Na^+ ions. Outside the axon, fluid contain more Na^+ and low K^+ions.
- The ionic gradient is maintained by Na-K pump which transport $3Na^+$ outward for $2K^+$ ions into the cells.

- Thus, outer surface is positively charged, while the inner surface is negatively charged. The state of resting membrane is called **polarised state**.
- The electrical potential difference across the resting plasma membrane is called as the **resting potential**.

2. Action Potential

- Due to the stimulation of nerve fibre, membrane become highly permeable to Na^+, leading to rapid influx of Na^+ and thus, polarity of membrane is reversed.
- The membrane is said to be **depolarised**.
- Action potential or nerve impulse is the electrical potential difference across plasma membrane. Nerve impulse is conducted along the whole length of axon.

3. Repolarisation

Soon, permeability of K^+ ion increases and membrane again become polarised due to the diffusion of K^+ ions outside the membrane, i.e., **repolarisation**.

Transmission of Nerve Impulse

- A nerve impulse flows from one neuron to another through **synapses** which is formed by the membranes of a pre-synaptic neuron and post-synaptic neuron, which may or may not be separated by a gap called **synaptic cleft**.
- There are two types of synapses present, which are as follows :
  - **Electrical synapse** In these, the gap between pre-synaptic and post-synaptic neuron is negligible and thus, the electric current flows at faster rate from one neuron to another. These are rare in human body.
  - **Chemical synapse** In these, pre-synaptic and post-synaptic membranes are separated by chemical filled synaptic cleft. These chemicals are called **neurotransmitters** which are responsible for generation of action potential. Its nerve conduction is slower as compared to electrical synapse.
- At a chemical synapse, when an impulse arrives at the axon terminal, the synaptic vesicles move towards the plasma membrane, where they fuse and release their neurotransmitters in the synaptic cleft.
- The neurotransmitters bind to receptors and post-synaptic membrane, open ion channels and allow the entry of ions, so as to generate action potential in post-synaptic neuron.

Divisions of Nervous System

- The components of nervous system can be divided into Central Nervous System (CNS) and Peripheral Nervous System (PNS).

Central Nervous System (CNS)

- It consists of the **brain** and the **spinal cord**.

(i) Human Brain

- It is the main coordinating centre of the body, which enables an organism to think and take decisions.
- It is protected inside a hard covering called **cranium**.
- The weight of human brain is about 1300-1400 grams.
- **Meninges** envelops the brain and the spinal cord. It has three membranes. The three membranes (dura mater, arachnoid and pia mater) lines the skull and the vertebral canal.
- **Cerebrospinal fluid** is located in **sub-arachnoid space**. The brain consists of two types of tissues **grey matter** and **white matter**.

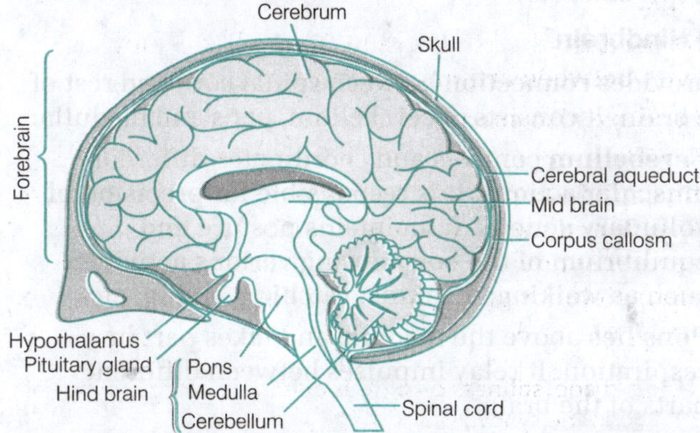

Diagram showing sagittal section of the human brain

- The three main regions or parts found in the human brain are as follows :

(a) Forebrain

- It is the largest, most developed and main thinking part of the brain. It comprises of cerebrum, thalamus and hypothalamus.
- **Cerebrum** acts as the main thinking part of the brain. It is responsible for reasoning, speech, intelligence sight, hearing and usage of information. Voluntary actions are controlled by cerebrum, e.g. movement of muscles of limbs.
- **Olfactory lobes** are a pair of very small, solid, club-shaped bodies widely separated from each other. These are responsible for detecting smell from different receptors.
- **Diencephalon** The main parts involved in diencephalon are epithalaums, thalamus and hypothalamus.
- **Thalamus** represents the lateral walls of diencephalon and mainly formed of grey matter. It is the relay station of sensory inputs and does not produce hormones.

- **Epithalamus** thin membrane tissue that acts as a posterior segment of the diencephelon.
- **Hypothalamus** contains a number of centres that control urge for eating and drinking. It is also called as **thermostat** of the body because it acts as thermoregulatory centre. It also integrates and controls the visceral activities. This part controls the body temperature, urge of eating, drinking, etc.

(b) Midbrain

- It connects forebrain to the hindbrain. It controls the movement of head, neck and trunk to locate sounds and visual reflexes that are involved in focussing on the objects.
- It also controls **reflex movements** of eye muscles, pupil size, etc.

(c) Hindbrain

It provides connection between spinal cord and rest of the brain. It consists of cerebellum, pons and medulla.

- **Cerebellum** controls and coordinates different muscular actions. It is responsible for precision of voluntary actions. It maintains posture and equilibrium of the body during various activities such as walking, drinking, catching, riding, etc.
- **Pons** lies above the medulla and takes part in respiration. It relay impulses between different parts of the brain.
- **Medulla oblongata** is found continuous with the spinal cord. It controls involuntary actions such as breathing, blood pressure (BP), etc. and regulates reflex responses like salivation and vomiting.
- **Spinal Cord** It is a long, tubular bundle of nervous tissue arising from medulla oblongata. A narrow cavity neurocoel filled with cerebrospinal fluid, lies in the central axis. Spinal cord functions primarily in the transmission of neural signals between brain and rest of the body.

Peripheral Nervous System (PNS)

- It consists of nerves that directly enter or leave the Central Nervous System (CNS) and connect different parts of the body.
- It consists of following types of nerves, which carry both sensory and motor neurons :
  - (i) **Cranial Nerves** These are the nerves, which emerge from brain and spread throughout the head.

    There are 12 pairs of cranial nerves.
  - (ii) **Spinal Nerves** These are the nerves, which arise from spinal cord along most of its length and spread throughout the body (except the head). There are 31 pairs of spinal nerves.

Autonomic Nervous System (ANS)

It was discovered by **Langley**. It is entirely motor and operates without conscious control.

It further consists of two divisions :

- (i) **Sympathetic nervous system** increases the defence system of body against adverse conditions. It is active in stress condition, e.g. pain, fear and anger.
- (ii) **Parasympathetic nervous system** provides relaxation, comfort, pleasure at the time of rest. It helps in the restoration and conservation of energy.

Reflex Action and Reflex Arc

- A **reflex action** is an automatic and rapid response to a stimulus. e.g. coughing, sneezing, blinking of eyes, etc. It protects the body from damage and does not involve conscious thought.
- The pathway taken by nerve impulses in a reflex action is called **reflex arc.**

Human Endocrine System

- The endocrine system is composed of hypothalamus, pituitary, pineal, thyroid, adrenal, pancreas, parathyroid, thymus and gonads (testis and ovary).
- In addition to these, some other organs, e.g., gastrointestinal tract, kidney, heart, etc., also produce hormones.

Hormones

- Hormones are specific non-nutrient chemicals, which act as intercellular messengers and are produced in trace amounts.
- These hormones regulate metabolism, growth and development of our organs, the endocrine glands or certain cells.
- The first hormone **secretin** was discovered by **Bayliss** and **Starling** in 1902.

Endocrine Glands in Humans

The description of endocrine glands in humans is given below :

(i) **Hypothalamus** It is the basal part of diencephalon, forebrain and it regulates a wide spectrum of body functions. It contains several groups of neurosecretory cells called **nuclei**, which produce hormones.

The hormones produced by hypothalamus are of two types :

- **Releasing hormones** They stimulate secretion of pituitary hormone, e.g. Gonadotropin Releasing Hormone (GnRH).
- **Inhibiting hormones** They inhibit secretion of pituitary hormones, e.g. somatostatin.

These hormones reach the pituitary gland through a portal circulatory system and regulate the functions of the anterior pituitary. The posterior pituitary is under the direct neural regulation of the hypothalamus.

(ii) **Pituitary Gland** The pituitary gland also referred as **master gland** is located in a bony cavity and is attached to hypothalamus by a stalk. Anatomically it is divided into an **adenohypophysis** (anterior pituitary) and a **neurohypophysis** (posterior pituitary).

(iii) **Pineal Gland** It is located on the dorsal side of forebrain. It secretes **melatonin** which functions to regulate biological clock, i.e. 24 hours sleep-wake cycle. It maintains sleep-wake cycle, body temperature, metabolism, pigmentation, menstrual cycle, etc.

Serotonin is also secreted by the pineal gland which helps in vasoconstriction of blood vessels.

(iv) **Thymus Gland** It is found between lungs behind sternum on the ventral side of aorta. It secretes peptide hormones called **thymosin.**

Thymosin plays a major role in the differentiation of **T-lymphocytes**, which provide **cell-mediated immunity** and production of antibodies to provide **humoral immunity.** It is degenerated in old individuals due to which the immune responses become weak.

(v) **Thyroid Gland** It is composed of two lobes located on either side of the trachea interconnected with isthmus. The thyroid follicular cells synthesise **tetraiodothyronine** or **thyroxine** (T_4) and **triiodothyronine** (T_3) and iodine is essential for the normal rate of thyroid hormones.

Thyroid hormones regulate the basal metabolic rate of body and influence water and electrolyte balance.

Hypothyroidism or **goitre** (enlargement of the thyroid gland) result due to the deficiency of iodine in diet.

(vi) **Adrenal Gland** Pair of adrenal glands are found at the anterior part of each kidney. It is composed of the centrally located adrenal medulla and the outer adrenal cortex.

Hormones secreted by **adrenal medulla** increase heart rate, respiration rate and are called **emergency hormones.** Adrenal cortex secretes **corticoids.**

(vii) **Pancreas** It is a composite gland, which acts as both exocrine and endocrine gland. Exocrine part includes acini, which secretes pancreatic juice.

Endocrine part consists of Islets of Langerhans. The two main type of Langerhans cells are :

- **α-cells**
- **β-cells**

α-cells secrete **glucagon** a peptide hormone, which plays an important role in maintaining blood glucose level.

β-cells secrete **insulin** which acts on hepatocytes and adipocytes and enhances cellular glucose uptake

- It converts glucose into glycogen known as **glycogenesis.**

(viii) **Testis** In male, individuals a pair of **testis** is present in the scrotal sac. It is primary sex organ and also functions as endocrine gland. It regulates the development, maturation and functions of male accessory sex organs like epididymis, vas deferens, seminal vesicle, prostate gland, urethra, etc.

(ix) **Ovary** It is the primary female sex organ located in the **abdomen.** It also acts as endocrine gland by synthesising two groups of steroid hormone **oestrogen** and **progesterone.** Each ovary produces one ovum during each menstrual cycle.

Various Endocrine Glands, Their Secreted Hormones and Their Functions

Glands	Hormones	Functions
Posterior pituitary gland	Oxytocin	Initiates labour and milk ejection
	Antidiuretic hormone	Stimulates water resorption by kidneys
Anterior pituitary gland	Growth hormone	Stimulates body growth
	Prolactin	Promotes lactation
	Follicle-stimulating hormone	Stimulates follicle maturation and production of oestrogen.
	Luteinising hormone	Triggers ovulation and production of oestrogen and progesterone by ovary.
	Adrenocorticotropic hormone	Promotes release of glucocorticoid and androgens from adrenal cortex
	Thyroid-stimulating hormone	Stimulates release of T_3 and T_4
Thyroid gland	T_3 (Triiodothyronine)	Increases metabolism, blood pressure and regulates tissue growth
	T_4 (Thyroxine)	Increases metabolism, blood pressure and regulates tissue growth
	Calcitonin	Childhood regulation of blood calcium levels through uptake by bone
Parathyroid	Parathyroid hormone	Increases blood calcium levels through action on bone, kidneys and intestine
Pancreas	Insulin	Reduces blood sugar levels by regulating cell uptake
	Glucagon	Increases blood sugar levels

Glands	Hormones	Functions
Adrenal medulla	Epinephrine	Short-term stress response: increased blood sugar levels, vasoconstriction, increased heart rate and blood pressure
	Norepinephrine	Short-term stress response; increased blood glucose levels, blood volume maintenance and immune suppression
Adrenal cortex	Glucocorticoids	Long-term stress response; increased blood glucose levels, blood volume maintenance. immune suppression
	Mineralocorticoids	Long term stress response; blood volume and pressure maintenance, sodium and water retention by kidneys
Pineal gland	Melatonin	Circadian timing
Thymus	Thymosin	Development of T-lymphocytes
Testes	Androgens	Reproductive maturation and sperm production
Ovaries	Oestrogens	Reproductive maturation and regulation of menstrual cycle
	Progesterone	Maintenance of programes and development of mammary gland.

Disorders of Endocrine System

All hormones secreted in our body are required in specific amount. Even a slightly more **(hypersecretion)** or less **(hyposecretion)** secretion of any hormone can lead to different disorders. Some common examples of hormonal disorders are given below:

- **Dwarfism** Deficiency of growth hormone in the human body (mainly in childhood), known as dwarfism.
- **Gigantism** Hypersecretion of growth hormone leads to abnormal condition known as **gigantism** or **excessive growth.**
- **Goitre** Iodine in diet is essential for the secretion of thyroxine hormone. In case, diet is iodine deficient there occurs a possibility of goitre characterised by swollen neck.
- **Diabetes Mellitus** It occurs when there is reduction in insulin secreted by β cells of pancreas. This leads to sugar accumulation in the body. If it is not secreted in proper amounts, the sugar level in the blood rises causing harmful effects.
- **Acromegaly** If an acidophilic tumour occurs causing high GH secretion after adolescence, it results in acromegaly in which jaw and limbs become abnormally large but the body do not attain giant structure.
- **Cretinism** It is caused due to the hyposecretion of thyroid hormone in infants. This leads to slow heart beat, lower blood pressure, low body temperature, stunted growth, mental retardation, retarded sexual development.
- **Addison's Disease** It is caused by deficiency of mineralocorticoids and glucocorticoids.
- **Cushing's Syndrome** It is caused by excess of cortisol which may result in high blood sugar, obesity, rise in blood volume and pressure.
- **Aldosteronism** It is caused by excessive production of aldosterone and form adrenal cortical tumour.
- **Adrenal Virilism** It is the appearance of male characters in female, which result in beard, moustaches, etc. It is caused due to excessive production of male sex corticoids (androgen) in females.
- **Gynaecomastia** It is the development of enlarged mammary glands (breasts) in males due to excessive secretion of female sex hormones (oestrogen) in males.
- **Precocious Puberty** It is early maturation of ovaries and testes with the production of ova before the age of 9 years in girls or sperms before 10 years in boys called sexual pseudoprecocity.
- **Eunuchoidism** It is a disorder which affects males due to failure of testosterone secretion. A eunuch has under developed and non-functional secondary sex organs, lacks external or accessory sex characters and does not produce sperms.

Reproduction in Animals

- The process of producing new individuals of the same species by existing organisms of a species, i.e. parents is called **reproduction.**
- Reproduction allows **perpetuation** of species, increase in population size and evolution.
- There are two main methods by which organisms give rise to new individuals, i.e. asexual reproduction and sexual reproduction.

Asexual reproduction

- It is the process of producing new organism from a single parent without the involvement of sex cells or gametes.
- Offspring produced *via* this method are identical copies of one another as well as their parents. Hence, they are called **clones.**
- This type of reproduction occurs in unicellular organisms, some lower plants and animals.
- It involves only **mitotic** cell division.

Modes of Asexual Reproduction

The modes of asexual reproduction are :

(i) **Binary Fission** It is the division of one cell into two similar or identical cells. In this nucleus divides first followed by cytoplasm.
Among animals, *Amoeba* and *Paramecium* reproduce through binary fission.

(ii) **Fragmentation** Multicellular organisms with simple body organisation such as **flatworms** which breakup into two parts upon maturity and each part develops into new individual.

(iii) **Regeneration** It is the ability of a fully differentiated organism to give rise to new individual organism from any of its body part.
For example, *Hydra* and *Planaria* can be cut into any number of pieces and each piece grows into a complete organism.
Organisms having complex structures cannot produce new progeny by regeneration as their cells have become specialised for certain functions and cannot divide, e.g. *Rhizopus*.

(iv) **Budding** In budding, a small part of the body of the parent grows out as a bud which then detached and becomes a new organism, e.g. *Hydra*.

(v) **Spore Formation** In many multicellular organisms spore is the reproductive cell that has the ability to germinate. Algae, ferns, fungi, reproduce by spore formation.
Different types of spores produced are :
(a) **Zoospores** *Oedogonium*, *Ulothrix* (algae), *Pythium* (fungi)
(b) **Conidia** *Fusarium*, *Penicillium*.
(c) **Cysts** *Vaucheria*
Similarly, in yeast a small bud arises as an outgrowth of the parent body. Later, the nucleus of the parent yeast separates into two parts and one of the nuclei shifts into the bud. This bud divides and outgrows as a cell.

Sexual Reproduction

- The mode of reproduction which involves the formation of male and female gametes (either of same or different individuals of opposite sex) is termed as sexual reproduction.
- These gametes fuse to form a new cell, **zygote** (by meiotic division) which grows and develops into a new individual.
- Sexual reproduction is exhibited by multicellular organisms, i.e. all flowering plants and most of the animals.
- In this type of reproduction, offspring produced are neither identical to their parent nor among themselves.

Sexual Reproduction in Animals

On the basis of gamete formation, animals can be :

(i) **Bisexual or Hermaphrodite** Animals in which both types of gametes are formed, e.g. earthworm.

(ii) **Unisexual** Animals in which male and female gametes are produced in separate bodies, e.g. cockroach.

Sexual dimorphism is the condition where two sexes of the same species exhibit different characteristics based on appearance, e.g. humans show sexual dimorphism.

Reproduction in Human Beings

- The changes, leading to reproductive maturity is called **adolescence**. It begins around the age of 11 and lasts up to 18 or 19 years of age.
- The human body undergoes several changes during adolescence. These changes mark the onset of **puberty**.
- The most important one is reproductive maturity.
- Other changes include in males-thick hair growth on face, armpits and genital area, oily skin, voice box (larynx) begin to grow, etc. In females-breast size increase, menstruation begin, etc.

Human Reproductive System

It consists of male and female reproductive system.

1. Male Reproductive System

Following organs comprise the male reproductive system :

Testes

- These are the primary male gonads in man.
- Each testis is oval in shape, with a length of about 4-5 cm and width of 2-3 cm. They develop in the abdominal cavity during early foetal life and descend in the scrotum in the later stages of life.
- Sperm formation requires a 2 – 2.5°C lower temperature as compared to the body temperature.
- Inside the testis, there are **seminiferous tubules.** These are site of spermatogenesis.
- Seminiferous tubules of testis open into a chamber of flattened channels called **rete testis.**
- Rete testis further give rise to **efferent ductules** which form the **epididymis.**
- Testosterone is secreted by cells that lie between the seminiferous tubules (Leydig cells).

Epididymis

- It is the male accessory duct.
- It is a coiled tube that connects testes to vas deferens.

- It remains divided into three parts–head, body and tail. It stores the sperms for maturation and transports it to **vas deferens**.

Vas Deferens

- It is a straight tube that carries sperm to urethera.
- It is also called **sperm duct**.

Seminal Vesicles

- These are accessory glands in humans (males).
- It consists of **fructose**.
- Seminal vesicle also add its secretions so that the sperm are in a fluid that makes their transport easier.
- It also produces nourishing fluid which makes part of semen.

Urethra

- It is also known as **urinogenital tract** as it provides common pathway for flow of urine and semen.

Penis

- It is the male external **genitalia**.
- It is composed of blood vessels. Penis facilitates copulation and transmits sperms into the vagina of the female.
  Hence, called **copulatory organ**.

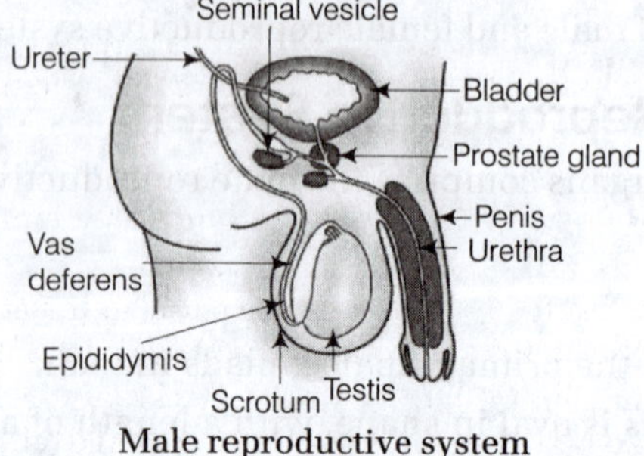

Male reproductive system

Accessory Glands

- **Prostate gland, seminal vesicles and bulbourethral gland** are considered as male accessory glands.
- These glands generate fluid which nourishes the sperm.

2. Female Reproductive System

Female reproductive system has the following parts :

Ovaries

- These are the primary sex organs of the female.
- They (a pair of ovaries) are located one on each side of the lower abdomen.
- Each ovary is 2 to 4 cm in length and produces ovum and ovarian hormones- **progesterone** and **oestrogen**.

Oviducts

- They are the part of the female reproductive system and are also called **Fallopian tubes**.
- A pair of Fallopian tubes connect the ovaries to uterus.
- The Fallopian tube is composed of three parts : **infundibulum, ampulla** and **isthmus**.
- The main function of Fallopian tube is to collect mature eggs from ovaries.
- These are also the site of fertilisation of male and the female gamete.

Uterus

- It is a muscular, inverted, pear-shaped organ also called **womb**.
- Uterus opens into the vagina from a narrow cervix.

Vagina

- It is a muscular tube (7-10 cm long) that connects cervix to the external body.
- It functions as the receptacle of penis during intercourse and also serves as birth canal to allow the delivery of the foetus.

External Genitalia

- It comprises of the reproductive as well as urinary tract structures.
- External female genitalia is inclusive of the following :
  - **Labia majora** These are raised skin folds.
  - **Mons pubis** This is the round area of the skin on which there is hair growth.
  - **Vaginal orifice** It is found in the posterior end of the vestibule. These are guarded incompletely by septum.

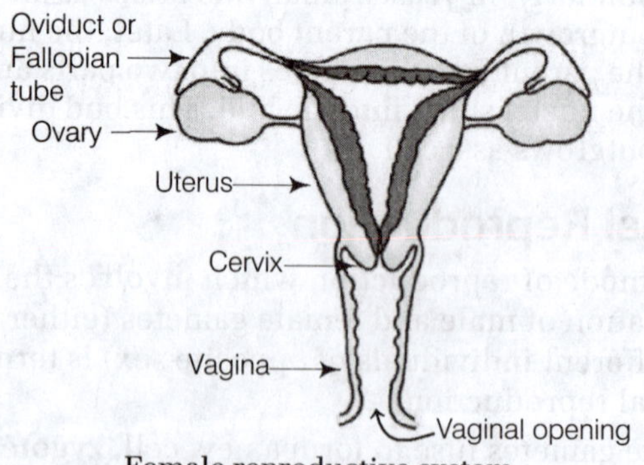

Female reproductive system

Accessory Glands

- **Bartholin glands** are present around the vagina. They secrete a substance that helps in lubrication.
- **Perineal glands** also secrete a special secretion in women.

Mechanism Involved with Human Reproductive System

Various process involved are given below :

Gametogenesis

- It is the process of formation of male and female sex cells or gametes, i.e. sperms and ova in the male and female gonads (testes and ovaries), respectively.
- It is divided into two main types :
  (i) **Spermatogenesis** The process of formation of a sperm is called **spermatogenesis.** It occurs in the seminiferous tubules of the testes.
  A spermatogonium (sperm mother cell) produces four functional spermatozoa.
  (ii) **Oogenesis** It is the process of formation of a mature female gamete (ovum). It occurs in the ovaries (female gonads).
  It consists of three phases :
  (a) Multiplication phase (b) Growth Phase
  (c) Maturation Phase

Fertilisation

- It is the fusion of a haploid male gamete (spermatozoan) and a haploid female gamete (ovum) to form a diploid cell the zygote. It is an internal process that occurs in the ampullary-isthmic junction region of the female's Fallopian tube.
- A glycoprotein fertilizin is secreted by ovum and the penetrating sperm also has a protein on its surface called **antifertilizin.**

Embryonic Development

- During embryonic development, different organs are formed from the three basic germ layers namely ectoderm, mesoderm and endoderm.

Parturition

- It is the act of expelling the fully formed young one from the mother uterus at the end of gestation period. This process is induced by both neural and hormonal system.
- Hormones are secreted by the endocrine glands of the mother. Oxytocin promotes the contraction of the uterine muscles.
- It is also called **birth hormone,** while relaxin increases the flexibility of the pubis ligaments and helps in the dilation of uterine cervix during labour pains (pains of child birth).

Lactation

- Production of milk in the mammary glands is called **lactation.** It starts towards the end of pregnancy and after the birth of the young ones. The first milk produced after the birth of baby is called **colostrum.**
- It is rich in proteins, calories and antibodies (IgA). It provides passive immunity for the newborn infant.
- Milk synthesis is under the control of prolactin hormone, while its release is controlled by oxytocin hormone and released by pituitary gland.

Extra Facts From Tamil Nadu Board and NIOS

- The nine essential amino acids are phenylalanine, valine, threonine, tryptophan, methionine, leucinr, isoleucine, lysine and histidine.
- Dr. Funk introduced the term vitamin. Vitamin-A was given the first letter of the alphabet, as it was the first vitamin discovered.
- In human females, the menstrual cycle starts at the age of 11-13 years which marks the onset of puberty and is called menarche.
- Menstrual cycle ceases around 48-50 years of age and this stage is termed as menopause.

08

Human Health and Diseases

[SOURCES]

Class-VIII NCERT Chap 2 (Microorganisms : Friend and Foe),
Class-IX Old NCERT Chap 13 (Why do we fall Ill?)
Class-XII NCERT Chap 7 (Human Health and Diseases)
Tamil Nadu Board (Class-IX), NIOS

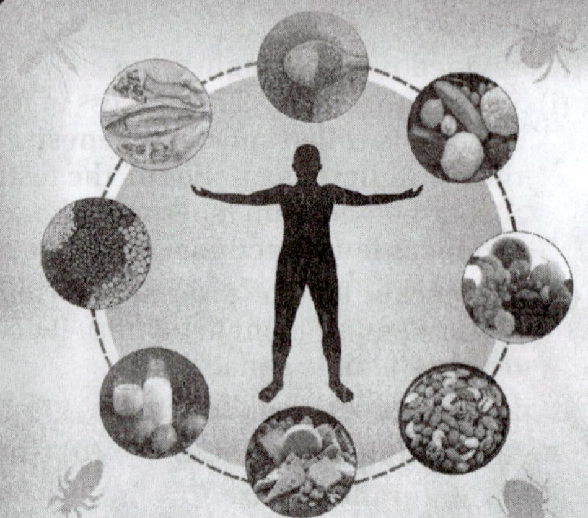

Health

- In 1948, **World Health Organisation** (WHO) stated that, 'Health is a state of complete physical, mental and social well-being and not merely the absence of disease or physical fitness.'
- **Balanced diet, personal hygiene** and **regular exercise** are very important to maintain good health.
- When the functioning of one or more organs or systems of the body is adversely affected, characterised by appearance of various signs and symptoms, we say that we are not healthy, i.e. we have a disease.

Disease

It is an uncomfortable state of body in which the anatomy functions of body or its parts are disturbed.

Symptoms

- There are specific organs in our body which perform important functions.
- In case of disease, several changes occur in the structure and functioning of one or more organs of our body which give rise to the symptoms of the disease.
- These symptoms indicate the illness, e.g. cold, headache, etc. They indicate that the body is sick. However, these do not specify the illness that one suffers from.
- These specific symptoms become the basis on which the doctor confirms a specific disease.

Types of Diseases

In living organisms, especially in humans, diseases are broadly categorised into two types :

1. Congenital Disease

- These diseases occur from the time of birth and include **anatomical** or **physiological abnormalities** in an organism.
- Their main cause are genetical, hereditary errors, etc. Birth defects like haemophilia, sickle-cell anaemia, congenital heart diseases.

2. Acquired Disease

- These diseases develop after birth of a child. They are also called **post-foetally acquired diseases.**
- Good health promotes our ability to work and enables us to bear mental and social pressure without much difficulties.
- Depending on the **duration of infection**, diseases may be of following two types :

  (i) **Acute Diseases** These are the diseases that last only for very short period of time. Thus, they do not cause long term harmful effects on human health. In these diseases, patients recover completely after the cure, e.g. common cold, cough, etc.

(ii) **Chronic Diseases** These are the diseases, which last for a long time, even as much as a lifetime. They cause drastic long-term effects on human health, e.g. elephantiasis (an infection caused by filarial worm), cancer, tuberculosis (TB), etc.

- Depending **upon the microorganism** causing the disease, These can also be of following two types :

(i) **Infectious Diseases** These are caused by infectious agents like microorganisms (bacteria, virus, fungi, etc). These diseases are easily transmitted from one person to another by various means such as water, food, insects (vectors) or by physical contact.
e.g. AIDS, malaria, etc. Thus, they are called **communicable diseases.**

(ii) **Non-infectious Diseases** These diseases are restricted only to the persons, who are suffering from them. These diseases are thus also called **non-communicable diseases.**
e.g. cancer, genetic abnormalities, etc.
Non-communicable diseases are of the following types :

- **Allergy** It is an exaggerated response of immune system to certain agents present in the environment. The agents which cause allergy are called allergens, e.g. dust, pollens, mites, etc. These often cause sneezing, itching, etc.
- **Nutritional Deficiency** It is a disease caused by the deficiency of a specific nutrient in the body. e.g. Kwashiorkor.

Nutrient Deficiency Diseases/Disorders

Nutrient	Deficiency disease/disorder	Symptoms
Vitamin-A	Loss of vision	Poor vision, loss of vision in darkness (night), sometimes complete loss of vision.
Vitamin-B_1	Beri-beri	Weak muscles and very little energy to work.
Vitamin-C	Scurvy	Bleeding gums, wounds take long time to heal.
Vitamin-D	Rickets	Bones become soft and bent.
Calcium	Bone and tooth decay	Weak bones, tooth decay.
Iodine	Goitre	Glands in the neck appear swollen, mental disability in children.
Iron	Anaemia	Weakness
Protein	Marasmus	Found in children, wrinkly appearance due to loss of moisture, retarded mental health.
	Kwashiorkor	Pot belly, stunted growth, skin losses its shine.

- **Degenerated Diseases** These are caused due to failure of any organ like heart, kidney, etc.
e.g. coronary arteriosclerosis.
- **Cancer** It is the uncontrollable growth of body cells leading to tumour. It can be malignant (spreading) or benign.
- **Mental Diseases** These are usually caused due to distortion in the nervous system. Depression is the main cause.
- **Respiratory and Skin Diseases** These are caused due to industrial and other types of pollution.

Infectious Agents

- These are organisms that can cause disease and are found in a wide range of categories of classification.
- Some of them are viruses, bacteria, fungi, single-celled animals or protozoans and multicellular organisms or helminthes (worms). They are also called **pathogens.**
- Some diseases are caused by several agents like air, water, sexual contact, vectors, etc. For example, dengue (*Aedes aegypti*), Chikungunya (*Aedes aegypti* and *Aedes albopictus*) and malaria (*Anopheles*) are caused by certain mosquitoes which act as **vectors.**

Communicable Diseases

Communicable diseases are of the following types :

Airborne Diseases

- Microorganisms associated with such diseases get transmitted by air whenever a sick person sneezes or coughs, droplets come out.
- These droplets may enter a nearby person while he/she breathes and makes him/her sick.
- Examples of airborne diseases include pneumonia, common cold, etc.
- Since, there are maximum chances of catching the infection from a person suffering from common cold, it is much advised to maintain an appropriate distance from the person and avoid using related belongings. Closed areas lack proper ventilation and hence, become a major cause of spreading airborne disease.

Water Borne Diseases

- These are the diseases caused by pathogenic microbes that are spread by contaminated water.
- Transmission of these pathogens takes place, while using water infected with microorganisms for drinking and cooking purposes, etc.
- When the waste (faeces) of a person infected with a communicable disease like cholera gets mixed with drinking water, it pollutes the water entirely and if consumed, makes the healthy population sick.

Sexually Transmitted Diseases

- These are diseases or infections that are acquired from an infected person to an uninfected one *via* sexual contact. They can be caused by bacteria, viruses or parasites.
- These microorganisms are transferred from one partner to another *via* body fluids exchanged during the sexual act.
- However, they are not caused by activities like shaking hands, playing, hugging, etc. e.g. AIDS and syphilis are the main sexually transmitted diseases.

Vector Borne Diseases

- These are infections or diseases transmitted by the bite of an infected species which surrounds us. These act as transmitting agents and transmit microbes from infected to a healthy individual, e.g. *Aedes*—Dengue, *Anopheles* (female) mosquito—malaria.

Bacterial Diseases

Diseases	Causative Organisms	Transmission	Symptoms	Prevention
Cholera	*Vibrio cholerae*	• Contaminated food and water • Spread by house fly.	• Reduction in body's water level. • Slowdown of blood circulation. • Incubation period 2-3 days. • Vomiting, acute diarrhoea, muscular cramps, etc.	• Drink pure water or boiled water, eat light food and careful disposal of wastes. • Vaccine is available for immunisation.
Diphtheria	*Corynebacterium diphtheriae*	• Droplets sprayed from mouth and nose during talking, coughing, etc.	• Mild fever, sore throat, patches on false membrane in the throat. • Incubation period of disease is nearly 3-5 days.	• Immunisation vaccine or take the injection of antitoxin diphtheria within 12-24 hours of its appearance in the system.
Plague	*Yersinia pestis*	• Through flea bite or accidental contact with infected rat. • *Xenopsylla cheopis* is a deadly flea that causes plague by entering in the human body.	• Acute body pain, reddish eyes, increase in body temperature, inflammation of glands in the neck, armpit and thigh.	• Remove infected rats from the diseased zone • Proper vaccination • Usage of sulphur drugs and streptomycin.
Whooping cough	*Bordetella pertussis*	• Through air and commonly occur in infants and children.	• Cough in night initially and after some time occur in day as well as in night.	• Immunisation of infants with the immune serum and vaccine such as DPT, etc.
Pneumonia	*Streptococcus pneumoniae*	• Through air borne droplets and the affected people suffer from a chronic fever and respiratory problems.	• Chills, chest pain, production of sputum, breathing problems, abdominal pain, etc.	• Protection from excessive cold must be taken. • Antibiotic drugs must be used.
Tuberculosis	*Mycobacterium tuberculosis*	• Inhaling infected droplets released in sneezes and cough	• Loss of appetite and weight, prolonged low grade fever	• Avoid over crowded areas • Isolation of patient • Maintenance of good hygiene
Typhoid	*Salmonella typhi*	• Contaminated food and water	• Headache • Subsequent high and low fever.	• Proper sanitation • TAB vaccination
Diarrhoea	*Escherichia coli*	• Contaminated food and water	• Frequent loose motions, vomiting, dehydration	• Avoiding stale food • Proper and personal sanitary conditions

Viral Diseases

Diseases	Causative Organisms	Transmission	Symptoms	Prevention
Influenza or flu	Influenza viruses (A and B)	• Air borne droplets into the respiratory tract.	• Fever, chill, muscular aches, uneasiness, etc.	• Vaccination with live attenuated virus vaccines • Antibiotics such as tetramycine, tetracycline, etc.
Smallpox	*Variola* virus	• Air borne droplets or indirectly through the infected articles.	• High fever, headache, backache, skin rashes on the third day passing through bright red spots, pustules, papules and vesicles scabs which fall on leaving pitted pock marks.	• Vaccination • Should remain isolated from healthy person.
Polio myelitis	*Poliovirus*	• Intestinal discharge, contaminated food, drink, etc.	• Effect on central nervous system, cells of the back bone and intestine become completely damaged. • Paralytic type of indication follows and reaches maximum within 2-3 days. Difficulty in forward bending movement of head.	• Vaccination, inoculation of salk vaccine invented by **Jonas Salk**, provide prevention for polio myelitis. • Oral vaccine invented by **Albert Sabin** in 1961 for polio eradication.
Rabies	*Rabies* virus	• Bite of animals like dog, wolf, fox, etc.	• Central nervous system affected. • Severe headache, high fever with alternating stages of excitement and depression. Difficulty in swallowing , Paralysis Convulsions	• Anti-rabies vaccine invented by **Louis Pasteur**. • Series of antibiotics are given. • Cleaning of wound with pure carbolic acid or nitric acid.
Chicken pox	(*Varicella zoster* virus)	• Infected person, clothing or other articles.	• Fever (appearing about 14 days after the contact of disease), headache, appearance of reddish spots turning into the pearly blisters on the chest, back and face, abdomen • Scabs from 4-5th day of the fever.	• Usage of calamine lotion on affected area. • Isolated from infected person.
Meningitis	Enterovirus, Herpes simplex virus.	• Through cerebrospinal fluid.	–	• Vaccination • Antibiotics
Dengue	Flavi ribovirus	• Bite of mosquito (*Aedes* sp.)	• High fever • Muscle and joint pain	• Use of mosquito repellant • Proper medication
AIDS	Retro virus (HIV)	• Blood transfusion • Sexual contact • Use of contaminated needles	• Swollen lymph nodes • Frequently occurring infections • Sweating at night	• Avoiding sexual contact with unknown person • Use of anti-viral drugs (only prolong lifespan)

Protozoan Diseases

Diseases	Causative Organisms	Transmission	Symptoms	Prevention
Kala-azar	*Leishmania donovani*	• Through bite of sand fly	• Enlargement of organs like spleen, liver • Fever, jaundice and skin pigmentation	• As directed by physician.
Sleeping sickness	*Trypanosoma brucei* (Protozoan parasite)	• Through the bite of tse-tse fly.	• Fever, headache. • Enlargement of glands at the back of the neck, rashes on the back and chest, pain in the joints, eyelid swelling in ankles and hands, mental disturbance, lethargy, etc.	• Benzimidazole
Amoebic dysentery or Amoebiasis	*Entamoeba histolytica*	• Through contaminated raw fruit and other food and drinks.	• Mild diarrhoea, in severe cases, mucosa and blood appears in the stools.	• Environmental sanitation • Drink filtered water. • No immunisation is available. • Effective medicines like, mexaform, etc.
Pyorrhoea	*Entamoeba gingivalis*	• Through Saliva	• Pus in teeth emerges through the gums of the teeth. Some time wounds also occur in the roots of the teeth.	• Regular dental check-up, regular cleaning of teeth gums, flossing and brushing, use of antiseptic mouthwashes.
Malaria	*Plasmodium* sp.	• Transmitted by *Anopheles* mosquito	• Headache • Nausea • High fever with chills	• Use of mosquito repellants. • Doses of quinine are prescribed

Fungal Diseases

Diseases	Causative Organisms	Transmission	Symptoms	Prevention
Athlete's foot	*Trichophyton*	• Through walking on infected floors and mats	• Skin problems	• Consult physician • Wear footwear
Scabies	*Acarus scabiei*	• Direct skin to skin contact • Contact with infected object	• Some irritation occur on skin making it dry with white rashes.	• Usage of permethrin, ivermectin.
Dhobie itch or crotch itch or Tinea cruris	*Candida albicans*	• Direct contact of the objects handled by infected person.	• Red rashes with itching usually in groin.	• Antifungal medication of the allylamine or an azole type.
Ringworm	*Micosporum trichophyton*	• Acquired from soil • Heat and moisture	• Dry scaly lesions, • Intense itching	• Avoiding the use of articles such as towel, clothes, comb of infected person. • Avoiding the direct contact with infected articles.

Rules for the Treatment of Infectious Diseases

Different medicines are prescribed by the doctor that work in different ways. Following are the two ways of treatment of infectious diseases :

Reducing the Impact of Disease

- It involves reducing the effect of the disease by a specific treatment so as to reduce the symptoms.
- Symptoms of a disease arise due to the response of the immune system and can be subsided by taking medicines.
- However, these medicines do not completely cure the disease as the microbes are not killed.

Death of the Causal Organism

- The best possible way of getting an effective treatment is to kill the microorganisms which causes the disease.
- Thus, it becomes important to take medicine which is specific to the pathogen that caused disease.

Methods of Prevention of Infectious Diseases

Method of prevention of infectious diseases are of two types :

1. Common Methods

They involve avoidance of contact with the patient. Public hygiene plays a major role in the prevention of infectious diseases. Some other general rules of prevention are :

(i) Having a **strong immune system** which fights with disease causing microorganisms and kill them. Thus, we do not acquire any disease.

(ii) **Balanced diet** An adequate balanced diet also plays a major role in the successful functioning of the immune system. Hence, all the mineral nutrients should be taken in the form of a balanced diet.

2. Vaccination and Immunisation

Vaccination and immunisation are based on the property of memory of the immune system.

Vaccination

- It is the process of introduction of weakened or inactivated pathogens or proteins (vaccine) into a person to provide protection against a disease.
- Vaccine is prepared from **dead** or **attenuated** infectious agents or their products which stimulates the immune system to form antibodies against a specific disease.

Immunisation

- It is the process by which the body produces antibodies against the vaccine (primary response) and develops the ability to neutralise pathogens during actual infection (secondary response), i.e. the body becomes immune to that antigen or infection.
- Vaccine generates memory B and T-cells that recognise the pathogens on subsequent exposure and produce an intense immune response by producing antibodies.
- Antibodies are **immunoglobulin** molecules. These are of five types **IgA, IgM, IgE, IgG and IgD.**
- Some common vaccines are :
  - DPT vaccine for protection against diphtheria, whooping cough (Pertusis) and tetanus.
  - BCG (Bacillus Calmette Guerin) vaccine for protection against tuberculosis.
  - Oral Polio Vaccine (OPV)
  - Typhoid vaccine
  - Measles vaccine
  - Hepatitis-A and Hepatitis-B vaccine
  - Coronavirus vaccine
- **Edward Jenner** discovered the first vaccine for **small pox** in 1796. Cowpox served as a natural vaccine until the modern smallpox vaccine came into existence.

- These vaccines should be administered at specific ages to children hence, to protect children from falling prey to infectious diseases. They are available under government health programs of India.
- The **Pulse Polio Immunisation** (PPI) programme in India was launched under the World Health Organisation's **Global Polio Eradication** proposal in the year 1995.
- India has been declared Polio free by WHO in the year 2014 although the programme is still on the run so that the possibility of its re-occurrence is eliminated.
- In case of requirement of quick immune response like tetanus infection, preformed antibodies are injected into the patient.
- Even in the case of snake bite, preformed antibodies called **antitoxin** is injected. This is called **passive immunisation**.
- Recombinant DNA technology has produced antigenic polypeptides of pathogen in bacteria or yeast. This allowed large scale production of vaccine, e.g. hepatitis-B vaccine produced from yeast, etc.

Antibiotics

- These are chemical substances produced by living organisms such as bacteria and fungi, etc. which can kill or stop the growth of some pathogenic microorganisms, e.g. **Penicillin, Tetracycline, Streptomycin** and **Chloromycetin**, etc.
- Famous antibiotic, i.e. **penicillin** was prepared by **Alexander Fleming** in 1928 while he was working on a culture of disease causing bacteria.

Autoimmunity

- It is the state where body loses the ability to distinguish between self and non-self cells. The body's immune system goes off the track and starts destroying self-cells and molecules.
- This results in autoimmune diseases, e.g. rheumatoid arthritis, Addison's disease, Hashimoto's disease, etc.

Immunity

It is the ability of an organism to resist or defend itself from the development of a disease. **Edward Jenner** is known as the **father of immunology** (the study of immunity). Immunity is of the following types :

1. Innate Immunity

It is present from birth and/or inherited from parents like skin, saliva, WBCs, interferons, etc. It is non-specific in nature.

2. Acquired Immunity

- It is not present from birth and develops during an individual's life time. e.g. lymphocytes, antibodies, etc.
- It is pathogen specific and can 'memorise' previous infections thus, providing immune responses in future.
- Acquired immunity is further divided into two types :

Active Acquired Immunity

It is the immunity developed by the body when it is exposed to antigens as a result, the body produces antibodies. It is of further two types :

(i) **Natural Acquired Active Immunity** It occurs when a person is exposed to a live pathogen, develops a primary immune response. A person's immune system is actively involved and produces immune cells.

(ii) **Artificial Acquired Active Immunity** Requires commercial production of antigens by various microbes. These antigens are used as :
  - **Vaccine** It is a biological preparation that improves immunity to a particular disease. It can be obtained from various bacteria and viruses.
  - **Bacterial Vaccine** It is obtained from inactivated bacterial cells and are directed against the pathogenic bacteria causing infection.
  - **Toxoids** These are bacterial toxins that have been weakened but are capable enough to induce antibody formation.
  - **Viral Vaccine** Such vaccines are prepared from viruses (live or weakened), e.g. Polio.

Passive Acquired Immunity

- It is the direct transfer of actively formed antibodies from one person (or other animal) to another. This type of immunity is short lived and is of the following two types :

(i) **Natural Acquired Passive Immunity** It occurs during pregnancy wherein, certain antibodies are passed from the maternal blood to the fetal blood stream *via* placenta or *via* colostrum (mixture of IgG , IgM and IgA).

(ii) **Artificial Acquired Passive Immunity** This type of immunity is a short-term immunisation achieved by the transfer of antibodies, which can be administered either as human or animal blood plasma or serum, e.g. tetanus, snake-bites, etc.

Extra Facts From
Tamil Nadu Board and NIOS

- Robert Koch (1876) discovered the bacterium *Bacillus anthracis* which causes anthrax disease.
- Streptomycin, tetracyline and erythromycin are some of the commonly known antibiotics which are made from fungi and bacteria.

09

Environment and Ecology

(SOURCES)

Class-VI NCERT Chap 6 (The Living Organisms-Characteristics and Habitats), Class-VII Old NCERT Chap 7 (Weather, Climate and Adaptations of Animals to Climate), Chap 11 (Air Around us), Old NCERT Chap 14 (Water), Class-VII NCERT Chap 12 (Forest : Our Lifeline), Old NCERT Chap 9 (Soil), Class-IX NCERT Chap 14 (Natural Resources), Class-X NCERT Chap-13 (Our Environment), Old NCERT Chap 16 (Management of Natural Resources), Class-XII NCERT Chap 11 (Organisms and Populations), Chap 12 (Ecosystem) Tamil Nadu Board (Class-IX), NIOS

Environment

- All the things and set of conditions that influence the life of an organism constitute the **environment**.
- It is composed of physical surrounding (e.g., air, water), living beings (e.g., plants, animals) and climatic conditions (e.g., rainfall, temperature) of the region. Environment comprises of biotic and abiotic components.
- **Biotic components** include plants, animals whereas **Abiotic components** include factors like soil, water, temperature etc.
- These affect our lives directly or indirectly.
- Resources provided by nature on Earth, which can be utilised by living organisms to sustain their life are called **natural resources.**
- These include air, water, soil, sunlight, minerals, etc.

Categorisation of Environment

All the resources are found accumulated in different layers of Earth, which are as follows

Atmosphere

- Air is a mixture of many gases like nitrogen, oxygen, carbon dioxide and water vapour.
- Photosynthesis process uses carbon dioxide (CO_2) and releases oxygen (O_2).
- The atmosphere covers the Earth like a protective blanket. The air is a bad conductor of heat.
- So, the atmosphere keeps the average temperature of Earth fairly steady during the day and even during the course of whole year. Eukaryotic and most prokaryotic cells require (O_2) to break down glucose molecule to obtain energy resulting in CO_2 production.
- Amount of CO_2 in atmosphere is less than 0.04% because it is fixed in two ways :
  - (i) Green trees convert CO_2 to glucose in presence of sunlight
  - (ii) Many marine animals make their shells out of carbonates dissolved in sea water.
- CO_2 comes in the atmosphere from respiration.
- Burning fossil fuel uses oxygen and releases CO_2.
- Rainfall patterns are decided by the prevailing wind patterns. In large parts of our country, rains are mostly brought by the South-West or North-East monsoons. In some areas, these are caused by the depressions in the Bay of Bengal.

Composition of Air

Component	% age	Component	% age
Nitrogen	78.09%	Carbon dioxide	0.03%
Oxygen	20.95%	Methane	0.0002%
Argon	0.9%	Hydrogen	0.00005%

Hydrosphere

- All water bodies existing on earth are collectively called **hydrosphere**.
- Water is an **inexhaustible natural resource.** It occupies very large area of the Earth's surface (both above and underground). Some amount of water exists in the form of water vapours in the atmosphere.
- It includes oceans, ponds, rivers, glaciers etc.
- The Earth is called the **Blue Planet** since 71% of it is covered by water.
- Water is essential for living beings as it provides a medium for all cellular processes to take place.
- All the organisms need to maintain the level of water within their bodies in order to survive.
- **Protoplasm** found in all the living organisms comprise of water. Jellyfish consists of 95% water. Human blood and brain contains 90% water.
- Human muscles, nerves and even the hardest substance found on teeth (enamel) contains water. Thus, making 70% of human body comprising of water.
- Rainfall is dependent on several factors like distance of a place from sea, topography, seasonal climate etc. This further decides the type of vegetation of that area.
- Areas with more rainfall and less temperatures, experience dense or evergreen rainforest, giving place of lichens, pine trees etc. whereas, areas where rainfall is less, small trees and deserts are found.
- Therefore, water is essential for the sustenance of life. The availability of water decides the number of individuals of each species that are able to survive in a particular area and also the diversity of life there.

Lithosphere

- It is the upper rough fertile surface of the Earth.
- It is made up of various mountains, plains, deserts etc., there are forests made by huge trees apart from terrestrial and aerial organisms.
- It covers about 29% of the earth and is mostly affected by geographical and climatic variation which cause biological development.

Soil

- It is one of the most important natural resources.
- It provides anchorage to the plants and supplies water and nutrients. It is the home for many microorganisms.
- Soil is a mixture of small particles of rocks, bits of decayed living organisms (humus) and partially decomposed plant and animal matter (detritus).
- Soil is formed by the breaking down of rocks by the action of wind, water and climate. This process is called **Weathering.**

Biosphere

Biosphere is the life supporting zone of earth where atmosphere, hydrosphere and lithosphere interact and make life possible.

Ecology

- The word ecology is derived from the Greek words '*Oikos*' meaning **habitation** and '*logos*' meaning **study.**
- Ecology is the branch of biology, which studies the interactions among organisms (biotic) and their physical (abiotic) environment. **Prof Ramdeo Mishra** is known as the **Father of Indian Ecology.**
- This science developed in response to the increasing awareness of inter-relationships between plants, animals and their physical habitats and how they make use of environmental resources including energy flow and mineral cycling.

Population

- It consists of all the organisms of a plant or an animal species, inhabiting in a given area. e.g., all individuals of tigers in an area constitute its population.
- The main reasons for the increase in population are **birth** and **immigration**. Whereas reason for the decrease in population are **death** and **emigration.**

Features of Population

The features of population are as follows

(i) **Population Density** It refers to number of people living in each block of land with a finite capacity to support the people who live on it. It can be shown by the following formula :

$$\text{Population Density (D)} = \frac{\text{Total Number of People (N)}}{\text{Area (S)}}$$

(ii) **Birth Rate** It is expressed as number of live births in a year per thousand of population.

(iii) **Death Rate** It plays an active role in population change, population growth occurs not only by increasing births rate but also due to decreasing death rate.

(iv) **Sex Ratio** It is the ratio between the number of women and men in the population.

(v) **Age Structure** It represents different age groups in a population. It can be of following types :

- **Expanding/Growing Population** This type of population pyramid is in a triangular shape with a wide base.

- **Constant/Stationary Population** It is shown in bell-shaped and tapered towards the top. The bell-shaped pyramid has birth and death rates almost the same and leading to a constant population.
- **Declining Population** A narrow base and tapered top of the pyramid shows the low birth rate and death rate.

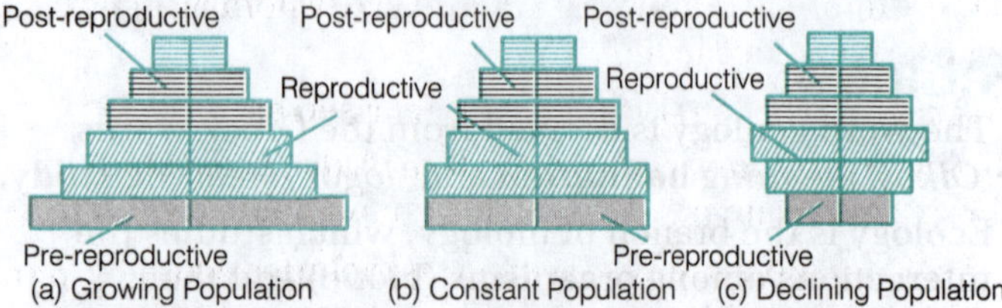

(a) Growing Population (b) Constant Population (c) Declining Population

(v) **Population Growth** This is the change of population expressed in percentage. **Natural Growth of Population** is the population increased by difference between births and deaths in a particular region between two points of time.

Ecological Interactions

In order to study the relationship between prey, predators, other interactions and phenomenon like competition, it is mandatory to study the theory of **population interactions**. It helps us to understand how biotic components have dependence over each other.

Types of Interactions

Interactions are of following three types

1. Positive Interaction

In these type of interactions, one or both the species involved is/are benefitted. It is further described as

(i) **Commensalism** In this type of interaction, one species is benefitted whereas, the other remains unaffected.
e.g., Clownfish and anemones.

(ii) **Mutualism** It is the interaction between two different species of living beings in which both are benefitted. However, individual survival is not possible.

2. Negative Interaction

In this type of interaction, out of the two species that participate, one is affected negatively. It is of the following types

(i) **Amensalism** It is the interaction in which one species is harmed while the other remains neutral.
e.g., *Penicillium* inhibits growth of various bacteria.

(ii) **Competition** It takes place due to lack of resources leading to a competition for resource.
It can be **intra or interspecific.**

(iii) **Parasitism** In this, one species benefits from the other and at the same time this process is harmful for other species.
e.g., *Plasmodium* species is transmitted by *Anopheles* mosquito, which causes malaria, in humans.

(iv) **Predation** This interaction involves predator-prey relationship in which prey is eaten up by the predator.

3. Neutral Interaction

- In this type, the two species neither benefit nor are harmed.
- One species mimics the other. The one who gets mimiced is called **model.**
- In mimicry (camouflage), one organism can imitate the other based on attitude, habits, shape, colour, etc. due to which they are left unharmed by the predators.

Ecological Adaptations

Structural, morphological, physiological changes in organisms due to environmental changes which lead to increased tolerance levels are called **ecological adaptations.**

Hydrophytic Plants

- Plants which are found in places which have sufficient water and may be wholly or partially submerged in water are called **hydrophytes.**
- They either have absence of roots or the roots, if present, are less developed.
- The stems are thin, soft and spongy and remain protected in the flow of water.
- Such plants have torn long and ribbon-like leaves. e.g., *Vallisneria* leaves that float on surfaces of water are large and contain a layer of waxy substance on upper surface.

Adaptations in Aquatic Animals

- Their body is streamlined so, they can swim easily.
- They have gills as respiratory organs.
- Their body is covered by scales meant for protection.
- They have fins as locomotory organs.

Xerophytes

- They are found in places where there is lack of water and arid (dry) conditions are constantly maintained.
- In these plants, root system is found to be highly developed with long root hair and root penetrate deeper into the soil in order to absorb more water.

- The base of these plants is short, woody and thick with bark and leaves have reduced to spines in order to minimise water loss.

Adaptations in Xerophytic Animals

- Certain animals like camel, have the capability to concentrate urine and thus, are able to sustain themselves when there is less water availability.

Adaptations in Plants in Mountain Regions

- Trees in mountain areas are cone shaped, so that the snow slides off easily without accumulating as it can cause damage.
- Their leaves are needle-like which allow rain water and snow to fall down easily.

Adaptations in Animals living in Mountains

- Animals living in mountains have thick skin or fur in order to retain their body heat thus, protecting them from cold. Such animals have shorter ears and limbs to reduce heat loss.
- Some animals also **hibernate** in colder conditions.

Ecosystem

- An **ecosystem** is the structural and functional unit of biosphere, comprising of all the organisms interacting among themselves and with the non-living constituents of the environment.
- It is a self-sustaining system where energy and matter are exchanged between living and non-living components. It has following two components :
  - **Biotic components** It means the living organisms of the environment-plants, animals, human beings and microorganisms like bacteria and fungi.
  - **Abiotic components** It means the non-living part of the environment, i.e. air, water, soil and minerals. The climatic or physical factors such as sunlight, temperature, rainfall, humidity, pressure and wind are part of the abiotic environment.
- A specific place or locality delimited by a combination of factors, physical features and barriers where a community dwells is called **habitat**. There are many types of habitats, however, these may be broadly grouped as **terrestrial** (on the land) and **aquatic** (in water).
- The **ecological niche** of an organism represents the physical space occupied by it, the resources it utilises and its functional role in the ecological system.
- **Migration** is the temporary movement from a stressful habitat to a more hospitable area and return, when the stressful period is over.

Types of Ecosystem

Ecosystem is of two types

1. Natural Ecosystem

The natural ecosystem are terrestrial (land) as well as aquatic.

(i) Aquatic Ecosystem

The common examples of aquatic ecosystem are ponds, lakes, rivers, ocean, etc.

Aquatic ecosystem is further categorised as

(a) **Freshwater ecosystem** It includes ecosystem in freshwater sources such as pond, lake, river, etc.

(b) **Marine water ecosystem** It includes ecosystem in marine water sources such as seas and oceans.

(ii) Land Ecosystem

The common examples of land ecosystem are forests, grasslands, deserts, etc.

2. Artificial Ecosystem

The artificial ecosystems are made by human beings. The common examples of artificial ecosystems are crop fields, gardens, parks, aquarium, etc.

Components in an Ecosystem

In an ecosystem, both biotic and abiotic components are found.

Biotic Components

Following are the biotic components

(i) Producers

- Those organisms which produce food by photosynthesis, i.e., organisms which can make organic compounds like sugar and starch from inorganic substances by using energy of the Sun in presence of chlorophyll are called **producers**.
- All green plants and certain blue-green algae are producers, e.g., *Nostoc*.

(ii) Consumers

- Those organisms which depend upon the producers for food, either directly or indirectly by feeding on other organisms for their survival are called, **consumers**. These depend upon those below them, in a food chain and are also called **heterotrophs**.
- Consumers can be classified into herbivores (primary consumers), carnivores, omnivores and parasites.

  (a) **Herbivores** are the animals that consume or eat vegetation or plants. These are also called **primary consumers**. e.g., cows, horses, etc.

(b) **Carnivores** are the animals that eat meat of other animals. They are called **secondary consumers**. e.g., tigers, wolves, etc.

(c) **Omnivores** or tertiary consumers are the animals that eat both plants and animals. e.g., humans, cockroaches, etc.

(d) **Parasites** are those organisms that live on (ectoparasites) or in (endoparasites) the body of another organisms, i.e., host from which it obtains its nutrients.

Decomposers

- Those microorganisms that obtain energy from the chemical breakdown of dead organisms, animals or plant wastes are called **decomposers**.
- These microorganisms are called decomposers as they breakdown the complex organic substances into simple inorganic substances that go into the soil and are used up again by the plants.
- Decomposers include bacteria and fungi. e.g., *Agaricus*.

Abiotic Components

- It includes all non-living components like temperature, water and soil. These affect biodiversity and number of organisms in an ecosystem.

Food Chain

- It is the sequence of organisms through which energy is transferred in the form of food, by the process of one organisms consuming the other.
- It shows the relationship of producer and consumer, i.e., 'who eats whom'. Thus, it is a series of organisms taking part at various biotic levels from the producer and ends in consumer.
- A simple generalised food chain operating in an ecosystem is shown as follows :

Producers → Herbivores → Carnivores

Examples of food chain are as follows :

- Food chain in forest or grassland ecosystems

Grass → Grasshopper → Frog → Snake → Eagle
(Producer) (Herbivore) (Carnivore) (Carnivore) (Top carnivore)

- Food chain in aquatic ecosystems

Phytoplankton→Zooplankton→Crustacean→Fish→Shark
(Producer) (Herbivore) (Carnivore) (Carnivore) (Top carnivore)

Types of Food Chain

There are three types of food chains in nature

(i) **Predatory Food Chain** This begins from green plants and goes upto higher animals *via* smaller ones.

(ii) **Parasitic Food Chain** This begins from higher organisms to lower ones.

(iii) **Detritus Food Chain** This begins from dead and decaying organisms and it end at microorganisms.

Food Web

- It is the network of various food chains which are interconnected at various trophic levels. Since, an organism can occupy position in more than one food chain, in a food web it occupies more than one trophic level.
- For example, grass may be eaten by grasshopper as well as rabbit or cattle and each of these herbivores may be eaten by many carnivores such as frog, bird or tiger depending on their food habits.

Flow of Energy in an Ecosystem

- The flow of energy through different steps in the food chain is **unidirectional**. This means that energy captured by autotrophs does not revert back to the solar input and it passes to the herbivores. It moves progressively through various trophic levels.
- Green plants capture 1% of energy of the sunlight that falls on their leaves and convert it into food energy.
- When green plants are eaten by primary consumers, a great deal of energy is lost as heat to the environment. On an average 10% of food eaten is turned into its own body and made available for next level for consumers.
- Thus, 10% can be taken as average value, the amount of organic matter present at each step and reaches the next level of consumers. This concept was given by **Lindemann** in 1942.
- As very less energy is available for next level of consumer, food chain consists of only three or four steps. The loss of energy at each step is so great that very little energy remains after fourth trophic levels.
- There are a greater number of individuals at lower trophic level, i.e., at the producer level of the ecosystem.
- In an ecosystem, the Sun's energy is transformed by producers into chemical energy by the process of **photosynthesis.**
- In herbivores and carnivores this energy is then transformed further at various trophic levels.
- The chemical energy is transformed into mechanical energy and heat.

- There is maximum energy at the producer level and further the energy goes on decreasing.
- The **herbivores** get more energy with food than **carnivores** at third and fourth trophic levels.
- At each trophic level large amount of energy is lost in maintaining the metabolic activities and lost as heat. The amount of heat lost is generally 90% and the amount of energy retained is 10% by trophic level.
- So, only 10% energy is available from previous trophic level to the next.
- The decline in energy level leads to :
  - Lesser number of organisms in each trophic level.
  - Limited number of trophic level in food chains.

Ecological Pyramids

- These are graphic representations, designed to show the connection between different trophic levels in terms of number, energy and biomass of an organisms.
- The base of each pyramid represents the producers whereas apex represents the tertiary consumers.
- There are three pyramids which are usually studied
  (i) **Pyramid of number** It represents the total number of organisms at each trophic level.
  (ii) **Pyramid of biomass** It represents the total weight of organisms at each trophic level.
  (iii) **Pyramid of energy** It represents the total energy of organism in each trophic level.

Biological Magnification

- It refers to the process of increase in the concentration of a toxic chemical with increasing tropic level in a food chain. These toxic chemicals are mainly pesticides.
- Harmful or poisonous substance such as DDT sprinkled to kill pests on plants enter the food chain.
- As human beings occupies the top level in any food chain, the maximum concentration of harmful chemicals gets accumulated in the body, the phenomenon of which is known as **biological magnification.**

Biogeochemical Cycles

- Biogeochemical cycles refers to the cyclic flow of nutrients between non-living components (soil, rock, air and water) and living organisms, which make the biosphere dynamic, but a stable system.
- Such cyclic flow involves transfer of matter and energy between the different components of the biosphere.
- Following are the biogeochemical cycles :

Water Cycle

- Water is one of the most important physical component which is essential for survival of life on Earth. Ocean is the biggest store house for water which on evaporation forms clouds and which after condensation fall down as rain. After rain it passes through rivers and gets collected again in the ocean. The circulation of water in this manner is known as **water cycle.**

Nitrogen Cycle

Nitrogen exists as free nitrogen in the atmosphere. In air N_2 is about 78%. This free nitrogen is fixed into compounds of ammonia and nitrates. Most of the organisms cannot utilise nitrogen as molecular nitrogen.

Steps involved in nitrogen cycle are as follows

(i) **Nitrogen fixation** It is the initial step of nitrogen cycle where atmospheric nitrogen is converted to unusable form ammonia. The process takes place by either of the following methods
  - With the help of certain blue-green algae and bacteria.
  - Atmospheric fixation with the help of lightening

(ii) **Assimilation** Plant intake nitrogenous compound from soil, available as nitrates, nitrites (ions) or as ammonia. This is called **assimilation.**

(iii) **Ammonification** Death and decay of plant and animals release N_2 back in soil. Decomposers namely bacteria or fungi present in soil, convert the organic matter back into ammonium, releasing NH_3.

(iv) **Nitrification** It is the process of conversion of ammonia into nitrate by the help of bacteria present in soil.

(v) **Denitrification** Ammonia and nitrates are converted into free nitrogen during this process. This takes place with the help of certain microbes.

- Nitrogen containing fertilisers produced artificially in factories are the fixed form of nitrogen.
- Plants take compounds containing nitrogen from the soil. From plants, nitrogen passes into food web. Decay of dead plants, animals and excreta like urine, faeces, causes return of nitrogen compounds to the soil.
- Denitrifying bacteria and fire cause liberation of free nitrogen in the atmosphere.

Carbon Cycle

- Carbon is a basic constituent of all living organism. It exists as carbohydrates, fats, proteins and nucleic acid.
- **Carbon dioxide** and **oxygen** are being continuously consumed and generated by the organisms. Steps involved in the carbon cycles are
  - (i) Green plants use CO_2 during photosynthesis and produce oxygen and carbohydrates. During respiration of organisms, oxygen and carbohydrates are consumed and carbon dioxide and water are formed.
  - (ii) Also, animals when consume plants, some part of the carbon, as CO_2 is released as a result of oxidation of carbohydrates.
  - (iii) When these animals die, the organic matter present in their bodies gets decomposed, producing and releasing CO_2 into atmosphere.
  - (iv) Thus, a balance of carbon dioxide and oxygen is maintained in the biosphere. But in recent years man is indiscriminately using fossil fuels. In this process, man is using more oxygen and producing carbon dioxide. This has resulted in increase of carbon dioxide in the atmosphere.

Oxygen Cycle

- Oxygen in gaseous form is present in atmosphere (21%). In water bodies, it is present in dissolved form. From these sources, plants, animals and decomposers take molecular oxygen for respiration.
- Burning of fuels such as coal, wood, petroleum also use atmospheric oxygen.
- Green plants utilise carbon dioxide and water during photosynthesis and release molecular oxygen in air and water.

Extra Facts From Tamil Nadu Board and NIOS

- Aerial animals include a small number of animals that are able to fly in air. True aerial animals are birds and bats. These animals exhibit adaptations to balance themselves and stay in air, soaring or flying. These adaptations include- streamlined body to steer through the air.
- Forelimbs are modified into wings to hollow bones to make them light.
- Bats use a remarkable high-frequency system called echolocation. In this, bats give out high-frequency sounds. These sounds are reflected back from its prey and bats use these echoes to locate and identify the prey.
- When the soil becomes too hot or dry, earthworms become inactive and undergo a estivation.

10

Biodiversity and Its Conservation

[SOURCES]

Class-VII Old NCERT Chap 1 (Weather, Climate and Adaptations of Animals to Climate), Class-VIII NCERT Chap 5 (Conservation of Plants and Animals), Class-X Old NCERT Chap 1 (Management of Natural Resources), Class-XII NCERT Chap 13 (Biodiversity and Conservation).

Biodiversity

- Biodiversity can be defined as the occurrence of different types of genes, gene pools, species, habitats and ecosystem in a given region at a given time.
- The term **biodiversity** was given by a sociobiologist **Edward Wilson.**

Levels of Biodiversity

The levels of biodiversity are as follows :

(i) **Genetic diversity** It is a measure of variety in genetic information contained in the organisms. It enables a population to adapt to its environment.
Greater the genetic diversity among organisms, more sustainable it is against environmental disturbances. e.g., India has more than 50,000 genetically different strains of rice.

(ii) **Species diversity** It is the diversity at the species level or the measure of variety of species and their abundance within a region. e.g., Western Ghats have more amphibian species diversity than Eastern Ghats.

(iii) **Ecological diversity** It refers to the diversity at ecosystem level due to the variety of ecosystem and habitat.
e.g., Flora and fauna found in deserts show differences with those found in grasslands.

Species Diversity on Earth and in India

- According to the **International Union for the Conservation of Nature and Natural Resources** (IUCN) (2004), the total number of plant and animal species described so far is slightly more than 1.5 million.
- According to **Robert May** the global species diversity is about 7 million. The global species diversity is with 70% animal species and 22% fungal and plant species.
- Among animals insects are the most species rich taxonomic group, making about 70% of the total. It means, out of every 10 animals, 7 are insects on the Earth.
- Although India has only 2.4% of the world's land area, its share of the global species diversity is 8.1%. This makes India one of the **12 megadiversity** countries of the world.

Patterns of Biodiversity

Following patterns of biodiversity are observed

Latitudinal Gradient

- Tropics (Latitudinal range of 23.5°N-23.5°S) harbour more species than temperate or polar areas.
- Tropical Amazonian rain forest in South America has the greatest biodiversity on Earth.
- It homes 40,000 species of plants, 3,000 of fishes, 1300 of birds, 427 of mammals, 427 of amphibians, 378 of reptiles and more than 1,25,000 invertebrates.

Species Area Relationship

- **Alexander von Humboldt** gave the concept of species area relationship based on his observations in the South American jungles.
- He observed that within a region species richness increases with increase in the explored area, but only upto a certain limit.
- The graph plotted between species richness and area of a wide variety of taxa gives a **rectangular hyperbola**.

Importance of Species Diversity to the Ecosystem

- An **ecosystem** is made up of all the plants, animals and microorganisms in an area along with non-living components such as climate, soil, river deltas, etc.
- According to ecologists, communities with more species tend to be more stable than those with less species.
- **David Tilman's** experiments on ecosystem showed that increased diversity contribute to higher productivity.
- **Paul Ehrlich** gave a **Rivet Popper Hypothesis** to explain the importance of biodiversity for the survival of species.

Loss of Biodiversity

- The biological wealth of our planet has been declining rapidly due to over population, urbanisation and industrialisation.
- Loss of biodiversity results in a decreased productivity (of that area) leading to environmental changes like drought, floods, cyclones, etc.
- The colonisation of tropical **Pacific Islands** by humans have led to the extinction of more than 2,000 species of native birds.
- The IUCN Red list, (2004) documents shows the extinction of 784 species (including 338 vertebrates, 359 invertebrates and 87 plants) in the last 500 years.
- Some latest examples of recent extinctions are **Dodo** (Mauritius), **Quagga** (Africa), **Thylacine** (Australia), **Steller's sea cow** (Russia) and three sub-species (Bali, Javan and Caspian) of tiger.
- The last twenty years alone have witnessed the disappearance of 27 species. Presently, 12% of bird species, 23% of all mammal species, 32% of all amphibian species and 31% of all gymnosperm species in the world face the threat of extinction.

Causes of Loss of Biodiversity

Major causes of the loss of biodiversity are as follows

- **Habitat loss and fragmentation** They possess a great threat to biodiversity as it is the major factor that contributes to plant and animal extinction.

  For example, lungs of the planet, i.e., **Amazon forests** are being cut for soyabean agriculture practices and other practices.
- **Overexploitation of resources** It has a major contribution towards environmental degradation as well as towards biodiversity loss. Plants and animals that have become **rare** or are now **endemic** (restricted to a specific area) were once over exploited for the resources that they provide.
- **Invasion of foreign species** The 'alien' species introduced, establish themselves in the new environment and spread unchecked. They affect the local population negatively. e.g Nile Perch, *Parthenium,* etc.
- **Coextinction** This phenomenon occurs when due to the extinction of one species, the other species dependent on it in a single or multiple ways, also become extinct.

The Red List

- The IUCN maintains a document called **Red List** or Red Data Book of taxa that are facing the risk of extinction.
- It divides species into nine categories :
  1. **Not Evaluated** (NE) It includes all those species that are not evaluated due to geographical barriers.
  2. **Data Deficient** (DD) A taxon is data deficient when there is inadequate information to make a direct or indirect, assessment of its risk of extinction based on its distribution and/or population status.

     A taxon in this category may be well studied and its biology is well known, but appropriate data on abundance and/or distribution are lacking.
  3. **Least Concern** (LC) A taxon is least concern when it has been evaluated against the Red List Criteria and does not qualify for critically endangered, vulnerable or near threatened. e.g., Giraffe, brown bear, gray wolf and house mouse.
  4. **Near Threatened** (NT) A taxon is near threatened when it has been evaluated against the criteria but does not qualify for critically endangered, endangered or vulnerable now, but is close to qualifying for or is likely to qualify for a threatened category in the near future. e.g., American bison, Jaguar, and tiger shark.
  5. **Vulnerable** (VU) A taxon is vulnerable when it is not critically endangered or endangered, but it is facing a high risk of extinction in the wild. e.g., African elephant, cheetah, polar bear and hippopotamus.

6. **Endangered** (EN) A taxon is endangered when the best available evidence indicates that it meets any of the criteria for endangered and it is therefore considered to be facing a very high risk of extinction in the wild. e.g., blue whale and tiger.
7. **Critically Endangered** (CR) A taxon is critically endangered when facing an extremely high risk of extinction in the wild. e.g., Bacteria camel and California condor.
8. **Extinct in the Wild** (EW) A taxon is extinct in the wild when it is known only to survive in cultivation, in captivity or as a naturalised population (or populations) well outside the past range.

   e.g., Hawaiian crow, Socorro dove and Scimitar Oryx.
9. **Extinct** (EX) A taxon is extinct when there is no reasonable doubt that the last individual has died. e.g., Javan Tiger, dodo and woolly mammoth.

Information in Red Data Book

- The Red Data Book contains colour-coded information sheets which are arranged according to the extinction risk of many species and sub-species.

  These are as follows :
  - **Black** represents species that are confirmed to be extinct.
  - **Red** represents species that are endangered.
  - **Amber** for those species whose status is considered to be vulnerable.
  - **White** is assigned for species that are rare.
  - **Green** for species that were formerly endangered but their numbers have started to recover.
  - **Grey** colour for the species that are classified as vulnerable, endangered or rare but sufficient information is not available to be properly classified.
- A study of the history of life on Earth through fossil records, shows that since (3 billion years) the origin and diversification of life on Earth, there were five episodes of mass extinction of species.
- Presently, the Earth is at the **sixth phase of mass extinction** which is mainly due to anthropogenic activities.
- The difference in the current species extinction rates and previous extinctions is that it is 100 to 1000 times faster than in the pre-human times.
- In general, loss of biodiversity in a region may lead to
  - Decline in plant production.
  - Lowered resistance to environmental perturbations such as drought.
  - Increased variability in certain ecosystem processes such as plant productivity, water use and pest and disease cycles.

Conservation of Biodiversity

- The plants and animals found in a particular area are termed **flora** and **fauna**. These are **endemic species.**
- They are not naturally found anywhere else. A particular type of animal or plant may be endemic to a zone, a state or a country.
- Biodiversity needs to be protected and conserved at all possible levels in order to derive sustainable benefits from it.
- Biodiversity conservation involves two main approaches i.e., *in-situ* and *ex-situ* conservation.

1. *InSitu* (On-site) Conservation

- This involves conservation of flora and fauna in their natural habitats and includes the following

Biodiversity Hotspot

- These areas were determined or brought into light by **Norman Myers** in 1988 as priority areas for *insitu* conservation.
- These are regions with very high levels of species richness and a high degree of endemism. There are 34 hotspots globally and cover less than 2% area of Earth's land.
- Hotspots which cover India's biodiversity regions are **Western Ghats** and **Sri Lanka, Indo-Burma** and **Himalayas.**

Protected Areas

- To protect our flora and fauna and their habitats, protected areas called **sanctuaries, national parks** and **biosphere reserves** have been setup.
- These are ecologically unique and biodiversity rich regions.
- Plantation, cultivation, grazing, felling trees, hunting and poaching are prohibited there.

Biosphere Reserves

- These are large areas of protected land for conservation of wildlife, plant and animal resources and traditional life of the tribals living in the area. A biosphere reserve may also contain other protected areas in it.
- A biosphere reserve consists of three zones :

  (i) **Core zone** It is a legally protected area which doesn't allow human intervention. It lies in the innermost side.

(ii) **Buffer zone** It is the area that surrounds core zone only research and education activities are allowed here.

(iii) **Transition zone** It is the peripheral area that allows human activities like cropping forestry and settlements can be found here.

- The **Panchmarhi Biosphere Reserve** of Madhya Pradesh consists of one national park named **Satpura** and two wildlife sanctuaries named **Bori** and **Pachmarhi**.
- There are 18 biosphere reserves in India as of 2021. Out of these 12 reserves are also part of United Nations Educational, Scientific and Cultural Organisation's (UNESCO), Man and Biosphere (MAB) programme established in 1986.
- These include Sunderbans, Great Nicobar Biosphere Reserve, Kanchenjunga Biosphere Reserve, Nilgiri Biosphere Reserve, etc.

National Parks

- The areas reserved for wildlife where they can freely use the habitats and natural resources.
- These are large and diverse enough to protect whole sets of ecosystems and are controlled by the central Government. They preserve flora, fauna, landscape and historic objects of an area.
- **Jim Corbett National Park** is India's first national park established in 1936. It is situated in Uttarakhand.
- **Satpura National Park** is the first Reserve forest of India. The finest Indian teak is found in this forest.
- Rock shelters are also found inside Satpura National Park. These are evidences of prehistoric human life in these jungles.
- There are 106 existing national parks in India covering an area of 44,402.95 km^2, which is 1.33% of the geographical area of the country according to **National Wildlife Database**, December 2020.

Wildlife Sanctuary

- Areas where animals and their habitat are protected from any rest of disturbance are called wildlife sanctuaries.
- These provide protection and suitable living conditions to wild animals.
- Sanctuaries are places where killing (Poaching) or capturing of animals is strictly prohibited.
- Some of the threatened wild animals like black buck, white eyed buck, elephant, golden cat, pink headed duck, gharial, marsh crocodile, phython, rhinoceros etc. are protected and preserved in our wild life sanctuaries.
- Indian sanctuaries have unique landscapes-broad level forests, mountain forests and bush lands in deltas of big rivers.
- There are 573 existing wildlife sanctuaries in India covering an area of 123762.56 km^2, which is 3.76% of the geographical area of the country (National Wildlife Database, December 2020).
- These include **Parambikulam wildlife sanctuary, Dandeli wildlife sanctuary, Gir wildlife sanctuary, Lockchao wildlife sanctuary**, etc.

Sacred Groves

- These are small groups of forests with special religious importance in a particular culture and are of mythological importance.
- These are undisturbed forests without any human interventions and remain protected by natures as a part of cultural traditions. e.g., **Khasi and Jaintia hills (Meghalaya) and Aravalli hills** (Rajasthan.)

Tiger Reserves

- Project Tiger is a tiger conservation programme launched in April 1973 by the Government of India and is still ongoing. It was launched in Jim Corbett National Park, Uttarakhand for the purpose of saving the tiger population from extinction in India.
- According to the **Tiger Census of 2018-2019** conducted in 20 states across India, 2967 tiger live in India. At present, there are about 53 tiger reserves in India.

2. *Ex-Situ* (Off-site) Conservation

- This approach involves placing the threatened flora and fauna in special care units so as to protect them.
- Zoological parks, botanical gardens, wildlife safari parks etc are examples of this method.
- Preservation of genes (in gene banks), seeds (in seed banks) and practices like cryopreservation (conservation of seeds, embryos, etc., at −196°C in liquid nitrogen) are a part of this method.

11

Agriculture Science and Animal Husbandary

[SOURCES]

Class-VIII NCERT Chap 1 (Crop Production and Management), Class-IX NCERT Chap 12 (Improvement in Food Resources)
Class-XII Old NCERT Chap 9 (Strategies for Enhancement of Food Production)
Tamil Nadu Board (Class-IX), NIOS

Agriculture Science

Agricultural science is a science that deals with food and fibre production and their processing. It is multi-disciplinary field of biology which include soil cultivation, crop cultivation, harvesting, processing, preservation and management. It basically deals with crop production and management.

Crops and Their Classification

When plants of the same kind are grown and cultivated at one place and on a large scale, it is called a **crop**.

Crops are classified on the basis of the following :

Types of Crops Based on Production

Crops are cultivated by human beings for their own benefit. The important types of crops are :

- **Cereal crops** These plants are cultivated to provide **carbohydrate** daily energy requirements. e.g., wheat, rice, maize, millets and *Sorghum* (provide carbohydrates for energy requirements).
- **Pulses** These are seeds of crops that can be eaten to fulfil **protein** requirement. e.g., gram (chana), pea (matar), black gram (urad), green gram (moong), pigeon pea (arhar), lentil (masoor), etc.
- **Oilseed crops** These plants provide necessary fats and oils. e.g., soyabean, groundnut, sesame, castor, mustard, linseed and sunflower, etc.
- **Vegetables, spices and fruits** These plants fulfill the requirement of a variety of vitamins and minerals with small quantities of proteins, carbohydrates and fats. e.g., cabbage, onion, pepper, etc.
- **Fodder crops** These plants are raised as food for the livestock. e.g., berseem, oats or sudan grass, etc.
- Different crops require different climate related conditions as well as different photoperiods. These conditions are required for completion of their life cycle.

Types of Crops Based on Seasons

Crops are classified on the basis of seasons as follows :

- **Kharif Crops** The crops which are sown in the rainy season are called Kharif crops. The rainy season in India is generally from June to September. Paddy, maize, soyabean, groundnut, cotton, etc., are the examples of Kharif crops.
- **Rabi Crops** The crops grown in the winter season are called Rabi crops. Their time period is generally from October to March. Examples of Rabi crops are wheat, gram, pea, mustard and linseed.
- **Zaid Crops** The crops grown in between Kharif and Rabi crops are called Zaid crops. e.g., watermelon, cucumber, pumpkin, etc.

Improvement in Crop Production

- The practices involved in farming to increase crop production can be divided into three stages :
  - The first is the **choice of seeds** for planting.
  - The second is the **nurturing of the crop plants**.
  - The third is the **protection of the growing and harvested crops from loss.**
- It is necessary to prepare soil by tilling and levelling. Plough hoe and cultivator are used for this purpose.
- Sowing of seeds is most important part of crop production. Before sowing, good quality seeds are selected. Then the seed drill are used for sowing with the help of tractors.
- There are two ways to incorporate desirable characteristics into crop varieties. These are

1. Hybridisation

- It is the crossing between genetically dissimilar plants to produce a new type (hybrid) or **High Yielding Variety** (HYV).
- It is further of following types :
  - **Intervarietal** The cross is made between two plants belonging to different varieties of crops. It is the most common method used in plant breeding.
  - **Interspecific** The cross is made between two plants belonging to different species of same genus.
  - **Intergeneric** The cross is made between plants belonging to different genera.

Genetically Modified Crops

- It involves the manipulation of crop plants for increasing their yield, improving quality, sustainability, etc.
- Genetic manipulation provides desired characteristics in the crop.

Factors for Crop Variety Improvement

Some of the factors for which crop variety improvement is done are as follows :

- **Higher Yield** Variety improvement is done to increase the productivity of the crop per acre.
- **Improved Quality** The definition of quality is different for different crops. e.g., baking quality is important in wheat, protein quality in pulses, oil quality in oilseeds and preserving quality in fruits and vegetables.
- **Biotic and Abiotic Resistance** Biotic stresses (diseases, insects and nematodes) and abiotic stresses (drought, salinity, water logging, heat, cold and frost) affect crop production to a great extent. Varieties resistant to such conditions are always preferred as they help to improve crop production.
- **Change in Maturity Duration** Short duration or period between sowing and harvesting makes a crop more economical. It allows the farmers to grow multiple rounds of crops in a year. It also reduces the cost of crop production. Uniform maturity makes the harvesting process easy. It also reduces losses during harvesting.
- **Wider Adaptability** Developing varieties that can grow and adapt to different conditions help in stabilising crop production. Thus, a single variety can be grown in different regions with different climatic conditions.
- **Desirable Agronomic Characteristics** These characteristics depict good growth and higher productivity in plants. Plants showing such characteristics are preferred more than others, e.g. tallness and profuse branching are preferred characters for fodder crops. Dwarfness is desired in cereals.

2. Crop Production Management

It involves the control of various aspects of crop production for the best yield. It requires skillful dealing with almost all aspects of crop production.

Preparation of Soil

- It is the first step before growing crops and involves **making the soil porous** so that roots can go deep into it in order to respire.
- **Turning the soil** and making it porous, also increases the growth of earthworms and other microbes.
- Process of turning of the soil and making it porous is known as **ploughing**. It is usually done with the help of cultivator.
- If the soil is very dry, it is watered first before ploughing.
- Earthen lumps found in the ploughed fields, should be broken.
- **Leveling of land** is done and time to time, manure is added before sowing.

Sowing

- It is the process of planting seeds in a moist humid soil.
- Usually, clean seeds which give high productivity are used and sowed at a regular distance so as to provides nutrients, sunlight and water in adequate amounts.
- Sowing is usually practiced with the help of seed drill conducted with the help of a tractor.

Nutrient Management

- Like animals, plants also require nutrients for their growth and development. Nutrients are the inorganic elements, which are supplied to plants by air, water and soil. There are sixteen essential nutrients for plants.
- Air supplies carbon, oxygen and hydrogen comes from water and soil supplies the other thirteen nutrients to plants. Amongst these thirteen nutrients, six are required in large quantities and therefore called **macronutrients** e.g., nitrogen, potassium, calcium, etc.
- The other seven nutrients are used by plants in small quantities and are therefore called **micronutrients** e.g., iron, manganese, boron, etc.
- Deficiency of any of these nutrients affects physiological processes in plants including reproduction, growth and susceptibility to disease.
- Nutrients can be supplied to the soil in the form of manure and fertilisers. It helps to increase the yield of crops.

1. Manures

- Manures are natural fertilisers. These are the organic substances formed by the decomposition of animal excreta and plant wastes.
- It supplies small quantities of nutrients to the soil.
- Based on the type of biological material used, manure can be classified as :
  (i) **Compost and Vermicompost** The process in which farm waste materials like cow dung, vegetable waste, domestic waste, sewage waste, straw, eradicated weeds, etc., are decomposed in pits, is known as **composting**.
  The compost is rich in organic matter and nutrients. Preparation of compost by using earthworms to hasten the process of decomposition of plant and animal refuse is called **vermicomposting**.
  (ii) **Green Manure** Some plants like sunhemp or guar are grown and mulched by ploughing into the soil before sowing of the crop seeds. These green plants turn into green manure. It helps in increasing nitrogen and phosphorus content in the soil. It also helps to improve hydration, aeration and crumb structure of the soil.
- Manure enriches soil with nutrients and organic matter (called humus). It increases soil fertility and decreases the harmful effects of pesticides and insecticides on soil.
- Manure helps in improving soil structure by increasing the water holding capacity in sandy soil. In clayey soil, large quantity of organic matter helps in drainage and avoiding water logging.
- Manure helps in the recycling of farm waste. By the use of biological waste material (manure), we can protect the environment from excessive use of fertilisers.

2. Fertilisers

- Fertilisers are commercially produced plant nutrients. They supply **Nitrogen**, **Phosphorus** and **Potassium** (NPK) to soil.
- Fertilisers are easily available, easy to use and store. They help in the higher yields of high-cost farming. They are used to ensure good vegetative growth (leaves, branches and flowers) and give rise to healthy plants.
- However, they have the following drawbacks :
  - Fertilisers need to be applied carefully in terms of proper dose, time and looking after the pre and post-application precautions for their complete utilisation.
  For example, excessive use of fertilisers can cause water pollution.
  - Continuous use of fertilisers can destroy soil fertility because the organic matter in the soil does not get replenished. Hence, microorganisms in the soil are harmed by the use of fertilisers. Thus, it provides short-term benefits.

Difference Between Fertiliser and Manure

Fertilisers	Manure
These are inorganic substances that are produced by man.	These are natural substances obtained by the decomposition of plant and animal remains by bacteria.
It does not provide humus to soil.	Provides humus to soil
Rich in plant nutrients such as nitrogen, phosphorous and potassium.	Less rich in plant nutrients.
e.g., Urea	e.g., Green manure

Organic Farming

- It is a farming system with minimal or no use of chemicals as fertilisers, herbicides, pesticides etc., and with a maximum input of organic manures, recycled farm wastes, use of bio-agents such as culture of blue green algae in preparation of biofertilisers.
- For storage purpose, biopesticides such as neem leaves or turmeric are used. These cropping systems are beneficial in insect, pest and weed control and in providing nutrients.

Irrigation

- The process of supplying water to crop plants in fields by means of canals, reservoirs, well, tubewells etc., is called irrigation.
- Most of agriculture depends on rain. Majority of the areas observe maximum harvest when there is maximum rainfall during monsoon.

- Timing and frequency of irrigation varies with crops, soil and season. Frequency of watering is relatively high in summer.

  Sources of irrigation are :

  (i) **Wells** are constructed wherever groundwater is present for irrigation. They are of two types:

  (a) **Dug wells** Water is collected from water bearing strata.

  (b) **Tube wells** Water can be drawn from deeper strata using pumps.

  (ii) **Canals** are an elaborate and extensively used methods of receiving water from reservoirs like dam or rivers. The main canal is further divided into other branches that have distributaries to irrigate fields.

  (iii) **River Lift Systems** is the method used in areas, where canal flow is insufficient or irregular due to insufficient reservoir release. Here, water is directly drawn from the rivers for supplementing irrigation in areas close to rivers.

  (iv) **Tanks** are small storage reservoirs. They catch and store the run-off of smaller catchment areas.

Modern Techniques of Irrigation

They include fresh initiatives for increasing water availability for agriculture by augmenting groundwater. They include :

- **Rainwater Harvesting** Rainwater is collected into ground by digging tunnels, etc. This water percolates into the soil, thus, maintaining the water table.
- **Watershed Development** Small check-dams are built to increase groundwater level. The purpose of check-dams is to stop the rainwater from flowing away and also to reduce soil erosion.

Irrigation Methods

Water available in wells, lakes and canals is transported to the fields *via* different methods in different areas as follows :

- **Traditional Methods of Irrigation** In these methods, cattle or labourers are made to work. These methods are cheap but less efficient.

  Following are the different traditional methods :

  (i) Pulley (ii) Chain pump
  (iii) Lever system (iv) Dhekli

- **Modern Methods of Irrigation** It involves economical use of water.

  (i) **Sprinkler System** It is a simple and an easy method of irrigation. Now-a-days water is provided to the fields by spraying water droplets, similar to rain, through pipes. This method encourages groundwater balance. It is required in areas where a change in temperature of earth, environment and humidity is seen.

  Continuous sprinkling of water improves physical conditions and composition of soil.

  (ii) **Drip System** This method involves dripping of water from small holes in the pipe lines laid down on fields. When water flows through the pipes, it drips at the place of the roots of the plants where it is absorbed and supplied further. No water is wasted in this.

Cropping Patterns

It involves raising crops so as to obtain maximum benefit from the same piece of land. It reduces the risk of crop failure, disease, etc.

For this purpose, crops can be grown in different ways. Some of them are

- **Mixed Cropping** In this practice, two or more crops are grown simultaneously on the same piece of land. e.g., Wheat + Gram, Wheat + Mustard, Groundnut + Sunflower, etc. mixed cropping improves soil fertility and avoids crop failure.
- **Intercropping** In this, two or more crops are grown simultaneously on the same field in a definite pattern. A few rows of one crop alternate with a few rows of other crop. The crops are selected as on the basis of their nutrient requirements.

  Two crops must have different nutrient requirements from each other. e.g., Soyabean + Maize, Finger millet (bajra) + Cowpea (lobia), etc. Intercropping ensure maximum utilisation of supplied nutrients and prevents the spread of pests.
- **Crop Rotation** In this type of practice, different crops are grown on a piece of land in a pre-planned succession. The crop combination depends upon the duration of crops.

  One crop is grown on a field and after its harvest, a second crop is grown on the same field. This can also follow a third crop. The crop to be chosen after one harvest depends upon the availability of moisture and irrigation facilities.

Crop Protection Management

It is very important to provide protection to crops from weeds, pests, insects, etc. Crop protection management reduces their chances as they harm the crops majorly.

Threat to Crops

- Weeds are the unwanted plants in the cultivated field. They compete with the crops for food, space and light. Examples of weeds are *Xanthium* (gokhroo), *Parthenium* (gajar ghas), *Cyperinus rotundus* (motha), *Amaranthus*, *Chenopodium*, wild oat, etc.
- **Weedicides** like 2, 4-D do not cause harm to the crop but kill the weeds.

- **Insect pest** affect the health of crop and reduce its yield. They attack the plants as they cut the root, stem and leaf. e.g., locusts.
- They suck the cell sap from various parts of the plant. e.g., aphids. They bore into stem and fruits. e.g., shoot borer larvae.
- Pests can be controlled by using resistant varieties and summer ploughing (i.e., fields are ploughed deep during summers to destroy weeds and pests).
- Diseases in plants are caused by pathogens such as bacteria, fungi and viruses. These pathogens are transmitted through the soil, water and air.

Plant Diseases Caused by Various Microorganisms

Plant diseases	Micro organisms	Mode of Transmissions
Citrus canker	Bacteria	Air
Rust of wheat (Wheat Rust)	Fungi	Air, seeds
Yellow vein mosaic of Lady finger	Virus	Insects
Bacterial blight of rice	Bacteria	Water

- Crop diseases can be controlled by the use of pesticides like herbicides, insecticides and fungicides.
- They are sprayed on crop plants in limited amounts. Excessive use of these chemicals is harmful to many species of plants and animals. They also cause environmental pollution.
- Harvesting of a crop is an important task. The cutting of crop after it mature is called **harvesting**.
- However, harvesting too early or too late both lead to crop loss.
- **Storing of grains** It can lead to loss of agricultural products. Following factors are responsible for these losses :
  - (i) **Biotic factors** These include rodents, bacteria, fungi, insects, etc.
  - (ii) **Abiotic factors** Because of lack of moisture and heat at the place of storage, there can be loss of grain. These have the following effects :
    - Deterioration of quality
    - Lack of germination
    - Loss of weight
    - Product discoloration

Animal Husbandry

- Animal husbandry is the scientific management of livestock. It can be defined as the science of rearing feeding, breeding, disease control and utilisation of animals. Animal based farming includes cattle, goat, poultry and fish farming.
- It is required to meet the increasing demands of animal based goods like milk, meat, eggs, leather, etc., according to the size of the population and living standards of the people.
- It sets guidelines for proper management and systematic approach to animal rearing.

Cattle Farming

- In India, cattle husbandry is done for getting milk and draught labour for agricultural work (such as tilling, irrigation and carting).
- Cattle in India belong to two different species :
  (i) *Bos indicus* (cows) (ii) *Bos bubalis* (buffaloes)
- On the basis of the workdone by cattle they can be divided into two categories :
  - **Milch animals** Milk producing females or dairy animals.
  - **Draught animals** Used for labour work in farms.

Breeds of Cattle

- These include **indigenous** or **local breeds** and **exotic** or **foreign** breeds.
  - Indigenous breeds are selected because of their high resistance to diseases. e.g., Sahiwal and Red Sindhi. These two breeds can be cross-breed to get both the desirable qualities in animals.
  - Exotic breeds are selected because of their long lactation period. e.g., Jersey and Brown Swiss.

Lactation Period and Requirements of Animals

- **Lactation period** is the period of milk production after the birth of a calf. Milk production largely depends on the duration of the lactation period. We can increase the milk production by increasing the lactation period.
- Food is required for dairy cattle maintenance and for producing milk. Food is required to support the animal to live a healthy life and for lactation period.
- Different types of animal feeds are roughage and concentrates. **Roughage** is largely fibrous and contain low nutrients, e.g., green fodder, silage, hay and legumes.
- **Concentrates** are low in fibre and contain relatively high levels of proteins and other nutrients for e.g., cereals like gram and bajra.
- Some feed additives containing micronutrients promote the health and milk output of dairy animals. Cattle should be given balanced ratios with all the nutrients in proportionate amounts.

Diseases in Cattles

Like other animals, cattles also suffers from a number of diseases. They are :

- **External Parasites** They live on the skin and cause skin diseases. e.g. lice, mites, etc.
- **Internal Parasites** They include worms that affect stomach and intestine and flukes that damage the liver.

Poultry Farming

- It involves rearing of domestic fowls for the production of eggs and chicken meat. Therefore, improved poultry breeds are developed and farmed to produce layers for eggs and broilers for meat.
- For the improvement of poultry breeds, cross breeding is done successfully between Indian or indigenous (e.g., Aseel) and foreign or exotic (e.g., Leghorn) breeds.
- These cross-breeding programmes focus to develop :
  - Desirable traits like quality and quantity (number) of chicks.
  - Dwarf broiler parent for commercial chick production.
  - Summer adaptation capacity/tolerance to high temperature.
  - Low maintenance requirements and reduction in the size of egg-laying bird with the ability to utilise more fibrous cheaper diets. This diet is formulated using agricultural byproducts.

Egg and Broiler Production

- Broilers and egg layers have different housing, nutritional and environmental requirements.
- Broiler chickens are fed with vitamin rich supplementary feed for good growth rate and better feed efficiency.
- Care is taken to avoid mortality and to maintain feathering and carcass quality. They are produced as broilers and sent to market for meat purposes.
- The diet of broilers is rich in protein with adequate fat. In the poultry feed, the level of vitamin-A and K is kept high.

Maintenance of Shelter

- It is done by proper cleaning, and sanitation of the shelter, maintenance of temperature and hygiene in the shelter, proper ventilation, prevention and control of diseases and pests.

Poultry Diseases and Their Prevention

- Poultry fowl suffer from various diseases caused by virus, bacteria, fungi and parasites.
- They also suffer from nutritional deficiency diseases. These diseases can be prevented by providing nutritional diet to poultry birds, proper cleaning and sanitation of shelter.
- Vaccination of poultry birds can prevent the occurrence of infectious diseases. Loss of poultry during an outbreak of disease can also be reduced by proper vaccination and spraying of disinfectants at regular intervals in the shelter.

Fish Production

- Fish is a cheap source of animal protein for humans. Production of fish includes both finned true fish as well as shellfish like prawns and molluscs.
- The two ways of obtaining fish are **capture fishing** (i.e., the method of obtaining fish from natural resources) and **culture fishery** (i.e., the method of obtaining fish from fish farming or pisciculture).
- Capture fishing is undertaken in both inland and marine waters. Culture fishery is undertaken mostly in inland and near seashore. Both methods can be used for fishing in marine and freshwater ecosystems.
- Marine fishery resources in India include 7500 km of coastline and the deep seas beyond it. Marine fishes are caught using many kinds of fishing nets from fishing boats. Popular marine fishes are pomfret, mackerel, tuna, sardines and Bombay duck.
- Marine fishes of high economic value that are farmed in seawater are finned fishes and shell fishes.
- Mullets, bhetki and pearl shots are **finned fishes**.
- Prawns, mussels, oysters and seaweeds are shellfish. Oysters are also cultivated for the pearls they produce. Yield of fishes can be increased by locating large school of fish in the open sea with the use of satellite and echo sounder.

Mariculture

- As marine fish stocks get further depleted, the demand for more fish can only be met by culture fisheries. This practice is called **mariculture**.
- The marine fishes are cultivated in coastal waters of India on commercial basis. It includes mullets, bhetki, eel, milk fish, etc.

Inland Fisheries

- It includes fishery in freshwater and brackish water. Freshwater resources include canals, ponds, reservoirs and rivers. Brackish water resources are those where sea water and freshwater mix together. e.g., estuaries and lagoons. These are also important fish reservoirs.
- The yield of capture fishing is not high in such inland water bodies. Thus, most fish production from these resources is done through aquaculture.
- Sometimes fish culture is done in combination with rice crops. In this, paddy crop gets ample of water and fishes get food.
- Fish production by cultivating a single species (monoculture) gives a low yield and demands higher cost.
- In composite fish culture, a combination of 5 or 6 fish species is cultivated in a single pond having different food habits. Due to this, they do not compete for food with each other. Thus, it helps in more intensive fish farming.

Fish Culture

- It is the process of raising desirable species of fishes in captivity and managing them in their environment to improve growth and reproduction.

Advantages of Composite Fish Culture

- Both local and imported fish species are used, due to different food habits all the food in pond is consumed by the fishes and the fish yield from pond is high as there is no competition for food.
- For example, *Catla* is surface feeder, Rohu feeds in the middle zone of the pond, Mrigal and common carps are bottom feeders, grass carp feeds on weeds in the pond.

Disadvantages of Composite Fish Culture

- Many of the fishes breed only during monsoon. Thus, one of the major problem of fish farming is the lack of availability of good quality seed.
- To overcome this problem, fishes are breed in ponds using hormonal stimulation. It ensures the supply of pure fish seed in desired quantities.

Beekeeping

- Honey is being widely used for various purposes. Thus, its production has become an agricultural enterprise these days. It is scientifically known as **apiculture**.
- It is the method of rearing, care and management of honeybees for obtaining bee products like honey bee wax (used in medicinal preparations) etc.

  For commercial honey production, apiaries or bee farms are established.
- Since, beekeeping needs low investments, farmers use it as an additional income generating activity. In addition to honey, the beehives are a source of wax which is used in various medicinal preparations.
- The local varieties of bees used for commercial honey production are *Apis cerana indica*, commonly known as the **Indian bee**, *A. dorsata*, the rock bee and *A. florae*, the little bee.
- An Italian bee variety, *A. mellifera*, has also been brought into increase yield of honey. This is the variety commonly used for commercial honey production.
- The Italian bees have high honey collection capacity.
- They stay in a given beehive for long periods and breed very well.
- For commercial honey production, bee farms or apiaries are established.
- The value, quality and taste of honey depends upon the pasturage or the flowers available to the bees for nectar and pollen collection.

Animal Breeding

- Animal breeding is an important part of animal husbandry.
- It aims to increase the yield of animals and improve the desirable qualities of produce.
- A breed is a group of animals related by descent and similar in most characters like general appearance, features, size, configuration, etc.
- Breeding can be of following types :
  - (i) **Inbreeding** It is the mating of closely-related individuals for 4-6 generations. Increasing homozygosity leads to the loss of variation and stabilisation of pureline. Continued inbreeding results in the loss of productivity, i.e., inbreeding depression.
  - (ii) **Outbreeding** The mating between two unrelated individuals is outbreeding. It is further of three types :
    - (a) **Out crossing** It is mating between unrelated members of same breed, but have no common ancestors in 4-6 generations. The resultant individuals is known as **out cross.**
    - (b) **Cross-breeding** It refers to the cross of superior male of one breed with superior females of another breed. e.g., Bikaneri (ewes) and Merino (ram) to give Hisardal (sheep).
    - (c) **Interspecific Hydridisation** It refers to the crossing between male and female animal of two different species. e.g., Mule and Hinny.

Extra Facts From Tamil Nadu Board and NIOS

- Earthworms and microbes are friends of the farmer since they further turn and loosen the soil and add humus to it.
- Hoe is a simple tool which is used for removing weeds and for loosening the soil.
- Sprinkler is very useful for lawns, coffee plantation and several other crops.
- Farmers with small holding of land do the separation of grain and chaff by winnowing.
- Farmers store grains in jute bags or metallic bins. However, large scale storage of grains is done in silos and granaries to protect them from pests like rats and insects.
- Dried neem leaves are used for storing food grains at home.
- In India, there has been a four times increase in the production of food grains from 1952 to 2010 with only 25% increase in the cultivable land area.
- Varieties or strains of crops can be selected by breeding for various useful characteristics such as disease resistance, response to fertilisers, product quality and high yields.

12

Environmental Issues

[SOURCES]

Class-VI Old NCERT Chap 16 (Garbage In, Garbage Out), Class-VII NCERT Chap 13 (Waste Water Story), Class-VIII Old NCERT Chap 18 (Pollution of Air and Water), Class-IX Old NCERT Chap 14 (Natural Resources), Class-X NCERT Chap 13 (Our Environment), Class-X Old NCERT Chap 18 (Management of Natural Resources), Class-XII Old NCERT Chap 16 (Environmental Issues) Tamil Nadu Board (Class-IX), NIOS

Pollution

- Any undesirable change in the physical, chemical and biological characteristics of air, water, land and soil is called **pollution.**
- **Pollutants** are agents that cause undesirable change in the environment.
- There are substances in the environment which can be completely degraded and some which do not. Based on this substances can be categorised as follows :
  - (i) **Biodegradable substances** These substances can be disposed off naturally by the action of microorganisms (e.g., bacteria, fungi) or can be put to treatment by waste management plants.

    In large quantity, they act as **pollutant**, release foul smell, serve as breeding ground for flies, etc. e.g., wood, animal bones, paper, fruit and vegetable peels, etc.
  - (ii) **Non-biodegradable Substances** These are toxic, inert substances that cannot be converted into harmless forms by the action of microorganisms or other means. They get accumulated in environment. e.g., radioactive waste, mercury, plastic, insecticides, heavy metals like lead, arsenic, aluminium, etc.

    The Government of India has passed the **Environment Protection Act, 1986** to protect and improve the quality of our environment (air, water and soil).

Types of Pollution

Pollution is of following types :

(i) Air Pollution (ii) Water Pollution
(iii) Noise Pollution (iv) Land Pollution
(v) Radioactive Pollution

Air Pollution

- It is an undesirable change in the physical, chemical or biological characteristics of air. It is caused due to an increase in the content of harmful substances (air pollutants) in air such as oxides of nitrogen and sulphur, etc.
- Air is the basis of life for every living being. Any change in its quality affects our lives immediately.
- The famous **Bhopal Gas Tragedy** had excessive release of methyl isocyanate gas which become a cause of hundreds of deaths across India.

Cause of Air Pollution

Following are the causes of air pollution :

- Combustion of natural and synthetic hydrocarbon based fuels which result in release of gases like CO_2, O_3, NO_2, CO, SO_2, etc.
- Various radioactive substances which are released into the atmosphere as a result of human activities.

- Chemicals used in agricultural practices to increase the yields of crops. However, their excessive use is responsible for air pollution.
- Deforestation (cutting down of trees) is a major factor which affects the CO_2–O_2 balance and hence, is responsible for increasing levels of harmful gases.
- Industrial waste which comprise of harmful gases, metal pieces and hydrocarbons.

Harmful Effects of Air Pollution

- Air pollution affects the respiratory system causing breathing difficulties and diseases such as bronchitis, asthma, lung cancer, tuberculosis and pneumonia.
- Burning of fossil fuels like coal and petroleum releases oxides of nitrogen and sulphur. Inhalation of these gases is dangerous. These gases also dissolve in rain to give rise to **acid rain.**
- The combustion of fossil fuel also increases the amount of suspended particles in air. These suspended particles could be unburnt carbon particles or substances called **hydrocarbons.**
- The presence of high levels of all these pollutants, reduce visibility in cold weather where water also condenses out of air forming **smog**. Smog is an indication of air pollution.
- Incomplete burning of coal and petroleum produce carbon monoxide (CO) instead of CO_2. CO has more affinity to bind with oxygen. Hence, if inhaled can cause death of the person.
- Other effects of air pollution are **global warming** and **ozone depletion.**

Ozone Depletion

- Ozone (O_3) is a molecule formed by three atoms of oxygen and is a deadly poison. It is found in the stratosphere, i.e., 20-30 km above Earth.
- Ozone at the highest levels of the atmosphere is a product of UV radiations acting on oxygen (O_2) molecules.
- The layer of atmosphere in which most of the atmosphere's ozone is concentrated is called **ozone layer.** It shield's the surface of the Earth from the harmful ultraviolet (UV) radiations of the Sun.
- These radiations are highly damaging to organisms. They can cause **skin cancer** in human beings, **damage eyes** (cause disease called cataract), **decrease crop yield, disturb global rainfall**, etc.
- Various man-made compounds like chlorofluorocarbons or **CFCs** (carbon compounds having both fluorine and chlorine) which are very stable and are not degraded by any biological process, reach the ozone layer. They react with ozone layer. It results in the reduction or thinning of ozone layer. It has already resulted in an ozone hole above **Antarctica** in 1985.

Methods to Control Air Pollution

- To prevent Taj Mahal corrosion, Supreme Court of India has ordered industries around Agra to switch to cleaner fuels like CNG (Compressed Natural Gas) and LPG (Liquified Petroleum Gas). Moreover, the automobiles should switch over to unleaded petrol in the Taj Zone.
- Cutting down the use of fossil fuels, improving efficiency of energy usage, reducing deforestation, planting trees, slowing down the growth of human population, etc.
- Taking international initiatives to reduce the emission of greenhouse gases into the atmosphere like **Kyoto Protocol.**
- **Montreal Protocol** was signed at Montreal (Canada) in 1987 (effective in 1989) to control the emission of ozone depleting substances.
- Use of Electrostatic Precipitator (ESP) and scrubbers in industrial exhausts.
- Use of catalytic converter in automobiles for reducing emission of poisonous gases like $_2$ and CO.
- Promoting practices for afforestation as plants/trees balance out the CO_2-O_2 ratio.
- Avoiding the use of private transport and using public transport.
- Use of biofuels, biogas, etc., in place of petrol and diesel.
- Heavy metals and Suspended Particulate Matter (SPM) particles can be separated by using cyclone filter and bag filter.

Water Pollution

- It is contamination of water of rivers and lakes with unwanted and harmful substances.
- Water is said to be polluted when there is any physical, biological or chemical change in its quality that adversely affects living organisms and makes it unfit for use.
- It affects the balance among various organisms that are found in water bodies.

Causes of Water Pollution

Following are the causes of water pollution :

- Agricultural substance such as fertilisers and pesticides are used to increase crop yield and some percentage of these are washed away into the water bodies that pollute the water.
- Sewage from homes and wastes from factories are dumped into rivers or lakes.

- Hot and cold water discharged from industries make a change in temperature, which is harmful for aquatic organisms.
- Presence of saline (high saline content) substances.
- Water that condenses from acid rain is also a major cause of water pollution.
- Mixing of polluted water and other chemicals released from industries with clean water.
- Oil spills.

Harmful Effects of Water Pollution

- The substances like fertilisers and pesticides used in farming and mercury salts used by paper industries could be poisonous.
- There could also be disease-causing organisms, like the bacteria which causes cholera.
- Industrial and household wastes reduce the dissolved oxygen in water bodies, thereby affecting the aquatic life.
- This can cause following effects :
  - **Algal Bloom** It is excessive growth of planktonic (free-floating) algae in aquatic bodies. In domestic sewage, nutrients like **nitrogen** and **phosphorus** favours the growth of algal bloom. It causes fish mortality and deterioration of water quality.
  - **Accelerated Eutrophication** It refers to accelerated ageing of lakes due to sewage, agricultural and industrial wastes or due to man's activities.
  - **Biological Magnification** It can be defined as an increase in concentration of toxicants at successive trophic levels in aquatic food chain. This is best described by the example of DDT transmission from pond to the hawk bird.
- Chemicals affect the reproductive rate of the organism and its calcium metabolism which results in thinning of the eggs shells and their untimely death leading to a decline in bird pollution.
- Aquatic organisms can stay alive in a certain range of temperature.
- Hot water released from industries can cause sudden change in temperature of water bodies, which is dangerous for aquatic organisms and can also affects their breeding.
- Fluoride water is a cause of dental problems.
- Due to heavy metals like cadmium, arsenic, lead, etc. deadly diseases like cancer occur.
- Reduction in the level of potable water (the water suitable for drinking). About 25% of world's population is without safe drinking water.

Method to Control Water Pollution

- Water treatment plants should be installed in all industrial areas.
- Laws for industrial units should be strictly implemented so that polluted water is not disposed off directly into rivers and lakes.
- At individual levels, people should consciously save water and not waste it.
- The rainwater can be used to recharge the ground water. This is referred to as **rainwater harvesting**.
- Implementing **water resource management** like building of dams, tanks and canals to minimise requirements for both agriculture and daily needs.
- Optimising cropping pattern based on water availability.
- Farmers can use water economically by **drip irrigation technique**.
- It is a technique of watering plants by making use of narrow tubings which deliver water directly at the base of the plant.
- The Government of India has passed the **Water Prevention and Control of Pollution Act, 1974** to safeguard water resources.

Ganga Pollution and Ganga Action Plan (GAP)

- Ganga runs over 2500 km from Gangotri in Himalayas to Ganga Sagar in Bay of Bengal.
- It is one of the ten most endangered rivers in the world.
- It is highly polluted due to several human activities like washing clothes, immersion of ashes, chemical effluents of industries, coliform bacteria of human intestine, etc.
- **GAP** was launched by Government of India in April 1985 in order to reduce pollution load on Ganga river.
- This plan failed to decrease the pollution level of river even after spending ₹ 901.71 crore over a period of 15 years.
- The Ganga at Kanpur in Uttar Pradesh has one of the most polluted stretches of the river. Kanpur is one of the most populated towns in Uttar Pradesh.

Soil Pollution

- Removal of useful components from the soil and addition of hazardous substances (both solid and liquid) into it, is called soil pollution.
- It destroys the soil structure by killing the microorganisms that recycle nutrients in the soil. It also kills the earthworms, which are helpful in making humus.
- Fertile soil can quickly become unfertile, if sustainable practices are not followed. One of the major cause of soil pollution is modern farming practices.

- They involve the use of large amount of pesticides and fertilisers. These substances adversely affect the soil fertility.

Soil Erosion

- It is the removal and thinning of the fertile top soil from a region due to climatic and physical processes, such as high rainfall and wind, etc.
- Soil erosion occurs easily where the soil is not covered by vegetation.
- Wind, heavy rainfall, improper farming, frequent floods and deforestation leads to soil erosion.
- Soil erosion can be prevented by :
  - Intensive cropping.
  - Providing proper drainage canals around the fields.
  - Terrace framing in hilly areas.
  - Planting trees and sowing grasses.
  - Construction of strong embankments along the river banks.

Harmful Effects of Soil Pollution

- Non-target organisms are killed in the soil due to pesticides.
- Soil becomes unfertile.
- Pesticides can result in biomagnification, as well eutrophication.
- Reduced crop productivity.
- Harmful chemicals when get involved in food chain become a cause of various diseases.

Control Methods of Soil Pollution

- Strict ways should be adopted by the industries and other sources for waste disposal.
- Use of organic farming is a cyclic zero waste method, where waste products from one process are cycled in as nutrients for other processes.
  It allows maximum utilisation of resources and increasing the efficiency of production.
- Reducing the use of chemical fertilisers.
- Establishing industries at lands which are not suitable for agriculture and are at a distance.
- Taking proper precautions while disposing radioactive substances.

Noise Pollution

- Noise pollution is undesirable high level of sound. In India, the **Air Prevention and Control of Pollution Act** came into force in 1981, but was amended in 1987 to include noise as an air pollutant.
- Sound is expressed in decibels (dB). A sound of over 115 dB is very harmful for ears. Prolonged exposure to noise level above 80 dB leads to permanent hearing loss.
- Use of loudspeakers and music system, jet planes and rockets during take off, industrial and factory noise contribute to noise pollution.
- Harmful effects of noise pollution includes sleeplessness, stress, increased heartbeat, breathing problems, damage to ear drums and impaired hearing ability.

Control of Noise Pollution

- By applying sound absorbent materials or by muffling noise in industrial units.
- Delimitation of horn-free zones around hospitals and schools.
- Strict laws for permissible sound levels of crackers and loudspeakers should be followed.
- Loudspeakers should be played up to a fixed time only.

Radioactive Pollution

- These are wastes that release radioactive particles (emission of α-particles, β-particles or γ-rays) from nuclides of their elements.
- These are invisible harmful radiations which result from the natural disintegration of atomic nuclei of radioactive elements like Uranium, Thorium, Plutonium etc.
- These radiations have serious effects on environment and living organisms.

Harmful Effects of Radioactive Pollution

- The most common disease that arises in people which have been exposed in radioactive pollution is **cancer**.
- α-rays cannot penetrate the skin but can cause damage to DNA.
- β-rays are capable of causing **cancer** and **cataract**.
- γ-rays cause **mutations**.
- X-rays cause **skin cancer**.

Control of Radioactive Pollution

- Prohibition of nuclear weapons.
- Reducing the number of nuclear power stations.
- Establishing nuclear power plants away from a densely populated area. Proper disposal of radioactive waste from nuclear power stations.

Solid Waste and Its Management

- These are discarded solid materials produced due to various human activities.
- These include wastes like paper, scraps, leather, rubber textile, glass, disinfectants, flyash and heavy

metals like lead, mercury, cadmium, etc. which are a part of e-waste.

- **Urbanisation development, increasing population** and several other factors result in generation of tonnes of solid waste every day.
- Solid waste can be divided into two categories :
  - **Biodegradable substances** e.g., vegetable peels, plants, flowers, etc.
  - **Non-biodegradable substances** e.g plastic, glass, etc

Methods of Solid Waste Disposal

There are various methods for solid waste disposal, which are as follows :

- **Recycling** It is done in specifically built facilities or manually. It is the only way to manage e-waste provided it is done in ecofriendly way.
- **Sanitary Landfills** These are areas where wastes are dumped in a depression or trench after compaction and covered with dirt. These are considered as an alternative to open-burning.
- **Composting** It is the rotting and conversion of biodegradable plant and animal waste, which also includes kitchen waste into organic manure in a controlled manner with the help of **bacteria** and **fungi**. It is environment-friendly practice.
- **Biogas Production** Sewage and other biodegradable substances are used for the production of biogas.
- **Open-burning** It involves burning of municipal waste in open dumps to reduce volume. This technique is suitable for infectious and toxic waste and involves two techniques :
  - **Incineration** It involves burning of wastes, specifically hospital wastes containing pathogens, disinfectants and other harmful chemicals at high temperatures of about 900 – 1200°C with release of various harmful gases.
  - **Pyrolysis** It is a thermochemical treatment where the material is burnt at temperature ranging from 600 – 800°C in closed vessel. However, it is done in anaerobic conditions i.e., oxygen is not involved.

Extra Facts From Tamil Nadu Board and NIOS

- The amount of ozone in the atmosphere began to drop sharply in 1980s.
- In 1987, the United Nations Environment Programme (UNEP) succeeded in forging an agreement to freeze CFC production at 1986 levels.
- It is now mandatory for all the manufacturing companies to make CFC-free refrigerators throughout the world.

13

Biotechnology

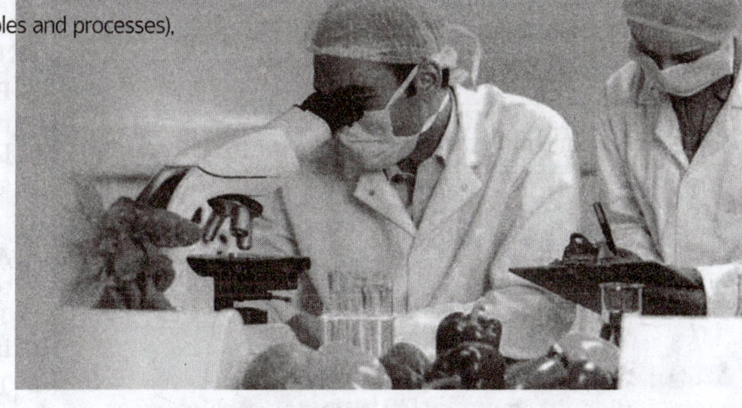

(SOURCES)

Class-XII NCERT Chap 9 (Biotechnology) : Principles and processes), Chap 10 (Biotechnology and Its Application).

- **Biotechnology** is an integrated branch of biology, which deals with the technique of using live organisms or enzymes from organisms in order to produce different products and processes useful to humans.
- The term (biotechnology) was coined by **Karl Ereky** in 1917. It encompasses both traditional and modern biotechnology.

Techniques of Biotechnology

Two core techniques that enabled birth of modern biotechnology are :

(i) **Genetic Engineering** It refers to the techniques used for modification of chemical nature of genetic material (DNA/RNA) and their introduction into another organism (host) to change the phenotypic characters of that organism. It is also called **Tailoring of DNA.** **Paul Berg** is known as the **Father of Genetic Engineering.**

(ii) **Sterilisation Methods** (Chemical Engineering) These methods are used to maintain microbial contamination free conditions in chemical engineering processes to enable the growth and manipulation of only the desired microbes or cells. It is used to get large quantities of products like vaccines, enzymes, antibiotics, etc.

Recombinant DNA Technology (RDT)

It is a technique of genetic engineering, which combines two genes from two different sources to create a new recombinant gene.

Recombinant DNA was first created by **Stanley Cohen** and **Herbert Boyer** in 1972.

Tools of Recombinant DNA Technology

The key tools involved in Recombinant DNA Technology are

Enzymes

Enzymes are involved in genetic engineering, which simplify this complex process. The various enzymes involved are

Restriction Enzymes (Molecular Scissors)

- These are enzymes, which are used for cutting of DNA at specific locations.
- Restriction enzymes belong to a larger class of enzymes called **nucleases**, which are of two types
  - (a) **Exonucleases** that remove nucleotides from the ends of the DNA (either 5′ or 3′) in one strand of duplex.
  - (b) **Endonucleases** make cut at specific position within the DNA.

DNA Ligases (Molecular Glue)

These enzymes repair broken DNA fragments by joining two nucleotides.

Alkaline Phosphate

This enzyme removes the phosphate group from the 5′ end of a DNA molecule, leaving a free 5′ hydroxyl group, which prevents unwanted self-ligation of vector DNA molecules during the formation of *r*DNA.

DNA Polymerases

This enzyme helps in *in-vitro* synthesis of complementary DNA (*c*DNA) strand on DNA templates.

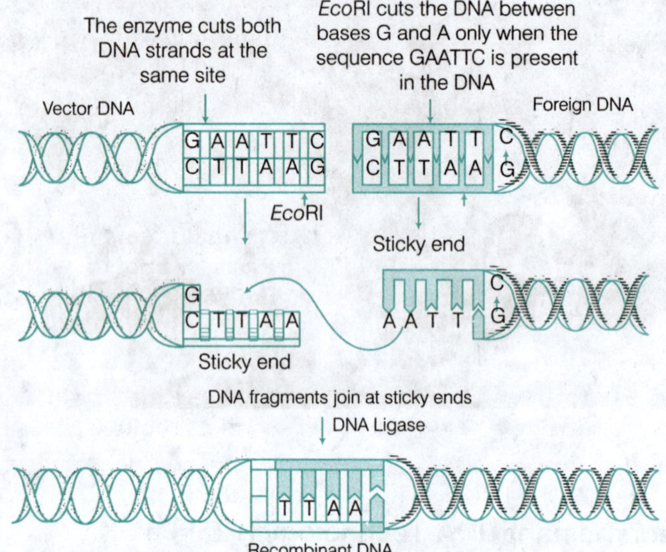

Recombinant DNA by action of Restriction Enzyme-EcoRI

Cloning Vectors

The DNA molecule that can carry a foreign DNA segment and replicate inside the host cell is called as a **vector**. These vectors have the ability to replicate within bacterial cells independent of the control of chromosomal DNA.

Following features are required for facilitating successful cloning into a vector :

Origin of Replication (Ori)

- It is a sequence from where replication starts and any piece of DNA when linked to this sequence can be made to replicate within host cells.
- This sequence also controls the copy number of linked DNA. It allows for autonomous replication and thus, the carrier can produce multiple copies of itself in host cells.
- Thus, it proves to be helpful in obtaining a high number of target DNA.

Selectable Marker

- It helps in identifying and eliminating non-transformants and selectively permitting the growth of transformants.
- Genes encoding resistance to antibiotics like ampicillin tetracycline, etc. are considered useful selectable marker for *E.coli*.

Cloning Sites

These are sites where DNA are inserted into the vector. **Restriction enzyme** recognises the site and makes cut in the DNA.

Usually, to avoid the process getting complex, there should only be one restriction site.

Following vectors are commonly used in recombinant DNA technology :

- **Plasmids** are small, autonomously replicating, usually circular, extrachromosomal double stranded DNA molecules that occurs in many bacteria and some yeast. e.g., *E.coli* containing vector p^{BR322}.
  p^{BR322} plasmid has tet^R. amp^R genes.
- A foreign DNA can be ligated at the BamHI site of tetracycline resistance (tet^R) gene in the vector p^{BR322}. This recombinant plasmid exhibits growth when kept in **ampicillin** rich medium.
- The recombinant plasmid do not increase in number when placed on tet^R medium and aids in selection of recombinants. Recombinants grow in ampicillin containing medium but non-transformants grow on both mediums.
- **Bacteriophages** are viruses infecting bacteria. They are used as the vector because of very high copy number of their genome within the bacterial cells.
- In plants, the Tumour inducing (Ti) plasmid of *Agrobacterium tumefaciens* (a pathogen of several dicot plants) is used as a cloning vector.
- This bacteria transfers a segment of *t*DNA to normal plant cells and converts them into tumour cells. These tumour cells produce chemicals for the pathogen.
- The proper vector for cloning in animal cells is SV40. Similarly, retrovirus, adenovirus, papilloma virus are also used as a cloning vector in animals because of their ability to transform normal cells into cancerous cells.

Competent Host Organism for Transformation with Recombinant DNA

- DNA is a hydrophilic molecule, so it cannot pass through cell membrane. In order to force bacterial cell to take up the plasmid, they must first be made competent.
- The cells can be made competent by following methods like heat shock, microinjection and biolistic/gene gun.

Process of Biotechnology or Recombinant DNA Technology

It involves the following steps in sequence :

- Isolation of the genetic material (DNA).
- Cutting of DNA at specific locations.
- Isolation of desired DNA fragment
- Amplification of Gene of Interest using Polymerase Chain Reaction (PCR).
- Ligation of DNA fragment into a vector.
- Insertion of recombinant DNA into the host cell/organism.
- The cell containing the foreign gene is cultured on an appropriate medium at optimal conditions.
- The desired protein encoding gene expressed in a heterologous host is called **recombinant protein.**

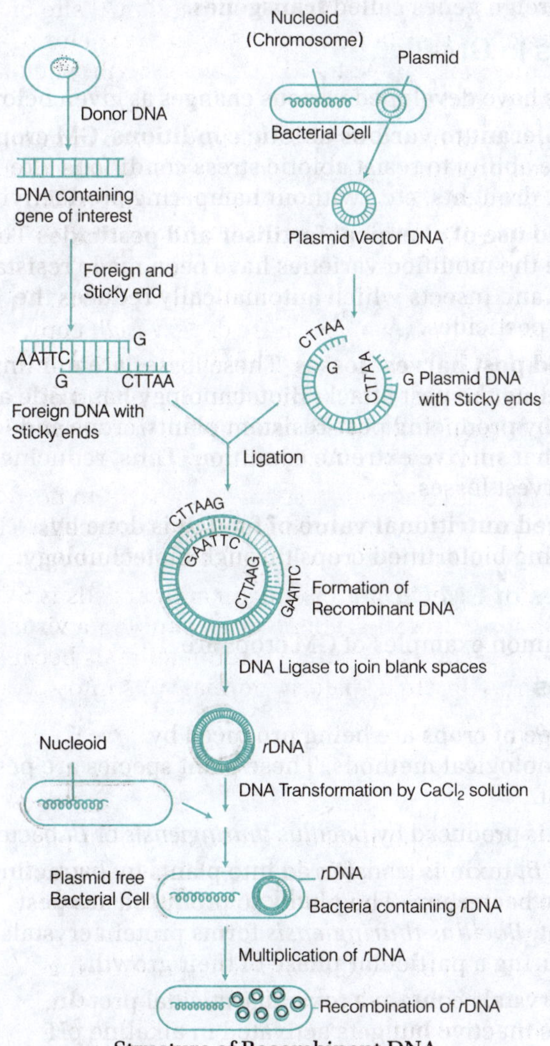

Structure of Recombinant DNA

Biotechnological Applications in Medicines

The recombinant DNA technological processes have made immense impact in the area of health care by enabling the mass production of safe and more effective therapeutic drugs.

Genetically Engineered Insulin

- Insulin is a short proteinaceous hormone secreted by the β-cells of the pancreas. It regulates glucose levels in blood.
- Deficiency of this hormone-leads to increased blood glucose levels as a result, the β-cells fail to synthesise sufficient glucose and the condition leads to **diabetes mellitus.**
- **Frederick Sanger** (1955) discovered that the insulin obtained from the pancreas of cow has two polypeptide chains α and β with 21 and 30 amino acid chain joined together by disulphide bonds.
- Mammals including human synthesise insulin as **pro-hormone** with an extra peptide 'C'. It gets matured by the action of proteases as C-peptide is removed.
- Human insulin was successfully produced for patients suffering with diabetes in the year 1983.
- Eli lily an American company, prepared two DNA sequences which were in correspondening to A and B chains of human insulin and introduced them into plasmids of *E. coli* to produce insulin chains.
- Chains A and B were separately produced, extracted and combined by disulfide bonds to form **human insulin.**

Gene Therapy

It is the replacement of a defective or faulty gene with normal healthy ones to correct a genetic disorder. It is used to correct ADA (Adenosine Deaminase) deficiency as follows

- Lymphocytes are isolated from the blood or bone marrow of the patient and grown in a culture outside the body.
- The normal functional ADA DNA is then introduced into the cultured lymphocytes, which are subsequently returned to the patient.
- These cells have a limited life, so the patient requires repeated infusion of such genetically engineered lymphocytes.

Gene therapy, was first used in 1990 to treat a four-year old girl who lacked enzyme **adenosine deaminase** essential for successful functioning of immune system.

Stem Cell Technology

The potential applications of stem cell include organ and tissue regeneration, bone marrow transplantation, brain disease treatment, etc.

Molecular Diagnosis

- For effective treatment of diseases, early diagnosis and understanding their pathophysiology is very important.
- By using conventional methods of diagnosis (serum and urine analysis), early detection of diseases is not possible.
- Recombinant DNA technology, PCR (Polymerase Chain Reaction) and Enzyme-Linked Immuno-Sorbent Assay (ELISA) are some of the techniques that serve the purpose of early diagnosis.
- **ELISA or Enzyme linked Immuno Sorbent Assay** is based on the principle of antigen-antibody interaction. Infection by pathogen can be detected by the presence of antigens or by detecting antibodies produced against the pathogen.
- **PCR or Polymerase Chain Reaction** is done when the bacteria or viruses are in small numbers. It multiplies their nucleic acids and thus, helps us identify them. The technique is also used to detect mutations in the genes of suspected cancer patients.
- **Blotting techniques** are used to detect DNA (Southern blotting), RNA (Northern blotting) or proteins (Western blotting).

  In this method, single stranded DNA or RNA having a radioactive molecule is hybridised to its own complimentary DNA from the one obtained in test cells. This is identified using auto-radiography.

Transgenic Animals

- Those animals whose genome has been modified by genes obtained from other species are called **transgenic** animals or **Genetically Modified** (GM) animals.

Benefits of Transgenic Animals

- Study of normal physiology and development.
- Study of diseases like cancer, cystic fibrosis, etc.
- To obtain biologically improved products, e.g., α-1-antitrypsin used to treat emphysema. **Rosie,** the first transgenic cow to produce protein (lactalbumin) enriched milk.
- To ensure vaccine safety and chemical safety.

Biotechnological Applications in Agriculture

- Green revolution succeeded in increasing the food supply however, it was not sufficient to feed the increasing population of the world.
- It managed to enhance our food production with the help of improved crop varieties, agrochemicals and better techniques.
- However, most of the agrochemicals are harmful to the environment and organic farming is expensive for farmers. The best solution to overcome these issues is to develop **Genetically Modified** (GM) foods or crops.
- The plants, bacteria, fungi and animals whose genes have been altered by manipulation are called **Genetically Modified Organisms** (GMOs). These are also called **transgenic organisms,** as they contain and express one or more foreign genes called **transgenes.**

Changes in GM Plants

GM plants have developed various changes as given below :

- **More tolerant to various abiotic conditions** GM crops have the ability to resist abiotic stress conditions like salinity, droughts, etc., without hampering productivity.
- **Reduced use of chemical fertiliser and pesticides** This is because the modified varieties have been made resistant to pests and insects which automatically reduces the need of pesticides.
- **Reduced post harvest losses** These losses are minimised by avoiding the pest attack. Biotechnology has made an impact by producing pest-resistant plants/crops and plants that survive extreme condition. Thus, reducing post harvest losses.
- **Enhanced nutritional value of food** It is done by generating biofortified crops through biotechnology.

Examples of GM Crops

Some common examples of GM crops are

Bt Crops

- Such type of crops are being produced by biotechnological methods. These plant species are pest resistant.
- *Bt* toxin is produced by *Bacillus thuringiensis* or *Bt* bacteria.
- Gene of *Bt* toxin is transferred into plants by extracting it from the bacterium. The plants so produced are pest resistant. *Bacillus thuringiensis* forms protein crystals (Cry) during a particular phase of their growth.
- These crystals contain a toxic insecticidal protein, which is inactive but gets activated in alkaline pH (pH of insect gut). Thus, it kills the pest.

(i) *Bt* **Cotton** *Bt* toxin gene is isolated from the bacteria and is transferred to the cotton/crops.
Bt cotton being resistant to bollworms increases its production. The gene forming *Bt* toxin is called *cry* **gene**. It is of two types :
- *cry* IAc and *cry* IIAb control cotton bollworms.
- *cry* IAb controls corn borer.

Pest Resistant Plants

- A nematode *Meloidogyne incognita* infects the roots of tobacco plants which reduces the production of tobacco.
- The strategy adopted to prevent this infection is based on the process of RNA Interference (RNA*i*), which occurs in all eukaryotic organisms as a method of cellular defence.
- This method involves silencing of specific *m*RNA due to complementary *ds*RNA that binds and prevents the process of *m*RNA translation.

Nutrient Rich Crops

- **Golden Rice** is a transgenic variety of rice which contains good quantities of β-carotene (provitamin-A inactive state of vitamin-A).

Ethical Issues in Applications of Biotechnology

- Genetic modification of organisms can have unpredictable results when such organisms are introduced into an ecosystem.
- Government of India has established **Genetic Engineering Approval Committee** (GEAC) to control the issues related with ethical concerns, validity of GM research, safety issues, patents, etc.
- A **patent** is the right granted by a government to an inventor to prevent others from making commercial use of his/her invention.
- Some nations are developing laws to prevent such unauthorised exploitation of their bioresources and traditional knowledge.

Biopatent

- The patents granted for biological entities and products derived from them are called as biopatent.

Biopiracy

- It refers to the use of bioresources by multinational companies and other organisations without proper authorisation from the countries and people concerned, without compensatory payment.

Bioreactors

- These are the large volume vessels (approximately 100-1000 L) which provide the optimal conditions for achieving the desired product by providing optimum growth conditions like temperature, pH, substrate, salts, vitamins and oxygen.
- The most commonly used bioreactors are stirring type bioreactor, simple stirred tank bioreactor and sparged stirred tank bioreactor.

Extra Facts From Tamil Nadu Board and NIOS

- Dolly was the first cloned female sheep, developed by Dr. Ian Wilmut and his colleagues at the Rosalin Institute, Scotland in July, 1996.
- Pharmaceutical products developed by *r*DNA techniques are
  - Human growth hormone used for treating children with growth deficiencies.
  - Blood clotting factor are developed to treat haemophilia.
  - Tissue plasminogen activator is used to dissolve blood clots and prevent heart attacks.
  - Development of vaccines against various diseases like hepatitis B and rabies.
- Transgenic sheep has been developed by inserting the gene for synthesis of amino acid (cysteine) for improved wool quality and production.
- Transgenic fish has been developed by inserting growth hormone gene for increased growth in fishes.

Appendix

Branches of Science

Branches of Physics

- **Astrophysics** It is the branch of astronomy that deals with the physics of the universe including the physical properties of astronomical objects such as stars, galaxies, and the interstellar medium as well as their interactions.
- **Atomic and molecular physics** The study of the structure and characteristics of atoms and molecules.
- **Biophysics** The science of the application of the laws of the physics to life processes.
- **Cryogenics** It is study of the extremely low temperatures.
- **Condensed matter physics** It is a branch of physics that deals with the physical properties of condensed phases of matter.
- **Cosmology** The study of the universe as a whole of the contents structure and evolution of the universe from the beginning of time to the future.
- **Electromagnetism** It is the branch of science concerned with the forces that occur between electrically charged particles.
- **Electrodynamics** It analyses the relationship between electrical and magnetic forces.
- **Fluid dynamics** It deals with the behaviour and movements of liquids and gases.
- **Geophysics** It is the study of the physical characteristics and properties of the earth.
- **Health physics** It involves the protection of people work with are radiation.
- **Mathematical physics** It is the study of mathematical systems that stands for physical phenomena.
- **Mechanics** The branch of physics concerned with the motion of the bodies in a frame of reference.
- **Molecular physics** It examines the structure properties and behaviour of molecules.
- **Nuclear physics** It is concerned with the structure and properties of the atomic nucleus and with nuclear reactions and their applications.
- **Optics** It is study of the nature and behaviour of light.
- **Particle physics** It is also called energy physics, analysis the behaviour and properties of elementry particles.
- **Plasma physics** It is concerned with the study of highly ionised gases that is, gases that have been separated into positively and negatively charged particles.
- **Quantum physics** It includes various areas of study based on quantum theory, which deals with matter and electromagnetic radiation and the interactions between them.
- **Relativistic physics** It is the physical theory of space and time developed by Albert Einstein. It is based on the postulates that all the laws of the physics are equally valid in all frames of reference moving at a uniform velocity and that the speed of light from a uniformly moving source is always the same, regardless of how fast or slow the source or its observer is moving.
- **Solid-state physics** It is also called condensed matter physics, examines the physical properties of solid materials.
- **Statistical mechanics** The branch of physics which deals with the properties of macroscopic systems to their atomic and molecular constituents.
- **Theoretical physics** The branch that uses mathematical abstractions and model of everyday life objects and systems to clarity, explain and predict natural occurrences.
- **Thermodynamics** It is the study of heat and other forms of energy, and of the conversion of energy from one form to another.

Branches of Chemistry

- **Agrochemistry** Concerned with the application of chemistry for agricultural production, food processing etc.
- **Analytical Chemistry** Concerned with qualitative and quantitative analysis.
- **Biochemistry** Concerned with chemical reactions related to the living organisms.

- **Environmental Chemistry** Concerned with chemical phenomenon in the environmental, especially related to pollution.
- **Food Chemistry** Concerned with chemistry associated with the chemical processes of food.
- **Forensic Chemistry** Concerned with chemical principles, techniques and methods to the investigation of crime.
- **General Chemistry** Concerned with the structure of matter and the reaction between matter and energy.
- **Geochemistry** Concerned with chemical composition, changes and processes associated with rocks, minerals etc, of earth or a celestial body.
- **Green Chemistry** Concerned with processes and products that reduce or eliminate the use and generation of hazardous substance and environmental pollution.
- **Inorganic Chemistry** Concerned with the study of all the elements (except C) and their compounds included CO, CO_2, carbonates and bicarbonates.
- **Medicinal Chemistry** Concerned with design, development and synthesis of pharmaceutical drugs.
- **Nanochemistry** Concerned with the assembly and properties of nanoscale assemblies of atoms or molecules.
- **Nuclear Chemistry** Concerned with the study of radioactive substances.
- **Organic Chemistry** Concerned with the study of compound of carbon and hydrogen (*i.e.,* of hydrocarbon and their derivatives).
- **Photochemistry** Concerned with interactions between light and matter.
- **Physical Chemistry** Concerned with chemical changes along with the energy consideration.
- **Polymer Chemistry** Concerned with the structure and properties of polymers and finds new ways to synthesise these molecules.
- **Quantum Chemistry** Concerned with the mathematical description of the motion and interaction of sub-atomic particles.
- **Solid State Chemistry** Concerned with the study of structure, properties and synthesis in solid phase of matter.
- **Stereochemistry** Concerned with the spatial arrangement of atoms in molecules and complexes.
- **Surface Chemistry** Concerned with the phenomenon that occurs at the surface or interfaces.
- **Thermochemistry** Concerned with the study of thermal effects of chemical reactions.

Branches of Biology

- **Aerobiology** Study passive tranport of organic (airborne) particles such as fungal spores, pollen grains etc.
- **Anatomy** Study of internal structure of an organism as revealed by dissection.
- **Arthrology** Study of joints.
- **Agriology** Study of customs of primitive man.
- **Agronomy** Study of management of farms and the science of crop production.
- **Anthropology** Study of the origin and development of human societies and cultures.
- **Anthology** Study of flowers.
- **Agrostology** Study of grasses.
- **Agrobiology** It is the quantitative science of plant life and p!ant nutrition.
- **Agrology** It is the soil science dealing with production of crops.
- **Andrology** Study of male reproductive organs.
- **Apicology** Study of honeybee.
- **Araneology** Study of spiders.
- **Agriculture** Study of cultivation of crops and the improved methods of farming.
- **Actinobiology** Study of radiation effect on living organisms.
- **Angiology** Study that deals with the branch of biology of blood vessels.
- **Bacteriology** Study of bacteria.
- **Bioinformatics** Study of development and application of computing system and technology in order to make novel observation about biological processes.
- **Biotechnology** Study of biological agents such as micro organisms or cellular components for beneficial use.
- **Biometrology** Study of effects of atmospheric changes on living organisms.
- **Bionics** The study of mechanical systems that function like living organisms or parts of living organisms.
- **Cytology** Study of structure and functions of cell.
- **Cryobiology** Study of effect of low temperature on living organisms.
- **Chronobiology** Study of biology of cyclic physiological or time dependent phenomena.
- **Conchology** Study of shells.
- **Chondrology** Study of cartilage.
- **Craniology** Study of skull.
- **Cardiology** Study of heart.
- **Dermatology** Study of skin.
- **Developmental Biology** Study of the processes by which an organism changes from a single cell into a mature, multicellular individual.
- **Development Morphology** Study of developmental aspects of organisms.
- **Desmology** Study of structures and anatomy of ligaments.

- **Biotechnology** Study of biological agents such as micro organisms or cellular components for beneficial use.
- **Biometrology** Study of effects of atmospheric changes on living organisms.
- **Bionics** The study of mechanical systems that function like living organisms or parts of living organisms.
- **Cytology** Study of structure and functions of cell.
- **Cryobiology** Study of effect of low temperature on living organisms.
- **Chronobiology** Study of biology of cyclic physiological or time dependent phenomena.
- **Conchology** Study of shells.
- **Chondrology** Study of cartilage.
- **Craniology** Study of skull.
- **Cardiology** Study of heart.
- **Dermatology** Study of skin.
- **Developmental Biology** Study of the processes by which an organism changes from a single cell into a mature, multicellular individual.
- **Development Morphology** Study of developmental aspects of organisms.
- **Desmology** Study of structures and anatomy of ligaments.
- **Embryology** Study of the stages of an organism that occur immediately after fertilisation.
- **Ecology** Study of inter-relationship between living organisms and their environment.
- **Ethology** Study of animal behaviour and conditions of animals.
- **Entomology** Study of insects.
- **Exobiology** Study of kind of life that may exist in outer space.
- **Environmental Biology** Study of the natural world, as a whole or in a particular area, especially as affected by human activity.
- **Evolutionary Biology** Study of the origin and descent of species over time.
- **Endocrinology** Study of ductless glands and their hormones.
- **Enzymology** Study of enzymes and their activities.
- **Eugenics** Study of science dealing with factors which improve successive generations of human race.
- **Food Technology** Study of processing and preservation of food is called food technology.
- **Forestry or Silviculture** Study of development of forests and the utilisation of their products.
- **Genetics** The scientific study of the ways in which different characteristics are passed from each generation of living things to next. The study of genes and heredity.
- **Genetic Engineering** Process of method of artificial DNA synthesis.
- **Herpetology** Study of reptiles and amphibians.
- **Horticulture** Study of plants cultivated in gardens and orchards.
- **Helminthology** Study of parasitic worms.
- **Hepatology** Study of liver.
- **Haematology** Study of blood and blood disorders.
- **Histology** Study of the structure and chemical composition of animal and plant tissue as related to the function.
- **Heredity** Study of inheritance of characters from parents to offspring.
- **Ichthyology** Study of fish.
- **Integrative Biology** Study of complex interrelationships between organisms and the physical and biological environment in which they live.
- **Limnology** Study of bodies of fresh water for their biological, physical and geological properites.
- **Lepidopterology** Study of butterflies and moths.
- **Marine Biology** It is the scientific study of organisms in the ocean or other marine or brackish bodies of water.
- **Morphology** Study of form and structure of organisms.
- **Microbiology** Study of microscopic organisms.
- **Molecular Biology** Study of formation, structure, and function of macromolecules found in living organisms, particularly nucleic acids and proteins.
- **Nematology** Study of nematodes (round worms).
- **Nephrology** Study of kidney.
- **Neonatology** Study of new borns upto twenty eight days in humans.
- **Neurology** Study of nervous system.
- **Nosology** Study of classification of diseases.
- **Ornithology** Study of birds.
- **Odontology** Study of teeth.
- **Ophiology** Study of snakes.
- **Ophthalmology** Study of eyes.
- **Osteology** Study of bones.
- **Olericulture** Study of agriculture dealing with vegetables.
- **Oncology** Study of tumours.
- **Physiology** Study of process and function associated with life.

- **Rhinology** Study of nose and olfactory organs.
- **Serology** Study of serum; interaction of antigens and antibodies in the blood.
- **Splanchnology** Study of visceral cavity and its organs.
- **Soil Science** Study of soil involving its structure, type and dynamics is called soil science.
- **Sitology** Study of food, diet and nutrition.
- **Structural Biology** Study of molecular structure of biological macromolecules.
- **Teratology** Study of developmental abnormalities during embryonic stages.
- **Taxonomy** Study of principles, identification, nomenclature and classification of the animals.
- **Taphonomy** Study of conditions conductive to fossilisation of organisms.
- **Toxicology** Study of poisons.
- **Therapeutics** Study of healing.
- **Traumatology** Study of injuries and wounds.
- **Urology** Study of excretory system.
- **Virology** It is the study of viruses.
- **Xenology** It is the study of alien life.
- **Zoology** Study of animals.
- **Zoopathology** Study of diseases of animals.
- **Zoophytology** Branch of zoology concerning zoophytes.
- **Zymology** Study of fermentation.
- **Zootechny** Science of breeding and domesticating animals.

Inventions/Discoveries and Principles

Inventions and Discoveries in Physics

Invention	Inventor
Adding machine [France]	Pascal [1642-44]
Aeroplane [USA]	Orville and Wilbur Wright [1903]
Air conditioning [USA]	Willis Haviland Carrier [1902]
Airplane (Jet engine) [Germany]	Ohain [1939]
Airship (Non-rigid) [France]	Henri Giffard [1852]
Atomic bomb [USA]	J Robert Oppenheimer [1945]
Ball-point pen [USA]	John J Loud [1888]
Barometer [Italy]	Evangelista Torricelli [1643]
Battery (Electric) [Italy]	Alessandro Volta [1800]
Bicycle [Britain]	Kirkpatrick Macmillan [1839-40]
Bicycle tyres (Pneumatic) [Britain]	John Boyd Dunlop [1888]
Bifocal lens [USA]	Benjamin Franklin [1784]
Busnen burner [Germany]	R Wilhelm Eberhard Bunsen [1855]
Burglar alarm [USA]	Edwin Holmes [1858]
Camera (Kodak) [USA]	Walker Eastman [1888]
Car (Steam) [France]	Nicolas Cugnot [1769]
Car (Petrol) [Germany]	Karl Benz [1988]
Cassette (Videotape) [Japan]	Sony [1969]
Cement (Portland) [Britain]	Joseph Aspdin [1824]
Cinema [France]	Nicolas and Jean Lumiere [1895]
Clock (Mechanical) [China]	I-Hsing and Liang Ling-Tsan [1725]
Clock (Pendulum) [Netherlands]	Christiaan Huygens [1656]
Compact disc [USA]	RCA [1972]
Compact disc player [Japan, Netherlands]	Sony, Philips [1979]
Computer (Laptop) [Britain]	Sinclair [1987]
Computer (Mini) [USA]	Digital Corp [1960]
Diesel engine [Germany]	Rudolf Diesel [1895]
Dynamo [France]	Charles F. Brush [1832]
Electric flat iron [USA]	H W Seeley [1882]
Electric lamp [USA]	Thomas Alva Edison [1879]
Electric motor (DC) [Belgium]	Zenobe Gramme [1873]
Electric motor (AC) [USA]	Nikola Tesla [1888]
Electric washing machine [USA]	Alva J Fisher [1906]
Electro-magnet [Britain]	William Sturgeon [1824]
Electroplating [Italy]	Luigi Brugnatelli [1805]
Electronic computer [Britain]	Dr Alan M Turing [1824]
Facsimile machine [Britain]	Alexander Bain [1843]
Fibre optics [Britain]	Kepany [1955]
Film (Moving outlines) [France]	Charles F. Brush [1885]
Film (Talking) [Germany]	J Engl, J Massolle and H Vogt [1922]
Galvanometer [France]	Andre-Marie Ampere [1834]
Gramophone [USA]	Thomos Alva Edison [1878]
Helicopter [France]	Etienne Oehmichen [1924]
Hydrogen Bomb [USA]	Edward Teller [1954]
Intelligence testing [France]	Simon Binet [1905]
Jet engine [Britain]	Sir Frank Whittle [1937]
Laser [USA]	Theodore Maiman [1960]
Launderette [USA]	J F Cantrell [1934]
Lift (Mechanical) [USA]	Elisha G Otis [1852]
Lighting conductor [USA]	Benjamin Franklin [1752]
Loudspeaker [Britain]	Horace Short [1900]
Machine gun [Britain]	Richard Gatling [1918]
Magnetic recording tape [Germany]	Fritz Pfleumer [1928]
Microphone [USA]	Alexander Graham Bell [1876]
Microscope (Comp.) [Netherlands]	Z Janssen [1590]

Invention	Inventor
Microscope (Elect.) [Germany]	Ruska Knoll [1931]
Microwave oven [USA]	Percy LeBaron Spencer [1947]
Motor cycle [Germany]	G Daimler [1885]
Movie projector [USA]	Thomas Edison [1893]
Neon lamp [France]	Georges Claude [1910]
Neutron bomb [USA]	Samuel Cohen [1958]
Optical fibre [Germany]	Narinder Kapany [1955]
Pacemaker [USA]	Zoll [1952]
Photoelectric cell [Germany]	Julius Elster, Hans F Geitel [1893]
Photography (On metal) [France]	J N Niepce [1826]
Photography (On paper) [Britain]	W H Fox Talbot [1835]
Photography (On film) [USA]	John Carbutt [1888]
Piano [Italy]	Cristofori [1709]
Pistol, revolver [USA]	Colt [1836]
Radar [USA]	A H Taylor and Leo C Young [1922]
Radiocarbon dating [USA]	Libby [1947]
Radio telegraphy [USA]	Dr Mohlon Lommis [1864]
Radio telegraphy (Trans Atlantic) [Italy]	G Marconi [1901]
Rayon [Britain]	Sir Joseph Swan [1883]
Razor (Electric) [USA]	Col Jacob Schick [1931]
Razor (Safety) [USA]	King C Gillette [1895]
Refrigerator [USA]	James Harrison, Alexander catlin [1850]
Rubber (Latex foam) [Britain]	Dunlop Rubber Co. [1928]
Rubber (Vulcanised) [USA]	Charles Goodyear [1841]
Rubber (Waterproof) [Britain]	Charles Macintosh [1823]
Ship (Steam) [France]	I C Perier [1775]
Ship (Turbine) [Britain]	Sir C Parsons [1894]
Steam engine [Britain]	Thomas Savery [1798]
Steam engine (Piston) [Britain]	Thomas Newcomen [1712]
Steam engine (Condenser) [Britain]	James Watt [1765]
Steel (Stainless) [Britain]	Harry Brearley [1913]
Stethoscope [France]	Laennec [1819]
Submarine [USA]	David Bushnell [1776]
Electronic calculator [USA]	J H Van Tassel [1976]
Tank [Britain]	Sir Einest D Swinton [1914]
Tape recorder [Denmark]	Fessenden Poulsen [1899]
Telegraph [France]	M Lammond [1787]
Telephone (Cellular) [USA]	Bell Labs [1947]
Telephone (Imperfect) [Italy]	Antonio Meucci [1849]
Telephone (Perfected) [USA]	Alexander Graham Bell [1876]
Telescope [Netherlands]	Hans Lipperhey [1608]

Invention	Inventor
Television (Mechanical) [Britain]	John Logic Baird [1926]
Television (Electronic) [USA]	P Farnsworth [1927]
Television (Colour) [Britain]	John Logie Baird [1928]
Transistor [USA]	Bardeen, Shockley and Brattain [1948]
Transistor radio [Japan]	Sony [1948]
Uranium Fission (Atomic reactor) [USA]	Leo Szilard [1942]
Vacuum cleaner (Elec.) [USA]	Spangler [1907]
Vidoe tape [USA]	Charles Ginsberg [1956]
Wireless (Telegraphy) [Italy]	G Marconi [1896]

Discoveries and Principles in Chemistry

Discovery/Theory	Scientists
Atomic theory	Dalton
Atomic theory based on quantum theory	Neils Bohr
Atomic number	Moseley
Avogadro's hypothesis	Avogadro
Artificial radioactivity	Irene Curie and Frederic Joliot
Activation energy, theory of ionisation	Arrhenius
Brownian movement	Robert Brown
Catalysis	Jons Jakob Berzelius
Dual nature of electron	L de-Broglie
Dobereiner's triads	Dobereiner
Dilution law	Ostwald
Dynamite	Alfred Nobel
Electron	J J Thomson
Gold number	Zsigmondy
Gun powder	Roger Bacon
Group displacement law	Fajan, Russel and Soddy
Hund's rule of spin multiplicity	Hund
Hess's law of constant heat summation	GH Hess
Helium	Frankland and Lockyer
Hydrogen gas	Cavendish
Heavy water	H Urey
Inert gas	Ramsay
Law of conservation of mass	Lavoisier
Law of constant (definite) proportion	Proust
Law of multiple proportion	Dalton
Law of reciprocal proportion, Law of equivalent proportion	Richter
Law of gaseous volume	Gay Lussac

Discovery/Theory	Scientists
Law of diffusion of gases	Graham
Law of partial pressure	Dalton
Law of octaves	John Newlands
Law of mass action	Guldberg and Waage
Le-Chatelier's principle	Le-Chatelier
Law of electrolysis	Faraday
Mass-energy relation ($E = mc^2$), Photoelectric effect	Albert Einstein
Mass spectrum, Mass spectrograph	Aston
Molecule	Avogadro
Modern periodic law	Moseley
Modern concept of acids and bases	Bronsted and Lowry
Manufacture of HNO_3 from air	Brikeland
Manufacture of steel	Bessemer
Meson field theory	H Yukawa
Neutron	James Chadwick
Neutrino	Frederick Reines
Negative meson, Positive meson	H Yukawa
Nylon	Wallace Carothers
Oxygen gas	Priestley
Optical isomerism	van't Hoff
Octet rule	GN Lewis
Periodic law and classification	DI Mendeleev
pH scale	SP Sorensen
Plastics	Alexander Parkes
Wave nature of electron (experiment proof)	Davison
Exclusion principle	Pauli
Proton	Goldstein
Positron	Anderson
Quantisation of angular momentum (experimental proof)	Stern Gerlach
Radium	Marie and Pierre Curie
Radioactivity	Henri Becquerel
Rubber (vulcanised)	Charles Goodyear
Rubber (waterproof)	Charles Macintosh
Stainless steel	Harry Brearley
Sulphur	Frasch
Synthesis of ammonia	Haber
Synthesis of hydrocarbons	Kolbe
Synthesis of urea	Wholer
Synthesis of higher alkanes	Wurtz
Terylene	J Whinfield, J Dickson
Theory of hybridisation	L Pauling
Theory of electrovalency	Kossel
Theory of covalency	GN Lewis

Some Important Compounds and Their Formula

Chemical Compound	Formula
Absolute alcohol	C_2H_5OH
Aspirin	*ortho* - $CH_3OCO—C_6H_4—COOH$
Baking soda	$NaHCO_3$
Baryta water	$Ba(OH)_2$
Black oxide	MnO_2
Bleaching powder	$CaOCl_2$
Blue vitriol	$CuSO_4 \cdot 5H_2O$
Borax (tincal)	$Na_2B_4O_7 \cdot 10H_2O$
Borazole (inorganic benzene)	$B_3N_3H_6$
Calgon	$Na_2[Na_4(PO_3)_6]$
Calomel	Hg_2Cl_2
Carbolic acid	C_6H_5OH
Carborundum	SiC
Caustic potash	KOH
Chloropicrin (Tear gas)	$CCl_3—NO_2$
Chrome yellow	$PbCrO_4$
Chromyl chloride	CrO_2Cl_2
DDT	Dichlorodiphenyl trichloroethane
Dry ice	Solid CO_2
Ferric alum	$NH_4Fe(SO_4)_2$
Freon	CCl_2F_2
Gammexame (BHC)	$C_6H_6Cl_6$
Glauber's salt	$Na_2SO_4 \cdot 10H_2O$
Grape sugar	$C_6H_{12}O_6$ (fructose)
Gun powder	KNO_3(70%) + S(12%) + charcoal(13%)
Gypsum salt (Gypsum)	$CaSO_4 \cdot 2H_2O$
Inorganic rubber	$(PNCl_2)_n$ (n = 3 to 7)
Hydrolith	CaH_2
Hypo	$Na_2S_2O_3$
King of chemicals (oil of vitriol)	H_2SO_4
Laughing gas	N_2O
Litharge	PbO
Lunar caustic	$AgNO_3$
Marshall's acid	$H_2S_2O_8$ (Peroxydisulphuric acid)
Marsh gas	CH_4
Milk of lime (slaked lime or lime water)	$Ca(OH)_2$

Discovery/Theory	Scientists
Sulphur	Frasch
Synthesis of ammonia	Haber
Synthesis of hydrocarbons	Kolbe
Synthesis of urea	Wholer
Synthesis of higher alkanes	Wurtz
Terylene	J Whinfield, J Dickson
Theory of hybridisation	L Pauling
Theory of electrovalency	Kossel
Theory of covalency	GN Lewis

Some Important Compounds and Their Formula

Chemical Compound	Formula
Absolute alcohol	C_2H_5OH
Aspirin	*ortho* - $CH_3OCO—C_6H_4—COOH$
Baking soda	$NaHCO_3$
Baryta water	$Ba(OH)_2$
Black oxide	MnO_2
Bleaching powder	$CaOCl_2$
Blue vitriol	$CuSO_4 \cdot 5H_2O$
Borax (tincal)	$Na_2B_4O_7 \cdot 10H_2O$
Borazole (inorganic benzene)	$B_3N_3H_6$
Calgon	$Na_2[Na_4(PO_3)_6]$
Calomel	Hg_2Cl_2
Carbolic acid	C_6H_5OH
Carborundum	SiC
Caustic potash	KOH
Chloropicrin (Tear gas)	$CCl_3—NO_2$
Chrome yellow	$PbCrO_4$
Chromyl chloride	CrO_2Cl_2
DDT	Dichlorodiphenyl trichloroethane
Dry ice	Solid CO_2
Ferric alum	$NH_4Fe(SO_4)_2$
Freon	CCl_2F_2
Gammexame (BHC)	$C_6H_6Cl_6$
Glauber's salt	$Na_2SO_4 \cdot 10H_2O$
Grape sugar	$C_6H_{12}O_6$ (fructose)
Gun powder	KNO_3(70%) + S(12%) + charcoal(13%)
Gypsum salt (Gypsum)	$CaSO_4 \cdot 2H_2O$
Inorganic rubber	$(PNCl_2)_n$ (n = 3 to 7)
Hydrolith	CaH_2

Chemical Compound	Formula
Hypo	$Na_2S_2O_3$
King of chemicals (oil of vitriol)	H_2SO_4
Laughing gas	N_2O
Litharge	PbO
Lunar caustic	$AgNO_3$
Marshall's acid	$H_2S_2O_8$ (Peroxydisulphuric acid)
Marsh gas	CH_4
Milk of lime (slaked lime or lime water)	$Ca(OH)_2$
Milk of magnesia	$Mg(OH)_2$
Mohr salt	$FeSO_4 \cdot (NH_4)_2SO_4 \cdot 6H_2O$
Muriatic acid	HCl
Mustard gas	$ClCH_2CH_2SCH_2CH_2Cl$
Oleum	$H_2S_2O_7$
Oil of winter green (Methyl salicylate)	*o*- $HOC_6H_4COOCH_3$
Pearl ash	K_2CO_3
Perhydrol	30% H_2O_2
Permutit (zeolite)	$Na_2Al_2Si_2O_8$
Philosopher's wool	ZnO
Phosgene	$COCl_2$
Plaster of Paris	$CaSO_4 \cdot \frac{1}{2} H_2O$
Prussian blue	$Fe_4[Fe(CN)_6]_3$
Prussic acid	HCN
Quick lime (lime)	CaO
Red lead	Pb_3O_4
Rochelle salt	$NaOOCCH(OH)CH(OH)COOK$
Rust	Fe_2O_3
Smelling salt	$(NH_4)_2CO_3H_2O$
Soda ash	Na_2CO_3 (Anhydrous)
Spirit of wine (Grain alcohol)	C_2H_5OH
Talc	$3MgO \cdot 4SiO_2 \cdot H_2O$
Teflon	$(C_2F_4)_n$
TEL	$(C_2H_5)_4Pb$
TNT	Trinitrotoluene (an explosive)
Turnbull blue	$KFe(Fe(CN)_6$
Urea	NH_2CONH_2
Vinegar	CH_3COOH (7 - 8%)
Washing soda	$Na_2CO_3 \cdot 10H_2O$
Water glass (quartz)	Na_2SiO_3

Important Medicines and Source Plants

Drug	Plants	Uses
Aconite	Monkshood (*Aconitum napellus*)	It is used externally for neuralgia and arthritis, and internally to relieve from fever and pain
Colchicum	Meadow saffron (*Colchicum autumnale*)	It is used in the treatment of arthritis and gout.
Gentian	Bitterwort (*Gentiana lutea*)	It is used for digestion problems such as loss of appetite, fullness, diarrhoea, heart burn etc.
Penicillin	*Penicillium notatum*	It is used for the treatment of bacterial endocarditis, gonorrhea, mastoiditis, local infections.
Streptomycin	*Streptomyces griseus*	It is helpful in treating tularemia, urinary infections and some forms of tuberculosis, meningitis and pneumonia.
Aureomycin	*Streptomyces aureofaciens*	It is helpful in treating diseases like pneumonia, whooping cough and eye infections etc.
Morphine/ thebaine/ Codeine /Papaverine/ noscapine	Opium Poppy (*Papaver somniferum*)	It is used as a pain reliever.
Tiotropium	*Atropa belladonna*	It is used in the treatment of chronic obstructive pulmonary disease.
Cannabidiol	Cannabis plant (*Cannabis sativa*)	It is used as a pain reliever.
Aloe (gel and latex)	Aloe barbadensis miller	It is used for osteoarthritis, bowel diseases, stomach ulcers, diabetes, asthma *etc*
Herb and Root Extracts	Ashwagandha (*Withania somnifera*)	Use for treating stress, tumor, tuberculosis, liver problems, swelling, ulcerations, etc.
Reserpine	Sarpagandha (*Rauwolfia serpentina*)	Used to treat high blood pressure.
Caffeine	*Camellia sinensis*	It acts as a CNS stimulant.
Chymopapain	*Carica papaya*	It acts as a proteolytic.
Aspirin	Bark willow tree	It is used as an analgesic, antipyretic and an anti inflammatory.
Curcumin	Turmeric (*Curcuma longa*)	It reduces swelling and might cure symptoms of osteoarthritis and rheumatid arthritis etc.
Quinine	Bark of cinchona tree	It acts as a antipyretic, antimalarial, analgesic and anti-inflammatory.

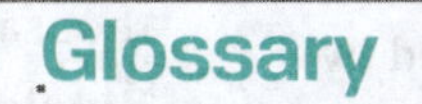

Glossary

Physics

- **Aberration** A defect in the image formed by a lens or curved mirror.
- **Absolute zero** The lowest imaginable temperature, at which all the particles in a body would be completely at rest. It is –273°C (–459°F).
- **Absolute error** The magnitude of the difference between the true value of a quantity and its individual measurement value. This is denoted by $|\Delta a|$.
- **Absolute humidity** The mass of water vapour per unit volume of air.
- **Absolute permittivity** It is permittivity of free space.
- **Absorptance** It is the ratio of the radient or luminous flux absorbed by a body to the flux falling on it.
- **Absorption spectrum** Spectrum of electromagnetic radiation absorbed by matter when radiation of all frequencies is passed through it.
- **Absorptivity** A measure of the ability of a substance to absorb radiation.
- **Accelerator** Machine for accelerating charged particles (protons, electrons, nuclei, etc.) to very high speeds.
- **Accelerometer** An instrument for measuring acceleration, especially of an aircraft or a rocket.
- **Accumulator** A device which acts as a source of electric current and can be recharged again after a long use.
- **Achromatic lens** Lens for which all light colours have the same focal length.

- **Adiabatic process** Any thermodynamic process that occurs at constant heat. In an adiabatic process, heat absorbed or released is zero.
- **Admittance** It is the reciprocal of impedance. It is measured in Siemens(S).
- **ADSL** It stands for asymmetric digital subscriber line. It is a mechanism in which broadband communication is available using telephone line with simultaneous use of line for normal phone calls.
- **Aerometer** Instrument for measuring the weight or density of air and gases.
- **Alternating source** It is a source of potential difference whose polarity changes with time.
- **Amplifier** Electronic device which increases the strength of an input signal.
- **Ampere hour** A practical unit of electric charge. It is equal to the charge flowing in one hour through a conductor passing one ampere. It is equal to 3600 coulombs.
- **Amplification** It is the process of increasing the amplitude (and consequently the strength) of a signal using an electronic circuit.
- **Amplitude** The maximum value (or maximum height of the waves) of anything that goes back and forth in a cycle.
- **Amplitude modulation** In this type of modulation, the amplitude of carrier wave is modified in accordance with the signal to be transmitted (modulating signal).
- **Analyser** A device used to observe plane polarised light.
- **Angular magnification** The ratio of the angle subtended at the eye by an image to that subtended by the object. It is denoted by *M*.
- **Aperture** A part of a lens or a mirror through which light is allowed to pass. The aperture is also the diameter of such an area.
- **Apogee** The largest distance of a satellite from the earth during its motion around the earth.
- **Armature** It is the coil of a dynamo or an electric motor.
- **Astigmatism** It is a defect of lens in which the horizontal and vertical object at same distance from the lens are not focused simultaneously.
- **Atmometer** It is an instrument for measuring the rate of evaporation of water. It is also called evaporometer.
- **Axial vector** A vector that does not reverse its sign when coordinate system is changed to a new system by a reflection in the origin.
- **Back emf** A potential difference that opposes the current that induces it.
- **Ballistic pendulum** A device for measuring the velocity of a projectile (*e.g.*, a bullet).
- **Ballistics** The study of the motion of projectiles.
- **Band gap** A range of forbidden energies between two allowed bands of energy. It is also known as energy gap.
- **Bandwidth** The frequency range over which an equipment operates or the portion of the spectrum occupied by the signal.
- **Bar** Unit of pressure in the CGS system; 1 bar $= 10^6$ dynes per sq. cm $= 10^5$ newton per sq. metre.
- **Barn** A unit of area defined as 10^{-28} square metre.
- **Barometric height** The height of liquid column in a barometer.
- **Barograph** Instrument used by meteorologists for recording on paper the variations in atmospheric pressure with time.
- **Beam balance** An instrument to determine the mass of an object. It consists of two pans suspended from a centrally pivoted beam.
- **Beckmann thermometer** Sensitive thermometer for measuring small changes in temperature.
- **Bias** It refers to the steady voltage inserted in series with an element of an electronic device.
- **Biconcave** (biconvex) **lens** A lens with two concave (convex) surfaces.
- **Binary star** A pair of stars turning around each other. They may take a few hours if they are very close, or thousands of years if they are far apart.
- **Bipolar transistor** A transistor that uses two types of charge carriers, electrons and holes, for its operation.
- **Biprism** A glass prism with an obtuse angle that functions as two acute angle prism placed base to base. By this prism a double image of a single object is formed.
- **Black hole** An object with such strong gravity that light waves cannot escape from it. Anything pulled inside a black hole is lost forever.
- **Blind spot** A small arc on the retina where the optic nerve leaves the eye and which is insensitive to light.
- **Blue shift** An apparent decrease in wavelength, when waves are received from a source moving towards the observer.
- **Breakdown** The sudden passage of current through an insulator.

- **Breakdown voltage** It is the reverse voltage at which the *p-n* junction breaks down with sudden rise in reverse current.
- **Bridge rectifier** A full wave rectifier consisting of a bridge made by diodes.
- **Brownian movement** It is the random motion of particles in fluid or gas.
- **Bulk modulus** The ratio of normal stress to the volume strain of the material of the body.
- **Bypass** It denotes a shunt path around some circuit element.
- **Bypass capacitor** A capacitor that provides a low impedence path over a range of frequencies and allow AC to pass through it.
- **Caesium clock** An atomic clock that depends on the energy, difference between two state of the caesium-133 nucleus when it is in magnetic field.
- **Capillary wave** These waves are ripples of fairly short wavelength-no more than a few centimetres-and the restoring force that produces them is the surface tension of water.
- **Carnot effciency** Ideal efficiency of heat engine or refrigerator working between two constant temperatures.
- **Carrier** It refers to the electrons or holes whose movements are responsible for current in any substance.
- **Carrier wave** An electromagnetic wave of specified high frequency and amplitude emitted by a radio transmitter in order to carry information. The information are superimposed by modulation.
- **Cathetometer** Instrument consisting of a telescope which can slide along a graduated vertical pillar, used for measuring lengths at a distance of a few feet.
- **Caustic** The curve surface formed by the reflection of parallel ray of light in a large-aperture concave mirror.
- **Centre of buoyancy** It is the point through which the resultant of the buoyancy force on a submerged body act, it coincide with the centre of gravity of the displaced fluid.
- **Charge carrier** Any particle that transport electric charge in an electric current. The type of carrier depends upon the nature of conductor.
- **Charge density** The electric charge per unit volume of a body or medium is called volume charge density.
- **Choke** A low resistance coil used for controlling current in an ac circuit without wasting much energy.
- **Chromatic aberration** Variation in focal length of lens with wavelength of light.
- **Chromatron** Type of cathode-ray tube having four screens, used in colour TV sets.
- **Closed circuit** A circuit in which electric current can flow without any interruption.
- **Coelostat** Device used with an astronomical telescope to follow the path of celestial bodies.
- **Coercive force** The magnetic field intensity needed to reduce the magnetic flux density in a magnetic material to zero. The maximum value of this force is known as coercivity.
- **Commutator** A part of the dynamo or generator through connection are made to external circuits.
- **Compression** When a vibrating object moves forward, it pushes and compresses the air in front of it creating a region of high pressure.
- **Cosmic dust** Extremely small particles of matter distributed throughout space.
- **Coulomb barrier** The atomic nucleus is surrounded by a strong electrostatic potential barrier that is called coulomb barrier.
- **Coupling constant** A physical constant that is the measure of the strength of interaction between two parts of a system or two or more systems.
- **Crest** A point of maximum positive displacement in a wave.
- **Cryometer** Thermometer for measuring low temperatures.
- **Cryophorus** Apparatus used for demonstrating the cooling effect of evaporation.
- **Cryostat** Apparatus in which a low temperature can be maintained.
- **Crystal lattice** Structure of solid consisting of regular arrangement of atoms.
- **Damping** A decrease in the amplitude of an oscillation as a result of energy loss from the oscillating system to overcome frictional or other resistive force.
- **Dilatometer** Apparatus for measuring changes in volume of substances.
- **Depolarisation** The prevention of polarisation in a primary cell.
- **Depolariser** Any substance that is used to avoid polarisation in a voltaic cell. *i.e.*, MnO_2.
- **Dielectric polarisation** The phenomenon that is explained by the formation of dipoles of elements of dielectric under stress.

- **Diffusion** The movement of charge carrier from a region of higher concentration to a region of lower concentration across the junction.
- **Dip circle** It is an instrument that is used to measure the angle of dip at a place. It consist of a magnetic needle mounted in such a way, that it can rotate in vertical plane.
- **Dopant** Small quantities of material added to semiconductor to increase electrical conduction.
- **Ductility** Property of substance due to which it can be drawn into wires.
- **Echolocation** Location of an object using an echo.
- **Electrified** If an object possesses an electric charge, it is said to be electrified or charged. When it has no charge, it is said to be neutral.
- **Electret** Dielectric having a permanent electric charge or molecular dipoles.
- **Electrodynamometer** Instrument for measuring current, voltage or power, in both dc and ac circuits.
- **Epicentre** The point on the surface of the earth which lies directly above focus of earthquake.
- **Epidiascope** Device for projecting images of opaque or transparent objects.
- **Epitaxy** The process of growing a thin layer of material upon a single crystal substrate so that the lattice structure is identical to that of the substrate.
- **Far infrared** The part of the spectrum towards the end of the infrared region of the electromagnetic spectrum which is near the radiowave region.
- **Ferrites** A group of compounds which have weak but permanent magnetism.
- **Fluid resistance** The force exerted by a fluid opposing the motion of a body moving through it.
- **Fluoroscope** Fluorescent screen on which X-ray images can be observed directly.
- ***f*-number** Term used for a lens to denote the ratio of focal length to diameter.
- **Frequency converter** The device, which converts frequency of the received signals to gigahertz. It is also called transponder.
- **Fresnel's biprism** A glass prism with a large angle (=179°) which produces two coherent virtual sources and interference patterns when monochromatic light is passed through it.
- **Gyration** The motion of a body around a fixed centre or axis.
- **Goniometer** Instrument for measuring angles, especially between crystal faces.
- **Gyroscope** Apparatus consisting of a heavy spinning wheel mounted in such a way that it is free to rotate about any axis.
- **Helmholtz coils** A pair of similar coils designed to produce nearly uniform field in the region between them when a current is passed through them. Separation between them is equal to their radius.
- **Hologram** The intermediate photographic record which contain the information for reproducing a three-dimensional image.
- **Inclinometer** Device for measuring the angle of inclination of an aircraft with the horizontal.
- **Infrared astronomy** The study of radiation from space in the infrared region of the spectrum.
- **Klystron** Electron tube used to generate or amplify microwaves.
- **Laevorotatory** A compound capable of rotating the plane of polarised light in an anticlockwise direction as viewed against the direction of motion of light.
- **Lag** The angle, time or phase by which one periodic quantity lags by another.
- **Lateral inversion** In an image formed by a mirror the left of the object appears on the right and the right appears on the left.
- **Linear charge distribution** When charge is uniformly distributed on a wire or rod, then it is called linear charge distribution.
- **Lodestone** Naturally occurring magnetic rock.
- **Mach number** The ratio of speed of body to the local speed of sound. The speed of body is therefore called supersonic if its mach number is greater than unity.
- **Machmeter** Instrument for determing the speed of an aircraft in terms of the speed of sound.
- **Magnetic bottle** This term is used in plasma physics and refer to the magnetic field applied to contain a plasma in controlled fusion experiments.
- **Magneton** A term used for atomic, molecular or nuclear magnets to represent their respective magnetic moment.
- **Magnetic storm** Sudden disturbance in the earth's magnetic field due to sunspot activity.
- **Magnetometer** Instrument for comparing strength of magnetic fields.
- **Magnetosphere** Space surrounding the earth or any celestial body, in which its magnetic field can be experienced.
- **Malleability** Property of being hammered out into thin sheets.

- **Mobility** The average drift velocity of a charge carrier per unit electric field.
- **Multimeter** An instrument which can be used to measure various electrical quantities like resistance, voltage, AC as well as DC etc.
- **Nephelometer** Instrument for measuring the scattering of light by particles suspended in a liquid.
- **Nephoscope** Instrument for determining the speed of celestial bodies (even clouds).
- **Nicol prism** A device made from crystals of spar used which produces plane-polarised light.
- **Octave** The interval between two musical notes whose frequencies are in the ratio 2 : 1.
- **Occulation** Interception of the light or radio emission from a celestial body when another celestial body comes between it and the observer.
- **Opaque** Material that does not transmit light.
- **Oscilloscope** It is a device that depicts on a screen periodic changes in an electric quantity, as voltage, current, using a cathode ray tube or any other similar instrument.
- **Panchromatic film** Photographic film sensitive to light of all colours.
- **Pentode** A thermionic valve with five electrodes cathode, anode and three grids between them.
- **Perihelion** The point in a solar orbit which is nearest to the sun.
- **Phasor** It is quantity that varies sinusoidally with time may be represented as the projection of a rotating vector.
- **Phonetics** It is the science of speech sound and their production transmission reception and their analysis.
- **Phonon** It is quantum of elastic vibration in crystals. It is given by $h\nu$ where h is the planck constant and ν is the frequency of vibration.
- **Piezo-electric effect** The production of a small emf across certain substance when they are subjected to external pressure.
- **Plumbline** A cord having a metal bob attached to one end. It is used for determining the depth of water.
- **Planimeter** Instrument for measuring areas.
- **Pleochroic** Certain crystals that exhibit different colours when observed from different directions.
- **Polarity of charge** The property which differentiates the two kinds of charges.
- **Precession** If a body is rotating about an axis, it is said to precess when the axis of rotation moves around another axis at an angle to it.
- **Pyroelectricity** Property of certain crystals of acquiring electric charges on opposite faces when heated.
- **Quadrupole** It is one of the multipolar system of charge and current which exhibit effect of electric and magnetic field outside the system.
- **Radial field** A field in which the field lines are radii that radiate from a centre. Point charges and masses and spheres have radial fields.
- **Radial velocity** Component of velocity which is along the radius of circle when an object is moving in circular path.
- **Radio telescope** It is a concave reflector is used and is used to gather radio waves given out by celestial bodies. It helps to bring all such rays to a receiver placed at its focus.
- **Refractometer** Apparatus for measuring the refractive index of a substance.
- **Recoil electron** An electron that has been set into motion by a collision.
- **Reference level** Location at which potential energy is chosen to be zero.
- **Regular reflection** Reflection from a smooth surface like that of a mirror is called regular reflection. Images are formed by regular reflection.
- **Rejector** It is a parallel resonant circuit comprising an inductance and a capacitor in parallel.
- **Resilience** It is the power to return to the original form or position after being bent or compressed.
- **Retentivity** The property measured by the residual magnetic induction corresponding to the saturation induction for the material.
- **Sensitometer** Instrument used for measuring the sensitivity of a photographic equipment to light.
- **Siphon** Bent tube for transferring a liquid from a higher to a lower level *via* a third level higher than either of the two levels.
- **Spectrometer** An instrument which is used for analysing the spectrum of source of a light.
- **Telephoto lens** Lens system used for photographing distant objects.
- **Threshold audibility** The threshold audibility at any frequency is the minimum intensity of sound at that frequency which can be detected.
- **Thyristor** It is a silicon controlled rectifier. Its anode-cathode current is controlled by a signal applied to a third electrode the gate.
- **Tokamak** It is an axially symmetric system in which the plasma suppresses the instability.

- **Tomography** Technique for using X-rays for photographing a desired plane of the body.
- **Tonometer** Instrument for measuring the pitch of a sound.
- **Transponder** Electronic equipment designed to receive a signal and transmit a reply automatically.
- **Turbogenerator** Electric generator with a steam turbine.
- **Tweeter** Loudspeaker for higher audio frequency sounds in the range 5-15 kHz.
- **Wave train** It refers to a series of successive waves which are spaced at regular intervals.
- **Wavemeter** Instrument for measuring the wavelength of a radiowave.
- **Yield point** When a rod wire of a certain material is subjected to slowly increasing tension, the point at which a small increase in tension produces a sudden and large increase in length.
- **Zodiacal light** Faint light seen in the sky before sunrise and after sunset.

Chemistry

- **Absorbent** Anything having the power of absorbing.
- **Absorption** A process in which gas is taken up by a liquid or solid, or a liquid is taken by a solid. It is a bulk phenomenon.
- **Adsorption** The accumulation of molecular species at the surface rather than in the bulk of a solid or liquid.
- **Aerosol** A colloidal system in which particles are dispersed in a gas as in smoke or mist.
- **Alcohols** Aliphatic compounds, which contains at least one OH group and have a general formula ROH.
- **Aldehydes** Derived from alkanes by the replacement of one hydrogen atom by aldehydic (CHO) group and have a general formula R CHO.
- **Alkaline earth metals** The group of chemical elements that are alkaline in nature and present in earth crust.
- **Alkali metals** A group of elements that react with water to form alkalies, and are found in group I A of the periodic table. e.g., lithium, sodium, potassium, rubidium, caesium, francium.
- **Alkanes** These are simple hydrocarbons that are commonly called paraffins and having general formula [CnH_{2n+2}]. The alkanes series begins with methane.
- **Alkenes** These are unsaturated hydrocarbons containing at least one double bond and having general formula [CnH_{2n}].
- **Alkynes** These are unsaturated hydrocarbons containing at least one triple bond and having general formula [C_nH_{2n-2}].
- **Allotropy** The property by which certain chemical elements exist in two or more different forms (as carbon in graphite, charcoal, diamonds, lamp black, etc).
- **Alloy** Metal consisting of a mixture of one metal with another metal or non-metal. e.g., brass is an alloy of copper and zinc.
- **Amalgam** An alloy of mercury with other metals. Silver amalgam is used as a dental filling material.
- **Amphoteric** Substances having both acidic and basic properties. e.g. alumina.
- **Aromatic compounds** There is a series of compounds based upon benzene ring structure. Many of which have an odour or derived from materials having odour.
- **Atom** The smallest part of an element capable of taking part in a chemical reaction.
- **Atomic mass** The atomic mass of an element is numerical number which indicates how many times an atom of an element is heavier than 1/12 mass of carbon-12.
- **Atomic number** This is equal to the number of protons present in the nucleus.
- **Atomicity** It is the number of atoms in a given molecule.
- **Avogadro's number** Number of molecules present in one mole of a substance is constant and is equal to 6.023×10^{23} at STP/NTP.
- **Base** A compound release hydroxyl ions (O^-H) in aqueous solution, having pH greater than 7.
- **Base metal** Non-precious metal, the main metal constituent of an alloy.
- **Bath salts** Salts used to soften hard water.
- **Benzene** A clear inflammable liquid obtained by the fractional distillation of coal tar. It is used as a solvent and has carcinogenic properties.
- **Biomolecules** Molecules of a high complex nature that are found in living systems. e.g., carbohydrates, proteins, fats etc.
- **Bleaching** Decolourisation by means of chemicals or by exposure to the sun's rays.
- **Borax** A white crystalline salt with an alkaline nature used in the manufacture of glass, soldering of metals, enamels, gems, soaps etc.
- **Boric acid** A white crystalline solid which behaves as a weak acid. It is used as a mild antiseptic and in the manufacture of cement, enamels, etc.
- **Brass** An alloy of tin and copper.
- **Brine** It is a saturated solution of NaCl in water.

- **Carbanion** Such a carbon species carrying a negative charge on carbon atom.
- **Carbocation** A positive species having a carbon atom possessing sextet of electrons.
- **Carbohydrate** A chemical compound made only of carbon, hydrogen and oxygen. Starch and sugar are carbohydrates.
- **Carbolic acid** Phenol is called as carbolic acid.
- **Carbon dating** A method of estimating the age of archaeological specimens of biological origin by using C-14 isotope.
- **Carbonyl group** Aldehyde and ketone groups jointly known as carbonyl group.
- **Carboxylic acid** Organic compounds containing —COOH group are called carboxylic acids.
- **Catalysis** The process by which the rate of a chemical reaction may be altered.
- **Catalyst** Any substance that changes the rate of a reaction without undergoing any chemical change.
- **Catenation** Property of atoms binding themselves to atoms of the same element. This property is exhibited by carbon.
- **Chemical bond** It refers to the attractive forces that keeps ions, atoms or group of atoms bound together.
- **Chemical energy** The energy stored by atoms and molecules and released during chemical reactions.
- **Chemical reaction** A process in which one or more chemical elements or compounds (the reactants) form new compounds (the products).
- **Coal tar** Thick, black, sticky substance which is produced, when coal gas is made by the destructive distillation of coal.
- **Coke** Light type of coal obtained when coal is heated in the presence of air. It is used as a fuel in stoves.
- **Colloid** A chemical substance with large molecules which disperse in liquid to form a solution that has different properties from a true solution.
- **Compound** A chemical substance that contains two or more elements combined together. e.g., salt (NaCl) consists of sodium and chlorine.
- **Coordinate bond** A bond formed by unequal sharing of electron pair between two atoms.
- **Covalent bond** A bond formed by equal sharing of electrons between two atoms.
- **Crystal** A solid substance that has a definite, symmetrical shape that is formed by the arrangement of its atoms and molecules.
- **Dehalogenation** Elimination of halogen.
- **Dehydration** Elimination of water.
- **Desalination** Removal of salt from sea water or saline water.
- **Diagonal relationship** The behaviour of lithium and beryllium is more similar with the second elements to next group, i.e., magnesium and aluminium in periodic table.
- **Diamagnetism** It is shown by those substances, in which all electrons present in orbitals are paired. These substances are repelled by a magnetic field.
- **Diffusion** General transport of matter whereby molecules or ions mix through normal thermal agitation.
- **Dilute solution** Any solution with small ratio of the quantities of solute to solvent or solution has low concentration of solute.
- **Distillation** A process involving both evaporation and condensation simultaneously, used for purifying liquids.
- **Double salt** A compound of two salts formed by the crystallisation of a solution containing them.
- **Electrolysis** The phenomenon of decomposition of an electrolyte by passing electric current through its solution.
- **Electrolyte** Ionic compounds, which on dissolving in water dissociate into ions.
- **Electrons** Negatively charged particles orbiting the atomic nucleus.
- **Electron affinity** The energy released or absorbed for one mole of neutral atoms in a gaseous state, when electron is accepted by each atom.
- **Electronegativity** A measure of the ability of an atom to attract the electron pair in a covalent bond to itself.
- **Electronic configuration** The distribution of electrons into orbitals of an atom.
- **Electroplating** The process of coating a solid surface with a layer of metal by the electrolysis process.
- **Electrovalent bond** The bond formed, as a result of the electrostatic attraction between opposite charged ions.
- **Efflorescence** Phenomenon in which some crystalline salts loose water of crystallisation on exposure to air and become powdery on the surface.
- **Emulsion** A colloidal dispersion of one liquid in another.
- **Enthalpy** The energy stored within the substance or the system that is available for conversion into heat.
- **Entropy** A measure of disorder or randomness in a system.

- **Ester** An organic compound obtained by the reaction of an acid with alcohol and has a fruity smell. In nature, esters give flowers their smell and fruits their flavour.
- **Ether** A class or organic compound made from alcohol. It is volatile, heavier than air, inflammable and is only slightly soluble in water.
- **Exothermic reaction** Reactions in which heat is liberated.
- **Fatty acids** Monobasic organic aliphatic acids occurring in living things in the form of glycerides in oils and fats.
- **Fermentation** The process of breaking down large molecules into simpler ones due to action of enzymes.
- **Filtration** A process of separation of insoluble particles from a liquid by passing the fluid through porous material.
- **Gasoline** Same as petrol it is obtained by the distillation of petroleum.
- **Grignard reagent** An organic compound of alkyl halide and magnesium used to synthesis of organic chemicals.
- **Halides** The halogen element compounds like fluorides, chlorides, bromides and iodides.
- **Halogen group** Non-metallic elements belonging to group VII A of the periodic table, comprising fluorine (F), chlorine (Cl), bromine (Br), iodine (I) and astatine (At).
- **Hard water** Water that contains salts of calcium and magnesium which does not lather easily with soaps.
- **Hydrates** Compounds containing water of crystallisation.
- **Hydrocarbon** Any compound made of hydrogen and carbon, e.g. methane, ethane, acetylene, ethylene, benzene, butane, toluene.
- **Hydrogenation** A process in which an unsaturated compound (generally hydrocarbon) is treated with hydrogen to produce less unsaturated or saturated compound.
- **Ideal gas** (perfect gas) The gas conforming accurately to the gas laws (Boyle's, Charles' and Gay Lussac's laws).
- **Indicator** A substance that changes colour in the presence of an acid or base.
- **Inert gas** These are inactive gases of group 0 in the periodic table. These are now called as noble gases.
- **Insoluble** Any compound that is insoluble in a particular solvent or all solvents.
- **Internal energy** It is the sum of all the atoms, molecules or ions contained in the system.
- **Invert sugar** A mixture of glucose and fructose, combined or mixed in equal proportions, e.g., sucrose.
- **Ion** An atom that has an electrical charge because it has lost or gained electrons.
- **Ionic bond** A type of chemical bond characterised by the transfer of electrons from one atom to another.
- **Ionisation** A process in which a neutral molecule splits into charged ions in the solution.
- **Ionisation enthalpy** The energy required to remove the most loosely bound electron from an isolated atom in the gaseous state for one mole of the substance.
- **Isobars** Atoms of different elements with the same mass number.
- **Isoelectronic species** The species which contain the same number of electrons.
- **Isomers** Different chemical compounds with same molecular formula but having different structural formulae. This phenomenon is called isomerism.
- **Isostructural** Substances have the same lattice type and crystal structure.
- **Isotope** An atom of an element having the same number of protons but different mass number.
- **IUPAC** It stands for International Union of Pure and Applied Chemistry. It developed a systematic chemical nomenclature method.
- **Joule-Thomson effect** The change in temperature produced, when a gas expands by flowing through some kind of obstruction (like a porous plug) from a region of higher pressure to one of lower pressure.
- **Kossel-Lewis theory** According to this theory, elements have a high tendency to attain stable (inert) electronic configuration.
- **Lamp black** A soft black carbon pigment prepared by incomplete combustion of natural gas or petroleum.
- **Lassaigne's test** A test for the detection of nitrogen, halogen and sulphur in organic compound.
- **Lauryl alcohol** A white crystalline solid used in the manufacture of detergents.
- **Lewis acid** Substances which can accept the electron pair.
- **Lewis base** Substances which can give a pair of electron.
- **Limiting reagent** In a reaction, the reagent which gets consumed first, limits the amount of product formed.
- **Liquefaction of gases** The conversion of a gas into its liquid form under pressure and at lower temperatures.
- **Liquid air** Air brought to the liquid state. It is used as a refrigerant and in the production of inert gases.

- **Lithophone** A white pigment made from zinc sulphide and barium sulphate. It is used in paints.
- **Litmus paper** A dye paper used as an acid-base neutral indicator. With acids, blue litmus paper turns red whereas, with bases, red litmus paper turns blue.
- **Mass number** The total number of protons and neutrons in the nucleus of an atom.
- **Metalloid** An element having both metallic and non-metallic properties.
- **Modern periodic law** The physical and chemical properties of the elements are periodic functions of their atomic numbers.
- **Mole** Amount of a compound equal to its molecular or atomic weight in grams.
- **Mordants** Substances used for fixing colours and dyes on textiles during the process of dyeing.
- **Mother liquor** The solution or liquid left after the formation of crystal.
- **Neutralisation** The process in which an acid reacts with a base to form a salt and water.
- **Neutron** A neutral fundamental particle which has a mass nearly equal to that of hydrogen atom.
- **Noble metals** Metals having low reactivity, show little affinity for air, moisture, carbon dioxide or other non-metals present in nature. e.g., gold, silver, mercury and platinum.
- **Non-metal** An element which has a tendency to accept electrons.
- **Nuclear fission** The disintegration of an atomic nucleus into two or more fragments. This process is used in the production of nuclear (electric) power in nuclear weapons.
- **Optimum temperature** It refers to that temperature where the yields of the products is maximum for a given reaction.
- **Orbit** An orbit, as proposed by Bohr, is a circular path around the nucleus, in which an electron moves.
- **Orbital** A region around the nucleus of an atom in which probability of finding electrons is maximum. There are one *s*, three *p*, five *d* and seven *f*-orbitals in corresponding subshells.
- **Ore** A mineral from which a metal can be extracted economically.
- **Organic compounds** Hydrocarbons and their derivatives are considered as organic compounds.
- **Oxidation** The addition of oxygen/electronegative element to a substance or removal of hydrogen/electropositive element from a substance or increase in oxidation number of an element in a reaction.
- **Oxide** A compound of oxygen with some other element.
- **Paraffin or paraffin wax** A white, waxy solid. It contains higher hydrocarbons and is obtained from petroleum (or crude oil).
- **Paramagnetism** It is shown by those substances in which all electrons present in orbitals are not paired. These are weakly attracted by a magnetic field.
- **Periodic table** A table of arranged chemical elements in the order of increasing atomic mass or atomic number to show the similarities of chemical properties.
- **pH** The pH of a solution is the negative logarithm to the base 10 of the hydrogen ion or hydronium ion cocentration.
- **pi bond** When atomic orbitals overlap in such a way that their axis remain parallel to each other and perpendicular to the internuclear axis, a pi bond is formed.
- **Plastics** Materials that are stable in normal use and easily moulded to any desired shape. These are cross-linked polymers.
- **Polymerisation** Process by which polymers and plastics are made from monomeric units.
- **Polymers** Substances which are made up of small molecules (called monomers) and are very large in size and weight. e.g., polythene, PVC, proteins, starch, rubber, etc.
- **Power alcohol** Ethyl alcohol, used for purpose of power generation in internal combustion engine.
- **Proof spirit** Solution of ethyl alcohol containing 49.28% alcohol by weight in water.
- **Propellant** A solid or liquid substance used to provide thrust in a rocket engine.
- **Proton** One kind of particle in an atom's nucleus. Protons have a positive electric charge.
- **Pyrolysis** Chemical decomposition by the action of heat.
- **Quanta** The energy of an electron is packed in small bundles.
- **Quicksilver** Another name given to mercury (because it is a liquid and looks like molten silver).
- **Radical** A species of one atom or group of atoms having either negative charge (acidic radical) or positive charge (basic radical).
- **Reactants** The substances which combine or react to give products.

- **Reagent** A substance which produces a chemical reaction with a certain chemical and can be used in testing for ion, radical or chemical substances.
- **Redox reaction** A chemical reaction in which oxidation and reduction process takes place simultaneously.
- **Reduction** A process which involves the addition of hydrogen to a substance or the removal of oxygen from it.
- **Salt** The chemical substance formed, when a base reacts with an acid.
- **Saturated solution** A solution in which no more solute can be dissolved at the same temperature and pressure.
- **Shell** Main energy level of electrons. e.g., K, L, M, N...
- **Sigma bond** A type of covalent bond formed by the end to end overlap of bonding orbitals along the internuclear axis.
- **Silica** A hard, insoluble, colourless solid with a very high melting point. It is chiefly made up of silicon dioxide.
- **Silicon** A non-metallic element used in the steel industry and in making alloys and electronic chips for computers, etc.
- **Soda ash** It is anhydrous sodium carbonate.
- **Soft water** Type of water that easily produces a lot of lather with soap.
- **Solubility** The weight of a solute present in 100 grams of the solvent at a particular temperature.
- **Solutes** Solids that dissolve in liquids to make solutions.
- **Solution** Homogeneous mixture of two or more than two components.
- **Solvents** Liquids used in making solutions. e.g., water in syrups.
- **Spectroscopy** The study of emission or absorption of spectra.
- **Stainless steel** Iron containing 4% chromium to resist rusting.
- **Steel** It is primarily iron, containing 0.25-2% carbon, traces of chromium and manganese.
- **STP** It corresponds to standard temperature and pressure.
- At this stage, properties of gas is observed at 273.15 K (0°C) temperature and 101325 Pa (or 760 mm of Hg or 1 atm) pressure.
- **Sublimation** The conversion of a solid directly into vapour, or the process of change from the solid to the gaseous state without becoming a liquid.
- **Subshell** In an atom, each shell (orbit) contains one or more subshells. These subshells are *s*, *p*, *d* and *f*.
- **Suspension** A mixture consisting of very small undissolved or partially dissolved particles of solid, distributed in a liquid dispersion medium.
- **Trace element** An element which is present in extremely small quantities (in traces) in the earth's crust. Also, that are required by organisms in very small quantities as essential constituents of enzymes, vitamins, or hormones.
- **Transuranium** The man-made elements that have a higher atomic number (number of protons in the nucleus) than uranium (atomic number, 92). e.g. plutonium (Pu, 94).
- **Trinitrotoluene** (TNT) It is a highly explosive, yellow solid. It detonates, therefore used in filling shells.
- **Triple point** The point at which (or temperature and pressure at which), the three states of a substance-liquid, solid and gas coexist.
- **Unshared electron** Electrons not utilised in covalent bond formation are unshared electrons, pair of unshared electrons in a molecule is known as lone pair of electron.
- **Valence electrons** The electrons present in the outermost orbit of an atom, which can take part in forming chemical bonds.
- **Valency** The combining capacity of an element measured by the number of hydrogen atoms which combine with, or are displaced by an atom of other elements.
- **Vulcanisation** This is a process of improving the quality and hardness of rubber by heating it with sulphur at about 150°C.
- **Wax** Thick, dull-yellow, sticky substance secreted by bees for making honeycombs.
- **Xanthate** A class of organic salts, formed by the treatment of an alcohol with in the presence of an alkali.
- **Zeeman effect** Splitting of spectral lines when the source of spectrum is exposed to a magnetic field.

Biology

- **Acclimatisation** Physiological adjustment to a change in an environmental factor.
- **Acrosome** An organelle present at the tip of a sperm cell that helps the sperm to penetrate the egg.
- **Actin** A globular multifunctional protein that forms microfilaments.

- **Active site** Specific portion of an enzyme that attaches to the substrate by means of weak chemical bonds.
- **Active transport** The movement of a substance across the membrane against its concentration gradient with the expenditure of energy and specific transport proteins.
- **ADP** Adenosine diphosphate, an important organic compound in metabolism and is essential for the flow of energy in living cells.
- **Adrenaline** A hormone produced by the medulla of the adrenal gland that increases the concentration of glucose in the blood, rises blood pressure and heartbeat.
- **AMP** Adenosine monophosphate, also known as 5′-adenylic acid. It is a nucleotide used as a monomer in DNA and RNA. It is produced during ATP synthesis by combining two ADP molecules.
- **ATP** Adenosine triphosphate, a nucleotide triphosphate used in cells as a coenzyme also called energy currency of a cell.
- **Aerobic** It refers to the presence of oxygen.
- **Aldosterone** An adrenal hormone that acts on the distal tubules of the kidney to stimulate the reabsorption of sodium (Na^+) and the passive flow of water from the filterate.
- **Allele** An alternative form of a gene.
- **Allopatric speciation** A mode of speciation induced when the ancestral population become segregated by a geographical barrier.
- **Allopolyploid** It is a common type of polyploid species resulting from two different species that are interbreeding and combining their chromosomes.
- **Alveoli** Small air sacs of the lungs through the walls of which gaseous exchange takes place between blood and air.
- **Amniocentesis** A technique used for determining genetic abnormalities in a foetus by the presence of certain chemicals or defective fetal cells in the amniotic fluid.
- **Amnion** The innermost membrane of extra embryonic membrane which is enclosed by a fluid filled sac in which the embryo is suspended.
- **Anabolism** Set of metabolic pathways that form molecules from smaller units by the help of energy input.
- **Anaerobic** It refers to the absence of oxygen.
- **Angiosperm** A flowering plant which forms seeds inside a protective chamber called an ovary.
- **Analogous** Organs or parts similar in function or appearance but not in origin or development.
- **Anoxia** It is a condition characterised by absence of oxygen supply to an organ or a tissue.
- **Antibody** A protein produced by the body's immune system when it detects some foreign substance called antigens in the blood or tissues.
- **Antigen** A foreign substance (usually protein occurs in nature) which elicits, the formation of specific antibodies within an organism.
- **Aorta** The major artery in blood-circulating system that sends blood to the other body tissues.
- **Apical dominance** Concentration of growth at the tip of a plant shoot where a terminal bud partially inhibits axillary buds growth.
- **Apoptosis** Programmed cell death brought about by signals that trigger the activation of a cascade of suicide proteins in the cells destined to die.
- **Autosomes** Chromosomes other than the sex-chromosomes, human have 22 pairs of autosomes. These are common in both males and females.
- **Bacteria** Simplest, single-celled living organisms that are found everywhere. They constitutes a large domain of prokaryotic microorganisms.
- **Basal metabolism** Amount of energy required by an individual in the resting state, for the functions such as breathing and circulation of the blood.
- **Biodiversity hotspot** A relatively small area with an exceptional concentration of species.
- **Biomass** The dry weight of organic matter comprising a group of organisms in a particular habitat.
- **Biome** A large naturally occurring community of flora and fauna occupying a major habitat. *e.g.*, forest or tundra.
- **Biosphere** An artificial structure enclosing a self contained ecosystem or ecosystems.
- **Blastocyst** A mammalian blastula in which some differentiation of cells has occurred.
- **Blastula** An animal embryo at the early stage of development when it is a hollow ball of cells.
- **Blood serum** Blood plasma without clotting factors.
- **Blood sugar** The concentration of glucose in the blood. *i.e.*, 100 mg/100 mL.
- **Bundle of His** It is a collection of heart muscle cells specialised for electrical conduction that transmits the electrical impulse from the AV node to the point of the apex of the fascicular branches.
- **Callus** A mass of unorganised parenchyma cells derived from plant tissue (explants) for use in biological research. These are actually cells that covers plant wound.

- **Calyx** Sepals of a flower.
- **Carcinogen** A chemical agent that causes cancer.
- **Cardiac output** The volume of blood pumped per minute.
- **Casparian strip** A water impermeable ring of wax around endodermal cells in plants that blocks the passive flow of water and solutes into the stele by way of cell walls.
- **Cell cycle** An ordered sequence of events in a life of a dividing eukaryotic cells. *i.e.*. It involves the sequence G_0, G_1, S, G_2 and M.
- **Cell differentiation** The structural and functional divergence of cells as they become specialised during a multicellular organism's development.
- **Cellular respiration** An efficient catabolic pathway for the production of ATP, in which oxygen is consumed as a reactant along with the organic fuel.
- **Cell sap** The solution of inorganic and some organic substances found in the vacuole of a plant cell.
- **Centriole** A small cylindrical cell organelle present near the nucleus in animal cells which is involved in the development of spindle fibres during cell division.
- **Chiasmata** The X-shaped, microscopically visible region representing homologous chromatids that have exchanged genetic material through crossing-over during meiosis.
- **Chromosomes** Self-duplicating rod-shaped or thread-like structures of nucleic acid and protein found in the nucleus of most living cells. It mainly carries genetic information in the form of genes.
- **Chyme** The partially digested food after leaving the stomach.
- **Commensalism** An association between two species in which one is benefitted and the other neither harmed nor benefitted by existing together.
- **Conjunctiva** The thin mucous membrane that lines the eyelids and the exposed surface of the eyeball.
- **Corpus callosum** A broad band of nerve fibres joining the two hemispheres of the brain.
- **Corpus luteum** A secreting tissue in the ovary that forms from the collapsed follicle after ovulation and produces progesterone.
- **Cytokinesis** The division of the cytoplasm to form two separate daughter cells immediately after mitosis.
- **Deoxyribonucleic acid (DNA)** It is generally a double helix structure (consisting of two long chains held together by hydrogen bonds) present in all living organisms.
- **Desmosome** A type of intercellular junction in animal cells that functions as an anchor.
- **Dicotyledon** A flowering plant having embryo that bears two cotyledons.
- **Dihybrid** A hybrid individual that is heterozygous for two genes.
- **Dimorphism** Displaying two separate growth form.
- **Diffusion** The movement of materials from higher concentration to lower concentration.
- **Ecotype** A locally adapted variant of a species. It is a biological community interacting organisms and their physical environment.
- **Embryo** The early developmental stage of an animal while it is in the egg or within the uterus of the mother.
- **Endometrium** The inner lining of the uterus which is richly supplied with blood vessels.
- **Epistasis** The phenomenon in which one gene alters the expression of another gene that is independently inherited.
- **Fertilisation** The proces of fusion of a male gamete with female gamete resulting in the formation of a zygote.
- **Fibrinogen** A soluble protein present in blood plasma from which the insoluble protein called fibrin is produced by the action of the enzyme thrombin.
- **Gastrulation** The formulation of a gastrula from a blastula.
- **Gene** The unit of heredity-a segment of DNA molecule in all living organisms and a segment of RNA in some RNA-viruses (because virus that do not have DNA).
- **Glycolysis** Anaerobic process of breaking down of glucose molecules by enzymes, releasing energy and pyruvic acid.
- **Guttation** Secretion of droplets of water through hydathodes at the tip and margins of certain leaves.
- **Haemoglobin** The iron-containing, red coloured respiratory pigment that transports oxygen in the blood of vertebrates.
- **Haploid** An organism or structure having a single set of unpaired chromosomes.
- **Heterozygous** Organisms having identical alleles at corresponding chromosomal loci. *e.g.*, Rr, Tt, Ww, and therefore, producing dissimilar gametes with reference to these particular genes.
- **Homeostasis** The tendency to maintain stability in the internal environment without changing the external environment.

- **Homologous** Structures (organs) of various animals which have similarity in basic structure and development but not necessarily in function.
- **Homozygous** An individual having identical alleles at corresponding chromosomal loci for *e.g.*, RR, rr, tt, etc.
- **Host** An organism, a plant, animal, or even a microbe like a bacterium on which—another organisms feeds (parasite).
- **Hydrolysis** Breakdown of complex molecules into simpler ones making use of water.
- **Hydroponics** The process of growing plants in sand, gravel or aqueous solutions containing all the essential mineral elements; soil-less growth.
- **Hymen** A fold of mucous membrane which partially covers the opening to the vagina.
- **Immunity** Tendency of a body by which an organism is safe from getting a disease.
- **Karyogamy** Fusion of nuclei of two cells, as part of syngamy.
- **Karyotype** A method of organising the chromosomes of a cell in relation to number, size and type.
- **Lactation** Process of milk secretion by the mammary glands.
- **Lichen** A symbiotic relationship between an algae and a fungus often growing on rocks and tree trunks.
- **Meiocyte** A cell that differentiates into a gamete through the process of meiosis.
- **Meiosis** A type of division in which a cell undergoes cell division in which the formation results in four daughter cells with half the number of chromosomes of the parent cell, as in the production of gametes and plant spores.
- **Menarche** The first occurrence of menturation in girls.
- **Meninges** Membranes enclosing the brain and spinal cord.
- **Mesosomes** Special structures formed by the infoldings of the bacterial membrane increasing its surface area.
- **Metabolism** The chemical processes that occur within a living organism in order to maintain itself and carry out the activities characteristic of the living state.
- **Metastasis** Transfer of disease from one organ or body part to another that is not connected to it. It is an important event in cancer.
- **Metamorphosis** A complete change in the shape and appearance of an organism during the course of its development. *e.g.*, when a caterpillar turns into a pupa.
- **Mitosis** Type of cell division in which the chromosomes within the nucleus splits into two daughter cells having the same number and kind of chromosomes as the parent nucleus.
- **Monocarpic** A plant which flowers only once in its life after which it dies. *e.g.*, the century plant (*Agave*).
- **Monosomic** A cell or individual that is basically diploid but has one copy of one particular chromosome types. It has chromosome number $2n-1$.
- **Mutation** A sudden, discrete and discontinuous change in the genome (genetic make up) of an organism which results in the creation of a new character or trait not found in the parent type.
- **Monocotyledon** A flowering plant constituting an embryo that bears a single cotyledon (seed leaf).
- **Mutualism** A relationship between two or more species in which both participants are benefited.
- **Myocardial infarction** A heart attack caused by the blockage of a coronary artery.
- **NADP** It stands for Nicotinamide Adenine Dinucleotide Phosphate. It is a coenzyme that functions as an electron carrier (acceptor) in various process like photosynthesis and respiration which reduces as $NADPH^+H^+$ or $NADPH_2$.
- **Nerve impulse** Transmission of a signal distally along the length of an axon (nerve fibre).
- **Nitrification** Process of conversion of ammonia into nitrites (NO_2^-) and nitrates (NO_3^-).
- **Nucleic acid** Macromolecule composed of many nucleotides linked in a long chain. *e.g.*, DNA or RNA.
- **Nucleoid** Nuclear material of bacteria.
- **Ovule** The part of the ovary of seed plants that contains the female germ cells. After fertilisation it becomes the seed.
- **Parasite** An organisms which lives in or on another organisms. *i.e.*, in host.
- **Parthenocarpy** The phenomenon of the development of fruits without the formation of seeds.
- **Passive immunity** Temporary protection against an infectious disease by the injection of antibodies taken from an animal or another human exposed to the disease.
- **Pathogen** Any organism that causes disease.
- **Phagocytosis** The engulfing of micro-organisms, other cells and foreign particles by phagocytes and amoeboid protozoans.
- **Plasma membrane** A delicate membranous layer of lipid (phospho-and glyco-lipids) and proteins which is selectively permeable in nature.
- **Pleura** The membrane that envelopes the lungs and lines the walls of chest and diaphragm.

- **Pseudopodia** Temporary protrusion of the protoplasm or any cell that usually functions in locomotion and feeding.
- **Puberty** The period of life when the gonads become functional, *i.e.,* an individual becomes sexually mature.
- **Purines** Nitrogenous bases (adenine and guanine) found in the nucleic acids RNA and DNA.
- **Radicle** The embryonic part of a plant which develops into the primary roots.
- **Recessive gene** A gene that is phenotypically expressed in the homozygous form but its expression becomes weak in the presence of a dominant gene.
- **Ribonucleic acid (RNA)** It is a single helix structure composed of ribonucleotides *i.e.,* ribose (a 5-carbon sugar; and hence, the name), a phosphoric acid molecule, and a nitrogenous base (or 4 types, as in DNA, but thymine of DNA is replaced by uracil in RNA).
- **Ribosomal RNA (rRNA)** An essential component for protein synthesis in all living organisms.
- **Skeleton** The supporting framework of bone, cartilage, or other rigid material which supports and protects the soft parts of the body.
- **Species** A group of organisms of similar individuals which can breed and produce more of their own kind. It acts as the basic unit of classification.
- **Sperm** Male gamete or sex cell in mammals including humans.
- **Stamen** The male fertilising organ of a flower, *i.e.,* pollen-bearing part of a flower.
- **Septum** A partition that divides a structure such as a fungal hyphae into compartments.
- **Sino-atrial (SA) node** Area of the vertebrate heart that intiates the heart beat. It is located where the superior vena cava enters the right atrium.
- **Somatic cells** Any cell in a multicellular organism except a sperm or egg cell.
- **Thermoregulation** The maintenance of internal temperature within a tolerable range.
- **Thrombin** An enzyme derived from prothrombin responsible for converting fibrinogen to fibrin and participates in blood clotting process.
- **Thromboplastin** An enzyme released from damaged cells which converts prothrombin (inactive enzyme) into thrombin (active enzyme).
- **Totipotency** Ability of embryonic cells to retain the potential to form all parts of the animals.
- **Uterus** A female reproductive organ where eggs are fertilised and/or development of the young ones occurs.
- **Vaccine** An antigenic substances which derived from the causative agent of a disease to administered a person in order to establish resistance to the particular infection.
- **Vector** An organism that transmits pathogens or parasites from one animal or plant to another.
- **Vascular cambium** A continous cylinder of meristematic cells surrounding the xylem and pith that produces secondary xylem and phloem.
- **Venule** A very small vein.
- **Vivipary** Phenomenon of reproduction inside the body of the mother eventually leading to the live birth as opposed to laying eggs.
- **Xylem** Tube-shaped, non-living portion of the vascular system in plants that carries water and minerals from roots to rest of the plant body.
- **Yolk** The stored food in egg cells that nourishes the egg.
- **Yolk sac** One of four extra embryonic membranes that supports embryonic development.
- **Zooplankton** A collective term used for the non-photosynthetic organisms present in plankton.
- **Zygote** The diploid product formed by the union of haploid gametes in conception. *i.e.,* a fertilised egg.